CADOGAN GUIDES

"Cadogan Guides are mini-encyclopaedic ... they give the explorer, the intellectual or culture buff—indeed, any visitor—all they need to know to get the best from their visit ... a good read too by the many inveterate armchair travellers.'
— *The Book Journal*

"The quality of writing in this British series is exceptional ... From practical facts to history, customs, sightseeing, food and lodging, the Cadogan Series can be counted on for interesting detail and informed recommendations."
— *Going Places* (US)

"Standouts these days are the Cadogan Guides ... sophisticated, beautifully written books."
— *American Bookseller Magazine*

"Entertaining companions, with sharp insights, local gossip and far more of a feeling of a living author ... The series has received plaudits worldwide for intelligence, originality and a slightly irreverent sense of fun."
— *The Daily Telegraph*

Other titles in the Cadogan Guides series:

AUSTRALIA
BALI
BERLIN
THE CARIBBEAN
ECUADOR,
   THE GALÁPAGOS
   & COLOMBIA
GREEK ISLANDS
INDIA
IRELAND
ITALIAN ISLANDS
ITALY
MEXICO
MOROCCO
NEW YORK
NORTHEAST ITALY
NORTHWEST ITALY
PORTUGAL
PRAGUE
ROME
SCOTLAND

SOUTH OF FRANCE: PROVENCE, CÔTE
   D'AZUR & LANGUEDOC ROUSSILLON
SOUTH ITALY
SOUTHERN SPAIN: GIBRALTAR &
   ANDALUCÍA
SPAIN
THAILAND
TURKEY
TUSCANY, UMBRIA & THE MARCHES
VENICE

Forthcoming:

AMSTERDAM
CENTRAL AMERICA
GERMANY
ISRAEL
JAPAN
MADRID & BARCELONA
MOSCOW & LENINGRAD
PARIS

D1343366

CADOGAN GUIDES

TUNISIA

BARNABY ROGERSON
&
ROSE BARING

From a fellow traveller

Bxxxxx

Sbeitla (Sufetula)
forum
October 1997

CADOGAN BOOKS
London

THE GLOBE PEQUOT PRESS
Chester, Connecticut

Cadogan Books Ltd
Mercury House, 195 Knightsbridge, London SW7 IRE

The Globe Pequot Press
138 West Main Street, Chester, Connecticut 06412, USA

Copyright © Barnaby Rogerson and Rose Baring 1992
Illustrations © Lucy Milne 1992
Maps © Cadogan Books Ltd

Cover design by Keith Pointing
Cover illustration by Povl Webb
Maps drawn by Thames Cartographic Services
Index by Meg Davies

Series Editor: Rachel Fielding

First published 1992

British Library Cataloguing in Publication Data
Rogerson, Barnaby *1960–*
  Tunisia.—(Cadogan guides).
  1. Tunisia
  I. Title   II. Baring, Rose
  916.110452
ISBN 0–947754 15–6

Library of Congress Cataloging-in-Publication Data
Rogerson, Barnaby
  Tunisia /Barnaby Rogerson and Rose Baring: illustrations by Lucy Milne.
    p.   cm.—(Cadogan guides)
  Includes bibliographical references and index.
  ISBN 0–87106–323–9
  1. Tunisia—Description and travel—1981–   —Guide-books.
I. Baring, Rose.   II. Title.   III. Series.
DT244.R63   1991   91–8895
916.1104′52—dc20   CIP

Photoset in Ehrhardt on a Linotron 202
Printed and bound in Great Britain by
Redwood Press Limited, Melksham, Wiltshire

CONTENTS

Acknowledgements *Page viii*

Introduction *Pages ix–xi*

The Best of Tunisia *Pages xi–xii*

Part I: General Information *Pages 1–34*

Getting to Tunisia *1*
Travel Agents *3–4*
Passports and Visas *4*
The Libyan Border *4–5*
The Algerian Border *5*
Customs *6*
Tunisian National Tourist Board *7*
Where and When to Go *7*
What to Wear *8*
A Traveller's Checklist *8*
Getting Around Tunisia *9*
Tourist Information *13*
Money *13*
Opening Hours *13*
Embassies and Consulates *14*
Police and Other Uniforms *15*
Tipping *15*
Alms and Beggars *15*

Guides *15*
Kif *16*
Lavatories *16*
Electricity and Gas *16*
Cameras *16*
Health, Chemists and Medicine *17*
Sex *17*
Public Holidays *18*
Festivals *20*
Newspapers, Cinema and Television *20*
Sports *21*
Shopping *22*
Where to Stay *27*
Eating Out *28*
Drinking *30*
Nightlife *32*
Itineraries *33*

Part II: Tunisian Culture *Pages 35–80*

History *35*
Islam *56*
Art and Architecture *60*
Literature *69*

Music *73*
The Land *73*
Wild Flowers *77*
Animals and Birds *78*

v

Part III: The Bay of Tunis *Pages 81–123*

Tunis *82*
  The New Town *89*
  The Souks and the Zitouna Mosque *90*
  The Upper Medina and Kasbah Quarter *94*
  The Southern Medina *97*
  The Northern Medina *100*
  The Belvedere Park and Al Jellaz Cemetery *103*
  The Bando Museum *104*

South of Tunis *111*
La Goulette *113*
Carthage *114*
Sidi Bou Said *121*
La Marsa *123*

Part IV: The Cap Bon Peninsula *Pages 124–47*

Hammamet *126*
Nabeul *133*
Kelibia *138*

Kerkouane *140*
El Haouaria *142*
The North Coast *144*

Part V: The Sahel *Pages 148–89*

Sousse *150*
Monastir *159*
Mahdia *163*
Sfax *167*

Kerkennah Isles *174*
El Jem *178*
Kairouan *181*

Part VI: The North Coast and the Mejerda Valley *Pages 190–232*

Utica *192*
Bizerte *197*
Tabarka *209*
Ain Draham *213*

Béja *219*
Bulla Regia *223*
Chemtou *229*
Ghardimao *231*

Part VII: The Tell *Pages 233–93*

Zaghouan *237*
Thuburbo Majus *240*
El Fahs *242*
Zama Minor *245*
Testour *247*
Ain Tounga *249*
Dougga *251*

El Kef *263*
Makhtar *272*
Sbeitla *280*
Haidra *287*
Kasserine *291*
Jebel Chambi *292*

Part VIII: The Chott El Jerid *Pages 294–318*

Gafsa *298*
Metlaoui and the Seldja Gorge *301*
Tamerza *303*
Midès *303*

Chebika *304*
Tozeur *305*
Nefta *309*
Douz *316*

Part IX: Jebel Demer and the Isle of Jerba *Pages 319–53*

Gabès *323*

Matmata *328*

Medenine *331*

Tataouine *334*

Jebel Abiod *338*

Jerba *342*

Houmt Souk *346*

Ajim *351*

Glossary of Historical, Architectural and Arabic Terms
Pages 354–9

Chronology *Pages 360–3*

Language *Pages 364–9*

Further Reading *Pages 370–4*

Index *Pages 375–84*

LIST OF MAPS

Key to Regional Maps *x*

Tunisia and her Neighbours *5*

Tunisia—Roads and Railways *10*

Bay of Tunis *82*

Central Tunis *86–7*

Carthage *116*

Cape Bon Peninsula *125*

The Sahel *149*

Sousse *150*

Sfax *168*

Kairouan *182*

The North Coast and the Mejerda Valley *191*

Bizerte *201*

The Tell *234*

Centre of Thuburbo Majus *241*

Dougga *252*

El Kef *264*

Makhtar *274*

Sbeitla *282*

Haidra *289*

Chott El Jerid *295*

Tozeur *305*

Nefta *310*

Jerba and Jebel Demer *321*

Gabès *324*

Houmt Souk *347*

ABOUT THE AUTHORS

Barnaby Rogerson is a historian who has been a tourist in North Africa for fourteen years. He has written a number of travel guides to the region, but earns a living laying ornamental floors in temples and hermitages. Rose Baring is a script writer and traveller, who speaks Russian and learned Mandarin during her lone wanderings in Central Asia. She is 6 feet 2 inches tall and met Barnaby while mourning her grandmother in a ruined Scottish abbey 10 years ago.

ACKNOWLEDGEMENTS

A number of people were instrumental in smoothing our passage in Tunisia, and pointing us in the direction of further information. We would like to thank the librarians of the School of Oriental and African Studies, M. Mardassi of the Tunisian National Tourist Office in London, M. Ennabli at the National Institute of Art and Archaeology in Tunis and Frej Chaouchane, director of the International Cultural Centre in Hammamet. Since returning, thanks are due to our editor, Rachel Fielding, for her advice and attention and for her exotic continental patisseries.

Among the many who have shared meals, enthusiasm and medicine with us are Mary Miers, Johnny Harley, James Graham Stewart, Derek Williams, Inger Eriksson, Henrik Silverstope, Jane Davey, Drifi Hachim in Metameur, Znaidia Moncef in Metlaoui, Noureddine Ben Arfa in Uzappa, Ali Ben Aluaya in Zaghouan, Samir Hermi in Djendouba, and his sister Helen at Samara Travel in London. Thanks are also due to Hugh Rochford for his notes on Tunisian wine. For the varied surroundings in which we have squatted with word processors since returning, our thanks to Keith and Kathy Rogerson, John and Sally Baring and Julian and Isobel Bannerman, and to Sue for providing a haven without them.

The publishers would also like to extend their warmest thanks to Jennifer Speake, Stephen Davies and Meg Davies for respectively copy editing, proof reading and indexing.

PLEASE NOTE

INTRODUCTION

Fishes are everywhere in Tunisia. They adorn lorries, pregnant mothers' and babies' necklaces, and lie glistening in ancient mosaics and in artful tableaux beside charcoal barbecues. They turn up in conversation, in modern painting, in casual greetings and in propitious dreams, particularly in groups of five. For the fish is both a symbol of good luck and fertility, and something of a national totem. Start your holiday auspiciously in a seafood restaurant beside the sea, and the country begins to reveal itself.

For it is the insular nature of Tunisia, caught between the Mediterranean and the Saharan sand sea, that lies at the heart of the country's character. Tunisia has had to swim with both, to master the caravan routes of the Sahara and the waters of the Mediterranean. Its position beside the narrow straits of Sicily has kept it constantly at the centre of the violent history of the Mediterranean. The country has been swept by army upon army and has learned not just to bend with, but also to adapt with, the wind. The Romans, Vandals, Byzantines, Spaniards, Turks, and most recently the French, have all left their imprint, while the Phoenicians and Arabs are cornerstones of the national identity.

This powerful cultural cocktail has produced the most liberal of Arab nations, a crossroads between Europe and Muslim North Africa. It offers thousand-year old mosques, Roman temples, Jewish synagogues and Christian churches to explore. And when the hurly-burly's done, isolated beaches and the perfect stillness of the desert night. Whether bargaining another dinar from your purse or proferring a bouquet of jasmine blossom, the Tunisians are welcoming and courteous, and their hospitality is likely to leave you in their debt.

Guide to the Guide

We have divided Tunisia into seven regions: Part III covers the capital Tunis; Part IV the Cap Bon peninsula; Part V the ancient cities of the Sahel coast; the rugged hills and coastline of the North with the fertile Mejerda Valley are described in Part VI; the high plateau of the Tell, filled with Roman ruins, in Part VII; the Chott el Jerid, a vast salt-flat surrounded by date-palm oases in Part VIII, and finally the island of Jerba and the Jebel Demer mountains which curve round to the Libyan border in Part IX.

The central attraction of **Tunis** is the medieval medina with its honeycomb souk, ancient mosques and magnificent hidden town-houses. Out in the suburb of Bardo an old Beylical palace now holds one of the greatest collections of mosaics in the world. On the coast are the ruins of Punic and Roman Carthage, the fish restaurants of La Goulette and the picturesque hill-top village of Sidi Bou Said.

The landscape of **Cap Bon** is barely distinguishable from that of southern Europe with its citrus groves and vineyards. It has a magnificent stretch of beach at the twin towns of Hammamet and Nabeul, which are well developed tourist resorts and can be very busy in summer. To the north, a distinctive light white wine is grown beneath Kelibia castle and there is a Phoenician city at Kerkouane and Roman underground quarries at El Haouaria.

The **Sahel** boasts four entrancing walled cities: Sousse, Mahdia, Sfax and Kairouan, which, between them, house some of the earliest and finest examples of Muslim architecture

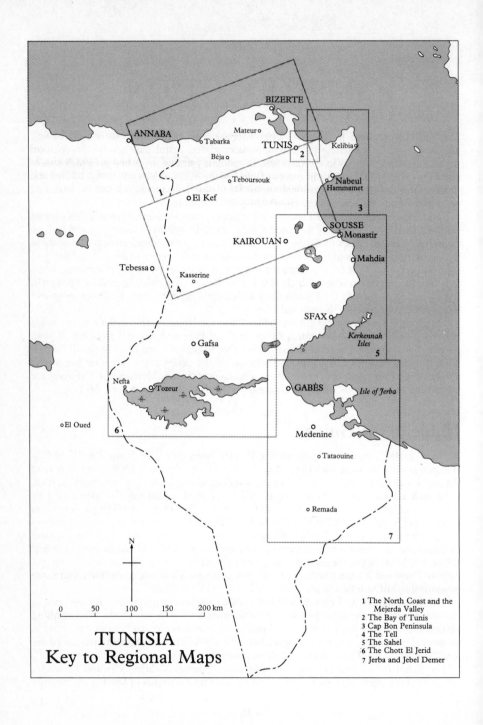

BIZERTE

ANNABA

Mateur○

TUNIS○

Kelibia○

Tabarka○

Béja○

2

Teboursouk○

Nabeul
Hammamet

1

El Kef○

3

SOUSSE
○Monastir

KAIROUAN○

Mahdia

Tebessa○

Kasserine○

4

SFAX

Kerkennah
Isles

Gafsa○

5

Nefta○

GABÈS○

Isle of Jerba

○Tozeur

El Oued○

6

Medenine○

Tataouine○

N

Remada○

7

0   50   100   150   200 km

TUNISIA
Key to Regional Maps

1 The North Coast and the
   Mejerda Valley
2 The Bay of Tunis
3 Cap Bon Peninsula
4 The Tell
5 The Sahel
6 The Chott El Jerid
7 Jerba and Jebel Demer

in the world. In contrast there are also quiet beaches, fish restaurants and the enduring skeleton of the Roman amphitheatre at El Jem.

The **North Coast** and the **Mejerda Valley** are a pair of opposites. A rugged chain of mountains shelters a national park, boar-hunting hotels and a series of isolated beaches that can be explored from the old corsair city of Bizerte or the quiet resort of Tabarka. The slow, serpentine bends of the Mejerda river flow across a prosperous agricultural plain. It snakes beside the Roman ruins of Utica, the underground villas of Bulla Regia and the marble quarries of Chemtou, as well as bustling market towns.

The **Tell** is an enormous corn-growing plateau, quite neglected by tourists but studded with some staggeringly beautiful Roman ruins, forested mountains and quiet traditional villages. El Kef, the ancient and modern citadel of the Tell, provides a central base for explorations, aided by hotels close to the magnificent Roman remains of Dougga and Sbeitla.

The desert fantasy, riding camels from well to well, pitching low brown tents and baking flat bread on an open fire, can be fulfilled from both Tozeur and Douz in the **Chott el Jerid**. The region offers largely undisturbed walks through palmery gardens, brick-built medinas, hot, open-air mineral baths and some spectacular, eroded canyons.

The island of **Jerba** and the **Jebel Demer** mountains contain all the ingredients of a holiday. Jerba is thought to be the enchanted island of the Lotus Eaters which Odysseus and his men were so reluctant to leave. Beaches surround this island of date palms served by one white-washed market town, Houmt Souk. On the mainland the communities of underground houses around Matmata and the extraordinary Berber architecture of the Jebel Demer, like the hill citadels of Chenini and Douiret, wait to be explored.

The Best of Tunisia

Unspoiled beach resorts: Tabarka, Kelibia, Mahdia and the Kerkennah Isles.
Deserted beaches: Sidi Ali el Mekki by Ghar el Melh, Ras Engelah by Bizerte and Plage Zouiraa near Tabarka.
Impressive Roman ruins: Dougga, the triple capitol and baptismal fonts at Sbeitla, the amphitheatre at El Jem and the underground villas of Bulla Regia.
Roman ruins to be alone in: Haidra, Chemtou, Medeina and Makhtar.
Finest Islamic architecture: the Great Mosque and Ribat at Sousse, the Great Mosque of Kairouan, the Zitouna Mosque in Tunis, the Great Mosque at Mahdia and the Ribat at Monastir.
Museums: the Bardo in Tunis, the Dar Jallouli in Sfax, archaeological museums at Sousse and El Jem and the Phoenician museum at Kerkouane.
Deservedly popular towns: El Kef, Nefta, Houmt Souk and Tamerza
Under-visited towns: Béja, Zaghouan, Sfax and Mahdia
Obscure towns to be the only tourist in: Sidi Bou Zid, Thala and Mahrès.
Overrated destinations: Gabès, Matmata, Douz and Hammamet
Carpet shopping: Sfax, Tunis, El Jem and Foum Tataouine.
Unlikely sports: sand-yachting on the Chott el Jerid, scuba-diving at Tabarka, hang-gliding from Jebel Ressas and sand-skiing at El Fouar.
Hotels: Dar Said and Bou Farès at Sidi Bou Said, Petit Mousse at Bizerte, Sable d'Or at Houmt Souk and the Hotel des Cascades at Tamerza.
Restaurants: Dar el Jeld in Tunis, Sicca Veneria in El Kef, Princesse d'Haroun in Houmt Souk, Hotel Florida in Kelibia and Restaurant La Sirène by Sfax port.

Bars: Oasis bar and Café de la Corbeille in Nefta, Hotel Cercina in Kerkennah, Brasserie Phoenix in Béja.

Nightlife: Tunis

Natural landscape: Jugurtha's Table, a steep-sided flat-topped mountain on the Algerian border, the Chott el Jerid salt-flats, Midès canyon and the village citadels of Chenini and Douiret.

Natural hammams: Tozeur and Nefta palmery pools, the Roman marble baths at Hammam Mellège near El Kef and the showers in Hotel Borj des Autruches, Kebili.

Spectacular walks: up the canyon to Midès, Jugurtha's Table, Jebel Sidi Abiod at El Haouaria, with views to Sicily on clear days.

Excursions: by four-wheel drive or camel to Ksar Ghilane, a day's fishing off the Kerkennah Isles and through eucalyptus forest and *maquis* to Cap Serrat.

Part I

GENERAL INFORMATION

Harissa Harvest in Cap Bon

Getting to Tunisia

By Air

From Britain

Direct 2¾-hour flights from Britain to Tunis are now run by Gibraltar Air and Tunis Air. Tunis Air currently fly from Heathrow on Fridays and Sundays, Gibraltar Air from Gatwick on Thursdays and Mondays. An **Apex** ticket, booked for a specific date two weeks in advance and unalterable, costs about £150 return. An open ticket is over £400. You can book through any travel agent or direct from Gibraltar Air at Gatwick, tel (0293) 644239, and Tunis Air at 6 Vigo Street, London W1, tel (071) 437 6236 or 734 7644.

Charter flights, from Gatwick, Manchester and Luton, usually go to Monastir and are less comfortable, more subject to delay and have a fixed return date between one and four weeks later. In midsummer, they may cost up to £200, but if you are prepared to risk it and wait to the last minute, you can sometimes pick up a return flight very cheaply. In winter they dip as low as £48. Your local travel agent should be able to find these for you, but if not, ring round the list of tour operators and agents given below or look up the bucket shops that advertise in the back pages of *Private Eye, Time Out, The Sunday Times* and *The Observer*.

From France

France has the best air connections to Tunisia, shared between Air France and Tunis Air. From Paris, there are over 20 flights a week to Tunis, 12 from Marseille, six from Lyon and eight from Nice, and there are at least twice-weekly connections from Paris to Jerba, Sfax and

1

Monastir. For more information ring Tunis Air, 17 Rue Daunou, 75002 Paris, tel 42–96–10–45 or Air France, 62 Rue Monsieur le Prince, 75006 Paris, tel 43–25–73–95.

From North America

There are no direct flights from North America to Tunisia. Fly instead to London or Paris and pick up a connection there. If you have a choice it might be more entertaining to combine a trans-Atlantic flight with a ferry trip across the Mediterranean, which means flying or making your way to Marseille, or to the Italian ports of Genoa or Trapani.

Overland

To catch a boat to Tunisia, you must head for either Marseille, Genoa or Trapani, the three ports which run regular car ferries to La Goulette, the passenger port of Tunis. This is undoubtedly the most expensive and laborious way of reaching Tunisia.

However, if you like ferries and trains and loathe airplanes and airports, the 50-hr rail journey from London Victoria to Trapani, at over £200 return, may be cheap at the price. Genoa is a mere 30 hours from London, Marseille barely a day. For more information visit the British Rail Travel Centre at Victoria Station, tel (071) 834 2345, and if you are under 26 or over 65 they will advise you which bargain tickets, like Eurotrain/TransAlpino or InterRail, you can use.

Travelling by coach from either London or Paris, use Euroways, which can be booked through any National Express ticket office and makes up in the reliability of service for any marginally higher fares.

By Ferry

Marseille

The 24-hr Marseille crossing is the most frequent, and easiest to book from Britain. There are, depending on the season, between a dozen and two dozen sailings a month, usually leaving between 10.00 and 12.00. In winter, tickets can be bought at the harbour, the Gare Maritime de la Joliette, on departure. In summer, you should book well in advance if you are thinking of taking a vehicle across.

From Britain you can book through Continental Shipping and Travel Ltd at 179 Piccadilly, London W1V 9DB, tel (071) 491 4968.

In Tunisia, reservations and tickets are obtained from the CTN, Compagnie Tunisienne de Navigation in Tunis at 126 Rue de Yougoslavie, tel (01) 242775, or from the marginally more efficient TourAfric office at 52 Av Habib Bourguiba.

In France contact SNCM, the Société Nationale Maritime Corse Mediterranée, either in Paris at 12 Rue Godot de Mauroy, 75009, tel 42–66–67–98, or in Marseille, 61 Blvd des Dames, 13002, tel 91–56–32–00. Second-class passenger tickets for midsummer 1990, return, cost £134, first class £235. A standard-sized car costs an additional £257.

Genoa

The direct Genoa–La Goulette boat, the *Habib*, is also run by CTN. During the high season, from July to September, there are sailings at least every five days, but outside that period the service is much more sporadic. There is no London booking agent, but Continental Shipping and Travel Ltd (above) have information on the schedule. To book a passage, call the CTN/SNCM office in Marseille, tel 91–56–32–00.

Trapani
Getting to the Trapani ferry on Sicily is an expensive marathon. There is only one sailing a week, currently leaving Trapani at 09.00 on Tuesday morning and returning on the same day at 20.00.

This route is run by Tirrenia Navigazione. Their agents in London are Serena Holidays, 40–42 Kenway Road, SW5, tel (071) 373 6548; in France SNCM; and in Tunis CTN (addresses and telephone numbers above). In Trapani the Tirrenia office is at 52 Corso Italia, Trapani, tel 27480.

In addition there is a new hydrofoil service that runs between Trapani and Kelibia, the chief port on the Cap Bon peninsula. It has its limitations, for travelling by hydrofoil is about as much fun as being in an airplane, and there is an erratic timetable which only operates in fine weather. At the moment return tickets, and return tickets only, can be bought from Tunis or Trapani, costing just under £100.

Some old maps and guides connect Malta, Cagliari and Annaba to Tunis or Bizerte, but none of these routes still operates.

Travel Agents

There are two well-established Tunisian specialist agents, who can give knowledgeable advice on hotels, itineraries, arrange car hire and the outward journey. The **Tunisia Travel Bureau**, 304 Old Brompton Road, London SW5, tel (071) 373 4411, leaves a bit to be desired on the efficiency front, and **Tunisia Experience** is at 29 Queens Road, Brighton, BN1 3YN, tel (0273) 202391. The latter, or its offshoot Panorama, also organize tours covering the main Second World War battlefields and war cemeteries. **Cadogan Travel** also know the area well and are at 159 Sloane Street, London SW1, tel (071) 730 0721.

'Adventure' Tours
Tunisia is scantily covered by the more specalist up-market tour agents, like **Serenissima** and **Swan Hellenic**, but is well represented on adventure tours which concentrate on the well-worn routes across the Tunisian Sahara. You will, of course, get much more adventure by travelling on local buses than tucked into a truck with a load of other fellow nationals and shepherded by a guide. Still, adventure tourism is a growing business and its glossy brochures make harmless browsing.

Topdeck runs a five- and a seven-week tour through Spain, Portugal, Morocco, Algeria, Tunisia and Italy. It is a whistlestop cultural skirmish, popular with Australians. Details from 64–65 Kenway Road, London SW5, tel (071) 373 5095. **Encounter Overland**, 267 Old Brompton Road, London SW5, tel (071) 370 6845, runs a four-week tour of the Tunisian and Algerian Sahara. **Guerba** has a similiar tour, plus a trans-Saharan special that starts from Tunisia; it is based at 101 Eden Vale Road, Westbury, Wilts, tel (0373) 826611. Other agencies include **Explore Worldwide** at 7 High Street, Aldershot, Hants, tel (0252) 319448, **Dragoman Travel**, 10 Riverside, Framlingham, Suffolk, IP13 9AG, tel (0728) 724184 and **Exodus** at 27/31 Jerdan Place, London SW6 1BE, tel (071) 385 0176.

Package Tours
There are several dozen tour agencies that offer a flight to Tunis or Monastir, a coach connection and a week or a fortnight in a large hotel in one of the four beach resorts, Hammamet–Nabeul, Sousse–El Kantaoui, Skanes–Monastir or Jerba. British tour operators are some of the most competitive in the world, and the real bargains are the last-minute discount holidays advertised in the windows of High Street travel agents. It is not exceptional to pick up a week's holiday for little over £100.

For those who need to plan ahead, ring the Tunisian National Tourist Board in London on (071) 224 5561 and they will send a list of holiday companies featuring Tunisia. These include **Airtours, Cadogan Travel, Club Mediterranée, Cosmos, Enterprise, Horizon, Skytours, Sovereign, Thomas Cook, Thomson, Tjaerebourg** and **Wings**. Booking in advance, prices range from £200–£400 for a week, depending on the season and standard of accommodation.

Passports and Visas

All foreign citizens require a valid passport to enter Tunisia. British, Canadian, Scandinavian and most EEC citizens are allowed to stay in Tunisia for three months without a visa, and US citizens get four months. The situation is different for Dutch, Australian and New Zealand citizens who, due to their own nations' restrictive immigration policies, should apply for a visa from a Tunisian consulate before departure. Holders of South African and Israeli passports are not admitted to Tunisia, and proof of travel in either country is a legitimate reason for denying entry.

Tunisian consulates are found at:

Great Britain: 29 Princes Gate, London SW7, tel (071) 584 8117;
Holland: 198 Gentsestraat, Den Haag, tel 512251;
Sweden: 73 Drottningatan, Stockholm 11136, tel 236470;
Italy: 7 Via Asmara, Rome, tel 839–0748;
USA: 2408 Massachusetts Av, Washington DC, tel 234 6644;
Canada: 515 Oscanner St, Ottawa, tel 237 0330.

There is a procedure for extending a stay beyond three months, but even the officials involved will counsel you against entering the confused world of North African bureaucracy. A short outing to Algeria or Sicily gives you a new three-month visa without this experience, which begins with a visit to the sheds of the Tunis Harbour Police station. Here you will have to prove you are spending satisfactory amounts of foreign exchange, provide a good reason for your extension and surrender your passport. It may reappear a few weeks later with the extension.

The Libyan Border

Libya is famous for its leader, its oil wealth and its xenophobic policies. It also has the most magnificent Roman ruins in North Africa at Leptis Magna, Orea and Sabratha, empty beaches, desert palmeries and continual sun. However, it is a country closed to tourism. The Libyans have no need of tourist revenue and their government is determined to maintain the country as a purely Arabic and Islamic state. At the moment the only reliable way to visit Libya is to get a job, or go on business. Philip Ward, a poet whose guides to Libya are still in print, got to know the country working as librarian for a British oil company.

The land frontier with Tunisia is currently wide open and the Libyan government has even disbanded its customs posts in an unreciprocated gesture of fraternity with Tunisia. The border area has become a series of bustling boom towns, with Tunisians moving east to find work and Tripolitanian Libyans crossing into southern Tunisia to shop, holiday and play the black-market currency exchange. Though Libyan wages and prices are level with the West and fuel and cars are in plentiful supply, there is a shortage of basics like food, cloth and ceramics.

But though the border is now busy for North Africans, the situation has not changed for Western visitors. Without an official invitation, even if you have got a visa you may be turned back. To try getting a visa, first have all the details of your passport translated into Arabic.

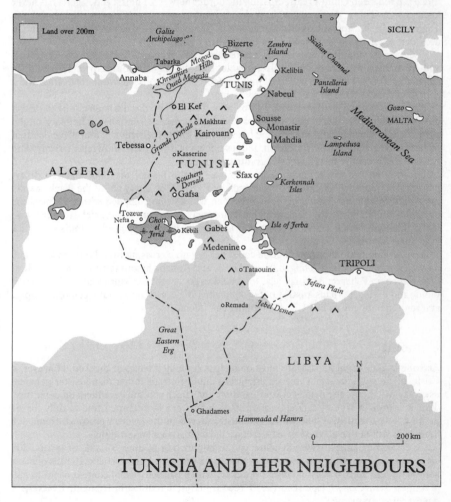

TUNISIA AND HER NEIGHBOURS

The British Consulate in Tunis has a rubber stamp with the appropriate headings and a hotel receptionist can usually be persuaded to fill in the rest. Your passport can then be presented to the Libyan People's Bureau at 48 Rue du 1er Juin, Tunis, or at the consulates in Cairo, Athens, Rome and Malta. There is no Libyan Embassy or Consulate in Britain. Once you get there, alcohol is prohibited, all street signs are in Arabic, maps are non-existent and food and accommodation uninspiring and expensive. Send us a postcard.

The Algerian Border

Since the Maghreb Unity Treaty, crossing the border between Tunisia and Algeria has never been easier. There are now almost a dozen border posts open, regular flights and the Trans-Maghreb Express train. In the centre of Tunis there are queues of yellow Algerian taxis that regularly ply the routes between the two capitals.

EEC citizens and Scandinavians do not require visas to enter Algeria, though Americans and Australians do. These are freely available from the Algerian Embassy at 136 Av de la Liberté in Tunis, where you will need four passport photographs with your application and a couple of days in hand to wait for its processing.

There are just two provisos to this rosy picture. The land border has been closed to British passport holders for almost two years now and the 'tourist tax' continues. The block on the British was in retaliation for the efficient but tactlessly swift repatriation of four plane-loads of Algerians illegally resident in London. It does not apply if you travel to Algeria directly from Europe and recent reports suggest a gradual relaxation.

The 'tourist tax' is the compulsory purchase at the border of 1000 Algerian dinars per person, roughly £100, at the official exchange rate. This is way above the black-market rates that are quoted elsewhere in Algeria. You will also be equipped with an official log on which you are invited to declare all hard currency and record any official exchanges you make. The only beneficial effect of the 'tourist tax' is to discourage coaches, tours and quick visits.

A week-long tour of eastern Algeria could begin with a crossing from Nefza to El Oued, moving north to Tebessa, Timgad, Souk Ahras, and Annaba before returning to Tunisia at Ghardimao or Tabarka. Alternatively, you could strike out for the Moroccan border posts at Oujda and Figuig, perhaps missing out on sprawling Algiers to concentrate on more compact and idiosyncratic towns like Cirta, Laghouat and Tlemcen.

Customs

Arriving by air, casual tourists are most unlikely to have their baggage checked. However, if Customs are suspicious that you are importing things to trade rather than just for personal use, they will record the details in your passport and check you still have them on departure. This is especially true of cars and motorbikes, which can be imported free of duty for six months for personal use, but are meticulously entered in the owner's passport. If you sell them, you will not be allowed to leave before paying massive import duty.

Customs' regulations currently allow you to import free of duty: 1 bottle of spirits, 200 cigarettes or 40 cigars or 400 grammes of tobacco, 2 cameras, 1 cine camera, 10 rolls of black and white film and 20 rolls of colour, jewellery with a precious metal content of up to 500 grammes, 1 wireless, 1 tape recorder, 1 record player, 1 musical instrument, 1 bicycle, 1 typewriter, 1 pram, etc.

When leaving, remember that the export of Tunisian dinars is forbidden, that the export of wildlife or hunting trophies requires the authorization of the Ministry of Agriculture, and that antiques require the authorization of the Ministry of Cultural Affairs.

Tunisian National Tourist Board

Practically every capital in Europe has a Tunisian National Tourist Board office. In London it is at 77a Wigmore Street, W1H 9LJ, tel (071) 224 5561. France has two offices, one at 32 Av de l'Opera, 75002 Paris, tel 47–42–72–67 and a second office in Lyon at 12 Rue de Seze, tel 78–52–35–86. In Belgium the office is at 60 Galerie Ravenstein, 1000 Bruxelles, tel 5112893; in the Netherlands at 61 Leidsestraat, 1017 Amsterdam, tel 22–49–71–72; in Germany at 100 Graf Adolph Strasse, 4000 Dusseldorf, tel 359414 and at 6 Am Haupt-bahnhof, 6000 Frankfurt am Main, tel 231891. The address in Sweden is 19 Engelbrekts-gatan, 11432 Stockholm, tel 206773, and in Switzerland, 69 Bahnofstrasse, Zurich, tel 2114830.

There is a sprinkling of Tourist Offices and *Syndicats d'Initiative*, signalled by an undistinctive red and blue sign, in every major tourist town. They are useful as a source of free posters and pamphlets, but are not informative about local history or any site not covered by a coach tour, though there are honourable exceptions. The Hammamet office has remained friendly and provides a good local map; Sousse has a good display of local travel information; Kairouan provides guides and sells the entrance ticket to the sites, and in the south you can book camel rides at the offices in Tozeur, Nefta and Douz.

Where and When to Go

Tunisia is about the same size as England and Wales and has an efficient transport system which allows you to cover a lot of ground in a two-week holiday. You should, however, allow the seasons to shape your itinerary.

Summer has its disadvantages. The Tunisian nation is also on holiday, the big cities are sultry, the fields are dead and the glare of the sun burns out the subtle colours of the monuments in the interior. It is the time for the beach, the boozy lunch and the long siesta. Avoid spending much time in Tunis or going further south than Sfax, for in summer the Saharan provinces are just too hot and debilitating to be enjoyed by anybody used to a northern climate. Concentrate instead on Cap Bon and the northern coast, broken by visits to higher, cooler towns like El Kef, Zaghouan and perhaps Ain Draham.

Spring, from March to May, and autumn, in October and November, are the ideal times for a general tour of Tunisia. It is off-season but warm enough to swim and get a tan, and not so stifling as to discourage walking, while the countryside buzzes with activity and the fields and hills are alive with flowers. The only disadvantage is the risk of hitting a patch of rain, in which case head straight for the animation of the capital, Tunis.

The real off-season, when you pick up travel bargains, is December, January and February. You can be lucky with the weather, but generally the coastal resorts, bar Jerba, are depressing, and cold winds can put much of the high interior out of bounds. These are the months to explore the Saharan provinces, enlivened by the date and olive harvests—and the odd flash flood.

What to Wear

North Africa has a different dress code to Europe and America, and it is important to respect it. It would be extremely rare for a Tunisian to express open disapproval, but be assured that they have a very low opinion of people who expose too much breast or thigh in public.

Bikinis and swimming trunks are perfectly acceptable on the beach, in a hotel garden or roof terrace, but never in a village or on the road. A pair of trousers and a T-shirt are the minumum for a man wandering around a town. The same will do for women, but if you are trying to be sympathetic pack a long, light skirt and a full shirt. Leave your black designer mini-skirts at home and bring out floral and colourful things that local Tunisian women can also admire. There is no need to go overboard and wear a haik, though a scarf loosely draped around the neck may keep the sun off.

In hammams, the public or open-air baths which are strictly divided between the sexes, both men and women strip down to pants or swimming costumes. Entering a private house it is customary to remove your shoes in the hall.

The one most notable difference between Tunisians and tourists is the crisp cleanliness of the former's clothes. You will not be turned away from any restaurant for not wearing a tie, but in the smarter places in and around Tunis you may find all the other tables thick with blazers.

The temperature charts below might be of some use for packing, though these are monthly midday averages which hide an often dramatic range in daily temperature. Even in midwinter you may need dark glasses and a strong sun cream, and a light sweater in midsummer is useful for evening coastal breezes, cool mountains and the desert nights. At the very least it can be moulded into a pillow for long bus journeys.

Average Air Temperature (in Celsius):

Month	Tunis	Bizerte	Hammamet	Sousse	Jerba	Tozeur
Jan	11°C	11°C	11°C	11°C	12°C	12°C
Apr	16°C	15°C	16°C	16°C	19°C	20°C
July	26°C	25°C	26°C	26°C	27°C	32°C
Oct	20°C	20°C	21°C	21°C	23°C	22°C
Dec	12°C	12°C	13°C	13°C	14°C	12°C

Average Sea Temperatures:

April	15°C	60°F		*October*	21°C	69°F
July	23°C	72°F		*December*	11°C	52°F

A Traveller's Checklist

A photocopy of the first four pages of your passport may come in handy if you lose it. A corkscrew and knife for picnics, a good lighter, a torch for caves and underground ruins, a suction bath plug, one roll of soft loo paper and a packet of Immodium and Nurofen provides a holiday survival kit.

To ease your passage through the country, an address book for Tunisian friends to write in, and a good stock of pens are useful. A different order of gifts and good trading items in themselves are printed T-shirts, strong shoes, pop cassettes and dark glasses.

Getting Around Tunisia

Distance (in kilometres) between principal places by road:

	Bizerte	Jerba	Kairouan	El Kef	Nefta	Sfax	Sousse	Tunis
Bizerte		575	215	210	540	330	205	65
Jerba	575		360	500	390	280	410	510
Kairouan	215	360		175	325	136	57	155
El Kef	210	500	175		345	290	230	175
Nefta	540	390	325	345		315	380	500
Sfax	330	280	136	290	315		127	270
Sousse	205	410	57	230	380	127		140
Tunis	65	510	155	175	500	270	140	

By Air

There is no need to fly within Tunisia, any more than you would within England and Wales. The country is well served by trains, buses and *louage* taxis. If you are in a real rush however, Tunis Air and Tunisavia operate a schedule of connections from Tunis to Jerba, Monastir, Tozeur, Gabès and Sfax with regional connections from Tozeur to Jerba, Monastir to Jerba and Gabès to Tozeur. Prices and schedules can be obtained from the Tunisavia office at 38 Rue Gandhi, Tunis, tel (01) 254875; and Tunis Air at Tunis airport, tel (01) 288000, at 48 Av Habib Bourguiba, tel (01) 259189 or at 113 Av de la Liberté, tel (01) 288100.

By Train

The SNCFT, the Société Nationale des Chemins de Fer Tunisiens, runs air-conditioned trains with smoked-glass windows on most of the main lines. The stations are elegant and well placed in the city centres, and the service is efficient and cheap by British standards with a much, much better line in sandwiches. Travelling by train is a little more expensive than by bus, but about the same as taking a *louage*.

Fanning out from Tunis' main Pl Barcelone train station are the four principal routes in Tunisia:

North to Bizerte: there are three trains a day, stopping at Mateur and Tindja, a journey of 1 hr 50 min.

West to Ghardimao: there are five trains a day to Ghardimao on the Algerian frontier, stopping at Béja, Bou Salem and Jendouba. The 11.55 is the Trans-Maghreb Express which crosses the border to Souk Ahras, Annaba, Constantine and Algiers.

Southwest to Kalaa Kasbah: there are three trains a day, seldom used by tourists, on the 6-hr journey through El Fahs, Gaafour, El Ksour to Kalaa Kasbah.

South to Cap Bon, Gabès and Gafsa: there are 10 trains a day to Bir Bou Regba, where you change onto a branch line for the frequent trains to Hammamet and Nabeul. Eight trains continue south to Sousse, a 2-hr journey, and five go a further 3 hr 40 min to Sfax, stopping at El Jem. The other three follow the coast to Monastir and Mahdia, a journey of 1 hr 45 min. From Sfax there are two trains a day south to Gabès, a journey of 2 hr 20 min. One train a day leaves Sfax for Gafsa and Metlaoui. From Metlaoui, Le Lézard Rouge, an ex-Bey's train makes daily excursions up through the dramatic Seldja gorge, though there is also a cheaper train used by commuting phosphate miners.

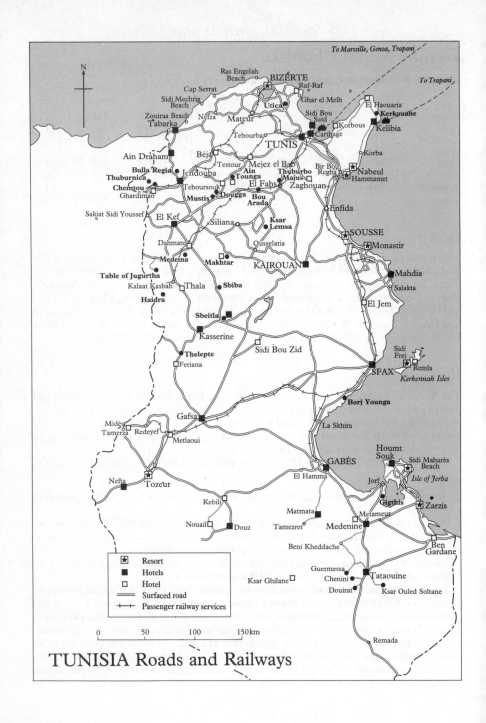

TUNISIA Roads and Railways

By Bus

Travel by bus is very cheap and all the large towns are well served by frequent departures. The Société Nationale de Transport, SNT, runs the majority of services to and from Tunis, stopping at major towns on the way. Local services are coordinated by a network of independent Sociétés Régionales de Transport, SRT, which also run some inter-city services. In the smaller towns both work out of a central bus station, but in Sfax, Tunis and Bizerte they operate separate termini. You have to be persistent in tracking down departure information, for although the SNT usually displays a departure board, there may well be an earlier regional departure to your destination, and you will only find out in the relevant office. Tickets should be bought from the offices before departure.

By *Louage*

One of the joys of independent travel in Tunisia is the network of large Peugeot 504s, known as *louages*, which have been specially adapted to carry five passengers at high velocity across the country. They are slightly more expensive than buses, but get you around more directly, with no waiting at intermediate stops.

Finding the departure point for *louages* can be difficult, and in large towns there may be several stations serving different directions; these locations are listed in the relevant section of the guide.

The name of the town written in red on top of a *louage* does not necessarily indicate its destination. When a tourist approaches, the waiting drivers usually shout their destinations, and once you have settled on a driver ask the price for one seat. If no one approaches you, make your own destination known. You can also negotiate with the drivers to hire them to take you to a specific site, but expect a lengthy discussion and a hefty first price.

By Taxi

There are small local taxis, known as *petits taxis*, which can either be hailed or tracked down at a taxi rank in all major towns. They take three passengers, and are useful for getting out to less crowded beaches and the less accessible Roman sites. Do not worry about the price, as all journeys are metered, and if you have taken a taxi in Europe recently the cheapness will astound you.

If there are more than three of you, there are *grands taxis*, but they are more expensive. Drivers of both small and large taxis are happy to negiotiate a price for your day's sightseeing itinerary, but always fix the price before beginning the tour.

By Car

Car rental in Tunisia is expensive, due to the relative cost of cars. Even the smallest Renault 4 will cost over 300 dn a week, before tax and insurance.

There are only two compelling reasons to hire a car. The first is if you are a 'ruin maniac', and want to visit all the sites in the Tell. Some of these are nowhere near a bus route, but they are all on perfectly negotiable tracks, particularly if you are in the carefree position of driving a rental. The other area in which it is a boon to have a car is in the south, where the bus routes are limited to the large towns, and some of the most interesting places are small, remote hill villages and natural formations.

11

All the big international agencies, Hertz, Avis etc. have offices in the major cities and in the tourist resorts, and compete with local firms. All you need is a licence that you have held for more than a year, though an international licence may be helpful if you are renting away from the tourist areas. Bear in mind that prices are marginally cheaper from local firms in the large resort areas, Hammamet, Sousse and Jerba, than in places that see few tourists. On top of the rental price, there is insurance and a 17% tax, and petrol costs around the same as it does in the UK.

If you are bringing your own car to Tunisia, as well as a valid driving licence you must have your registration document, or *Carte Grise*, and proof of insurance. It is very difficult to find a UK insurer that will cover you for North Africa, but you can get third-party insurance at La Goulette port and at the Algerian border posts.

The roads in Tunisia are generally good and are right-hand drive. Seat belts are not obligatory, almost all signposts are in French and Arabic, and the speed limit is 100 kph on the open road and 50 kph in towns. However, as there are relatively few cars, the population has a much less developed traffic sense. Be extremely careful in towns and villages, as children regularly run straight into the road. It is almost worth avoiding driving at dusk for this reason.

The traffic police do a lot of spot checks, and if you are stopped you should have your passport as well as the car's papers on you. A smile and a single Arabic greeting help avoid fines.

By Bicycle and Motorbike

Tourist hotels in the resorts rent out bicycles and mopeds, but you are not usually allowed to take the mopeds far. If you are bringing your own motor or pedal bike to Tunisia, bring everything you need with you. There are no spare parts, except for mopeds, and not many of those either.

Hitching

In many parts of Tunisia, hitching is an integral part of local transport. On small roads many cars will stop, and payment is only necessary in the Peugeot half-trucks which serve as *taxis rurals*. Women alone or in pairs should be wary.

Maps

All maps of Tunisia have inaccuracies, as much to do with the constantly improving road system as cartographic error. The Tunisian National Tourist Office distributes a free 1:1,000,000 and a 1:800,000 map of Tunisia which is as good as anything you can buy. They also print town plans of Kairouan, Bizerte, Sousse, Hammamet, Nabeul, Monastir and Jerba with varying degrees of accuracy. All other more detailed maps are under the control of the *Direction de la Topographie et de la Cartographie* on Rue de Jordanie, Tunis, and are restricted.

If you want to buy a map before you go, the most useful is the **Michelin Algerie–Tunisie**, no. 172, which has an 1:500,000 enlargement of the region around Tunis. Others include **Hallwag: Algeria–Tunisia** and **Kummerly and Frey Tunisia**.

In London, these can be found at the Travel Bookshop, 13 Blenheim Crescent, London W11; at Stanford's, 12 Long Acre, Covent Garden WC2; or in McCarta's at 122, Kings Cross Road, WC1. In the USA, Forsyth Travel Library, 9154 W. 57th Street, PO Box 2975, Shawnee Mission, KS 66201, lists a wide range of maps in its mail-order catalogue. In Paris, try Itinéraires, 60 Rue Saint Honoré, 75001; L'Astrolabe at 46 Rue de Provence, 75009; or Ulysée, 35 Rue Saint Louis en l'Île, 75004.

Tourist Information

Money

The Tunisian dinar is a soft currency, one whose rate is fixed by its own government at an artificial level and not dealt in on the international exchange. In order to maintain the quoted rate and frustrate any lower prices being offered outside the country, it is strictly illegal to import or export dinars. There is no black market, though hard currency is often happily accepted. In mid 1991 £1 was exchanged for 1.6 Tunisian dinars and US$1 at 1.2 dinars.

Dinars come in notes of 20, 10, 5 and singles, which are increasingly being superseded by a dinar coin. The dinar is broken down into millimes, or thousands, which can cause some initial confusion as 1.5 dn can also be written as 1500 ml. Small change includes silver half-dinar coins and brass 100, 50, 20 millimes, and the light, almost worthless aluminium 5 millimes.

You can bring in and take out as much hard currency as you like. Major European currencies are all acknowleged but US dollars remain the number one. In every big city or resort hotel, travel agents and the smarter shops accept credit cards and there are facilities for changing traveller's and Eurocheques. But off the tourist trail, even in large provincial towns, you will find banks distinctly reluctant to change anything other than cash.

In banks, you can cash up to 175 dn on each Eurocheque. Bear in mind that you can only cash back a third of the dinars that you can prove to have brought. So if, miracle of miracles, you spend fewer dinars than you thought on your holiday, you will need to have kept your exchange slips.

Opening Hours

There are no standard opening hours in Tunisia, though you can expect the bigger department stores to stick quite close to a 08.00–12.00 and 15.00–19.00 timetable.

Banks

Tunisian banks have their own working hours, with different winter, summer, Ramadan and Friday schedules. They are closed over the weekend, though in major tourist areas there is a rota, notified by a photocopied sheet stuck on the front door, which keeps one bank open from 08.00–12.00 on Saturday mornings.

Summer officially begins on 1 July and ends in the middle of September, when banks are open Mon–Fri, 08.00–11.00. In winter, hours are Mon–Thurs, 08.00–11.00 and 14.00–16.15, Fri, 08.00–11.00 and 13.30–15.15. Over Ramadan the hours change again, and the banks are open Mon–Fri, 08.00–11.30 and 13.00–14.30.

Post Offices

The Post Office is known in Tunisia as the PTT which stands for Poste, Téléphone, Télégraph. It is well distributed, usually in imposing modernist blocks in the centre of town and easy to spot. They are open for business Mon–Fri, in summer from 08.00–13.00, in winter from 08.00–12.00 and 15.00–18.00, and on Sat from 08.00–12.00. Over Ramadan, hours are 08.00–15.00.

Stamps are also sold by newsagents, postcard booths and tobacconists. Post boxes are small and yellow, and letters to the UK usually arrive within a week.

For receiving mail the most reliable PTT is at Tunis, and letters should be addressed clearly to Tunis R.P, Rue Charles de Gaulle, Tunis. Get people to write your surname in block capitals, since in Islamic countries the surname goes first, and there may be some filing confusion.

Telephone calls are much cheaper from a PTT office than a hotel, but are often housed in a separate office or nearby building. From the larger PTT you can dial direct, feeding 1 dn coins into your machine. In others a switchboard does the dialling and you pay at the end of your call.

The international code is 00, followed by 44 for Britain, 1 for the USA and Canada, 46 for Sweden, 37 for Germany, 47 for Norway and 45 for Denmark, remembering to leave out any initial 0s in the town codes.

Local pay phones take 100 ml coins, and the area codes are 01 for Tunis, 02 for the North and Cap Bon, 03 for Sousse to Mahdia, 04 for Sfax, 05 for Gabès and Jerba, 06 for Gafsa, 07 for Kairouan and 08 for El Kef.

Museums and Sites

In theory these are open from Tues to Sun, 09.00–12.00 and 14.00–17.30 in winter, and 15.00–18.30 in summer. Most are closed on Mon, and sometimes in the afternoon on Sun, Tues, Fri, and on Muslim and public holidays.

Admission and permission to photograph are granted on separate tickets, but to use a tripod or flash you may need the permission of the Institut National d'Archéologie et Arts, in Tunis medina. Only the most important sites have tickets and fences, the lesser sites having a resident guardian but no entrance charge. Here you are free to wander in any time during daylight.

Mosques

According to a 1972 law, a non-Muslim is allowed to enter any mosque in Tunisia but not to proceed into the prayer hall. In practice you will find that you are only welcome in the inner courtyard of the big four ancient mosques of architectural interest, the Great Mosque of Kairouan, the Zitouna in Tunis, and the Great Mosques of Sousse and Mahdia; the rest are quite firmly closed to tourists.

Some of the tombs of saints and old religious colleges, known as zaouia and medersa, have been converted into museums and to these you are, of course, welcome. But for those that are still in use or have been converted to a modern secular use, you should not enter without a local escort. A modicum of interest and polite enquiry are often enough to guarantee you a complete tour and a cup or two of tea.

Embassies and Consulates

All embassies and consulates are in Tunis, at:

Great Britain: 5 Pl de la Victoire, tel (01) 245100.
France: Pl de l'Indépendance; the consulate entrance is 1 Rue de Hollande, tel (01) 245700.
Canada: 3 Rue Didon, tel (01) 286577.
Holland: 6 Rue Meycen, tel (01) 287455.
USA: 144 Av de la Liberté, tel (01) 282566.

14

Belgium: 47 Rue du 1er Juin, tel (01) 282650.
Sweden: 87 Av Taieb Mehri, tel (01) 283433.
Norway: 7 Av Habib Bourguiba, tel (01) 245933.
Algeria: 136 Av de la Liberté, tel (01) 280082.
Egypt: 16 Rue Essayouti, tel (01) 230004.
Morocco: 39 Rue du 1er Juin.
Libya: 48 Rue du 1er Juin.

Police and Other Uniforms

The Tunisian police force is modelled on the French, with twin forces, both armed, under the direction of the Ministry of Interior. The police proper dress in blue-grey uniforms with leather belts, and the 4000 strong Gendarmerie concerned with state security wear khaki. The most conspicuous branch of the police are the traffic cops, the Police de Circulation, who wear white cuffs and caps.

The Customs service in their light grey uniforms can be spotted at harbours, airports and border posts. There are 7000 National Guards, the 'anti-tourists', who turn up at the most isolated beaches, tracts of desert and mountain tops, and have the slightly irritating habit of rushing off with your passport to radio details to their headquarters.

Other rarer uniforms include helmeted military police who guard the barracks of the 30,000 part-conscript army, the blue of the 3000-strong navy at their base outside Bizerte and about the same number of air force grey. The smallest numerical group, but on conspicuous display as conclusive evidence of modernism, is the small corps of women police in Tunis.

Tipping

Tipping practice is similar to Europe. Taxi drivers, waiters and hairdressers should be given 10–15%. The only extras are the odd 100 ml to barmen, petrol pump attendants and car guardians. If you have been given a present, invited in for tea or a meal, rather than sullying the generosity by proffering money, reciprocate with a present when you return home.

Alms and Beggars

Compared to Morocco and Egypt, there are very few beggars in Tunisia, which befits the country's relative prosperity and disciplined civic spirit. In city centres, at bus stops and after the midday Friday prayers, you will see Tunisians giving alms to the less fortunate. One hundred to 300 millimes is standard practice, but the Koran gives the best counsel. The prophet Mohammed was always being badgered by the question, 'What shall we bestow in alms?' and replied, 'What you can spare. For thus does God instruct that you might think more deeply . . . but if you turn away from them, while you yourself hope for help from God, at least speak to them in a kindly manner.'

Guides

Apart from Kairouan, where the commission on bringing a tourist to buy a carpet is irresistible in a town of chronic unemployment, there are practically no guides, touts or hasslers in Tunisia. Many Tunisian men will go out of the way to show you where to go, if you ask, but then depart with a handshake and not so much as a thought for a reward. Only at the

15

Roman ruins of Carthage, Dougga, Sbeitla and Thuburbo Majus will you find a few prospective guides-cum-coin-sellers, who can either be politely shaken off or employed. In the rest of the country the most you can expect is a little enticing salesmanship as you walk through the souks of Tunis, Sousse or Sfax.

In minor sites throughout the country you may be escorted by the official guardian, whose job it is to check that you do not take any illicit photographs or pinch anything. They will very rarely accept tips. Only the tourist office in Kairouan is in a position to offer guided tours.

Kif

Tunisia's drug habits are again in contrast to the rest of North Africa. In Egypt, southern Algeria and Morocco the smoking of cannabis, or *kif*, is deeply rooted in popular culture. Before the introduction of tobacco in the 18th century, this was also true of Tunisia, but under both the French colonial regime and since independence it has been illegal, and driven underground. There it remains, as a discreet, illegal and private habit that is publicly invisible. There are strong punishments for dealing and possession, though inevitably in the big cities and tourist resorts market forces are at work. Despite Tunisia's proximity to France and Sicily, opiates are unknown.

Lavatories

There are no public lavatories in Tunisia. Urban cafés and houses have a crouch hole, no paper, a bottle for sluicing and a tap for washing with your left hand. Elsewhere, harbour walls, rocks, dung heaps and ruins are freely used. Anglo-Saxon flush bowls are found in hotels, licensed restaurants, airports and trains. These are in no way indigenous, and in all but specifically tourist hotels the 'rat trap' plastic seat can never be persuaded to stand up, the plumbing leaks, and odours and insufficient flushing power are common. Unless you are in the middle of an attack of the runs, it is sensible and cheaper to choose a bedroom without a WC and use the public loo down the corridor.

Electricity and Gas

A 220 volts AC system has now almost completely replaced the old 110 volt AC. Machinery that operates on the British 240 volt AC is quite happy on 220, but dies if plugged into the 110. There is rumoured to be some of this voltage still in Tunis, but it is hard to find.

On or off the grid, cooking is rarely electric, but done on charcoal or gas. The 13-kg bottles of government-subsidized Bottogas, Agipgas and Primagas are available throughout the country.

Cameras

Tunisians are genuinely surprised to see a tourist without a camera, and no visit to any house is complete without an hour or two pouring over football, summer hols, circumcision and especially marriage snaps. It is, of course, insufferable to photograph anybody, particularly a rural lady, without permission. Do not go anywhere near anything remotely military, which includes airfields, with a camera. The Tunisian sense of national security appears absurdly fragile.

Reliable filmstock can be bought and developed in most towns, but do not expect to find fast film, or a selection of black and white.

Health, Chemists and Medicine

Next to baby talk, one of the easiest ways to start a conversation and win friends in Tunisia is to have a health problem. Health, medicine and herbal or thermal cures and regimes seem to touch some deep national obsession. Pharmacists are knowledgeable and respected, their shops well stocked and busy. Always French-speaking, rarely English-, they can recommend a good local doctor for problems beyond their remit. Unlike their English counterparts they will prescribe drugs for common complaints—runny tummy, flu, sore throats—themselves, and also sell Immodium, Tampax, condoms known as 'Chapeaux Americains' and some brands of contraceptive pills, 'La Pilule'. Remember that in bad cases of diarrhoea the pill loses its effectiveness. Loo paper, soaps, scents and shampoo are all found in general stores.

No inoculations are required when travelling to Tunisia though for peace of mind your typhoid, cholera, tetanus and polio immunization should be up to date, and you could talk to your doctor about the pros and cons of a hepatitis jab if you are spending long in the south.

What is worth while is a travel insurance policy which can be bought in Britain from banks, travel agents and airports, and costs under $20 for a month's cover, which includes repatriation costs.

Sex

For a lot of tourists, both male and female, romance and sex are a vital ingredient of a good holiday. The example set by tourists in the past, and by many of the Western films shown in Tunisia, means that you will not be able to avoid propositions. Understanding something of the Muslim attitude to sex may not stop them, but it will hopefully reduce the irritation caused to many women.

Islam, until this century, has always had a more liberal sexual ethic than the Judaeo-Christian cultures. It never diminished female sexuality or created an image of women as pure asexual beings. In fact, quite the opposite. According to one anthropologist, 'the conception of woman as a lust-driven animal that must be kept under lock and key is one of the sickest and most disgusting aspects of Arab culture'. This vision of womankind helps to explain the strict segregation of Muslim women enforced by their menfolk. The honour of women, judged by their modesty and virginity at marriage, is a vital concern to the family and they are protected from themselves by their separation from strange men.

This unbridgeable division between the sexes is perhaps the most remarkable feature of Muslim societies. Young children scamper around as free as the birds, but as adolescence approaches a rigid social separation appears. Though you will see many women in the street they are usually only hurrying from home to their place of work. Public spaces, the markets, streets and cafés are a male domain, and most Tunisian women intrude only when 'invisible', covered by a large sheet known as a *haik*. Without this article, a woman in a public space is considered to have little modesty and possibly no honour.

For this treatment of women, there is sanction in the Koran. Sura 414 declares, 'God desireth to make your [women's] burden light, for men have been created wiser ... men are superior to women.' Elsewhere is the prayer, 'Blessed art thou, O Lord God, who hath not made me a woman.' These might be interpreted gnostically, but male Arab attitudes are less equivocal.

17

On top of that, in contrast to the asceticsm of Jesus, the prophet Mohammed was a sexual athlete of the first order. Arab men cannot hope to equal his performance, but they are firmly convinced that they are immeasurably more resilient lovers than European men. If the confessions of the French author André Gide's first night of homosexual love or those of the prostitutes of Earls Court are anything to go by, there may be some truth in this belief. Nor does a Muslim suffer from a confused and guilt-laden sexuality. The Koran cautions against celibacy—'as to the monastic life they invented it themselves . . . many of them were perverse', and freely acknowledges sexual appetite—'your wives are your field . . . go in therefore to your field as you will, but first do some act for your soul's good.' It is only mildly disapproving of homosexuality—'come ye to men instead of women lustfully. You are indeed a people given up to excess.'

So what does this all mean for a traveller? You are in Tunisia, and are bound, at some level, to be judged by the standards of that society. If you flout convention by, for example, appearing scantily dressed in public, it immediately suggests loose morals, and you may well be put to some fondling test. Although some leeway in behaviour is given to Western women, this is counteracted by the Muslim perception of our promiscuity. Playing one of the recognized 'unavailable' roles—the wife, the mother, the stern intellectual teacher—may help. A firm but immediate slap is more effective, but do not expect to be thanked for it.

For their part, foreign men should be wary of talking to Tunisian women alone, not out of fear for themselves but because of the complications it can cause the ladies. A single man is also likely to receive a number of homosexual propositions. These are easily brushed aside or consummated.

Without being too cynical, bear in mind that either as a man or a woman your greatest attraction is your ability to provide a foreign passport through marriage. This small book assures a lifetime of easy travel and opportunities for well-paid work, neither of which are at all certain for the average Tunisian.

Time

Tunisia is one hour ahead of GMT, so in the summer there is no need to change your watch.

Public Holidays

Since independence a secular calendar of public holidays has been created. This has been part of a conscious attempt to wean the population away from their pure religious loyalty and forge a new nationalism and political consciousness. For visitors, they provide little entertainment, being state-directed, with a profusion of bunting, speeches, presentations and parades, but they will interrupt shopping hours and services. The dates are:

1 January	Beginning of the Gregorian year
18 January	Anniversary of the Revolution
20–21 March	Independence Day, followed by Youth Day
9 April	Martyrs' Day
1 May	International Labour Day
1 June	National Day
13 July	Women's Day
25 July	Day of the Republic
7 November	Anniversary of the Events of 1987

Ramadan and Other Muslim Holidays

The main event of the Islamic year is Ramadan, a month of fasting. Unlike the Christian Lent it has remained a great institution and is cherished as an act that binds all Islam together in a month of asceticism. Apart from the sick, travellers, children and pregnant women who are all excused, Ramadan involves abstaining from food, sex, drink and cigarettes during the hours of daylight.

Non-Muslims are not involved, but outside the resorts you will find many cafés, bars and licensed grocers closed. It is obviously insensitive to smoke, eat or drink in public and more rewarding to join Ramadan as a quiet volunteer, sharing the exuberance at dusk when the fast ends with a bowl of soup and the streets explode into life. A wave of relief, and often music, breaks out and continues deep into the night.

Ramadan has an added poignancy in Tunisia, as an annual assertion of the power and importance of tradition. President Bourguiba, aware that little work was done over the fast, attempted one year to cancel it. The people, led by the city of Kairouan, quietly persisted and he backed down in the face of universal opposition.

The end of Ramadan is celebrated with a feast called Aid es Seghir. The feast of Aid el Kebir commemorates Abraham's sacrifice of a lamb instead of his son and like the English Christmas is a great excuse for family reunions. Muharram is the feast of the Muslim New Year and Mouloud, celebrated with fire crackers, is the Prophet's birthday.

The Muslim Calendar
The Muslim calendar is based on a lunar rather than a solar cycle, and has years of 354 or 355 days. In practice this means that each year the Muslim calendar starts 10 or 11 days earlier than our solar Gregorian calendar. The Muslim equivalent of year 1 took place when Mohammed left Mecca for Medina 1411 years ago, a journey known as the Hegira (hence [a.h.] rather than [a.d.]).

	1991/1411	1992/1412
Ramadan	18 March	7 March
Aid es Seghir	17 April	6 April
Aid el Kebir	24 June	13 June
Muharram	13 July	2 July
Mouloud	13 Oct	2 Oct

The 11-day calculation is not a hard and fast rule, as Muslim leap years are common. In a 30-year period there are 19 years with 354 days, and 11 years with 355 days. In other ways the calendars are similar, for both follow the Babylonian tradition of dividing the year into twelve months, originally based on the 12 stations of the zodiac with weeks of seven days based on the seven planets of the solar system. Because of the 11-day yearly shift however, the Muslim months have not got our consistent seasonal association.

The year starts with the month of Muharram (30 days), then Saphar (29 days), Rabia (30 days), Rabia II (29 days), Gamada I (30 days), Gamada II (29 days), Rajab (30 days), Shaaban (29 days), Ramadan (30 days), Shawwal (29 days), Dhulkaada (30 days) and ends with Dhulheggia (29 or 30 days).

Festivals

As well as the national holidays and Muslim feast days, there are local festivals which are largely held in July and August. Most have genuine local origins, though they are increasingly being directed at the tourist market:

Date	Place	Festival
April	Nabeul	Festival of Oranges
May/June	El Haouaria	Falconry Festival
June	Testour	Festival of Malouf Music
July	Tabarka	Coral Festival
July/August	Sousse	Festival of Theatre and Music
July/August	Dougga	Festival of Classical Theatre
July/August	Kerkennah	Folklore Festival
July/August	Hammamet	International Cultural Festival
July/August	Carthage	International Cultural Festival
July/August	Jerba	Folklore Festival
July/August	Tabarka	International Cultural Festival
July/August	Gabès	Festival of Sidi Boulbaba
3 August	Monastir	Theatre and Poetry Festival
August	Sousse	Festival of Baba Aoussou
August	Sidi Bou Said	Kharja Celebrations
October (biennial)	Carthage	Cinema of the Third World
December/January	Tozeur Oasis	Folklore Festival
December/January	Douz	National Saharan Festival

The Falconry festival in El Haouaria is unusual, and takes place in spectacular natural scenery. To see a play performed (in French) in Dougga's ancient theatre is a must if you are nearby, and the Hammamet and Douz festivals are also worth a detour.

Newspapers, Cinema and Television

European newspapers are sold in the central avenue in Tunis, and at Hammamet, Nabeul, Sousse and Jerba, at least a day after publication. As literate Tunisia is almost totally bilingual, there are three French language dailies and two Arabic. The French ones, *La Presse*, *L'Action* and *Le Temps* all tow the party line and follow world events. *Le Temps* is useful for its listings of cultural events and a daily timetable of planes, boats, trains and express buses leaving Tunis, as well as advertisements for restaurants, weekend specials, nightclubs, villas and flats for rent.

In addition, there are two good weekly magazines, *La Maghreb* and *Jeune Afrique* which follow a *Time/Newsweek* format and have gained credibility by being occasionally banned by the government.

There is a wide choice of radio stations to pick from, so you can arbitrarily switch from Egyptian music, to pop from Radio Monte Carlo, to catch the BBC's World Service on 15.07 Mhz or 19.91 m.

Tunisian television is not good. It is a mixture of painful Egyptian soaps, football matches, badly dubbed films and a home-produced news programme, 'Téléjournal', which daily shows what the President has been up to. It has recently been outflanked in the north by Italian channels which can be picked up, and throughout the country by the French channel Antenne 2. When no important football match is on, Antenne 2 is watched by all.

There is little temptation outside of a rainstorm to visit a cinema in Tunisia, though different attitudes to humour, violence and romance always make foreign audiences a fascinating study. In Tunis you can usually find one or two good French language films, particularly at the cinema in the Hotel Africa. General releases in Tunisia fall into three types: violence either by an American rogue cop or an Asian martial artist, Indian/Egyptian saccharine romance and adolescent porn, on the lines of *Porky's IV* or *Confessions* movies.

Sports

As a conversational ploy, **football** hardly ever fails to attract an enthusiastic response. Tunisia has its own football league and the national and city teams compete in a plethora of international competitions, including the World Cup and various Mediterranean, Maghreb, Arab and African leagues. All over the country organized matches kick off at 13.00 on Sunday afternoon. Most large hotels have their own pitch, and organize regular games, including staff vs visitor matches. These resort hotels also have a wide range of water and other sports to occupy their guests.

Resort Sports

Hammamet, Monastir and Port el Kantaoui all have **golf** courses, and another is being built at Tabarka. Most large hotels have a selection of **tennis** courts, **volleyball** pitches, **basketball** courts and **crazy-golf** courses. Nearby, there will also be facilities for **riding** donkeys, camels and horses.

At Hammamet and Nabeul, Port el Kantaoui, Sousse, Monastir and Jerba, the beaches are littered with equipment for **windsurfing**, **water-skiing** and **para-gliding**. For the more sedate there are pedalos and the sea itself to swim in. Compared to the water of Italy and Spain, it appears delightfully clean, safe and invigorating.

Boar Hunting

Boar hunting takes place in the winter in the hilly areas of Tunisia, but requires several months' advanced planning. Hunting parties use the Cilium Hotel at Kasserine, the Sicca Veneria at El Kef, and the Hotel Morjane at Tabarka, though Les Chênes Hotel at Ain Draham is undoubtedly the most popular. You can either contact them direct, or go through the Tunisian National Tourist Board in your country.

Camel Treks

For a first taste of the camel's back, away from a beach resort, Nefta and Tozeur in the Jerid are convenient bases. The Tourist Offices run trips from an hour to several days. However, the more intrepid and cheaper possibilities tend to run from Douz and Ksar Metameur. You can ride for several days from well to well, pitching your own tents and cooking on camp fires with responsible guides, or ride from one ruined hill fortress to the next, camping in grain stores. More information can be found in the body of the guide.

21

Fishing

There is no river fishing in Tunisia, but plenty of fish in the sea. No permit is required for fishing from a boat or with a line, and in every harbour there are fishermen to give advice or negotiate a day's chartering. At Kerkennah, where no one does anything much else, a lazy day in a boat is a must.

Hang Gliding

The Federal Gliding Centre at Jebel Ressas, outside Tunis, has instructors and equipment. Telephone (01) 906712 or (01) 255762 for more information.

Hill Walking

There are no mountains in Tunisia to lure serious climbers, but Zaghouan, Kasserine, Ain Draham and El Kef all make convenient centres for some spirited hill walking.

Sand Yachting

A club has recently been established on the Chott el Jerid, 60 km from Tozeur on the road to Kebili. For information, call the Hotel Jerid in Tozeur, on (06) 50488.

Snorkelling and Scuba Diving

The Mediterranean coastal waters off North Africa are in a much healthier state than off Europe, and as a result the reefs and marine life are colourful and exotic. It is well worth bringing a snorkel with you and hunting out rocky pockets of coastline for an absorbing few hours. The best place for both learners and accomplished scuba divers is Tabarka on the north coast. An ancient centre of the coral trade, it now has a highly professional diving club which you will find detailed in the Tabarka section.

Shopping

Souks

At the heart of a traditional North African town lies the market quarter known as the souk, a buzzing network of covered alleyways and narrow streets, lined with shops selling vegetables in one area, spices in another, blankets here and cosmetics there. Even with no intention of buying, to wander through these traditional quarters is an absorbing occupation, dodging between barrows of vegetables, identifying strange, long-familiar smells and marvelling at the tottering piles of olives, herbs and henna.

Bargaining

To enter into the spirit of the souk you must learn the art of bargaining, an amusing process as long as you take your time and keep your head. It involves a mixture of praise for the goods and the salesman, and veiled aggression in pursuit of the right price.

Above all, do not be swayed by free cups of tea or coffee, or by salesmanship: decide exactly what you want, and how much you would be willing to pay for it. Praise the other objects in the shop first before ending up with your chosen object. If there are two of you, one should feign disinterest and mild dislike for the object. Delay quoting your first price for as long as possible

Perfume Seller

and then do not weaken or the price will be ratcheted away to dizzy heights with mutual drops from him and advances from you. However well you think you are doing, look crestfallen; and it is in the highest order of gamesmanship to praise the salesman's ruthless bargaining skills when clinching a highly advantageous deal.

Rural Souks
Throughout Tunisia, both in large towns and tiny rural communities, one day a week is market day. The more remote the area, the more socially important the market. In the least populated areas, these get-togethers are still held in empty fields in the middle of the countryside, known by the day on which the souk takes place. Travelling past a sign to *Souk el Jemma* on a Friday, you should stop and take a look. Sunday markets are known as *El Had*, the first, Monday the second, *El Tnine*, and so on through the week: Tuesday *El Tleta*, Wednesday *El Arba*, Thursday *El Khemis* and Saturday *Es Sebt*. Merchandise includes everything from hollow sheeps' horn finger-muffs for olive picking to blue Chinese Mao suits.

Crafts

The Tunisian government has established a network of shops selling craftwork to tourists under the banner of the Office Nationale de l'Artisanat Tunisien (ONAT). These prominent spaces have all the atmosphere of a supermarket, quite failing to evoke any of the intimate, localized atmosphere which is at least half the charm of handicraft buying. Prices are displayed in the ONAT so there is no bargaining. Use it for establishing your maximum price before venturing out into the souks or workshops where, whatever you pay, your object will at least come home loaded with associations. Buying from a production area also means greater quality and choice.

Camels

On your flight back from Tunisia there will be more camels on board than people. Like a nightmare they cascade from the overhead lockers, poke their heads out from behind every seat and duty-free bag. Their pesky nylon begins to look mighty forlorn by Gatwick, so think long and hard before you buy one.

Carpets, Killims and Mergoums

Throughout the world there are carpets and killims and some confusion over which is what and what is which. Carpets are expensive and last longer as they are composed of thousands of separate knotted strands. Killims are cheaper as they are woven, though the difference in price and look is confused by embroidering over a killim which, in Tunisia, produces something known as a mergoum.

Carpets

Tunisian carpets were first mentioned in the 14th century, being exported to Venice by Ahmad ibn Maliki, a trader in Tripoli and Jerba. From the 15th century there was also an equal trade in raw silk and wool to the new carpet-manufacturing centre of Lyon.

Tunisian carpet manufacture, once in the hands of individuals, is now controlled by the ONAT who have produced a number of uninspiring standard patterns, based on adaptations of traditional tribal specimens and Persian carpets. The majority of these carpets, recognizable by their white or light background against which warm-coloured lozenges are offset, are known as 'Berber' with some added regional name like Dougga or Sbeitla. This refers to the pattern only and has nothing to do with its place of manufacture. The carpet salesmen's patter has the same relationship to the product as the term 'Highland' does to most shortbread. Popular romantic selling notions include 'nomad' or 'Touareg', but do not believe a word of it.

Carpets are valued and given a government tag according to the number of knots tied per square metre. Whereas the finest Persian carpets may have 1200 knots per square inch, those of Tunisia rarely exceed 50. On the international market they are of little esteem. Buy Tunisian carpets for your own pleasure, as back in Britain you will get back only a fraction of what you paid for them. As a general guideline, the firmer the pile, the thinner the thread and the sharper the definition of the pattern, the more knots, which means the carpet will last longer and cost more. When you see women knotting carpets in the factories, you appreciate the labour that goes into producing even the smallest piece.

Killims and Mergoums

Tunisia's traditional killims remain in the unorganized, erratic, individual state that first attracted the 19th-century buyers of Kairouan carpets, though even these are getting increasingly rare. They are characterized by geometrical motifs, lines broken by diamonds, lozenges and zigzags. In mergoums, these details are set off and developed by overstitching, often with added tassels and sequins. The ONAT has developed its own line in mergoum, a rigid, one-colour lozenge grid with not a breath of individuality, picked out by a black and white stitch pattern that resembles long roles of film.

In the south of the country, centred on Gafsa, there was a tradition of pictorial weaving. This has been developed and codified by the ONAT into cartoon images of humans and animals in bright colours arranged on a background of squares. As well as these lifeless pictograms, they have increased their repertoire with woven killims with scenes from Muslim legends, used in 19th-century glass paintings, designs from Roman mosaics and contemporary desert landscapes.

All tourist carpet shops contain the same ONAT selection but do often keep odd piles of traditional killims for you to look through. The best places to shop for these are specifically detailed in the guide, in Tunis, Sfax, El Jem, Foum Tataouine and Tozeur.

Ceramics

Tunisian ceramics range from the modelled Sejnane figures, natural terracotta amphora, through sets of traditional Moorish wall tiles, a southern tradition for half-green and yellow ceramic (a colour combination supposedly derived from the palm tree—green for the leaves, and yellow for the date) to imitations of Chinese and European plates. They are all widely distributed thoughout the country.

If you want to go to working potteries, visit Nabeul, Moknine or Jerba. For wall tiles, Nabeul is the place; for plain terracotta, Jerba, with its new line in magic camel jugs. The water goes in, the camel is inverted but the water remains. For more details on the pottery tradition look in the Art and Architecture section.

Clothes

The most tempting clothes to buy in Tunisia are second-hand children's suits of embroidered velvet, which were traditionally worn on the day of circumcision. In the same shops, adult waistcoats and bustiers covered with sequins, amusing for dressing up, are sold. You may also be tempted by the local everyday clothing, brown burnous coats and jellabas for men. Tunis, and specifically the Souk des Chechias, is the best place to buy the traditional red felt hats worn by most Tunisian men. With an eye to the tourist trade, they can now be found in a range of bright turquoises, pinks, yellows and greens.

Coins and Antiquities

These are the preserve of hawkers, often disarmingly small children, who find you at every Roman site. Complete oil lamps and terracotta statues are without exception fakes, bought in large quantities from factories. The same applies to many of the coins, though at all the sites you may be offered originals. Most of the fakes are easy to spot, over-large, over-detailed in gleaming modern metal. Look closely at a fake and you will see small bubbles left by the casting process. Real coins, now as then, were stamped, leaving no such traces. Silver Roman coins are rare, bronze ones quite common. In parts of Algeria they remained legal tender well into the 19th century. The genuine ones are likely to be small bronze denominations, green in colour from the 4th century AD with the stamp often offset from a perfect circle.

Contemporary Art

If you are interested in modern art, there are a number of galleries which regularly exhibit and sell works by modern Tunisian painters and sculptors. The majority of these are in Tunis, and amongst the best are:

Galerie Yahia, 1 Av de Carthage, Tunis
Espace Alif, 20 bis Rue de Yougoslavie, Tunis
Galerie de l'Information, Pl de l'Indépendance, Tunis
Galerie Ammar Farhat, 3 Rue Sidi el Ghimrim, Sidi Bou Said
Galerie Sophonisbe, Carthage Dermech, Carthage
Galerie at 21 Souk el Kaid, Sousse

Food and Picnics

Olive oil in Tunisia costs 1.5 dn a litre, and can either be bought early in the year direct from the presses or from Monoprix supermarkets. Monoprix is also the place to head for provisions for picnics. They sell cheese, tuna fish and mineral water, which can be supplemented with tomatoes and cucumbers from the markets. Crusty French bread is best brought direct from the bakers. You can usually smell them a mile off. Taking home a tube or jar of harissa guarantees you a culinary souvenir of Tunisia, and Tunisian saffron is also good value.

Fossils and Minerals

Down in the south of Tunisia, you will be offered tempting selections of crystals, minerals and fossils at prices it is hard to resist. The most distinctive minerals, the *Roses du Sahara*, are made of crystallized gypsum dug out of beds of sandy local clay or, as the salesmen like to hint, from the heart of sand dunes. If you walk up any southern river beds, you will see rock seams made of fossilized crustaceans. Just after the rains, smaller pieces, individual fossils and many minerals, lie in the muddy river beds, waiting to be taken home as souvenirs.

Jewellery

Jewellery making was traditionally the preserve of Tunisia's Jewish population, but the skill survives despite the emigration of the majority of craftsmen to Israel. It is still advisable to buy in the old Jewish areas, like Tunis and Houmt Souk on the Isle of Jerba. Two of the most popular designs bring the wearer good luck. The fish is originally derived from that harbinger of fertility and hence luck, the phallus, and to Tunisians a group of five fishes is particularly lucky. Fish shapes are painted on houses, and sewn into clothes, particularly wedding dresses.

The Hand of Fatimah, *muchta*, wards off evil spirits. Fatimah was the favourite daughter of the Prophet Mohammed, and her stylized palm, its five fingers outstretched, is worn by women throughout the Muslim world. In fact, it has an even older history and must be one of the most frequently produced images in the world. In museums you will see headdresses decorated with scores of them.

Some of the best native Berber jewellery is sold opposite the entrance to the amphitheatre at El Jem. If you do not manage to agree on a reasonable price there, at least you will known what standard you should aim to find.

Leather

Everywhere you turn, you are assailed by cascades of leather goods. In tourist-frequented towns this needs to be checked carefully. If you come across a genuine craftsman elsewhere, his saddles, belts, leads and killim handbags will be found sturdy and fashionable even when you get them home.

Metalwork

The tap-tap-tap of chisels on brass is a familiar sound in the souk. Small boys are accomplished in the art of putting camels and palm trees on ashtrays and plates almost before they can walk. Many do an individual service, applying your and your friends' names to the metal which make original and useful presents. Just watch to make sure the spelling is going right, and perhaps try to cut down on camels and go for something more geometric.

The community in Sidi Bou Said have adapted their metalworking skill, which shows in the profusion of window grills, into a useful little earner. Their plain and white-painted birdcages are sold throughout Tunisia, and are hard to resist. Be warned that they do not fit in the luggage rack of any aircraft.

Wood

As you will see when you walk past carpenters, modern standards of furniture-making in Tunisia are remarkably low. The exception to this is carved olive wood, turned into bowls, spoons, chess boards, boxes and sculptures. As you would expect, Sfax, the capital of the olive oil business, has the greatest selection. When buying, always check that the knots in the piece are not cracked.

Where to Stay

Hotels

The Tunisian National Tourist Board awards all tourist hotels stars, between 1* and 4****
Luxe, but the criteria for these awards are so mysterious that it is best to ignore them altogether. Instead, this guide classifies hotels as:

EXPENSIVE from 30dn to 150 dn a double, bed and breakfast, in summer
MODERATE between 15 dn and 30 dn a double, bed and breakfast, in summer
CHEAP less than 15 dn a double in summer

Between October and May, prices are considerably lower.

The recommendations tend to be hotels used by discerning French or the Tunisians, where size and character are more important than clinical plumbing. They are often old colonial establishments whose architecture, situation, atmosphere and staff make them more enjoyable than a state-of-the-art modern deluxe. Where expensive hotels are recomended, unless a price is quoted they tend to be at the bottom end of the price range.

Because of the prevalence of package tourism, small hotels with character are few and far between, especially on the coast. Below the starred hotels are a number of *pensions familiales*, often the best bet for independent travellers. Prices in these are around 8 dn per person. They are usually small, with immaculate rooms and friendly proprietors. Non-classified hotels range from charming forgotten establishments in the interior to little more than knocking shops in the city centres, which women alone should certainly avoid. You pay upwards of 5 dn a person in these. Remember that in establishments where you pay for a bed, usually around 3 dn, you may find yourself sharing a room.

Even in the popular resorts in the height of summer, it is very rare not to find a bed. Should you be unlucky enough not to, Tunisian hospitality is such that it is hard to imagine not being offered a bed somewhere by someone.

Campsites

There are suprisingly few official campsites in Tunisia, but you are free to pitch your tent or doss down in most places, though it is wise to inform the police. The only places where the practice is frowned upon is on the major resort beaches, but at Nabeul there is a campsite and in Sousse there are several cheap and clean medina hotels to choose from. Inland, it is both the law and good manners to seek out the local land owner and ask his permission to camp.

Average charges in official campsites are 1 dn a person, 2 dn for a caravan and 1 dn for a car. If you are a connoisseur, there is one campsite you should not miss. In Degache, the local police chief has a palm-shaded haven on the edge of the oasis, where you camp amongst fruit trees and vegetable gardens.

Eating Out

Tunisian cooking is based on a small traditional repertoire in which harissa, a hot red pepper and olive oil sauce, plays a dominant role. Finding good, honest Tunisian cooking outside of a home is difficult and most of the tourist-orientated restaurants serve bland versions of traditional cuisine or a mish-mash of international dishes. In the licensed restaurants, French and Italian cooking are as dominant as Tunisian, and the basic ingredients, particularly fish, are exquisitely fresh. However, if you are not yet in the habit of double-checking restaurant bills, start in Tunisia. Mistakes in addition are common, rarely in the customer's favour, but seldom seem to embarrass or upset the management. **Throughout the guide we give prices for a three-course meal for two, with wine, in licensed restaurants, which tend to be between 15 dn and 20 dn.**

Eating in local restaurants, *gargottes*, is both cheap and satisfying, though they are not places to spin out a meal for much over half an hour. **Prices for these are quoted per head, and a three-course meal can be as little as 1.5 dn.** The restaurant might stock mineral water but will never have a licence. Alternatively, eat on the hoof, picking out snacks from sandwich barrows, patisseries and grill-cafés which cluster around bus stations and along the main street in every town.

The place to stretch out a meal over an hour or so, enjoying both good food, wine and tablecloths, is at local licensed restaurants. The best of these are on the coast, offering mouth-watering squid and prawns cooked in garlic, and you can rely on fresh fish plainly grilled on charcoal and served with chips and a salad. This is not freezer and microwave land, and restaurants pride themselves on elegant arrays of the freshest catch which naturally change with the season. Fish is reasonably expensive and usually sold by the 100 g. It is wise to check on the price before eating, when evidence of weight has disappeared.

Vegetarians

As in all countries where meat is an expensive luxury, vegetarians will find it difficult to make their position understood. It is almost inconceivable to a Tunisian that anybody who is relatively rich, like a foreigner, would forego meat on principle. A lot of dishes which sound as if they contain not a jot of meat will be garnished, for your benefit, with a nice chunk of mutton or chicken. The only advice is to make your distaste for meat abundantly clear. There are salads on every menu, and most cheaper restaurants have a pot of spicy tomato and chickpeas or haricot beans constantly on the fire. The one dish that people seem to be happy to serve with just vegetables is couscous, the best of all.

Below is a list of the most common local dishes you will be offered. For the more basic translations of menus from French, see p. 368.

Brik: At their most basic, which is the way they are served in tourist restaurants, a *brik* is an egg wrapped in a triangular envelope of filo pastry and deep-fried. It can only be eaten with the hands and everybody has their own technique for coping with the runny yolk which can get everywhere. On the street, *briks* are often more · exciting, containing a whole galaxy of additional stuffings, which include spiced potato, anchovies, prawns, spinach and tuna fish, pepped up with a dash of harissa.

Chakchouka: If not too oily, this is a delicious spicy vegetable stew, made from tomatoes, pimentoes and onions, usually with an egg on top.

Cheese does not feature much in the Tunisian diet. The best, which is not saying much, is a *camembert* made in the northern town of Mateur, and available sometimes in Monoprix. Otherwise, you can buy processed cheese in silver foil and a kind of Edam in most local shops, and may be lucky to find a good curd cheese sold off a barrow.

Chorba means soup, and *Chorba Tunisienne*, which features on most menus, appears to have no set recipe. Most of the time it contains tomatoes, onions and harissa, with rice-shaped grains of pasta, but often with a thick layer of oil on top. Do not miss the chance of eating *chorba de poisson*, fish soup, which is often a real treat.

Complet de poisson: Fish are most often served in this way, grilled or fried, with salad, chips, pimentoes and strangely, a fried egg. In restaurants which specialize in seafood, you will be offered a bewildering selection of species. A translation of the French names for the most common types appears on p. 369.

Couscous is the national dish. The grains are made by half-baking flour and water, and grinding it into semolina-like grains. These should then be steamed, over stewing vegetables, and oiled at least three times, to allow each grain to retain its distinct granular texture. The vegetables are ladled onto the grains and a piece of meat or fish added. In good restaurants or in the home, the experience can be sublime. Never turn down the generous offer of home-made couscous, and take a present that suitably reflects the work put in on your behalf.

Fèves is French for broad beans, and you may be offered these if you stop for a bottle of wine or beer. Independent salesmen bring them round in buckets, and offer helpings sprinkled with cumin.

Kaftaji are spicy fried meat balls, served with chopped liver, peppers, onions and courgettes.

Kamounia is a slow-cooked meat stew, strongly flavoured with the eponymous cumin. It is delicious, and all too rarely on menus.

Knef is Tunisia's most subtle meat dish. A piece of lamb on the bone is delicately braised with rosemary, and served in the cooking juices.

Koucha is again rather rare. It is lamb, roasted with chillies and potatoes.

Marcassin is wild boar and the only pork you will meet in this Muslim country. When eating it, as when drinking wine, you may sometimes find a screen erected between you and the locals, so as not to offend their sensibilities. It has a strong taste, but is usually well cooked in a tasty sauce, and served only during the winter hunting season.

Mechoui usually refers to a plate of grilled meat, typically a pair of lamb chops, some liver and a few *merguez* sausages. As a French corruption of an Arab word for grilling or roasting, it can have odd variants.

Mechouia with an 'a' at the end changes grilled meat into grilled vegetables. In this case, chopped onions, peppers and tomatoes are grilled, mixed with olive oil and garnished with tuna and hard-boiled eggs. Beware, as this can be very fiery.

Merguez are small, hard mutton sausages, whose red colouring gives away the quantity of chilli used in their preparation.

Ojja is offered '*nature*', or '*merguez*'. The former is onions and peppers fried with tomatoes and harissa, into which eggs are scrambled. The latter includes slices of hot sausages.

Patisseries abound in every town, and appeal to a very sweet tooth. *Baklawa* is a delicious mélange of nuts and honey, baked between layers of filo pastry. Almonds feature strongly in biscuits, and freshly baked macaroons are a meal in themselves. In Kairouan particularly, but also elsewhere, you will see mountains of stodgy-looking pastry, stuffed with a small layer of date. Called *makrud*, they can be delicious, or distinctly lardy. You can usually get sweet lemonade or fresh orange juice at patisseries as well.

Tajine in Tunisia is not the slow-cooked stew of Morocco and Algeria but a sort of meat quiche without the pastry. Delicious when hot, it is less impressive when served as a cold slice of cake with a sauce dribbled over the top.

Drinking

The Koran has this to say of alcohol: 'O believers, come not to prayer when you are drunk but wait till you can understand what you utter;' also: 'they shall ask you concerning wine and games of chance. Say that in both there is a great sin and also an advantage to man, but their sin is greater than their advantage.'

Adorno, a Spaniard visiting Tunis in the 15th century, reported that 'the Moors know no other drink but milk and water. The rich and great sometimes drink a wine made of dried grapes. On occasion they also drink sweetened water or syrup and at the end of dinner poppy seeds are served to help sleep.' Times have changed and bars and licensed restaurants do a roaring trade. In matters of drink, Tunisia follows its Mediterranean rather than its Muslim heritage, though town bars are closed on Friday and throughout Ramadan.

Tunisian Wine

The area suitable for vines in Tunisia seldom extends more than 50 km from the ruins of Carthage, and the Carthaginians were ingenious viticulturists. The Romans continued the Punic tradition, but it was broken by the Muslim invasion in the 7th century, though grapes were still grown for eating and drying into raisins and sultanas, and unfermented grape juice remained a popular drink. It was also considered permissible to drink wine that had been heated to evaporate off the alcohol, which gave a thick, slightly cooked tasting drink reminiscent of today's sweeter Madeiras.

The revival of wine-making came with the vinous French 'colons', and the White Fathers' agricultural estate at Thibar was the centre for research and development. Disaster struck in 1957 when the phylloxera virus wiped out both the recent imports from Italy and France and the surviving original strains. A continuation of sorts was provided by grafting the old stock on to resistant roots imported from California. All purists, however, claim that post-phylloxera wine has a foxy undertone.

Practically all Tunisian wine is strong, 11–12% alcohol by volume, drunk young in the home market with nothing left over for export, though the bottles travel well. The largest and best distributed label is **Chateau Mornag Rosé**, known affectionately in bars and restaurants as 'Chateau'. According to an 11th-century legend, Mornag was the last Byzantine governor of Carthage. It was he who betrayed the city in 692 to a besieging Arab army under the command of Hassan ibn Numan. Whilst Carthage was sacked, its citizens slaughtered or enslaved, he took possession of his reward, an estate of 360 villages that has ever after borne his name. There are now two official Mornag regions. Grand Cru Mornag lies to the west of Bizerte and Mornag proper is in the strong vine country around the towns of Grombalia and Mornag.

With seafood, try the dry Blanc de Blanc. Domaine Karim is a slightly drier, more astringent clear white. Muscat de Kelibia is luscious but not sweet, straw-yellow in colour with a heady muscatel flavour. It is produced on Cap Bon, just south of Kelibia Castle. Sidi Rais is a slightly more idiosyncratic muscatel, grown on the north coast of Cap Bon. There is a Tunisian champagne type, known as Vin Mousseux, which is made on the Thibar estate and best left on the shelves.

The red wines of Tunisia are robust, strong in colour and taste, perhaps a bit overbearing to be drunk alone, but excellent with hot meaty sauces. They are also the ideal picnic wine, for they are happiest when warm which is almost inevitable. It is worth keeping an eye out for the labels: Chateau Ferrien, Lamblot Bonne, Magon Superieur are rare and good, therefore worth stocking up on. Sidi Saad, in its amphora-shaped bottle, is disappointing even if you take no notice of the inflated price. Thibar, marketed as Vieux or Clos Thibar, is the standard, and is produced on the Thibar estate where the rougher Khanguet also grows. Koudiat and Turki are both bubble-gum wines and should be indignantly refused.

Rosé tends to mean Chateau Mornag and in second place Gris de Tunisie and Gris de Tebourba, the great standbys of drinking in Tunisia. They are refreshing when cool, easy with any meal and ideal to fill the odd watchful hour. There are other labels, Haut Mornag, Royal Tardi, Côte de Hammamet and Côteau d'Utique, but the last two are quite hard to find. Koudiat and Turki both have a rosé version which should be treated just as the reds.

Tap and Mineral Waters

Tunis tap water tastes almost as bad as London water though, like all tap water in Tunisia, it is perfectly safe. The only time to watch out is during floods when drains and water supply do not always remains separate. The only other curiosity is the tap water of Makhtar, which seems to induce a half-day ethereal high after a burst of diarrhoea.

Keep an empty bottle handy for bottling your own spring water. There are memorable springs at Bulla Regia, Zaghouan, Oued Zit, Ain Draham, Medeina and two on the road to Dougga. There are five bottled mineral waters. Ain Garci is fizzy, but not available everywhere. Ain Koutine, Ain Melliti and Ain Safia are the three most common flat mineral waters. Safia comes from the limestone hills at El Ksour, south of El Kef, and Melliti from just north of the Roman ruins of Dougga. Ain Oktor is a thick very mineral-rich water which will not appeal unless you find Badoit too light for your taste. It comes from a spring just south of Korbous, on the north coast of Cap Bon.

Beer and Soft Drinks

Bottled Celtia is the Tunisian brew, stranded somewhere between a light ale and lager, a touch gassy and cloying but nonetheless refreshing when cold. Smarter bars may stock imported beers but you will pay for the difference.

Boga have pride of place in the bottled lemonade sales, trailed by Seven Up and Sinalco. There are also the inevitable Pepsi and Coca Cola, various sweet, fizzy orange drinks and a local enthusiasm for fizzy, or straight apple juice like Juspomme, Apla, Pomdor and Boga Cidre.

The more sophisticated patisseries serve their own brands of *sirops* and soda, mixed from tubs of liquid colour, which usually include a traffic-light array of red grenadine, white almond milk and green *menthe*. Better than any of these are the vats of astringent home-made lemonade, Magimixed carrot juice, and freshly squeezed orange juice that is given that extra twist with judicious additions of grapefruit and lemon.

Tea and Coffee

Coffee reached North Africa from Arabia in the 17th century. Father Dan, who travelled through Tunisia in 1637, described the new habit: 'outside the shops they chat and drink coffee out of tiny porcelain cups . . . it is a kind of drink, black as ink which they consider very healthy. They drink it in small sips and indulge in this charming occupation for two to three hours a day, the rest of which is spent taking tobacco in smoke.'

Modern coffee comes in three varieties, all sugared unless you specifically ask for '*sans sucre*'. First there is a weak chick-pea mixture that hotels habitually serve in the morning for breakfast. Fortunately, even in the smallest towns, you will be able to find a café with an expresso machine. These turn out strong cups of real coffee, with delicious gurgles and smells, and are only marginally more expensive. In some towns chocolate is added to a cappuccino in quantities that create a hybrid drink. Lastly, there is Turkish coffee which is cooked fresh in small pots, so you can reasonably ask for it unsweetened and flavoured with cardamom.

Tunisians are also great tea drinkers. No workmen's tent, kitchen or beach picnic is complete without a battered enamel teapot gently roasting on a charcoal fire. The tea produced by continual heating is a thick, tannin-rich syrup poured with panache into small glasses. Liking it is a difficult but vital social grace. In cafés you will also be able to find a mild mint tea, a longer drink made from sweetened gunpowder or green tea, with a fist-full of mint crammed into the glass. In the south the local variations on mint include verbena, peanuts or fresh almonds. European tea is also produced in the major cities, a yellowish brew served with lemon. For tea with milk ask for '*thé anglais*' or '*thé au lait*'.

Spirits and Liqueurs

Thibarine is made on the Thibar estate, an invention of the White Fathers who produced a liqueur modelled half on Benedictine and half on cough mixture. It is thick, brown and treacly with the usual monk-like secrecy over its ingredients, though the basis is distilled fig wine. *Boukha* is a clear, but heavy white spirit. It is another distilled fig wine and has nothing to do with dates as popularly supposed. *Laghami* is the fermented sap of the date palm, made locally and only to be taken judiciously. There is also Tunisian Pale Gin, Whisky and Curaçao, which are worth tasting once to justify forever the expense of better stuff.

Nightlife

You can go to hotel discos in all of the resort towns, but the only place with an indigenous nightlife is Tunis.

Beyond local music, drinking and dancing, the best way to find out about theatres and concerts is to buy a copy of *Le Temps* or *La Presse*. Both have daily listings of one-off events in the capital and other major cities.

It is worth going once to a *Soirée Folklorique*, where all manner of exotic dancing and feats of dexterity are performed, but do not rush straight to another venue, as all performances are very similar. If you happen upon a cultural festival of course, your choice will be immeasurably widened.

Itineraries

Tunisia is small enough to travel almost anywhere in under 24 hours, so it is possible to cover a lot of ground.

Winter

If you are here in winter, stick to the south of the country. For a one-week, general picture of Tunisia through the ages, spend the first night in Sousse, and visit the architectural glories of the 9th-century city. Move on to Kairouan, the ancient Islamic capital with its famous Great Mosque. From there travel to Sbeitla and the ruined Roman town, before heading for Tozeur. Stay in either Tozeur or Nefta to examine life in a working oasis, and cross the barren Chott el Jerid to Douz, where the sand dunes begin. Take a ride on a camel and spend a night under canvas before returning to Sfax or the Kerkennah Isles, and thence to the airport.

If you would like to spend more time in the arid south, head straight for Gabès, and spend a night there, taking in the museum, before heading on to the underground dwellings of Matmata. Spend a couple of nights in Foum Tataouine, exploring the nearby hilltop citadels, and then move on to the fertile Isle of Jerba, with its whitewashed mosques and relaxed market town, Houmt Souk.

With two weeks in winter you could combine these itineraries, following the first to Douz, and then picking up the second in Gabès.

Summer

In summer, concentrate on the north of the country, and while you will want to spend time on the beach, think about visiting some of the Roman sites in the Tell, such as Makhtar and Dougga, and the town of El Kef. North of El Kef, near Jendouba are the magnificent underground villas of Roman Bulla Regia, after which you can reward yourself with a couple of days in the sleepy resort of Tabarka.

With more time on your hands, continue to Tunis, the Bardo Museum and the Cap Bon peninsula. Here the beaches may seduce, but at Kelibia, Kerkouane and El Haouaria Tunisia's earlier inhabitants have left their mark in spectacular ways. If you still have time, visit Sousse and the holy city of Kairouan.

Roman and Punic Tunisia

Arriving at Tunis, spend the first day visiting the city and Carthage. Head on to Teboursouk and the majestic ruins of Dougga, before continuing to Bulla Regia. Stay at El Kef, and explore some of the many nearby Roman sites—Makhtar, Haidra, Medeina. Spend a night in Sbeitla, move on to Kairouan and El Jem before heading north to Thuburbo Majus and Zaghouan. From there it is a sidestep to Cap Bon and the Punic ruins of Kerkouane and the magical Roman quarries at El Haouaria. Before leaving, visit the myriad mosaics in Tunis' Bardo Museum.

Islamic Tunisia

Most of the important Muslim monuments of Tunisia are found on the coast. A north-south tour might begin in Tunis, continuing to Sousse, Monastir, Mahdia, Sfax and Jerba, before returning via the holiest mosque in the country, at Kairouan. Some of the most worthwhile secondary Islamic sites are the mosques and zaouia of Bizerte, Gabès museum, the Old Mosque in El Kef, the Sufi shrines of Nefta and the 17th-century Moorish town of Testour.

Part II

TUNISIAN CULTURE

Mosaic of Venus at Bulla Regia

History

Tunisian Prehistory

The history of man in Tunisia began a million years ago when *Homo erectus* first travelled north over the Sahara. Some of the oldest traces of his simple chipped pebbles were discovered outside Kebili, a Tunisian oasis on the edge of the Sahara, though the earliest bone fragments only date from around 200,000 BC. They were found with improved, bifaced stone tools at Metlaoui, Redeyef, Gafsa and El Kef. The El Kef excavations showed the Atlas men (*Atlanthropos*) living in temporary hunting encampments in the pine-wooded mountains, sited near a water source and protected by rocky escarpments.

By the last major ice age, about 70,000 years ago, Neanderthal man had appeared, and in Tunisia there are rich veins of his diverse stone-tool culture, known as Mousterian, at Oued Akarit and El Guettar, dated to 40,000 BC.

The Ibero-Mauretanian and Capsian Cultures

A subsequent rise in the level of the Mediterranean Sea, which conclusively separated North Africa from Europe, gave rise to the development of two indigenous North African cultures which provide a crucial record of the evolution of man. First, between 18,000–8000 BC the northern coast of Tunisia was part of the domain of the Ibero-Mauretanians. They gleaned the seashore and hunted the hills from camps made on sand dunes or sheltered by overhanging cliffs. Their dead were buried in a crouched position with stones to mark the graves, and the male skulls can be identified because of the cultural tradition of plucking out the two front teeth.

The later Capsian culture, around 7000–4500 BC, evolved in the southern Tunisian interior, and is named after the first discoveries made around the oasis of Gafsa, ancient Capsa. The perfection and aesthetic beauty of the stone tools found here show a considerable evolutionary advance, and Capsian man was also beginning to model human and animal bone into knives and needles and to make ostrich eggshell into necklaces and hanging baskets. Archaeologists have even found a limestone carving of a female head, its face veiled behind two cones of hair.

Capsian camps are surrounded by heaps of snail shells and burnt stones, used for boiling food. Food was placed in animal-skin containers and the heated stones dropped into it, a style of cooking practised by Indian tribes on the Pacific coast within the last few centuries. Burial ritual included anointing the corpse with red ochre powder, and the skulls are graceful and regular with a high forehead, an early form of *Homo sapiens*, the women this time distinguished by the removal of a pair of molars. There is even speculation that Capsian man may have been the first hunting society to learn to herd, supported by the mythology of Ammon, the ancient ram-headed Egyptian god, who came with herdsmen from the west.

The Neolithic Revolution

Whatever the contribution of the Capsians, the replacement of hunting and gathering by agriculture and herding was one of the most profound revolutions to affect mankind. It allowed for a massive rise in food production, a corresponding growth in population and the formation of the first settled communities. The full force of this new stone age, the Neolithic, reached Tunisia sometime after 5000 BC and is distinguished by modelled pottery, polished stone axes to clear woodland for planting and stone millstones for grinding grain.

Saharan cave painting also testifies to this revolution. Earlier depictions of man show aboriginal hunter-gatherers, but between 6000–4000 BC when a wet period turned the desert into a vast pastoral territory, a cultured black race from the southern Nile depicted themselves with great herds of cattle and goats, agile dread-locked herdsmen and well-clothed women with distinctive crimped hair.

The Berbers

As the Sahara returned to desert, it came into the hands of the chariot-driving North African tribes, who from the Atlantic to the Nile were known to the early civilized world as 'Berbers', a word derived from the Greek slang for foreigner, *barbaroi*. For 3000 years they lived undisturbed in huts, dressed in animal skins, and whilst the men herded sheep and goats, the women performed most of the agricultural labour. They were also fierce and renowned for their bellicosity and polygamy. The Romans later distinguished between the eastern, coastal inhabitants of Tunisia, the Libyans, and the Numidians whose flocks grazed the interior steppe land.

The Arrival of the Phoenicians

By 1000 BC the Phoenicians, great Mediterranean traders from the Lebanon, had established a series of anchorages along the Tunisian coast, separated by a day's rowing (approximately

20 miles). They formed part of the four-year round trip to the silver mines of southern Spain. Over the centuries, small sampan-like boat communities grew up around the safe harbours, and the first permanent shore settlements were established in the 8th century BC. As the Phoenicians traded and married with the Berbers of the interior, so their useful baggage— the alphabet, metalworking, dyeing, weaving, new crops, the pottery wheel and improved agricultural techniques—was disseminated. In 550 BC faced with aggressive Greek competition over Mediterranean trade and the loss of the Lebanon to the Babylonians, these colonists formed a protective league under the leadership of the city of Carthage.

Magonid Carthage, 550–396 BC

The Carthaginians, led by the Magonid dynasty, came to dominate the western Mediterranean, routing the Greeks and establishing colonies on Sicily, Corsica, Sardinia, the Balearics and in southern Spain.

This loosely-structured empire was shattered in 480 when a Carthaginian army was destroyed by Greek colonists from Syracuse in Sicily, at the battle of Himera. For 70 years Carthage abandoned her Mediterranean island empire and concentrated instead on new trade routes down the Atlantic coast of Africa, and the long conquest of the Tunisian interior. Fortresses at Tebessa and El Kef eventually came to mark the far western frontier, enclosing seven Carthaginian provinces, which produced wine, oil, corn and fruit on great agricultural estates.

In 410 Carthage broke from its isolation and sent an army of 50,000 to Sicily in a savage war of revenge. Greek temples and tombs were despoiled, and 3000 prisoners were tortured to death to appease the ghost of Hamilcar the Magonid. By 396 this expeditionary force had been destroyed, and Carthage faced a widespread Berber revolt at home.

Aristocratic Carthage and the Sicilian Wars, 396–241 BC

Following a series of defeats, the Carthaginians banished the last of the Magonids and established a republic much admired by Aristotle. At the same time Carthage welcomed an influx of foreign workers, who brought with them new styles and techniques of architecture and ceramics, and introduced new gods, Demeter, Core and Persephone to name a few, to the Punic (Carthaginian) pantheon.

Sicily continued to play its part as the Rhineland of the ancient world, a perennial battlefield where Carthaginian generals struggled to retain their foothold against charismatic Greek leaders of Syracuse like Dionysius, Timoleon and Agathocles. Apart from a single Carthaginian regiment, the sacred band, which functioned as a school for officers, the Carthaginian army was entirely made up of mercenaries recruited largely from North Africa and Spain. Not until Agathocles' invasion in 311 BC did the Sicilian war come to Africa. Following the maxim that the best method of defence is attack, Agathocles landed on Cap Bon, sacking a string of defenceless Carthaginian cities before being forced to return by problems at home.

It was not until the Carthaginians' former allies, the Romans, began to flex their muscles that the great maritime Empire's days were numbered. A titanic struggle between them over Sicily, from 264–241 BC, became known as the First Punic War. The Romans took the offensive, and, following in the footsteps of Agathocles, Regulus landed at Cap Bon, fermenting a Berber revolt and laying siege to Carthage. The war however was finally decided at sea, when a single Roman naval victory in 242 BC forced the Carthaginians to surrender Sicily.

The Barcids and the Second Punic War, 241–202 BC

In the succeeding five years, Carthage's mercenary army revolted, Rome seized Sardinia and the corruption and inefficiency of the aristocratic government of Carthage was exposed. Hamilcar Barca, the pre-eminent military commander, rose to dominate the state with popular backing. He extended the empire up into Spain, and was succeeded by his 25-year-old son, Hannibal, in 221 BC.

Increasing Roman interference in Spain encouraged Hannibal to launch a pre-emptive attack on Rome. He left Spain in 218 BC and crossed the Alps with his elephants, marching south to destroy a series of Roman armies in the ingenious battles of Trebia, Lake Trasimene and Cannae. The war in Italy extended into tussles in Spain and the Mediterranean islands, but was eventually settled in North Africa. General Scipio invaded Tunisia in 204 BC and in a risky move sent half of his troops to support Massinissa, his Numidian ally. In return, his army was bolstered by cohorts of Numidian cavalry, whose superiority at the battle of Zama against Hannibal proved decisive (see p. 245). Carthage surrendered, her territory was restricted to Africa and her fleet to ten ships, and the city was made to pay an indemnity of 200 talents a year for 50 years.

Massinissa's Numidia, 201–146 BC

After the battle of Zama, Massinissa made himself king of Numidia, and was supported by Rome as a useful check on Carthage. He had been educated at Carthage, and employed Punic officials and encouraged the spread of the Punic language, culture and religion throughout his kingdom. When the Romans began to rearm against Carthage, Massinissa's aim of creating a strong African state by absorbing Carthage was shattered and he was noticeably

Three Numidian Kings—Massinissa, Jugurtha and Juba I

reluctant to assist Rome. He died before the end of the Third Punic War, and the Romans weakened the Numidians by dividing the kingdom between his three heirs, Micipsa, Mastanabal and Gulussa.

The Third Punic War, 149–146 BC

The final Roman victory over Carthage came in 146 BC a year in which the world held its breath as Rome also obliterated Corinth in pursuit of empire. When the Carthaginians first became aware of Rome's aggressive intentions, they immediately sued for peace, surrendering hostages and arms to the army disembarking at Utica. But when the Romans demanded that Carthage be abandoned and rebuilt ten miles from the sea, her citizens prepared to defend themselves. Several Phoenician cities took the opportunity to make peace with Rome, and those which remained loyal to Carthage were systematically sacked. The three-year siege ended with the city looted, burnt and levelled, its citizens sold into slavery and the ground cursed and ploughed with salt.

The Roman Province

At first the border between Numidia and the new Roman province of Africa Proconsularis was sharply defined by Scipio's *fossa regia*. But when Jugurtha, Massinissa's grandson, reunified Numidia in 112 BC the Romans responded with a seven-year war, at the end of which Jugurtha was captured and Marius, the Roman commander, secured Roman gains by planting half a dozen military colonies on the border zone.

In 46 BC the Roman civil war spilled into the African province. Julius Caesar landed to face the alliance of Cato, Sextus Pompey and King Juba I of Numidia, and defeated them at the battle of Thapsus (see p. 163). Caesar plundered the province, extracting enormous fines and implementing wholesale land confiscation. He annexed much of Numidia and renamed it Africa Nova before giving it over to the tender mercies of its first extortionate governor, the historian Sallust. Caesar's successor, Augustus, continued his work, refounding Carthage as a colony for landless Romans and disbanded soldiers. The provincial frontiers were progressively extended south and west in a series of bloody campaigns, briefly resisted by the indigenous revolt of Tacfarinas from AD 17–24. By the end of Tiberius' reign in AD 39 only two legions were required to safeguard the desert frontier. By the 2nd century only the Third Augustan Legioh remained.

The High Roman Empire, AD 37–235

The next 200 years, to the reign of Alexander Severus, was a period of peace, marked by a steady growth in trade, population and civic amenities. The hundreds of ruined Roman towns, with their magnificent temples, baths and mosaic-strewn villas, all date from this era. At the time, North Africa's population of eight million provided Rome with two-thirds of the corn it needed and a third of its Senators.

Africa Proconsularis was ruled by a governor in Carthage with a permanent staff of 400. He toured the country, acting as an appeal court, overseeing municipal administration and the collection of taxes. The *annona*, a corn tax, was collected in town granaries, and then taken to state silos at the shipping ports. The provincial council provided a platform on which grievances could be aired before the governor, as well as coordinating loyal imperial cults.

A fifth of the province was occupied by imperial estates, administered by a separate procurator. The land, both in imperial and private hands, was cultivated by *coloni*, share-cropping tenants. The *conductores*, as the powerful landlords were known, built opulent townhouses and served as magistrates; their names, like the Memii of Gigthis and the Gabini of Dougga, are preserved in numerous dedicatory inscriptions.

The Late Empire

The overthrow of the Severan dynasty in 235 heralded a 50-year period of anarchy. Dozens of generals contended for the throne, though Tunisia fielded only one.

In 238 a group of wealthy landowners from El Jem and Sousse plotted against Emperor Maximinus. They fostered tax riots and persuaded the provincial governor, Gordian, to claim the throne. However they failed to win over Capellianus, the commander of the Third Augustan Legion, who marched up from the frontier, crushed the revolt and sacked both towns. The province was then so effectively plundered by imperial tax collectors that not a single inscription dated between 244 and 270 has been found.

In 284 Diocletian restored order and calmed the rampant inflation with a new gold-based coinage. He created separate civil and military hierarchies, rationalized provincial boundaries and reformed the frontier defences. Africa Proconsularis, one of the three wealthiest provinces of the empire, was expanded westwards and Byzacena, a new province, was created from southern Tunisia and Libya. Maximian, Diocletian's co-Emperor, campaigned in Numidia and added new forts to the desert frontier. This was now manned by a static frontier force, the *limitanei*, a militia of farmers who could be reinforced by a 20,000-strong mobile field army.

In 308 Diocletian's complicated succession system, the tetrarchy, broke down and the empire fell back into anarchy. In 311 Maxentius' army landed, destroyed the frontier army, sacked Carthage and began to hunt down landowners. His successor Constantine could send no more welcome gift to Carthage in 312 than Maxentius' head.

Christianity

The lack of a strong central authority in the 3rd century allowed Christianity to gain ground. It attracted believers with its combination of a mystery cult that promised personal salvation and a moral code of conduct. But despite the fact that a Christian council held at Carthage in 256 was attended by 80 North African bishops, it was not until the long reign of Emperor Constantine (306–337), that the religion became legal and that purpose-built churches were constructed.

Diocletian's persecution in 303–5 divided North Africa's Christians between those who obeyed the imperial edicts (the Catholics) and those who did not. The followers of the martyrs formed a schismatic doctrine known as Donatism, which was opposed to those priests who were compromised by their political temporization. This doctrinal division dominated provincial life throughout the 4th and 5th centuries, and was brought to a head in 411 when the Council of Carthage condemned the Donatists, who had their strongest support in the Numidian hinterland. However, the practical differences between the churches were slight—both promoted cults of the early martyrs and insisted on a three-year probation period with exorcism before baptism. This ceremony of immersion marked entry into an often chaste community, under the moral direction of a bishop, who had the power to forgive sins only once before death. Strong pockets of pagan belief survived as well, and there were riots in Carthage when the temple of Dea Caelestis was closed in 399, and again in 421 when it was levelled.

By the 4th century, Carthage was one of the strongest intellectual centres of the empire. Its grammar and rhetoric teachers were in demand and well-paid by the state. The divisions amongst the Christians fuelled a literary war in which St Cyprian, Tertullian and St Augustine defined the faith. Their style of Latin was to dominate medieval Christendom for the next thousand years. Monasticism was unknown in Tunisia before the 5th century, when a famous community was founded in Carthage by Anicia Prola, the mother of three consuls, with other noble refugees. From here her granddaughter, Demetrias, corresponded with St Jerome, the translator of the Bible.

Vandal Rule, 429–533

In 429, 80,000 Vandals pillaged their way through France and Spain, crossed the straits of Gibraltar and destroyed the small Roman army. By 431 the entire province had capitulated, save Carthage which held out for another eight years. Though the principal cities had been sacked in the Vandal conquest, small towns and estates were untouched, their leaders and owners replaced by a warrior class, which was separated by racial pride and its faith in the Arian heresy from the local Christians.

Genseric, the Vandal leader, overturned the traditions of tribal government to make himself king. He maintained his position with executions and popular campaigns. Each spring a Vandal fleet left on a raiding tour of the Mediterranean, including in one year the notorious 14-day sack of Rome, from which they returned with vast treasure. In 477 the Vandal crown passed to Hilderic, a mildly homosexual, pro-Roman bachelor of orthodox faith who was, through his mother, a grandson of the Emperor Valentinian III. During his weak reign the interior fell into the hands of allied Berber chieftains.

Byzantine Tunisia, 533–698

The 150 years of Byzantine rule in Tunisia were a period of energy and achievement. The piratical Vandal fleets were destroyed, the nomad tribes quelled and a vast building programme initiated.

In 533, just after the main Vandal army had set sail for Sardinia, the Byzantine general Belisarius landed at Ras Kaboudia on midsummer's day with a 15,000-strong army of Huns and Scandinavians. He marched north and easily defeated Gelimer in two battles outside Carthage. The Berber chieftains and desert tribes took much longer to subdue (see Cillium, p. 292), but with a mixture of bribery and force the Byzantines gradually imposed their authority.

The port of Carthage was restored, dozens of magnificent churches built and the interior guarded with 80 forts and over a thousand local defensive works. Christian missions were sent out to the desert tribes, the last temples were closed and Jews, Arians and Donatists persecuted. The Byzantine Exarch of Carthage was one of the most important rulers of the Mediterranean, controlling the trade in corn and ruling Corsica, Sardinia and the Balearic Isles. Heraclius, the son of an Exarch, became Emperor in 608 and thought highly enough of the prosperity of Carthage to contemplate moving the capital there from Constantinople in 620.

41

The Arab Conquest, 647–698

Islam was imposed on Tunisia during the second half of the 7th century by a series of Arab invaders. When the Prophet Mohammed died in 632, his theocratic state controlled all Arabia, and within a decade his successors had made Persia, Syria and Egypt part of the Muslim Empire. In 647 a raiding force penetrated deep into southern Tunisia and destroyed the army of the Exarch Gregory at Sbeitla. A bitter succession dispute in Arabia occupied Muslim energy for the next few decades, while Constans II ruled Byzantium from Sicily. In 670 the newly established Omayyad dynasty despatched an army under the command of Oqba ibn Nafi to North Africa. A near-legendary Arab hero, he subdued Libya, Jerba and southern Tunisia and established a forward base at Kairouan before being repelled in 682 by the Christian Berber tribes.

The final conquest was achieved by Hassan ibn Numan between 694–8. He was almost driven out of Tunisia before he defeated the formidable Berber queen, Al Kahena, at a battle near Gabès. He pursued her westwards, finally destroying her during a heroic last stand, possibly in the amphitheatre at El Jem. Byzantine Carthage fell to the Arab siege, betrayed by its governor, just a few days before the arrival of reinforcements sent by Emperor Leontius. Hassan ibn Numan then ordered the construction of the first Arab fleet, which captured the last of the Byzantine ports.

In 705 Kairouan was made capital of the Wilaya of Ifriqiya, the African province of the Muslim Empire. Its Emir, appointed by the Omayyad Caliphs, came to rule the area from the Pyrenees to the Sahara, after Spain was conquered in 711 and the Arabs launched their first raid on the Sudan in 734.

The Kharijite Revolt

In 739 a Berber garrison in Morocco mutinied against its contemptuous Arab overlords, and within a few months a revolt against the Arab ruling class had swept across North Africa. The Berber tribes united behind the puritan Kharijite creed, which held that political authority should only be obeyed if it were truly Islamic, and that the leadership should be elective, regardless of race and colour. The province degenerated into an anarchic jumble of local wars between Berbers and the Arab military caste, the Jund, led by the descendants of Oqba ibn Nafi, until an Abbasid army reimposed order in 761.

The Golden Century of the Aghlabids

The century of Aghlabid rule was one of the great eras of Tunisian achievement. It began in February 800 when an Abbasid general, Ibrahim ibn al Aghlab, imposed his personal authority after subduing another Jund revolt. He was welcomed by the Caliph in Baghdad, Haroun al Rashid, who had tired of the expense and difficulty of ruling North Africa. The Aghlabids, for their part, offered tribute and were scrupulous in paying lip-service to Abbasid suzerainty.

In 812 an understanding was patched up with the Kharijite tribes in the south. In exchange for respecting the trade routes and the coastal cities they were left to control their own affairs. Relations with the previous Arab leaders were far from easy, however. The religious scholars of Kairouan objected to Aghlabid tolerance of wine, singing and banking, while the Jund regularly rebelled. The Aghlabids never felt safe in Kairouan, and ruled from palaces outside the city, protected by negro and European slave regiments. The invasion of Sicily in 827 was partly launched to divert the Jund from internal politics. The Aghlabids also constructed fortified ribats on the coast, not only to defend it from Christians and Vikings, but also to serve as bases for diversionary raids, like the one in 846 which managed to sack St Peter's in Rome.

Despite this, Aghlabid rule created stability, which allowed for agricultural productivity and economic expansion, aided by new crops and techniques brought by the Arabs from the East. Sugar was produced at Kairouan, silk woven at Gabès and cotton and woollen cloth produced in Tunis and Sfax. The export of corn and olive oil, formerly the mainstay of the economy, took second place to the enormous profits made from Saharan trade in slaves and gold. Kairouan was the centre of the trade, supplying the coastal markets at Tunis, Sousse, Sfax and Tripoli.

The reign of Abu Ibrahim Ahmed (856–63) marked the halcyon period. He organized nightly processions during Ramadan when alms were distributed to the poor, and oversaw the completion of the Great Mosque of Kairouan, the Zitouna Mosque in Tunis and the Great Mosque of Sousse. His 13-year-old son Mohammed II inherited the throne, but he developed such debauched tastes, along with a passion for hunting cranes, that he died before he was 24. He was succeeded by Ibrahim II, an enlightened despot who ruled with a 10,000-strong negro slave army from his palace at Reqqada.

Ninth-century society was affected by a complex blend of influences; on the one hand Sunni orthodoxy of the Malikite school was being defined in Kairouan, whilst the pre-Islamic learning from Byzantium, Persia and Mesopotamia was also imported. Latin remained in use in rural areas, and there were still 40 towns with Christian communities and bishops, under the authority of a resident Primate of Carthage.

The Fatimids

The Fatimid Caliphs, for all their glory, do not deserve to be remembered with affection. They used Tunisia as a mere stepping-stone for their ambitions, and brought about the ultimate disaster of the Hilalian invasion in the 11th century. The Fatimid Empire was the creation of the Ismailis, who in this period were an extreme, Shiite, underground organization. They believed that the descendants of the Prophet's son-in-law, Ali, who married Fatimah (hence the name), were the divinely appointed Caliphs, and planned to seize control of the Muslim world in their name.

By 902 one of their agents, Abu Abdullah, had created an embryo state amongst the Kabylie Berbers in Algeria. From this base he conquered Tunisia, ejecting the last Aghlabid from the palace at Reqqada in 909. He then rescued his Ismaili superior, Ubayd Allah, who had been imprisoned in a distant oasis. Ubayd Allah proclaimed himself Mahdi, the 'rightly guided', assassinated Abu Abdullah and built a coastal citadel at Mahdia as the new capital of the Fatimid Empire. Orthodox Sunni scholars in Kairouan were persecuted. An efficient tax system allowed a succession of fleets and armies to be despatched from Mahdia, capturing Sicily in 912, Alexandria in 913 and Fez in 917, but these early victories were followed by prolonged campaigns.

The unpopularity of Fatimid rule was demonstrated in 943 by the unsuccessful Berber revolt led by Abu Yazid, 'the man with the donkey' (see p. 297). However, in 969 they succeeded in conquering Egypt, and the Fatimid court left for Cairo, which from 973 became its capital.

The Zirid Emirs

Before he left for the East, the Fatimid Caliph al Muizz appointed a viceroy to rule North Africa. He chose Buluggin, a Berber chief from Algeria, whose father Ziri had been one of the best Fatimid generals. For four generations the Zirids faithfully ruled the province for the Fatimids, from a palace outside Kairouan. However, by the 11th century they identified themselves with the prevailing orthodox Arab culture, and had lost control of both Libya and Algeria.

In 1016 the simmering rivalry between the Shiite and Sunni aristocracy exploded into nationwide rioting and the massacre of some 20,000 Shiites. Though order was restored, by 1044 the Zirids had renounced the Fatimids and pledged loyalty to the orthodox Abbasid Caliphs, only to face the wrath of their former overlords.

The Hilalian Invasion

In revenge, Al Mustansir, the Fatimid Caliph in Cairo, encouraged two Bedouin Arab tribes, the Beni Hilal and Beni Sulaym, to invade the rebellious North African provinces. The destructive appetite of their 50,000-strong army, fed by a simple desire for grazing land, devoured cities, villages, orchards and farmland. The devastation they wrought put the assertive Muslim culture of Tunisia back hundreds of years.

They advanced westwards in 1050, the Beni Sulaym settling in Libya; the Beni Hilal, having destroyed a Zirid army near Gabès, preyed on the central plains of Tunisia. Kairouan was overrun and the Zirid court retreated to Mahdia where, impotently, it watched the destruction.

The Normans

In the anarchy that followed, the Normans seized a number of Tunisian coastal cities. Roger II, 1102–54, a capable and tolerant prince, ruled Sicily with a half-Arab court. He commissioned a Muslim scholar, Al Idrissi, to write a report on North Africa, and by 1148 he had quietly taken control of Tripoli, Jerba, Mahdia, the Kerkennah Isles, Gabès and Sfax. The cities, threatened by complete destruction from the Bedouin Arabs, had welcomed any protection, even that of a Christian.

The Almohad Empire, 1159–1230

The Almohads were the only indigenous dynasty to have united the Maghreb. Their period of authority in Tunisia was short but decisive, humbling the Bedouin Arabs, expelling the foreign garrisons and introducing the sophisticated Moorish culture of Andalucia.

The Almohads, literally the unitarians, originated as a religious reform movement in the High Atlas mountains of Morocco. The empire's privileged ruling class of warriors and doctors of law was drawn from a few Berber mountain tribes. The military genius who led them to power was Abdel Moumen. In 1152 he subdued Algeria and crushed the Bedouin Arab army at the battle of Setif. By 1160 the last Norman garrison had been expelled from Tunisia.

Almohad authority was continously challenged by the Beni Ghaniya, an able dynasty of Muslim rulers from Spain. They fermented a succession of revolts amongst dissident tribes in North Africa. By 1183 they were based in southern Tunisia and waged a 40-year guerrilla war which at times verged on victory.

In 1229 a civil war in the Moroccan heartland of the Empire allowed Al Ma'mun to take the throne in Marrakesh. He had been totally discredited by his reliance on Spanish Christians and his renouncement of Almohad religious doctrines. Abu Zakariya, the governor of Tunisia, took the opportunity to discard Almohad authority, and seven years later was confident enough to style himself Caliph. His claims were not disputed for he was a Hafsid, a direct descendant of Abu Hafs Umar, the tribal chief of the High Atlas tribes who had played a vital role in the foundation of the Almohad power.

Three Centuries of Hafsid Rule

Despite continuous threats from Bedouin tribes and from Christian Spain, the Hafsids preserved Tunisian independence for 300 years. Their chronicles tell of a bewildering succession of palace intrigues, complicated by rival Hafsid princes with power bases at Tripoli, Constantine and Bejaia. And yet it was during this period that Tunis became the country's capital, and that the foundations of today's sophisticated urban culture were established.

It was also under the Hafsids that the Saharan trade (in gold, slaves, ivory, ebony, ostrich feathers, precious oils, gums and kola nuts) really came into its own. Christian merchants who flocked to Tunisia were only allowed to stay in fondouks in the port cities, to keep them ignorant of the details of Saharan trade, which resulted in much furious fighting to control key oases and ports. In the 14th century the routes across the desert used by Moroccan and Algerian merchants were increasingly blocked by tribal warfare. Ghadames, the Libyan oasis due south of Tunisia, and the new direct crossing from Tripoli, became all the more important.

Beneath the confusion of Hafsid rulers, three distinct eras are discernible: an initial glorious half-century, a hundred years of decline and a long period of stability.

Abu Zakariyya and Al Mustansir, 1230–77

Abu Zakariyya extended his rule over Algeria and sent a naval expedition to the aid of Muslims in Spain. He and his wife built the first medersas, teaching colleges, in North Africa, augmenting the standing of Tunis's Zitouna university. By the end of his reign he realized that he could not rely on an entirely Almohad army, and began the Hafsid practice of employing Andalucians and freed Christians, who were recruited into two rival corps.

His son, Al Mustansir, pursued a more peaceful policy and is remembered for the exquisite gardens and parks he created outside Tunis and Bizerte. He allowed a Dominican college, the 'Studium Arabicum' to be established in Tunis, which housed the theologian Raymond Martin from 1250–69. Other Europeans—merchants and government emissaries—began to flood to Tunisia, to the court of the most powerful Muslim monarch of the era, recognized by the troubled Meccan sherifs as Caliph.

Hafsid Decline, 1270–1370

The weakness of the Hafsid state was exposed in the summer of 1270 when the Eighth Crusade, led by King Louis IX of France, landed at Carthage. This detour was undertaken at the instigation of Louis's ambitious brother, Charles of Anjou, who ruled Sicily and hoped to see Al Mustansir reduced to the status of client king. Two desultory battles were fought before both armies collapsed with dysentery and St Louis's life literally drained away on 25 August. Charles, unaware that Al Mustansir was on the point of abandoning Tunis, then concluded a favourable peace. Complete chaos descended after Al Mustansir's death, the kingdom dividing as Bedouin tribal chiefs supported rival claimants to the throne. In order to counterbalance the power of the Bedouin tribes, Abu Hafs (1284–95) and his successor Ibn al Lihyani became dangerously dependent on the Spanish, who received the islands of Jerba and Kerkennah and ran the customs and the royal bodyguard. Abu Bakr (1318–47) restored a level of national sovereignty by expelling the Spaniards, but his achievements were destroyed by invasions, in 1347 and 1357, by the Merenid rulers of Morocco.

Late 14th-Century Renewal

Abu Abbas (1370–94) began the restoration of Hafsid authority by creating a loyal professional army, which he expanded by the skilful manipulation of tribal rivalries. His efforts were triumphantly realized in 1380, when a series of popular revolts against local dynasties allowed him to reimpose Hafsid rule in the south.

His internal authority was mirrored by his steadily increasing profits from the corsair war. Mahdia was one of the principal Hafsid bases, and proved such a nuisance that in 1390 it was besieged by a combined French, Aragonese and Genoese fleet. The next year Abu Abbas broke this powerful alliance, concluding treaties with Genoa and Venice. By the reign of Abu Amr Othman (1435–88), both Morocco and Algeria recognized Hafsid suzerainty.

The Hapsburg-Ottoman War, 1520–1580

The 'holy war at sea', *al Jihad fil Bahr*, was in fact just warming up. The simmering rivalry between Muslims and Christians was intensified by the fall of Muslim Granada in southern Spain in 1492, igniting a 60-year war between Hapsburg Spain and Ottoman Turkey. In the process Hafsid Tunisia, with its cities and industries, was devastated.

On overcoming the Muslims at home, Spanish raiders seized control of a dozen North African ports. Muslim resistance relied on two celebrated corsair captains, the brothers El Uruj and Barbarossa, whose career began with the transport of Muslims fleeing from Spain. They had been born on the Isle of Lesbos, the children of a Turkish janissary and Greek mother, and Barbarossa had been a potter before taking to the sea. He spoke Greek, Turkish and Arabic and learned French, Spanish and Italian from the renegade pirates who made up his and El Uruj's fleet. At first they operated in partnership with the Hafsids, using La Goulette and Jerba as bases. By 1516, they had established their own pirate city-state around Algiers, but were constantly under threat from local tribes, the Spaniards and, in 1520, a Hafsid army.

El Uruj died and Barbarossa appealed to Suleiman the Magnificent, the Ottoman Sultan, for help. His prompt assistance secured the Algerian coast, and in 1534 Barbarossa invaded Hafsid Tunisia and seized it in the name of the Sultan. It was not to be so easy, however, for the following year the Hapsburg Emperor Charles V led a counter-invasion, captured Tunis and put a puppet Hafsid prince on the throne, backed by Spanish garrisons.

In 1541 the Spanish began another offensive. Southern Tunisia was occupied by Admiral Andrea Doria, but his success was overshadowed by a disastrous Spanish assault on Barbarossa's Algiers. Three years later Barbarossa felt secure enough to retire. He delegated the Tunisian waters to Dragut, whom he had ransomed from a Genoese galley in exchange for the fortress of Tabarka. Dragut, the drawn sword of Islam, was worth the price. He reconquered Tripoli in 1551, destroyed a Spanish fleet off Jerba in 1560, made a new Ottoman province out of southern Tunisia and Libya and died directing the great Ottoman siege of Malta in 1565.

Over the next 15 years, Tunis changed hands three times. In 1569 the Pasha of Algiers succeeded in expelling the Spanish garrison, but after the battle of Lepanto, in which three-quarters of the Ottoman navy were sunk on 7 October 1572, the Spaniards reoccupied Tunisia without firing a shot. Within two years the Ottomans, under the command of Sinan Pasha, had recaptured it, astonishing the world by building a new fleet of 230 galleys. It was the last great campaign of the war, for the Turks had become heavily embroiled on their Persian frontier whilst Spain had become preoccupied with the Netherlands and England. The two empires signed a truce in 1580.

The Corsair War

This did not, however, signal an end to hostilities on the high seas. A second stage of the Corsair War continued until about 1680, by which time the stronger naval powers, France, Holland and England, were in a position to blast Barbary pirates out of the water.

Oar-power for the corsair galleys was supplied by teeming Christian slave markets in Algiers, Tunis and Tripoli, and equally notorious auctions of Muslim galley-slaves in Livorno, Malta and Marseille. This was the era of individual captains, many of whom were adventurers from England and Holland, who in their northern frigates could lead raids deep out into the Atlantic. Captain Mainwaring flew the colours of Tunis (three silver crescents on a green ground), the Duke of Tuscany or the Venetian Republic, depending on the identity of his prey. Simon Danser, alias Simon Rais, switched masters once too often and on falling back into the clutches of the Bey of Tunis was hanged. John Ward, who operated from Tunis, boasted that 'If I should meet my own father at sea I would rob him and sell him when I was done.' Tunis was 'the Shanghai of the 16th century', a financial centre where prizes and captives were sold, contraband exchanged and ransoms negotiated. When financial go-betweens were needed, the Livorno Jews resident in Tunis provided a direct link with Italian banking houses.

Ottoman Pashas, Turkish Deys and Muradite Beys, 1574–1705

When the Ottomans recaptured Tunis in 1574, their authority was vested in an appointed Pasha, supported by a small Turkish military caste. The 4000 Turkish troops housed in elegant barracks in Tunis were divided into units of 100, under the command of Deys, 'uncles'. The Deys, with a few local notables and corsair captains, formed the Diwan, the ruling council of 40. After a coup in 1590, the Deys elected a Pasha from their own ranks, and the Sultan's government in Istanbul was acknowledged as an honoured but distant suzerainty.

The 17th century saw a period of growth and restoration. The vigorous central government began to pacify the tribes and established the present frontiers of Tunisia. Muslim Andalusians, expelled from Spain in 1610, were welcomed to Tunisia with grants of land and a three-year tax holiday. They brought with them sophisticated agricultural techniques and new industrial skills, particularly in the field of ceramics. Wealth from these and from the corsair war was chanelled into an extensive programme of national reconstruction. Tunis was rebuilt, ancient mosques were restored and numerous dams, fountains, bridges, forts, aqueducts, mosques and medersas constructed throughout the country.

During the capable rule of Youssef Dey (1610–37), the meritocratic regime, open to any foreign man of talent, threw up a new dynasty, the Muradites. Ramadan Bey, the official in charge of taxing the interior, fell in love with Murad Osta, a Corsican slave boy. Trained to succeed Ramadan, Murad had such success in the south and brought the office of Bey to such repute and power that his son, Hammouda Pasha I, was appointed co-ruler to the ageing Youssef Dey. In 1665 Hammouda reopened direct trading links with Europe, appointed the first consuls, established state monopolies and reaped the resulting customs' dues. His son, Murad Bey II, strengthened the southern frontier, but the dynasty began to weaken and died with the assassination of Murad ibn Ali in 1702 and the massacre of the entire family.

The Establishment of the Husseinite Dynasty

The Husseinite Beys ruled from 1705 to 1881, the first 50 years of which were dominated by dynastic struggle. During the Algerian invasion of 1705 the ruling Dey was captured and Hussein ibn Ali Turki, his deputy, was left to organize national resistance. Hussein was particularly successful with the native tribes, for he spoke Arabic as his first language and had a Tunisian mother. However to the Turkish military, he was a half-caste, a *kurughlis*. After the defeat of the Algerian invasion they rose in revolt, but Hussein mastered the coup and had the last Dey dragged from the sanctuary of Sidi ben Arous and executed. He continued to maintain the Turkish regiments at full strength but balanced their power with an equally large corps of *kurughlis* and Zuwawa tribal cavalry.

In 1728 Ali, the nephew of Hussein ibn Ali Turki, rebelled after he lost his position as heir to Hussein's young son. This succession dispute intensified into a widespread civil war, with national divisions between the Husseinite and Bashia factions. For 30 years the country was disrupted, until the enlightened reign of Ali II, who reformed agricultural leases in favour of the tenants and encouraged export trade with interest-free loans.

Society in the Reign of Hammouda Pasha II

The long reign of Hammouda Pasha II (1781–1813) was the zenith of the Husseinite dynasty. He encouraged domestic industry by refusing to wear any cloth that was not of Tunisian manufacture, managed his own farms, personally examined complaints against government officials and frequently consulted local leaders. He was assisted by a remarkably outspoken and constructive vizier, Yusuf Sahib et Tabaa who was noted for his philanthropic works. His court officials were Mamluks, recruited as slave boys from the Christian territories of the Ottoman Empire. His 8000-strong army was kept well-trained and helped to resolve the long-running Algerian border war in 1812. At the summit of native society sat the *ulema*, a collective body of judges, government clerks, Sufi sheikhs and doctors of law. They made occasional remonstrations to the Bey and were exempt from taxation, whilst the more influential members might receive a salary from the Bey.

A third of the state's revenue was raised from a poll tax and a tithe on crops, trees and herds. Customs' duties netted another third, with additional revenue scraped together from a sort of VAT, a rent tax and monopolies on corn, oil, hides and wool. The productive base of the nation was the 400,000 tenants and share-croppers who cultivated the coast, the oases and the Mejerda valley. In addition, there were perhaps 450,000 nomads in the steppe with innumerable herds of sheep and goats. This hinterland was administered by a twice-yearly military progression, known as the *mahalla*. It was led by the Bey du Camp, the heir apparent, who collected taxes, administered justice, bestowed gifts and confirmed tribal leaders in office. In June he marched west to Béja, in November south to Tozeur and returned to the capital by March. On the outer limits of the state were the Ouerghamma, Drid and Khroumir tribes, who were exempted from taxation in return for guarding the frontiers.

Towns harboured 15% of the population, about 160,000, of whom half dwelt in Tunis. The capital boasted 300 mosques, some 200 zaouia and 15 medersas, housing the 800 students of the Zitouna university. Townsmen occupied a relatively privileged position, immune from military service and the grosser tax abuses. The manufacture of perfume, chechia hats and cloth were the three most prestigious urban trades. These commodities were exported, whereas the jewellery, rope, baskets, leather and pottery were produced only for the domestic market. Towns were governed by a Caid, who was usually a local notable. They 'had to pluck the fowl without making it squeak', for changes of office amongst rival families were frequent. The Caids appointed Khalifas for the outlying villages and tribes, kept local fines and added 10% on to the taxes. The Jewish communities were outside the main current of society but provided most of the skilled artisans and financial officials. They paid additional taxes but were governed by their own Caids.

In every principal town a Cadi administered Islamic law and could call on a Mufti or a regional council for advice. The Bey, advised by a ten-man judicial council, the *majlis al Shari*, sat every Sunday to give justice. Even in the sentence of death, the graduation of society was maintained. Turks and Mamluks were strangled with a silken rope dipped in soapy water, townsmen were beheaded, tribesmen were hanged and Jews drowned.

The Growth of European Influence, 1813–81

The successors of Hammouda Pasha II became increasingly exploitative and corrupt, providing a feeble foil against the imperialist ambitions of the great powers of Europe. This was matched by a decline in traditional industries which could not compete against the flood of cheap goods from industrialized Europe.

The growth of European naval supremacy allowed a French and British naval squadron to force Mahmoud Bey to renounce the corsair war in 1819. It was confirmed by the destruction of the Turkish fleet (supported by one Tunisian vessel) at Navarino in 1827. The French invasion of Algiers in 1830 destroyed an old Husseinite enemy, and was initially welcomed by Hussein II who became heavily involved in intrigues to annex western Algeria.

Growing French pressure for free trade (especially from the olive-oil-buying soap boilers of Marseille) resulted in the abolition of state monopolies. The capitulation treaties, granted by Hussein II, were an even greater blow to national sovereignty. European consuls were given the right to judge all cases that involved their nationals. This privilege was abused as consuls increasingly extended their 'protection' over hundreds of native agents. The Beys had developed the ploy of playing off the European powers against the Ottoman Empire, their technical overlord. This tactic ended abruptly in 1835 with the Ottoman military occupation of Libya, which left Tunisia even more dependent on Europe.

Ahmed I, who reigned from 1837–54, attempted to reassert some sovereignty by creating a modern army of 26,000. This half-trained, badly-equipped, conscript force failed to impress any observer and was only paid for by extortionate taxes. Other extravagances, like a fledgling navy, a state visit to France, a new palace at Mohammedia and military aid given to the Ottoman Empire during the Crimean War completely bankrupted the state. In the last few years of his reign Ahmed's army melted away and his chief minister absconded to Paris with the remaining state funds. Though much of Ahmed Bey's reign was tinged with farce (the cruiser built at La Goulette was too large to pass up the canal to the sea) he deserves credit for the abolition of slavery, some two years before the French in Algeria.

Ahmed was succeeded by M'hammed, a more traditionalist and popular ruler. The new Bey battled against the growing power exercised by the British and French consuls, Richard

Wood and Léon Roches. Despite fostering their rivalry, he was forced in 1857 to publish a new law that gave non-Muslims equal legal rights, which for the first time allowed Europeans to own land.

The Collapse of Sovereignty under Mohammed es Sadok, 1859–1882

When Mohammed es Sadok acceded to the throne, Tunis was still a walled Muslim city. His reign witnessed the growth of Tunis's 'New Town', an orderly city filled with European settlers, symbolic of the complete shift in power that occurred during his reign.

In an attempt to stall calls for reform from foreigners and Tunisians, the government devised a new constitution in 1860. It was mere window-dressing however, and made not the slightest difference in practice. A more vital concern to the Bey's court was the exhaustion of all sources of domestic credit by 1862. The next year a foreign loan was floated in France, a fraudulent financial adventure that benefited the Parisian Banque d'Erlanger, the prime minister and a motley collection of financial agents. To meet the interest payments of the new loan the government doubled the poll tax, provoking an immediate and bloody rebellion in 1864. European troops were rushed to the principal cities to protect their nationals. By cancelling the new tax and manipulating tribal rivalries the Bey was eventually able to reassert his authority, and then imposed swingeing fines and confiscations. He went on to contract additional loans abroad, in a hopeless and fast-escalating debt cycle. By 1868 he had exhausted his foreign credit and the European owners of near-worthless Tunisian government bonds clamoured for direct European intervention.

The Bey was forced to surrender his financial authority to an International Financial Commission, run by the British, Italian and French. By 1870 the commission had consolidated the national debt at 160 million francs and negotiated a new interest rate based on government expenditure of under 7 million and an annual revenue of 14 million. Further investigations exposed the scale of corruption at the Bey's court and the prime minister, Khazandar, was sacked in 1874. He was replaced by Kherredine, a great Muslim reformer who had overseen the shortlived 1860 constitution and now set about a thorough overhaul of the government. This included the creation of Sadiki College, an enduring monument which he set up to train government servants in a modern curriculum. His dismissal in 1877 sealed Tunisia's fate.

In 1878 the rivalry between Britain and France was settled at the Congress of Berlin, where the European powers carved up the crumbling Ottoman Empire between them. In return for Cyprus, Britain gave the French a free hand in Tunisia. However, newly unified Italy began to challenge the French position. The Italians had historical claims, geographical proximity and three times as many settlers as the French in Tunisia. With the encouragement of the Bey they also began to buy up the old British interests—gas works and the railway system. The French government of Jules Ferry decided to act before Italian influence grew any stronger. Using the pretext of incursions by Khroumiri tribes into Algeria, the French marched into Tunisia on 30 March 1881. The Bey meekly ordered his garrisons to surrender, though in cities like Sfax the French faced active resistance.

The French Protectorate, 1881–1956

The Protectorate was formally established by the Treaty of the Bardo in 1881 and further developed by the La Marsa Convention of 1883. It left the Bey and the traditional administrative structure intact, though all effective power was placed in the hands of a French resident-general and his *contrôleurs civils*. French courts assumed judicial control of the European population whilst Tunisians remained under a modernized Islamic code. Most of the European population lived in Tunis New Town, governed by an elective municipal council, and had token national representation on a *Grand Conseil*.

Compared to the previous regime however, the mass of the population found the autocratic rule of the French a model of honesty and diligence. They disciplined the Bedouin tribes of the interior and created an efficient grid of roads. To eradicate the periodic and infectious plagues of North Africa, a minumum standard of health care and sanitary reforms covered the whole country. This was the Protectorate's greatest gift. In the 70-odd years of French rule, the native population grew from one to four million.

Unlike in Algeria, the French did not confiscate any land, and despite a colonization fund it was only a wealthy minority of the European population that owned land. Apart from the development of vast olive orchards around Sfax, the coast, the steppe and the south were left in native hands. European estates concentrated in the northwest and the Mejerda valley, land previously owned by the Bey, his courtiers or nomad tribes. In Cap Bon and around Tunis and Bizerte, citrus groves were established, and European farmers successfully introduced mechanized dry-farming of wheat beside the Mejerda. The encouragement of capitalist enterprise led to the discovery of substantial mineral deposits, particularly the vast phosphate deposits at Metlaoui. The mining companies then built an extensive railway system and new deep-water harbours for the transport of their goods.

However, most of the rewards of imperialism—new schools, hospitals, railway carriages, theatres, galleries and restaurants—were reserved for European settlers and a tiny minority of privileged Tunisians. The first signs of a re-emerging nationalism surfaced in 1911. A rumour spread that the French planned to quarry the holy burial ground of Al Jellaz. Mass demonstrations in Tunis led to the deaths of nine settlers and dozens of Tunisians. The next year an Italian tram driver ran over a Tunisian child, and the native tramway workers went on strike. They demanded equal pay with the European workers and the sacking of all Italians. The Young Tunisians, the reforming heirs of Kherredine, came out in their support. The French crushed this incipient opposition by exiling the leaders and imposing martial law which was not lifted until 1921.

In 1921, political agitation was revived with the foundation of the Destour (Constitution) Party. It campaigned for a government responsible to an elected assembly, with equal working conditions, a free press and universal education. However, this admirable programme was far removed from the concerns of the masses, and the leaders lacked interest in extending its influence beyond its Tunis-based, middle-class constituency.

The Neo-Destour Struggle for Independence, 1934–1956

The Destour leaders were increasingly challenged by a younger generation of militant intellectuals from the Sahel. Habib Bourguiba was typical of this group. He was born at Monastir, educated on a scholarship at Sadiki College in Tunis and went on to study law in France, returning in 1928 with a French wife. By March 1934, the radical wing could no longer be accommodated within the Destour Party, and at a conference held in Ksar Hellal it broke away to form the Neo-Destour. By the end of the year the new party had been made illegal, but the arrest of its leaders only helped its popularity. Underground cells were established throughout the nation and began to recruit cadres.

In the late 1930s the Neo-Destour mobilized a series of street demonstrations and in the resulting disorder there were hundreds of deaths. By the outbreak of the Second World War political activity had been stifled and most of the leadership were behind bars. From November 1942 to May 1943 the **Tunisian Campaign** turned the country into a battlefield for European armies. The campaign was a turning point in the war: before it the Allies were in retreat on every front, after they were everywhere on the offensive. It was launched to take pressure off the Russians who bore the full weight of German aggression. British and American troops landed in Vichy-occupied Morocco and Algeria, and the Germans responded by rushing troops into Tunis. The two armies met west of Tunis, with fighting concentrated around Mejez el Bab, until a second front was opened at Mareth on the Libyan border, as Montgomery advanced after his October victory against Rommel at El Alamein.

February and March saw three German counter attacks: an early victory against the US II Corps at Kasserine, another bloody battle against the British First Army at Mejez el Bab and a costly defeat against the Eighth Army at Medenine. Fighting a series of running battles, Montgomery's Eighth Army advanced up the Sahel coast. They were halted by Axis defences at Enfida and the campaign switched back to the Mejez el Bab area. Meanwhile, in April 1943, a successful Allied sea and air blockade stopped even a single German supply ship getting to Tunisia. The Axis position was hopeless and after a massive Allied assault both Tunis and Bizerte were occupied on 7 May 1943.

The campaign was no great turning point for the Tunisians, however. Moncef Bey used the period of uncertainty to promote a number of moderate nationalists and reduce French power. But when de Gaulle's Free French took over from the Vichy administration, Moncef was unfairly accused of Nazi collaboration and forced to abdicate.

The postwar period witnessed a hardening of the French colonial position. From 1945 Bourguiba was outside the country soliciting foreign aid. The brunt of political activity and violent police repression was now borne by the UGTT, the newly formed national trade union, led by Farhat Hached. Salah ben Youssef, Bourguiba's Neo-Destour deputy, was attracted to the radical Arab nationalism of Nasser's Egypt and began calling for immediate and uncompromising independence. By comparison, Bourguiba began to appear more attractive to the French. He was invited to return to Tunisia to negotiate a new political framework. As a result, the 1950 cabinet of the French resident-general was led by a nationalist and even included Salah ben Youssef.

The 250,000 European colonists in Tunisia, their livelihoods and prejudices under threat, reacted by forming the right-wing Rassemblement Française de Tunisie in 1951. The next year a change of policy brought the arrest of Bourguiba and the Neo-Destour leadership, causing rioting and the imposition of a state of emergency. In December 1952 Farhat Hached, the UGTT leader, was assassinated, ostensibly by the Red Hand, a terrorist organization of right-wing colonists, but the complicity of the French police soon became apparent. It was the spark that lit the flame of revolt. Mass protests spread across the whole of North Africa.

By 1953 there was a virtual civil war in Tunisia, the *fellagha* (peasant rebels) began attacking French farms from their bases in the highlands whilst terror and counter-terror spread through the towns. In November 1954 the Algerian rising began. In order to concentrate resources and hold on to Algeria, the French decided to let Morocco and Tunisia go. On 2 June 1955 Habib Bourguiba accepted the French government's offer of autonomy. This tactical move was bitterly opposed by Salah ben Youssef, but at the crucial Neo-Destour party conference that November Bourguiba was confirmed as leader and Salah ben Youssef expelled. In January the party was purged of Youssefites, who used their strong regional support in the south to mount a guerrilla campaign. Habib Bourguiba employed French troops to crush their rebellion, and was able to negotiate complete independence from the French on 20 March 1956.

Habib Bourguiba, 1956–1987

A week after independence a Constituent Assembly was elected to draft a new constitution. Like the cabinet, it was entirely composed of Neo-Destour members, the first in an endless succession of one-party parliaments. Habib Bourguiba immediately started to create his vision of a modern secular Tunisian state. Many of the Sufi brotherhoods were disbanded, while mosques and the wealth of the religious institutions, the *habous*, were brought under government control. The Personal Status Code abolished polygamy and gave women equal civil rights. They could now vote, contract their own marriages, sue for divorce and marry non-Muslims, whilst the provision of universal education was enshrined in a later bill.

In July 1957 the last Bey was deposed and a republic established. The next year, in a series of show trials, Habib Bourguiba removed his political rivals from both the right and the left. Crown Prince Chadli and the old moderate nationalists were convicted of corruption and treason, and over 50 Youssefites were convicted of conspiring with Egypt and Libya to overthrow the state. Bourguiba's pre-eminence was affirmed when the constitution of June 1959 gave him enormous presidential powers.

Relations with France were dominated by the nationalization of colonial land and businesses, and by the savage struggle in Algeria. Flash points occurred when the French hijacked five Algerian resistance leaders in Tunisian airspace in 1956, and bombed the village of Sakiat Sidi Youssef in 1958. Actual fighting between them broke out in 1961 at Bizerte (see p. 200) and in the Sahara, when Habib Bourguiba ordered an attack on Fort Garat el Hamel in support of territorial claims. Only after the Algerian ceasefire in March 1962 did they agree on compensation for nationalization, the complete French withdrawal from military bases in Bizerte and continued French aid.

In July 1961 Habib Bourguiba invited the UGTT union leader, Ahmed ben Salah, to head a Planning Ministry which would oversee a socialist economy. By 1964 nationalization had brought over 400,000 acres of prime farming land under government control. In the same year the Neo-Destour changed its name to the Socialist Destourian Party. During the next five years Ahmed ben Salah made some notable achievements, like the development of a tourist industry, a fishing fleet and the creation of heavy industry away from Tunis. His downfall was over agriculture. Hitherto productive French farms proved expensive and inefficient when run as state communes. An attempt to extend collectivization over smallholders and the Sahel olive groves brought intense resistance. By 1969 government policy was in tatters, and Habib Bourguiba neatly sidestepped responsibility by having Ahmed ben Salah tried and disgraced in September.

The 1970s saw a return to a mixed economy, boosted by a series of good harvests and the discovery of small but useful oil fields. A political shift to the right was marked at the party conference in 1974, which elected Habib Bourguiba President for Life. As the gap between rich and poor widened, so state oppression of the left-wing opposition increased. In January 1978 the UGTT called a general strike against the growing dictatorship. The strike was severely put down, with hundreds of deaths, and was followed by the trial of union leaders. On the second anniversary of the strike, Libyan-backed guerrillas briefly seized control of Gafsa in a coup attempt known as the Gafsa incident.

53

A growing trade deficit forced the government to turn to the IMF and the World Bank for assistance. Their loans were tied to conditions, one of which was that the government should cut down the crippling cost of subsidizing basic foodstuffs. Subsequently, in January 1984 the price of bread more than doubled. Violent riots began in the south and spread all over the country, necessitating a state of emergency and the reimposition of corn subsidies. As the 1980s rolled on, it became more and more apparent that the educated society which Bourguiba's social reforms had produced was frustrated by the lack of jobs and of a political voice. Though some nominal recognition of other parties was given, the restrictions imposed on them and the continual succession of 100% Destour election victories led to a boycott of the 1986 elections. Bourguiba felt a particularly violent antipathy to the fundamentalist Muslim party, the *Mouvement de la Tendance Islamique* (MTI) and had 3000 of its activists arrested.

President Ben Ali

On the evening of 7 November 1987, the prime minister Ben Ali, with the agreement of many leading party members, despatched seven doctors to the palace at Carthage, and they declared Habib Bourguiba senile and unfit to rule.

In accordance with the constitution, Zine el Abidine ben Ali was sworn in as President. He was a senior Tunisian general, trained at the military academies of Saint-Cyr and Châlons-sur-Marne as well as in the USA. His political career began with the efficient repression of the bread riots in 1984, and in April 1986 he had been promoted to Minister of Interior following a series of strikes and MTI disturbances.

But despite Ben Ali's authoritarian background, his presidency inaugurated a period of national reconciliation. Before the end of the year, opposition papers were back in publication, new legislation limited police powers of custody and detention and the infamous State Security Court, used for the political treason trials, was abolished. Within two years over 10,000 of Bourguiba's political victims were either pardoned or released from jail. Ben Ali even talked of a multi-party state, and in preparation the Destourian Socialist Party changed its name again in February 1988, to the Democratic Constitutional Assembly (RCD). A new constitution limited the presidency to two elected five-year terms and endorsed a multi-party system. Bourguiba's personality cult was dismantled and consultations began with all political parties, even the fundamentalists.

When the elections were held in April 1989, the outcome was less hopeful. In the presidential elections Ben Ali, the only candidate and chairman of the RCD, received a 99% vote. The RCD also took all the parliamentary seats with its 80% share of the vote, despite six opposition parties. In September Ben Ali dismissed his prime minister and replaced him with Hamed Karoui, an economic hardliner who began to press on with the World Bank/IMF reforms.

In June 1990 the local elections were boycotted and the RCD remained in complete control. Two days later elections in Algeria saw a massive victory for the fundamentalist Islamic Salvation Front. This confirmed suspicions that the most effective opposition to the RCD in Tunisia is from the fundamentalists, now known as Hizb el Nahda, the Renewal Party. Ben Ali has refused to allow them to register as a political party until they define their social policies, though they have been allowed to publish their own newspaper.

Tunisia Today

The Debt Crisis

Tunisian exports are only two thirds the value of the country's imports. For many years this shortfall was filled by two great invisible earners of foreign currency—tourists and the pay sent home by half a million Tunisians working in Europe and the Arab world. Since 1975, however, they have proved inadequate, and the widening deficit has been serviced by loans. Today, Tunisia's debt has reached the dangerously high figure of over 6 billion US$.

Aided by IMF/World Bank loans, the government is currently pursuing a solution through the development of agricultural self-sufficiency, a restructuring of the monolithic state sector (which accounts for 60% of the economy) and the encouragement of foreign investment.

The Economy

In Tunisia there are two economies. There is a sophisticated business community, based in Tunis and half a dozen lesser coastal cities, which trades with the EEC countries. At the same time more than half the population is primarily dependent on subsidized food and subsistence farming. During the last hundred years this population has expanded from 1 million to over 7 million, and agricultural production has not been able to keep pace. Tunisia is dependent on grain imports, and when bad weather reduces local yields by up to 90%, grain bills soar. In 1989 it was 360 million US$. Soil stabilization, damn and irrigation schemes are all underway to promote self-sufficiency in wheat.

Investment in new ports, boats and processing plants, coupled with an admirable policy to prevent over-fishing, has produced a successful fishing industry. Recently fish exports have toppled olive oil as the main agricultural earner, with fruit in third place.

Since the late 19th century the export of crushed phosphate rock and acid, used in fertilizers, has provided the backbone of the national economy. It still accounts for over a third of all exports though the state corporations which run the mines and the chemical processing plants have become increasingly monolithic and unprofitable. The much smaller deposits of iron, lead and zinc ore are becoming increasingly unprofitable, but there has been a recent growth in cement production. Oil was first dicovered in Tunisia in 1970, and has provided a small but welcome surplus of about 1 million tons, but unless new fields are discovered Tunisia will soon be importing again. As it is, she already receives 5% of the oil and gas which crosses the country in a pipeline from Algeria.

Cheap labour and new laws in 1974, which reassured foreign investors of the security of their financial commitments, have produced a dramatic expansion of the textile industry.

Foreign Affairs

Tunisia's relationship with her Maghrebi neighbours, Libya and Algeria, has a vitality and volatility of its own. Since the resolution of border disputes involving oil fields in the 1960s, relations with Algeria have been largely good and stable. However, the conflicting personalities and stances of Habib Bourguiba and Libya's leader Colonel Gadhafi led to the Gafsa incident in 1980 (see p. 299), border closure and near war in 1985. Bourguiba was conspicuous in his refusal to condemn the US bombing of Tripoli in 1986. Under President Ben Ali relations dramatically improved, allowing for the creation of the 'Great Arab Maghreb' in 1989, a unity treaty signed by Libya, Tunisia, Algeria, Morocco and Mauretania. This has opened all frontiers and communications, but has yet to produce anything more substantial.

For 20 years, Tunisia's standing in the Arab world was low, largely because of Habib Bourguiba's public support of the USA, fuelled by jealousy of Egypt's dominance in North

Africa. The signing of the Camp David agreement between the USA, Egypt and Israel in 1979 provided the opportunity to reverse the situation. Bourguiba vociferously joined the Arab condemnation of Egypt, and the Arab League headquarters were moved from Cairo to Tunis, only to return in 1990. A similar rapprochement occurred with the PLO, who moved their headquarters to Tunis after being ejected from Beirut in 1982. While improving friendships within the Arab world, this has also had its downside. Two PLO leaders have now been assassinated in Tunis and in 1985 Israeli aircraft bombed the PLO headquarters, causing an international scandal.

Whatever the prevailing international rhetoric, Tunisia's relationship with the EEC is perhaps the most vital. Until the end of the Algerian war, relations with France were turbulent, but since 1964 there has been a warm accord. France, Italy, West Germany and Belgium are Tunisia's principal trading partners, and are also indirectly responsible for the bulk of invisible earnings from migrant workers and tourism. They are the chief suppliers of foreign investment, loans, credits, arms and a large measure of technical, cultural, financial and educational collaboration. French language and culture remain conspicuous, boosted recently by the satellite transmission of the French TV channel, Antenne 2.

A further reinforcement of western influence, particularly in terms of aid and finance, is provided by the USA and also by the Gulf states. The understanding between Tunis and Washington set up by Habib Bourguiba continues, though the days of outspoken support are now replaced by an agreement to differ. The effect of Tunisia's support for Saddam Hussein and the Palestinian cause in the recent Gulf War has yet to be felt, though there is certain to be a considerable downturn in important Kuwait-financed projects.

Islam

la ilaha ill'Allah, Muhammed rasul Allah.
There is no God but God, and Mohammed is his Prophet.

With this short creed, all Muslims profess the basic tenets of their faith. Islam literally means 'submission', and implies the submission of believers to God, whom they call Allah. Through the Archangel Gabriel, the word of God was passed to the Prophet Mohammed who recited it aloud. His utterances were later collected in the Koran, the holy book of Islam.

To Mohammed, Islam was not a new religion. It was a reformation of the monotheistic tradition of the Old and New Testament, the books of the Jews and the Christians. Mohammed was the last in a long line of prophets which stretched back to Adam, and included Abraham, Moses, John the Baptist and Christ. This reformation presented an opportunity for the squabbling Christian and Jewish sects to unite under one religion. However, the task of coverting all the Christians and Jews was impossible, and towards the end of his life Mohammed realized that Islam must stand alone. Muslims began to pray facing Mecca rather than Jerusalem, and though all Muslims are enjoined to respect the 'peoples of the book', as Christians and Jews are called, the Prophet's attitude hardened. Early in his teaching he had asked, 'Will you dispute with us about God? When he is our Lord and your Lord! We have our words and you have your words but we are sincerely his.' Towards the end he enjoined, 'O believers! Take not the Jews or Christians as friends.'

The Prophet Mohammed

Born in 570, the young Mohammed was orphaned and brought up by a succession of relatives from the influential Koreisch clan in Mecca. As a young man he worked for Khadijah, a wealthy widow 15 years his senior, whom he later married. Mecca was the centre of pagan Arab spiritual life, and Mohammed and his wife joined the circle of Hanyfs, who sought enlightenment through some form of monotheism and were familiar with Jewish, Christian and Persian doctrines.

Mohammed received his first revelation in 610, when he was 40 years old. The Archangel Gabriel appeared to him in a cave, which he frequently used for prayer and meditation, outside Mecca. Doubtful at first about these revelations but encouraged by his wife, he risked ridicule and shared the word of God. His ardent monotheism and criticism of the pagan worship that centred on Mecca won him some followers but even more enemies. Eventually the protection of his Koreisch clan proved inadequate, and to avoid assassination he fled to the city of Medina on 15 June 622.

This date marks the beginning of the Muslim era, known as the **Hegira**. Mohammed was welcomed to Medina and invited to become its ruler. He established a theocratic state and developed practical moral and legal codes for his community. From Medina he waged war on the Meccans and gradually subdued the surrounding Jewish and pagan tribes. By 630, two years before his death, his authority extended over all Arabia.

The question of Mohammed's successor, the Caliph, has rent the Muslim world to the present day. Over the centuries, this mantle was assumed by a variety of conquering Muslim heads of state, a succession which the Sunni majority, including most Tunisians, accept. However the Shiites believe it should have been passed down by birth from the fourth Caliph Ali, Mohammed's cousin and husband of his daughter Fatimah. Lesser Shiite sects like the Ismailis, Druze and Kharijites are divided by their own interpretations of the rightful succession.

The Koran

The Koran means recitation, for the illiterate Mohammed was enjoined by Gabriel to recite the word of God as it was dictated to him. It was delivered by Mohammed between 610 and 632, memorized by his followers and collected into the first written version 18 years after his death, in 650. The Koran is divided into 114 unequal chapters or **suras**, which are arranged in order of length starting with the longest. Each sura is known by a name—the cow, the bee, the ant etc.—which has no significance other than as a memory aid, for Muslims are themselves taught to recite the Koran by heart. The very beauty of the language of the Koran is taken as proof of its divine inspiration: 'you will never understand . . . until you can feel in your heart the poetry and music of the noble Kor..n.'

In content, the Koran divides roughly into four: the worship of Allah, the Day of Judgement when every soul will be sent either to heaven or hell, stories of earlier prophets and proclamations and social laws. Koran 17:22–39 contains a set of commands similar to the Ten Commandments, encouraging kindness, charity, sobriety and humility and prohibiting murder, adultery, idolatry and meanness. Muslims are also beholden to the collected sayings and traditions of the prophet, known as the Hadith.

From the Koran and the Hadith a legal system, known as sharia, was created. Traditional Islamic countries have no civil code, and criminal acts as well as spiritual sins are judged according to **sharia**. In Tunisia and a handful of the more progressive states, however, civil codes have been introduced as well. At the forefront of the fundamentalist campaigns in these countries is a return to sharia laws.

Religious Life

The Koran sets out the five pillars of Islam, the prerequisites of Muslim religious life. These are the profession of faith, prayer five times a day, giving alms, fasting during Ramadan and pilgrimage to Mecca.

The first **prayer** of the day is known as Moghreb, and is held four minutes after sunset, Eshe when it is quite dark, Soobh Fegr at dawn, Dooh at noon just after the sun has passed its zenith and Asr midway between noon and sunset. At each mosque the muezzin announces prayers by calling 'God is great. I testify that there is no God but God. I testify that Mohammed is his prophet. Come to prayer, come to security. God is great.' Before the morning prayer an extra inducement, 'prayer is better than sleep,' is added.

Before prayer all believers ritually purify themselves by washing with water or sand. Facing Mecca they stand with hands held up and open to proclaim God's greatness. With hands by their sides they recite the opening verse of the Koran, the *fatiha*, before bowing with hands on knees and then fully prostrating themselves. Kneeling again, the *chahada*, a prayer for the prophet, is recited. The three positions of prayer, standing, bowing and prostrating, symbolize the superiority of man's rational rather than his animal nature, a servant before his master and submission to the will of God. Friday is the chief day of prayer, when the community gathers for noon prayers at the most important local mosque, followed by a sermon, *khutba*.

Almsgiving was originally enshrined in Muslim law, and assessed at a fortieth of income, known as *zakat*, though nowadays the practice is purely voluntary.

The **fast of Ramadan** proscribes sex, smoking, drinking and eating during the daylight hours of the ninth month of the Muslim year. Only children, the sick, nursing or pregnant mothers, old people and travellers are exempt. The fast commemorates the month in which Mohammed received his first revelation, but is also based on pre-existing Christian and Jewish spiritual practices. Tunisia is the only Muslim country in which the fast is not a legal obligation, but Habib Bourguiba gave up attempts to stop it all together in the face of religious protest.

Pilgrimage to the Kaaba stone in Mecca, revered as the altar of Abraham, takes place between the seventh and tenth days of the last month of the Islamic year. It is governed by a set of rules which begin six miles from the Holy City and last for the three days' observances. For a poor man it may be the journey of a lifetime, partly paid for by friends who will themselves receive merit by their contribution. He will return to his community with the proud title of 'Haj'. The distance of Mecca from Tunisia gave rise to the hope that seven visits to Kairouan might equal the journey to Arabia.

Sufism

The spread of Islam was greatly assisted by mystical Sufi brotherhoods, who set up religious complexes, known as **zaouia**, throughout the Muslim world. The word comes from 'suf', meaning wool and signifying the coarse woollen cloth worn by some adherents next to their skin. Sufis are not satisfied merely to worship God by obeying Islamic law, but aspire to a direct spiritual experience. Celebrated local mystics, beginning with Ali, the son-in-law of Mohammed, attracted followers and became masters (*sheikhs*). Each established a set of rituals to achieve the desired union with God, which is passed down through generations, by disciples becoming in their turn masters.

Most Sufi regimes are simple and ascetic, and include outward features, such as charity and teaching, as well as the inner search for *wajd*, the ecstatic experience of the divine. They often prescribe a repetitive physical action, such as recitation, music or dancing, as a tool in their quest (for instance, the whirling dervishes). To outsiders, the best-known Sufi trait is indifference to worldly concerns, which led to the practice of self-mutilation to show indifference to pain. More off-beat Sufis practised prolonged contemplation of a beautiful young man, an ephebus, who was believed to embody the divine.

The most important Sufi master to be associated with Tunisia is Sidi Belhassen ech-Chadli, who taught in Tunis in the 13th century in a cave which is still revered on Al Jellaz hill. Born in Morocco, he travelled east to Mecca and on his return stopped in Tunisia, though the brotherhood was only set up after his death in Egypt. Fifteen other Sufi groups now quote Chadli as their spiritual mentor. He united local Sufi practices with the teachings of the great eastern masters Al Jilani and Al Ghazzali.

Nefta is Tunisia's centre of Sufism, and there the most important zaouia follows the teachings of the early 12th-century Abd el-Kader el Jilani. He was the first sheikh to set up a brotherhood, the Qadriya, with associated zaouia in far-off countries, and is therefore father of the Sufi tradition of disseminating the faith. Taking El Kef at the turn of the century as an example, you would have found eight Sufi brotherhoods: two purely local cults, four Qadriya zaouia, as well as one Tijania and one Aissaouia. The Tijania followed the teachings of an 18th-century Algerian, Ahmed al Tijani, and were a brotherhood of courtiers and intellectuals, whilst the Aissaouia were founded by the Moroccan Sidi Mohammed ben Aissa in the 16th century.

Christianity and Islam

Muslims see their religion as a reformation of Christianity, which, with the evidence of the cult of the Virgin, the sacrifice of the Cross, odd celibate monks, doctrines about the Trinity, original sin, sacraments, priests and saints, they see as a corrupted version of monotheism. Christianity for its part has always found it difficult to venerate Mohammed whose wives, wars and very human dilemmas contrast sharply with the poor, celibate, pacific and miracle-working Jesus.

However, the alarming antagonism between these two religions stems as much from their proximity and continual history of conflict as from doctrine. Early struggles in the Middle East between Byzantium and Islam were institutionalised with the First Crusade in the 11th century, and continued through the Hapsburg-Ottoman and Corsair Wars of the 16th-17th centuries. The establishment of Christian colonial regimes in every Muslim country except Saudi Arabia and the creation of Israel compounded the mutual mistrust. Daily, the newspapers carry proof that the age-old war continues largely unabated.

Islam and Tunisian Celebrations

The main religious event of the Muslim year is the fast of **Ramadan**, which is still adhered to, in public at least, by much of the population. For the entire month, productivity drops and a sense of lassitude descends during the day. When Ramadan falls in the summer, tempers are notoriously frayed, but everything is forgotten at the setting of the sun, when cafés fill with hungry customers, who traditionally break the fast with a bowl of steaming soup. Deep into the night towns reverberate to the sound of revelling, as families take to the streets after their communal meal. Musicians, story-tellers and puppet-shows monopolise the pavements. After a few hours' sleep and a nourishing breakfast before sunrise, the fast begins again. The feast of **Aid el Seghir** at the end is a time for new clothes and sumptuous banquets.

Most of the rites of passage celebrated by Christians in the church are secular events in Tunisia, embroidered with folklore and earlier pagan practices. On the seventh day after **birth**, children are named and presented to the family, adorned with amulets for good luck and to chase away the 'evil eye'—fishes, coins and teeth. **Circumcision**, performed between the ages of 5 and 7, begins with the young boy's first visit to the mosque, accompanied by his male relations. The surgery is now usually performed by doctors, but the local barber still plays his traditional role in country areas. At the moment of circumcision, other children break a jar of sweets on the ground, to distract the wicked spirits, *jinnis*, from entering the child through the wound.

Tunisian **weddings** are often signalled by a cavalcade of hooting, decorated cars. Preparations begin some weeks before with a visit to the lawyer's office, where the marriage contract, concerned with dowries and the terms of both marriage and divorce, is drawn up and signed by bride and groom. The old week-long festivities are nowadays concertinaed into a couple of days. The bride's bodily hair is all waxed off and the palms of her hands and soles of her feet covered with auburn henna. Sumptuously dressed, she is shown off to family and friends, sitting on a dais, before men and women separate to eat the marriage dinner. Traditionally, the bride then walked seven times around her father's house, bidding farewell, before being taken to her husband's bed. The husband returns from the town with a group of friends who leave him at the door. Proof of virginity, the bloodied sheet, is still often displayed by the couple's mothers.

Death in Tunisia is greeted with frenzied ululations from female relatives and friends. Muslims are buried quickly, borne to the cemetery on a bier carried by male friends, in a cortège of male mourners, often headed by a man reciting the Koran.

Art and Architecture

Little in the way of artefacts and even fewer buildings remain to testify to Tunisia's 500 years of Phoenician domination. The Romans, on the other hand, left a handful of magnificent ruined cities and a vast collection of mosaics to posterity, while a number of impressive Byzantine fortresses still stand.

Roman Amphitheatre at El Jem

When Islam conquered Tunisia, so did its two dominant art forms, architecture and the purely Muslim innovation, calligraphy. Figurative art, the art of idolaters, was discouraged, and Islam developed a complex tradition of decorative art. Using geometric, floral and calligraphic patterns they sought to ennoble earthly surfaces by evoking the word of God as revealed in the Koran. This quite distinctive Islamic form embellishes buildings and books, and fuels the lesser arts of ceramics and coinage. In crafts like jewellery and carpet-making pre-Islamic symbols linger on.

Architecture

Phoenician Remains

Carthaginian rule is architecturally represented by two hip-high excavations, an area of housing in Carthage on the Byrsa hill, and a walled town, called Kerkouane on Cap Bon. Only the Punic-influenced mausoleum of Prince Ateban at Dougga allows the imagination to roam. Otherwise, knowledge of the era rests on excavations of intact tomb chambers, often with stairwells cut deep into the living rock. Haouanets, above-ground rock tombs which are only found in the north of the country, are also believed to be Punic-influenced. The 2nd-century BC megalithic tombs of the interior, like those at Elles, Hammam Zouakra and Makhtar, have similar rectangular chambers, but are made from massive blocks of roughly dressed stone.

Roman Grandeur

Although Tunisia was a Roman province from 146 BC the vast majority of Roman buildings were built, or rebuilt, between AD69 and 235. The hall-marks of Roman architecture arrived fully formed, and were little influenced by Tunisian traditions. Only in the construction of temples was there respect for the indigenous tradition of worshipping in an open-air enclosure before a small shrine. Even then, as at the sanctuary of Saturn at Dougga, the outer wall was dressed with a classical portico.

Impressive though the temples, and particularly the Capitoline temples at Dougga and Sbeitla seem however, Rome's great architectural contribution was in the development of the arch and concrete. This shows itself repeatedly in Tunisia's triumphal arches, scattered across the country, in the magnificent ruins of Carthage aqueduct, the amphitheatre of El Jem, the bridges at Chemtou, Thuburnica and Thuburbo Majus and the almost needless extravagance of the free-standing theatres at Medenine, Chemtou and Bulla Regia. For a discussion of Roman theatrical productions, see Dougga (p. 253).

The construction of arches was further refined in the great vaulted and domed halls for public bath houses and law courts. Nowhere are these intact, but in Carthage, Bulla Regia, Makhtar, Dougga, Thuburbo Majus and Sbeitla enough remains for us to imagine their scale and grandeur.

Christianity and Byzantium

It was these public buildings, not pagan temples, that were models for the first churches built in the 4th century. Even the name of a Byzantine church, a basilica, was borrowed from the law courts. Ruined naves, complete with mosaics, tombstones, altars, pillars and baptisteries—particularly fine at Sbeitla—can be seen in many of the Roman sites, but only at Haidra and at El Kef can you see a surviving apse. El Kef also boasts the most intact Roman building in the country, later transformed into a mosque.

As well as churches, the Byzantines left fortresses throughout Tunisia. There is not a Roman site without one, built hastily from the spoils of the town to fortify the forum, temple, bath or arch, inadvertently doing much to preserve the Roman buildings for archaeologists. The most impressive forts are seen at Ksar Lemsa, Mustis, Borj Brahim, Ain Tounga and, above all, at Haidra.

The Architecture of Islam

Islam and the West approach buildings from opposite standpoints, more because of climate than philosophy. Islamic architecture aims to enclose a space, to domesticate an area of wilderness, and create a suite of rooms facing on to a serene interior courtyard. Western architecture creates interiors sealed from the environment, and stresses the exterior views, enhanced by landscaping. Both traditions share the same classical influences, though, whilst Europe tends to look to pagan Greece, Islam is more informed by the domes and arches of Byzantium.

The oldest Islamic buildings in Tunisia are fortified monasteries, *ribats*, at Monastir and Sousse. In the reused stone of their formal gateways, one can already see the beginnings of the horseshoe-shaped arch, which was to become the leitmotif of North African Islamic architecture. The reworking of Roman and Byzantine materials into recognizably Muslim forms continues with the Great Mosques of Tunis and Kairouan, whose prayer halls and colonnades are supported by rows of horseshoe arches resting on salvaged pillars. The tapering, angled walls of the minaret at Kairouan suggest an Iraqi prototype, whilst the domes in both mosques were copied from Byzantine church architecture in Syria.

The Great Mosque of Sousse, built in the same period, is a much purer Islamic space. The clutter of borrowed columns and capitals is discarded in favour of clean, freshly-dressed pillars and arches. It relies for its effect not on size and a sea of columns but on proportion, simplicity of form and elegant stonework, not least in the sober dignity of its calligraphic frieze. This new independence and confidence can also be seen in Kalaout Koubba at Sousse, the Great Mosque in Sfax and particularly in the Fatimid Great Mosque at Mahdia.

The 11th-century Hilalian invasion all but stopped this promising line of development. Under the Almohad and Hafsid Caliphs, the architecture of Muslim Spain was introduced to Tunisia, though the full Moorish exuberance was toned down by the more puritanical North Africans. Nothing from this great period remains except the Kasbah Mosque in Tunis, for the Ottoman-Hapsburg War in the 16th century destroyed much and left nothing but a string of squat coastal artillery fortresses at Tabarka, Bizerte, La Goulette, Mahdia and Jerba.

The 17th-century Muradite Beys imported the Ottoman style, in octagonal minarets, marble inlay and wall tiles, to the mosques of Tunisia. In more domestic interiors, this was combined with hectic Moorish carved plaster, Andalucian tiles and painted woodwork. For all its enthusiasm, exuberance and fun, the sense of proportion and relationship of decoration to structure was increasingly lost, and Tunisian architecture never really recovered. The Husseinites added a few Western details such as external windows and decoration to the mix, and Dar ben Abdallah, Tourbet el Bey, the Mosque des Teinturiers, the Bachiya Medersa and the Sahib et Tabaa Mosque are all slightly lighter in feel. The Bardo Palace however, is turn-of-the-century, bordello excess.

Wast al Dar—the Courtyard Plan

The plan of a North African house, be it in a Punic citadel, a Roman insula, a quarter of the medina or in a 20th-century suburb has always been the same. Rooms for eating, cooking and sleeping enclose a courtyard, the *wast el dar*, used by the women of the house. The scale can be expanded to palatial proportions, repeated to allow for an extended family or reduced to the size of a *bidonville* shack.

The courtyard, often with a well or cistern, is a private space, screened from public gaze by a hall (*driba*), a dog-leg passage (*skifa*) or by a simple screen. Larger houses have a room off the hall where male visitors can be received without disturbing life in the central courtyard. Traditionally the courtyard contained an arcade, and the rooms had tiled lower walls, carved plaster above and painted wooden ceilings. Today, whitewashed concrete is the norm. More public buildings, hammams (bathhouses), fondouks (merchants' hotels), hotels, medersas (religious colleges) and zaouia (tomb complexes) simply repeat the plan on a larger scale. The zaouia tend to exaggerate the halls and passages to give pilgrims a sense of distance from the concerns of the outside world, and to heighten expectations on the journey to the shrine. They also have to provide lodging-rooms.

Mosques

A new religion instituting the practice of mass communal prayer, required a new architectural form—the mosque—literally the place of prostration. At its simplest it is just a defined open space with a marker to show the direction of prayer towards Mecca. The next development was to enclose the space with a wall, and create a more elaborate *mihrab*, a niche shaped like a white sugarloaf, to indicate Mecca. A hundred years ago these were commonplace in the south of Tunisia, and early travellers mistook the mihrab for evidence of a phallic cult. In modern mosques the mihrab and part of the prayer area is roofed, leaving a courtyard called a *sahn*. In the courtyard or an adjoining building are basins for the ritual washing and from the minaret the faithful are called to prayer by the haunting call of the *muezzin*.

Apart from the mihrab, modelled on Byzantine altar apses, of the building itself, only the pillars are sometimes decorated, with simple carving. Otherwise, decoration is confined to reed matting pinned along the wall and floor, overlaid carpets, chandeliers and the wooden marquetry of the doors and the pulpit-like minbar, from which the local religious leaders deliver the Friday noon sermon.

Mosaics

Tunisia's astonishingly rich collection of coloured, figurative mosaics, displayed to dazzling effect in the Bardo Museum, date from the 2nd and the 6th centuries AD. These were preceded by the mosaic traditions of the Punic and early Roman period, examples of which are well represented in archaeological sites.

Punic and Early Roman Pavements

The elegance of Punic pavements was commented on by early Roman writers. Excavations at Carthage and Kerkouane have revealed three basic types. The most common is *opus signium*, a pink-coloured cement floor made from crushed terracotta and flecked with fragments of glass and marble. In a few examples the marble pieces have been set in simple symbolic patterns, such as the sign depicting the Carthaginian godess Tanit. The Carthaginians knew how to cut *tesserae*—the component marble cubes from which a mosaic is formed—and occasionally constructed plain white floors from them. *Opus figlinium* was composed of small upturned ceramic tiles arranged in simple herringbone or dog's-tooth patterns. Similar floors have been found in the earliest layers of Roman settlement at Utica, Oudna and Carthage. They are contemporary with two new imports: the simple black and white mosaics of the Italian tradition and *opus sectile*, multicoloured floors of skilfully cut marble shapes.

The Hellenistic Tradition

The mosaic discovered in the baths at Acholla (top floor of Bardo Museum) is the earliest coloured, figurative mosaic to be found in Tunisia. It was composed by a Greek master craftsman and finished by his pupil between AD 115–130. One glance at its extravagant Dionysian theme and complex design is enough to see the sophisticated level at which Hellenistic mosaics were imported into Tunisia.

Tesserae mosaics developed out of the ancient tradition of pebble paving, which as early as the 8th-century BC included the key patterns, lozenges, interlocking triangles and swastikas seen in later mosaics. The earliest figurative pebble floor, at Pella in Macedonia, has been dated to the 4th century BC. By the mid-3rd century BC *tesserae* mosaics were widespread, some of the earliest examples found in the Greek cities of Syracuse, Alexandria and Pergamon. Mythological and literary subjects familiar from wall paintings were represented. The finest mosaics, which matched the detail and sense of depth of paintings, were known as *emblemata*. They were composed of small *tesserae*, known as *opus tessellatum*, and even finer slivers of stone, *opus vermiculatum*. The *emblemata* were often small enough to be portable, or were set in the centre of a room to be admired but not walked over. The functional area of the floor was covered by larger cubes in simpler tones, which created ornamental borders.

North African Mosaics from the 2nd and 3rd Centuries AD

Workshops at El Jem, Sousse and Carthage grew to cope with the escalating local demand for mosaics in public baths and opulent town-houses, though they were never laid in temples and only rarely in the largest country villas. Native craftsmen were soon producing sophisticated designs that reflected the soaring walls, arches and domes of the great public bathhouses. They employed typical Hellenistic subjects like the triumph of Neptune/Oceanus, the birth of Venus, the four seasons and the triumph of Dionysus. Together with the more intimate mythological scenes, still lives, bird and animal portraits theirs was an opulent and majestic body of work. Accurate dating is still in its infancy though there are some useful guidelines: early 2nd-century work had large areas of white around its finely executed figures and as the century progressed the designs became more crowded and complicated. By the end of the 2nd century most large cities had their own workshops. Some can be identified by recurring motifs, such as the laurel-leaf borders of Thuburbo Majus.

A distinctive North African approach first appeared in 3rd-century private houses. The standard classical scenes were gradually replaced by vivid images drawn from the circus, the arena and the hunting field, reminiscent of 18th-century English sporting painting. These contemporary scenes frequently focussed on a particular incident, naming favourite horses, hounds and gladiators. There were also rural and marine views, stocked with accurate details, that replaced imaginary landscapes. The development of circular compositions acknowledged that mosaics were rarely seen in totality and, without breaking the unity of the design, could be admired from a number of angles. Improvements in technique and design meant larger areas of detail could be composed, and *emblemata* panels were increasingly rare. None of these developments was matched in the rest of the Roman Empire: western Europe was too provincial, Italy remained loyal to its simple black and white mosaic floors and the Hellenistic east to its own traditions.

The 4th Century and Early Christian Mosaics

Although North Africa was spared the destruction of the 3rd-century civil wars, the 4th century was nevertheless a period of artistic decline, except amongst the craftsmen of Carthage who continued to produce elegant mosaics into the 6th century. The use of space was ambiguous and exaggerated, isolating figures in a plain background. The careful gradations of colour and fine details disappeared, to be replaced by an unsubtle use of light and shade. By the late 4th century mosaics had a cartoon-like quality, with emphatic dark outlines filled by solid blocks of colour, enlivened just occasionally by an attenuated almost humorous elegance of line.

The 4th century also saw the steady advance of Christianity and the first purpose-built churches with mosaic floors. Until the late 5th century Christians followed the Jewish prohibition on images, but made use of existing geometrical designs, combined with specific Christian motifs like the PIX monogram, the letters alpha and omega, and more ambiguous symbols such as fishes, Dionysus's chalice and Venus's peacocks. The Christian cult of martyrs and their strong belief in an afterlife saw graves for the first time inside religious buildings. Tomb mosaics, like those on display at the Bardo, Enfida and Sfax, were the predominant art-form of the 5th century.

The most remarkable Christian relics in Tunisia are the baptismal fonts, like those at Sbeitla, with their voluptuous, mosaic-decorated curves. The Byzantines introduced cut glass and a strong figurative vein into the 6th-century church mosaics but only a shadow of this survived the Arab conquest, and lingers on in the fine, decorated marble floors found in some of Tunisia's zaouias and medersas.

Calligraphy—The Art of the Pen

The development of calligraphy stems from the fact that Arabic is considered to be a holy language. Muslims believe that it did not exist before the Prophet Mohammed received the first verses of the Koran in AD 610. Linguists have traced its evolution from Nabato-Aramaic, a successor to Phoenician. The earliest Arabic inscription, found near Aleppo, has in fact been dated to 512. There appear to have been at least four distinct Arabic scripts in existence before the Islamic era, but Caliph Abdel Malik (685–705) reduced them to the two schools of calligraphy which still exist. These are **kufic**, an angular, solid, hieratic script suitable for carving and ornamental texts and **cursive**, the more rounded, flowing script of everyday use, which is sometimes referred to as *nashki*.

The most obvious development of calligraphy is found in early copies of the Koran. The oldest to survive is from the 8th century, and is written in a pronounced cursive known as Al-Mail, the slanting. Kufic became the preferred religious script in the 9th century, and quickly developed regional variations. A strong black or gold kufic written with short vertical strokes and marked horizontal elongations developed in Kairouan and spread throughout North Africa. As a result, Korans came to be written on long shallow pages to suit the structure of the script. Red dots indicated vowels, short black commas differentiated letters of similar shape and gold ornaments marked verse endings. More complex and decorative symbols developed: an endless knot marking the end of verses, a tear-drop at the end of every five verses, an almond-shaped lozenge as a mark for readers, for the Koran was divided into 60 equal parts for the purposes of recitation. A domed square frame marked an important passage that required a prostration from the reader.

The Bedouin invasions of the 11th century decimated Kairouan as a scholastic centre. During the Almohad Empire a script used by the new class of government secretaries from Moorish Spain became dominant, and remained almost standard until the 18th century. It preserved an ancient synthesis of kufic and cursive, and is characterized by deep sublinear flourishes and a rigidly horizontal principal line. This Maghrebi script was traditionally written in black ink made with scorched wool from a sheep's belly. The standard pen was composed of 24 donkey hairs though dried reed was a common substitute. A red copper pen was used for marriage documents, a silver or stork-beak pen when writing to a friend and a pomegranate sliver to an enemy. In the 18th century, printing rationalized the scripts and halted any further developments.

Outside North Africa a multitude of other scripts were used. The rich field included graceful Persian Taliq and the variant cursives of Rihani and Thuluth. Muhaqqaq is a flowery development of copy clerks, Tughra the cryptic lettering of the Tartars. Nastaliq was developed in Central Asia in the 15th century and became the script of Mughal India. Riqa was an early stout script of the Turks, Sayaquit the secret script of the Seljuks whilst the opulent decrees of the Ottoman court were written in Diwani. The different tones of Manachir could indicate reprimand or satisfaction before even the first letter had been read. Ghober ('dust') was a miniature script which allowed for a pigeon post and miniature Korans, some so small they could be hidden under a signet ring.

The Art of the Book

The most striking difference between the books of the northern and southern shores of the Mediterranean is that they open at opposite ends, since Arabic is written from right to left. Traditional Islamic books have a flat spine and the edges of the covers exactly cover the pages with no overlap. To protect the pages from sand and dust, a leather flap can be wrapped around them. In old libraries books were stored flat not upright, the titles inscribed on the head or tail of the book. Pages were sometimes tinted, blue, rose and ochre being favourite colours.

Geometric, Floral and Calligraphic Decoration

The philosophical basis for Islamic decoration lies in drawing attention away from the real world to the divine world of pure form. In this it borrows from earlier Semitic traditions in Egypt and Syria, which believed that sacred art must be geometrical and mathematical in essence. Within the infinitely repeating geometrical patterns, the lattices, interlaces, overlays and borders, there is also an aesthetic echo of the human ritual of Islam: the endless chanting of single phrases, the recurring ritual of daily prayer and the repetitious nature of the koranic verses themselves.

The tradition of floral art was initially borrowed from Persia and Byzantium. They are exempt from the koranic threat that on the Day of Judgement every artist will be challenged to breathe life into his work and on inevitable failure will be condemned. For floral motifs—

acanthus, peonies, tulips, roses, pine cones, vine leaves, pomegranates and palmettes—are themselves a reminder of the rewards of paradise. The Koran is full of references to the overhanging trees and fruits in heaven, and the symmetry of flowers and seed pods reveal the geometrical hand of the creator.

Calligraphic decoration usually takes the form of plain or floral kufic. In Tunisia, the minaret of the Great Mosque of Sfax and the courtyard of the Great Mosque of Sousse are mesmeric examples. The square kufic used in Sousse became popular from the mid-13th century, but is heavily stylized, without any markings and awkward to read.

Ceramics

The production of ceramics in Tunisia goes back way before Islam, to the Carthaginian era. The best pottery was in fact imported from Egypt, Greece and southern Italy, but home production churned out simple tableware and mass-market copies. The only indigenous artistic contribution to the art of ceramics was the grotesque devil masks used in ceremonies of child sacrifice.

In the Roman era, a number of production centres developed on the Sahel coast, and Tunisian lamps, characteristic red slipware and amphorae for shipping wine, dates and olive oil were exported. Today, of those centres, only Moknine and Jerba continue to manufacture earthenware pottery. Alongside these relatively sophisticated centres is a self-sufficient rural tradition of modelled pottery, made by women and baked in local bread ovens. Their simple geometrical decoration is unchanged since Neolithic times. The collection at the Bardo, gathered from villages in the northern hills, is the country's most extensive. There are also smaller collections near ancient production centres at museums in El Kef, Moknine, Gabès and Houmt Souk.

Sadly, the more sophisticated ceramics in the Islamic galleries at the Bardo, Monastir and Reqqada are all imported. The oldest pieces are Nishapur slipware, clear white plates decorated on the rim with the dark eastern kufic of the 11th and 12th century, from Iraq. Fatimid lustreware was made in Fustat, south of Cairo. The lustre decoration, often of hares, was protected by an opaque tin glaze, usually white but sometimes tinted turquoise or purple. Raqqa ware, sometimes known as Irabi technique, was made in the 12th century on the banks of the Euphrates in northern Syria. It is characterized by boldly drawn birds and harpies in blues, greens and browns and grooved to prevent the colours running under the glaze. Pottery from Andalucia in the same period avoided the figurative and concentrated on lustre arabesques, calligraphy and heraldry, set against a striking deep blue.

In the 14th century, Chinese blue and white porcelain was copied for the mass market, and Islamic styles increasingly neglected. There was a revival in Islamic taste in the 16th century, led by Damascus Cuenda-Seca ware, blue and black tiles painted under a turquoise glaze. In the same period the Ottoman potters of Iznik developed 'Damascus ware' a vigorous fusion of chinoiserie and arabesque. In the 17th century these promising developments were halted as Muslim taste became obsessed by wall tiles. Syrian centres produced a floral design with combinations of manganese purple, blue and green, and from the mid-16th century Iznik tiles shone with a range of bright new colours—cobalt blue, emerald green and bole or tomato red.

Tunisia, as a province of the Ottoman Empire from the 16th century, faithfully followed these changes in style. Domestic innovation was revived by the arrival of skilled exiles from Andalucia in the 17th century. Wherever they settled, at Tunis, Zaghouan, Testour and Nabeul, they disseminated their distinctive ceramic heritage. This included swirling floral designs in yellow, blue and green, separated by bands of thin black tile and the geometric *zellig* tradition of Morocco. In response to growing European influence, figurative themes began to appear framed by false arches. Every 17th-century zaouia or palace betrays this Andalucian influence, though by the 19th century cheap Italian imports took their toll. Today, however, the modern potteries of Tunis and Nabeul have returned to the Andalucian tradition, though they lack some of the fluency of form and colour.

Coinage

Coinage is a vital political barometer, for *sikka*, the right to issue coinage in his own name, was one of two actions by which a ruler proved his independent status (the other being invocation in the mosques). Displays of gold and silver coins have a prominent place in Tunisian museums. They conjure up the lost luxury and sophistication of the old dynasties, the Aghlabids, Fatimids, Zirids, Almohads and Hafsids, when it was Muslim, not Christian, merchants who controlled the trade routes to India, the Spice Islands and black Africa.

The first purely Islamic coin was struck in 696, before which the Caliphs had used Persian and Byzantine coinage. In that year images were abandoned and replaced by a bold declaration of faith in kufic script: 'Allah is one, Allah is the eternal. He did not beget nor is he begotten'. Using earlier models, the gold coins were known as dinars, from the Latin *denarius*, silver dirhams were based on Persian drachm and copper fals on Byzantine follis. All later Muslim states used the same design, though the quotation from the Koran was later framed and surrounded by more profane details like the date, the sovereign and the mint, in decorative calligraphic borders. In Tunisia, the 100, 50 and 20 millime coins still retain this style.

Modern Art

With the invasion of the French, the tradition of figurative art and of painting on canvas were firmly established in Tunisia. Ever since, there has been a struggle to resolve the marriage of European aesthetics and the Islamic cultural environment. Even today, some of the painting seems lost in a trans-Mediterranean limbo, but when it works, contemporary Tunisian painting has a vibrancy, a newness that makes it refreshing after the often well-trodden feel of European painting.

Modern artists are dependent on the Gulf of Tunis, for its dozen commercial galleries, state exhibition halls and art school. The Museum of Modern Art in the Belvedere Park holds occasional summer exhibitions, but has yet to open properly (for other addresses, see Shopping section, p. 25).

What little tradition of figurative painting existed in Tunisia in the 19th century consisted of Islamic folklore scenes painted on glass and formal court portraits of the Beys, commissioned from visiting Western artists. The first native court painter was Ahmed ben Osman, who worked in the late 19th century and was succeeded by Hedi Khayouchi.

Under the French, painters such as Paul Klee flocked to the light and architecture of Tunisia and a Tunisian salon, with an annual exhibition, was established in 1894. At first it was dominated by colonial painters and orientalism, but by 1912 it was also showing a handful of Tunisian painters. In the 1920s, the Tunis School, founded by Pierre Boucherle, welcomed Tunisian members and has acted as a solid foundation to the present day. Early members Yahia Turki and Abdelaziz ben Rais are now considered the fathers of Tunisian painting. Yahia's paintings show naive, colourful street scenes, focused on real day-to-day Tunisian life, while Abdelaziz used the heritage of Persian miniatures, glass painting and elements of folk culture in his peaceful native landscapes.

The struggle for independence in the 1940s and 1950s influenced the artistic debate as well. Hatem el Mekki was a strong but mercurial character who experimented with realism, expressionism, surrealism and primitivism before investigating the role that calligraphy should play in national art. He became the iconographer of independent Tunisia, creating a new national image for stamps, currency and posters. Ammar Farhat is a more populist figure from a poor, labouring background, who painted detailed scenes of street-life and canvases dominated by symbols and metaphors drawn from folk wisdom. The inclusion of these two elements, calligraphy and folk art, was central to the future development of Tunisian painting. For some, however, the dichotomy between European and Islamic tradition could never be resolved. Painters like Amara Debbech left Tunisia in the 1940s for the greater freedom of France. He returned in 1967 for an exhibition in Tunis, but sensing an unbridgeable gulf within himself he returned to France and later took his own life.

A third generation of painters took painting further into the bosom of Tunisia. Their subject matter was drawn from the traditional way of life, sentimental family loyalties and folk culture. Abdel Aziz Gorgi turned Islamic miniatures away from elegant court scenes to address the common man. Ali Bellagha further developed calligraphy, painting powerful forms on glass, while Zoubeir Turki's canvases, devoid of colour, follow the outlook of a cynical café philosopher. Jellalah ben Abdallah explores the daydream of the intimate, domestic interiors, the realm of beautiful women. In reaction, the late 1960s and 1970s saw the rampant abstraction of Habib Chebli and Hedi Turki, and the more interesting work of Nejib Belkhodja and Naj Mahdaoui who added bold calligraphic forms and themes drawn from Islamic architecture. As you can see for yourself in Tunisia's galleries, the debate continues.

Literature

The people of Tunisia have had a literate culture for over 2500 years, using four successive languages, Phoenician, Latin and Arabic, and recently some French. When Carthage fell to the Romans in 146 BC the language of high culture in the Mediterranean, including Rome, was Greek. However Roman Carthage thought in Latin, and within a couple of hundred years produced the pure Latin of the pens of Tertullian, St Cyprian and St Augustine, which dominated early Christian literature. Arabic conclusively supplanted Latin in the 10th century, and Tunisia contributed three great figures to the wider Islamic literary culture: the 11th-century poet Ibn Rashiq, the 14th-century historian Ibn Khaldoun and the 20th-century poet Abu el Kacem al Shabbi. If you remember only one name, let it be Ibn Khaldoun, of whose work Arnold Toynbee wrote that it is 'the greatest of its kind that has ever been created by any mind in any time or place'.

Phoenician

The earliest surviving example of Phoenician script anywhere dates from a 10th-century BC coffin, and the language was first translated at Oxford in 1750. The earliest Tunisian sample is inscribed on a 5th-century BC gold pendant. Though we know that there was a great library in Carthage, Tunisia's contribution to Phoenician literature has only survived in translation. This includes a 600-line passage in Greek describing Admiral Hanno's voyage of African exploration, and a scattering of quotations, in authors like Pliny, Varro and Columella, from Mago's 28-volume agricultural encyclopaedia, initially translated on the orders of Scipio. The intellectual vigour of Phoenician Carthage is attested by scholars who survived the destruction of the city. Chief of these is Hasdrubal, better known as the philosopher Clitomachus, who became head of the Athenian Academy, wrote over 400 books, many of them in Phoenician, and struggled all his life against belief in magic, divination and astrology.

Tunisia's only indigenous written language, Libyo-Phoenician, was a fusion of Phoenician and Berber used from the 2nd century BC for a few hundred years, but only a few carved stone inscriptions are left to testify to it. In the 19th century however, it was discovered that the Berber Touaregs, who live deep in the Sahara, continue to use a non-Arabic alphabet, known as Tifinagh, Libyo-Phoenician's lone heir.

Latin

The first Latin writer Tunisia can lay claim to is Terence (185–160 BC), the great comic dramatist. As a young Berber slave, his precocious talent was recognized by his Roman master, who freed and supported him while he produced six 'drawing-room' comedies adapted from Greek plays, before an early death. His plays, *The Eunuch, Phormio, The Girl from Andros, The Mother-in-law, The Self-tormentor* and *The Brothers* are still performed today, and inspired both Congreve and Molière.

Through the succeeding centuries, Tunisia provided academics and tutors to Rome, including Salvius Julianus who advised the Emperor Hadrian and Marcus Cornelius Fronto, tutor to the philosopher-emperor, Marcus Aurelius. The country's most lasting contribution to literature, however, came in the sphere of Christian theology, with the formation of ecclesiastical Latin, the language of the Christian West for a thousand years. Tertullian, born in Carthage in 155, is the father of this creation. Using a lively, bold and witty style, he invented new words and phraseology as well as developing those characteristic aspects of medieval Christian writing, destructive invective and an authoritarian tone. He was also an important theologian and moralist, covering every aspect of Christian behaviour from the use of cosmetics and the wearing of military decorations to the resurrection of the flesh.

St Cyprian was also born in Carthage, in 200, and lived, worked and died within its influence. He was a pagan rhetorician who brought his polished literary style to the service of Christianity after his conversion in 246. He became a bishop two years later, was criticized for hiding during the persecution of Christians under Emperor Decian in 250, but redeemed himself by being beheaded during Valerian's persecution. One of the great martyrs of the Catholic Church, his literary reputation is based on a surviving collection of 65 letters and 13 pamphlets which include his most famous work, *On the Unity of the Church*.

Two Tunisians contributed to the Christian opus in the early 4th century, Arnobius, whose *Adversus Nationes* is a violent attack on pagan beliefs and customs, and Lactantius. As well as tutoring Emperor Constantine's son Crispus, he wrote a number of historical and ecclesiastical works. One of his most charming is an 85-line poem, 'The Bird Phoenix', a history of the bird viewed as a symbol of Christian resurrection.

Although St Augustine was born at Souk Ahras in eastern Algeria, he was educated and taught for a long time at Carthage. He was a Manichaean for nine years before drifting back to the faith of his mother, St Monica, after he had moved to Rome to establish his own school of rhetoric. Baptized by St Ambrose in 387, he became a priest in 391, bishop of Hippo in 397 and was adviser to Aurelius, Catholic bishop of Carthage, and everybody else worth knowing in the late 4th century. His immense literary output—500 sermons, 200 letters, 113 books have survived—was mostly polemical in origin. Favourite campaigns were against Donatism in North Africa, the heresy of the Welsh monk Pelagius and his own former Manichaean beliefs. His great work, *The City of God*, responded to the sack of Rome by urging Christians to look inward and attend to the state of their souls rather than that of frontiers. His most accessible work is his *Confessions*, a vigorous spiritual autobiography that is constantly reinterpreted.

Apuleius, whose *The Golden Ass* is still studied in school Latin classes, was born in Madaura, Algeria, but was educated at Carthage before leaving for Athens where he spent the last of his considerable inheritance. He rescued his fortune and health by marrying his best friend's mother, an act suitable for the author of a magical tale of transformation, farce and sexual adventure written in a popular style.

The only Tunisian literature of the Vandal period to come down to us are the works of Dracontius Blossius Aemilius. He composed poems on classical myths for the court, but was imprisoned at least once by King Gunthamund. His chief works are a tragedy on the theme of the Oresteia, an *Apologia* addressed to the King and three books of hexameters entitled *De Laudibus Dei* which were admired by Milton.

Arabic

From the 7th century, Tunisia gradually adopted the literary culture of Islam. This was nurtured at centres of power throughout the Muslim world, and biographies of the early Arabic writers are full of travel, intrigue and hurried departures to the court of a more lavish and sophisticated monarch. The pilgrimage to Mecca served to bind the intellectual world of Islam closely together and a poet or a doctor of religious law was welcome in any princely court from Marrakesh to Baghdad.

In Tunisia, therefore, literature was produced first in Kairouan, then Mahdia and later Tunis, the three capitals. It was chiefly concerned with praising rulers, disparaging rivals and arguing points of theology. The four categories of poetry express this perfectly. *Madith* is the eulogy, *ritha* the elegy, *hija* the satire and *zuhd* the poetry of piety and asceticism. But Tunisia was far from the intellectual forcing-ground of Islam in Baghdad and Damascus, and isolated in a sea of non-Arabic speech. In the 14th century Ibn Khaldoun looked back at the literature of his homeland and concluded, 'there have been no famous poets in Ifriqiya except for Ibn Rashiq and Ibn Sharaf. Most of the poets there have been recent immigrants. Down to this day their eloquence has inclined to the inferior'.

In the first 300 years, Tunisian Arabic writing was largely derivative of the Middle East, both in style and subject matter. Two Aghlabid poet-emirs, Ibrahim and Abu Abbas, boosted Kairouan's literary reputation, and encouraged Hammad al Zanati al Tiharti (816–919), a scholar of religious law, who produced much-lauded personal verse as well as the requisite satires, eulogies and elegies. At the court of the Shiite Fatimids at Mahdia, Ibn Hani al Andalusi (937–972) used the potent atmosphere of royalism and revolution to fuel his eulogies on the dynasty and their cause. His best-known poems exult in the power of the Fatimid army and fleet, which had captured Egypt just before he died, but as Ibn Khaldoun would point out, he hailed from Spain.

It was under the Zirid dynasty in the 11th century, and back in Kairouan, that Ibn Rashiq and Ibn Sharaf emerged. Ibn Rashiq's fame rests on his *Kitab al Umda fi Mahasin al Shir wa Abadith*, which studies the nature of argument, the role of poetry and its contribution to civilization. His position at court was continually threatened by Ibn Sharaf, which stimulated a sniping war of diatribe and satire between them. With the mid-11th-century Bedouin invasion, Kairouan's scholars dispersed to the four winds: to Andalucia, to Cairo, to Sicily or to Mahdia, which held out for a few more years. Ibn Sharaf and Ibn Rashiq both followed Sultan Al Muizz to Mahdia, but on his death apparently became firm friends and left to live together in Sicily. Sherif el Idrisi was also part of this exiled Sicilian culture. He was commissioned by Roger II, the Arabic-speaking Norman King of Sicily, to compile a great geographical description of North Africa, often referred to as the *Book of Roger*.

Unfortunately for Tunisia, literary action under the Almohads (1159–1230) centred on their court at Marrakesh. In 1238 Ibn al Abbar left Valencia after the fall of the Almohads there and sought service under Tunisia's Hafsid Caliphs. He served as head of chancellery for two monarchs, meanwhile compiling a major study of the Andalucian poets, *Tulifat al qadim*. One of his humorous works ironically led to his execution. A satirical poem about his second master Caliph Al Mustansir fell into the wrong hands.

The revered Ibn Khaldoun was born in the Khalduniyah quarter of Tunis on 29 May 1332, of noble Sevillian Arab descent. He was educated at the Zitouna University and served for three years at the Hafsid court before a tempestuous political career as a minister in practically every court of North Africa, and twice in both Fez and Granada. By 1375 he had exhausted any chance of further employment and retired to a castle in Algeria to write a history of North Africa. In 1379 he returned to Tunis where he restricted himself to scholarship, but left for Cairo in 1382. The second great tragedy of his life (his mother and father had both died of the black death when he was 17) occurred when his entire family and library drowned at Alexandria. His last great adventure, bar being left for dead by Bedouins and the usual court intrigues, was a dramatic meeting with Tamerlane, the Tatar leader, during the siege of Damascus.

His history of North Africa is still a primary source, but it is on its long introduction, 'The Muqaddimah', that his fame rests. It is a work of unparalleled originality, in which he outlines, for the first time, a sociology and philosophy of history. His work was neglected after his death, and it was not until a French translation in 1860 that it was fully appreciated.

In the early 16th century, a Christian corsair ship returned from Jerba with a certain Al Hassan ibn Mohammed el Fasi (1483–1554) in its hold. A Spanish Muslim, he was presented to Pope Leo X, who freed him, baptized him with the ridiculous but heroic name Leo Africanus and sponsored his work on *A History and Description of Africa*. It was published in 1526 and Leo returned to Tunis, where he died a Muslim. The book was first published in English in 1600.

After a period when Tunisian literature was obscured by the mystical tendencies of Sufism, and the lead taken by Tlemcen in Algeria, the French invasion stimulated Arabic by giving it a cause. With their traditionally calm political temperament, Tunisian poets and writers were not engulfed by nationalism like their Algerian colleagues. However, poems like Husain al Jaziri's *Wonders of Prison* added a new dimension of pain to the Tunisian palette, and just as earlier poets had glorified courts and rulers, so some now turned their pens to the glory of the *ulema*, the Muslim community.

The acknowledged genius of modern Arabic poetry in the Maghreb, Abu el Kacem al Shabbi, was Tunisian and died at the tragically early age of 25 in 1934. He was educated in the Islamic tradition at the Zitouna, never learned a foreign language and appeared only to be influenced by Arabic literature, involving himself in the heated debate taking place in both Cairo and amongst Syrian immigrants, like Khalil Gibran, in New York. Yet though his poetry is traditional in form, it introduces new complex elements of uncertainty and theme, and is clearly affected by his country's fate. His poem 'Will to Live', written as he fought fatal heart disease, is directed also at the Tunisian nation, struggling to emerge intact from the yoke of colonialism.

The French also introduced their language and culture to Tunisia, as well as alien literary forms such as the novella and plays. The first Minister of Education in independent Tunisia, Mahmoud Messadi, was a graduate of Sadiki College, which offered a European-style education. In 1940, he wrote a play called *The Dam, al-Sudd*. It is an allegory of the problems facing Tunisia at the time and tells of the hero's struggle to build a dam in a dry valley and his failure. The later work of Ali Ben Ayad, Tunisia's most famous dramatist and director, transcended national boundaries, travelling to France as well as other Arab nations, and his death in the early 1970s is still mourned.

Recently in Tunisia the novella has been fashionable amongst liberals seeking to challenge the establishment. Laila ben Mami leads the feminist voice, seeking an end to the oppression of women which cripples both them and society, and Izz al Din al Madani tries to encourage a more rational approach to the country's Islamic heritage. Naturally, the traditionalists deplore these new elements. Equally typical, the best-known Tunisian contemporary writer, and the only one regularly translated into English, is Albert Memmi, a Tunisian Jew who lives in Paris and writes entirely in French.

Music

Music is a constant feature of street life in Tunisia, blaring from the tape recorders of shops and cafés. To the untrained ear, popular Arabic music can sound generic and repetitive. It is based on a five-note, pentatonic scale, which makes it difficult for those used to the octave to discern the harmony. After a few days, however, you will begin to recognize the song of the moment, usually sung by a Egyptian, Syrian or Palestinian *chanteuse* and played countless times everywhere. In the more cosmopolitan areas, you will also hear Western pop and reggae.

The Institute Rachidia on Rue du Dey in Tunis medina was established to protect the musical and poetic culture of Tunisia, and funds the Rachidia orchestra. The orchestra's repertoire consists of Moorish classical music, and it plays regularly in Tunis theatre (see press for listings). They also perform at the June festival of malouf music in Testour. Malouf originated in the Moorish states of Andalucia in the 8th century, and sung in local dialect rather than classical Arabic, hauntingly evokes memories of the early cultural heritage of the Maghreb. Throughout the year in the evenings it can also be heard in the cafés of Sidi Bou Said.

A number of restaurants in Tunis have resident local bands playing in the evenings, and are listed in the Tunis restaurant section. A large part of Tabarka's summer festival consists of musical acts, both European rock bands as well as more traditional music.

The Land

The Tunisian landmass is easy to visualize, rising gradually from east to west, from the coastal plain onto the steppe plateau and then up to the pine-forested hills of the Algerian border. The east coast has a uniform maritime climate, but the interior of the country gets progressively drier as you move south towards the Sahara.

The Interior

Tunisia's northern coast is isolated by the Khroumir and Mogod mountains on which settlement is sparse. To the south snakes the country's largest river, the Mejerda, flowing east from Algeria through a wide fertile valley. Still further south begins the high steppe land, the Tell, divided by a line of hills known as the Grande Dorsale, which provides Tunisia with its finest scenery. It is the eastern end of the Atlas range, which begins in Morocco, and includes Tunisia's highest mountain, Jebel Chambi near Kasserine, and Jebel Bargou and Jebel Zaghouan near Tunis, before extending into the sea as Cap Bon.

The hills also mark a rough climatic divide. To the north it is wet enough for grain, to the south the land is only suitable for grazing. The Tell ends with the Southern Dorsale and its lucrative phosphate mines. South of these hills, in the sub-Sahara, cultivation and human settlement are restricted to oases fed by springs, where the main cash crop is dates. The region is divided by a series of salt flats or chotts, part of a chain of depressions that runs deep into Algeria. South of the chotts the land contains still fewer springs and the oases peter out in the sand dunes of the Great Eastern Erg.

The Coast

Apart from the limestone spine of Cap Bon, the coastal plain of Tunisia is largely featureless from Bizerte to Libya, broken only by lagoons and *sebkhet*, seasonal brakish lakes. Offshore, the Island of Jerba and the Kerkennah Isles are remnants of the old coastal plain, which 15,000 years ago stretched 100 km east into the Mediterranean.

Up to 100 km wide in places, with a mix of sand, clay and limestone soils, the coastal plain contains the country's most productive and populous regions. Good rainfall between Bizerte and Sousse allows for mixed farming typical of the Mediterranean, while around Sousse and Sfax average annual rainfall of 12 in is perfect for olive cultivation. South of Gabès the Jefara coastal plain sustains only arid grazing, though the crescent of Jebel Demer which runs deep into Libya supports small terraces of land cultivated by dry-farming techniques.

Land Holding

Tunisian land divides into three categories—tilled and irrigated land, grazing land and dead land—of which ownership of the first, known as *ashir*, is by far the most complex. These two million hectares are either state-owned or freehold. After Independence the best land, which had been farmed by the colonists, and all land owned by religious institutions, was national-ized, and some of it redistributed. Plough land is measured in 10 hectare units, called *mashia*, and irrigated land, such as in oases, in *merja* of a sixth of a hectare.

Khamsa and Enzel Tenancies

Two separate systems of leasing land operate in Tunisia, one largely governing agricultural land, the other the specialized arboriculture of olives. Most agricultural tenancies operate on the principle that there are five (*khamsa*) equal components to farming: land, seed, equip-ment, labour and plough animals. A tenant who provides just his labour is known as a *khames*, and theoretically receives a fifth of the crop, after tax, as payment. In practice the *khames'* proportion of the harvest fluctuates with supply and demand and the type of crop. Dates, which require comparatively little labour, pay a seventh, fruit orchards a quarter and grain or vegetables a third. The problem with this seemingly just system arises from the yearly payment, at harvest time. In the intervening months, labourers often need loans, the interest on which binds them forever to the landowner. All contracts are annual, finishing after the harvest.

The Sahel townships operate the more favourable system of *enzel* tenancies. The poorer half of the rural population own orchards of 40 trees or less and survive by taking on long-term tenancies from the handful of big landowners. Rents are fixed at between 3% and 10% of the value of harvest. In days gone by the creation of new orchards was encouraged by a system called *mugharsa*. Until the first crop was picked, which could be up to 15 years, the labourer had free use of the land beneath. He then surrendered half the trees to the original landlord and kept the other half for himself.

Cultivation

A wheat ear, a sack of olives and a branch of dates are the heraldic symbols of Tunisian agriculture. Add to this trinity a bunch of oranges and a cascade of grapes, both grown commercially around Cap Bon, and you have the major crops of the entire country.

Alongside these, irrigation techniques and in the south, the shade of palm trees, allow fruit and vegetables to be grown everywhere. As well as vegetables like the common potato, okra, cumin, red pimentos, bananas, pomegranates, apricots, figs, melons, strawberries, peaches, oranges, lemons, clementines, grapefruit, mandarins, pistachios and almonds all proliferate. The country also harvests crops of indigo and madder roots for vegetable dyes—indigo around Mahdia and madder outside Gabès. Gabès is also known for its superior henna, used not only as a dye but also for magic. The leaves of the henna tree are burned to expel evil spirits, to attract loved ones and are scattered before the feet of a traveller when he leaves home.

Cornland

Wheat dominates the northern Tell, whilst barley predominates in any land ploughed south of Mahdia. In the shade of orchard trees, maize, sorghum, millet, rye and oats are also planted. The Tunisian growing season is short. The fields are ploughed after the first autumn rain. Two weeks later a second ploughing, perpendicular to the first, takes place and the land is seeded, weeded and kept free of birds while the farmer prays for rain. A host of proverbs like 'March rain, pure gold', and 'The rain of Nissan (between 25 April and 5 May) fills glasses' testifies to the anxiety of the growing season. By June, the corn is harvested, and the fields given over to nomadic herds, welcome for their manure.

Though many of the nationalized ex-colonial estates use modern machinery, the small irregular plots of Tunisia's subsistence farmers still employ the techniques of their ancient fore-fathers. The Carthaginians first introduced the light plough, pulled by anything from mules to camels, which cuts a shallow turf thus protecting soil from becoming over-dry, exhausted and wind-eroded. It can tackle hill slopes and patches of land between rock outcrops denied to a tractor or a heavier team. It is also cheap to make, from wood and crude metal blades, and requires no bank loans. The harvested stooks are taken to the *mandra*, a stone threshing floor sealed with mud and dung. Here teams of oxen drag *jaarush*, sleds fitted with blades and stones to thresh the seed, which is then hand-winnowed from the chaff.

A few embers of the rural cults still glow. Before ploughing, men assemble for a meal of wheat and pomegranate, of which a portion is put aside for the fields. The senior ploughman anoints the draught animals and yoke with a wheat gruel and crushes a pomegranate on the handle of the plough. A corn dolly made from the last stook of the previous harvest is ploughed into the first furrow.

Here and there on the grazing land of the southern Tell, a cash crop, wild alfa or esparto grass, is harvested by the women. About a million and a half acres produce some 70,000 tons a year, and it is bundled into bales for paper-makers or sent to the factory at Kasserine to be made into cellulose.

The Sahel Olive Orchards

Two-thirds of all Tunisia's olive trees grow in the Sahel, which produces most of the export-quality oil. It has become a lucrative business for the large growers, producing some 100,000 tons of oil a year. The total number of trees has grown from 300,000 in 1678, 3 million in 1840 to about 21 million trees today.

In a well-run orchard, trees are planted about 20 m apart and about 15 years later produce a first crop. Olives have a recognizable cycle of one good and one bad crop in any four years. The ground between the trees is ploughed twice a year, cultivation kept at a minimum and grazing forbidden before the harvest begins in November. The olives are either gathered by beating the trees or hand-raking the branches with rams' horn finger guards. The fruit is then carted off to the oil press, which has separate storage bins for each of its customers. In a normal year a good tree might give 50 kg of raw fruit. Pruning occurs just after or during the harvest and provides a valuable supply of firewood and wattling.

At the press, the olives are first crushed in a mill and then packed into *scourtin* bags which are stacked on top of one another and mechanically pressed three times. The first pressing produces *shamlali*, superior oil, the second common oil, and the third local cooking oil and oil for processing into soap. The liquid drains off into tanks and is mixed with water. The oil floats and is tapped off, while the vegetable residues sink to the bottom. These, and the material left in the *scourtins*, are either fed to animals or used as fuel.

Date Palms

It is said of the date palm that it requires its head to be in the fire and its feet in water. Only the palmeries around the Chott el Jerid are hot enough to produce good eating dates. Once the trees are established, they require little attention apart from irrigation, and pollination, which entails removing the male flowers and brushing the female clusters with their pollen. Dates are harvested by fit young boys who shin up the trunks and drop the clusters, which weigh up to 15 kg each. Inferior varieties are either fed to animals or dried in the sun, crushed into flour and eaten diluted with water. Softer dates are packed into jars whence date honey oozes from a hole in the base.

All parts of the tree are used in this otherwise unproductive region. The flowers are prized as an aphrodisiac and the heart and young fronds are eaten, dressed with salt, vinegar and oil. The trunks provide beams as well as firewood, which burns slowly with hot embers. The fronds can stripped and used as canes or softened in water and ground to produce fibre for rope and shoes. The trees are also milked for their sweet white sap, tapped from a deep incision, which turns quickly into alcohol. However this is a destructive process practised only on old or male trees.

Forests and Hedgerows

Much of the mountainous northern and western part of Tunisia is covered by forests, principally of Aleppo pine and cork, from which about 7000 tons of bark are gathered a year. The hills are grazed by goats, and in small clearings cash crops, like tobacco, sugar beet and vegetables are grown.

Hedgerows of cypress, acacia, eucalyptus, prickly pear and agave cactus play a vital role throughout the country, as a defence against the two agents of desertification, goats and the wind. They also provide shade, fruit and incontestable boundaries. Beware the prickly pear, known as Barbary fig, with its tempting mango-coloured fruit. Imported by the Spanish from the Caribbean, it was planted as early as the 16th century as an extra defence around their forts. Unlike its importers, it has successfully colonized North Africa, but the fruit is covered in hundreds of tiny spines, impossible to extract from fingers and tongue. If expertly peeled, it is an antidote to diarrhoea.

Parks and Gardens

Some of Tunisia's modern hotels and parks borrow from the refined tradition of Moorish gardening, based on a harmony of flowing water, shady trees and delicate, scented plants. Generally however, Tunisia seems to have lost the art, which once fed the country's reputation for flower essences and perfumes. Hardy modern imports, like mimosa from Australia, bougainvillaea from Brazil and boulevard palm from the Canary Isles, are now more common than white *nesri* roses, violets, hollyhocks and jasmine.

Wild Flowers

Pressure exerted by the rising human population has seen increasing encroachment by herds and agriculture on the habitat of wild plants in Tunisia. However, the country still contains a wide variety, from heather in the northern hills to water-retentive desert blooms. To see the desert in flower, the best time to come is in winter, but you have to be lucky and catch some rain as well. For the rest of the country spring is the ideal time to visit, for by summer all but the highest hills are burned out. Autumn sees a miniature resurgence amongst the bulbed species.

Distribution Summary of Trees and Plants

Mountains and forests: cork oak (below 800 m), holm oak, juniper, Aleppo pine (below 1000 m), walnut and almond. In the northern hills you may find *arbutus unedo*, the strawberry tree with its laurel-like leaves. The bright fruit appears in winter, but *unedo* means eat one, and by implication that one is enough. The leaves and bark are used medicinally, and the wood is good for turning and charcoal and is also used for making flutes. Flowers in the mountains include various crocuses, *Narcissus bulbocodium, Orchis laxiflora, Asphodelus fistulo-sus, Matthiola, Polemonium caeruleum, Echium diffusum, Genista* and *Ononis speciosa* and other orchids in lush places.

Lower slopes: fig, carob, whose long bean pods are boiled to make a soft drink, the food of hermits like St John the Baptist, olive (not above 600–800 m or anywhere where the temperature averages less than 3°C in the coldest month of the year), cypress, almond, prickly pear, trefoils, medicagos, vetches, dwarf prickly oak, gum ammoniacum and oleander, which produces a blast of colour along river beds. It is said to have been created from Fatimah's tears, when she discovered that her husband Ali had taken a second wife, and like them is unbearably bitter.

Maquis and scrubland: pink or white cistus or rock rose, two sorts of broom, mastic, lavender, sage, wormwood, rosemary, lentisk, acacia/mimosa, and under bushes or in limestone clefts orchids and irises.

Lagoons, lakes and coast: white alyssum (*Loburia maritima*) a sprawling plant with clusters of white flowers, hottentot fig, a low fleshy plant with bright pink or yellow flowers, Virginia stock (*Malcolmia maritima*) with its pinky purple four-petalled flowers, sea lavender (*Limonium latifolium*) with delicate white or blue flowers, and masses of grasswort, low fleshy shrubs dotted with tiny flowers.

Spring meadows: bright yellow chrysanthemums, lupins, crimson adonis, deep orange marigold, Bermuda buttercups, poppies, campions, common borage, blue pimpernels, pink-tubed valerian (*Fedia cornucopiae*), dwarf palm (*Chamaerops humilis*), iris, mugwort and the odd gladiolius, squill, honeywort (*Cerinthe major*), lots of inedible asphodels sending flowering spikes from an extruding bulb, blue-tinted daisies, orchids, esparto, saffron, and a number of convolvulus, including the tricolor with its blue, white and yellow flowers.

Sub-Sahara: acacia, tamarisk, jujube, date palm, eucalyptus, sea lavender, *Cladanthus arabicus*.

Animals and Birds

In spring and autumn, Tunisia serves as a funnel for a wide variety of migrating birds, who use the short sea crossing between Cap Bon and Sicily. In winter the country is home for some of the summer birds of Europe, particularly water birds, and in summer, birds from central Africa migrate here to escape the heat.

Animals graze even the most distant and desolate stretches of land, but most of these are domestic herds of goat, sheep and camel. There are an estimated seven million herd animals in Tunisia, many of whom are moved by their nomadic owners between seasonal pasture, heading north in summer and south in early spring. Wild animals are much more difficult to spot, but if your are lucky you may catch a glimpse of wild boar, mongoose, jackal, fox, desert fox and a range of rats and, less luckily, snakes. Most of these animals do their foraging by night, however.

Domestic Animals

Sheep, goats and donkeys have been part of the North African scene since the Neolithic age, while horses arrived here around 1600 BC and one-humped dromedary camels have only been succesfully bred since AD 200. Over five million sheep dominate the farmland of the Tell and Steppe, while over a million goats graze the mountains, in the north, west and southeast of the country. Cows are also farmed, but only around Mateur and Bizerte, where butter and cheese are made. Camels, once the 'ship of the desert', are much less numerous than formerly, and though found throughout the country are only bred, for meat, in the sub-Sahara.

Wild Animals

The list of mammals that used to live in Tunisia before the French shot them to extinction is impressive. It includes lions, panthers, moufflon, addax and oryx antelope, hyenas, baboons, cheetahs and all manner of gazelles.

The distribution sheets of the Ministry of Forestry and Water claim that the following animals are resident in Tunisia. Generally speaking, the smaller the more likely you are to see them, though most are invisible to the casual observer.

Large Mammals: Barbary deer, wild sheep, dorcas gazelle, dune gazelle (*leptocerus*), oryx, addax, ostrich (these three reintroduced in an animal reserve near Maknassy), jackal, wild boar, fox, porcupine, genet (a small striped half-cat/half-stoat with a long ringed tail), fennec (a small fox with large bat-like ears) (*Fennecus zerda*), Mediterranean monk seal, cheetah, lynx, Libyan polecat and otter.

Small mammals, snakes and reptiles: hedgehog, gerbil, desert rat, jerboa, rabbit, hare, Saharan hare (*Lepus capensis pallor*), mouse, shrew and great rat. Reptiles and amphibians are most common of all: lizard, skink, frog, toad, salamander, the meat-eating desert lizard (*Varanus griseus*), and dozens of snakes like the horned viper (*Cerastes cornutus*).

Birds

Any evening or morning, a walk in the Tunisian countryside will churn up some birdlife. For those dedicated to more active bird-spotting and identifying, there are a number of particular places to visit at certain times of the year. Check under El Haouaria and Jebel Ichkeul for details, and also consider visiting Ghar el Mehl during the migration periods, the Kerkennah Isles and the Sebkhet el Melh below Zarzis for waders, and Zaghouan, Ain Draham and Kasserine for woodland and mountain birds.

Plains and farmland: finches, goldfinches, linnets and chaffinches, are common and are caught and caged as song-birds. There are also quail, Barbary partridge, fan-tailed warblers and brown corn buntings. Perched or hovering predators include marsh harriers, kites and shrikes, including the resident great grey shrike and in the summer the red-headed woodchat shrike.

Woodland and mountains: unmistakable hoopoes with their crests and striking black and white wing feathers (in Fardi ad Dir Altar's classic *Discourse on Birds* they lead the search for God), woodpeckers, nightingales, wagtails, Moussier's redstart, stonechats, rock buntings, blue rock thrushes, warblers, wrens, jays, tits and finches. Resident birds of prey include buzzards, eagles, vultures, kites and falcons.

Coast: gulls, terns, cormorants, Cory and Manx shearwaters, and on tidal mudflats pink flamingoes, avocets, spoonbills, sandpipers, dunlin, stints and redshank.

Desert: larks, wheatears, trumpeter finches and hoopoe larks.

Butterflies

Lastly, you could well see some butterflies that do not live in Britain. In spring, look out for painted ladies, the deep yellow and black-tipped wings of clouded yellows, Moroccan orangetips, small and yellow with orange wingtips, the large and striking cleopatra, with orange patches on its yellow wings and two types of swallowtail.

Part III

THE BAY OF TUNIS

*A 17th-century view
of the Sidi Youssef Mosque*

The Bay of Tunis is the undisputed centre of the nation. It has cradled three distinct civilizations—the Phoenician state of Carthage, which later became the second city of the Roman Empire and the Muslim capital of Tunisia. Each of them evokes dramatic images: of Dido the forsaken suicidal queen of Carthage, of Christian martyrs thrown to wild beasts in the amphitheatre and of a walled city grown fat on piracy, ruled by regents for the Ottoman Sultan.

While Carthage has all but disappeared, Tunis has broken out beyond its walls in the last hundred years, spreading through a landscape of lagoons against a backdrop of mountains. Contemporary realities like a deepwater port, a Metro line and an airport have drawn businesses away from the medieval centre, distributing them, Californian style, along the main highways. The Bay of Tunis is now a virtual metropolis, where a future is being built amongst relics of a 3000-year past.

For a visitor Tunis offers fine restaurants, idiosyncratic shopping and nightlife, as well as the intimate Islamic architecture of the medina and one of the world's great museums, the Bardo. Its cafés, art galleries and street life are sophisticated in comparison with the rest of the country. In summer the inhabitants desert the heat, humidity and diesel fumes of their capital for the nearby beaches. Lured north by the ruins of Carthage, you can stop off at one of La Goulette's fish restaurants on the way, and continue to the dazzling whitewashed village of Sidi Bou Said, before returning to the city in the cool of dusk.

TUNIS

History

The Gulf of Tunis serves as a funnel, channelling contact between Africa and Europe through the city. Tunis grew as both an entrepôt to lure traders and a fortress to repel invaders. It still functions as a valve, filtering the exchanges between Christendom and Islam.

An Arab Port

Until the Arab invasion in the late 7th century, Tunis was little more than a hillock between two inland lakes, invariably chosen as a base for armies besieging nearby Carthage. This cycle was broken when Hassan ibn Numan, the conqueror of Tunisia, set out to create a new Muslim centre from his encampment. He imported workmen from Egypt to build the first Arab fleet, and 'made the sea come to Tunis' by digging a canal out to La Goulette. Tunis became the chief port of trade between Africa and Europe, with buildings like the 9th-century Zitouna Mosque attesting to its wealth.

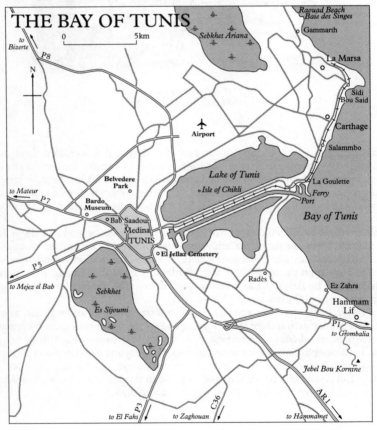

THE BAY OF TUNIS

0   5km

to Bizerte

P8

N

Airport

Raouad Beach
Baie des Singes

Gammarth

La Marsa

Sidi
Bou Said

Carthage

Salammbo

Sebkhet Ariana

Lake of Tunis

Isle of Chikli

La Goulette
Ferry
Port

Bay of Tunis

Belvedere
Park

to Mateur

P7

Bardo
Museum

Bab Saadoun
Medina
TUNIS

El Jellaz Cemetery

Radès

Ez Zahra

Hammam
Lif

P1

to Grombalia

P5

to Mejez el Bab

Sebkhet
Es Sijoumi

Jebel Bou Kornine

AR1

to El Fahs   to Zaghouan   to Hammamet

P3   C36

The Khorassan Principality of Tunis

During the 11th-century Bedouin invasion of Tunisia, Tunis fell under the sway of the Riyah tribe. Her desperate citizens appealed to the Emir of the Beni Hammad, a Berber mountain kingdom, who sent one of his sons, Abdelhaq ibn Khorassan, to Tunis' rescue. He freed the city, reinforced its defences, developed factories and opened new trade routes to Europe. The rule of his two sons continued this golden era of prosperity and independence, while the rest of the country suffered under either nomad or Norman rule. The Khorassan rulers built the Mosque of the Ksar and the Koubba of the Khorassan, and lived not fearfully behind the fortified walls of the kasbah but amongst their citizens, in a palace now known as the Dar Hussein.

The Capital of Ifriqiyya

In 1159 Tunisia was absorbed into the Moroccan Almohad Empire, and Tunis became the country's capital. Under the Hafsid dynasty, which ruled from 1230 to 1574, the city expanded to the north and south, where new quarters known as the ribats were founded. In the same period half a dozen medersas were built around the Zitouna Mosque, which became one of the great universities of North Africa. The 14th century saw five invasions, as the Hafsid's succession to the Almohads in Tunisia was challenged by Moroccan and Algerian dynasties. In the 15th century, however, the population rose to 100,000 and the city boasted 1200 mills, 700 spice dealers and 4000 workers employed just to make its daily bread. Its woven goods, leather work and scent-makers dominated the North African markets, and Europeans came to buy precious goods from across the Sahara—gold, ivory and ostrich feathers.

A Pawn in the Hapsburg-Ottoman War

Tunis was almost destroyed in the 16th-century conflict between the Hapsburg and Ottoman Empires, and its role as a Saharan market decimated by Portuguese discoveries of new routes to West Africa and the Indies. In August 1534, the corsair admiral Barbarossa captured Tunis kasbah for the Ottoman Sultan. The following year, as Emperor Charles V landed with an army and defeated him in battle, Christian slaves seized control of the kasbah. Some of his troops had been promised three days of pillage, but the Emperor personally intervened to stop this massacre of innocents, which is still remembered as 'Black Wednesday'. For 35 years the rule of Charles V's puppet prince was upheld by a chain of forts, until the Ottoman Pasha of Algiers took the city in 1569. Three years later a second Spanish army landed and the entire population fled to the slopes of Jebel Ressas. In the empty city Christian cavalry were stabled in the Zitouna Mosque, its great library was trampled into the street and the tomb of Sidi Mahrez desecrated, after which it is said that the saint haunted the dreams of the Ottoman Sultan. In 1574 a great Ottoman fleet under the command of Sinan Pasha recaptured Tunis.

Ottoman Restoration

Tunis was effectively restored by two energetic Ottoman officers, Dey Othman and Youssef Dey who ruled the country from 1594 to 1637. Dey Othman welcomed both Muslim refugees from Spain and Italian Jews, and, using pirates like 'Issous Rais', an English renegade, made Tunis into a corsair boom town. Tunis and Algiers were the New York of the 17th century, cities open to any ruthless man of talent, with fortunes to be made speculating in ransoms and by deals in contraband, risk-insurance and captured shipping. Youssef Dey built the first of Tunis' 'Turkish' Hanefite mosques, complete with medersa and mausoleum, as well as rebuilding the souks.

The Husseinite City

Hussein ibn Ali Turki founded the Husseinite dynasty, which occupied the throne for 350 years, when he led the defence of Tunis against an Algerian invasion in 1705. Under his successors, Tunis was increasingly neglected in favour of a succession of new palaces built at Mohammedia, La Mornaghia, Hammam Lif, La Goulette, La Marsa and the Bardo. The beys only spent time in the medina when deposited in their mausoleum, the Tourbet el Bey.

In the 19th century competition from European factories began to cut into Tunis' traditional markets. The death-knell of the medieval city was sounded in 1861, when the Bey ordered the internal city walls dismantled and Europeans had already begun to lay out the New Town on land recovered from the lake. On 10 October 1881 two battalions of French infantry marched into the kasbah and began to level the ancient citadel.

20th-Century Tunis

By 1935, 150,000 Europeans were living in the clean, well-lit New Town complete with schools, banks, theatres and hospitals, while 300,000 Tunisians packed into the old city, an increasingly dilapidated and overcrowded Muslim ghetto. After independence in 1956, the *beldi* merchant class moved out to take possession of the New Town flats and villa-strewn suburbs. Medina society became almost rural, as it filled with immigrant farmers from the Tell.

Architectural details were taken away from old family houses in the medina to furnish new villas, and the houses themselves were broken up by subletting. The abolition of the *habous*, religious endowments, in 1956 deprived the city's numerous shrines, medersas and zaouia of their funds. The burden of their maintenance is only now beginning to be taken seriously by the state.

A strong central government ensures that Tunis' influence over the country is set to continue. Her population nears 1.5 million, a fifth of the nation, and the city is the centre for everything other than the oil and phosphate industries.

GETTING AROUND

Arriving in Tunis

By Air: Tunis-Carthage Airport is on the northern shore of Lake Tunis, 9 km from the city centre. The no. 35 bus plies the route to central Av Habib Bourguiba, or it is a 3-dn metered taxi ride.

By Boat: All boats dock at La Goulette, a 1-dn taxi ride from the centre of Tunis, or a 200-ml ride on the light railway, the TGM, to the bottom of Av Habib Bourguiba.

By Train: Travelling to Tunis by train, you arrive at the central Pl Barcelone station, which also has a local bus terminal and Metro station, and is at the heart of the hotel quarter.

By Bus: Coming from El Kef and all points north, you will be dropped at Bab Saadoun station on the northwest corner of the medina. Flag down a taxi for a 1-dn ride into the centre of town, or go straight to the other bus station on the no. 50 link bus. Coming from anywhere south of El Kef you will be dropped at the new Bab Alleoua terminal, a short taxi ride or straightforward walk to the city centre. Leave through the exit for *louages*, turn left and walk 1 km down shady Av de Carthage to Av Habib Bourguiba.

By Car: Head for the carpark beside the Hotel Africa and leave your car there throughout your stay in Tunis. It will be guarded for 1.7 dn a day, and washed if you want. Parking on the streets by day is safe enough but by night Tunis is the one place in the country where you can expect a car to be broken into. Locals all leave their cars visibly empty to avoid the annoyance of shattered windows.

Travelling around Tunis

It is almost as quick and certainly more enjoyable to walk everywhere in central Tunis. Nothing is more than a half-hour walk from Av Habib Bourguiba. The only exception is the Bardo, an hour by foot or a 240-ml ticket on the no. 3 bus. Other local buses of use are the no. 1 and no. 2 which circle the medina, the no. 5 and no. 7 for the Belvedere Park (Parc Belvedère).

Going out to the north coast for a day, a meal or just for the ride across the lake, use the TGM railway with stations at La Goulette, Carthage, Sidi Bou Said, La Marsa and points in between. The TGM station is at the eastern, coastal end of Av Habib Bourguiba, open from 05.00 to midnight, and tickets are as cheap as the buses.

Riding the Metro, more of a tram, as it rumbles through the centre of town is fun but it does not yet take you anywhere very useful. The track is being extended round the northern edge of the medina to the Bardo which will make a perfect excuse for a trip.

For Hammam Lif and Jebel Bou Kornine to the south of the city, use the Pl Barcelone railway station.

Travelling from Tunis

Tunis is the centre of the national transport system and there is not a sizeable town in the country that you cannot reach by bus or train in a day. For details of boats and planes to Europe see the 'Getting Around' section at the beginning of this book (p. 9). In addition, the daily papers, like *La Presse*, publish a listing of airplanes arriving and departing from Tunis, all the train departures and a complete timetable of the SNTRI express coaches, a government-backed network for towns not on the railway.

By Air: There is no need to fly within Tunisia, though there is a network of connections linking Tunis to Jerba, Monastir, Tozeur, Gabès and Sfax. Prices and schedules can be obtained from the Tunisavia office at 38 Rue Gandhi, tel (01) 254875, and Tunis Air at the airport, tel (01) 288000, at 48 Av Habib Bourguiba, tel (01) 259189 or at 113 Av de la Liberté, tel (01) 288100.

By Train: Fanning out from Tunis' Pl Barcelone station are the four principal railroads in Tunisia. Going north to Bizerte there are three trains a day, stopping at Mateur and Tinja, a journey of 1 hr 50 mins.

Travelling west there are five trains a day to Ghardimao on the Algerian frontier, stopping at Béja, Bou Salem and Jendouba. The 11.55 is currently the Trans-Maghreb Express which crosses the border to Algiers, though it does not yet link up with Morocco. Few tourists use the line southwest to Kalaa Kasbah though there are three trains a day, a 6-hr journey broken at El Fahs, Gaafour and El Ksour.

The most popular route is south to Cap Bon, the Sahel coast and Gabès. There are 10 trains to Bir Bou Regba, where you change on to a branch line for frequent trains to Hammamet and Nabeul. Eight trains go on to Sousse, a 2-hr journey, five of which carry on to Sfax stopping at El Jem on the way. The other three follow the coast on from Sousse to Monastir and Mahdia. From Sfax two trains continue south to Gabès, and one crosses from there to Gafsa and Metlaoui.

By Bus: Beyond looking out in the press for the express connections there is no need to worry about bus timetables as there are plenty of departures. Just go along to the right station and catch the next bus. The Bab Alleoua covers all destinations south of Tunis up to El Kef,

CENTRAL TUNIS Medina an

to Bab Saadoun

to Bab el
Souika
Quarter

0   200m

Pl Bab
Souika

Rue   Bab   Souika

10
9

11   Pl Bab
Carthagena

16

12   15

13

Rue de la Noria

Rue du Tribunal

14

Rue de la Hafsia

Zarkoun

Rue

Rue Karamed

Douan

A Souk des Orfèvres
B Souk Kebajin
C Souk Berka
D Souk Leffa
E Souk el Bey
F Souk Dziria
G Souk des Femmes
H Souk el Trouk
I Souk el Kachachine
J Souk du Coton
K Souk de la Laine

Rue   du   Pacha

de   l' Agha

Souk el   Grand   Kasbah

la

Pl
Vi

Rue du   Diwan

Rue   Dar   Sidi   ben   Jeddi

Rue

Rue de Tunis

de   Rue   el Attarine

Rue   Jamaa   ez   Zitouna

27

17

Pl du
Gouvernement

19
20

21   Souk   el Attarine

Pl de la
Kasbah

18

22   Souk el Bey   E

Souk el   Trouk

24

Rue   des   Librairies

Rue   el   Bey

Souk   des   Sidi

Souk el Kachachine

Pl Cheikh
el Barzouli

28   2 Mars   1934

23

32

C

H

36

K J

Rue du   2 Mars

Souk   Sekkine

F   C
B

I

Souk el Kachachine

30

F

A

G

Rue   du   Dey

Rue   Souk   des   Femmes

Bd

Souk

Rue des   Andalous

Rue   Sidi   Kassem

Rue   du   2 Mars   1934

31   29

35   34

Rue du
Château

33

38

37   42

39

Rue   de   la   Vérité

Rue   Tourbet   el   Bey

41

Bab

Menara

Pl de la Résidence
du Leader

40

Bab
Jedid

to Marché de Blé
& Gorjani Pk   Souk des Armes

to Bab el Djemilla Quarter

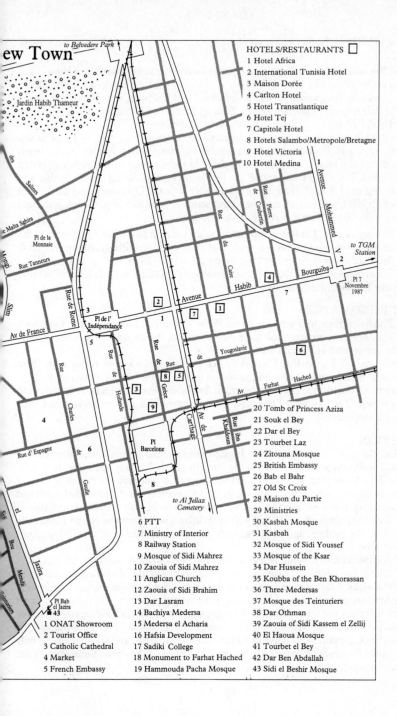

ew Town

to Belvedere Park

Jardin Habib Thameur

HOTELS/RESTAURANTS □

1 Hotel Africa
2 International Tunisia Hotel
3 Maison Dorée
4 Carlton Hotel
5 Hotel Transatlantique
6 Hotel Tej
7 Capitole Hotel
8 Hotels Salambo/Metropole/Bretagne
9 Hotel Victoria
10 Hotel Medina

Pl de la Monnaie

Rue Tanneurs

Av de France

Pl de l' Indépendance

Rue de Rome

Av de France

Pl Barcelone

to Al Jellaz Cemetery

Pl Bab el Jazira
43

to TGM Station

Pl 7 Novembre 1987

20 Tomb of Princess Aziza
21 Souk el Bey
22 Dar el Bey
23 Tourbet Laz
24 Zitouna Mosque
25 British Embassy
26 Bab el Bahr
27 Old St Croix
28 Maison du Partie
29 Ministries
30 Kasbah Mosque
31 Kasbah
32 Mosque of Sidi Youssef
33 Mosque of the Ksar
34 Dar Hussein
35 Koubba of the Ben Khorassan
36 Three Medersas
37 Mosque des Teinturiers
38 Dar Othman
39 Zaouia of Sidi Kassem el Zellij
40 El Haoua Mosque
41 Tourbet el Bey
42 Dar Ben Abdallah
43 Sidi el Beshir Mosque

6 PTT
7 Ministry of Interior
8 Railway Station
9 Mosque of Sidi Mahrez
10 Zaouia of Sidi Mahrez
11 Anglican Church
12 Zaouia of Sidi Brahim
13 Dar Lasram
14 Bachiya Medersa
15 Medersa el Acharia
16 Hafsia Development
17 Sadiki College
18 Monument to Farhat Hached
19 Hammouda Pacha Mosque

1 ONAT Showroom
2 Tourist Office
3 Catholic Cathedral
4 Market
5 French Embassy

tel (01) 490358/391574. El Kef and everywhere north are serviced by Bab Saadoun station, tel (01) 562299.

By *Louage*: **For towns close to Tunis catching a** *louage* is straightforward. For Bizerte and the north go to the station at 14 Av Ali Belhouane, opposite the Esso garage at Bab Saadoun. For places due south like Zaghouan, El Fahs, Nabeul and Kairouan go to the station under the flyover at Bab Alleoua. The Sahel cities, Sousse, Mahdia and Monastir are served from Garage du Bois at 37 Rue al Jazira, opposite Rue d'Angleterre.

For more distant destinations it is no use pretending foolproof locations, as Tunis' *louage* stations move regularly. Even tourist offices, guides and hotel porters become vague when asked, though the city taxis are usually up to date. At the moment all the yellow Algerian *louages* for Algiers, Bone and Constantine use the Av de France; *louages* for Medenine and Tataouine collect at 11 Rue al Jazira; those heading for Béja and Djendouba use the Café El Hana on Av Bab Jedid, and *louages*; and the longer southern routes to Sfax, Gabès, Jerba and Tripoli leave from Garage Soudan at 6 Rue du Soudan.

Car Hire: Having a car in Tunis is a hindrance, so do not rush to the car hire booths at the airport the moment you land unless you wish to avoid the city completely. Along Av Habib Bourguiba there are a number of firms: Hertz at no. 29, tel (01) 248529, Topcar at no. 17, tel (01) 241462, CarthaRent at no. 59, tel (01) 254304 and Avis at 90 Av de la Liberté, tel (01) 282508. Prices are fairly uniform (see p. 11).

TOURIST INFORMATION

The main **Tourist Office** in Tunis squats on Pl du 7 Novembre and is well stocked with booklets. Otherwise it is amongst the least informative in the country. There are branch offices at the airport and in Pl de la Victoire.

Tunis' principal **PTT** is on Rue Charles de Gaulle. Stamps and poste restante are dealt with in the main hall, telephones round the corner in Rue Gamal Abdel Nasser.

Banks are freely distributed along the length of Av Habib Bourguiba and take it in turns to stay open on Saturday morning. Otherwise the big hotels will change money and cash traveller's or Eurocheques.

ORIENTATION

The medina, the old city studded with Islamic monuments, is the principal attraction of Tunis, and is also the physical centre of the modern city. It is a busy but traffic-free core, with a maze for a street plan, and is enclosed by a ring road following the circuit of the old walls, of which only the odd gateway survives. In the 13th century the city expanded north and south, throwing up two new quarters, known as the ribats of Bab el Souika and Bab el Djemilla. They were originally enclosed within their own walls but now merge seamlessly with the bulk of the medina, and in places with the rigid grid pattern of the 19th-century French New Town.

It is still possible to find yourself in a genuinely medieval space, wandering through quiet residential alleys, the sunlight broken by spanning arches or the darkened animation of barrel-vaulted souks. Craft workshops, government ministries, popular markets, cafés, restaurants, hammams, houses, shops and mosques exist in tight proximity. This animated street life is at least half the joy of the medina, for there are only two historical buildings that a tourist can expect to get inside—the **Museum of Dar ben Abdallah** and the **Zitouna Mosque**. All the state buildings, mosques and active zaouia are closed to tourists, and are appreciable only from the outside. If you are persistent, charming or lucky you will be allowed into some of the medersas and mausoleums.

To see all the principal sites of Tunis in one go is an exhausting and confusing experience. Therefore we have divided the city into five areas, starting from Pl de la Victoire, the square that divides the medina from the New Town: the first goes east down Av Habib Bourguiba to point out the few things of interest in the New Town; the second follows the main artery of the medina into the souk, that maze of shop-lined alleys surrounding the Zitouna Mosque; the third tour cuts across the medina, avoiding the souk, highlighting buildings of interest on the way up to the old kasbah, now as ever the government quarter; the fourth takes you through the southern end of the medina; the fifth explores the little-visited northern end.

I: The New Town

Place de la Victoire's most prominent feature is **Bab el Bahr**, the Sea Gate or Porte de France, which now sits stranded in the centre of the square. The arch dates from the last comprehensive restoration of the medina's defences in 1848. The square is now the place to watch the medley of Tunis' citizens: its earnest students, aged European residents, sharp-eyed touts, besuited men of affairs, parcel-clutching tourists or elegant conservatives dressed in white gellabas and crimson skull-caps.

Until 1859 the square was a warren of slums, clustering at the foot of the medina near the festering rubbish-strewn shores of Lake Tunis. Since Europeans were allowed back into Tunis in the 17th century, it had been the **Christian ghetto**. But from 1860 they began to build a European city to the east by reclaiming land from the lake. All the consuls moved from their cramped medina quarters, leaving only the **British Embassy**—one suspects for reasons of economy—which was rebuilt at the turn of the century with the tall, handsome stucco façade that now lines the north of the square. The ground floor is occupied by a well-stocked British Council library which is closed throughout the summer.

Av de France stretches east, a row of bookshops on its northern pavement and a bustle of yellow Algerian taxis in the centre. The areas to its north and south, the parts of the European city closest to the medina, were the **'poor white' quarters**, housing communities of Maltese, Sicilians, Sardinians and Greeks. Though these settlers have long since left Tunis, their intimate terraced streets are still the liveliest in the New Town. To the north Rue de Rome leads past the Greek Orthodox church, where you get the best **shoeshine** in Tunis, to baobab-shaded Pl de la Monnaie. There's a raffish secondhand furniture trade in the surrounding streets, Rue des Tanneurs and Rue Malta Sghira. South of Av de France, Rue Charles de Gaulle leads to an enormous **covered market** where every imaginable variety of fish, fruit, vegetable, tree and picnic basket can be found. The streets surrounding the market, as well as being favoured by street hawkers, are lined with grocers selling dates, nuts, spices, pickled olives and sauces.

Av de France ends at the small Pl de l'Indépendance where a stern statue of Ibn Khaldoun, the medieval historian (see p. 72), flies the respectable flag of Islamic scholarship between two flanking memorials of the colonial era. To the north rises the **Catholic cathedral of St Vincent de Paul**, built in 1882 of course. What other age could build a porch in such a scrapbook of Gothic, Romanesque, Byzantine and Moorish architectural styles? It is crowned with an offensive bust of God the Father, though fortunately few Muslims would think of connecting this protrusion with Allah. The interior is grey and monumental, only partially enlivened by representations of the local St Augustine and St Cyprian. Immediately to the south of the statue is the old colonial seat of power, the offices and garden of the French Resident, now the **French Embassy**.

From Pl de l'Indépendance the main commercial artery of the city, Av Habib Bourguiba, stretches east. Apart from its cafés, restaurants and all-pervading air of business, the chief delight of 'Habib' is its long **central promenade**, shaded by a double line of ficus trees under which newsagents and jasmine salesmen have their stalls. At dusk it reaches a crescendo of activity, the cafés and the evening *passeo* reach their social height, starlings take flight to perform showy acrobatic turns above the city and florists illuminate their opulent displays of gladioli.

On the south side of the avenue, look out for the bulging rococo façade of the **theatre**, and further on the heavily guarded, monolithic Ministry of the Interior. It is from here that recent bouts of unrest in the country have been controlled, and it is the one government building in Tunis that emanates a sense of power. Pl du 7 Novembre, the former Pl d'Afrique, punctuates the eastern end of the promenade and beyond cheaper shops, carparks, garages and insurance offices line the way to the **TGM station**, where trains set off north across the lake.

II: The Souks and the Zitouna Mosque

The Zitouna Mosque is the physical and spiritual heart of Tunis, a startling 9th-century survivor. Around it spreads the souk, one of the world's great marketplaces, a colourful, exuberant and confusing network of covered streets. It is an easy area to reach—from Pl de la Victoire just drift up Rue Jamma ez Zitouna with the human flow.

Some of the best hours in Tunisia can be lost here, haggling over velvet circumcision suits, Roman lamps, painted mirrors, olive-wood bowls and killims. Trading is most brisk in the morning but the hours before dusk are more social, when even the broader streets are packed with crowds that move as one.

Rue Jamma ez Zitouna

This street is lined by glittering, nest-like tourist bazaars, including Youssef Ayoub's collection of antiquities at no. 45. Over the hammering of brass plates break cheery welcomes in the half-dozen major European languages.

The large stucco building at the beginning of the street housed the International Financial Commission, a sort of 19th-century IMF that took charge of Tunisian finances when Bey Mohammed threatened to declare the country bankrupt. It was deeply resented by the man on the street, who rightly saw it as a surrender of national sovereignty, which led to the French invasion of 1881.

Just beyond, a series of Romanesque doorways on the left belong to the old Catholic **church of St Croix**, whose nave now serves as municipal offices. It was built by Father Jean Le Vacher, of the order of St Vincent de Paul, a society which redeemed European slaves. He was the first Christian, since the Hapsburg occupation, to be allowed into Tunis medina. In 1635 he was allowed to build a small chapel, and in 1662, three years after he was made the first French consul, Hammouda Pasha I gave him leave to build this substantial church. The adjoining rectory, no. 12, is now the El Hanout pottery shop.

Rue Sidi Ali Azouz on the left was named after a celebrated mystic from Morocco. He was adopted into the pantheon of Tunisian saints and a zaouia, where his spiritual discipline was taught, was established in the medina. The present building, no. 7, was restored in the 19th century. Just beyond the zaouia, down a passage to the left, is a magnificent town house now used as a workshop for producing painted tiles.

One of the best places for buying carved and turned olive wood is at 25 Rue de Tamis, the alley to the right at the next crossroads. The street to the left, Souk el Belat, is predominantly a food market. Further up on the right you pass the **National Library**, almost entirely hidden by bazaars. Through its doors you can glimpse its elegant interior, built by Hammouda Pasha II as a Turkish barracks. Squeeze past the tables of one of the best-placed café-restaurants in Tunis and emerge into the daylight in front of the high walls of the Zitouna Mosque.

The Zitouna Mosque

The Zitouna, or 'olive tree' Mosque is supposed to be open from 08.00–12.00, every day except Fri, but it is not unusual to find it closed within these hours. When you get in you will only be allowed into a viewing enclosure looking over the magnificent *sahn*, an expanse of paved stone, broken only by a sundial and four ancient well-heads.

The contrast between the anarchic animation of the souk and the ordered serenity of the mosque's colonnaded interior has an almost mystical impact. Outside the hours of prayer it is filled only by pigeons and the resonance of a thousand years of incessant prayer. A sense of great age emanates from the outer wall, made from stone first used in the Roman city of Carthage. According to tradition, the Zitouna was at that time occupied by a temple to Athena, later dedicated to St Olive. The first mosque was supposedly founded by Hassan ibn Numan, the Arab conqueror of Carthage, though the earliest proven Muslim building here was a ribat, built on the orders of an Omayyad governor in 732. The present mosque dates from the reign of the Aghlabid Abu Ibrahim Ahmed (856–63). In the midst of completing the Great Mosque in Kairouan, he set about the contruction of the Zitouna, symbolically making Tunis' mosque a third the size of that in his capital.

The prayer hall, and its 15 rows of Roman columns crowned by horseshoe arches, is virtually as he left it. The wider central aisle was further emphasized by the addition of a 'bahu' or entrance dome, by the 11th-century Khorassan Emirs of Tunis. The three niches of the square lower storey combine with the horseshoe arch to create a triumphal entrance, capped by a cylindrical Byzantine layer and a white gadrooned dome.

The Hafsids added a minaret in the northwest corner of the *sahn*, which was replaced in 1894 by the heavy tower which stands today. They also built a separate ablutions hall, the Midhat Soltane, and the first medersas to house the students who had for centuries flocked to the Zitouna to study the Koran and Islamic jurisprudence. This brought teaching at the Zitouna to the level and prestige of that of Egypt's Al Azhar and Morocco's Qaraouyine Mosques. The prayer hall doubled as a lecture hall where knots of students clustered around teachers who leant against the columns. Those favoured by the teachers have an extra polish. Teaching continued at the Zitouna until the 1960s, when the government brought theological studies under the control of the new National University of Tunis.

Souk el Attarine and Souk des Etoffes

The four streets surrounding the Zitouna make a good further introduction to the souk.

Souk el Attarine, the perfumers' souk, was built against the north face of the Zitouna by Abu Zakirayya, the first Hafsid in the 13th century. Until the 20th century, **scent-making** was the noblest of all trades and no city in North Africa could match the reputation of Tunis. It required not only the finest olefactory sensibilities but precise knowledge of when to harvest, distil and preserve any of a hundred vegetable components, let alone the more arcane techniques required for milking the glands of whales and wild cats. At one point a single civet cat was valued at 50 negro slaves. The souk is still lined with the booths of scent sellers, and stalls offering kitsch cushions and baskets, the Islamic eqivalent of wrapping paper.

Detail from Bachiya Medersa, Tunis

The alley to the right, Souk el Blaghia, used to be the old haunt of the slipper-makers. The Bab el Bouhour gate to the Zitouna has a fine 11th-century inscription and almost immediately opposite is a smelly alley with stairs leading up to the handsome gate of the **Midhat Soltane**, the lavish white marble ablution courtyard built by Abu Yahia in 1316 for ritual washing before prayers. It is now firmly closed.

To the left Souk des Etoffes, with its striking line of red and green barley-sugar columns and more formal double row of boutiques, was first laid out in the 15th century. It is still awash with cascades of clothing, light fabric and shawls. It seems a world away from the Zitouna, but now and then an open door gives an entrancing view straight into the inner courtyard. Opposite no. 37 is the black and blue gate of the **Medersa el Muradia**, built by Murad II in the 17th century. It is in good condition, its yellow stone courtyard occupied by a school teaching traditional crafts. Turn left down the narrower Souk de la Laine, where at no. 21 is the **Gate of the Imam**, a stunning entrance to the mosque made with 2nd-century AD carved Roman lintels.

Three Medersas: En Nakhla, Bachiya and Slimanyia

From Rue Jamma ez Zitouna it is a short walk to Rue des Librairies, a street housing three medersas. This succession of connecting courtyards, prayer halls and tomb rooms was built by the first two Husseinite Beys in the early 18th century and are the most important group in the city. Pupils' rooms were arranged around an interior courtyard, and the more lavish foundations had their own prayer hall.

At the **Medersa en Nakhla**, the medersa of the palm, 13 Rue des Librairies, sunlight still filters through palm fronds into the small courtyard of yellow stone arches suspended on white columns, built by Hussein ibn Ali Turki in 1714. He was deposed by his nephew Ali Pasha I who built the much larger **Bachiya Medersa** next door in 1752, named after the victorious faction that had supported him in the long war against his uncle. It has two blue gates at no. 27 and no. 29 which may be open due to restoration work. The courtyards are still in a bad state but the mausoleum, with its squashed green hat of a dome just visible from the street, is girded by an elegant band of calligraphy picked out in blue. On the opposite side of

92

the road is an old Turkish bath, the **Hammam Kachachine**, entered through the barber shop, open from 05.00–17.00.

The third, **Es Slimaniya Medersa** was commissioned by Ali Pasha only two years later, on 8 December 1754, to celebrate the birth of his son Sliman. Its Andalucian tiled entrance projects into Rue es Slimaniya, just round the corner. The small tiled and arcaded courtyard now houses a para-medical training centre. The uphill continuation of Rue es Slimaniya is known as Souk Kachachine, an area where tailors and embroiderers can easily be persuaded to add arabesque swirls to your sleeves or lapels.

Souk et Trouk

Uphill from Souk des Etoffes is Souk et Trouk, built in the early 17th century, its name a shortened slang for the Turkish tailors who used to make Ottoman caftans here. On the corner, the **Bazaar ed Dar** is a civilized and elegant shop that is almost halfway to a museum. A rival neighbour, the 'Musée des Turcs', is also worth a browse, not least in order to climb to the roof terrace for a fine view into the 17th-century Mosque of Sidi Youssef. Further up the street is the **Mrabet Restaurant**, its upstairs dining-room inundated by large tour groups, but its ground floor a popular local café with sugar-twist columns, raised matting floors, hubbly-bubblies and good coffee.

Souk des Femmes

The densest network of alleys is above and below Souk des Femmes, the southern continuation of Souk des Etoffes, which later turns into Rue Tourbet el Bey. It drips with coloured scarfs and neatly packed white haiks. Below, around Souk du Cotton and Rue el Beji, is a labyrinth of tailors, cutters, stitchers and looms.

Above Souk des Femmes, Souk des Orfèvres, the goldworkers' souk, is still the centre for **jewellery**. Each trade in the medina was ruled by an *amin*, an elected guild-master who between them elected the Sheikh of the Medina. Each *amin* inspected the quality of goods of his trade before they were allowed to be sold. The *amin* of the jewellers also fixed prices, based directly on the weight and purity of the precious metal used. The jeweller added only a small percentage, seldom over 20%, for the actual work.

Souk Sekkajine

Souk Sekkajine is another great thoroughfare. It leads uphill from Souk des Etoffes, passing a network of alleys to right and left before emerging into the traffic and sunlight of the medina ringroad. On your first trip it is difficult to pass the Palais d'Orient (or the two neighbouring shops) without being lured up to their ornately tiled roof terraces. The famous view south takes in the minaret of the Zitouna and the two white domes of the prayer hall before panning out over the green squashed hat of the Bachiya Medersa and down to the twin cathedral towers in the New Town. On your way down you may be shown a 19th-century 'Beylical' gilt bed and are unlikely to avoid the lavish display of carpets from one of the most comprehensive stocks in the country.

Walking further up Souk Sekkajine you enter an area long renowned for skilled **embroidery**, both elaborate female costumes covered in sequins and ornate velvet 'circumcision' suits. A second right leads into Souk el Dzira, the source of some of the finest **leather work** and slippers. Running off it are elaborately painted jewellers' booths in Souk el Berka, built by Youssef Dey as a centre for Turkish workmanship. At its centre is a small dome supported by six green and red striped columns which served as an occasional **slave market**. Kairouan was always the important market for trans-Saharan slaves, and corsair ports, like La Goulette, Ghar el Melh and Bizerte, held markets for Christian galley slaves. Souk el Berka was for the domestic end of the market–casual dealing in servants, clerks, skilled artisans and concubines. It was also a centre of ransom speculation. Christian captives who looked worth a ransom were initially sold in groups, at three times the going rate for galley slaves, by corsair captains keen to turn a quick profit. Their price then fluctuated as individual details such as their religion, nationality, family ties and wealth became available, and sometimes the gamblers were rewarded for risking their capital by ransom payments.

Back on Souk Sekkajine look out for Souk Leffa on the left. It is a good street for **killims** and has a secretive but noisy café, the Dar Mnouchi, at no. 54. The upper reaches of Souk Sekkajine are the best place for rougher leather work. At no. 12 and opposite at no. 25 is a dedicated saddle-maker with a stock that includes mule and donkey packs, high Arab and open European saddles and a side-line in killim handbags. Further up, by the mid-street saint's tomb, are belt- and dog-collar-makers. Where Sekkajine meets Rue Bab Mnara look out for the low tomb of Abdallah al Tourjoumane, better known in the west as Anselm Turmeda. He was a famous Majorcan convert to Islam who composed *'La Dispute de l'Oré'*, a diatribe in Catalan against the men of Barcelona, as well as a number of more sober works in Arabic expounding on the superiority of Islam to Christianity.

III: The Upper Medina and Kasbah Quarter

This exploration avoids the souk to get to the upper medina without getting lost. It begins with a visit to the tomb of Princess Aziza, then passes the Hammouda Pasha Mosque and dips into the Souk el Bey for coffee. Emerging by the Sidi Youssef Mosque, it passes the Dar el Bey and the Kasbah Mosque before going up to the Mausoleum of Sidi Kassem el Zellij and back down again to look at the Koubba of the Beni Khorassan at the top of the souk.

Take **Rue de la Kasbah**, a narrow alley which enters the medina from the corner of the British Embassy. Paved in black stone and empty of tourist bazaars, it is packed with the needs of contemporary Tunisians—cascading displays of blue jeans, black leather jackets, handbags and high-heel shoes.

Walk uphill for 350 m keeping a sharp look out on the left for Rue Djeloud. About 15 m along this road there is an unpromising-looking turning, the Impasse Echemmahia, named after Tunis' first medersa, built here in 1249. At the top of the impasse is an innocuous brown door on the right, no. 9. Knock loudly with the Hand of Fatimah shouting, 'Tourist'. You will then be welcomed in by the custodian family, escorted under the washing and shown the **tomb of Princess Lalla Aziza Othman**. The dark koubba still bears the remains of its decorative carved plaster and tiled walls, though all attention is drawn to the floor, a sea of delicately carved white marble tombs. Aziza's tomb is the humble low marble plaque in front of the closed door, flanked by her sisters. To her left, second turban along, is that of her father the great Dey Othman, who ruled Tunisia from 1594–1610, and whose house you can see in the southern quarter of the medina. The princess's real name was Fatimah; Aziza means beloved, an affectionate nickname that she won for her charitable works. She established a trust to free debtors, another to provide dowries for poor girls and another to ransom good Muslims held as galley slaves by wicked Christian rulers like the King of France and the Grand Master of the Knights of Malta. The koubba was built by Hussein ibn Ali Turki, founder of the Husseinite dynasty, who had good reason to cherish Princess Aziza, his mother-in-law.

Return to Rue de la Kasbah and approach the elegant octagonal minaret of the **Hammouda Pasha Mosque**. It was built in 1655 by the Pasha to honour his father, Muradide, an Italian who had embraced Islam and risen to become Bey du Camp, or military commander, under Youssef Dey. Italian craftsmen were employed to carve the mihrab arch and the columns in the prayer hall, though non-Muslims must be satisfied with looking at its minaret. Its buttressed gallery, from which once the muezzin and now a loudspeaker call the faithful to prayer, supports a light-roofed pavilion, a Turkish rather than North African feature.

Looking left down Rue Sidi ben Arous, this thin Turkic minaret contrasts strongly with the bulky tower of the Zitouna Mosque, and between them lurks the green-tiled roof the **Hammouda Pasha Mausoleum**. It is an unforgiving building that has taken the Tunisian penchant for coloured marble to unpalatable extremes. The basis for each face is a processional arch, but so embellished with geometrical, floral, classical and Egyptian themes that its structure is lost in a confusion of coloured stone. Further down the street are two zaouia, firmly closed to non-Muslims. The one next door to the Hammouda Pasha koubba is the **Zaouia of Sidi ben Arous**, a Tunisian mystic educated by the celebrated Moroccan Sufi master, Al Jazuli. Opposite is the **Zaouia of Sidi Kelai** built by the Hafsid Caliph, Abu Yahia, during his brief reign from 1490–94.

Further up Rue de la Kasbah two yellow stone arches give entrance to an elegant covered rectangular market, known as the **Souk el Bey**. This Tunisian Burlington Arcade was built by Mohammed el Hafsi, a Muradite Bey who ruled from 1675–84, as a commercial venture directly below his house, the Dar el Bey. It is spanned by two covered alleys, the Petit Souk des Chechias and the Grand Souk des Chechias, joined by a short street entirely overtaken by a café. It is a calm, meditative place, with a mixed clientele of hat-makers and civil servants, disturbed only by low chatter and air rattling through hubbly-bubblies. The Souk el Bey is still dominated by makers of *chechias*, the red felt hats that adorn male heads. It is a thrilling 19th-century medley of painted wood, gilt mirrors, framed photographs and ornamental calligraphy, and though hat-making has plummeted from its once prestigious position, the souk remains a dignified place. Instruments of work, tweezers, needles, expanding calipers and teazle brushes lie around displays of *chechias* of every colour and size.

Back on Souk el Bey the minaret of **Sidi Youssef Mosque** rises above on the right. It is entirely detached from the prayer hall, and is the oldest of the four Turkic, octagonal minarets of Tunis, with a simple, elegant gallery and pavilion. It was built by Youssef Dey in 1616 immediately below the military kasbah quarter and symbolically placed above the Zitouna Mosque. At this time the Ottomans had only ruled Tunisia for a generation, and their religious traditions were quite different. Here the Turkish troops kept to the predominantly Turkish Hanefite rite, and in 1622 a medersa was added to keep Hanefite teaching quite separate from the Malekite Zitouna University. The complex was further augmented by a **mausoleum** built for Youssef and his immediate descendants, a monumental square koubba covered by a green tiled pyramid roof. Its marble façade, a pair of diminishing arches flanked by twin sets of niches, is influenced by the Roman triumphal arches that still scatter the countryside of Tunisia. Above the mosque rambles the hospital named after Lalla Aziza Othman, incorporating pleasant garden courtyards and gates from an earlier 17th-century barracks.

Returning to Rue de la Kasbah walk up between the high walls of two government buildings. On your left is the **Dar el Bey**, built by Hammouda Pasha I as the town house of Tunisia's rulers. The first gate, to the offices of the Prime Minister, is patrolled by the red-uniformed Beylical guard; the second, with a mere blue-uniformed sentinel, is the Foreign Ministry. Its magnificent audience chambers are not open to the public, though they were put at the disposal of the Prince Regent's, later George IV's, estranged wife, Princess Caroline, when she took refuge in Tunis in the early 19th century. Across the central garden of Pl du Gouvernement is the 19th-century façade of the Treasury and Planning Ministry with two clock faces. One shows the usual 12-hour clock and beneath it is a much rarer Muslim lunar clock, which when working gives the date and size of the moon.

Above Pl du Gouvernement, **Tourbet Laz** is a delightful koubba with a squashed-hat roof of green tiles, the mausoleum of the last Turkish Dey to challenge the Muradite Beys. Below it hides the Café Jawaher, tucked away in a corner. The café makes a shaded vantage point from which to look out over the large modern square that crowns the high point of Tunis. This is the site of the old kasbah—the road marks the line of walls that once separated the enclosed government fortress from the rest of the city. It was levelled by the French within months of seizing power, in a graphic but ugly demonstration of the new order. Recent excavations for an underground carpark have revealed sedimentary layers of history, an Aghlabid palace, and fortresses of the Zirids, the Beni Khorassan and the Turks. In the centre rises a classic piece of 'new nation monolithic', a **monument to Farhat Hached**, the Tunisian trade unionist whose assassination united the Maghreb in the independence struggle against the French. On the summit of the hill rests the two-storey *Maison du Parti*, an appropriate site for the headquarters of what was for a long time the only political party, with a recent 100% poll to its credit.

Of the old kasbah quarter there are only two traces: the 13th-century Kasbah Mosque and the 19th-century **Sadiki College**. The latter, founded by the reformer Khereddine with estates confiscated from his corrupt rival, teaches a successful mix of traditional Muslim education and a western liberal curriculum, and has become an enduring legacy. Sadiki provided Tunisia with most of its post-independence leadership, and its class lists are a Tunisian Who's Who. On the other side of the square is the **Kasbah Mosque** built by the first Hafsid ruler, Abu Zakariyya, in the middle of the 13th century. Its minaret is a perfect example of the indigenous North African tradition. The tower is decorated with a tracery of entrelacs, pierced by Moorish double windows and crowned with a lantern, a fifth the size of the tower. The spire, with its three golden balls, reminds the faithful of the basic minimum of daily prayer. As the highest minaret in the city, it is always the first to signal the call to prayer.

Walk up Rue du 2 Mars 1934 to reach a surviving artillery bastion of the kasbah defences. A garden walk decorated with archaeological oddities is being built here amongst piles of carved marble tombstones removed when the old kasbah cemetery was ploughed up. Slip down the dual carriageway to the crossroads known as Bab Sidi Kassem and you reach the pyramidal roof of the 16th-century **Zaouia of Sidi Kassem el Zellij**. The Sidi was a revered Sufi teacher from Andalucia, and Zellij in his title refers to a form of cut tile mosaic, for he was also a master potter, and the zaouia is built over his pottery. It has recently been restored and turned into a museum that exhibits carved Muslim gravestones (open 09.30–16.30, except Mon). It is a subject of minority interest, but has an attractive shaded garden with Spanish seats and a view south over the *sebkhet* to the bubbly silhouette of Jebel Zaghouan and the twin peaks of Jebel Bou Kornine.

Beside the zaouia is a tree-shaded square, Pl du Résidence du Leader. No. 6 Rue Jamma el Haoua is an old haunt of Habib Bourguiba's, and the stumpy minaret of the **El Haoua Mosque** all that is left of an originally Hafsid foundation, complete with medersa, that was built by the wife of the first Caliph.

Take Rue de la Verité, in the lefthand corner, to cut down through the winding back streets to Blvd Bab Menara, the busy medina ringroad below the Kasbah Mosque. Taking the back entrance to the souk, Rue Souk Sekkajine, and a first right brings you to a green door marked **Musée du Sidi Bou Khrissan**. Knock and put on your best smile, for the resident guardians may then let you into their courtyard filled with the odours of olive, fig, lemon and jasmine. In a corner, surrounded by carved tombstones, is the 11th-century koubba of the Beni

Khorassan Emirs. It is North African Muslim architecture at its austere best–an elegant arched kiosk, decorated with vestigial pillars and bands of alternating yellow and white stone. The squinches that support the dome in the corners are vigorously carved and joined by blind arches. On the summit of the exterior wall a band of Kufic script attests that the two sons of Abdelhaq ibn Khorassan raised the dome over their father's grave in 1093.

From here you can either wander down Rue Souk Sekkajine into the heart of the souk, or catch a no. 1 bus or taxi back round to Pl de la Victoire.

IV: The Southern Medina

This walk does not pass a single souvenir stall but takes you through local markets, past a number of historic mosques and town houses, around the Tourbet el Bey and into the Dar ben Abdallah, a palatial town house turned museum.

In Pl de la Victoire turn left at Restaurant Semaphore on to Rue de la Commission which follows the line of the old medina walls. Passing a house used by Garibaldi whilst plotting the invasion of Sicily, continue through baobab-shaded Pl Cheikh el Barzouli. Beyond lies Rue de la Menzil, a high, shady street filled with the odour of long strings of red pepper. It ends in a burst of sun and traffic at Pl Bab al Jazira, dominated by the free-standing minaret of **Sidi el Beshir Mosque**. Built by the Hafsids in the 14th century and recently restored, it has a classic Maghrebi silhouette, a square tower with the crowning lantern a fifth its height.

A sharp right turn leads up Rue des Teinturiers, the street of the dyers, through its perpetual **street market** selling fish and vegetables. On the right is a small **mosque**, known as Harmal, that was built in the 1600s—a deliberate piece of archaic simplicity to harmonize with the minaret of el Beshir. Keep an eye out for the dyers' alleys (opposite nos. 92 and 104), the last remnants of the medieval trade that once dominated this long thoroughfare. They are often strung with gay bolts of wool, drying from a session in the vats. Just beyond is the **Hammam des Teinturiers**, one of the best advertised and most accessible of the medina bathhouses.

Mosque des Teinturiers

Looming ahead is the unmistakable minaret of the Mosque des Teinturiers, which is affectionately known by the locals as 'El Jedid', the new mosque, though it was finished in 1716. It was commissioned by the founder of the Husseinite dynasty, Hussein ibn Ali Turki, who was Cretan by ancestry. He belonged to a world that looked to Ottoman Istanbul for its cultural references, and the minaret, with its octagonal high pointed spire and hanging balcony, mirrored by an interior awash with Iznik and Damascus tiles, creates a distinctly Turkish look. Hussein also built a **mausoleum** next door where he prepared suitable company for his grave by burying two holy men, Sidi Kacem el Beji and Sidi Kacem es Sebati. Unfortunately he was deposed by a nephew and though he kept his life, he lost his grave. The new Bey, Ali Pasha, buried his own father there instead.

Dey Othman

Just after the mosque dive right through a barrel-vaulted alley to reach a small sun-baked yard in front of 16 Rue M'bazza, the **palace of Dey Othman**. It was something of a country cottage for the Dey, a quiet sanctuary in one of the poorer quarters of the medina away from the intrigue of the government councils over which he presided from 1594–1610. Built at the height of corsair prosperity, it survived the centuries as a government storehouse. The black and white marble gate is impressive but illustrates the architectural decadence which even then allowed the triumph of decoration over form. The traditional horseshoe arch has been corrupted to the shape of a key-hole and disturbed by a riot of geometrical bands. The tiled and carved plaster interior is in the long process of restoration, but if work is in progress the men are happy to let you admire their skills. A tiled bayonet hall leads into a small colonnaded garden courtyard flanked by four T-shaped halls.

Museum of Dar ben Abdallah

Returning to the Mosque des Teinturiers, turn right beyond it down Rue Sidi Kassem and then left to reach the **Museum of Arts and Traditions** installed in an 18th-century palace, Dar ben Abdallah (open daily except Sun, 09.30–16.30; adm).

The Dar ben Abdallah is one of the most delightful spots in the medina, a palatial house that in its heyday ranged far over the local area. The entrance hall is dark and cool, a tiled corridor of a room which was known as the **driba**, and lined with benches where clients, friends and petitioners would wait. The favoured were led through an even narrower passage, the *skifa*, to the dazzling sun-baked courtyard at the heart of the house. A marble fountain plays in the centre and surrounding reception rooms are enclosed behind a colonnade, with an upper gallery whose blue beams and balustrade presage a pure square of blue sky. In Islamic countries, the cosy interiors contrast agreeably with the aggressive public life of the streets. Even here the kitsch floral tiles and central fountain subdue the interior space with their domesticity.

The four T-shaped rooms that surround the court are a traditional arrangement that fitted well with the Koranic injunction for men to treat their wives equally. They have been given 19th-century interiors and filled with dressed dummies. One room has a **male tea party** with an exhibition of appropriate trinketry: beads, belts, books and snuff boxes and the different styles of dress worn by the cadis of the Malekite and Hanefite schools of law. The second salon shows a **bride** being prepared for her wedding, though in a truly traditional house she would have been blindfolded, to be released from her splendour and darkness only by her new husband. The third room shows **family life**, no depressing haiks here but brief silk day suits of pantaloons and short-sleeved shirts.

In the fourth room sits a tableau of young girls learning their roles from a grandmother, though it is chiefly dedicated to babies and the various baths, rituals and herbal cures prescribed for infertility. Modern medicine has largely superseded this quackery, but the exhibition of **baby paraphernalia** is echoed in the streets of today. The seventh day after birth the new child is named and presented to its family, decked in embroidery and charms to ward off the evil eye: five fishes, Hands of Fatimah and teeth. The larger sequined suits were worn for circumcision celebrations, when a boy at the age of five or so passes from babyhood to the first stage of manhood. After his first visit to the mosque, the foreskin of his penis was clipped, without anaesthetic and usually by the barber. This ceremony, though not mentioned in the Koran, is at the heart of popular Muslim culture and with female depilation and a taboo on pork is a legacy of the earliest Semitic cultures.

Out of the museum, turn left onto Rue Sidi Kassem again and walk through a tunnel lined with carpenters' workshops to pop out in front of the Tourbet el Bey.

Tourbet el Bey

The Tourbet el Bey, the mausoleum of the Husseinites, was built by Ali Pasha II (1758–81) opposite the tomb of his grandfather Hussein ibn Ali Turki, the founder of the dynasty. It is fashionable to despise the mausoleum with its Italianate exterior, classical proportions, windows and pilasters. It is a brave attempt, however, to marry the architectural traditions of the south and north coasts of the Mediterranean, a role for which Tunisia is uniquely well placed. The carving on the pilasters is North African—pine cones, arabesques and cypress motifs. The exterior wall for all its classical regularity is surmounted by a confusion of Islamic domes, the squashed green hats indigenous to Tunisia.

The mausoleum is more often than not closed, but if you are lucky the custodian or workmen may be there. Wander into its two open courtyards, surrounded by half a dozen funerary chambers with sumptuously decorated ceilings, their tiled floors virtually invisible under a sea of raised marble tombs. The oldest ones have carved turban headstones, but the majority boast a marble fez, the result of a mid-19th-century Sultan's decree against the wearing of turbans.

Beside the mausoleum runs Rue Tourbet el Bey, the central thoroughfare of the southern medina. At no. 56 is the first of three shops run by el Haj Amor el Aouadi, an antique dealer. They conjure up the *fin de siècle* world of the Husseinite regency, in their confusion of Beylical portraits, Moorish gun racks, art nouveau and civic medals. The prices and imperturbable nature of the proprietor, puffing contentedly on a hubble-bubble, maintain it as an almost static collection. If you want a rest, follow Rue Tourbet el Bey south and leave the medina through double white gates to meet the ringroad and its cafés.

Rue de Riche and Rue des Andalous

The most elegant and mysterious quarter of the city lies along these two streets, where buttress arches, vaulted tunnels, high arched gateways and elegant studded doors are a visual treat. A tapestry of carved stone, crumbling pillars and riveted wood completely hide the legendary splendours of dozens of 17th-century palace gardens.

Walk north up Rue Tourbet el Bey, past no. 33, the **birthplace of Ibn Khaldoun** (see p. 72), and continue to the **Msid el Koubba**, a handsome 14th-century dome supported on three yellow stone arches, traditionally the entrance to the mosque where Ibn Khaldoun taught as a young man. Retrace your steps, and turn left down Rue du Riche, branching on to Rue des Andalous to the right. The last wave of Andalucians arrived in 1610 after Philip III of Spain banished all his Muslim and Jewish subjects. The more vengeful provided the boarding parties for corsair fleets, both at nearby La Goulette and at Ghar el Melh and Bizerte.

At the end of Rue des Andalous turn left up Rue du Dey. Just beyond the vaulted arch is the **Institut Rachidia** behind its closed blue doors. Named after Tunisia's great 11th-century poet, the institute protects the musical and poetic culture of Tunisia as well as funding the Rachidia orchestra. This orchestra conserves the pure heritage of Moorish classical music.

Dar Hussein

The next left, Rue du Chateau, feels more like a square, and contains Dar Hussein and the Mosque of the Ksar. Dar Hussein has a dull white façade surmounted by battlements hiding a spacious 18th-century courtyard with a confusion of painted wall tiles, a serene marble floor and a richly carved plaster colonnade. It now houses the National Institute of Archaeology and Arts, and unless you want to use their library the porter will keep you at bay.

Mosque of the Ksar

Opposite is the much older Mosque of the Ksar. The minaret, built in the 17th century from fine yellow stone, is broken by three decorative bands, different for each face, on which discordant black and white marble inlay has intruded. Glance down at the outer wall of the prayer hall with its simple dignified span of three arches, imposed in double relief to create a powerful play with shadow. This is the earliest portion of the mosque, which was built in 1106 by the Berber dynasty of Ahmed ben Khorassan. Under the wing of a Muslim friend it is possible to enter the courtyard and look into the simple prayer hall, decorated with columns taken from the ruins of Carthage. Passing through the passageway beside the mosque you emerge into a space known as Bab Menara, overlooked by the busy ringroad and the balconies of the Hotel de la Victoire and Elemessa.

Bab Jedid
Turn left and walk down the ringroad, lined with canopied cafés and ornate 19th-century stucco terraces. After about 200 m is a Hafsid gate, a survivor from the 13th-century walls inappropriately known as the new gate, the Bab Jedid. Walk through its bayonet passage to find a cheap **restaurant** inside, at the start of Rue des Forgerons. The road still resounds to a cacophony of hammer blows as blacksmiths forge arabesque iron screens, for use at home or on the Peugeot, and repair anything from cooking pots to oil sumps.

Bab el Djemilla Quarter
The medina's southern suburb is of interest only for its packed **street market**. Directly across the ringroad from the Bab Jedid, is a broad café-lined street known as Souk el Aassar. From here the road, now known as the Souk des Armées, twists uphill between fruit and vegetable stalls overlooked by the 14th-century **El H'laq Mosque**, whose squat minaret and green surroundings have something of an English village church about them. Beside the mosque the narrow Rue et Tohma leads into two contiguous wedge-shaped squares known as Pl des Cheveaux and Marché de Blé. 'Horse Square' is now largely devoted to football, the corn market transformed into a flea market. Climbing the steps of Rue Dar el Gorjani you come out into shady **Sidi Ali el Gorjani park**, once the cemetery of the Almohad rulers of Tunisia. Above the park, over the carriageway there is a view over **Sebkhet Essijoumi**. At dusk the lake, carrying the reflection of Jebel Zaghouan amongst clouds of pink flamingoes, turns gold in the sun.

V: The Northern Medina

The two celebrated monuments in the northern end of the medina, the **Mosque of Sidi Mahrez** and **Youssef Sahib et Tabaa Mosque**, are both closed to non-Muslims, and as a result no tourists visit the area. It appeals, however, to those who are happy to spend a half-day walking through quiet 17th-century streets and packed street markets, and watching everyday life from tables in local cafés.

The area immediately north of Pl de la Victoire is one of the most alarming and fascinating in the medina. It is a dark warren of half-covered alleys, filled with neglected junk shops, over-used hotel bedrooms, street hawkers, pimps and prostitutes.

A right turn immediately beside the British Embassy takes you down Rue des Glacières, where ice storage was provided in dark subterranean cellars. Now the alley resounds to continuous disco-funk, its cavernous halls filled with piles of secondhand clothing and 19th-century junk.

The parallel **Rue de l'Ancienne Douane**, right a few metres up Rue de la Kasbah from the square, is a thin alley of towering dark tenements. It is a poor area, but these courtyard houses are surprisingly elegant, with fine carved cedar pillars and beams. This is all that is left of the old Christian quarter, on the dirty and unfashionable lakeside edge of the medina.

Here, from 1675–1859, lived the merchants, agents, consuls and customs officers of the European powers. A plaque on no. 5 commemorates the first French Consulate.

North from the British Embassy, Rue Mongi Slim follows the line of the old medina wall. It is also lined with antique shops, whose plaster busts, daguerrotypes, art deco statuettes, solid colonial furniture and Indo-Chinese watercolours are preserved by outrageous prices. An amusing group of book dealers have colonized the area by Rue des Tanneurs, which commemorates a medieval tannery.

Rue Mongi Slim and Rue des Glacières both issue into Pl Bab Carthagena, an unremarkable swirl of dust and traffic 500 m north. The eponymous Carthage Gate survives only in name, and the Hafsia, the area of the medina inside the gate, was demolished in the 1950s. The plan for its redevelopment, which won the **1983 Agha Khan Prize for Architecture**, is like so many plans in Tunisia 'en procès de réalisation'. It used to be the medieval Jewish ghetto, an introverted self-regulating community, but by the end of the 19th century it had become a criminal slum, its more talented inhabitants moving to the New Town. The Hafsia was strictly divided between native North African Jews and those from Livorno, who came in the 16th century to finance ransoms and negotiate the release of hostages and cargoes taken by the corsairs. Later they provided most of the Beys' treasury officials. The native Jews, many originating from the Isle of Jerba, performed less profitable services such as tailoring and metalwork. This division was carried into the New Town: Av de Paris was settled by Livorno Jews, whilst the locals settled on the less prestigious Av des Londres.

Opposite the old entrance to the Hafsia, at 195 Rue Mongi Slim, is the **Anglican church of St George**. It is an incongruous mid-Victorian granite chapel and vicarage, hidden in a walled garden littered with tombstones and war memorials. Generations of British, Dutch, Swedish and American residents are commemorated in this Protestant ghetto. There is Thomas Reade, who influenced Hemet Pasha Bey (Ahmed I) to abolish the slave trade and the Gibsons, whose family tragedy can be pieced together from three gravestones propped up against the garden wall. The church and graveyard are open on Sunday morning for the service at 10.00 hrs (09.00 during July and August) or by appointment with the Rev. Daniel Sealy, tel (01) 243648.

Some 450 m further Pl Bab Souika, the old pottery quarter, has been given a dramatic facelift. Two underpasses have turned the square into a pedestrian space, bordered not by French stucco but by a gleaming new Islamic façade replete with arches, terraces, hanging windows, pools and fountains.

Bab el Souika Quarter

This area to the north was a separate walled quarter built in the 13th century. Walking up Rue Souk el Halfaouine, a street market, you pass the square minaret of the Hafsid **Mohammad Pasha Mosque**, before reaching shady Pl el Halfaouine, dominated by the **Mosque of Youssef Sahib et Tabaa**. Youssef Sahib et Tabaa, originally a humble slave from Ottoman Rumania, became the trusted minster of the enlightened Hammouda Pasha (1781–1813). After his master's death, this venerable old statesman attempted to curtail the excesses of succeeding Beys, but was assassinated for his pains in 1815. He built the mosque as the focus of his restoration of the area and it is one of the most handsome in the city. Its Turkish minaret (only finished in 1971), open courtyard, loggia and high terrace are directly modelled on the Mosque of Sidi Youssef. The ground-floor arches give entrance to shops whose rent goes directly to the upkeep of the mosque. The side doors into the main prayer hall are a striking demonstration of Italian influence, their heavy white baroque curves picked out in black marble.

Using Pl el Halfaouine as a base, explore the minor sights of the quarter. Rue Souk Bel Khir leads east to Bab el Khadra, the celebrated and much-painted double arch that heralds Pl Ali Belhouane, a bustle of buses, *louages* and overladen passengers surrounded by cafés and snack shops. Due north of Pl el Halfaouine, about 500 m along Rue de Miel is Bab el Assel, an artillery bastion of the city's defences, restored in 1848. Immediately west of Pl el Halfaouine is **Souk Jedid**, a covered market also built by Youssef Sahib et Tabaa. Rue Sidi Abdessalem leads straight from the souk to Bab Sidi Abdessalem, now the dusty focus of an occasional flea market but once an important entrance to the city. Here Youssef Sahib et Tabaa restored the 15th-century open koubba, its green dome sheltering a holy man who protected the local well from his reused Roman sarcophagus. Today, it is in a sad state of disrepair.

To complete your perimeter tour, walk west down Blvd Hedi Saidi to Bab Saadoun, a restored triple arch, stranded in the middle of a roundabout. Rue Bab Saadoun passes blacksmiths and musical instrument-makers on its journey back to Pl Bab Souika.

Sidi Mahrez

The best view of the **Mosque of Sidi Mahrez**, or rather its domes, is from Pl Bab Souika. From the medina down Rue Sidi Mahrez, the mosque is entirely obscured up to the right, but a concentration of candle- and perfume-sellers at least gives an odour of sanctity. The interior of the mosque is one of Tunisia's most remarkable, a piece of Istanbul transported to North Africa. The domed prayer hall is supported by four faience pillars and was built by Mohammed el Hafsi, who reigned from 1675–84. It is still incomplete, as the original plan called for four needle minarets to reflect the minor supporting domes.

The **Zaouia of Sidi Mahrez** is immediately opposite the mosque at street level, and gets rebuilt, on average, every century. Brass gates frame a colonnade leading to a sunny courtyard flanked by a prayer hall and the saint's tomb. This open space, complete with a well from which boys drink before circumcision, is never without a cluster of squatting supplicants, predominantly old and female, who firmly escort interlopers out of the precinct. They have some reason to mistrust Christians, as the Sidi's grave was desecrated by Spanish soldiers in the 16th century. Sidi Abu Mohammed Mahrez es Seddiki is the patron saint of Tunis, and over the centuries a bewildering tangle of legends have accumulated around him. Historically, he was a marabout forced to play a public role during the troubled decades of the mid-10th century. The orthodox Sunni city of Tunis was caught between the devil and the deep blue sea, between Abu Yazid, leader of the puritanical Kharijite rising, and Ubayd Allah, the Shiite Mahdi who founded the Fatimid dynasty. Having saved the city, rebuilt its walls, reformed its politics and modernized its industry, he returned to his arduous spiritual disciplines and was rewarded with the title El Abid, the ascetic.

About 50 m beyond the mosque, turn right up Rue Monastiri, a street that climbs gently into the more elegant quarter of the medina, revealed in impressive vaulted arches and studded gates. A 17th-century palace, **Dar el Monastiri**, hides behind the large green gate at no. 9. At 62 Rue Monastiri the **Medersa el Acharia**, one of the five medersas built by Ali Pasha I, is usually closed but you might catch a glimpse of rich columns in the small lemon-shaded courtyard.

Rue Monastiri turns into Rue Sidi Brahim and reaches a whitewashed arch. Pop under this to glance at the green dome and brass doors of the **Zaouia Sidi Brahim**, then back and left down Rue du Tribunal. On the right is **Dar Lasram**, an extensive 19th-century palace that houses the offices of the ASM, the Association for the Safeguard of the Medina. It plans to open shortly to visitors on Saturdays.

Take a right turn up Rue de la Noria, past its **ladies' hammam**, and left on to the wider Rue de la Pacha. This elegant street once boasted the official residence of the Ottoman governor, though the line of Pashas appointed by the Sultan only lasted 16 years, after which the title became a prestigious and expensive honour. At no. 40 stands the **Bachiya Medersa**, built by Ali Pasha II (1758–81), its dedication stone, a piece of Italianate baroque, contrasting strikingly with the traditional Moorish gateway. It now serves as a day nursery, though the main courtyard is locked and increasingly ruinous.

Turn left down Rue de l'Agha, and 100 m later take a right into Rue du Divan. At no. 3 the Diwan, a council of 40 senior Turkish officers who monopolized political life from 1574–1705, used to meet. Return to Rue de l'Agha until you meet the covered Souk el Grana, one of the busiest commercial thoroughfares, a long tunnel illuminated by thousands of bolts of bright-coloured cloth. A left turn on the Souk el Grana puts you on a fairly direct 500-m walk back to Pl Bab Souika, and a right brings you to Rue de la Kasbah, thence down to Pl de la Victoire.

The Belvedere Park and Al Jellaz Cemetery

Old Tunis is flanked by these two green spaces, their symmetry symbolic of the conflicting influences on modern Tunisia. The French turned the northern hill into a park for the bourgeois to take the air, while the southern is crowned by a fort from the corsair years and the tomb of a 13th-century Sufi master. When the French were suspected of wanting to develop the cemetery in 1911, a riot, in which over 40 died, began.

Belvedere Park
Beside the Catholic cathedral on Pl de la Indépendance, Rue de Rome leads to Rue des Salines, the smaller left branch at the Y-junction. Rue des Salines is a long **street market**, animated by crowds, cheap cafés, displays of fish you have never seen before and barrows of flowers. It ends at Jardin Habib Thameur, a small paved garden square, which connects with Av de la Liberté. Continuing north you pass the space-age **synagogue** with its armed guards and further up the road, the **Bourguiba School of Living Languages**, which runs cheap intensive Arabic courses in the summer. A kilometre from Jardin Habib Thameur, Av des Etats Unis leads off to the entrance to the Belvedere Park.

There is a popular café on an island in the middle of the lake near the **zoo** (open daily, 10.00–16.00; adm). It houses a large selection of wild cats, birds and mammals reasonably and is a useful place to check up on the small mammals, wild boar, snakes and raptors that you might meet in the Tunisian interior as well as functioning as a human courting ground. The stars of the show, apparently content, are the marabout storks, some savage-looking Shetland ponies and a pair of two-humped Asian or Bactrian camels.

Above the zoo and lake rise the neglected acres of the rest of the park, partly planted with flowering shrubs, figs and cacti, partly with a mixed woodland of pine, palm, olive and eucalyptus, intersected by serpentine tarmac roads. A 17th-century **garden pavilion** of marble and carved plaster, shaped like a koubba and moved here in 1901, makes a good picnic spot though again it is in need of restoration. The other Moorish building that peeps above the treeline is the French-built Casino du Belvedère. It has been designated the **Museum of Modern Art**, but has yet to open its doors to the public.

On the western edge of the park is Pl Pasteur, where an open-air **swimming pool** functions in summer. The square is named after the still-functioning Institut Pasteur, arguably France's most influential legacy to Tunisia. During its heyday under the direction of

Charles Nicolle (1886–1936), periodic devastations by the plague, influenza, typhus, smallpox, rabies and malaria were checked, allowing the population of Tunisia to increase 700% in the last hundred years.

Al Jellaz Cemetery

Rising immediately south of central Tunis, down Av de Carthage, is the rough wooded slope of Al Jellaz hill. Its summit is crowned by a 17th-century artillery fort, Sidi Ali Rais, still garrisoned by the army and inaccessible. The entire northern slope of the hill bristles with whitewashed graves. A constant stream of visitors flits in and out of the gates, cleaning and visiting tombs, laying wreaths or escorting groups of koranic reciters to a recent grave.

On the eastern summit is the sprawling **Zaouia of Sidi Belhassen ech-Chadli**, whose meditation cell is protected by a minor labryinth of terraces, gravestones, arches and courtyards. Though the earliest part of the zaouia dates from 1815, it has been a site of pilgrimage since the Sidi's death in the 13th century, for he is one of the central figures of Maghrebi Sufism. He united North African practices with the teaching of the great eastern masters like Al Jilani and Al Ghazzali and founded the Chadli brotherhood from which at least 15 separate Sufi brotherhoods claim descent. During travels in the Yemen, he discovered the tonic effects of coffee on lengthy sessions of prayer, and imported the habit to Tunisia. During the first week of summer and for the following seven Saturdays, the zaouia is the centre of an enormous *fête*.

The Bardo Museum

The Bardo (open daily except Mon, 09.30–16.30; adm) is Tunisia's National Museum, the repository of the country's rich archaeological collections, and particularly renowned for its mosaics (see pp. 63–9 for a more detailed discussion of mosaics, Islamic art and ceramics). What you see in the museum's 30 or so rooms is nothing to the collection in its storage cellars, known by one French archaeologist as 'the last great dig in the Mediterranean'.

There is little choice of restaurants in the immediate area. The **Complexe Café Touristique** opposite the back entrance to the museum contains the undistinguished Relais Bardo Sport. Bringing a picnic, or buying one from the fruit stalls and supermarket on the nearby roundabout, allows you to take a break in the museum's garden, itself littered with carvings and stelae from Punic and Roman Tunisia.

The museum is housed in a mid-19th-century Beylical palace, whose interiors are a strange mix of Moorish and a sugary pastiche of classicism. The Islamic collection, known as the **Arab Museum**, occupies galleries around an older, more traditional tiled courtyard.

The Hafsids first built here in the 13th century, and by the 19th century the area was awash with palaces, and housed a court of 2000 when the Bey was in residence. Here were harems, viziers' houses, the palaces of princes and an entire bazaar for the inhabitants of this town within a town. The Beylical court was always a hive of sexual gossip. Several of the Turkish rulers were known to prefer men to their wives, and one's dalliances with beautiful boys became legendary. The newcomers, stolen off the street or from the bosom of their families by a Circassian pimp, were placed on the Bey's specially waxed saddle. When lifted from this contraption, they were hairless, as the ruler preferred. Little of this warren of political intrigue survives, though **Tunisia's Parliament** still occupies the building to the left of the museum's main entrance. Its steps are guarded by a pair of marble lions and sabre-swinging guards, dressed in the old scarlet Beylical uniform.

The Bardo is never all open, as areas are modernized and rearranged. Nevertheless there is always plenty to see, and the following itinerary picks out the highlights of the collection.

GETTING AROUND
The no. 3 bus runs from Av Habib Bourguiba directly to the Bardo. The Metro line marked on maps is still being laid.

The Museum
Rooms I and II contain artefacts from the 6th-4th centuries BC, mostly excavated from the Salammbo Tophet in Carthage (see p. 117), where Carthaginian children were sacrificed in fires to the god Baal Hammon. A tall pointed stele, carved with an elegant simplicity of line, shows a priest cradling in his arms a small babe.

Room A displays 5th-century BC statues of a trinity of fertility gods, Core, Pluto and Demeter, evidence of early Greek influence. The small terracotta statue of Baal Hammon, Carthage's principal deity, seated on a throne and wearing a high feather headdress is exceptionally fine, as befits a sculpture from 1st century AD. Though the Romans conquered Tunisia in 146 BC, the ancient gods continued to be worshipped. This statue, together with the perennially smiling goddess Tanit disguised behind a lion's face, was found at Thinissut, a sanctuary high on the hills behind Hammamet.

Room IV provides a useful contrast between the crude pottery made by the Carthaginians, from African red clay, and what they imported from the rest of the Mediterranean. The red and natural-coloured group is from Greek Corinth, the black from Campania, the red on black from Athens and the translucent alabaster jar from Egypt. The painted designs on the inside of the display cabinets are copied from Punic tombs and show stages in the journey of a soul to heaven.

Terracotta figurines and amulets were buried with the Carthaginian dead to protect them from evil spirits. Those which show traces of African influence are representations of the healing god, Ptah-Patèque. The grotesque masks had a ritual not a theatrical purpose.

Corridor B/D: This contains a large selection of sarcophagi and stelae, of which the **sarcophagus of the Muses**, almost opposite the door into Room V, is particularly fine.

Room VIII: The chief glory of the Thuburbo Majus collection is a polished marble statue of Hercules, and a good small statue of Jupiter. The two enormous arms on the floor are part of the massive cult statue of Jupiter in the city's Capitoline temple. Inexplicably, his feet reside upstairs in a room devoted to treasures from Sousse.

Arab Museum—ground floor: Not far from the entrance to Room VIII, a narrow corridor leads into a display of Tunisian ceramics, the best collection of indigenous modelled Berber ware, domestic pottery and imported tiles.

Room V: Back down the corridor, the Christian exhibits in this room include the baptismal font from El Kantara on Jerba, a stark marble cruciform tub in which the whole body was immersed, and if you visit the house of George Sebastian in Hammamet's Cultural Centre, you will see that he used this as a model for his four-man bath. Above a sarcophagus is a mosaic from Tabarka, showing the schematic representation of a 4th-century church, vital for our knowledge of early church architecture.

Corridor C: These terracotta tiles were used to cover the walls and ceilings of Christian basilicas throughout Tunisia. The scenes depict a mixture of episodes from the Testaments and pagan myths and symbols. Pegasus and nymphs appear by peacocks, long a symbol of immortality. The man with the serpent is St Theodore, a martyred Roman soldier to whom the battle with the dragon was attributed before it became attached to St George. Christ's bearded face shows strong local influence in its wide eyes and Egyptian hairstyle. The most lively representation is of Eve handing Adam an apple, a voluptuous and attractive vision of Original Sin.

Room VI: Bulla Regia's wealth in the 3rd and 4th centuries has left a crop of beautiful remains. The mosaic of Perseus and Andromeda from one of the underground villas is arrestingly direct. Only the sacrifice of Andromeda to the sea monster can save her father's kingdom from the wrath of the Nereids. But when Perseus sees Andromeda he immediately falls in love, kills the sea monster and rescues her.

In niches along the opposite wall stand three magnificent statues. In the centre is a superb long-haired Apollo whose unapproachable, supine grace mocks our earnest morality religions. His lyre bears a carving of the flayed Marsyas, the mortal who dared to measure his musical skill against an Olympian. Traces of paint can be seen on the knife-edged creases of the god's robe, for the Roman temples would originally have been gaudy with colour. To Apollo's left stands his son Aesculapius, the god of healing, and a rather-severe looking Ceres on his right.

Room VII has a collection of Imperial busts found all over Tunisia. There is a mean-mouthed Vespasian, the arriviste founder of a dynasty, and a deceptively boyish and innocent-looking Augustus, perhaps the world's most successful power politician. The philosopher Marcus Aurelius looks his familiar disdainful self and Hadrian has allowed us an intimate portait of his jaded fat face enlivened by penetrating eyes. Septimius Severus appears without a trace of his Libyan ancestry and Gordian I looks a suitably weak, elderly pretender with a fashionable two-day's growth.

The **main staircase** leads from Room V through a forest of palaeo-Christian tomb mosaics.

Arab Museum: Turning right at top of stairs, you reenter the older palace and the Arab Museum, moving through a display of Tunisian applied arts to the main courtyard, with its geometric tiling and carved plaster. At one end lies a T-shaped reception room, filled with 19th-century gilt; other smaller rooms contain European watercolours and a Jewish alcove. During the 19th-century reign of Ahmed Bey the walls were lined with paintings of Napoleon, the conqueror of Egypt, an unusually quirky obssession for a Muslim ruler.

A staircase leads down to a collection reflecting the wider Islamic civilization. It includes damascene swords, glass weights, astrolabes, enchanting Fatimid lustreware, the blue and gold plates of Andalucia, as well as the black and white calligraphic pottery from Iraq, known as 'Nishapur'. There are also vellum pages from early Kairouan Korans, showing gold-leaf calligraphy on Giotto blue, and samples of 'Le Tiraz', Coptic fabric woven with calligraphic inscriptions.

Room IX: This large, gilt-colonnaded room to the left of the stairs is devoted to statuary from Roman Carthage. On the left is a striking black marble herm with a Libyan hairdo. In the centre of the room is a square altar, carved at around the time of Christ. It shows Aeneas fleeing Troy with his father and son, Rome personified as an Amazon siting on a pile of weapons, the sacrifice of a calf by the Emperor Augustus and Apollo, the Emperor's protector, with his zither, griffon and tripod.

The mosaics are from the ruins of Oudna. One shows Bacchus giving the vine to Ikarios, king of Attica, the corners occupied by representations of the four seasons. Below it is a hunting scene, in which the owner's two favourite hounds, Ederatus and Musteia, are immortalized.

Room XIV: This room of treasures unearthed at Oudna holds some of the finest work of the museum—a rare fresco of Bacchus, young and seductive, lying on a leopard's back, and a mosaic of Orpheus, his eyes gouged out by Christian iconoclasts, literally charming the birds off their perches. Two *emblemata*, detailed mosaic still-lifes, flank the door, reminiscent of the techniques of the pointillists, constructing pictures from tiny dots of paint.

Room XV holds Tunisia's most famous mosaic, of Virgil with Clio, the Muse of History, and Melpomene holding a tragic mask, symbol of her inspiration of tragedy. It was found in Sousse and dates from the 3rd–4th century AD, but is thought to be a copy of a contemporary portrait of the poet, who was born in 80 BC. His significance in Tunisia lies in Book IV of the *Aeneid*, which borrows and elaborates on the story of Dido, Queen of Carthage.

The room centres on a 3rd-century mosaic which depicts Saturn, the god of the year and of Saturday, at its centre, surrounded by the other days of the week. Monday is symbolized by the moon, holding halo and torch, Tuesday by helmeted Mars, Wednesday by Mercury with his wings and Thursday by the bearded figure of Jupiter with a golden wreath. Friday comes in the guise of Venus with her peacock feathers and Sunday as the golden rays of Sol Invictus, the unconquerable sun, whose day had become holy well before St Paul decreed it so for Christians.

The room itself is a jewel-like Moorish womb, exceptionally decorated with faience tiles and a plaster roof. From its traditional balcony window you can look down on the lion statues and pantomime soldiers who guard the entrance to the National Parliament next door.

Rooms XVI–XXII are currently being restored. XVI holds cases of stone tools. Room XVII holds a startling collection of sub-erotic human lamps and Room XVIII the famous statue of Agon, all recovered from a wreck off Mahdia.

Room XIII: The central mosaic in this gaudily painted concert room was discovered at Medeina, in the hall of the sanctuary of Aesculapius. It is an important technical document, revealling 23 of the different types of boat used in the 4th century AD, and naming them in Latin and Greek. Bobbing on a sea which teems with sea creatures, are horse carriers, pirate ships, troop carriers and grain vessels.

Room X: Beneath a large painted ceiling and hideous pink chandeliers, lies a vast mosaic depicting the Triumph of Neptune, unearthed in Sousse. Round the top of the wall are semi-circular architectural studies of villas, set in fecund and rather idealized country landscapes. In another, known as the mosaic of Master Julius, the master and mistress sit outside their house to receive produce from their workers, and are seen indulging in various country pursuits round the edge of the work. The massive disembodied feet of Jupiter come from the capitol at Thuburbo Majus.

Room XI: The Thugga (Dougga) room is dominated by a mosaic of the Triumph of Venus combined with the Four Seasons. The fleshy tones of the mosaic depicting three giant cyclopes forging Jupiter's thunderbolts came from a neighbourhood bathhouse.

Room XII: This combination of mosaics from El Jem gives an idea of the concerns of the villa-owning classes of Roman North Africa. On the floor, a mosaic celebrates Bacchus, god of wine. On the wall are the nine Muses, but most striking are the mounted coursing scenes and still-life scenes of game birds.

Rooms XXV–VIII: This series of rooms displays mosaics on a number of levels, including the famous mosaic showing Ulysses tied to a mast, awaiting the call of the Sirens. Amongst the best are the wild boar hunt, the lion attacking the zebra or the scene from Bacchus' travels when he metamorphoses a boatload of pirates.

Room XXX: At the top of the stairs is the bestiary, a room filled with scenes involving wild animals, many being killed in the amphitheatre, as well as a simple tigerskin mosaic which has the advantage over a skin in the North African climate for its ability to be sluiced with cold water. The striking non-animal scene in this room shows a poet, deep in meditation, flanked by a pair of tragic masks.

Room XXXIII: Almost all these mosaics come from the Trajanic baths at Acholla, a Roman town 40 km north of Sfax, and are the earliest set yet discovered. They present a typical picture of the recurrent themes of North African mosaics—Bacchus, the Four Seasons and the riches of the Ocean—as well as giving a flickering insight into the sumptuousness of the public baths. The striking image of Bacchus triumphant would have been instantly recognized as a reference to Trajan's triumph over the Parthians.

Room XXIX: The upper gallery of the Roman Carthage room is lined with cabinets containing grave goods, principally from Sousse and El Jem. The larger glass jars were used as urns filled with the ashes and fragments of bone gathered from a funeral and buried beneath a stele, while the more domestic phials and jugs were buried to support the dead in their journey through the afterlife. There are also earthenware grave talismans and grotesque masks crafted to ward off evil spirits. Do not miss Bess, the pot-bellied Punic dwarf-god, or the unusual depiction of Venus on a camel.

FESTIVALS

Tunis' festivals are not geared for tourists, but if you are there in February there is a **music festival**, and a **theatrical festival** in March and April. The **Festival of the Medina**, an Islamic event, takes place during Ramadan, and a **Festival of Youth Music** in November. Every other year in October, Carthage hosts the **International Festival of Third World Cinema**.

SHOPPING

The medina souk lies at the heart of any shopping tour. Recommendations for more unusual buys include a good selection of **carved olive wood** in two shops, at 38 Rue Sidi ben Arous, tel (01) 264990, and at 25 Rue de Tamis. The only licensed trader in **antiquities**, Younes Dejoui, also has two shops, the Boutique des Amisin at 55 Souk el Leffa, tel (01) 263536, in the medina, and one on Av Habib Bourguiba. For the most elegant display of traditional Tunisian goods, of manners, and a virtual museum in itself, go to **Bazaar ed Dar** run by three brothers, Ali, Youssef and Rachid ben Hedi Chammaki with doors at 7 Souk et Trouk and 8 Rue Sidi ben Arous, tel (01) 261732.

In the New Town at 88 Rue de Yougoslavie you will find the **atelier of Ayed Abdelkader**, an engagingly friendly painter and ceramicist, tel (01) 247797. **Espace Alif**, at 3 Rue de Hollande, have commissioned their own series of up-market postcards, large, well-printed vignettes of Tunisia, and sell them in their gallery, alongside a good selection of historical and cultural books.

HAMMAMS

The Dar ben Abdallah Museum has a complete list of the 20-odd hammams in the medina. Three easily accessible ones are on Rue des Teinturiers, the Kachachine Hammam on Rue des Librairies and a ladies' hammam on Rue de la Noria. They are often sited near mosques and form part of the ablutions before Friday prayers. Your hotel will be able to direct you to the nearest that welcomes non-Muslims.

RELIGIOUS SERVICES

For non-Muslims, these take place in the synagogue at 107 Av de la Liberté, in the French Protestant church at 36 Rue Charles de Gaulle, the Greek Orthodox church at 5 Rue de

Rome, the Anglican church on Pl Bab Carthagène and in the Roman Catholic cathedral on Pl de l'Indépendance.

SPORTS
There is an 18-hole **golf course**, and club house with licensed restaurant at the Golf Club de la Souakra, tel (01) 903081/902025. An open-air municipal **swimming pool** opens for the summer by the Pl Pasteur entrance to the Belvedere Park, and you will find **tennis courts** at the sports complex opposite Mohammed V Metro station. Professional pools, courts and football pitches litter the area around Stade Olympique Metro station. **Horse riding** takes place both at Club de la Souakra and the Kassar Said racing stadium, tel (01) 223252, out of Tunis on the Tabarka road.

WHERE TO STAY
Most of Tunis' hotels and restaurants are found in the New Town just on or off Av Habib Bourguiba. The smaller hotels can fill up at any time of the year, so it is as well to find a room early in the day.

EXPENSIVE
The two most prominent de luxe hotels are the **Africa**, in the skyscraper at 50 Av Habib Bourguiba, and the **International Tunisia Hotel** at 49 Av Habib Bourguiba. They are businessmen's hotels and correspondingly expensive, but soulless for holiday-makers to stay in. Both have ground-floor cafés which form part of the everyday bustle of the avenue, as well as bars and night-clubs, well-stocked bookstalls in the lobby and money-changing facilities. The Africa also has an open-air swimming pool and bar on its eighth floor, officially open to residents only.

Considerably cheaper is the **Tej**, 14 Rue Aziz Taj, tel (01) 342666, a small, clean hotel on a quiet back street not far from the Africa.

MODERATE
The **Maison Dorée** at 6 Rue de Hollande, tel (01) 240632, is a discreet, unpretentious but efficient hotel, with the feel of a bygone era. The hotel linen is a relic of the French protectorate, and the good breakfast a treat. It also has one of the best restaurants in town. More popular, but not of quite the same standard, is the **Carlton Hotel** at 31 Av Habib Bourguiba, tel (01) 258167, where you can choose between rooms with or without baths/ showers. Dropping again in quality, there is the **Transatlantique** at 106 Rue de Yougoslavie, tel (01) 240680, with its tiled passages and big, dark, often noisy bedrooms. The **Hotel Capitole** at 60 Av Habib Bourguiba, tel (01) 244997, has double rooms overlooking the tree-lined centre, and a cheap restaurant.

CHEAP
The edge of the medina and particularly its ringroad is the place to look for cheap local hotels. Graduate to these rougher dives after a couple of nights acclimatizing in either the **Hotel Victoria**, 79 Av Farhat Hached, tel (01) 342863, the **Bretagne**, the **Metropole** or the **Salambo** on Rue de Grèce, tel (01) 242146, or the **Hotel Medina** in the Pl de la Victoire. The last-named might already be raffish enough for your taste.

EATING OUT

The Best

For Tunisian cooking at its best, in a magnificent medina town house with elegant service and sophisticated traditional music, try the **Restaurant Dar el Jeld** at 5 Rue Dar el Jeld just off the Pl du Gouvernement, tel (01) 256326. You will need to dress up and book a table in advance, but prices are still not astronomical. Dinner for two with wine starts at 30 dn. Of the two other restaurants in the medina, Le Chateau is now closed, and the **M'rabet** dedicated to block-booked tour groups, tel (01) 263681. Two other restaurants recommended for Tunisian cooking are **L'Etoile du Sud** in the Hotel Africa and **La Sofra** in the International Tunisia Hotel. They are considerably more expensive and suffer from the institutional hotel atmosphere.

Licensed Restaurants with Music

Going down-market, but becoming considerably more lively in the process, there are a number of restaurants where live Arabic music accompanies your meal. There is normally a heady atmosphere of heavy drinking, jazz-like improvisation and unapproachably cool female soloists, and often the intense experience of Tunisian *joie de vivre*, all too rare at staged folk evenings. Three places within a few minutes' walk of each other should be tried. **Restaurant le Malouf**, across a patio courtyard at 108 Rue de Yougoslavie, tel (01) 243180, is the smartest. **Le Palais** at 8 Av de Carthage, opposite the big ONA store, tel (01) 256326, has the atmosphere of a nightclub, and just round the corner on a side street is the smaller and rowdier **Restaurant Savarin**.

Licensed Restaurants

For a quieter evening with a menu drawing on fresh grilled seafood, French, Italian and Tunisian cooking, there are dozens of licensed restaurants in the centre of Tunis to sniff out. Dinner for two with wine will cost around 20–25 dn. **Le Cosmos** at 7 Rue ibn Khaldoun, tel (01) 241610, is a deservedly popular and animated bistro, and **La Petite Hutte** at 102 Rue de Yougoslavie, tel (01) 244959, a quieter place to spin out an evening over, amongst other things, a delicious *tajine*. **Restaurant Chez Slah**, reclusively tucked away at 14 Rue Pierre de Courbetin, is popular with resident French, but apart from its puddings rests on old laurels, tel (01) 258588. The best cooking, though in rather quiet and over-decorated surroundings, is in the **Restaurant Margaritas** at Hotel Maison Dorée, 6 Rue de Hollande.

Cheap Unlicensed Restaurants

Restaurant Semaphore, tucked away at the medina end of Pl de la Victoire, is ideally placed for lunch. Its quick and honest staff serve a good selection of traditional Tunisian dishes, piping hot. The first-floor restaurant at the **Hotel Capitole** does a good meal for 3 dn, though being unlicensed it is a bit dull at night. Rue de Caire, off Av Habib Bourguiba almost directly opposite the Hotel Africa, is lined with popular restaurants. Try the **Restaurant du Caire** at no. 6, which serve four-course meals for under 2 dn.

Cafés

On your first promenade through central Tunis the city seems to be lined with cafés. Once you have cut out the stand-up patisseries, however, serious street-watching happens at five distinct locations on the Av Habib Bourguiba. The chairs of the café below the **Hotel Medina** in Pl de la Victoire get the most sun. Further east is the enclosed café of the **Hotel Tunisia International**, and further on the two poles of café society, the tables of the **Café de**

Paris and the **Café de Tunis**, with waiters in blue and red respectively. If you want an alcoholic drink or to avoid boot-blacks, take a table inside. Lastly, enclosed in a glass corner and air-conditioned, sit the smart clientele of the **Café Africa**, next to the Hotel Africa.

NIGHTLIFE
There are half a dozen nightclubs in central Tunis, unmemorable places all with their international decor of strobes, neon and far too many men. A tour of the more serene of these would include **Lafayette** at Hotel Ibn Khaldun, 30 Rue du Koweit, **Tunis Club** by the Café de Tunis on Av Habib Bourguiba and the **Joker**, beside the Hotel Tunisia International at 49 Av Habib Bourguiba. Smarter Tunisians invariably drive out to the coast, either to **La Plaza** at La Marsa or **La Baraka** just outside Sidi Bou Said.

South of Tunis

The area immediately south of Tunis is an industrial wasteland, summed up by notices discouraging swimming at Radès, warning 'Danger of Death'. Beyond, a string of towns line the bay right to Cap Bon, including **Hammam Lif**, an old spa town of decaying streets and palm-lined boulevards. For the energetic there is the sacred mountain of **Jebel Bou Kornine** just behind. It commands a magnificent view, and has a convenient licensed restaurant at its foot.

Jebel Bou Kornine

The silhouette of Jebel Bou Kornine is an unmistakable double horn, its shoulders rising up from the shore. Its steepness exaggerates its true height, for its 576 m and 496 m summits are lower than neighbouring, lumpen-shaped Jebel Ressas and only about a third the height of Jebel Zaghouan.

Bou Kornine was the sacred mountain of Carthage, the beacon by which the black ships of the Phoenicians steered into the Gulf of Tunis. The cleft between the two peaks formed an ancient altar, dedicated to Baal Karnine, Lord of the Two Horns. No temple was built, but footings cut in the living rock defined an inner sanctuary. Worship continued here throughout the time of the Roman Empire, and sacrifices dedicated to Saturn Balcarnesis took place well into the 4th century AD. Excavations recovered 365 fragments of carved stelae, with the god depicted as bearded, veiled and carrying a scourge and a sacrificial saucer.

The mountain is officially a national park but that has not stopped quarrying at its foot or the construction of a rough track to the relay aerials and National Guard post at the summit, which completely destroyed the temple in the process. The view over Tunis and the Gulf is superb. The wind whistles through the peaks and moans in imitation of the answer of a god. A pair of Bonelli's eagles nest each year on its cliff edge and in spring the forested slopes are covered in cyclamen, heather, rosemary and cistus, and hoopoes flit through the Aleppo pines in search of caterpillars.

111

The route up the mountain is not well advertised. After Bou Kornine railway station, between Ez Zahra and Hammam Lif, look out for the Mobil garage and a battered sign to the Restaurant Chalet Vert which is up a 1-km drive. Beyond the restaurant, the rough track continues to the peak, or you can leave it and cut up through the pine woods.

Hammam Lif

Squeezed between the slopes of Jebel Bou Kornine and the sea, Hammam Lif's regular avenues, pseudo-Moorish architecture and palm-lined avenues give it a thoroughly turn-of-the-century look. In fact the therapeutic quality of the local hot-water spring has been appreciated for 3000 years. Its name derives from Hammam en Alf, the Bath of Noses. The nose is a common Arabic euphemism for penis, and this hot spring, Ain el Ariane, has long been a recognized cure for the pains of tertiary syphilis. Ali Pasha II built a villa here at the end of the 18th century, and it was a popular summer station for succeeding members of the dynasty.

The villa has gone but the baths remain in a porticoed roadside **Hotel des Thermes**. Sufferers are soaked for half an hour in private baths of hot water, and vaginal douches, enemas and massages are all on offer. Five glasses of cooled water are recommended as a mild purgative. For a more pleasant experience try the Pl du 19 Avril, the palm-shaded centre of café life, especially busy on Sunday, market day. On the beachfront there is a bar in the defunct **Casino Hotel** and a restaurant, **La Sirène**, though much the smartest place to eat and drink is **Restaurant Le Chalet Vert**, with wide sweeping views over the bay, stained carpets, dinner-jacketed major domo and not unreasonable prices—see above for directions. And if the Fates strand you in Hammam Lif, there is the **Hotel Bon Repos**, which lives up to its kitsch suburban name, on the hill opposite the *Hotel des Thermes*, and charges 9 dn for a double room, tel (01) 291458.

Cedria Plage

South of Hammam Lif is Cedria Plage, named after the colonial village of Borj Cedria just inland. The PLO established their headquarters here after being forced out of Beirut. Despite US backing for the move to Tunisia, the PLO compound was attacked in a precision bombing raid by Israeli jets in 1985, since which time staff levels have been kept down to an administrative minimum. Opposite the turning to the beach is one to the German military cemetery, the **Deutscher Soldaten Friedhof**. It is a grim and thoroughly depressing morgue, built in 1975 when 8562 soldiers were dug up from scattered war graves and their remains placed in communal concrete bins, lined with a veneer of grey stone to resemble fridges. It is appropriately sited, for even after the surrender of Tunis and Bizerte the Germans defended Hammam Lif with vigour. They only surrendered after being surrounded by British tanks which had driven through the surf along the beach, the only avenue that the Axis defence plan had overlooked. At this stage in the campaign it was impossible to predict the actions of the British cavalry regiments which had become quite recklessly drunk.

Leaving Borj Cedria you enter the wine and citrus country of Cap Bon, passing villages familiar from wine labels, like Khanguet, Grombalia and Mornag.

112

North of Tunis

A string of seaside suburbs line the north of the Bay. They are neither the cleanest nor the quietest place for a beach holiday but make a perfect day's break from the city. The port of **La Goulette** has some delightful fish restaurants, **Sidi Bou Said**, despite the tourists, is still the prettiest village in the country and **Raouad**, just north of Gammarth, has a long sandy beach. The suburb of **Carthage** marks the site of two of the greatest cities of the ancient world, but you should come supplied with your own enthusiasm. Carthage's fragmentary ruins, hedged in by suburban villas, have been disappointing visitors for generations. Travel on the TGM, a light railway that runs from Av Habib Bourguiba to La Marsa every 20 minutes until after midnight.

The Lake of Tunis and La Goulette

The Lake of Tunis, also known as *El Bahira*, the Little Sea, is a brackish lagoon, the home of shoals of mullet, migratory waders and flocks of pink **flamingoes**. In its natural state it was connected to the sea by a number of shallow creeks which were periodically cleared to allow the lake shores to be used as an extra anchorage. The Arab conqueror Hassan ibn Numan altered its geography by cutting a wide mouth out to the sea and dredging a 10-km canal from, there to present-day Tunis. The capital thus has two harbours, one where it meets the lake and one at the Halk el Oued, the throat of the canal, which in the pidgin esperanto of the Mediterranean became Goletta and then La Goulette. La Goulette now handles the majority of cargo ships, visiting yachts and all the passenger ferries from France, Sicily and Italy.

A free ferry plies across the mouth of the canal to Radès which has been developed into an additional dock. In the northern half of the lake, visible from the causeway, is the **Isle of Chikli**, on which the Spanish built the small artillery fort of St James which was enlarged by the Turks and later used as a prison before decaying into a bird refuge. The TGM causeway was built in the 19th century for Bey Mohammed by a British company, who quarried the ruins of Carthage for hard core.

The TGM railway passes on one side of the old **walled town** of La Goulette, the road on the other. This dates from the prosperous centuries of the corsair war when La Goulette housed a large Jewish community, only partly supplanted in colonial times when the town became known as Little Sicily. As well as bypassed it is now run down, its blue-painted balconies peeling alongside the whitewash from the high stuccoed façades. Life now follows the main road past a mounted statue of Habib Bourguiba and the port gates, yacht harbour and old kasbah fortress before reaching the main drag, Av Franklin Roosevelt, lined with cafés, shops and fish restaurants.

The **kasbah** has been in the front line for four centuries, most recently defended from Allied bombing in 1943 by German anti-aircraft guns. It is partly inhabited by squatters whose washing lines do something to soften the depressing, almost haunted, aura of the massive artillery walls. The foundations date from a double-moated Spanish fortress built by the Emperor Charles V of Spain after the capture of Tunis in 1535. It survived a long siege in 1569 (the author of *Don Quixote*, Miguel Cervantes, was in the garrison) after all other Spanish forts had fallen, and was the bridgehead from which Don Juan of Austria briefly reoccupied Tunis three years later. In 1574, faced by the enormous Ottoman fleet of Sinan Pasha, the garrison meekly surrendered. As a hated symbol of Spanish power it was first slighted and later rebuilt with cellars to house the thousands of manacled slaves required to power the corsair galleys. Over the 17th and 18th centuries its walls were battered by many a Christian fleet but the fortress always succeeded in barring the way to Tunis, succumbing at last not to the cannon but to the threats of Lord Exmouth's fleet in 1816.

WHERE TO STAY AND EAT

Both the **Restaurant Monte Carlo** and the **Restaurant Gordoue,** opposite one another on Av Franklin Roosevelt, have elegant displays of freshly caught fish which they grill perfectly, and which with wine will cost around 10 dn per head. The **Brasserie de l'An 2000** on the same road has the camaraderie of a café and is much cheaper for a drink and a snack. If you are charmed by La Goulette and want to stay, the **Beau Rivage Hotel**, next to the Restaurant Monte Carlo charges 6 dn per person, in summer only.

Carthage

Few names are as pregnant with a sense of past greatness and tragedy as that of Carthage. Founded by a Phoenician princess, it became the capital of the great Carthaginian Empire. In 146 BC the city was annihilated by the Romans and ploughed over, only to rise again to become the chief city of Imperial North Africa and one of the cradles of early Christian philosophy. Carthage has often kindled the creative imagination. Turner painted a series of fantastic Carthaginian landscapes, a city of layer upon layer of classical pillars and pediments, rising like clouds to a crowning heavenly temple. Flaubert's picaresque *Salammbo* describes the revolt of the mercenaries against their violent plutocracy amidst a world of religious fanaticsm, sumptuous feasts and imaginative tortures.

Today's reality is disappointing. The ruins of Carthage are cut through by tarmac and buried by smart suburban villas. However, since the name and history will inevitably lure you, pack all the imagination you can muster in your bag, and come ready to create your own romantic picture. The complete tour starts at the Tunis end of the suburb, and will take all day. If you had rather spend less time, make an itinerary that includes the Salammbo Tophet, the Punic harbours, the Roman and Palaeo-Christian Museum, the Byrsa Museum and the Antonine baths. The sites are open from 08.00–19.00 in summer and 09.00–17.00 in winter, every day except public holidays, unless otherwise specified in the text.

History

Mythological Origins

Virgil's *Aeneid* provides the most familiar literary account of Carthage's origins, though his Latin epic introduced some subtle distortions. Dido fled the great Phoenician city of Tyre when King Pygmalion, her brother, killed her husband Acerbas. She sailed west with a group of supporters and founded Kart Hadasht, 'New City', on a piece of land cunningly prised from a North African prince. Dido asked for as much land as could be covered by an ox-hide, cut the hide into shoe-lace strips and managed to enclose all the land from the sea to the back of the Byrsa hill—the word *byrsa* derives from the Greek for hide. Virgil then altered the story and made her fall in love with his stiff-upper-lipped hero Aeneas. Abandoned by Aeneas, to whom the task of founding Rome was more important than love, Dido committed suicide. In the older myth the queen offered herself up to a funeral pyre as a royal sacrifice that dedicated the city. Some corroboration is given by a single urn enclosed by a terracotta shrine, found in the earliest layer of the Salammbo Tophet. Carthage's foundation date is 814 BC,

Punic glass faces from the 4th–3rd century BC

though archaeologists have yet to date anything before 750 BC, probably because the early Phoenicians lived largely afloat, like the sampan communities of Hong Kong.

Punic Carthage

By the end of the 6th century BC Carthage was a permanent city, well placed on the trade route between southern Spain and Lebanon. Colonies were established at Ibiza, Sicily, Sardinia and Spain. Faced with aggressive competition from the Greeks, the other Phoenician cities along the North African coast were brought in as junior members of a defensive league. For centuries Carthage led this maritime empire and yet continued to pay rent to Berber princes. The conquest of Tunisia only began in 408 BC, after which the agricultural provinces contributed to the city's prosperity. The Carthaginians were most celebrated as sharp-witted traders. Their great wealth was based on firm control of Spanish mines, an Atlantic trade in Cornish tin and West African gold, and they also used a trans-Saharan route, known as the Garamantian way. In manufacturing they were known for their woodwork, dyeing and weaving of textiles. These are all perishable goods, so that apart from a few specimens of jewellery, Carthage is represented in museums by carved stone, and pottery imported from Egypt and Greece.

After an isolationist period in the 5th century, Carthage's xenophobic monarchy was replaced by a republic, whose constitution was admired by Aristotle. Though open to foreign influences and craftsmen, the city was conservative in religious matters. The Moloch, the fire sacrifice of children, was notorious even in the ancient world. Nevertheless, the city was probably more in touch with the currents of Hellenic civilization than Rome.

The three Punic Wars ended with the obliteration of Carthage in 146 BC. Plutarch was speaking with the voice of a Roman propagandist when he described the Carthaginians as 'a hard and gloomy people, submissive to their rulers and harsh to their subjects, running to extremes of cowardice in times of fear and of cruelty in times of anger: they keep obstinately to their decisions, are austere, and care little for amusement or the graces of life'.

115

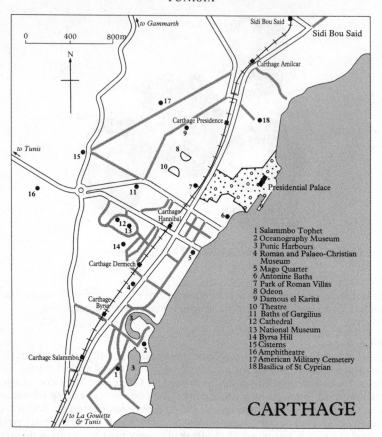

0   400   800m

N

to Gammarth

Sidi Bou Said

Sidi Bou Said

Carthage Amilcar

●17

Carthage Presidence
9

to Tunis

15 ●

8

10

7 ●

11 ●

16 ●

●18

Presidential Palace

Carthage
Hannibal

6 ●

12
13

14 ●

Carthage Dermech

5

4

Carthage
Byrsa

3

Carthage Salammbo

2

1   3

to La Goulette
& Tunis

1 Salammbo Tophet
2 Oceanography Museum
3 Punic Harbours
4 Roman and Palaeo-Christian
    Museum
5 Mago Quarter
6 Antonine Baths
7 Park of Roman Villas
8 Odeon
9 Damous el Karita
10 Theatre
11 Baths of Gargilius
12 Cathedral
13 National Museum
14 Byrsa Hill
15 Cisterns
16 Amphitheatre
17 American Military Cemetery
18 Basilica of St Cyprian

CARTHAGE

Roman Carthage

A mere century after the Romans had cursed the smoking ruins and symbolically sown the site with salt, a new city was founded here by Julius Caesar. It grew quickly, becoming the provincial capital within a century and by the 2nd century was the third city of the empire, after Rome and Alexandria, with a population estimated at 700,000. Its greatest era was in the 3rd–4th century when a handful of scholars from its university, St Cyprian, Tertullian and St Augustine, shaped the empire's new Christian faith and formulated ecclesiastical Latin, the language of European scholarship for the next thousand years.

Carthage held out for three years against a Vandal siege (436–439) and though it was initially sacked, treasure from King Genseric's other raids, like that from the sack of Rome, poured into the city. Carthage kept faith with the empire, however, and aided Belisarius' conquest of Tunisia in 534. The baths and churches were restored, a new cathedral and port built, and one Byzantine emperor even toyed with the idea of leaving Constantinople to make his capital at Carthage. Towards the end of the 7th century refugees from the Arab invasion poured into the city, which fell in 692 before the 40,000-strong army of Hassan ibn Numan.

116

Ruined once again, Carthage's supremacy was forever eclipsed by the new Muslim foundation of Tunis.

GETTING AROUND
The TGM light railway leaves the station at the end of Av Habib Bourguiba in Tunis and stops at six Carthage stations, cutting down on the need for taxis, horse-drawn *calèches* or walking in the midday heat.

The Site

The Salammbo Tophet
Following signs from the main road to Hotel Résidence Carthage, the entrance to the tophet, where children were sacrificed, cremated and buried, is beyond the hotel on Rue Hannibal. The earliest of all discoveries in Carthage have been made in this enclosure, where urns containing the ashes and milk teeth of mid-8th-century BC children have been unearthed. The first thing you will see is a forest of *stelae* or gravestones.

Here, in moonlit ceremonies, boy children from important families, aged between two and 12, were killed and ceremoniously carried by priests and deposited in the arms of a massive bronze statue of the Carthaginian God Baal Hammon. Beneath the god's outstretched arms burned a raging fire. Parents, musicians and dancers, many wearing grotesque terracotta masks, watched as the body slipped from the god's embrace. A ferment of drums, flutes and cymbals drowned the cries of the parents and encouraged ecstatic dances celebrating the promise of help in the forthcoming trials.

The guardian of the site may show you into the excavation hut to add credence to his fake oil lamps and figurines by showing them amongst real *stelae*. The thin, pointed ones in hard grey limetone bear the triangular sign of Tanit, the goddess who became almost synonymous with Carthage, and date from the 5th–4th centuries BC. She is also symbolized by the cresent moon above the Punic inscriptions. At the far end of the sanctuary the **underground chamber** is a later Roman silo, built in the reign of Commodus to store grain.

The Punic Harbours
A right turn at the end of Rue Hannibal leads to the **Museum of Oceanography**, a dusty display of marine and river life, which is open every afternoon except Mondays.

Admission to the harbours which surround it (signed *Les Ports Puniques*) is on the same ticket as the tophet. The rectangular black lagoon south of the road was the original commercial harbour, the hub of Punic Carthage. To the north, the round lagoon centred on an island was the military port, linked by a narrow channel to the commercial harbour, with no sea entrance of its own.

On the island is a small **antiquarium** erected by the British UNESCO task force who excavated here, containing scale models of both the Punic and Roman military harbours. The Carthaginian admiral directed proceedings from the tallest building, whence he could see over the concealing walls to the beseiging enemy on the open sea. The navy's 220 flat-hulled rowing boats were pulled out of the water when not in use, into hidden berths each entered between two Ionic pillars.

The Roman military harbour was considerably more grandiose, and by AD 200 it had its own entrance. This is currently blocked, while piles are sunk around the harbour to stabilize its banks. In AD 193 Commodus set up a special corn fleet, which operated out of both harbours and was vital for the supply of the empire. The majority of the foundations you can still see on the island are Roman, apart from the runners of a Punic boat berth. Just next to the bridge are the low bases of a triumphal arch.

The Roman and Palaeo-Christian Museum
Just to the left of the main road, behind a bright orange fence, is a museum laid out by the American UNESCO team of archaeologists. It sits at the crossroads of two ancient Roman streets, over an intact Roman cistern where rainwater from the museum's guttering still collects.

The sensual 5th-century marble **statue of Ganymede** gazing lovingly at Zeus, his amorous kidnapper in the guise of an eagle, was found in the cistern as well. It is quite unlike anything else in Carthage, where sculpture tends towards the imperial and military.

From the Christian period date the two **peacocks mosaics**, the saint carved from bone and a fine 6th-century bronze cross. Carthage also produced the terracotta tiles with which the early basilicas were decorated.

One final striking mosaic shows four victorious charioteers at the start of a race. The Carthaginians were well known for their 'insane passion' for horse-racing, and Carthage race-track was second only in capacity to Rome, seating 40,000.

Under the roof covering the outside excavations lie the ruins of a Byzantine church and baptistery, the 6th-century **basilica of St Agileus**, built over a smaller 4th-century chapel, and some villas.

The Mago Quarter Architectural Park
From Carthage-Hannibal station, take the wide Av de la République towards the sea. The entrance booth is on the right. This patch of excavation has exposed a level of the Punic city suprisingly similar to later Roman development. The Augustan settlement did not change the orientation of the streets, nor the Carthaginian style of architecture.

In the first of two small exhibition rooms is a model of the limestone quarry at El Haouaria on Cap Bon, from which Punic, Roman and Byzantine Carthage were largely built. There is also a display of mosaic pavements, showing the level of Punic influence on Roman methods, and an extraordinarily fresh piece of Punic *trompe l'oeil*, a painted egg and dart frieze from the 3rd–4th century BC.

Down towards the sea lie traces of the monstrous, weathered grey boulders which formed part of Carthage's 3rd-century BC **defensive wall**. During the Roman era the town spread into what is now the sea, and its defences still hide beneath the waves. A second area of excavation is best examined from a viewing platform on Rue Septimius Severus. It consists mainly of the remains of **Punic villas**, complete with wells, cisterns and courtyards, and areas of leopard-skin mosaic. The Carthaginian villas were later used as foundations for a row of Roman artisans' workshops.

The Antonine Baths
Turn seawards from the main roundabout with the massive (fake) capital at its centre, to get to the most dramatic ruin from Roman Carthage, a huge bathhouse complex lapped by the Mediterranean.

The surrounding archaeological park also includes Punic tombs and later churches. It is Tunis' equivalent of a drive-in movie for saccharine courtship, and has large numbers of fake oil lamps and coins for sale.

The entrance to the park follows an old Roman street, lined with Punic stelae and ossuary boxes. Turn left at the first crossroads to a **7th-century underground funerary chapel**.

It has been moved here from elsewhere, but its charming fish and bird mosaics have been preserved. Diagonally opposite are the ruins of a *schola*, a meeting-place for members of the imperial cult. The damaged mosaic of children dancing beneath a canopy shows part of the cult's annual rituals.

Turn right a little beyond the *schola* to reach the **basilica of Douimès**, a square Byzantine church with three rows of double pillars and an almost uniform geometric mosaic floor. In the far corner, a round font in the floor marks the baptistery, with bases for the four-pillared canopy that once covered it. Beyond the basilica are some **Punic graves**, the most impressive topped by a wigwam of limestone, and entered down a short flight of steps.

Back towards the sea, you may not enter the **Antonine baths**, but can study them from the viewing platform. The plan is initially confusing as what is left is little more than the cellars. The baths were commissioned during the reign of Hadrian, and completed under Antoninus Pius (138–61). They are the largest outside Rome, but it is now difficult to imagine the massive, cathedral-like vaults which would have spanned the central cold room, the *frigidarium*, marked out by the single highest column. A sense of scale is given by the Corinthian capital on the roundabout above the baths, a plaster-cast of the capitals which crowned these pillars.

The symmetrical layout of the baths allowed both sexes to bath at once in privacy. The normal routine saw people undressing in the *vestibularium*, oiling their skin in the *unctuarium*, having a work-out in the *palaestra*, being scraped down in the *destrictarium*, and sweating it out in the *sudarium* before taking a warm bath, a cold one and finally a warm one.

The Park of Roman Villas
Crossing the main road from the Antonine baths, a right turn leads to the *Parc Archéologique des Villas Romaines*, an area of Roman housing built over a Punic graveyard. An elegant 3rd-century Roman terrace is littered with beautiful sarcophagi, torsos and mosaics and has excellent views of the Gulf. It is known by the elderly guides as **Hannibal's Palace**, despite the fact that the Carthaginian general lived at least 400 years before the house was built. To the north, towards two modern blocks of flats, lies a set of earthworks which sketch out the shape of Carthage's **Odeon** theatre.

Walk to the right of the modern flats, to an ecclesiastical complex known as **Damous el Karita**, an Arabization of *domus caritatis*, the house of charity. It shows evidence of several different churches and orientations, and a plethora of outbuildings. Though it is not central enough to have been Carthage's cathedral, it was obviously an important Christian site, perhaps dedicated to the town's martyrs and an object of pilgrimage.

The Theatre
The turning to Carthage's Roman theatre, much in use today, comes just after that to the Archaeological Park of Roman Villas. Built in the early 2nd century, it has been completely restored and is barely worth visiting outside of a performance.

Byrsa Hill: Punic Houses and National Museum of Carthage
Take the road beside the ruinous site of the **baths of Gargilius**, recognizable by a number of tall double pillars, to Carthage's main museum, beside the French cathedral on Byrsa hill.

During the Punic period, Byrsa hill served variously as a cemetery, a place of metal-smelting and coin-minting, and finally as the site of a citadel and temple to the god Eschmoun, protected by a wall and a warren of houses on its slopes. Augustus considerably enlarged the hilltop, and planted a Capitoline temple and forum here, which were fortified by the

Byzantines in the 6th century. In the spirit of French colonialism, the cathedral of St Louis for the 'Revived Diocese of Africa' was added in the late 19th century.

Inside the gates of the Carthage Museum which are next to the cathedral main door, is an area of excavated hillside. At the far end of the terrace lie the foundations of Punic housing. Appian, using the eye-witness accounts of Polybius, describes these houses as six storeys high in 146 BC. 'As the tall narrow houses which crowded the slopes were cleared by fire, there fell with the walls many bodies of those who had hidden in the upper storeys and been burnt to death, and others who were still alive, wounded and badly burnt . . . and dead and living were thrown together into pits.' Protected by a wall, the area would have felt just like an Arab medina. The houses let in a little light through their central courtyards, and had blank whitewashed outside walls. They were built of mud bricks on a foundation of Cap Bon stone. Many of the houses were decorated with stuccoed Ionic pillars, some carrying carved entablatures. You can still see areas of the pink stucco which covered floors and walls, long thin cisterns and complex drainage systems.

The museum itself is housed in a new building, next to the monastery once occupied by the White Fathers, a missionary organization set up to teach Christian values by example, putting little stress on conversion. To the left of the entrance are a number of fine Roman sculptures; Victory, her arms full of produce, was sculpted in the 2nd century. More sensual and repulsive is the group showing Silenus, his skin mottled with drink and indulgence, being carried home legless by a pair of satyrs. Silenus was a man of great wisdom, Bacchus' tutor, and was said to be able to reveal their destiny to those who succeeded in tying him up during one of his drunken slumbers.

The 4th-century BC carved marble sarcophagi of a priest and priestess are the treasures of the museum. The noble tranquillity of their faces reveals strong Etruscan influence, and in the priestess' clothing, and her bird-like wings, flit echoes of Egypt. There are many plainer sarcophagi on show, and miniature versions for ashes. Those sculpted show a heroic depiction of the deceased.

An overblown vision of Roman Byrsa painted by one of the White Fathers dominates the stairs, which lead to an eclectic collection of smaller objects found in Punic graves: incense burners, plates, containers and prophylactic figures. The wafer-thin petal-design bronze 5th-century jug was imported from Corinth. The finest ceramics are also imported: the black 'bucchero' ware is Etruscan, the glazed red, orange and black ware is Corinthian. More popular exhibits include the diabolic green figurines in glass paste, apparently two Nile gods and a monkey, each protecting a large pot and covered in unsightly black spots and the kitsch putti asleep in the saucer.

The ostrich-shell masks, razors and grimacing terracotta masks were made in Carthage. Ostrich masks, like the evil eye or Hand of Fatimah were used to ward off evil spirits. The swan-neck Punic razors were used for ritual shaving. The vast terracotta mask with its hideous gaping mouth adorned a Punic tophet.

The wall in front of the museum, made from broken statuary, mosaic fragments and pieces of architectural decoration has the feel of a Renaissance studio. The garden it encloses delights in torsos stretched out in the sun, sugar-twist pillars, and pieces of entablature thrown down by giants. St Louis, who died near here during the Eighth Crusade, is commemorated by a turn-of-the-century relief and a dull, pious 19th-century sculpture. Nearby is a sculpted symbol of Punic Carthage, as seen on her coins, a horse against a palm tree, and a larger-than-life, decapitated goddess, her body sensuously veiled by drapery.

The Amphitheatre and Cisterns

East of Byrsa hill, beyond the roundabout, an amphitheatre hides in a bowl of trees to the left of the road, opposite cisterns on the right. Here lies the final stretch of the Roman Zaghouan aqueduct, just a pipe running along and feeding 15 massive cisterns, some still in use as stabling.

The amphitheatre, its atmosphere concentrated by the oppressive forest around it, is an eerie ellipse of stone, punctured by rebuilt arches. In its time it was the largest amphitheatre in North Africa, and in the 11th century was cited as the most impressive monument in Carthage. Part of the exposed central trench was turned into a chapel in 1903, dedicated to the memory of Felicity and Perpetua, two Christians martyred here on 7 March 203. On that day the banks of spectators watched as Perpetua was gored by a heifer, Felicity by a gladiator's sword. Debates, not unlike those today on television violence, raged in Roman times over the effect of the amphitheatre. Cicero believed they were 'incomparable training to make the spectator despise suffering and death,' while St Augustine believed the opposite. In June 1943, it rang to a quite different sound—the sure and steady rhetoric of Winston Churchill, addressing Allied troops in the presence of the King.

Lesser Sites

The Basilica of St Cyprian

Right at the end of Carthage, shortly before Sidi Bou Said, Rue Cyprian opposite a Fina petrol station leads directly to a quiet, shaded field, the site of a 4th–5th-century church. Little remains, except a reconstructed apse wall, filled with broken pillars, and the memory of St Augustine's mother, St Monica, crying here the night her son left for Rome. With a good view over to Cap Bon, and plenty of trees, it makes a secluded picnic spot.

The American Military Cemetery

To the left of a small road leading from the Roman cisterns to Sidi Bou Said stretches a testament to human folly and American efficiency, a memorial to the 6564 Americans who died in North Africa during the Second World War. Four fountains are surrounded by a sea of 2840 neatly tended tombstones, and a Wall of Remembrance, engraved with the names of the 3724 men whose bodies were never recovered. In the far pavilion are ceramic and mosaic maps of the North African campaign and of the war as a whole.

WHERE TO STAY AND EAT

EXPENSIVE

The **Hotel Résidence Carthage**, a small family-run hotel at 16 Rue Hannibal, tel (01) 731072, is just by the Salammbo Tophet. It is open April–Oct. The hotels recommended in nearby Sidi Bou Said are infinitely preferable to the others in Carthage.

There are a number of restaurants, like the signposted **Neptune** and **Hannibal**, in Carthage, but they tend to be overpriced. Alternatively you can buy the ingredients for a picnic in the shopping centre by Carthage-Hannibal station. Better still, combine your sightseeing with a meal in La Goulette.

Sidi Bou Said

Sidi Bou Said, a waterfall of white houses cascading down Jebel Manar, beckons visitors to its web of cobbled streets, bazaars and shady restaurants. For many years, coachloads of tourists have tramped up the central shopping lane, sat in cafés and even ventured into some of the back streets. And yet this village remains breathtaking. Its uniform whitewashed walls, carved stone doorways, blue doors and delicate window grills are interrupted here and there by sunbursts of magenta bougainvillaea, bright violet morning glories or a mustard-painted door. Arrive early in the morning, before the salesmen begin their ceaseless patter, and watch the village waking—each raised blind and opened door offering glimpses of cool courtyards and exquisite works of art.

The village takes its name from Abu Said Kalafa ben Yahia el Temimi el Beji, a 13th-century sufi who settled here following his pilgrimage to Mecca, and is credited with curing rheumatism and scorpion bites. The **mosque** and his **zaouia**, hidden at the centre of the village, are holy ground and forbidden to non-Muslims. Legend has it that St Louis, the French king who misdirected a crusading army to Tunisia and died of dysentery in 1270 at Carthage, had a second life as Sidi Bou Said. The King was secretly converted whilst at Carthage and only pretended to die in order quietly to abandon his crusade and his throne. He settled at Jebel Manar, married a passing Berber beauty and became a great holy man. Sadly, the chronology is off: Louis IX only arrived in Tunisia 34 years after Abu Said had died.

At the top of the village, a squat 19th-century black and white **lighthouse** sits on the foundations of a 1000-year-old ribat. This housed a Spanish garrison for half the 16th century, but from 1574 to 1820 no Christian was even allowed into the village. You can now climb up the lighthouse, and examine its satisfying brass lantern. The view from here, and from the cliff-edge cemetery below, ranges across Tunis, backed by Jebel Zaghouan, and right along the promontory of Cap Bon. The **cemetery**, still inaccessible to non-Muslims, contains the body of Sidi Dhrif, a follower of Sidi Bou Said and scholar of the Andalucian tradition of malouf music. At night, many of the restaurants and cafés in Sidi Bou Said are enlivened by malouf.

SHOPPING

The bazaars and shops in Sidi Bou Said sell goods from all over Tunisia, but the local speciality is bird cages. They are made using the same technique as for the half-fig-shaped grills which cover the village's windows. As the village has for so long been the centre of Tunisia's artistic community, it is worth looking in at **Galerie Ammar Farhat**, halfway up the main street down a street to the left.

WHERE TO STAY

EXPENSIVE

The **Sidi Bou Said Hotel**, on the road to La Marsa called Av Sidi Dhrif, tel (01) 7272153/196/411, is the only hotel near the village with a swimming pool.

MODERATE

A certain Baron Rodolphe d'Erlanger arrived in Sidi Bou Said in 1912 and pressed the government to legislate for the village's preservation. The fruits of this can be fully admired, if you are lucky enough to get a bed, at the **Dar Said Hotel**, a converted palace to the right at the top of the main street. It is open from March to November, tel (01) 270792/4. Alternatively, there is the quiet, family-run **Hotel Bou Farès**, at 15 Rue Sidi Bou Fares, tel (01) 740091, left at the top of the main street.

EATING OUT

At the top of Sidi Bou Said's main drag sits Tunisia's trendiest cafe, the **Café des Nattes**. Prices are high but it has an alluring steep staircase and shaded balcony. Beneath the Dar Said Hotel, set in palace gardens, the **Dar Zarrouk Restaurant** is expensive but beautiful. To eat more cheaply turn right at the Café des Nattes and carry straight on to a cheap café-*gargotte* on the left or the moderately priced **Restaurant Typic**, where they serve a 10-dn meal of the day in the garden. The port-side **Pirate Restaurant**, down a cliff-side staircase, lives off its once considerable reputation and now serves overpriced and unattractive seafood.

La Marsa and Gammarth

La Marsa has retained its cachet as the smartest resort on the Bay. The town centre abounds with stylish boutiques, ice-cream parlours and exquisite French patisseries. Its discreet **villas** and **palaces**, buried deep in luxuriant gardens, shelter a community of diplomats, old Mamluke families and Europeans working in the capital.

It is a population curiously in keeping with its history which began promisingly enough as a rich suburb of Punic Carthage known as Megara. It later became known as Marsa er Roum, Christian Marsa, after it was settled in the 8th century by Copts, the skilled Egyptian Christians who were imported by Hassan ibn Numan to build the first Arab fleet. Its current revival began as a favourite summer residence and building site of the Husseinite Beys, whose efforts were imitated by Mamluke courtiers and consuls. Two of the finest summer palaces were built by Mohammed Bey who presented them on completion as embassies for France and Britain.

Though none of these 19th-century palaces is accessible it is still worth wandering into the town centre, a short walk from the TGM station. A well-proportioned Hafsid-type mosque, capped with green tiles dominates the leafy square, surrounded by cafés and snack bars including the famous **Café Safsaf** now peeling and well warped with age. Here you can savour a coffee and in the summer watch a camel padding round the tiled Hafsid well, drawing up water which no one seems keen to drink. Opposite is the old palace of Ahmed Bey (1837–54).

Gammarth town is of no interest though there is an extensive view of Jebel Zaghouan and the Bay of Tunis from the hilltop Free French war cemetery. Leaving La Marsa, fork up Av Farhat Hached, an avenue of trees sculpted with military uniformity to the hill also known as Jebel Khaoui, the 'Hollow Mountain', a reference to the deep graves found here dug by the Jewish community of Roman Carthage.

Further along the coast there is a shoal of hotels and restaurants, before the cliff-fringed *Baie des Singes*, the Bay of Monkeys, reputedly first named by a local fisherman in scathing reference to the mixed naked bathing of the French colonists. Try the **Restaurant Le Pêcheur** here for a seafood lunch. The 10-km-long stretch of Raouad beach is the most inviting place to swim in the Bay.

Part IV
THE CAP BON PENINSULA

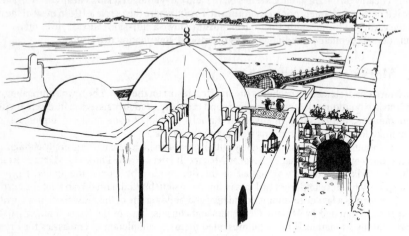

Hammamet Medina

The Cap Bon peninsula is a finger of land stretching out into the Mediterranean, which in the Palaeolithic era formed part of a bridge between Africa and Italy. It has a mild climate and at times the citrus groves, vineyards and scattering of old villages seem more European than North African. In spring and autumn the skies are full of birds, particularly honey buzzards, which use the short crossing to Sicily for their migration between the continents.

The central limestone escarpment of Cap Bon divides the Bay of Tunis from the Sahel. The driving force of national history has always alternated between these two coastal regions, leaving Cap Bon as no more than a prosperous province. It was at its most influential during the Punic era, 6th–2nd centuries BC, when it was on the front line between warring empires.

Agathocles, the tyrant of Syracuse, took the maxim 'the best method of defence is attack' to its logical conclusion. In 310 BC he escaped the Carthaginian siege of his city and, landing at Cap Bon, sacked the Phoenician cities of the coast. His example was followed in the Second Punic War by the Roman general, Regulus, who arrived from an Italy almost totally controlled by the Carthaginian, Hannibal. The end of this cycle came at the end of the Third Punic War, when the cities of Cap Bon which had remained loyal to Carthage were ruthlessly sacked.

Many of these settlements were refounded during the long centuries of Roman prosperity. The region, defended by the Byzantine navy, was one of the last to succumb to the Arab invasion, at the end of the 7th century. In their turn, prosperous Muslim trading communities were wrecked by Christian raiders, the Spanish, Italians and the Knights of Malta, in the warfare of the 16th century. There was an accelerated restoration of prosperity in the 17th century, with the settlement of skilled Andalucian refugees in Cap Bon. The principal towns, Nabeul, Korba and Soliman, were now built safely inland, though the coastal fortress of Kelibia and the walled medina of Hammamet continued to play an active role in Mediterranean piracy.

124

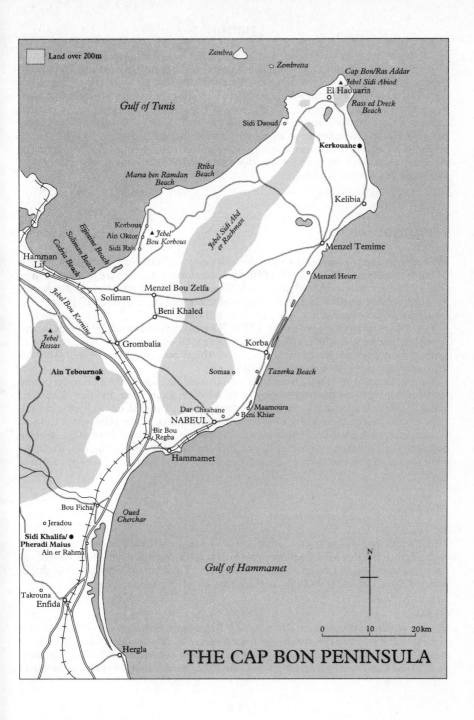

THE CAP BON PENINSULA

The beach between Hammamet and Nabeul is the most magnificent in the country, a continuous swathe of white sand, clean turquoise sea and a palm-lined shore which puts any comparable European package resort to shame. Nabeul, with its larger population, active commercial life and small *pensions*, is the more interesting place to enjoy the sea, and from which to explore the peninsula. The real joys of Cap Bon are to the north, the unspoilt markets in Korba and Menzel Temime, staying in a beach hotel in the lee of Kelibia Castle, and visiting Kerkouane, the most impressive Carthaginian site in Tunisia. At the tip of the peninsula is Cap Bon itself, concealing the magical subterranean quarries of El Haouaria. On the north coast there are miles of deserted beach and the distinctly quirky charms of a 19th-century spa town, Korbous.

Hammamet

Most package tour brochures offer a selection of holidays in Hammamet, at one of the resort's 60 hotels. Unlike the concrete jungle of the Spanish resorts, hotels here are mostly no higher than a palm-tree, surrounded by gardens which lead directly on to the beach. However, this has not prevented what was once a self-contained fishing and farming community from being swamped by European tourists, souvenir shops and coaches.

The tourist invasion began in the 1920s. The bay was colonized by European and American aesthetes, led by a millionaire Rumanian, George Sebastian. Twenty years of privileged indolence was interrupted by the North African campaign, but at the end of the war the community slowly took up where it had left off.

Some of elegant, pre-1960s Hammamet has survived. Standing on the walls of the central kasbah, listening to the constant lapping of the Mediterranean below, the view skims over coloured fishing boats pulled up on white sand to the gardens beyond, in which some of these villas remain hidden. Sebastian's now forms the centrepiece of the Hammamet Cultural Centre, others the nucleus of larger hotels. And despite the fact that most of the working population of Hammamet has never known anything but mass package tourism, life in the whitewashed medina continues unaffected, beguilingly veiled from the tourists by a forest of studded doors.

GETTING AROUND

By Train
Hammamet's train station is at the end of Av Habib Bourguiba, 1 km from the town centre. It is on a branch line that joins the main Tunis to Sfax line at Bir Bou Regba. Nine trains a day run to the main line, picking up regular connections to Tunis, Sousse, Monastir, Mahdia, El Jem and Sfax. The first train in the morning runs direct to Tunis.

By Bus
The bus station is opposite the PTT on Av de la République. Buses leave every half-hour for Nabeul, and it is from there that connections continue up into the peninsula. There are at least ten buses to Tunis a day, and at least two morning departures for Sousse, Monastir, Mahdia and Kairouan. There are five buses a day for Zaghouan, some of which continue to El Fahs.

By *Louage*/Taxi

There are no *louages* from Hammamet, but local taxis for Nabeul, the hotels along the coast or anywhere else can be picked up from the taxi rank in front of the medina walls.

Car/Moped and Bicycle Rentals

There is a glut of car hire firms, and competition has pushed prices lower than elsewhere in Tunisia. You should be able to find a Citroen Visa for under 300 dn a week, unlimited mileage. Topcar organizes rentals through most of the hotels, but otherwise the best place to go is Route Dag Hammarskjoeld, where you will find Avis, tel (02) 80303 and Azur Car Hire, tel (02) 80233. All the hotels rent out bicycles and most of them mopeds too. The going rate is 6 dn a day for a bicycle and 15 dn for a moped.

TOURIST INFORMATION

The **Tourist Office**, tel (02) 80423, is one of the very few helpful ones in the country. It is in the town centre, on Av Habib Bourguiba, and hands out good maps of both Hammamet and Nabeul.

All the hotels in Hammamet will change money at the standard rate, as will all of the numerous **banks** in the centre of town. The **PTT** is 100 m from the medina, on Av de la République, tel (02) 80598. It is far cheaper to telephone abroad from one of its numerous booths than from your hotel. There is a large **police station** beyond the Tourist Office on Av Habib Bourguiba.

Hammamet's weekly **market**, which starts on Wednesday evening but really takes off on Thursday morning, sells everything from make-up to saddles. It takes place 2 km up Av de la République and left on to Av Hedi Ouali.

The Medina

It is impossible anywhere in Hammamet to escape entirely from tourists, but at least the medina remains steeped in its own culture. The houses, their whitewash bruised with watery blues and purples, are adorned for good luck with fishes and Hands of Fatimah. The original entrance is the crooked arch in the northern wall. The street to the left passes the restored 15th-century minaret of the Great Mosque. Opposite its main entrance are the green and red striped door of the Turkish Bath—men welcome in the mornings, women in the afternoons.

Look out for the shop known as *Maison Arabe*, which contains an exhibition of Hammamet marriage costumes, intricate tunics weighed down by the gold and silver embroidery. For an impromtu dip, signs to 'The Brother's Shop' also lead to a small sea gate. The medina ends in cemeteries, a large, exposed Muslim one, and a small Christian enclave founded in the summer of 1881 for French soldiers who died locally during the invasion.

The Kasbah

(Open 08.00–21.00 in summer, 08.30–18.00 in winter; adm)

The Kasbah, approached up a monumental ramp, is crowded and soulless, but useful as an observation tower from which to peer into the street pattern of the medina, and take in the broad sweep of the Mediterranean.

The villas beneath the walls on the sea are mostly owned by foreigners, including the Italian ex-Prime Minister Craxi, and their walls, staircases and domes form a Cubist 'White on White'. Avoid the packed Café Turk, on the kasbah's highest turret. Instead, descend and follow the walls of the kasbah round to the sea wall, and the **Café Sidi Bou Hadid**.

International Cultural Centre

Three kilometres out of the town centre on the southern beach road, the grounds of George Sebastian's sumptuous villa have been converted into a Cultural Centre which hosts, in July and August, an international **festival of the arts**. Perched on dunes, the seats of the open-air theatre command magnificent views of the sea and stage. Tickets for events can be purchased from the box office at the Cultural Centre itself on Av des Nations Unis, tel (02) 80030, at the Tourist Office or in the larger hotels.

At other times of the year, the villa and gardens are open on Mon, Wed and Fri, 10.00–12.00 and 15.00–17.00. Ali, who used to work for Sebastian, will show you his four-man marble bath, based on a 6th-century Byzantine font found on Jerba. Ali can cap any name-drop, as he shows the English where he served tea to Mr Eden, and the Germans where he made up a bed for Rommel. The entire house, built for less than £1000, is a meditation on the possibilities of traditional Tunisian architecture. A marble swimming pool occupies the centre of an arcaded courtyard, and stairs leading to bedrooms are hidden behind studded Andalucian doors. In these encouraging surroundings, the painter Paul Klee and writer André Gide found their parched artistic souls rejuvenated.

During the war, the villa was put to less creative ends. In early 1943, as the struggle for Tunis intensified, the villa was requisitioned by Rommel's general, von Arnim, though Rommel himself only stayed here for three nights. It was from this very place that von Arnim cabled news of the total defeat of the Axis troops in North Africa to his superiors.

Roman Pupput

(Open daily except Mon, 08.00–sunset.)

Hammamet's other site is the mosaics and cisterns unearthed by an archaeological dig at the ancient town of Pupput, signposted on the Sousse road, some 6 km from the town centre between the Samira Club and Tanfous Hotel. Pupput was a small place until the 2nd century AD. Thanks to the patronage of the provincial governor, Salvius Julianus from a prosperous Soussi family, it grew rapidly to become an important stronghold of Byzantine Christianity.

The mosaics on the wall are a fine collection of 4th-century Christian tomb mosaics. The public baths, inland from the wall, contain well-preserved mosaics on the floors and the subtle sand and white pieces used in one of the pools hint at a decorous, clean interior.

Step down into the housing area, and the courtyard of the first house, with a fountain opposite the entrance to the dining-room. Roman dining-rooms can often be identified by the inverted T-shaped mosaic, in this case a 2nd-century black and white example. The servants would come right up the centre of the room with brimming dishes, whilst the diners lay around the walls. Beside the dining room, notice too the mosaic featuring the head of Dionysus. The most fascinating aspect of the house, however, are the cisterns into which you can slither. With a torch, or matches, you can see the terracotta pipes which led rainwater down from the roofs, and inspect the well-preserved plaster seal, strong enough to prevent nearby salt water from contaminating the supply.

The courtyard of the large house to the southwest contains an extraordinary mosaic, designed to look like distorted shadows of the colonnade. To the north of the house are its own private baths, decorated with warped lumps of magenta lava imported from Sicily.

SPORTS

There is an 18-hole **golf course** 10 km from Hammamet, just off the main Tunis-Sousse road.

The beach south of the town is more sheltered than that to the north and, though more crowded, is prettier. Camel and horse rides can be picked up at regular intervals along the sand, at a cost which averages out at 8 dn an hour. All the large beach hotels have facilities for waterskiing, sailsurfing and some parascending, and also offer tennis courts, ping-pong tables and ugly clock golf courses.

WHERE TO STAY
If you decide to stay in Hammamet rather than continue to Nabeul or beyond, where the accommodation is marginally more idiosyncratic and cheaper, be warned that even by spending 40 dn a night it is difficult to escape the package mentality.

EXPENSIVE
The **Hammamet Sheraton**, Av Moncef Bey, tel (02) 80555/546, is certainly the best of the beach hotels, decorated with some fine Tunisian antiques and an amusing selection of puppets. Be warned that prices go through the roof in summer (up to 130 dn a double). Not far from there is the much cheaper **Hotel Tanfous**, tel (02) 80213.

MODERATE
The best value hotel out of town, 3 minutes from the beach, is the **Pension Bennila**, Av des Hotels, tel (02) 80356.

The least institutionalized hotels are in town, though none of them is cheap. Try the **Hotel Alya** on Rue Ali Belbouane, tel (02) 80218, first. The beach is only 100 m away and its rooftop bar commands a sea view across the Muslim cemetery. If this is full, the larger **Hotel Sahbi**, tel (02) 80807, on Av de la République is a bit cheaper. Ask for a room with a big terrace.

CHEAP
The campsite, a little further up Av de la République and across the road, is really little more than a parking lot with showers, known as the **Ideal Camping**.

EATING OUT
All the hotels have their own dining-rooms, but Hammamet has a plethora of good licensed restaurants scattered throughout the town and along the beach roads. The **Restaurant de la Poste**, tel (02) 80023, right at the head of the taxi rank opposite the medina, is an excellent spot for people-watching from the roof. Fresh fish and salad cost 4.5 dn. Next door is the **Restaurant Berbère**, tel (02) 80082, more expensive, but serving excellent fish couscous in its clean and airy dining-room. Out on the road to the south of town, the garlic squid at the **Restaurant du Théâtre**, opposite the Cultural Centre, is mouth-watering. Good cheap food can also be found, particularly in the area around the train station.

NIGHTLIFE
All the big beach hotels have their own nightlife, in the form of organized entertainments, barbecues, cabarets and discotheques. The independent nightclubs are all some distance from the town, and the **Mexico**, near the Hammamet Sheraton on Av Moncef Bey, is the best. A little closer to town, the **Scheherazade Restaurant** on Av des Nations Unies combines dinner with belly-dancing, fire-eating, jug-dancing, snake-charming and other displays of bodily dexterity.

Around Hammamet

For a peaceful escape from Hammamet, walk or ride up the valley of the **Oued Fouara**, which crosses the road to Bir Bou Regba just outside the town. Horses and guides can be found in front of the Hotel Fouarti. To get there by car, turn right just before crossing the railway line at Bir Bou Regba, and head up to the National Guard school. On your right, you pass white gates leading to a small farmyard which is built from the scant remains of Roman Siagu. Skirt round the school to the left and head up the valley on a dirt track, clambering down to the river where you will.

A spring-fed stream trickles down through the floor of its narrow valley. Above extend crumbling limestone cliffs marked with the sharp veins of soil erosion or transformed into terraced gardens watered from deep wells. It is an almost biblical scene with its intimate combination of wild hill grazing and the quiet husbandry of the cultivators. One of the spurs high above the valley held the sanctuary of Thinissut, a temple built in the Roman period but dedicated to the Punic god Baal Hammon and his consort Tanit, the face of Baal. The terracotta sculptures discovered here can be seen in both the Bardo and the local museum in Nabeul. The half-dozen statues of Tanit are particularly haunting; she is represented as a lion-faced woman, whose savage jaws contrast disturbingly with the rigid stance of her formal female figure.

Several kilometres up the river bed, small boys sell river cooled Coke and Fanta just before a waterfall which flows over a neglected bed of Roman dressed stone, once the start of an aqueduct. Beyond, where recent concrete shores up the older stonework, a series of springs emerge, the natural focus of water-fetching and washing expeditions by the local inhabitants.

The Agricultural Hinterland of Cap Bon

Southwestern Cap Bon is fertile farming land, not a place of great inspiration though pleasantly untouched by tourism. It bears a strong colonial imprint in the red-tiled farmhouses crowning each hilltop, and the hedgerows of cypress which divide the land, but the French and Italian farmers have left their strongest legacy in two particularly dominant crops, citrus fruit and vines.

The area's wine production centres on Grombalia, and is celebrated in a **wine festival** in September. In late autumn, the range of reds given off by the dying vine leaves can almost rival a New England 'fall' and the smell of burning fills the air. Vine roots and prunings make particularly good charcoal.

There are some Roman ruins at **Ain Tebournok**, a possible picnic detour some 8 km from Grombalia. Take the small road opposite the STB bank in the centre of town and wind through wine country to this hamlet at the foot of the rougher hill country. The houses extend in an arc around the modern pumping station and the ancient shrine. A low stone wall in the stream bed once held back a sacred pool from which stairs run up to the water shrine. It was converted into a colonial farmhouse but is now a cattleshed ringed with debris and a cluster of beehive bread ovens.

At the twin towns of Beni Khaled and Menzel Bou Zelfa citrus fruit and in particular, the orange, is king. **Beni Khaled** has a busy local market on Saturday from where you might be proudly shown a, for once, quite elegant new mosque with its impressive dome covering acres of faience and marble. There is an **orange festival** staged at neighbouring **Menzel Bou Zelfa** in April to catch the blossom, though the various species of fruit are picked in the months after November. Citrus fruits were first brought by the Arabs to Europe from China but large-scale cultivation was a colonial innovation. The Tunisian orchards were only firmly established in the late 1930s when the Spanish Civil War ruined the groves in Andalucia and Valencia.

Hammamet to Sousse

There are no hotels on the 80 km between the resorts of Hammamet and Sousse, though there are things to see around Enfida and at the Roman ruins of Pheradi Maius.

Bou Ficha

Halfway to Bou Ficha, in an enormous military camp, is the Roman mausoleum, marked **Ksar Menara** on some old maps but now strictly *interdit*. Console yourself with a fleeting glance of the ruined **Roman bridge** at Oued Cherchar, 4 km before Bou Ficha. The main road sweeps past the village, a favourite stop for *louages* and trucks as it is halfway from Tunis to Sousse. Try the black and yellow tiled local restaurant at 47 Av Habib Bourguiba. Dish of the day, chips and salad cost 1.5 dn.

Pheradi Maius

At the village of Ain er Rahma, 9 km south of Bou Ficha, a tarmac road leads inland to the village and shrine of Sidi Khelifa. Just after the saint's tomb, a dirt track on your left leads 500 m to the ruins of Pheradi Maius, a Roman settlement. It is currently being excavated (you are free to explore), and some of the digging has already been done by a stream which has cut a small gorge through the centre of the ruined town.

Through the fence you first meet a low, enclosed compound, one of the town's **markets**, and then the more impressive walls of the **baths**. The rich, late Roman mosaic floor has only recently been revealed. It has yet to be stabilized but you can peer over the walls into the bright apsidal pools and central hall.

A tall, thin **triumphal arch** stands beyond in almost pristine condition. The side niches which once held statues are still decorated with carved scallop shells and on the other face are bold half-relief columns with palm-leaf capitals. The arch gives onto a large **forum** paved in fine white stone across which the stream deposits offerings of ceramic and bone. Immediately to your left are two small sanctuaries and across the forum an arcade is being carefully restored. Stairs from here mount into a higher courtyard that preceded a **temple** which was entirely enclosed by a colonnade. A collection of inscriptions on the far wall preserves addresses to the emperors and gods. These include a stone incised with the rough shape of a pair of feet. It is a symbol that has been variously interpreted, either as an instruction to take off your shoes or as a gentle reminder that the gods walk here but are only visible to a chosen few. The more prosaic think they may have been footings to hold life-size statues.

The unexcavated city rises on the slopes to the west and the east. Above, on the summit of the hill, tower the remaining foundations of a **temple to Baal**, Lord of the High Places. The warm orange stone has been skilfully jointed and requires no mortar. The view from the top is exalting. To the east, surf pounds on the thin spit of shore that separates a lagoon from the ocean. To the north, over Bou Ficha you can search the hills above Hammamet, discarding the centuries to imagine the sister temple of Baal Hammon at Thinissut.

Jeradou

From Sidi Khalifa the road runs inland to the hilltop village of Jeradou 6 km away. Like the nearby village of Takrouna, this is an old Berber village crowned by a green-domed zaouia of Sidi Abdel Kader and a mosque. It is less striking, more populous but also less visited than Takrouna, though you will still need to be in the mood to enjoy an escorting band of children. Below the village is the shell of an old Roman temple.

Enfida

Back on the main road you pass the enormous 250,000-acre Enfida agricultural estate. In 1880 the future of this estate was at the heart of every diplomatic conversation in Tunis and Paris. Once the property of the Vizier Khereddine it passed in a complicated succession of deals to a French company. The difficulties that this company experienced in getting hold of their purchase suggested that independent Tunisia was not 'safe' for international capital and that direct control was required. Four years later, the French Protectorate began.

For the 7000 estate workers and the surrounding hinterland, Enfida is the chief market, attracting crowds of sturdy farmers and their wives to the Sunday **market**. Fruit and vegetables can be brought any day of the week at the covered market of the main street, almost opposite the old colonial church. Appropriately, this has been turned into a museum for Christian mosaics unearthed in the 4th- and 6th-century churches at the site of old Uppena, 6 km north of Enfida.

The Museum

(Open 09.00–12.00 and 14.00–17.30, except Mon.) No admission is charged but you may have to dig the guardian out of the old clothes shop just to the left of the Banque de Tunisie opposite the church.

Uppena was known about for centuries from a literary source which records that one Bishop Honorius of Uppena was exiled by the Vandal King Huneric. His mosaic tomb cover, and that of another local bishop, Baleriolus, flank a central mosaic dedicated to six Christian martyrs where the altar would once have stood. In the apse is the stone memorial to a priest of Saturn from the second century AD and there are other pagan memorials ranged around the wall. These stones marked the burial of pots of ashes following a pagan cremation, whilst the Christian mosaics covered bodies buried in churches. Some of the earlier Christian tombs are dated by the pagan calendar: 'the seventh day of the Ides of March', 'the fourth day of the Ides of May'. This precision over the day of death shows that the custom of an anniversary graveside meal continued. It also allowed for the later creation of a holy Christian calendar, filled with saints' days. In the west floor there is another reminder of Vandal history. The Bishop of Mauretania, who came to Carthage for the church council of 484, was also prohibited from returning to his diocese by King Huneric, and ended his days at Uppena.

The Enfida and Oued Abdallah War Cemeteries

There are two Second World War cemeteries beside the road to the hill village of Takrouna. The **Commonwealth War Cemetery** is on the edge of town beside a ruined colonial cemetery. Here are buried 1551 dead from the last three months of the Tunisian campaign beneath three banks of pale headstones. The Eighth Army under Montgomery repeatedly attacked the well-prepared Axis positions that ran from Enfida up into the hills to the west.

Though there are only two members of the Indian Army buried here, the Nepalese Gurkha regiments, specialists in night assaults on hill positions, were involved in some of the bitterest fighting.

The **French Military Cemetery**, distinguished by rows of green painted helmets, is in the village of Oued Abdallah, 3 km from Enfida. The Christian and Jewish dead lie around a Cross of Lorraine carved from red stone, many with Senegalese names. Thirty-four local Muslim soldiers from Leclerc's Free French Army lie in a separate plot around a koubba of honour. Exotic battle honours like Fezzan, Ksar Ghilaine and Cyrenaica recall the lesser-known skirmishes of the desert campaign when the 'Touareg' legion fought its way up from Chad to join the Eighth Army.

Takrouna

Takrouna village, heart of some of the fiercest fighting from April to May 1943, looms enticingly over Oued Abdallah on its craggy limestone outcrop. Over-visited as it is, it is nevertheless a remarkable survivor, a good example of the old pattern of Berber hilltop villages. A Berber community, though spread widely over farmland, often shared a central village which acted as a hill fort, where they could safely store the harvest. Crowned by the green domed tomb of local holy man Sidi Ali Bou Qaddida, at the heart of the zaouia of Abdel Kader, the village also boasts a number of disintegrating farm houses. Come prepared to be guided and well-armed with small change.

Hergla

The coastal village of Hergla, 17 km south of Enfida, marks the beginning of the Sahel. It occupies the site of a Roman town, Horres Caelia, which was turned into a Byzantine stronghold and held out for a long time against Arab attacks from Kairouan. When it fell, it fell completely. The inhabitants were massacred and the fort was pulled down. There is a beach to the north, a sweep of sand dotted with palms, and a fishing port has recently been built. Weaving alfafa grass into bags for pressing olive oil, known as *scourtins*, was the village's traditional occupation and there are usually one or two hanging up for sale as mats to any passing tourist. A new speedboat factory by the port ties in with the habits of the local patron saint, Sidi Bou Mendil, a 10th-century sage with magical powers which included flying to Mecca on a pocket handkerchief.

On to Sousse

The coastal road from Hergla to Sousse is not pretty. Market gardens and shabby villages are gradually displaced by a gathering storm of package holiday hotels. This is at its most absurd at **Port el Kantaoui**, a new marina development complete with a golf course, estate agents, bogus towers and, despite their astonishing exteriors, some quite tacky hotels. The only possible reason for coming here is to be taken out for a boating day-trip or to go scuba diving. For that see the sports section in Sousse (p. 157).

Nabeul

Hammamet's neighbour, Nabeul, is the main town of the Cap Bon peninsula and the seat of local government. Founded slightly inland in the 12th century, out of the grasp of Christian raiders, it has also resisted the worst depredations of the tourists, absorbing them in its natural trading patterns. It is a centre of light industry, nationally renowned for its pottery, stone-carving and wrought-iron work, and smothered to the north by brick factories, which give some balance to the hotels which line the beach, and the tourist bazaars which have colonized the centre of the town. This is upset every Friday, when the **camel market** causes traffic to be diverted from the town centre, making way for a continual stream of tourists, bussed in to the largest souvenir emporium in Tunisia.

For the rest of the week, locals and tourists meet on an equal footing in the town's cafés and restaurants. The handful of cheap *pensions* allows independent travellers to enjoy the town, its beach and excellent museum.

GETTING AROUND

By Train
A direct service leaves the train station in the centre of Nabeul, tel (02) 8505, for Tunis at 05.30, but otherwise there are eight trains a day on this branch line, travelling through Hammamet to Bir Bou Regba. Mainline trains from Bir Bou Regba are detailed in the Hammamet section (p. 126).

By Bus
There are two bus stations in Nabeul, both on the main Av Thameur which turns into Av Farhat Hached. Frequent departures for all destinations further up Cap Bon, including five buses a day for Kelibia, leave from the eastern end of town, almost opposite the enclosure for the camel market. Buses for the rest of the country leave from the western station, near the Office National de l'Artisanat. There are two a day for Kairouan, two for Sousse and connections to Monastir and Mahdia, six for Zaghouan and two for El Fahs, with hourly departures for Tunis.

By *Louage*/Taxi
The *louage* stations are attached to the bus stations and serve the same areas—most of Cap Bon from the eastern, Hammamet and the rest of Tunisia from the western station. Small red and white or blue and white taxis, which you can pick up in the centre of town, will take you where you wish in the local area. As always, they charge according to the meter.

Car, Moped and Bicycle Hire
A company called Express Car monopolizes the hotel lobby trade, but its main offices are at 146 Av Habib Thameur, tel (02) 86873 or 87014. Their rates are competitive with the rest of the companies in the area, but if they have nothing try Hertz, Av Habib Bourguiba, tel (02) 85027. All the big hotels rent out bicycles and mopeds, at rates of around 6 dn and 15 dn a day respectively.

TOURIST INFORMATION
The **Tourist Office (ONTT)**, tel (02) 86800, is on Av Taieb Mehiri, just up from the beach. The main **Post Office (PTT)** is on Av Habib Bourguiba, opposite the **Tunis Air** office, tel (02) 85193, and the **police station** is also up there, tel (02) 85474. All hotels operate their own *bureau de change*, and most of the banks in town will also change money.

The Museum
(Open daily 09.00–16.30, except Mon.) Nabeul's courtyard museum is opposite the train station on Av Habib Bourguiba, close to the pot-encased tree that marks the centre of town. The statuettes in the first room on the left, in particular that of the naked man, are Carthaginian, around 2500 years old, but could almost have been sculpted yesterday. Whether these were made in North Africa or imported is not certain, but the style of many of the items shows a fluid interchange of ideas amongst Mediterranean cultures of the time. Some of the amulets, charms and scarabs on display in the same room, mostly worn to ward off evil spirits, depict Egyptian-looking beaked gods, birds and fishes. The statuette of a woman shows definite Greek influence.

The second room contains some of the most important evidence relating to Carthaginian religion ever found. These extraordinary sculptures were unearthed at a temple sanctuary called Thinissut, high in the hills above Hammamet, in 1948. They depict the main goddess of Carthage, Tanit, with the half-smiling, half-fierce head of a lion, wearing draped clothing which covers the plumage of a bird. The human feet which protrude at the bottom come as something of a surprise. The date of these finds, 1st century AD, 200 years after the Roman conquest, shows the strength of belief in the Punic deities. The dedicatory stones in the temple, which you can also see, are in both Punic and Latin. The other sculptures in the room further illustrate the shared ancestry of Mediterranean worship. The seated Tanit and the Greek-looking goddess beside her both wear a 'polis', such as is still worn today on the heads of Greek Orthodox priests.

The third room holds a collection of Roman domestic pottery and fittings, of which the ornate pieces of bronze casting are particularly high quality. For once, the collection of Roman oil lamps and the moulds from which they were made is well-displayed and the lamps themselves quite fine.

The impressive mosaics in the courtyard come from a local series that illustrates episodes from the *Iliad*. Do not miss the black stone carving of Bacchus on the back of a leopard, sitting in the courtyard. The other empty rooms are earmarked for Islamic exhibits which are not yet in situ.

Neapolis
(Open daily, dawn to dusk.) Southwest of present-day Nabeul stood a city which thrived for 1200 years, from the 5th century BC to 7th century AD, known to us as Neapolis, the Greek name used by Thucydides.

The site only shows slight traces of the Roman town established here, which has been partly excavated in an enclosure opposite the Pension Monia Club, at the Hammamet end of town. Follow the path and turn left to find the foot-high remains of a palace, with a vast courtyard and opulent dining-room flanked by smaller fountain courtyards. More intriguing is the sanctuary across the paved street, its entrance marked by two pillars. On the mosaic floor, otherwise completely plain, the word 'Artemonis' is crowned between two candelabra. The building was associated with the Artemisian Games, held in honour of the virgin huntress. They were performed all over the Roman Empire, with men taking part in running and javelin competitions.

By the beach at the far corner of the site enclosure, there is a series of pits, the remains of a Roman factory, tiled with a patterned terracotta floor. When excavated in the late 1960s amphorae, still full of the rotting fish paste, *garum*, manufactured here, were found. It was made by sealing the blood and guts of tuna fish, with salt, into an airtight container and waiting. After several months a hole was punctured and the putrid mixture flowed out. In taste, *garum* had something in common with *blachan*, the fish paste commonly used in Southeast Asian cooking.

SHOPPING AND SUNBATHING

The least crowded beach is at the southern edge of town, down by the Pension les Oliviers and the Hotel Jasmine campsite. There is a stall there selling drinks and sandwiches, and sand and sea to your heart's content.

The other great Nabeul pastime is shopping, but before you head off it might be an idea to go to the Office National de l'Artisanat (ONAT) on Av Habib Thameur to see the maximum prices you should aim to pay.

Every Friday morning, Nabeul's *marché aux chameaux*, or **camel market**, converts a large dusty enclosure into a massive tented supermarket. The scale of the market is worth seeing, and the local food and clothes market is more interesting than the glittering display of brass ashtrays, 20th-century harem wear, leather, pottery and stuffed camels, arranged for the tourists. On the way, look in at the warehouse on the left of Rue el Arbi Zarrouk, which houses the *Poterie Artistique*, covered head to toe in tiles.

Nabeul did not turn to pottery until the 16th century, when potters from Guellala on Jerba were attracted by the quality of Cap Bon clay as well as the fertility of its land and sea. They were followed, in the 17th century, by Andalucians who brought with them the art of producing faience wall tiles. Tunisia particularly developed the use of transparent lead glazes, green and yellow, which still decorate the more traditional of Nabeul's pots.

The other Nabeulian speciality is distilled **flower essence and perfume**, made from local jasmine and citrus blossoms. Though the products are not easily transported, do not miss going to see Nabeul's **stone carvers** in the suburb of Dar Chabaane, just beyond the Friday market enclosure. Worked in soft limestone, pillars and door surrounds carved here are to be found gracing houses all over Tunisia.

SPORTS

Nabeul Plage (beach) is the place to head if you want a ride. Horses and camels wait in droves on the hot sand and should cost 8 dn an hour.

All the beachfront hotels provide watersports equipment and instruction, including water-skiing and wind surfing. The Hotel Lido at the northern end of town has waterskiing, tennis courts, a football pitch and ping-pong tables, all available to non-residents. The nearest golf course is the other side of Hammamet.

WHERE TO STAY

EXPENSIVE
If you want a beach hotel with a swimming pool, try the smallest, **Hotel Club Ramses**, tel (02) 86363/644.

MODERATE
Nabeul has an unusual collection of *pensions familials* on offer however, all clean and much friendlier than the sea-side, package affairs. **Pension les Oliviers**, Rue Aboul Kacem Chebbi, tel (02) 86865, is close to a relatively quiet stretch of beach and set in an olive grove. A little more expensive, at 32 dn a double, is the **Pension Monia Club**, tel (02) 85713, closer still to the beach down the same road and to the left.

136

CHEAP
Cheaper, and right in the centre of town, the **Pension les Roses**, Av Farhat Hached, tel (02) 85570, is clean, and close to the best and cheapest restaurants in town. If both of these are full, which they may well be in summer, try **Pension les Hafsides**, on Rue Sidi Maaouia, tel (02) 85823. The **campsite** by the Hotel Jasmine in the same area is shaded and popular, but gets very busy in summer.

EATING OUT
The cheapest and best food in Nabeul is to be had right in the centre of town, in the cafés around the Pension les Roses. For a longer meal with wine, one of the best restaurants is at the Pension Monia Club. The **Rotonde Restaurant**, tel (02) 85782, overlooking the sea on Nabeul Plage, has a good terrace for beer and light lunches, though you would be wise to steer clear of anything complicated. They do a very good, hot mechoui salad.

Around Nabeul

Although there is nothing specific to attract your attention in the peninsula's hilly spine, it can make a good antidote to grilled bodies on a beach. The southern end of the peninsula centres on rolling farmland, reminiscent of southern Spain and Italy, and on the minor roads life is conducted at donkey's pace. In the north, the geography is more rugged, and the scenery less intimate.

North of Nabeul

The coast between Nabeul and Kelibia is one long white beach, backed, like much of Tunisia's coast, by marshy salt lakes, known as *sebkhets*. The market towns of Korba and Menzel Temime service both the coast and a large agricultural community in the centre of the peninsula. Although you will probably only treat these as day-trips from Nabeul, there are hotels at Korba and Menzel Temime. Local buses for all destinations leave from Nabeul's eastern bus station.

Maamoura and Tazerka
These two beaches between Nabeul and Korba are signposted right off the main road. Maamoura, just beyond the wool-weaving Nabeul suburb, Beni Khiar, is served in summer by the Restaurant de la Mer. To the west of the beach are an extensive group of rock-cut tombs and an underground necropolis, where niches in the walls of a series of low rounded caves would once have held coffins and urns.

The second beach, 4 km before Korba, only sports a small *buvette*.

Korba

The town of Korba, straddling an intermittent river, occupies the site of the now invisible Roman Curubis. Arriving for the Sunday **souk**, walk off further into the twisting alleys of the whitewashed medina, and recuperate in the citrus shade of the café opposite Korba's main mosque. Alternatively, on the spotless beach thirst can be slaked at the **Café Restaurant Sidi Maouir**, beside the blue and white domed koubba of the same name.

Menzel Temime

Between Korba and Menzel Temime, the bumpy road continues straight through country-side which has changed little since Roman times. Now, barrel-vaulted farm buildings hide heaps of hot red peppers and other vegetables, and the wooden workings of stone well-heads decay, outmoded by the small electric pumps which crouch beside them. Salty lagoons and marshes are colonized by flamingoes, standing unperturbed by darting wading birds, avocets and spoonbills. **Lebna's** main street wafts with hot harissa and the subtle smells of cumin and coriander, issuing from the Warda spice factory.

Menzel Temime has a *Monoprix*, in a smart new building on the road into the centre of town, which can be raided for picnic supplies. There is also a **Café Restaurant** at the beach, a kilometre from the town.

On the way to the beach you pass beneath an ancient burial site, the hill crowned by the green and white striped domes of the tomb of Sidi Salem. The koubba on the way out of town towards Kelibia is that of his son, Sidi Bou Salem.

WHERE TO STAY AND EATING OUT

On the outskirts of Korba, there is a **Club Med Hotel** open in the summer which takes in non-members if you ask politely at the gate. Club Meds are usually hyper-efficient and packed with boisterous children, but this place is pleasantly run down and situated on a clean, fresh stretch of beach. As well as the hotel restaurant, there is the **Café Restaurant Sidi Maouir** on the beach.

The 48-room **Hotel Temime** on Rue Mohammed Ben Fadhel, Menzel Temime, tel (02) 98296/62, has moderately priced clean rooms and a bar. The hotel also has a good restaurant where you can eat fresh grilled fish washed down with wine for 6 dn a head.

Kelibia

Stretching in both directions beneath the walls of Kelibia Castle, a laid-back stretch of beach offers accommodation, excellent food, a fishing port and a nearby town, the perfect basis for some quiet seaside relaxation.

In the evening stroll into Kelibia town, some 2 km inland from the port. The minarets of the old town's 10 mosques are lit up with copious bulbs, and the streets seethe with the activities of weavers and tailors, carpet-makers, iron-workers, carpenters, hairdressers by the dozen, mechanics and wool merchants.

GETTING AROUND

Constant taxis buzz up and down the short open road between the port and the old town.

By Hydrofoil

The hydrofoil to Trapani, Sicily, is run by a company called Tourafric, who do *not* have an office in Kelibia. Buy tickets and reserve seats from Tourafric at 52 Av Habib Bourguiba, tel (01) 341488, in Tunis, or 14 Av Khaled ibn el Oualid, tel (03)24277/509, in Sousse. Crossings depend on good weather, but there are at least five a week in the summer and three in winter. You can only buy return fares, which cost over 125 dn.

By Bus

The bus station is on the main road, near the roundabout with the central pillar. Minibuses leave frequently for El Haouaria, and there are nine buses for Nabeul between 04.30 and mid-afternoon. For most of the rest of the country, travel to Nabeul first, though there are three buses a day direct to Tunis.

By *Louage*
Louages leave from the bus station as well, and are most useful after the majority of buses have left by mid-afternoon.

TOURIST INFORMATION
On the main road between town and port, you will find **banks, chemists, PTT** and **police station.**

Kelibia Castle

A steep drive twists up to the castle and its heavily defended entrance gate. The interior is a jumble of historical fragments; a central Roman bastion surrounded by anti-aircraft gun emplacements. Roman capitals, a French lighthouse, chickens and washing lines are all enclosed in restored 6th-century Byzantine walls, which give a commanding view over beaches and hills. The castle was sacked thrice by the Spaniards between 1535–1547, but current restorations are repairing bomb damage from 1943, when the Allies sought to rout Axis troops from both the fortress and the port.

One of the most enthusiastic guardians in Tunisia, a mine of accurate information on local history and archaeology, watches over the castle armed with a whistle. He lives in the Turkish barracks he restored himself in the middle of the massive courtyard.

Roman Ruins

Roman Clupea occupied the area around the base of the castle, its houses clinging to the steep incline which would have culminated in a capitol and temples, now buried beneath the courtyard of the castle. Beside the main road from the town are the remains of a Roman temple. Several massive pieces of marble entablature, their decoration as good as new, lie strewn beside pillars the size of redwood trunks. Attention to detail shows in the way that the entablature's frieze has been carved at an angle, so as to preserve the correct perspective from the front of the building.

The site guardian will take you round the side of a fishing school to the remains of a large 4th-century villa. The rooms flank a large courtyard which was once shaded by a double colonnade. Later, graves and the shrine of a Muslim saint were built on top. Behind the Roman fountain you can make out the mihrab of a small mosque.

Past wool-dyeing vats and over the road lies a Byzantine church. Broken pillars are mirrored by a palm tree which now grows beside the remaining mosaic-covered tombs.

Punic Rock-Cut Tombs

North of the castle, opposite the entrance to the defunct Mansourah Hotel, a small road leads off beside a pipe depot and ancient quarry. A set of over 20 Punic tombs, cut deep into the rock, were discovered here. Each has a flight of narrow steps, bounded by thin ramps on either side, leading straight down through the golden rock into a square burial chamber some 2 m below ground. Seen at sunset, the sculpted tombs invest Punic gravediggers with the skill and dignity of artists.

There is another group of tombs, the **Haouanets of Harouri**, at the village of Oued el Khatef, up a signposted road at the Nabeul end of town. The sight of a dozen gaping entrances, cut into ancient banks of rock above the river course, is impressive. Some are three chambers deep, with rock walls almost plaster smooth.

WHERE TO STAY

EXPENSIVE
At the far end of the southern beach, the **Hotel Mamounia** offers a choice of rooms with terraces or bungalows. It also has a discotheque and facilities for watersports.

MODERATE
Beside the port road are two smaller hotels, with restaurant terraces overlooking the sea. The rougher of the two is the **Hotel En Nassim**, tel (02) 86737. The **Hotel Florida**, tel (02) 96248, is next door, a fraction more expensive but it has a delicious restaurant.

EATING OUT
The **Hotel Florida** offers an excellent four-course menu for 4 dn. The other hotel restaurants come a good equal second. There is the split-cane-shaded dining-room of the **En Nassim** and, halfway between the port and town, the lively **Bar Restaurant Relais du Kelibia**, or the **Café Restaurant Sidi El Bahri** above the port with snack shacks right by it. The local wine, *Muscat de Kelibia*, is light, refreshing and fairly dry, made with grapes normally associated with sweet dessert wines.

Kerkouane

Nine kilometres north of Kelibia, a right turning leads to the excavated site of Punic Kerkouane. When the town was discovered in 1952 our knowledge of the Carthaginian era was based on the excavation of burial sites. Here, for the first time, was the opportunity to discover how the Carthaginians lived. After its sacking by Regulus in 256 BC the town never recovered, and no later civilization was tempted by the isolated site.

The knee-high ruins lie on the very edge of the sea. The museum contains some fascinating exhibits, and the site makes a peaceful and thought-provoking half-hour walk, with the chance of a swim in the midday heat. Both are open every day except Mon, 09.00–12.00 and 14.00–17.00; adm.

Carthaginian Life

Kerkouane existed by the 6th century BC, since a bowl, imported at that date from the Ionian islands in Greece, has been found. That date suggests that it was settled by Phoenician refugees fleeing from Nebuchadnezzar's invasion of Tyre in 574 BC. The Tunisian *Institut National de l'Art et de l'Archéologie* claims that the inhabitants were indigenous and merely influenced by the Punic civilization, but it is a view that smacks of retrospective nationalism.

The site shows a dense, compact town, encircled by the sea and a double landward wall. There are no traces of a port, but many fishing weights and vats, in which 'Tyrian Purple' dye was extracted from murex shellfish, have been found. It is assumed that the inhabitants simply drew their boats up on to the beach for safe harbour. Exhibits in the museum show that, as is characteristic of Carthaginian settlements, the inhabitants traded with other parts of the Mediterranean, and that the cross-fertilization of skills and beliefs was prolific. Kerkouane emerges as an intensely urban society, having little relationship with the land around it. Its 2500 inhabitants were whitewashers, dyers, fishermen, stonemasons, iron-workers, glass-blowers, plasterers, sculptors and painters, but there is no sign of a stable or barn in the town.

The Museum
In one corner of the central courtyard, the steady downwards gaze of a larger than life-size cow's head hides a drainpipe, and beside it are some terracotta paving tiles, in hexagonal and lozenge shapes. The collection of small square altars, some modelled and others carved from blocks of stone, would have been used to hold sacrifices to various household gods. On the far wall is a coffer of spiny murex shells, displayed beside fishing weights and obsidian, a shiny stone quarried from the island of Pantelleria in the Sicilian straits.

The majority of the exhibits inside the museum are grave goods excavated from four Punic necropolises outside the town. The etched black pottery was imported from the Greek colony of Capua in southern Italy, and is known as Campanian ware. There is a bread oven on display which hints that the Carthaginians ate the same delicious flat bread as is still produced in the Tunisian countryside today.

The jewellery is more likely to be local work, and includes carving on imported stones such as jasper and cornelian, and some highly detailed amulets of Greek and Egyptian design. The metalwork is in parts so intricate that large magnifying glasses are provided to appreciate it. The etched metal razors with swan neck handles were used for ritual shaving before ceremonies.

Throughout the exhibition rooms, there are numerous gods and votive figures. An aristocratic revolution in 396 BC marked the introduction of Demeter/Ceres, the goddess of corn, to a celestial circle previously dominated by Baal Hammon and his female alter-ego, Tanit. In the collection you will notice a couple of statues of a goddess with several rows of fertile breasts, similar to the Artemis of Ephesus, and strange Campagniform figures, round-headed, blank-faced terracotta statues with prominent male genitals, which are thought to have been offered to Baal, though in return for what particular favour is not known. Excavations of a sanctuary at Kerkouane have show that kilns within the religious buildings were used to manufacture these figures.

The 'Princess of Kerkouane' is the most striking of all the sculptures, a life-size wooden sarcophagus cover. It was painted red, and carved in the shape of the Carthaginian goddess Ashtarte, the guardian of the dead. The disembodied arm has not broken off, but was, for some unkonwn reason, carved separately, and laid across the figure as shown.

The Site
Wandering through Kerkouane, it is obvious that the wide streets and regular islands of housing were built to an urban plan. The construction techniques are very varied; some, such as *Opus Africanum*, the practice of strengthening small stone walls with large upright dressed blocks, were, until the discovery of Kerkouane, thought to be a Roman invention.

The plan of the **houses** is remarkably uniform, with variety only in size and orientation. A dressed stone doorstep leads into a narrow corridor, bounded by drains, which in turn leads to a courtyard, offset so as to be invisible from the street. The courtyard normally contains a well, and off to one side a **bathroom**, often equipped with a built-in hip bath and basin, all connected to a complex system of overflow and drainage. A staircase would have led up to bedrooms above.

141

One of the most conspicuous elements of the housing is the fine pink cement which coats the floors and walls, produced by adding ground bricks and crumbled terracotta which keeps it cool and prevents cracking. The floors are sometimes flecked with fragments of white marble and blue glass. In one house the marble chips have been set in the sign of the goddess Tanit, a triangle with round head and arms. As in Tunisian houses today, the principal rooms are ranged around the courtyard. Some of these were decorated with mosaic floors, their walls painted yellow and grey, or even in imitation marble.

At the centre of the site, on the crossroads of the Rue des Artisans and Rue du Temple, the stumps of two pillars announce the entrance to Kerkouane's **sanctuary**. The long room to the right of the entrance hall is surrounded by benches. Beyond it is the kiln room, in which votive statues and figurines of the gods were made. In the first courtyard stands an altar, a crude square block, and beyond it the more intriguing sacrificial courtyard. In the corner is a collection of small boulders, as found in countless sacred places from the earliest times, and thought to symbolize a favour asked or prayer addressed to one of the gods. From figurines found here, the sanctuary appears to have been dedicated to the trinity of Tanit, Baal and Cid, god of hunting and fishing.

El Haouaria

Sheltered from the Mediterranean in the lee of Jebel Sidi Abiod, El Haouaria at a distance looks like a cluster of terraced boxes connected by a web of aerials and wires. But once past the official end of town with its smart double carriageway and falcon statue, it reveals itself as a charming confection of whitewash, blue paintwork, long, slow coffee drinking and absorbed hookah smoking. On the headland beyond there are spectacular cavernous **quarries**, whose stone was used from the 6th century BC for building the great cities of the Gulf of Tunis. El Haouaria holds a **festival of falconry** in mid-June, and in spring and autumn Jebel Sidi Abiod is a key point on migration routes.

GETTING AROUND
El Haouaria is served by a fleet of red and white minibuses, and there are thrice daily services down the south coast of Cap Bon to Nabeul, and along the north coast to Tunis.

TOURIST INFORMATION
There is no tourist office in El Haouaria, but **banks**, **police** and the **PTT** are all clustered around the entrance to the town.

Roman Quarries

Two kilometres beyond the town, following signs to the *Grottes Romaines*, is the coast where Agathocles, invading from Sicily in 310 BC, demonstrated his determination by ordering his men to burn their boats. No escape from a new expression. It is an easy half-hour walk. For three centuries the Carthaginians had already been quarrying the soft orange limestone which forms the tip of Cap Bon. It was used then and throughout the Roman and Byzantine period for decorative carving. The Byzantines added the fort whose ruins can be seen on the hill.

A *buvette*, the **Café des Grottes**, and some woven parasols provide welcome shade in the car park, an open patch of orange ground that drops vertically into the sea beyond. The view looks out over the gently heaving Mediterranean to the islands of Zembra and Zembretta, and there is the military delivery of the octogenarian *Guide des Grottes* to look forward to. He will lead you into the main *Ghar el Kebir*, the large cave, in the centre of which an effective camel has been sculpted. And with encouragement he will show you cave after extraordinary cave. The stone was excavated from these underground quarries to leave a series of interior pyramidal voids, lit by sunlight which cuts through holes in the ceiling above. It was through these that the quarried stone was laboriously hauled to the surface and thence transferred to ships for the journey across the Gulf of Tunis. The walls have a severe man-made beauty; the pools of sharply defined light which pick out wedges of the undulating quarry floor give the whole place the feel of a natural stage, on which some epic play is about to begin. Capers are the only flora to disturb the rock's hegemony. They cascade from the ceiling holes and their strange, bitter buds are culled in April before being treated in brine.

There are a number of tales about whole communities of manacled slaves who lived their entire lives underground, breeding children who were unable to tolerate the light of day. Archaeologists have found no evidence to support this, though it was usual for mines and quarries to be worked by slave labour in the ancient world.

Falconry

The **Club des Fauconniers**, which you pass on the way to the quarries, is run by the helpful *Cellule Nature et Oiseaux* and is a mine of information on wildlife and particularly falcons. This far point of Cap Bon serves as a funnel through which many migrating birds, and particularly falcons, pass before using the short Mediterranean crossing to Sicily. The local falconers catch peregrine falcons and sparrowhawks when young in March or April, and train them up for the **falconry festival** and its competitions in June, when they are set after partridge and quail. The sparrowhawks are reputedly released into the wild after that, but at any time of the year there is someone in El Haouaria willing to show you their falcon. Friday, **market day**, is of course the best day for meeting people, and the bar of the Hotel Epervier, the place.

Peregrine Falcon

143

Jebel Sidi Abiod and Rass ed Dreck Beach

Jebel Sidi Abiod, and the headland, Rass Addar, which it masks, make breezy and deserted walking locations. For those who prefer their swimming a little less adventurous, Ras ed Dreck beach is sandy and remote, and a small shop and bar restaurant are open there in summer. The sea laps langorously at the beach, unaware of the oil pipeline station hidden to the west, and to the northeast butts up against the dramatic rising headland. It is 4 km out of town. To get there take a right before the mosque and turn right again on to the beach road.

WHERE TO STAY
The **Hotel Epervier** in the centre of the town has been in gestation for over 10 years now, but this pretty establishment, its courtyard decked in jasmine and orange trees, has still not quite opened. Follow instead the tortuous route signposted from the central Place de la République to the **Hotel Dar Toubib**. Here you will find seven bungalows, each with bathroom and shower, costing 18 dn a night (for up to three people). Otherwise, you could camp out at the beach, and take yourself to the Bain Mauré (men in mornings and women in afternoons) when you want a wash. To get to it, follow the signs from Place de la République for Restaurant des Fruits de Mer. You cannot miss its green and red striped entrance on the right.

EATING OUT
For a cheap meal, any one of the small grill restaurants round the central Place de la République will serve salad and fresh charcoal-grilled fish, but to drink as well try the **Hotel Epervier**. Both here and the **Restaurant des Fruits de Mer**, signposted from the central Place, on Rue Hedi Chaker, tel (02) 97078, are used by day-trippers at lunchtime, but at night they transform into a noisy riot of local eating and drinking. For fresh seafood, including rock lobster, the Fruits de Mer is the best, and a meal with wine (but without lobster) should not cost more than 8 dn a head.

The North Coast

The north coast of Cap Bon runs from heathland and virgin beach in the northeast through the mountain-backed spa town of Korbous to Soliman, on the edge of Tunis' suburbs.

GETTING AROUND
It is easy to explore the area in day-trips from El Haouaria or Nabeul. There are frequent buses and *louages* from Nabeul's eastern station to all destinations on Cap Bon's north coast, and a *louage* station in Soliman which also serves the area well. Three buses a day leave and return to Tunis' Bab Alleoua station to El Haouaria via Korbous, though to take full advantage of the deserted beaches it might be worth hiring a car, moped or taxi for the day.

Sidi Daoud

The coast road 13 km from El Haouaria passes the turning for Sidi Daoud, an unprepossessing huddle of mean houses, clustered round a green domed mosque. Apart from a very ruined fortress to the north, superbly weathered into a parody of a crenellated defence tower, there is really nothing to draw you.

The port and ugly canning factory have a curious and macabre fascination. Tuna fishermen congregate here for *La Matanza*, around spawning time in May and June. A huge straight net, known as the *madrague*, runs 2.5 km out to sea from the beach, stretching from seabed to surface. As the tunny try to migrate round this, they swim out to sea and are corralled into ever smaller and more inescapable nets, until finally they reach the *corpo* or death chamber. When the head of the hunt commands, the gate in the death cell is shut and from their flotilla of boats the fishermen heave the catch bodily to the surface. As the sea boils with lithe flashes of silver, men jump into the nets, spearing the fish which sometimes weigh over 100 kg. The sea turns red, the catch is loaded on to the boats and canned within hours. It is a bloody scene, the ideal subject for a lost Hemingway novella. The technique has changed little since Pliny recorded the migration, and the Romans set out from their port here, Missua.

Rtiba Beach

From Sidi Daoud the north coast is increasingly hemmed in by the mountainous spine of the peninsula, first by Jebel Ben Oulid (637 m) and later by the long striding escarpment of Jebel Sid Abd er Rachman and its three peaks. Consequently the road travels through more rugged scenery, sometimes supporting olive groves and vines, at other merely scrub grazing. Half way to Korbous the magnificent beach of Rtiba comes into view. Seven isolated kilometres of clean white sand, backed by dunes and lapped by a gentle blue sea, are accessible by numerous tracks, including a signposted one 2 km before the road crosses the Oued el Abid. It is a 2-km walk through pine plantations to the sea.

Marsa ben Ramdan Beach

Following the new Korbous road, a signed right turn to Bekakcha 3 km after the village of Bir Meroua leads through an old colonial vineyard, 8 km to the beach of Marsa ben Ramdan. The 300-m sweep of sand beach is dominated by a small fort on the cliff, now a private house. During the high summer a café/restaurant operates from the terraced hut, and throughout the year the bamboo-shaded shed and pier house a clam factory. The shellfish hang in bags off the pier's struts into the sea, and are periodically sieved for size. Those large enough make the long journey to a Frenchman's stomach.

Korbous

Ain el Atrous

The road to Korbous climbs dramatically from this turning, only to plunge towards the sea over the Col du Douala. Where the road meets the sea, a restaurant and a number of grill cafés signal the most impressive of the area's many natural hot springs. **Ain el Atrous**, as it is known, gushes steaming water out of a pipe beneath the road, and after flowing through a bathing channel it falls naturally down the rocks into the sea. Said to be 'mildly purgative', the smell of sulphur and the fairytale mineral deposits it leaves on the rocks suggest a stronger effect.

But if it is your skin, not your insides, that needs a good clean out, the mud at the spring known as **Kalaa Sghira**, 1.5 km walk along the coast from Ain el Atrous does wonders. It is a beautiful walk, sometimes hundreds of feet above the clear sea. Look out for hot springs bubbling up into the sea itself.

Korbous Spa

The spa town of Korbous, 1.5 km along the coast road, comes as a total surprise. It nestles in a narrow valley beneath the towering peak of Jebel Bou Korbous, a small whitewashed settlement of pseudo-Moorish houses, shaded by palms, that looks like a touched-up sepia photograph from the turn of the century. Until the arrival of the French there was no road and Korbous was only accessible by boat. It was a popular trip in Roman times, from Carthage to the spa known as *Aquae Calidae Carpitanae*.

The spirit of the hidden valley is, however, cramped by the long faces of the patients, the white-coated officials of the *Etablissement Thermal* and the dusty souvenirs that line the main street. It was the spa-obsessed Ahmed Bey who constructed a palace, now the *Etablissement Thermal*, in the middle of the 19th century. This was expanded in 1901 by a French engineer, Lecore Carpentier, who designed the spa complex, and built himself the precarious-looking house beside the old spring, above the Hotel des Sources, now a neglected presidential palace. The Zerziha rock beneath it, down which hot water and women seeking a cure for sterility used to slide, is dry, and sanitized by concrete repairs.

If you are game to join the world of *thermalisme*, a private bath in the *Etablissement Thermal* costs 2 dn, and you can follow it with an all-over massage for 4 dn, afternoons only. A less clinical alternative is to sweat it out in **Ain el Arraka**, just up the hill on the right. Despite its modern entrance, this has changed little since the Romans used it. The dark stairs lead down into an unlit cave, transformed into a sauna by natural emissions of steam. Otherwise, Korbous' other spring, **Ain es Sbia**, the spring of the Virgin, trickles forlornly from a neglected fountain beneath the terrace café nearby.

Jebel Bou Korbous makes a challenging climb, perhaps entailing a stay at the Hotel des Sources, otherwise best used for lunch. The set menu costs 5 dn, for which you can also use the pool.

Ain Oktor

Four kilometres beyond Korbous, the mineral-laden waters of Ain Oktor are bottled in a factory which brings to mind the dislocated environment of a Jacques Tati film, an industrial see-through bottling plant in a world of mountains and sea. The hotel next door is hideous, and the concrete teepee in the carpark is broken so it no longer cascades free samples of the disgusting water.

Sidi Rais

The village of Sidi Rais beyond has fallen into disrepair and the beach is often dirty, which is a pity as its clapboard houses on stilts are charming, and the wine made from the surrounding vines is light and refreshing. Sidi Rais, the patron of corsair captains, is entombed in the koubba which crowns the hill behind the village. The tree-lined road leads into citrus country and past the Hotel Restaurant Chiraz, where the cooking is simple but delicious, though it has no licence. This region was heavily colonized, and the remains of villas and farmhouses, tucked away down drives and behind high gates, still haunt the orchards.

Soliman and its Beaches

Soliman is an inland agricultural town, which hosts a **market** every Friday. It prospered greatly under the influx of Andalucian refugees in the 17th century, who left behind a pretty tiled mosque, its **square minaret** typical of western Moorish style. In stark contrast, though of the same age, is the town's Hanefite mosque built by Turkish officials with a thin **hexagonal minaret**.

A swampy lagoon separates Soliman town from the sea. The beach road crosses it and branches out to reach three patches of sand. Straight ahead is **Plage Ejjenine**, a collection of seaside villas with a restaurant whose central avenue has been orientated directly across the Bay of Tunis to Sidi Bou Said. The left branch takes you past a seasonal colony of beach huts before reaching **Soliman Plage** and its two down-market package hotels, the Solymar and the El Andalous. From here, it is only a few hundred metres to the four hotels and a riding stable at Cedria Plage, described in 'South of Tunis' (p. 112).

WHERE TO STAY
There are a number of places you can stay on the north coast of Cap Bon, but apart from **camping** *sauvage* on the beach at Rtiba none of them is that attractive.

MODERATE
If you have to use a hotel, the best value is the **Hotel Chiraz**, tel (02) 93230, crouched on the edge of a never-ending orange grove south of Sidi Rais. The **Hotel des Sources** in Korbous, tel (02) 94533, is functional but has a swimming pool.

Part V
THE SAHEL

A Muslim cemetery

The Sahel, meaning 'coast', is coloured by deep red clay, dirty white broken limestone and varying shades of olive green. Olive trees, half a dozen aged trunks in a walled family plot, or hundreds of thousands in regular plantations, distinguish an otherwise bland, undulating landscape. If Amsterdam is built on herring bones and London on wool, then the Sahel towns, from Sousse to Sfax, rest on a firm foundation of olive stones.

An unparalleled concentration of urban communities is sustained here by the enduring fertility of the hinterland and the shallow sea. Many of the 50 smaller towns and five major cities have a continuous history of settlement that stretches back to their foundation by Phoenician traders in the 6th century BC. This stability has allowed the population to maintain crafts and to pass down a tradition of industry and learning from generation to generation.

Though largely untouched by colonial settlement, the Sahelians quietly began to provide the staff for the new secular society created by the French. They became doctors, teachers, lawyers and in particular translators, from which the French created the junior ranks of the civil service. Habib Bourguiba and Ben Ali, the two presidents since independence, are typical products and the Neo-Destour Party and the trade union movement also originated from the Sahel. Independence has been described as 'the fruit of the olive tree', a metaphor for the new supremacy of the men of the Sahel over the traditional Tunis-based ruling class.

The Sahel's attractions are its long sandy beaches, fish restaurants and the monuments of its ancient walled cities. On the coast, Sousse, close to Monastir-Skanès international airport, is a relaxed city, with a walled medina containing some of Tunisia's earliest and finest Islamic monuments and a beach to the north. For a quieter time, Mahdia combines monumental proof of its history with a much less developed beach. Sfax, to the south, has always been a busy, self-centred city, but has an untarnished and battlemented medina, two museums and

148

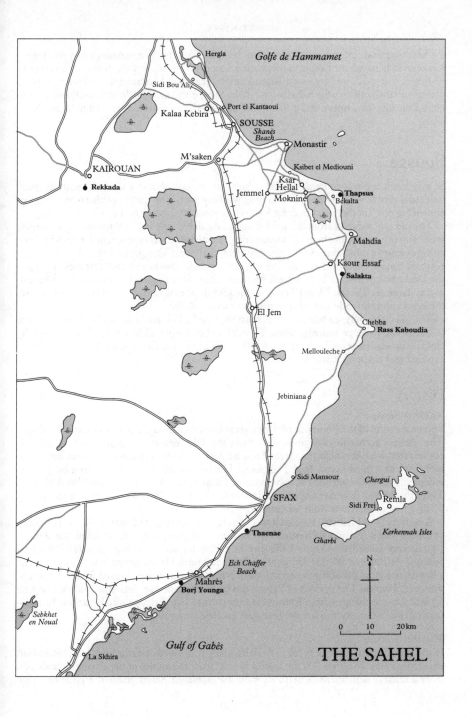

THE SAHEL

the best souk and restaurants of the region. Its lack of beaches is compensated by the nearby Kerkennah Isles, where fishing in the shallow waters is the only activity. Inland, the village of El Jem is overshadowed by a vast Roman amphitheatre and Kairouan, the ancient capital, perches on the border of the Sahel, between the Steppe and the Tell. Within the medina is the holiest mosque in Tunisia and a handful of other religious sites hidden behind ochre brick walls.

Sousse

Sousse has a triple identity as a beach resort, an ancient Islamic walled city and the gritty industrial centre for the Sahel, with a busy working port. The three worlds coexist happily, enhancing one another, and making Sousse the most interesting of Tunisia's resorts.

The old city survives from the golden age of Aghlabid rule in the 9th century. Its streets teem with mercantile life beneath a smattering of early religious monuments, including three of the country's most impressive sites: the ribat, the Great Mosque and the Museum of the Kasbah. Sousse medina has a number of small, friendly hotels with roof terraces. They are the ideal place to watch a Soussi dusk, when the cries of the muezzin echo from the minarets, and as darkness falls the Khalef Tower on the kasbah takes up its mournful role as lighthouse, the beam intermittently sweeping across the medina skyline.

The old city is only ten minutes' walk from the beach. The sands are packed with a mixture of locals and package tourists. Stout Tunisian ladies ignore all beach fashion and sit fully clothed in shaded tents brewing tea for their immense families within yards of tonnes of exposed and ripening European flesh.

History

Ancient Sousse

Sousse was one of the Phoenicians' three great coastal cities, a sister to Utica and Carthage. The earliest archaeological finds date from the 6th century BC, when the Phoenicians consecrated a tophet, near the Great Mosque, where children and animals were burned in sacrificial fires to the god Baal Hammon. Though an ally of Carthage, Sousse kept its independence and controlled its own territory, following a wise policy of neutrality during the Third Punic War. The city was spared destruction by Rome, its position further enhanced by being a free city exempt from taxation.

A century later Hadrumetum, as it was known, was incorporated into the Roman province of Africa Nova by Julius Caesar. Two centuries of prosperity ended when the Roman commander Capellianus sacked the city in 238, after an attempted meddle in imperial politics. At the end of the 3rd century the chastened Hadrumetum was chosen as the administrative capital of the new province of Byzacena, which was formed from what is now southern Tunisia. The periods of Vandal and Byzantine rule have left little evidence beyond egoistical name changes, from Roman Hadrumetum to Hunsericopolis to Byzantine Justinianopolis, when the city was for the first time encircled by walls.

Muslim Sousse

In the late 7th century, the city fell to Arab invaders, who killed or enslaved its citizens and left the city in ruins. In about 790 the ribat was built from the stones of the Byzantine wall, and from a nuclear settlement beneath its walls the Aghlabid Emirs planned a great new city.

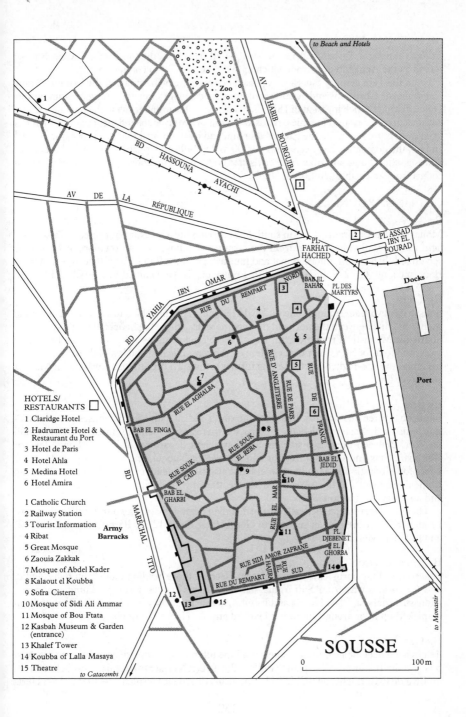

to Beach and Hotels

Zoo

AV HABIB BOURGUIBA

BD HASSOUNA AYACHI

AV DE LA RÉPUBLIQUE

PL-FARHAT HACHED

PL ASSAD IBN EL FOURAD

Docks

BD YAHIA IBN OMAR

RUE DU REMPART NORD

BAB EL BAHAR

PL DES MARTYRS

Port

RUE D'ANGLETERRE

RUE DE PARIS

RUE DE FRANCE

RUE EL AGHALBA

BAB EL FINGA

RUE SOUK EL REBA

RUE SOUK EL CAID

BAB EL JEDID

BAB EL GHARBI

RUE EL MAR

BD MARÉCHAL TITO

Army Barracks

PL DJEBENET EL GHORBA

RUE SIDI AMOR ZAFRANE

RUE EL HAJRA

RUE DU REMPART SUD

to Monastir

HOTELS/RESTAURANTS □

1 Claridge Hotel
2 Hadrumete Hotel & Restaurant du Port
3 Hotel de Paris
4 Hotel Ahla
5 Medina Hotel
6 Hotel Amira

1 Catholic Church
2 Railway Station
3 Tourist Information
4 Ribat
5 Great Mosque
6 Zaouia Zakkak
7 Mosque of Abdel Kader
8 Kalaout el Koubba
9 Sofra Cistern
10 Mosque of Sidi Ali Ammar
11 Mosque of Bou Ftata
12 Kasbah Museum & Garden (entrance)
13 Khalef Tower
14 Koubba of Lalla Masaya
15 Theatre

to Catacombs

SOUSSE

0   100m

Today's ramparts, kasbah and Great Mosque all date from the 9th century, when Sousse served as the Aghlabid port from which an Arab fleet sailed to conquer Sicily.

From the 11th century Sousse was poised between the twin threats of the bedouin Arabs and seaborne Christians and became an enthusiastic supporter of any strong Muslim power. Only after the French invasion in 1881 did it emerge as the premier city of the region, with the construction of new port facilities, roads and a rail network. Since independence growth has been even more rapid. On the back of tourism, and its traditional role as a processor of wool and oil, the population has risen from 40,000 to 230,000, and it has become the third city of Tunisia, after Tunis and Sfax. The city's star is still in the ascendant, for President Ben Ali comes from an established Soussi family.

GETTING AROUND

By Air

Monastir-Skanès Airport is 15 km south of Sousse on the Monastir bus route, and also has a light railway station just 100 m from the terminal building. For information, or tickets for scheduled flights, both international and internal, go to the Tunis Air Office at 5 Av Habib Bourguiba, tel (03) 27955/21951, or Air France on Av Mohammed V, tel (03) 22409.

By Train

Sousse has two train stations, one on Blvd Hassouna Ayachi, which deals with the mainline trains, and one between the port and the medina walls, where the Sahel light railway departs hourly for Monastir. From the main station there are five trains a day for Tunis, two hours away, and four for Sfax, stopping at El Jem on the way. The first and last of these continue on to Gabès, the late-night departure going further to Gafsa. Three trains a day head for Mahdia via Monastir.

By Bus

Sousse has three bus stations. Buses for the south and all national SNT buses leave from Pl Bab Jedid on the eastern wall of the medina, but there are also some useful departures from Pl du Port. Between these two stations there are eight departures a day for Tunis, five for Kairouan, Sfax and Gabès, three for El Kef, two for Nabeul, one for Bizerte, and regular buses for Monastir and Mahdia. Bab el Jedid also runs a daily service to Jerba, two buses to Medenine, one of which goes on to Tataouine, the other to Zarzis, one bus a day to Matmata and an overnight bus to Douz.

The Sidi Yahia station, beneath the north wall of the medina, serves only local destinations. From here there are regular services to Hergla (nos. 8 and 12), to Port el Kantaoui (no. 12) and to Chott Meriem (no. 16).

By *Louage*/Taxi

Louages travelling north leave from Pl Farhat Hached, those heading south from Bab el Jedid, and for local towns from Sidi Yahia station. Drivers regularly run to Tunis, Kairouan, Monastir, Mahdia, Sfax, Hergla and Enfida. Sousse local taxis are blue and yellow, and can be picked up in or around Pl Farhat Hached and Av Habib Bourguiba.

By Car

There is no need of a car in the Sahel, as all the interesting destinations are easy to reach by bus or train. If, however, you plan to explore the Tell, it is easier to organize a car here at Avis, on Blvd de la Corniche, tel (03) 20911; Europcar, Blvd de la Corniche, tel (03) 22152; Hertz on Av Habib Bourguiba, tel (03) 25428; or Africar in the Tourafric offices on Rue Khaled ibn Walid, tel (03) 24277.

TOURIST INFORMATION
At the heart of Sousse is a confusion of roundabouts, small gardens, statues and kiosks, known variously as Pl Farhat Hached, Pl des Martyrs, Pl du Port and Pl Sidi Yahia. To add to the mêlée of buses, taxis and policemen, trains go right through the centre, blowing whistles in warning as they part the seething crowd. The port, southeast of the square, is so close that empty cargo vessels riding high at the docks, their decks ablaze with lights, add a final inimitable touch. The medina walls rise to the southwest with the new town avenues stretching north towards the beach and its row of hotels.

A helpful regional **Tourist Office** at 1 Av Habib Bourguiba is backed up by a **Syndicat d'Initiative** kiosk on Pl Farhat Hached. They are both open from 07.30–19.30 in summer, 08.30–13.00 and 15.00–17.45 in winter, half day Fri and Sat, closed on Sun.

The **PTT** lies a short walk up Av de la République on the left. There is another place for international telephone calls, open 08.00–22.00, near the Catholic church at the end of Blvd Hassouna Ayachi. Otherwise, everything you need is on, or just off, Av Habib Bourguiba: the **police**, tel (03) 25566, on Rue Pasteur just beyond the Hotel Claridges; **banks** all along the street; foreign language newspapers sold in a bookshop opposite the **Monoprix**, which sells picnic ingredients and wine. Any of the beach hotels will change money when the banks are closed.

The Medina

Sousse's historical monuments and its main tourist souk all lie within the crenellated walls of the medina, which originally stood right on the seashore. An inscription on the southern wall dates their construction to 859, probably founded on the original 6th-century Byzantine walls. They were restored in 1205, and over the years have been fortified by strong internal arcades. The breach by Pl des Martyrs was caused by Allied bombing of the port during the Second World War.

The Great Mosque
The courtyard is open from 08.00–14.00 every day except during Friday prayers; tickets from a booth beside the Hotel Ahla. Non-Muslims should not enter the prayer hall.

The low plain crenellated walls and strong round corner towers of the Great Mosque make it look like a fortress. There is no minaret as the muezzin originally issued the call to prayer from the neighbouring ribat tower. In the supremely elegant courtyard, decorative features like the koranic frieze which runs around the walls, the stairs up to the tower and the rigid calligraphy of the courtyard floor merely serve to emphasize the proportions and simplicity.

Though parts of the prayer hall have been altered since the mosque's foundation in 850, the courtyard is original. It signalled the start of a new architectural order for the triumphant expression of Islam. No Roman columns are used, nor any Byzantine or Persian decoration, but rather a colonnade of dignified horseshoe arches crowned by the holy words of the Koran. The arcade in front of the prayer hall was added by the Turks in the 17th century, and its higher arches break the severity of the earlier arrangement and obscure the koranic carving. The central arch, marked by double pillars, carries a rededicatory stone from work completed in 1965.

Looking into the prayer hall, the central nave, leading to a mihrab niche which signals the direction of Mecca, is noticeably wider and more richly decorated. The first three rows of columns belong to the original 9th-century prayer hall, but the three furthest were added in 980, a change best appreciated from the top of the ribat tower where the first dome signals the position of the original mihrab. To the right of the mihrab rise the 10 steps of the lectern or minbar. The screen on the left defines the women's space.

The Ribat

Open every day except Mon, from 09.00–12.00 and 14.00–17.30 in winter, 15.00–18.30 in summer; adm.

The Ksar er Ribat is Sousse's oldest monument, built in the late 8th century some 60 years before the Great Mosque. It was one of a chain of fortresses along the North African coast, designed to protect the Islamic state from the threat of Christians, pagan Vikings and heretical inland Berber tribes. These ribats, which now read like a list of resorts—Sidi Bou Said, Hammamet, Sousse, Monastir—were defended by volunteer warrior monks, known as *murabitin*, who also organized raids from here, both by sea and land. Their combination of militancy and religion has always been a feature of Muslim belief, and still lies at the heart of Islamic politics. Serving in the ribat for a certain number of days was said to guarantee a place in Paradise.

Sunken beneath the rest of the city at its original 8th-century level, the ribat we see today is close to the 790s original, but incorporates the Aghlabid restoration of 821. Built on and with the ruins of the Byzantine fortress, it is almost square, like the Byzantine forts of the time, and its gateway incorporates classical pillars, but also shows the first hesitant development of the horseshoe arch, the leitmotif of Islamic architecture. The characteristic 'bite' above the capitals is provided by two wedges of stone.

The interior courtyard is lined by small rooms, the cells of the *murabitin*. A stairway leads up to the first-floor prayer hall in the south wall. A mere two bays deep, it is plain and barrel-vaulted, with a simple mihrab niche flanked by two pillars. Speculation suggests that its construction was based on the most enduring of classical remains, the water cistern. The crenellated battlements and koubba above the gatehouse are entirely 20th century, though modelled on the Great Mosque. The ribat's Nador tower has a narrow, unlit staircase, which leads up and out into an explosion of light and a magnificent view over the medina.

The Kasbah Museum of Antiquities

Uphill from the ribat, an attractive Turkish octagonal minaret, decorated with strips of coloured tile, signals the Zaouia Zakkak. Turn left in front of it, and begin climbing up Rue el Aghalba. The Mosque of Abdel Kader is on the left between nos. 50 and 52. The road ends at Bab el Fingha, where a left turn on to Blvd Maréchal Tito leads 400 m to the Kasbah Museum, open every day except Mon, 09.00–12.00, 15.00–18.30 in summer, 14.00–17.30 in winter; adm.

Even if the very word 'museum' fills you with horror, the one at Sousse should be visited as it houses some of the country's most delightful mosaics, around a small series of courtyard gardens. The kasbah was built at the highest point of the town between the 11th and 15th centuries, round the great Khalef el Fata tower. This tower was built in 859 and replaced the ribat tower as a signal and observation point or *manar* to protect the coast. Unfortunately, the tower is not open to the public as it is now a fully functioning lighthouse. The eastern battlement terrace of the kasbah gives fine views over the medina and the sea.

The entrance hall leads into a colonnade. To the right, up three steps is a floor mosaic from a 3rd-century *tepidarium*, the hot room of the public baths, with a transfixing medusa head. It is surrounded by a number of fragmentary sculptures including a victorious general in a chariot with the headless male torso of one of his prisoners.

Returning to the courtyard, walk clockwise, to the striking mosaic face of Oceanus, god of the sea, his hair wild with crustaceans. Like many other maritime designs it would once have rippled from the bottom of a pond. The next wall is covered with Christian tomb mosaics, which include such sugary dedications as the one to 'truly a gentle wife of the rarest sort'. The terracotta tiles once covered the walls and ceilings of Byzantine basilicas with their images of Adam and Eve and St Theodore (not yet St. George) slaying the dragon. The last wall of the colonnade is resplendent with a striking apse mosaic, shaped like a preening peacock's tail.

Two rooms open off the courtyard of which the larger holds the museum's best mosaics. To the left of the door is a joyous 3rd-century depiction of the Triumph of Bacchus. The young god of wine, pulled in a chariot, is seen with the usual entourage of drunken satyrs, putti, panthers and leopards. He wears Indian dress, alluding to his conquest of the East, an analogy for the spread of the vine and the supremacy of wine over beer. It seems likely that it was in fact the West that was conquered, for the vine is thought to have originated on the foothills of the Caucasus and in Afghanistan.

The mosaic to the right of the door depicts Apollo surrounded by the nine Muses. On the opposite wall, two mosaics show the Rape of Ganymede, but give the event a different slant. In one, the young shepherd seems totally unconcerned at Zeus' attempt to ravish him while disguised as an eagle. In the other, earlier (2nd century as opposed to 3rd) and less fine, Ganymede is struggling, exposing an erotic rippling torso as he does so. The symbol mosaics on the same wall acted as doorstep charms. There is a yin and yang device of a circle divided in two by a langorous S, a penis-shape ejaculating between two female triangles, and a phallic fish pointing at the female eye. They all express a balance between the separate spiritual powers of man and woman, a belief which underlies much of the ritual life in the Mediterranean, be it Christian or Muslim.

The smaller room off the courtyard contains Punic stelae and ex-votos discovered during the excavation of Sousse's tophet, where child and animal sacrifice was practised from the 6th century BC to the 1st AD, though there are no children's milk teeth found to date from after the fall of Carthage in 146 BC. They are carved with dedications in Punic script, the sign of the godess Tanit, represented by a triangle with arms, often beneath a crescent moon and a triple column. This symbol is still disputed: a trinity or just the supreme god in the form of his throne?

The corridor to the left of this room is filled with cases of terracotta funerary figures from the 3rd century BC–2nd century AD, representing divinities who welcome or protect the dead. It leads to three further rooms devoted to grave goods—the first Punic, the second early Roman and the third Christian. The Punic tomb in the first room was found here when the museum was established, and many of the nearby grave goods had been buried inside it. Of the three sets of Soussi catacombs mapped out in the final room only the Catacombs of the Good Shepherd (du Bon Pasteur) are open to the public (see p. 157).

There are three rooms on the far side of a second garden courtyard. The floor of the first is covered by a *triclinium*, or dining-room, mosaic. It is decorated with a sumptuous banquet complete with cushions. This is the area where servants would have passed with the dishes, serving guests who lay on benches on the U-shaped blank area. To the left of the door, a large mosaic depicts the months of the year, beginning with March/Martius, symbolized by a festival of Mars. A hot-food booth, for some lost reason, represents June, and Mercury, son of Maia, symbolizes May. Diana, whose birthday is on 13 August, represents that month and

September is represented by the grape harvest. December saw the festival of Saturnalia, when for a day slaves became masters and masters slaves, and which the Christians have turned into Christmas.

The third room contains an almost perfect mosaic of four gladiators preparing to kill the assembled wild life—including ostriches, wild ass, deer and gazelle. Three tired-looking Amazons stare down from the wall, and the headless statue of Priapus, has had his unmistakably massive penis broken off (in disgust or jealousy?), so we are left merely with a burgeoning apron of fruit to symbolize his fecundity. To the right of the door is a famous mosaic with appearances by Diana and Dionysus which commemorates a set of amphitheatre games sponsored by one Magerius, who rewarded the Telegemi team with 1000 dinars apiece for their skill in killing leopards.

The Souks and Shopping
The centre of Sousse medina is a warren of brightly hung, partly covered souks. The principal shopping thoroughfare runs east–west up to Bab el Gharbi, changing name half way from Rue Souk el Reba to Rue Souk el Caid. It is primarily a place for café life, walks and bargaining. If you are looking for more unusual souvenirs, there is an **art gallery** at 21 Rue Souk el Caid, run by the painter Moncef Noureddine, selling a good selection of the work of N. I. Belajouza and some charming hand-painted cards from around 15 dn. Visit 54 Rue de Paris, which starts by the Hotel Medina, to look at an old **fondouk**, a merchants' hotel. The building has great charm, with its corner well and towering courtyard, and now sells a comprehensive range of pottery.

The Hidden Medina
For those with more time to explore, there are a number of lesser buildings to be tracked down in the medina.

From the crossroads of Rue d'Angleterre and Rue Souk el Reba, the first right turn off the latter reveals **Kalaout el Koubba**, a handsome 11th–12th century stone building, thought to have been either the audience chamber of the neighbouring palace or one of the rooms of a hammam. The façade of the palace next door shows influences from Moorish Spain, and is most likely a 13th-century facelift. The surrounding walls are now used to display killims and carpets.

Walking up Rue Souk el Reba from Rue d'Angleterre, after the last arch an immediate left leads to dusty Pl Sofra. Beneath the square, entered through a rusty metal door in the wall, is the non-too-sanitary **Sofra Cistern**. Originally Roman, but restored before the 11th century, it is like a vast subterranean cathedral, held up by a forest of pillars dimly reflected in a dark pool of water.

Taking the small street opposite the entrance to the cisterns, you arrive on Rue el Mar, the continuation of Rue d'Angleterre. Turn right and shortly on the left appears the whitewashed façade of the 11th-century **Mosque of Sidi Ali Ammar**, pitted with varying niches, just after the dome of a hammam. The **Mosque of Bou Ftata**, further on down Rue el Mar on the left, is 200 years older. It is a tiny building with a bold and unusual band of kufic inscription. A little further on the right is the domed shrine of one Salah bin Ahmed.

Turning left down Rue Sidi Amor Zafrane after the Bou Ftata Mosque, you arrive in the southeastern corner of the medina, at **Pl Djebenet el Ghorba**, the Cemetery of Strangers. Its holiness is attested by the proximity of three koubba, that of Lalla Masaya now housing a nursery school. On the western wall is a plaque, by the Café Malouf, commemorating a speech made on the spot by President Habib Bourguiba in 1962, 10 years after 10 Soussi men died in demonstrations against the failure of negotiations for independence.

Walking back towards the new town along Rue de France, the medina tower marked no. 3 is a private house but the owners are happy to let you visit for a small tip.

The Catacombs of the Good Shepherd
Open daily except Mon, 09.00–12.00 and 15.00–18.30 in summer, 14.00–17.30 in winter; adm.

The catacombs are only just worth the walk or taxi ride through the suburbs. A small, badly restored section is open and even if you have a torch and ignore the keep-out notices, the other 6000 graves in a mile of tunnels beyond lie ruined by savage excavations. A marble plaque at the entrance, placed here in 1907, says that the inhabitants 'dormiunt in pace', sleep in peace, which could hardly be further from the truth. The only bones left in the whole place are a few dry old fragments in the first room on the left, opposite the ticket office.

Sousse's catacombs date from the 2nd–4th centuries, and were rediscovered by the French in 1888. There are better examples, for those interested, at Salakta (p. 167). The word 'catacomb' derives from the particular name of a famous martyrs' cemetery in Rome though there is nothing specifically Christian in the practice. Niches were professionally dug into the tunnel wall ready for the dead. The corpses, wrapped in linen, were placed into the space with their grave goods and packed in with lime and clay. A simple dedication could be etched, or a fresco or marble plaque added to the seal of wet clay.

FESTIVALS
Sousse's *fêtes* are nothing special. The most entertaining is the Festival of Baba Aoussou at the beginning of August, which culminates in a carnival procession. From mid-July to mid-August there is also an International Festival of Theatre and Music, and in mid-March there is a Festival of Local Popular Arts, mostly dance and music. Port el Kantaoui has its own tourist festival in July.

SPORTS
All the beach hotels provided **watersports**, including windsurfing, sailing, waterskiing and paragliding. There is a **riding club** on Av du 3 Septembre 1934, and a **tennis club** on Blvd Abou Hamed el Ghazali, tel (03) 20160, by the catacombs. Port el Kantaoui, the massive marina and holiday centre 9 km north of Sousse, arrived on this earth complete with an 18-hole **golf course**, and boats from the Port offer 25-dn day-trips with drinks, barbecue and **fishing** on the open sea. Look out for the *Mona*, and be there before 09.00 on weekdays. There is also a chance to learn to **scuba dive** from here.

HAMMAMS
The **Turkish baths** next to the Mosque of Sidi Ali Ammar are easy to find and accept men in the mornings, women in the afternoons, but are nothing by comparison with the **Grand Bain Maure Sidi Bouraoui**, behind the Mosque of Abd el Kader on Rue el Aghalba. Take the turning beside the mosque and the green and red pillars of the baths appear ahead. It is open to men from 04.00–15.00 and women from 15.00–24.00, and has a loyal local following.

RELIGIOUS SERVICES
French-language Roman Catholic Mass is celebrated in the church at the northern end of Blvd Hassouna Ayachi at 18.15 on Saturday evening and 09.30 on Sunday morning. An English language service takes place on Sundays at 10.00 at 16 Rue de Malte off Rue d'Angleterre, east of the Ribat.

157

WHERE TO STAY
There is no point missing out on the life of the town by staying in one of the beach hotels to the north, isolated in a charmless international vacuum.

MODERATE
For comfort, and, in winter, heating, there are two good places in the new town. The **Hotel Hadrumète**, by the port on Pl Assed Ibn el Fourad, tel (03) 26291, has a striking lobby with a statue of a Roman emperor and superb late 1950s balustrade, and a pool in summer. The bedrooms are run down, but have their own bathrooms. The **Hotel Claridges** on Av Habib Bourguiba, tel (03) 24759, is cheaper. Each of its two dozen large, comfortable rooms has its own shower or bath, and a balcony over the noisy street. There is a popular bar downstairs, where breakfast is served in the mornings, and which gets sleazier as the day goes by. The best known of the medina hotels, the **Hotel Medina**, on the southwestern corner of the Great Mosque, tel (03) 21722, also comes into this catagory. Its rooms surround an attractive old courtyard, with a bar that stays open until 23.00, often filled with adventure tour groups.

CHEAP
Less pretentious, scrupulously clean and with a large roof terrace is the **Hotel de Paris** at 15 Rue du Rempart Nord, tel (03) 20564. The monastic cells are compensated by the communal showers and loos, which are spotless and have plenty of hot water. If it's full try the **Hotel Ahla** which looks straight on to the Ribat and Great Mosque, tel (03) 20570, or the **Hotel Amira**, at 52 Rue de France, tel (03) 26325. Its roof terrace has an excellent view east over the market to the sea. Slightly further downmarket but near the Hotel de Paris, at 19 Rue de l'Eglise, is the **Hotel Tunis** which has even cheaper beds and a roof terrace.

EATING OUT
Licensed Restaurants
The ugly glass building in front of the Hotel Hadrumète by the port houses the **Restaurant du Port**, its tables filled with blue-jacketed dock workers, and buzzing with cigarette vendors and drunks hawking the clothes off their backs. The service is friendly and erratic, the menu largely fictional, but freshly grilled fish, brochettes and *merguez* deliciously real. A meal of fish and salad with wine costs about 6 dn a head, with the live theatre of the place thrown in free. The **Complexe Café de Tunis**, on Av Habib Bourguiba, tel (03) 24642, is next to one of the best bars in town. After a couple of Ricard apéritifs, slip next door to eat *tajine* for 3.5 dn, or a *salade niçoise* for 1.2 dn. There are tables on the pavement and a dining-room within. The **Tip Top** is considered to be the best restaurant. It is out on the Blvd de la Corniche north of the centre. Dinner starts from around 10 dn a head, and you should book a table on (03) 20158. Avoid the restaurants looking onto Pl Farhat Hached which cater for tourists and have become bland and over-priced.

Café Restaurants
Excellent, simple Tunisian food is to be had in the **Restaurant du Peuple**, beside the Hotel de Paris just inside the north wall of the medina. The restaurant is unlicensed and has a number of different dishes to chose from every day, including couscous, *tajine* and spicy vegetable stews. Lunch for two costs about 5 dn. **Le Cappuccino** on the corner of Av Habib Bourguiba and Pl Farhat Hached is the place to head for a leisurely breakfast of orange juice, *pain au chocolat* and coffee. If you are in more of a hurry, eat on the hoof from the hexagonal booth on the north side of Pl Farhat Hached.

BARS AND NIGHTLIFE
The best place in town for a drink is the **Café de Tunis**, on Av Habib Bourguiba. The bar below the **Hotel Claridges** gets full and smoky early on in the day and is something of a pick-up joint in the evening. All the large hotels have their own nightclubs, those nearest the town gathering the most interesting mix of people. Both the **Hotel Justinia** and the **Boujaafar** have late-night bars and lively discotheques. There are two independent discos on Av Habib Bourguiba, the **Topkapi** and the **Atlantic**, and the more elaborate **Le Douar** on Blvd de la Corniche opposite the Hotel Jawhara. The **El Oukala**, just inside the Bab el Gharbi at the top of the medina, puts on floor shows in the evening and is very popular with tour groups. Avoid mistakenly walking inside the walls to the northwest corner of the medina, which is a red-light area full of drunk customers.

All the big hotels organize trips to out-of-town evening **spectaculars**. For around 10 dn you are whisked off by bus to mysterious locations in the heart of the Sahel, where a well-prepared Tunisian feast, with wine, and an entertaining floor show offer an enjoyable night out.

Monastir

Only the headland of Monastir, covered with an ancient cemetery and crowned by an 8th-century ribat, is worth a visit. There is a dull esplanade below them, complete with a new marina complex and separated from the dozen large hotels on Skanès beach to the north by a line of low cliffs. The rest of the town has been gutted by town-planners and turned into a package tourist shopping centre and a monument to Habib Bourguiba.

History

Monastir's geography, with sheltered anchorage provided by two offshore islands, made it an ideal outpost for the Phoenicians trading along the coast. They knew it as Rous and it was

Nador tower of the Ribat of Harthema, Monastir

renamed Ruspina by the Romans in 146 BC. In the last years of Byzantine rule, at the end of the 7th century, walls were erected to defend the imperial fleet which held on to the coast while the Arab invasion conquered the Tunisian interior. The ribat was built a hundred years later, a fortress of Arab orthodoxy with a triple role of defending the coast, crushing the heretical Ibadite Berbers and launching raids against the Christian lands to the north. The cemetery beside the ribat became a favoured burial place for the entire region, further enhanced by its miraculous wells which drew fresh water so close to the sea. The ribat continued to play a military role during the 16th-century Hapsburg-Ottoman war, when it was briefly garrisoned by the Spanish before the Turks chased them out, rebuilt the city walls and restored the city.

Monastir's most famous son, ex-President Habib Bourguiba, was the son of a Tunisian army officer and was born at Monastir in 1903. He described himself as coming 'from a modest family, one that toiled and suffered' but soon left this milieu when he joined Sadiki College in Tunis, the country's top school. After his rise to power he returned to the neighbourhood where a palace was built on the beach to the north of town. A growing personality cult caused the destruction of the old town, added a gold statue, a Bourguiba family mosque and a massive mausoleum which uprooted many a lesser mortal from his place of burial in the process. The town also received more practical gifts like the dentistry college in the suburbs. On the night of 7 November 1987 the President for Life was deposed, declared senile and sent back in retirement to the palace at Monastir, where he lives on behind its rustic walls.

GETTING AROUND

The major transport centre in this region is Sousse, 20 km up the coast, with trains, buses and *louages* for all over Tunisia.

By Air: See Sousse for information about Monastir-Skanès airport. Tunis Air, on Rue de l'Indépendance, tel (03) 61758/61922, will book seats on both domestic and international scheduled flights.

By Train: Monastir's train station is on Rue Salem B'chir, behind the medina. It sees frequent Metro departures for Sousse and twice daily departures to both Tunis and Mahdia.

By Bus: There are frequent buses to Sousse, leaving from behind the medina by Bab el Gharbi, the West Gate. There are also daily buses to Mahdia, Sfax, Gabès, Medinine, Tataouine and Tunis.

By *Louage*/Taxi: Both *louages* and taxis can be found at the bus station. *Louages* heading south leave Monastir from beside the market on Av Habib Bourguiba. If you are trying to get to Mahdia and cannot find a *louage*, jump on one to Ksar Hellal and change car there.

By Car: Hertz, Avis, InterRent and Europcar all have offices at the Airport, tel (03) 61314.

TOURIST INFORMATION

Monastir's **PTT** is off Av Habib Bourguiba, south of the medina. There is also a rash of **banks** nearby and on Pl de l'Indépendance.

The Ribat of Harthema

Open every day except Mon, 09.00–12.00 and 14.30–18.00 (14.00–17.30 in winter); adm. The Ribat of Harthema is a massive, square building with a tapering tower above the harbour. It was founded in 796 by Harthema ibn Aiyan, built from yellow stone quarried from the island of El Gadamsi opposite and strengthened in the 9th and 11th centuries. Its garrison was drawn from the Arab ruling caste who as well as planning their own raids had to defend the coast against a number of seaborne enemies—Sicilians, Vikings and a revitalized Byzantium. The lofty main gates were added in the 9th century and incorporate Roman columns into an early version of a Moorish horseshoe arch. The dark entrance corridor emerges into a dazzling sun-baked courtyard, surrounded by a warren of towers, passages, ramps and battlements.

On the right of the courtyard, the original 8th-century prayer hall is now occupied by a **Museum of Islamic Art**, squatting beneath the later Nador tower. The strong outer walls, which surrounded this original building, turning it into a central keep, were added in the 9th and 11th centuries. The corner towers of the outer walls were remodelled in the 16th century, and in the 18th century the seaward defences were strengthened and the northeast tower given the sloping walls and wide portals of an artillery bastion. Beyond the museum, a second courtyard, known as the Women's Ribat, after a reference in early histories, conceals a prayer hall, with seven aisles, in its southern wall.

The collection housed in the museum comes from all over the Islamic world. There are samples of Arabic calligraphy (see p. 65 for more details) as well as pieces from an 11th-century minbar from Kairouan. The fragments of 12th-century weaving incorporate a plethora of animal motifs and were made by the Christian Copts in Egypt, a community celebrated for their skilled embroidery and weaving. A cabinet of lustreware, from Abassid Iraq and Fatimid Egypt, is one of the gems of the collection. There is also gold jewellery and a collection of Persian and Mughal miniatures, an art form that seems all the more lively in North Africa where figurative art was largely prohibited. The mihrab niche, decorated with framed koranic calligraphy recalls these rooms' first use as a prayer hall.

Climb the Nador tower for a liberating view, bathed by sea breezes, over the remains of Monastir's other early buildings. Directly south is the **Great Mosque** with a square minaret. It was built in the 9th century, at the same time as the ribat was encrusted in its outer wall, and expanded by the Zirids in the 11th century. The inhabitants of the ribat would proceed directly between the Roman columns of the horseshoe southern gate into the forest of Roman pillars in its prayer hall.

The small yellow stone blockhouse on the corner of the palm-shaded square is the **Mosque of Sidi Ali el Mezzeri**, now closed. Sidi Ali is buried in a koubba on the eastern corner of the cemetery, and was much visited by the mothers of sick children whom the saint was reputed to cure. Discouraged from worshipping in mosques, women centred their religion on such koubbas, where unorthodox cults often developed. The women claimed that on Friday the saint's presence was manifest in a pleasing aroma, and that the name Monastir originated from the poetic compliments paid by Sidi Ali to a certain princess, Mona.

Near the Mosque of Sidi Ali el Mezzeri, backing on to the white arcaded cinema, is another large ribat, known as the **Zaouia of Sidi Douib**. Its round towers and gate house have been carefully restored in the last 15 years. During the building of the Hotel Esplanade, the foundations of a third ribat, beneath the **Koubba of Lalla Saida**, a female saint, were discovered. This is more likely to be the site of the Women's Ribat, mentioned by the historian El Idrisi, than the second courtyard in the Ribat of Harthema.

The Bourguiba Family Mausoleum

The minarets, gold dome and green cupolas of this grandiose mausoleum, a 1960s pastiche of traditional Islamic architecture, are approached up a processional avenue which cuts right through the local cemetery of Sidi el Mezzeri. The right-hand koubba at the beginning of the avenue houses the graves of seven martyrs who fell in the struggle for independence.

Two small koubbas within the mausoleum's perimeter fence house the bodies, on the right, of Sidi Bou Zid, and on the left those of Bourguiba's parents and his French first wife Matilda, the mother of his sons.

The Medina
The Bourguiba Mosque, which dominates the front of the medina, was built in 1963. The grand marble steps are rarely used, the popular entrance being from Rue de l'Indépendance. Inside is an opulent courtyard with fountains leading to the prayer hall. The **medina** itself is a disappointing grid of regular streets lined with tacky souvenir stalls. The old sea gate, Bab Derb, has been replaced by a state-run craft shop, and brickwork indigenous to the Saharan oases lines the colonnaded Rue de l'Indépendance. On the right, there is a small exhibition of traditional costume, before the Tourist Office. Any of the next few left turns leads out through restored surviving gates in the medina wall, to Av Habib Bourguiba and a bogus hexagonal tower. The gold statue of Bourguiba as a gifted student nearby is the ultimate in personality cult.

WHERE TO STAY
If you decide to stay here, avoid both the hotels of Skanès and Monastir's esplanade, and go to the **Hotel Yasmin**, 1.5 km north of the Ribat, along the coastal Route de la Falaise, tel (03) 62511. It has 23 bedrooms, some facing the sea, and is well managed by Nouredine Abdel Latif, with an excellent restaurant. In high season, a double here will cost 26 dn.

EATING OUT
The licensed restaurant at the Hotel Yasmin has an interesting menu, and costs around 18 dn for two. Try the *Crêpe Bonne Femme* followed by a spicy *merguez* kebab.

Eating in the centre of town, **Le Rempart**, on Av Habib Bourguiba, is licensed and locally popular—two courses, wine and coffee for around 5 dn a head. Signposts lead to the **Restaurant des Emirs** in the medina, which is rather overpriced, or there is the **Restaurant Bonheur**, in a hole in the wall at the gate on Rue du 2 Mars.

The three sea-front restaurants and cafés in the marina are rather soulless, but the **El Farik**, further south overlooking one of the old fishing bays, is more raffish.

Ksar Hellal and Moknine
Almost halfway between Monastir and Mahdia, the twin towns of Ksar Hellal and Moknine capture something of the real spirit of the Sahel: industrious, political, cultured and fertile. Ksar Hellal, a prosperous mill-town of 30,000, has a tradition of weaving, particularly in silk, but now mostly practises its skills on the manufacture of jeans. A massive socialist-realist **statue** dominates the main square. It was here in March 1934 that Habib Bourguiba led a group of the more militant members of the Destour (Constitution) Party to form the Neo-Destour. *Louages* congregate at one corner of the square, leaving regularly for Mahdia, Monastir and El Jem, and in another a shady café beckons.

To the southeast, but now almost indistinguishable from Ksar Hellal, sits Moknine, a vibrant market town (market Wed), with a small **Museum of Local Art and Folklore**. Open every day except Mon, 09.00–12.00 and 14.30–18.00 (winter 14.00–17.30), it occupies a tiny mosque, known as the Mosque of Sidi Bou Abela, which was built in the early 14th century. To find it, first locate the town's central roundabout, adorned with a tasteless modernist arch. The *louage* station is 100 m down the road to Monastir, and a right turn next to it leads to the museum.

In the main prayer hall, among bridal costumes and jewellery, made by the town's Jewish population, are an unusual baby's cradle, made from the shell of a sea turtle, and a curved and carved wooden stick, held by the groom during the wedding ceremony to symbolize his power over his spouse. The other rooms round the courtyard contain examples of the red and black pottery, known as *chaouat*, which the Berbers of Moknine have been making for thousands of years; hollow goats' horns worn to protect the fingers during the olive harvest; the mosque's well and some good Roman coins.

Lamta
This village just north of Ksar Hellal is the site of ancient Leptis Minor, sister to the famous Leptis Magna which still rises in ruined splendour from the sands on the Libyan coast. The few objects excavated here have yet to be housed in the long-promised museum.

Thapsus
East of Moknine is the site of the battle of Thapsus which finished the Roman Civil War in 46 BC. From the roadside town of Bekalta take the coast road that winds through 6 km of dark red fertile gardens dotted with palms to the fishing port. There is a mound of masonry from the Roman town's baths, south of the harbour, and a section of the Roman harbour wall near the present-day mole, both of which take second place to the sandy beach which makes a good picnic spot while you meditate on the past.

On New Year's Day, Caesar landed with the first of his troops in a province that was entirely in the grip of the Republicans, supported by King Juba I of Numidia. His greatest problem was not the enemy, who kept avoiding battle, but a continual shortage of food. Thapsus, a garrisoned port known for its stores, was an obvious target. Whilst Caesar besieged the town, Juba advanced from the south and the Republican general Scipio came down from the north to trap him. Their plan miscarried, and Caesar's hungry legions attacked with such ferocity on the morning of 6 April that the battle was decisively won in the first rush. In the bloody aftermath 10,000 prisoners were killed and senators, knights and officers from both armies hunted down. Rather than accept Caesar's mercy, Scipio stabbed himself at sea, and Juba and the Roman general Petreius arranged to dine together before fighting a duel, with a slave at hand to finish off the wounded victor.

Mahdia

Mahdia is a quietly industrious town, with thriving fishing and weaving industries, and straddles the rocky promontory which shaped its history. This peninsula, easily defendable from land and sea, was chosen as the capital of the Fatimid dynasty in the 10th century, and was subsequently much fought over. There is a brooding atmosphere but comparatively little to show from this important national role, apart from a Great Mosque, a gate, a fort and some sea-eroded walls.

This makes just enough to do to occupy a restless mind between bouts of swimming and reading on one of Tunisia's least exploited beaches. If you are coming just for a day try to coincide with the Friday souk, famed for its colourful market in second-hand marriage costumes.

History

The Fatimids who founded Mahdia as their capital in the 10th century were Shiites. They were isolated from orthodox Islam by their insistence that the only legitimate heirs to the Caliphate were the descendants of Fatimah, the Prophet's daughter, and they aspired to convert the entire Islamic world to their belief. Mahdia was built between 916–21 as a safe retreat for the Caliph's family and as a secure harbour for his expeditionary forces. The neck of the peninsula was defended by a 30-ft wall, separating the royal palace on the peninsula from Zawila, a town in which the rest of the community lived, coming into the palace enclosure to work by day. As the first Caliph, Ubayd Allah, had predicted, Mahdia survived an eight-month siege by the puritan Abu Yazid, 'the man on the donkey', in 945. After Yazid was defeated, he was flayed and his skin stuffed with straw as a plaything for the Caliph's pet monkeys.

In 969 the Fatimids appointed the Zirids as governors of North Africa and moved to Cairo. The massacre of Shiites in Mahdia in 1016 marked the Zirids' complete independence from their former masters. Fifty years later the Hilalian invasion unleashed by the Fatimids forced the Zirids to retreat behind the city's stout walls, where they survived by trading with Sicily.

For the next seven centuries, the prosperous city, often known as Cape Africa, was juggled between Christian and Muslim hands. Between 1088 and 1549 'the richest city in Barbary' was attacked by the Sicilians, the Genoese with English knights, the French and by the Ottoman corsair Dragut. Charles V took the town in 1550, and when the Spanish garrison left four years later they burnt the town and blew up the Fatimid defences. These were never rebuilt, but were replaced by a series of Turkish forts and artillery bastions which faced a final assault from the Knights of Malta in the 17th century.

GETTING AROUND

By Train: Three trains a day leave the train station on Av Farhat Hached for Tunis, stopping at Monastir and Sousse.

By Bus: The bus station occupies the open ground between market and port. There are four buses a day to Monastir, and almost hourly buses for Sousse, Sfax and El Jem. There is also a daily service for Nabeul on Cap Bon.

By *Louage*: Beside the Esso garage by the port on Av Farhat Hached, *louages* leave for most of the towns in the Sahel, including Monastir, Sousse and El Jem. Departures further afield are less regular.

TOURIST INFORMATION

The *Syndicat d'Initiative* is just inside the medina gate. It is in the arcaded building, an old koubba, first on the right.

The Medina

Main roads pass through the new town at Mahdia, with its fishing port, banks and government buildings, and end at an open square at the neck of the peninsula. This is overlooked by an imposing gatehouse the **Skifa el Kahla** which guards the way into the old medina. The 140-ft passageway is part of the original 10th-century fortifications and provided the only entrance into the Fatimid palace. It was closed with a wrought-iron gate, followed by six successive portcullises. It was massive enough to withstand the Spanish attack of 1554 though the outer gate was destroyed. This was rebuilt by the Turks who also added an upper artillery bastion with a commanding view of the town, which can be reached by stairs in the south wall.

Rue Obeid Allah el Mehdi leads from the gate past a covered souk of jewellers and tailors at no. 14. Keep an ear out for the clack of silk looms which rings out from deep within whitewashed walls all over the medina. Mahdia has long been renowned for its simple, bright, woven silk, a skill introduced by Jews from Libya in the 19th century. The road leads on to **Pl du Caire**, dappled by the sculpted shade of four massive trees and the walls of Mosque Hajji Mustapha Hamza. It is the best place in the town for a reflective cup of coffee, sitting on one of the whitewashed gypsum benches round the walls, gazing, in winter, at the sight of gourds growing in the trees. Beyond, the street opens out into a square between the Great Mosque on the right and the minaret of Mosque Slimen Hamza.

The Great Mosque

Mahdia's Great Mosque was heavily restored in the 18th century but had disappeared by 1960. Between 1961 and 1965 a perfect copy of the original 10th-century building was re-erected. It has a plain façade, with no minaret to betray its identity. The unusually prominent main entrance, an Islamic triumphal arch, is evidence of the preeminent position the Caliph held in the faith; as El Mehdi, the Rightly Guided, only he could use it. For hundreds of years the Shiites had waited for this prophesied saviour, destined to return the Caliphate to its legitimate heirs.

Inside, a massive plain courtyard leads to the studded doors of the prayer hall. It is surrounded by an elegant stone colonnade, whose simple but austere lines reflect the integrity of the Fatimids, whose architecture throughout North Africa gives equal importance to defined space and visible stone.

The south and west walls of the original 10th-century mosque rose directly above the sea on reclaimed land, and formed part of Mahdia's defences. As a result, cisterns, which are normally concealed beneath a mosque's courtyard, would have been polluted by sea water, and two hidden rooms at either end of the entrance walls were constructed in their place. Water from the courtyard still runs into them, though rubble from the dredging of the fishing port now separates mosque and sea.

During the Spanish occupation of the town between 1550–4, the mosque was used as a church, and Christian gentlemen given pride of place in graves beneath the courtyard. Subsequently the Christian corpses were removed, but the burial practice continued, particularly with Muslim victims of a 1689 plague.

Borj el Kebir

Take the seaside road south of the Great Mosque to Borj el Kebir (open every day except Sun, 09.00–17.00; adm.), a Turkish fort built in 1595 by Abu Abdallah Mohammed Pasha. Originally completely square, the artillery bastions on the four corners of the fort were added in the 18th century. A monumental passageway leads to the central courtyard, with a dwarf plantation of Roman pillars and a rickety stage, behind which is a small prayer hall. Stairs lead up on to the battlements and a series of magnificent views. Looking back towards the town, the remains of both Fatimid and Zirid palaces lie confused on the ground below. The headland, with graves on every feasible piece of ground, is crowned by a **lighthouse**, on the site of a Fatimid tower in the sea wall. Near it are some **Phoenician rock-cut tombs**.

On the way to the lighthouse, fishing boats on the right rock gently in what looks like a natural harbour. This was the original Fatimid **rock-cut port**, its entrance protected by two towers and a massive chain that could be lifted between them. All along the rocky shore, ghosts of the defensive wall crop up. In 1907 the sea beyond divulged spectres of the Roman era, when sponge fishermen found a Roman galley, full of art treasures, which had sunk in

81 BC. The dig, which raised pillars, bronze statues and busts, was the first of its kind to be undertaken, and took five years. The best of the pieces are in the Bardo.

WHERE TO STAY

EXPENSIVE

If you do not mind the risk of a crowd, the **Hotel Cap Mahdia,** Route de la Corniche, tel (03) 83300, has a swimming pool, windsurfing boards, tennis courts, but will set you back a considerable sum.

MODERATE

The smallest and cheapest hotel on the beach in Mahdia is the **Sables d'Or**, Route de la Corniche, tel (03) 81137. Its 53 bungalows are scattered between palm trees.

CHEAP

There are two cheap small hotels in town, which tend to have dicky drains. Neither is far from the beach. The **Hotel Jazira**, in Rue ibn Fourat, tel (03) 81629, is on the northern shore of the old town. Ask for a room looking over the sea. The **Hotel Er Rand**, at 20 Av Taieb M'hiri, tel (03) 80039, has rooms with showers and a good licensed restaurant next door.

EATING OUT

Apart from the restaurant attached to the **Hotel Er Rand**, Mahdia's restaurants cluster opposite the port, on Av Farhat Hached. Both the **Restaurant du Quai** and the **Restaurant du Lido** are licensed and serve freshly grilled fish, salads and a variety of Tunisian dishes at reasonable prices. The **Restaurant des Sportifs** next door is cheaper and unlicensed, as is the popular **Restaurant Medina**, hidden behind the market and Banque de Tunisie nearby. For those who crave the camaraderie of all-male drinking haunts, **Le Corsaire** on Av Farhat Hached is the place. **Pl du Caire** in the old town and the **Café de la Grotte** perched above the sea below the Grand Mosque both serve good coffee.

From Mahdia to Sfax

Salakta

Salakta is a fishing village on the coast 16 km south of Mahdia. It is built over ancient Sullectum which was resettled with Roman colonists after being destroyed during the Thapsus campaign in 46 BC.

The Museum

The museum, marked by a standing column, stands between the port and a sand-covered Roman cemetery. It houses a magnificent mosaic of a lion, one of the most vivid in the country, full of subtle distortions that exaggerate its head, talons and teeth. It was commissioned for the villa of Leontius, a successful manufacturer of armour. There is also a copy of the Sullectum mosaic discovered at Ostia, the ancient port of Rome. It is decorated with black and white symbols of the principal African ports that supplied the capital with corn and oil. The room to the left houses an exhibition detailing the joint research into Tunisian pottery by the British Academy and the National Institute of Archaeology and Art.

The Catacombs

Salakta's catacombs are not signposted, and you will need your own torch/matches to explore them. From the port, take the coastal road south, and following it inland. Turn left up the dirt track lined by pylons. About 500 m further on there is a collapsed Roman underground cistern, and the second path on the left leads to a sunken pit filled with fig trees, the entrance to the burial site. It is an evocative, mysterious place, complete with rats and the odd stagnant pool. The underground tunnels are lined with layers of carved niches where the dead were placed, wrapped in linen and packed tight with lime and clay. The smaller niches held urns and children, the larger entire sarcophagi. Whole rooms were set aside for families and religious fraternities.

Chebba

Along the C82 coast road to Sfax, 16 km south of Ksour Essaf, look out for **Kechafa Echaabma**, a roadside hamlet beside a 1-km drive to a magnificent stretch of white beach backed by pine forest. A second beach, **Plage Douiria**, is down a drive about 2 km before you reach Chebba, a modern town fringed with beach villas. Chebba is named after the Chabbia brotherhood who set up a zaouia here in the 15th century. A ringroad takes in Ras Kaboudia peninsula to the east of town, once called Caput Vada, where Count Belisarius landed his mixed army of Huns, Scandinavians and Greeks in 533 for the conquest of Vandal Tunisia. Beside the modern lighthouse there, the ruined round tower is all that remains of the Ribat Kahdija, built on the foundations of a Byzantine fortress.

Some 20 km south of Chebba the coastal road passes the site of **Acholla** on Ras Bou Tria. It was founded in the 3rd century BC by Phoenicians from Malta, and it was here that the magnificent bathhouse mosaic of the Triumph of Bacchus, displayed on the top floor of the Bardo, was found.

SFAX

Sfax is the second largest city in Tunisia with a population of a quarter of a million, and sprawls along 20 km of coastline. It sits in lonely dominance, surrounded by a vast sea of olives with not a single town of interest before you reach Gafsa, Sbeitla or Gabès. This isolation has bred a strong civic identity, partly through intermarriage, which is mixed with equal measures of commercial acumen and pride. Sfaxis are the clannish heart of Tunisia's business community, just as the men of the northern Sahel dominate national politics.

The walled medina, with its gates, battlemented towers, souks and minarets, is the city's central attraction. The lack of beaches has kept Sfax off the tourist map, though the Kerkennah Isles are just a 1½-hour boat trip away.

History

Sfax has not always been so dominant or so isolated. For the thousand years of Phoenician and Roman rule this area was dotted with towns. Traces of ancient Taparura lie buried beneath Sfax though the now deserted ruins of Thaenae, 10 km to the south, and Acholla, 40 km north, were both larger and richer cities. A ribat, built from the ruins of Taparura, had by the 9th century grown into a town, trading in the Sahelian staples of fish, wool and olive oil. It was

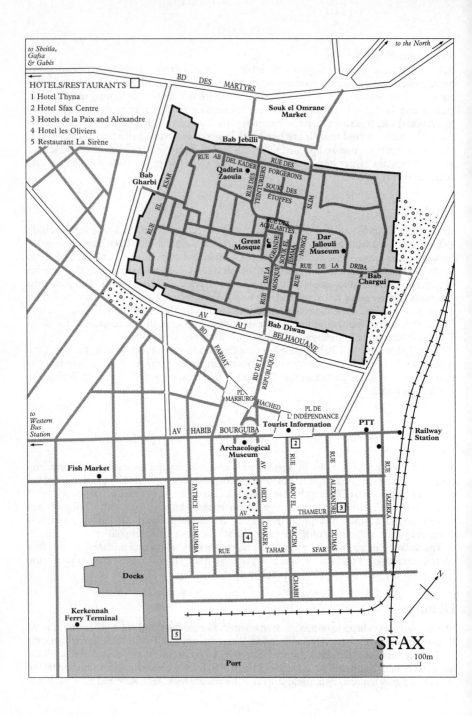

HOTELS/RESTAURANTS □
1 Hotel Thyna
2 Hotel Sfax Centre
3 Hotels de la Paix and Alexandre
4 Hotel les Oliviers
5 Restaurant La Sirène

to Sbeitla,
Gafsa
& Gabès

to the North

BD   DES   MARTYRS

Souk el Omrane
Market

Bab Jebilli

RUE AB DEL KADER
Qadiria
Zaouia

RUE DES
FORGERONS

Bab
Gharbi

RUE DES TEINTURIERS

SOUK DES
ÉTOFFES

RUE EL KSAR

SLIM

RUE DES
AGHLABITES

Great
Mosque

GRANDE MOSQUE

SOUK EL HEMMA

Dar
Jallouli
Museum

MONGI

RUE DE LA   DRIBA

RUE DE LA

RUE

Bab
Chargui

AV   ALI

Bab Diwan

BELHAOUANE

BD
FARHAT

BD DE LA
REPUBLIQUE

PL.
MARBURG
HACHED

PL DE
L' INDÉPENDANCE

Tourist Information

PTT

to
Western
Bus
Station

AV   HABIB   BOURGUIBA

2

Railway
Station

Archaeological
Museum

AV

RUE

RUE ALEXANDRE

RUE IAZERKA

Fish Market

PATRICE

LUMUMBA

HEDI

ABOU EL

THAMEUR

3

AV

CHAKER

KACEM

DUMAS

4

RUE

TAHAR

SFAR

CHABBI

Docks

Kerkennah
Ferry Terminal

5

SFAX

0   100m

Port

enclosed within walls and given a Great Mosque by the Aghlabids, when it came to resemble the medina of today. The name Sfax inexplicably derives from the Arabic for 'city of cucumbers'.

Sfax became dominant when it was the only urban centre to survive the Bedouin invasion of the 11th century. It fell under a succession of tribal chiefs, interspaced with periods of rule by Norman, Almohad or Hafsid governors. The greatest of the local dynasties were the Beni Makku, who throughout most of the 14th century controlled a state that stretched from Sfax to Tripoli. Only the great corsair Dragut improved upon this in the 16th century, when he also held Gafsa and repopulated the empty city of Tripoli with 40 families from Sfax. By the 17th century, when its population numbered 10,000, Sfax was firmly under the control of governors appointed from Tunis, though local corsairs like Sheikh Ali Nouni still won great fortunes and renown.

Sfax was the only Sahel town actively to oppose the French occupation in 1881. This militant stance was produced by a fragile alliance between an urban mob who had seized power during the sacking of the European quarter and local Bedouin tribes like the Neffat and Methalith. The Caid of the Neffat, Ali ben Khalifa, was acclaimed defender of the faith and led the resistance. On 16 July, French marines stormed the defences after a 24-hour naval bombardment, prolonged through the night by searchlights.

The colonial period added a precious new commodity, phosphates, to Sfax's and the nation's prosperity. It also witnessed a great reversal in power when the local bedouin grazing grounds were replanted with olive groves. A glittering new town of colonial mauresque was built between the medina and the port, only to be flattened by Allied bombs in 1943. Resources between 1944 and 1953 were directed at the construction of a new deepwater port and land reclamation schemes, rather than the total rebuilding of the new town. At the same time two local men, Hedi Chaker and Farhat Hached, were establishing an indigenous trade union movement and preparing the way for the independence struggle.

GETTING AROUND

By Air
Sfax airport, tel (04) 40879, is 10 km out of town on the road to Gafsa. Tickets for internal flights or flights to Paris can be bought from the Tunis Air office at 4 Av de l'Armée Nationale, tel (04) 23691, or Air France on Av Taieb Mehri, tel (04) 24847.

By Boat
The SONOTRAK Kerkennah ferry terminal is along Av Mohammed Hedi Kechafa, which runs beside the inner docks, tel (04) 22216. In summer there are six 1½-hour crossings a day, and from Nov–Mar there are four.

By Train
Sfax train station dominates the eastern end of Av Habib Bourguiba. Four trains a day go north to Tunis four hours away, stopping at El Jem, Sousse and Bir Bou Regba on the way. Going south there are three daily services, two to Gabès some two hours away, and one to Gafsa and Metlaoui, a four- and five-hour journey respectively.

By Bus
The principal bus station is on Rue Iazerka, opposite the train station. There are five buses to Tunis, five to Sousse, three to El Kef, two to Kairouan and one to Ksar Essaf whence *louages* run to Mahdia. There are eight buses south to Gabès, of which two continue to Houmt Souk in Jerba, two go on to Medenine and one to Tataouine. There is also a night departure for

TUNISIA

Douz. Travelling west to Gafsa or Sbeitla use the bus station beside the disused colonial church on Av Commandant Bejouane.

By Louage/Taxi
The principal *louage* stations, where you should find cars for most major destinations and many minor local towns are by the Post Office and on Pl de la République. Town cabs are best caught on Av Farhat Hached and by Bab Diwan.

By Car
Rue Tahar Safar has an Avis office at no. 48, tel (04) 24605, and a few local competitors. The Hertz office is at 47 Av Habib Bourguiba, tel (04) 23553; Africar at the Tourafric office at 35 Av Hedi Chaker, tel (04) 22287.

TOURIST INFORMATION
The *Syndicat d'Initiative* is in a circular booth on Pl de l'Indépendance, tel (04) 24606; it is closed on Sat morning and all day on Fri and Sun. The central **Post Office** is opposite the train station on Av Habib Bourguiba. **Banks** are all in the new town, Banque de Tunisie on Av Habib Bourguiba, Banque Nationale on Rue de Tyna and Banque Centrale on Rue Abou el Kacem Chabbi. **Foreign papers** can be brought in Pl Marburg. There are half a dozen French language bookshops in the new town and a French cultural centre at 48 Av Taieb Mehri, tel (04) 21533. A Catholic chapel, with mass at 18.30 Sat and 09.30 Sun, remains in business at 4 Rue Dag Hammarskjold, tel (04) 20779.

The Medina
The old ramparted city is filled with workshops, markets, cafés and quiet residential quarters. Ideally, it should be explored at random, but the description below introduces the major sites of historical interest.

Blvd de la République leads from the centre of the New Town straight up to Bab Diwan, the Council Gate and main entrance to the medina. It is surrounded by cafés and stalls. Just inside, in front of the old mosque, was the site of the fish market, and prisoners used to be locked inside the carved door to the left. Rue Mongi Slim, the principal thoroughfare, hung with jeans, leather jackets and modern goods, is right and left. About 130 m up look out for an arch and a left turn into the cluttered courtyard of Souk el Jemma, surrounded by workshops and a double layer of precarious wooden balconies, and an incongruous central pylon. From the souk the minaret of the Great Mosque is visible, but it is best seen from a café in a whitewashed courtyard off the Rue des Aghlabites.

The Great Mosque
This interior is closed to non-Muslims, leaving only the exterior of the eastern wall (that nearest Souk el Jemma) and the minaret to hint at its splendours. The first mosque was built here by the Aghlabids in the mid 9th-century, exactly a fifth the size of the Great Mosque of Kairouan. The current minaret and eastern wall both date from its Fatimid replacement, half the size, built in the 10th century. In the 18th century the mosque grew back to its original dimensions, discovered in excavations.

The eastern wall is decorated with an eyebrow dentil lintel that binds together an alternating arcade of horseshoe arched niches and skylights. The varied depth of the carving plays with the strong North African light to cast shadows that enhance the elegant forms. Set

170

into the wall are an intriguing collection of dedication stones. The kufic lettering is to be expected, but the Byzantine stone, with Greek lettering and the Christian device of two peacocks on either side of an eroded chalice, comes as an ecumenical surprise.

The minaret is celebrated for its bands of rich carving, including a band of kufic script, reminiscent of the Fatimid mosques in Cairo. Structurally, it straddles the transition from multi-staged Mesopotamian towers as at Kairouan to the simpler two-storey North African minaret. Its position on the northwest corner of the mosque, not centrally aligned with the mihrab, and the pierced turban arch of the lantern on the summit, both follow trends developed in Andalucia.

Souk des Etoffes
Sfax's covered souk lies between the Great Mosque and the Rue des Forgerons which runs inside the far battlements of the medina, by Bab Jebilli. At its heart is the cross-shaped Souk des Etoffes, between Rue Mongi Slim and Rue des Teinturiers. These few dozen stalls are one of the best places to shop in Tunisia, with heaps of killims, striped blankets, embroidered haiks which cover up women in public, old wedding dresses and cushion covers. Though rarely made with muted vegetable dyes or more than 20 years old, you can still find a variety of traditional and individual designs unaffected by the stereotypes produced by the ONAT. In particular have a look at Zribi Ahmed ben Taher's stock at 30 Souk des Etoffes, tel (04) 22224.

Bab Jebilli and the Kasbah
Bab Jebilli, at the far end of the medina away from the danger of naval bombardment, is the oldest surviving gateway set in an ancient stretch of wall. The stone facing retains a wall of packed mud, strengthened by vertical lines of clamping bond. Inside precarious wooden balconies face the white walls and corner minaret of the **Qadiria Zaouia**, whose carved kufic inscription is now almost hidden by years of whitewash. The great iron doors of Bab Jebilli are stuck open and frame the central artery of **Souk el Omrane**, a modern covered vegetable cum dry goods market which occupies its traditional place. The external face of the gate is pure 9th century, with Roman columns supporting an early horseshoe arch, and a band of carved script separated from the battlemented attic by a dentil frieze.

Other areas of wall have been rebuilt though they still follow the original plan. The last major overhaul was in the 18th century, when the corner artillery bastions and Bab Chargui were enlarged, thickened and given angled walls the better to survive an artillery bombardment. They are best appreciated from the outside as the inner walkway is dank and rubbish-strewn. There is a pleasant café in the garden just outside Bab Chargui. The red-light quarter just inside to the right should be avoided by women.

From Bab Jebilli you can walk inside the medina, down Rue Abdel Kader and along Rue el Ksar to the quiet shaded square outside the **kasbah**, overlooked by a mosque. The kasbah itself is a simple courtyard enclosed by high walls and barrack sheds, but is slowly being converted to house an exhibition hall and an open-air theatre.

Dar Jallouli Museum
Open 09.00–16.30 every day except Mon; adm. Walk up Rue Mongi Slim from Bab Diwan, take the third right, walk 100 m along Rue de la Driba past some elegant gates and turn left at a new mosque. The green and black doors of no. 5 on the left lead into the Dar Jallouli Museum, tel (04) 21186.

This is a typical, handsome, 17th-century town house, which belonged to one of the chief families of Sfax, the Jallouli. They claimed, perhaps snobbishly, to be Andalucian, though very few refugees had settled in the Sahel. Mohammed Jallouli, a Caid of Sfax in the 18th century, acted as both a commercial agent and moneylender to Hammouda Pasha II. He built and part-owned corsair ships and, apart from his extensive holdings in the medina, had olive groves in at least 24 Sahel towns. One day he was chided by the Bey for not entertaining, upon which he promptly invited his sovereign to the Jallouli country house outside Tunis. One dish was served. The lid was lifted to reveal a pile of gold and an enormous diamond nestling on its summit, a gift of 500,000 piastres. The Bey returned to the Bardo for lunch.

A double hallway maintains the privacy of the paved interior courtyard, flanked by two T-shaped reception rooms, resplendent with black and white paved floors, tiled walls and carved and painted wooden ceilings. The rooms are furnished with simple but elegant wooden benches, raised beds, screens and chests, often painted or ornamented with turned wood. On display are some 19th-century jewellery and cosmetics, painted glass, a kif pipe and some elegant embroidered male costumes. The small kitchen contains an alembic for distilling floral essences and the storehouse, as it would have been until this century, is stocked with amphorae full of specimens of dried food and spices.

The three first-floor rooms contain a high-quality display of traditional dress for both men and women of the region, and of the costumes and jewellery worn during the week-long celebration of a traditional marriage. On the second floor there is an exhibition of calligraphy (see p. 65), showing not only the end result but also the tools of the trade. The examples on painted glass are some of the best you will see in Tunisia. The myth of the Seven Sleepers inspired the corsair galley, and a sura of the Koran forms the Prophet on Boraq, the winged beast who bore him to the temple in Jerusalem after his death.

The New Town

Between medina and port lies this regular grid 'whose streets seem too wide and whose squares appear too spacious for the number of its inhabitants' (A. Broderick). Cutting it in two, Av Habib Bourguiba leads from the train station down a palm-lined vista that frames mountains of grey phosphate spoil in the far distance. An elaborate façade of colonial mauresque offices lines the street to Place de la République, where to the right the arcaded Blvd de la République frames the medina.

Archaeological Museum
Opposite, and set back from the square is the town hall, an unmistakable colonial building combining a clock tower and dome. The ground floor houses the **Archaeological Museum**, open every day except Mon, 08.30–13.00, 15.00–18.00; tickets from a voluble custodian who never has any change.

His tour begins in Room III, with magnificent funerary glass from Thaenae and delicate frescoes from Acholla. The Roman coins are from a 4th-century hoard found hidden in the *calidarium* of the baths in Thaenae. The central funerary urn is a mysterious, elaborate construction, painted with scenes of the soul's journey through the constellations. The collection of lamps ranges from Phoenician (4th century BC) through to the 10th century, impressive archaeological evidence of cultural continuity broken not by the Arab conquest but by that of the Bedouins in the 11th century. Above them are two 4th-century pagan funerary mosaics, the flowers, feast and music performed by winged figures presenting a familiar image of the afterlife. The mosaic on the far wall was found in Sfax, a 3rd-century work showing the poet Ennius surrounded by the nine Muses. The 3rd-century mosaic of children wrestling, their topknots indicating that they have not yet been circumcised, is particularly vivid. Above the cabinet of African slipware is a mosaic of Silenus, in the black and white style popular in Italy.

Amongst its mosaics, Room VI contains a fine head of Oceanus and a nymph riding a dolphin. Room V houses a collection of Roman tombs found at Sfax. The headstones are complete with the trough and hole through which libations of blood or wine could drain down into the amphora that held the loved one's bones.

The entrance hall, Room I, contains a schist sphinx, some Muslim tombs and examples of 10th-century binding and calligraphy (see pp. 65–6). To the left of the stairs there is a collection of stone tools from the two indigenous Stone Age cultures of Tunisia. The Ibero-Mauretanian tools were found at Oued Akarit, north of Gabès and the three eras of Capsian tools, including pieces of decorated ostrich egg, were found outside Gafsa (see p. 35).

Room II is filled with Christian funerary mosaics from Sfax, Thaenae and La Skhira. The 4th-century floor mosaics are geometric, and in the Semitic tradition carefully avoid any representational art. By the 5th century reworked pagan symbols like lambs, peacocks and chalices are used, leading up to a series of spectacular 6th-century Byzantine mosaics, like that of Daniel in his Phrygian cap being thrown to the lions. Three pagan ossuary boxes were discovered on the Kerkennah Isles, the central one with its finely carved ram-horned deity the most elegant object in the museum. Upstairs there are a few more mosaics, like the one of Arion riding a dolphin, though the main attraction is peeping in at the opulent council chambers. The principal hall has a gilded dome and a 2nd-century mosaic of the Triumph of Bacchus underfoot.

The Harbour
On the southwestern edge of the new town stands the old inner dock, bordered by the fish market and beyond it Souk Remla, the souk of the poor. Filled with sunken ships and a small shipbuilding yard, it gives a false impression of Sfax. The modern 65-hectare outer port of Tunisia's busiest harbour, with its deepwater channel and outer breakwater, can only be seen from the Kerkennah ferry.

The Coast
There's a moussem in the honour of Sidi Mansour held at the village of the same name 12 km north of Sfax in September. Without the bustle of pilgrims and air of merriment, however, it's a depressing ride on a no. 3 bus to a coastal terrace with koubba and mosque built beside the remains of a Roman lighthouse. The closest beaches are Plage Es Chaffar, 25 km south, and Chebba, nearly 70 km north, and both are colonized by the villas of successful Sfaxis. All the more reason to take the ferry across to the Kerkennah Isles.

WHERE TO STAY
EXPENSIVE
The swish international **Hotel Sfax Centre** on Av Habib Bourguiba is used by visiting businessmen. It has a swimming pool and balconied bedrooms with fine views.

MODERATE
The **Hotel des Oliviers** on Av Habib Thameur, tel (04) 25188, has much more character—a charming piece of colonial architecture in the heart of the new town. Social life centres

around the swimming pool in summer, and the olive-wood bar in winter, but avoid the restaurant as the food is very dull. **Hotel Alexandre** at 21 Rue Alexandre Dumas, (04) 21911, is well maintained and has a friendly downstairs restaurant. Otherwise, try **Hotel la Colisée**, Av Taieb M'hiri, tel (04) 27800, a tall thin building with a ground-floor bar.

CHEAP
Hotel de la Paix at 15 Rue Alexandre Dumas, tel (04) 21436, is a well-worn old colonial hotel, with cool, dark bedrooms. Moving into the medina, there are several small, very cheap hotels on Rue Mongi Slim. Try the **Hotel de la Medina** at 53 Rue Mongi Slim or the **Hotel du Jerid** with its courtyard and terrace in Souk el Jerid.

EATING OUT

Licensed Restaurants
Eating in Sfax is a treat. **Le Corail**, with its black marble entrance, is traditionally the town's smartest and can be found at 39 Rue Habib Maazoun, tel (04) 27031. Even here a lunch of fish soup and stuffed sole is under 10 dn. If you like low ceilings, sloping floors, drinking and fresh charcoal-grilled fish try **La Sirène** opposite the docks (see map), tel (04) 24691. **Le Printemps** is a small, recently established French restaurant at 57 Av Habib Bourguiba, tel (04) 26973. An elegant dinner for two here with wine costs around 15 dn. Also to be recommended are the **Bagdad** (closed Fri) at 63 Av Farhat Hached, tel (04) 23856, and the **Triki**, tel (04) 96277, on the corner of Rue Patrice Lumumba.

Snack Cafés
There are a number of delicious snack cafés along Blvd de la République and in and around Bab Diwan, including **Le Carthage**, on Av Ali Belhouane opposite the gates. There is a state-of-the-art steel and smoked glass **pizzeria/coffee shop** behind the Hotel Sfax Centre, and you can also grab a snack lunch from the **Restaurant Colombia**, opposite the station as you come straight off the bus or train.

NIGHTLIFE
There are small noisy bars scattered throughout the new town, though Europeans will probably be more relaxed in the Hotels Thyna, Oliviers or Sfax Centre. The latter also has a nightclub, open every day except Mon, 21.00–02.00.

Kerkennah Isles

The Kerkennah Isles are flat, featureless and flooded, but coloured by that combination of white sand, green palms and varying intensities of blue in sky and sea that immediately melt the northern soul. Ten thousand years ago they were part of the mainland but now they form an archipelago, set in a shallow sea and pierced by tidal lagoons. The highest point on the islands is under 12 m, which strengthens the impression that they are within an ace of permanently submerging into the marine horizon. Good cooking and the amicable nature of the islanders conspire to make them the perfect antidote to a week spent scampering around the Sahel cities.

History

There is no evidence that the islands were inhabited before Phoenicians founded a settlement here known as Cercina. Hannibal sailed here in 195 BC when he slipped away from his enemies in Carthage. He was quickly recognized, for many of the fishermen had at one time or another served under his command. To delay the news being carried back to Carthage, he ordered a great midday feast to which all the ships contributed their sails for a sun awning. Having guaranteed himself at least a day's start he slipped away from the bucolic reunion and headed east to Tyre.

Viking raids in the 9th century were succeeded by those of the crusaders, Sicilians, Spanish and the Knights of St John from Malta, who were only suppressed by Napoleon at the end of the 18th century, making permanent settlements impossible. Throughout this 1000-year war, strong mainland rulers fortified the islands, turning them into an early-warning station, whilst in periods of weakness Christian raiders used them as an advanced base. Otherwise they were inhabited by fishermen, farmers and herdsmen from Sfax during periods of peace. Permanent settlement dates from the 18th century, a period when the Beys began to use the islands as a dumping ground for excess concubines. In 1945 Habib Bourguiba followed in the footsteps of Hannibal by escaping from the island. As is the tendency when two heroes cross paths, the tales of their exploits are becoming inextricably fused. The most famous islander is Farhat Hached, the trade union leader whose assassination by Frenchmen in December 1952 was the spark that spread nationalist agitation from Casablanca to Cairo.

Island Life

The islands now support a population of 15,000 divided amongst 12 villages and the town of Remla. There are reckoned to be about 2000 boats on the isles, for fishing has always been a more important occupation than farming. It is too cool and damp here for date palms to fruit, the soil is poor and the water supply irregular so that wheat, olive and almond harvests are consistently meagre.

The sea is much more reliable: sponges are gathered and unbaited ceramic pots, known as *carour*, are an irresistible attraction to octopus from October to April. Along much of the shore and far out to sea, the tapering palm-frond walls of mullet traps are visible. Kerkennah also specalizes in weaving alfa, reed and split palm fronds to produce nets, baskets and ropes for the boats, as well as selling mats, sacks and baskets on the mainland.

The third traditional resource is emigration. Even in the mid-19th century about a fifth of the men left to work on the mainland. Just as Jerba is famous for its tight-fisted grocers, the natural charm of the Kerkennans has allowed them to carve out a niche as waiters and receptionists. Emigration in the last few years has shown a more amorous inclination—half a dozen marriages a year to girls from southern England after holiday romances.

Gharbi and Chergui

Kerkennah is largely made up of two islands, Gharbi, the 'western' island, and Chergui, 'eastern' or Grand Kerkennah. Ferries land at **Sidi Youssef**, on the western end of Gharbi. A track leading off along the north coast stops at a **look-out tower** built by Dragut in the 16th century. The islands' single tarmac road and bus route passes through the village of Melita before crossing El Kantara, a causeway first built by the Romans. There is a good stretch of beach here, but watch out for the currents when the tide turns.

A turning 1.5 km on to Chergui, at the hamlet of Ouled Yaneg, leads down to the beach of **Sidi Frej** and the main hotels. From the beach in front of the Grand Hotel, a coastal path leads 2 km along to the ruined walls of **Borj el Hissar**, a fort surrounded by sherds and bumps in the ground that mark the Roman town of Cercina.

The main road carries straight on to **Remla**, with its secondary school, post office, UIB bank, two chemists, 20-room hotel and Thursday market. The nearest beach, **Sidi Fankhal**, is one of the most beautiful on the islands, a few kilometres out of town, but the dirt road that leads there needs a guide first time round.

North of Remla, in the village of El Abassia a sign points out Farhat Hached's birthplace. The road leaves Chergui and splits a little further, the right fork leading to the larger coastal village of **El Attaia**, facing out to the deserted island of Gremdi. Ask around for a fisherman willing to take a trip across to the island or a fishing trip.

The road's left fork leads to the village of **Ech Chergui**, where there is a craft centre and a signposted turning to Bounouma beach. The road continues past the koubba of Sidi Salem, which looks out on to the deserted island of Charmadia, accessible by foot at low tide. It ends up at the new fishing port of **Kraten**, where sponge fishers still operate.

ACTIVITIES

Bicycles, the best way of getting around, can be rented from the Hotel Farhat for 4 dn a day. The sea is too shallow and sandy to make Kerkennah much of a base for scuba diving or even snorkelling. The Hotels Grand and Farhat do offer **windsurfing, sailing, horse riding** (4.5 dn an hour), **camel rides** for 3 dn an hour, and **tennis** at the Farhat. Otherwise, the only available sport on Kerkennah is a lazy day's **fishing,** grilling your catch either at midday on a deserted island, or on the shore at dusk. Either make your own arrangements or inquire at the Hotels Grand or Farhat. In July and August there is a *Festival de la Sirène,* when the events, dances, music and costumes of the traditional marriage season are put on for the tourists.

WHERE TO STAY AND EAT

Sidi Frej: If you are coming in July and August, ring in advance as rooms can be sparse and prices are up by half. The Hotels Farhat and Grand, which both have swimming pools, also have a strong English presence, due to two Brighton-based tour agents.

EXPENSIVE

The **Farhat,** tel (04) 81042, is a quieter and better looking, more upmarket hotel.

MODERATE

The **Grand Hotel,** tel (04) 81565, has a better beach and a nightclub. The **Cercina,** tel (04) 81028, sits at the far end of the beach and is the smallest and scruffiest of Sidi Frej's hotels, but has the best restaurant. From a table on its shaded terrace you look out over the sea-lapped fishing pier, washing down island specalities with wine.

Remla: Kerkennah's main town has a number of cafés and two restaurants, the licensed **Restaurant La Sirène,** beside the bank, and the **bar-restaurant-hotel Algeçiras,** tel (04) 81058, at the centre of town by the bus stop. The island's only off-licence, **Chez Krida's,** is to the right of Restaurant La Sirène, looking out to sea.

El Attaia: there are two café-restaurants here, by the port: **Restaurant Archipel** run by Madame Chedli, tel (04) 81314, and the **Regal** run by Nayet Ouarda.

Sfax to Gabès

Travelling from Sfax to Gabès by train is to doze through a forest of olive trees. On the road, green Tripoli number plates are as regular as the olives, usually attached to erratically driven cars. The combination of the recently opened border, a Libya awash with more money than consumable goods and Sfaxi enterprise has turned the roadside into one long broken souk.

There are a couple of minor archaeological sites and a swimming beach just off this road, and a good restaurant in Mahrès for lunch.

Thaenae

The Roman ruins of Thaenae (also spelt Thyna and Thina) are signposted 10 km south of Sfax, after the hideous superphosphate workings and industrial suburbs. A red and white striped lighthouse, about 4 km from the main road, stands at the centre of the ruins. Thaenae was originally a Phoenician settlement, which passed into Numidian hands after the fall of Carthage, only to become part of the Roman Empire in 46 BC. Its barely visible prosperity dates from the turn of the 2nd–3rd centuries under the North African Severan dynasty. They had a curious connection with the town, for it was a knight from Thaenae who assassinated the tyrant Commodus and helped Pertinax, the patron of Septimius Severus, to the throne.

Most easy to identify are the foundations of a 2.5-km Byzantine perimeter wall, with towers and gatehouses. The principal site is known as the Baths of the Months (to the right of the sea path from the lighthouse). Only the figures of January, February, April and December survive in its colourful mosaic floor. In its heyday the baths were lit by windows of translucent gypsum. The confusion of plaster-lined rooms on the landward side of the baths were hot rooms, complete with a service passage and blackened furnace. This is where the coin hoard displayed in the Sfax museum was found, dated to AD 397–8 when Gildo's Berber revolt in Algeria was in full swing. Just to the south are two further bathhouses, and to the north some excavated villas. In the necropolis, outside the city walls, is a sunken octagonal mausoleum, full of tombs.

Ech Chaffar and Mahrès

There is a turning to Plage ech Chaffar and a swim 15 km later. The beach is 4 km from the main road, and has a couple of cafés but no hotel. Mahrès, a little further on, does have one, but the coast here is jagged wave-cut rock covered in green weed. The Hotel Marzouk's licensed restaurant is good, and there is a market on Mondays, a curious whale skeleton in the middle of town and a knot of cafés by the pier.

Ribat of Sidi Ahmed

The Ribat of Sidi Ahmed, 10 km south of Mahrès, is also known as Borj Younga. It is the only one of many coastal fortresses built by the 9th-century Aghlabids to have survived. A dirt track opposite a couple of lonely shops just before the 89 km Gabès/45 km Sfax milestone leads through an olive plantation to its impressive walls.

The fortress and koubba of Sidi Ahmed stand alone above a sea dotted with fishing boats. The ribat rests on Byzantine foundations, of which a few finer stone courses can be seen by the cistern. Of its gates, only the smaller sea gate survives, its narrow portal enclosed in a strong gatehouse with a bayonet passage. Immediately south and west of the fortress are the scant ruins of two cities, Roman Junci and Byzantine Macomades Minores.

On to Gabès

La Skhira is now a deepwater petrol port for Algerian and Tunisian crude oil. It was created in the 19th century by British merchants wanting to export bales of alfa grass for paper-making without paying Sfaxi middlemen.

About 24 km south of La Skhira you cross the banks of **Oued Akarit**, the site of a battle in 1943, and since 1958 subject to almost continuous digs into the estuary's rich prehistoric deposits. Ghannouche, north of Gabès, is a mire of phosphate, electricity and chemical works.

El Jem

The Roman amphitheatre at El Jem is the most surprising sight in Tunisia. Neither photographs nor descriptions can prepare you for the first glimpse of the vast bulk of this monument as it looms out of a horizon of olives. Its serried mass of stone arches rises in threatening silhouette, composed of dazzling reflections of the African sun and deep pools of shade. For centuries a succession of travellers have sneered at the low cloth tents of the nomad tribes squatting beside this grandiose architectural achievement. Before adding your own glib cultural comparisons, read below and remind yourself of the 'high culture' embodied in the shows that were staged here.

El Jem itself is a nondescript market town, which appears remarkably unaffected by the amphitheatre, apart from the one or two good souvenir shops by the entrance. At the other end of town there are some restaurants and a museum with an excellent display of mosaics. Those who want to see the amphitheatre glow blood red at dawn and dusk can stay at the Hotel Julius.

History

We first hear of Thysdrus, the old name for El Jem, in the 5th century BC as the centre of one of the seven agricultural provinces of Carthage. It received a draft of colonists after the Roman conquest in 146 BC, but remained deeply parochial, despite exporting 300,000 bushels of corn in 46 BC.

By the 3rd century, Thysdrus had grown into a town of 30,000, encrusted with the villas of landlords and the centre for a large rural population who packed into town for the market and great agricultural festivals celebrated at the racetrack and amphitheatres. This was a halcyon age, when a third of the Roman senate and the imperial family were of African descent. It ended with the assassination of Alexander, the last Severan, in 235 when Thysdrus' new, largest amphitheatre in Africa was almost complete. The political confusion in Rome encouraged a cabal of local landowners to plot a coup against Maximinus, the usurping Emperor. In 238, a province-wide tax rebellion was fermented and led to the lynching of the procurator, the chief financial official of the province. The plotters proclaimed Gordian, an old senator serving as governor in Carthage, Emperor. However they failed to buy the support of the Third Augustan Legion and their coup was easily crushed by its loyal commander, Cappellianus. He made a particular example of Thysdrus which was burnt and sacked.

The town revived, but never recovered its old position, so that when Diocletian reformed the Empire at the end of the 3rd century, he choose Sousse as the capital of the new province of Byzacena. The amphitheatre was turned into a fortress in the 6th century and is traditionally thought to be the site of the Berber Queen Al Kahena's last stand against the Arab invasion. Whatever the truth of this legend, the proximity of the new Muslim city of Kairouan finished Thysdrus. By the end of the 11th century this once prosperous farming region was grazing land, the amphitheatre serving as a useful landmark under which the nomads could hold a weekly market. It remained almost intact until used by rebel forces in 1695, when government artillery blasted down a section of the wall.

GETTING AROUND

The town centres on the leafy square opposite the **train** station and the Hotel Julius, where there is a *louage* rank and the Monday market takes place. Five trains a day head south to Sfax, with connections to Gabès and Gafsa, and six go north to Sousse, Bir Bou Regba and Tunis. Frequent but often full **buses** pass through between Sousse and Sfax, so one is usually better off going by *louage*.

The Amphitheatre

Open daily 8.30–18.00; adm. The half-ruined amphitheatre, a mass of exposed arches and concrete vaults, is convincing testimony to the wealth of 3rd-century Africa and the enduring solidity of Roman architecture. It was the sixth largest amphitheatre in the Empire, a faithful copy of the Colosseum, whose elliptical arena was governed by the same 3:5 proportion, surrounded by tiers of seats supported on banks of arches rising above three concentric corridors. It is not known if all the tiers were ever completed, but if they were the amphitheatre could pack in a crowd of 31,700. Immediately above the arena a metal screen separated the privileged marble seats of the *podium* from the next two tiers reserved for the mass of free citizenry. Behind them there was a separate enclosure for women and then a terrace without seats, used by slaves. All were shaded from the midday sun by canvas sails. Admission was controlled by *tesserae*, entrance tokens with specific gate, tier and row numbers. The arena had opposing processional gates, a number of ground-level entrances, ramps and four elevators to raise wild beasts and props from the cellars, now exposed by the long central trench.

The outer wall of three progressively diminishing tiers of arches is embellished with engaged columns and a simple dentil entablature. The capitals are carved with palm fronds rather than acanthus leaves, a popular substitution in Severan monuments. This wall acted as a buttress to the inner structural arches, its colonnade a cool foyer where the audience could take a break, strolling amongst snack barbecues, wine shops, bookies and prostitutes.

GLADIATORIAL SHOWS

There were hundreds of different festivals and imperial jubilees celebrated in the Roman calendar. The most important, such as the games in honour of Ceres from the 12–19 April, might be celebrated with gladiatorial shows that lasted from dawn to dusk. These included circus turns, fights between gladiators, fights between gladiators and animals and the slaughter of common criminals by wild beasts and by each other.

The magistrate presenting the show dealt through the *lanistae*, managers who ran stables of gladiators and provided wild beasts. Some of the gladiators, like the *bestiarii*, equipped with capes, Scottish hounds and firebrands, fought only wild animals and were professionals not far removed from modern matadors.

The night before a fight between gladiators, a symbolic duel with muffled weapons was followed by a lavish public banquet. The gladiators were either *scutarii* who fought with broad shields and slashing swords, *parmularii* who used smaller round shields and daggers or *retiarii* who were armed with helmets, nets and tridents. At the start of the next day they paraded in fine embroidered cloaks, their weapons carried by valets, before giving the famous collective greeting to the presiding magistrate *Ave, morituri te salutant*, 'Hail, we who are about to die salute you'. A fanfare of flutes, horns and trumpets announced the first round and some frantic last-minute betting before the crowd roared out its mixture of invective and support. Assistants dressed as Charon used to finish off the mortally wounded, cart away the corpses and rake the sand for the next round. Famous gladiators, when wounded, could usually appeal to the crowd, who would wave their handkerchiefs and either shout *Mitte*, 'Let him go', or *Iugula*, 'Slay him'.

Those sentenced to death in the arena by the magistrates usually met their fate at dawn. They would be exhibited first, and then thrown to wild beasts or tortured to death. At noon, when most of the audience had broken off for lunch, it was the turn of robbers, arsonists and murderers to kill each other. In the words of Jerome Carcopino: 'the first pair was brought forth, one man armed and one dressed in a tunic. The business of the first was to kill the second which he never failed to do. After this feat he was disarmed and led out to confront a newcomer armed to the teeth and so the butchery continued until the last head rolled in the dust.'

Archaeological Museum

The museum with its banana-filled courtyard (open every day except Mon 08.30–12.00, 14.00–18.00; adm) is 200 m from the Hotel Julius on the road to Sfax. It sits beside an elegant dovecot and koubba that shades a drinking fountain, built by Sahib et Tabaa, the philanthropic chief minister of Hammouda Pasha II in the 18th century.

The exhibits are currently being rearranged in preparation for the opening of a new gallery. The central attraction is a magnificent display of 3rd-century mosaics. The sacking of Thysdrus in 238 could not have been better timed for archaeologists, as it preserved some of the most exuberant and characteristic of Africa's mosaics when they were almost brand new. Here the pagan deities appear for the last time with the full vigour of belief, using symbolism soon to be usurped by Christianity. Apollo in his chariot provides a prototype for Christ triumphant, Minerva a model for the Virgin Mary, Orpheus a type-cast Good Shepherd and the man who conquered death. The interlocking tendrils of vines, the harvest and the goblets of Bacchus are all familiar items of Christian iconography.

Nor are the Four Seasons the powerless women of Erté posters, for Thysdrus lay at the centre of an agricultural region, which enacted the ancient seasonal rituals and sacrifices. Mosaics of wild animals still bring the amphitheatre alive with flickering images of carnage. One of the smallest mosaics, undeniably a favourite, is a gladiatorial good-luck threshold talisman showing five fish and five Roman numerals. Today in Tunisia a few days after its birth a baby will be decorated with a necklace of fish charms and fives, still considered the luckiest of emblems.

The museum also houses some sculpture fragments including a headless Isis with robes rubbed to a fine polish by centuries of worship, a fine pair of male thighs, an imperial torso and a priapic statuette. Just by the entrance to the first gallery is a tablet that thanks Emperor Septimius Severus for a new water supply; inside are some pagan grave goods—terracotta statuettes of Eros and Venus Impudica. Below the museum terrace is an area of excavation, of which the two geometrical mosaic courtyards of a palatial villa, partly shaded by cedars, have been stabilized and opened to the public.

Directly across the road and railway from the museum are the remains of an old Turkish cemetery and El Jem's **second amphitheatre**, a more modest and ruinous 1st-century structure that held an audience of about 7000. Its chief admirers these days seem to be goats.

WHERE TO STAY AND EAT
Hotel Julius, the town's only hotel, is cheap, unfussy and charming. Good meals in the licensed restaurant or the central courtyard start from 4 dn. It is calm by day but lively when evening drinking gets under way. There are also a number of cafés, grills and *brik*-makers in town, and the licensed **Restaurant du Collisse**, just up from the Julius on the Sfax road, with an eclectic collection of bric-a-brac.

Kairouan

Arriving from the east, the view of Kairouan fulfils every expectation. The minaret of the Great Mosque, the oldest place of prayer in North Africa, looms above a skyline of sculpted domes and ochre battlements. It was the dominant city of Tunisia from 670 until its destruction in 1057, when only the Great Mosque was spared, and the city has been living off this relic ever since.

Its role as a pilgrimage centre was reinforced by legends of its foundation, a familiar litany of buried gold cups, miraculous springs and the banishment of noxious beasts and reptiles. In the centuries when the journey to Mecca was an impossibly expensive dream, Kairouan served as a North African surrogate. Like Mecca, it was forbidden territory to Jews and Christians and a tradition developed that seven visits to the Great Mosque were considered equal to the Mecca pilgrimage. Pious Muslims would even take off their shoes in reverence as they entered the city. It was ranked, by local tradesmen at least, as the third holiest city in Islam, an enthusiastic claim that ignores Jerusalem and at least a dozen more deserving rivals.

Whatever its current holiness rating, Kairouan offers an unrivalled opportunity to appreciate Islamic architecture in Tunisia. Equipped with a single ticket from the Tourist Office you can get inside the Great Mosque, the Zaouia of one of Mohammed's companions and the bizarre Zaouia of Sidi Amor Abbada, where gigantic constructions praise the name of God, and more. It is a city accustomed to vistors, and has a reputation for carpets and hassle, which are both largely undeserved. For most of the year it is extremely hot and busy, but precious and rewarding enough to take time over.

History

Military Origins
Kairouan, 'the caravan', was founded as a military base in 670 by Oqba ibn Nafi who led the third Arab expedition into Tunisia. His was a quest for glory, a free-booting slave raid and a proselytization of Islam. Kairouan had been a Roman settlement, supplied by a number of deep wells and was a good site for an army almost entirely composed of cavalry. From here Oqba could control the steppe which provided safe pasture for his mounts, and launch raids against the fortified Byzantine cities on the coast and the Berber tribes in the mountains. Twelve years later Oqba was ambushed in Algeria, Kairouan was sacked and the Arabs driven clean out of Tunisia.

Kairouan was refounded in 694 by Hassan ibn Numan who led the final Arab invasion. It was deliberately isolated from the cosmopolitan culture of the coast, a purely Arab and

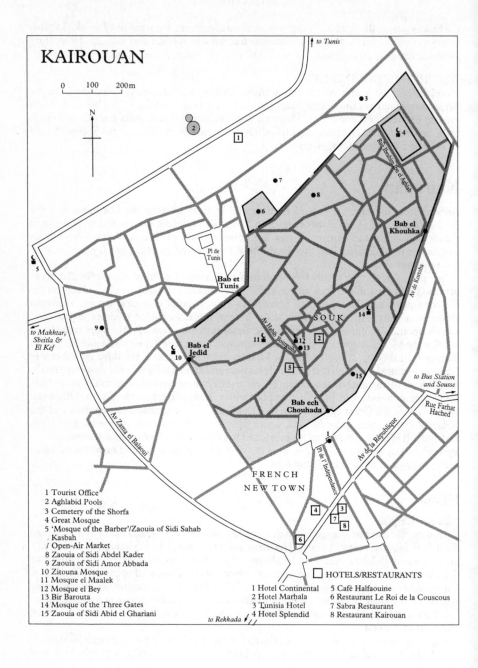

KAIROUAN

0   100   200m

N

to Tunis

to Makhtar,
Sbeitla &
El Kef

Pl de
Tunis

Bab et
Tunis

SOUK

Av Habib Bourguiba

Bab el
Jedid

Bab el
Khouhka

Rue Ibrahim Ibn el Aghlab

Av de Kortoba

Bab ech
Chouhada

to Bus Station
and Sousse

Rue Farhat
Hached

FRENCH
NEW TOWN

Pl de l'Indépendance

Av de la République

Av Zama el Balaoui

to Rekkada

1 Tourist Office
2 Aghlabid Pools
3 Cemetery of the Shorfa
4 Great Mosque
5 'Mosque of the Barber'/Zaouia of Sidi Sahab
  Kasbah
7 Open-Air Market
8 Zaouia of Sidi Abdel Kader
9 Zaouia of Sidi Amor Abbada
10 Zitouna Mosque
11 Mosque el Maalek
12 Mosque el Bey
13 Bir Barouta
14 Mosque of the Three Gates
15 Zaouia of Sidi Abid el Ghariani

1 Hotel Continental
2 Hotel Marhala
3 Tunisia Hotel
4 Hotel Splendid

5 Café Halfaouine
6 Restaurant Le Roi de la Couscous
7 Sabra Restaurant
8 Restaurant Kairouan

HOTELS/RESTAURANTS

orthodox citadel from which armies could be despatched against flickering patches of dissidence. In 740 a Berber revolt, inspired by a heretical Muslim creed, spread like wildfire across North Africa, but Kairouan held out, protected by an army sent from Egypt. Orthodox rule was only fully restored in 767 by an army sent west by the Abbasid Caliph of Baghdad.

The Capital
In 800 Ibrahim ibn Aghlab established his family as Emirs of Tunisia with a proclamation in the Great Mosque. The century of Aghlabid rule was the golden age of Kairouan, though it was deeply resented by the rest of the Arab ruling caste. As none of the Aghlabids ever felt secure in Kairouan, they ruled from luxurious palaces protected by slave bodyguards outside the walls. The city boomed, not just from the profits of government but as an entrepôt for the lucrative trans-Saharan caravan trade. It set the standards in poetry, doctrine, calligraphy, architecture and dress for the rest of North Africa. Even during the Shiite reign of the Fatimids from Mahdia in the 10th century, its doctors of law continued to define Muslim orthodoxy. In 973 the Zirid Emirs returned the court to Kairouan for a last glittering century before its complete destruction by the Hilalian Bedouin in 1057.

The Holy City
In the 13th century, the Hafsids restored the Great Mosque, though religious life in the holy city was dominated by more esoteric Sufi brotherhoods. It became a quixotic alternative to Tunis, its role in the national consciousness defined when Abu Yahia retired from the throne to join the Chadlia brotherhood at Kairouan. From the 16th century it was Tunisia's second largest city though it had no agricultural base or industry, and Saharan trade was in gradual decline. Trade in kola nuts and slaves continued into the mid-19th century, and Kairouan survived as the market for wool from the steppe, on profits from pilgrims and on the great endowments settled on the city's mosques and zaouia. This was offset by its continual embroilment in national politics. In the 1725–40 succession war Kairouan was the mainstay of the Hassaniya faction, who lost when Bey Hussein ibn Ali Turki was killed defending Kairouan.

GETTING AROUND
Kairouan is a black spot for finding your way around, not just in the narrow alleys of the medina but on the major roads out of the city as well.

By Bus
Kairouan bus station is on Rue Farhat Hached, the Sousse road running southeast out of town, tel (07) 20321. There are hourly buses to both Sousse and Tunis, five to Gafsa, of which two continue to Tozeur, and four to El Jem, Sfax and Sbeitla. The three buses for Makhtar and El Kef all leave in the morning, as do those to El Fahs. There are also two direct buses for Hammamet.

By *Louage*/Taxi
Louages for Tunis and northern and eastern destinations leave from the square in front of Bab ech Chouhada, the main gate into the medina from the new town. For Sfax and Sousse, they solicit on the roundabout at the end of Av de la République. *Louages* for inland destinations, Makhtar, Sbeitla and El Kef, leave from a forlorn T-junction beyond the Mosque of the Barber, the site of a Monday souk on the Gafsa road.

TOURIST INFORMATION
All offices and banks are in the drab French-built new town south of the medina. The **Tourist Office** is opposite the principal medina gate, Bab ech Chouhada, tel (07) 20452, and is open daily, 08.00–17.00. It is efficient, as all visitors must buy their admission tickets here. They will provide you with a guide if you wish, but it is certainly not necessary.

Kairouan's main **PTT** is on the roundabout at the end of Av de la République. International telephones do not operate here, but a little way up Av Zama el Balaoui from the roundabout, opposite the Hotel Ettaoufik. There are **banks** all over the new town as well as one just inside Bab ech Chouhada on Av Habib Bourguiba. The **police station** is opposite the Hotel Splendid on Av du 9 Avril 1939. Kairouan's market day is Monday, when the areas outside the north walls of the city and over to the west are packed with traders. The **Hammam Sabra** by the hotel of the same name is men only, and open 05.00–15.00 hrs.

Great Mosque of Sidi Oqba

Open 08.00–12.30, 16.30–17.30 in summer, 14.45–16.30 in winter, except Fri after 12.00, tickets from the Tourist Office on Pl de l'Indépendance. Those looking for a clear and quick route should walk 600 m east outside the walls, turning left through Bab el Khouhka and straight down Rue Ibrahim ibn el Aghleb.

The site of the Great Mosque has been used by Islamic worshippers for longer than any other in North Africa, since Oqba ibn Nafi chose to build here in 670. Nothing remains of the original mosque or its four successors, but the present structure was finished by the Aghlabid Emir Abu Ibrahim Ahmad in 863, and has been lovingly restored ever since.

The Sahn
This marble-paved courtyard is large and serene enough to silence even the most garrulous of tour groups. Its surface is broken by two sundials that cast the hours of prayer, and seven well-heads. These are made from column bases, now deeply incised by a thousand years of bucket ropes, originally hauling up water for ritual ablution. The underground cisterns hold

Mihrab and minbar in the Great Mosque, Kairouan

rainwater, filtered through the elegant central drain and its diminishing circles of pools, which recall the hoof marks familiar to every shepherd on the surrounding steppe.

The courtyard is enclosed by a shaded colonnade. In the original design, the outer arcade was supported by a single pillar, the façade by pairs of columns. The addition of extra columns, piers and struts has given it a more eccentric appearance. The columns and capitals were carted from Byzantine buildings in Carthage and Sousse, many of which had been quarried from Roman ruins. They make a disparate collection, an unlikely museum in which to hunt out tell-tale details such as stags' heads, pagan symbols and crosses.

The Prayer Hall

The actual prayer hall is closed to non-Muslims, but you can admire the marquetry of the great wooden doors as you wander along the higher, more pronounced and secure colonnade in front of them, remodelled by the Hafsids. The *bahu* cupola, rather clumsily repaired in the 19th century, rises above the main entrance, its interior structure clearly showing the Aghlabid debt to Byzantine architecture.

The central door gives a view down into the satisfactory gloom delineated by a forest of 16 serried rows of ancient columns. The larger, decorated main aisle leads the eye to the mihrab on the far wall. Its outer arch, illuminated by another dome, is decorated with a diamond pattern of lustre tiles from Iraq, the inner alcove covered with carved marble panels decorated with blue and gold tracery. To the right is an 11th-century *maksoura* screen and the original *minbar*, the oldest in the world.

The Minaret

Though it occupies the middle of the north wall, the minaret is not aligned with the mihrab, as the courtyard veers east. The 114-ft structure towers above the city with the brooding solidity of its secondary, defensive role. The lower seven courses, made from a jumble of reused Roman stone, and the crude gate date from the mid-8th century, the main body of the tower from the 9th. Its strong angled walls and three diminishing sections echo even older minarets in Iraq. The windows expand in a subtle reversal of the proportions of the tower. The crowning kiosk with its noticeably lighter vertical walls is a 13th-century Hafsid addition. The 128 steps up to the summit are occasionally open to non-Muslims.

Around the Great Mosque

The mosque's exterior wall, once bleak and utilitarian, has over the centuries received a charming confusion of porches and buttresses. The most admired gate is the Hafsid **Bab Lalla Rihana** on the eastern wall, built in 1294 and named after a local saint buried nearby. Its double horseshoe arch is almost deliberately antiquarian for the period, in keeping with the tone of the mosque. South of the mosque, a garden occupies the site of Dar al Imara, the original government palace. To the north, on the corner of the city wall is an 18th-century artillery bastion, and beyond it lie whitewashed sugar-loaf headstones, the cemetery of the Shorfa, descendants of the Prophet. From the bastion you can walk along the parapet for a good view of the domes of the mosque.

The Medina

Pl de l'Indépendance faces Bab ech Chouhada, the Martyrs' Gate, which has become the main entrance into the medina since the French built the administrative quarter to the south.

The martyrs commemorated are 10th- rather than 20th-century for a change. They were Kairouani teachers of orthodoxy who were burnt alive on the orders of the Fatimid Shiites.

Evidence of the original 8th-century earth **walls**, despite reinforcement in 1052, is sparse. The current circuit was built by Bey Hussein ibn Ali Turki after he had repelled an Algerian invasion in 1706. All the gates and stronger bastions date from the reign of Ali Pasha II (1758–81), who repaired the damage inflicted during the succession war. When the French came to occupy the city in 1881 they were unopposed, but arrived so early in the morning that a squad of hussars had to wake up the governor and find the keys before General Etienne could be ceremonially led through Bab el Khoukha.

The central thoroughfare of the medina was only named Av Habib Bourguiba in 1969, after an official visit. For the previous nine years there had been a distinct frost between Kairouan and the President, for the city had led the nationwide passive resistance to his plan to phase out the annual fast of Ramadan.

The **Zaouia of Sidi Abid el Ghariani** is 100 m up the first alley on the right after Bab ech Chouhada. In the 14th century the zaouia followed the teachings of Sidi Jadidi, but his fame was eclipsed in the next century by Abu Samir Abid bin Ya'ish el Ghariani, a Sufi from Tripolitania who studied, taught and died here. The El Ghariani family remained influential, and completely restored the zaouia in the 17th century. The building now houses the offices of the ASM, the association for the preservation of the medina.

A profusely decorated bayonet hall leads into the galleried interior courtyard with its intricate inlaid black and white marble floor and mihrab. Doors lead into a more austere triple-bayed prayer hall and the tomb room, with its central green-grilled catafalque. The two secondary courtyards were used for teaching, and are plain but for their Byzantine columns.

To get to the **Mosque of Three Gates**, take the first left after the zaouia, bear right under a violet arch and right again at a T-junction. After some weavers' workshops the mosque appears on the right. It has a 9th-century façade with bands of kufic script separated by floral and geometric medallions. It is more of a pattern book for carving than a harmonious design, but is of passing interest as a lone relic from the old city. It was built by an Andalucian exile, Mohammed el Maafiri, in 866, chopped around over the centuries and until independence was used as a lodge by the Aissaouia brotherhood.

At Av Habib Bourguiba's natural centre stand a knot of prominent buildings: the mid-street terrace of Café el Halfaouine, the Mosque of the Bey and the green tiled roof of **Bir Barouta**. The latter houses a first-floor pump room where you can drink holy water brought out of the well by a wheel and a mad camel.

Beyond it, three arches lead into thoroughfares of the **covered souk**, which was largely laid out by the Muradite Beys in the 17th century. It is a comparatively small area but still dark and intriguing enough to get briefly lost. It houses both tourist stalls and tailors, cobblers and saddle-makers, practising their craft cross-legged on the raised threshold of their booths. The street names Souk Lekka and Souk Attarine recall drapers and scent-makers who once dominated the commercial life of Tunisia's cities, but were ruined by cheap European imports in the late 19th century. On the other hand Souk Sekkajine's leather workers remain comparatively active. Tunisian leather is now better value than it was in the 18th–19th centuries, when a state monopoly, shared between the Beys and a Jewish clan called the Ghurnata, operated in raw hides. Along Souk el Blaghijia look out for the Hotel Marhala which has a rooftop view over the souks.

Continuing along Av Habib Bourguiba you pass a number of mosques: the Maalek on your left, then Sidi Bou Misra inscribed 'There is no God but God', and just before Bab Tunis the koubba and prayer hall of Sidi el Wuheishi. The gate and its gatehouse are unchanged, complete with vast iron-studded doors, antique columns, inscriptions and a guards' fondouk. The alley to the left, half concealed by the ramparts, was traditionally the red-light district.

Through the gates is Pl de Tunis, a dusty marketplace piled with amphorae, cafés and taxi ranks. The medina walls to the east run to the kasbah, a simple, increasingly ruinous walled enclosure that used to house the military garrison. Between the kasbah and the Great Mosque, the white ribbed dome and stumpy minaret of the Zaouia of Sidi Abdel Kader fills a gap in the walls made by the Germans, who built an airstrip with wall rubble in 1943.

The Zaouia of Sidi Amor Abbada

This zaouia, crowned by five domes and nicknamed the Mosque of the Sabres, can be suprisingly awkward to find. Leaving the medina via Bab Tunis, take the second street left, veering right at the first Y-junction and sharp left at the second. The entrance is 30 m down this alley, on the right. A third of the crumbling mid-19th century complex is open, filled with an extraordinary collection of wrought iron and wood furniture all deeply etched with kufic script.

The tomb room contains a gigantic catafalque and a display of candelabras, chests, chairs, swords and scabbards fit only for the most enormous jinni. It was the cult centre of an illiterate and prophetic blacksmith who had some of his revelations, mixed in with quotations from the Koran, inscribed on 18 massive plaques, a few of which still lie around. The arcane Sufi humour which led to these giant tasks is now lost on the modern visitor, but Sidi Amor predicted the peaceful French occupation of Kairouan. Another prediction, that 'three great serpents, covered with scales and vomiting iron and fire, will encircle Kairouan with their tracks and finding no defenders will penetrate into the city as a punishment for the number-less crimes there committed for centuries past,' is thought to refer to local tank warfare in 1943.

The Zaouia of Sidi Sahab

This zaouia, even more than the Great Mosque, is a place of active pilgrimage. It contains the grave of Abu Zama Balawi, a Sidi Sahab or companion of the Prophet, which has much the same connotations as being one of Christ's disciples. Its mosque is sometimes known as the Mosque of the Barber, since Abu Zama wore a locket round his neck containing three hairs plucked from the Prophet's beard. The zaouia spreads itself on the corner of Av de la République, behind the new formal square and fountain dedicated to martyrs of the national-ist struggle in the 1950s.

A zaouia was first built here in the 14th century, but the present building is largely 17th century, the work of Hammouda Pasha I and Mohammed el Hafsi. Escaping the souvenir salesmen at the gate, you find yourself in a large brick-paved outer courtyard. While the medersa teaching area is closed for repairs, take the door below the square minaret decorated with tiles, a faithful copy of an earlier Hafsid tower. Beyond lies worn splendour in the shape of a tiled entrance corridor, an open marble hall and an intricately carved vaulted chamber, before you reach the sun-drenched sanctuary courtyard. It is a delightful place to rest, leaning against cool, tiled walls under the shade of a yellow stone colonnade and watching the activities of passing sparrows and pilgrims. Leave the saint's catafalque, loaded down with scarves, to his devotees, who bring newborn babies here to be anointed with oil.

The Aghlabid Basins

Aerial photography has revealed a large number of cisterns and pools around Kairouan, for adequate water storage here has always been a problem. In winter wells, which are preferred to cisterns for drinking water, are fed by the spate rivers of the Tell which drain into the Kairouan depression. At the same time the cisterns, which in emergency provided summer drinking water, were threatened with contamination by flash floods. At the 9th-century Aghlabid Basins a 35 km aqueduct from the foothills of the Tell fed water into a small filtering pool and thence into a vast circular reservoir with 64 rounded buttresses. Ever since their excavation they have been almost continually undergoing repairs, and when watertight and surrounded by the envisaged walled garden will be worth the walk.

FESTIVALS
Thanks to its holy status, Kairouan has always attracted big crowds for Ramadan and the principal Islamic feasts, in particular Mouloud. Check p. 19 for the dates, which change each year.

SHOPPING
The goods in the cafés and patisseries of Kairouan are consistently more alluring than those in the craft shops. There is a good selection of leather and traditional metalware but Kairouan is over-stocked with carpet bazaars. Here you will be entertained with tea in a glittering sales room, shown embarrassingly large quantities of killims, mergoums and carpets and exposed to some sophisticated patter. Be prepared to bargain hard as prices are often unreasonable and the stock dominated by ONAT designs (see p. 24). An exception is the shop on the corner of Av Habib Bourguiba and the turning to the Zaouia of Sidi Abid el Ghariani, which has a good stock of killims.

WHERE TO STAY
Kairouan's expensive hotels, the Continental and the Aghlabites, are drab and continuously used by coach tours.

MODERATE
Hotel Splendid, on Av du 9 Avril 1939, off Av de la République, tel (07) 20522, makes up for them. It is a good-looking mauresque building, with green painted windows and shutters, and also has a bar and licensed restaurant. If it is full, try the nearby, new **Tunisia Hotel**, on Av de la République, tel (07) 21855. Though noisy, it has both heating and air conditioning, and all rooms have their own bathrooms.

CHEAP
Kairouan's other special hotel is the **Hotel Marhala**, an ancient hostel in the middle of the medina on Rue el Blaghijia, tel (07) 20736. Ask for a room near the roof terrace, but in winter bear in mind that there is no hot water. The **Hotel Barouta** in the medina is rather down-market and not for women on their own.

EATING OUT
Licensed Restaurants
Excluding the dull restaurants in the two smart hotels, Kairouan has only two licensed restaurants. One, in the **Hotel Splendid**, has a good set menu for 4 dn and the other, known variously as the **Restaurant des Sportifsr**, or the **Roi de Couscous**, is on the junction between Rue du 20 Mars and the PTT roundabout, tel (07) 21237. Ring first as the opening hours are erratic but the food is good and a meal for two should not cost much more than 10 dn with wine. Next door there is a busy drinking bar.

Unlicensed Restaurants and Snack Cafés

There are three good restaurants in this category, where a 3-dn meal can sometimes turn into a gastronomic experience. The **Restaurant Kairouan**, on Rue Soukeine el Houssein, tel (07) 22556, is very friendly and has a daily range of stews and other Tunisian dishes as well as omelettes and salad. The **Sabra Restaurant** is right beside the Tunisia Hotel, an immaculate, popular place with quick service. **Restaurant Fairouz** is in the middle of the medina, up Rue des Tailleurs, which runs off Av Habib Bourguiba opposite Mosque el Maalek. It is very cheap and includes some original spiced dishes. Their couscous is always worth a try.

Cheaper still, Av de la République is lined with booths selling roast chicken, barbecued kebabs, chips and salad. For breakfast, search out Kairouan's speciality, a scone-like flat bap with honey, orange juice and coffee. They are for sale in most off the medina patisseries, hidden behind mounds of Kairouan's speciality, date pastries called *makhroud*. The terrace of the trendy **Café Halfaouine**, in the middle of Av Habib Bourguiba, is the best place for medina watching.

Rekkada

Rekkada, 9 km south of Kairouan, is the site of the 9th-century palace of the Aghlabids. In its heyday it was a glittering suburb of walled gardens, pools and audience chambers, complete with its own Great Mosque and barracks for the rival regiments of negro and European bodyguards. Habib Bourguiba built some university buildings and a presidential palace here, just beyond the excavations, in 1970. The latter has recently been turned into the National Museum of Islamic Art, but despite the promising name is only of interest to keen Islamicists.

The archaeological dig is to the right of the road, signalled by a custodian's house which guards some Roman mosaics and tombs found below traces of the Aghlabid palace walls. A mound of decayed brick marks the centre of Ksar es Sahn, the Courtyard Palace, and the large rectangular basin was the core of the Water Palace, Ksar el Bahr.

The museum (open every day except Mon, 09.00–12.00, 14.30–17.30; adm) is down a palm-lined avenue that leads to a walled enclosure. The pride of the collection are the pages of a 10th-century Fatimid Koran made from blue gazelle-skin parchment and written in gold kufic script. Also handsome is the black Raiharni script, three of the 9th-century Iraqi tiles from the mihrab of the Great Mosque at Kairouan and some 13th-century glass. The coin collection is largely 11th-century, from a hoard of gold and silver coins found 6 km away at Cabra Mansouria, where the Fatimid El Mansour built a palace in 950 to celebrate his defeat of Abu Yazid.

Part VI

THE NORTH COAST AND THE MEJERDA VALLEY

Ruined Roman baths at Sidi Mechrig

A chain of limestone mountains, broken by sandy beaches, runs parallel to Tunisia's northern coast. This area of forests and rocky scrubland has an indigenous Berber population with all the traditional pride and poverty of a highland people. They have also proved fiercely independent and resilient to change. Many a civilization has established colonies and trading bases on this coast, leaving behind only the odd coastal ruin. Phoenician traders, Roman colonizers, Pisan fishermen, Genoese bankers, Turkish corsairs, Spanish crusaders and French miners have all come and gone.

The slow-running Mejerda river runs to the south and east of the mountains. Its wide, fertile valley is a prosperous agricultural region open to outside influences. It is studded with the ruins of ancient cities, dilapidated colonial farmhouses and a chain of quietly prosperous market towns.

From hotels in Bizerte and Tabarka, you can enjoy the coast, its isolated beaches and seafood restaurants, which offer spicy prawns, stuffed crayfish and *spaghetti aux fruits de mer*. Bizerte, despite a pretty medina and ancient port, is the larger and less attractive of the two. It is a good base for visiting the nearby corsair port of Ghar el Melh, the ruins of Utica and the Jebel Ichkeul nature reserve, where 15,000 water birds from Eastern Europe choose to winter. Tabarka, on the Algerian border, is a small, beguiling port complete with an island fortress. It is also closer to the chief attractions of the Mejerda valley: the sumptuous underground Roman villas of Bulla Regia, with their mosaic-paved and colonnaded court-yards, and the imperial marble quarries at Chemtou. In contrast, a walk in the hill villages above the Mejerda or stopping off at old market towns like Béja takes you into the Tunisia of contemporary Tunisians.

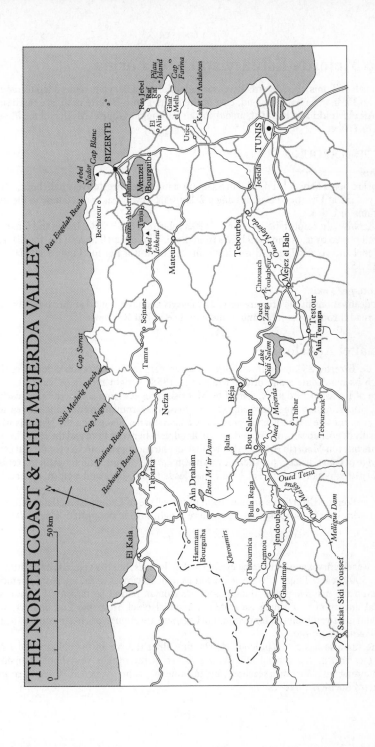

THE NORTH COAST & THE MEJERDA VALLEY

50 km

N

Coastal features (north to south):
Ras Engelah Beach
Sidi Mechrig Beach
Cap Serrat
Cap Negro
Zouiraa Beach
Bechouch Beach

Locations:
Jebel Nador Cap Blanc
Bechateur
BIZERTE
Menzel Abderrahman
Menzel Bourguiba
Timija
Jebel Ichkeul
Mateur
Tamra
Sejnane
Netza
Tabarka
El Kala
Ain Draham
Beni M'tir Dam
Hammam Bourguiba
Khroumirs
Thuburnica
Chemtou
Ghardimao
Bulla Regia
Jendouba
Sakiat Sidi Youssef
Mellègue Dam
Oued Mellègue
Oued Tessa
Beja
Balta
Bou Salem
Oued Mejerda
Thibar
Teboursouk
Lake Sidi Salem
Oued Zarga
Chaouach
Toukabeur
Testour
Ain Tounga
Mejez el Bab
Oued Mejerda
Te, Tebourba
Jedeida
TUNIS
El Alia
Ras Jebel
Raf Raf
Ghar el Melh
Pilau Island
Cap Farina
Kalaat el Andalous
Utica

The Mejerda Estuary and Cap Farina

Just north of Tunis, the Mejerda River meanders across a flat plain to the Mediterranean. On the Cap Farina headland beyond, east of the main Tunis–Bizerte road, are the beaches of **Sidi Ali el Mekki** and **Raf Raf**, an old corsair harbour at **Ghar el Melh** and the Phoenician ruins of **Utica**.

GETTING AROUND

By Bus

There are buses between Tunis' Bab Saadoun station and Bizerte every half-hour, which can drop you off at **Utique** village, leaving a 2-km walk down a signposted lane to the museum and ruins of Utica.

Otherwise, the important destination is **Ras Jebel**, as both Raf Raf beach and Ghar el Melh are well served by taxis and local buses from there. There are 10 buses a day for Bizerte from Ras Jebel and six for Tunis. Buses leave directly from Raf Raf for Tunis every day at 06.00 and 15.15.

By *Louage*/Taxi

Most destinations in the area are served by *louages* and taxis, found at the roundabout on the main road through Ras Jebel and at the entrance to Raf Raf town.

Kalaat el Andalous

Pont de Bizerte, 28 km north of Tunis, was an early area of French colonial settlement, though its handsome stone bridge dates from 1858. A right turn here leads 11 km to the village of Kalaat el Andalous, settled by Moorish refugees from southern Spain early in the 17th century. At that time the village sat on a coastal escarpment overlooking the sea, and had once been the site of the Roman port, Castra Corneliana. Since then the Mejerda River has gradually deposited silt and created a 5-km floodplain between here and the sea. There are no antique or even Moorish ruins to admire, just an entrancing view north over the flat estuary to the ridge of Cap Farina. The Andalucian ancestry of the villagers still shows in the remarkable number of fair-haired children. A new road leads to the shore and a clean, deserted, sandy beach.

From Pont de Bizerte, its another 6 km to the village of Utique (sometimes referred to as Zana), with its Thursday market. From here a right turn is signposted '*Utique Ruines*'.

Utica

Utica was the first known city to be established in Tunisia, but has comparatively little to show for its 3000 years. There are only a few tombs to bear witness to the ancient Phoenician city and even the massive public buildings of the Roman period lie destroyed or buried. The central attraction is a single excavated residential block from the 2nd century AD. The museum is currently closed for restoration but there are enough open-air exhibits to make it a remarkable picnic site.

The site also has a romantic air. Adobe huts litter the site of the old city and a Muslim cemetery crowns the central hill. With a flicker of the eyelids you should transform the surrounding flat plain into a seashore, and imagine the scenery which 3000 years ago attracted the first Phoenician traders.

History

Archaeologists dispute the foundation date of 1101 BC given by Pliny, as the earliest traces they can find date some several hundred years later. However, recent discoveries in Libya suggest that the Phoenicians may have lived for centuries in boat-cities, like the floating sampan communities in Hong Kong, before they bothered with any substantial buildings ashore.

What is undisputed is that for the first couple of centuries Utica was the chief port in North Africa, succeeded by the nearby foundation of Carthage. An uneasy rivalry existed until an outside threat, from the Greeks in Sicily, brought Utica into a subservient alliance with Carthage in 408 BC. This inferior position was confirmed a century later, when Agathocles, having failed to capture Carthage, destroyed Utica. The diminished city attempted to regain its independence in 240 BC, but sided with the losing mercenaries against Carthage and was forced into unconditional surrender. The final act in this Phoenician rivalry occurred in 146 BC when Utica allied itself with the Romans who used the city as headquarters for the destruction of Carthage. Half a dozen lesser rivals perished in this war and Utica emerged pre-eminent, a free city and the provincial capital of the new Roman province of Africa.

These were, however, just glittering titles masking a new subservience. Utica's Phoenician identity was literally buried under a tide of militant colonialism. The city's old temples and street pattern were overlaid by the regular grid of a Roman city. In AD 82, a Roman governor was roasted alive in Utica for failing to further the colonial cause more effectively. There was one irony left. Utica served as the last base for the Pompeian party in the civil war of 49–45 BC under the command of Cato—the grandson of the Cato who had so repeatedly called for the destruction of Carthage. Though the city suffered little direct damage, its connection with the losing Pompeian party encouraged the first Emperor, Augustus, to rebuild Carthage. Roman Carthage became the provincial capital and Utica merely a prosperous neighbour.

The surviving town houses mostly date from the 2nd century AD. Deposition of silt by the Mejerda gradually banished the sea—and hence commerce—from Utica, but it was the Arab invasions of the 7th century which dealt its death blow. Its ruins were quarried by nearby villages but most damage was inflicted in the 19th century when it was plundered by antiquarians and at least one commercial excavation.

Museum

The museum is currently being restored, mosaics are being mounted on walls and even a café is promised. When finished, it will be open 08.00–12.00, and 13.30–17.30; adm.

The museum has objects recovered from the excavations of 1948–58, mostly imported goods—white marble statues of Ariadne asleep and a musical satyr—and some fine imported Greek ware. Notice particularly a *skyphos* or wine goblet painted with a number of scenes: a maenad chasing a satyr; Achilles saying farewell to Thetis, his mother; Laodamia parting from her bridegroom; and Protesilaus, who had the honour of being first to die in the landings at Troy.

One of the earliest pieces is a flat-bottomed pot, or pyxis, from the 7th century BC. Otherwise the red figurative pottery is from the 4th century BC, and the black from the 6th century BC. The indigenous Phoenician products here were all recovered from tomb excavations: funerary stones with their angular Punic script, and oil flasks whose flat disc-like bottoms could be rubbed on the skin. Roman remains from 1st century BC onwards are represented by domestic lamps, nails and glass.

The principal attraction in the garden is the mosaic of the head of Oceanus, surrounded by fishermen and sea creatures. Set in a tank, the colours can be quickly brought to life by half a

193

bucket of water. There are lesser mosaics, capitals and columns scattered around and an elegant worn marble bottom from the 2nd century AD. Look out for a sarcophagus with some of its original mural intact—poppy flowers, a suitable motif for the long sleep of death. The most practical item is the massive lid of a Punic sarcophagus which forms a picnic table under the shade of a baobab tree.

The Site

Five hundred metres down the road, with a separate entrance and admission charge, are the ruins. From the small roundabout, step down through the remains of a house on to a paved road, named Decumanus A and enter **Maison de la Cascade** through the back door. The central courtyard contains a lobed pool and has been planted with a garden of cypress, pomegranate, rosemary and geranium. From here the principal dining-room, the *triclinium*, opens out prominently, its floor a grid of coloured marble, of circles set in coloured squares. Notice the relatively plain U-shaped area of grey and white flooring. This would have been the area covered by the tables and couches of the diners. Refuse was thrown behind to be swept up by slaves, while new courses were ceremoniously brought up the centre. This middle area also served as a stage for intimate floor shows.

The house gets its name from the room to one side of the *triclinium*, where the caretaker will lift wooden boards and sprinkle water on to the mosaic below—the cascade of a fountain. Fish of carefully variegated tones and a livid red prawn stand out against a green sea. Just above the cascade are the traces of a flanking pair of mosaic peacocks. This was not a room but an internal garden, awash with scent from vibrant blooms and echoing with the sound of running water.

On the other side of the *triclinium* part of the stone flooring has been restored to give an idea of just how busy and fresh the floors must have appeared in their heyday. By the massive front gateway of the house is another mosaic fountain. Part of the staircase which led up to the living quarters survives. On the roof terrace one can imagine the women of the house, catching a cool coastal breeze in the evening and looking out beyond the forum to a forest of masts at the docks, ships from Cadiz, Ostia and Corinth gathered to collect the corn of Africa Proconsularis.

The rest of the houses are less interesting. The **Maison du Trésor**, the House of Treasure, gets its name from a small hoard of coins, thought to have been hidden when the house was destroyed at the end of the 4th century. The central enclosed chamber is puzzling to archaeologists, and could be a grain silo. Notice the carved troughs in the long room. These appear all over Roman North Africa and no one can agree on their function. Explanations range from animal troughs, the side holes used for tethering; to bakeries, laundries and warehouses. The most intriguing, and increasingly favoured, suggestion is that they were dole rooms, where the servants of a rich man would find their rations of bread, wine, oil and water.

The **Maison des Chapiteaux Historiés**, is named after the two columns and their decorative capitals, all that remains of a 12-columned courtyard. Made from crumbly coastal stone, originally plastered, they are now so eroded that they are difficult to make out. They depict various historic and mythical figures between the corner scrolls. Facing into the courtyard is a figure with a lyre, Apollo, and to his left is a long-haired Minerva, holding her distinguishing spear. At the back of the pillar you can make out Hercules, his sword resting on his shoulder, and a flower decorates the other side.

The **Maison de la Chasse**, named after a mosaic that is no longer there, is neglected and empty, though there is one good mosaic floor left. Its four floral wreaths, showing sprigs of bay leaves enclosed by a circlet of palm, represent the cycle of the four seasons.

Across Decumanus B, stairs lead 6 m below the level of the Roman city to the older **Punic necropolis**, the only remnant of Utica's first urban period. The massive sarcophagi date from after the 8th century BC. Cuttings can be seen in the lids, which would have allowed them to be lowered on to the recumbent body with ropes. In one grave the skeleton was found with its hands bound and its head severed—a criminal perhaps. In another, a footrest and pillow had been carved. A child's grave held feeding bottles and amulets, whilst one was so well sealed that on first opening it the skeleton was seen perfectly shrouded with a glass vase beside it. On contact with the air, both the shroud and the vase instantly crumbled.

A street called Decumanus Maximus runs from the necropolis past a new grove of trees. On the right you can make out a rough, excavated square, scattered with grey pillars, which used to be the **forum**. Opposite, a wall and high bank are all that remain of the **Capitoline temple** to Jupiter, Juno and Minerva. Beyond the forum, on the summit of a slight rise, are the partly excavated traces of a palace with extensive private baths.

Return to the car park, and turn right through the village, a riot of washing, prickly pear hedges and TV aerials, to the great **public baths**. They are now a pile of crumbling boulders, composed of courses of brick-like yellow stone mixed with some low courses of schist blocks, punctuated by gaping holes and studded with palm trees. The site is recognizably on the old shoreline, and the baths must once have had something of the splendour of the Antonine baths at Carthage, and even now make gargantuan ruins.

Ghar el Melh/Porto Farina

Continuing on the main GP8 road past Utica, take a right fork to Ghar el Melh after the village of **Aousja**. The route buzzes with farming activity, running between smallholdings, divided by tall hedgerows of cypress and scented brushwood. The sandy local soil grows excellent potatoes, smooth and large, which are displayed on the roadside for the attention of wholesalers who drive up from Tunis. As you approach the village, the road dips to run beside a calm shallow lagoon. This used to be open sea and Ghar el Melh an important port. But silt, carried downstream and deposited by the Mejerda, and the formation of a sand spit to the east, have left the village with a relatively useless lake, and only a distant 50-m entrance to the sea.

Sandwiched between this lagoon and the mountain of Jebel Nadour, the village boasts three prominent **forts** which bear witness to its past as one of the chief bases of the Barbary corsairs. Ghar el Melh was well appointed for piracy, being just off one of the narrowest and busiest shipping lanes in the Mediterranean. Over the centuries, the lagoon saw a steady succession of merchant ships being towed across it by the sleek corsair galleys. In 1541, Emperor Charles V of Spain brought a vast armada into this bay for his great siege of Tunis. A century later, in 1654, an English flotilla under Admiral Blake bombarded the port. As a result, British shipping was left alone and in return the corsairs were sold munitions to enable them to attack other European nations more effectively.

Throughout the 18th century the rebuilt port still reaped massive rewards from piracy and continued to do so until 1834 when a pirate arsenal exploded, taking most of the town with it. Ahmed Bey, aware of the new expansionist spirit in Europe after the invasion of Algiers, brought the harbour under tighter state control. A grandiose scheme in 1837 attempted to turn Ghar el Melh into a major naval port but the plan failed due to competition from the more suitable port of La Goulette.

The first of the three forts, a massive squat structure, built from local orange stone, now houses the National Guard. The main road, Av Habib Bourguiba, passes through a white and blue vaulted tunnel at the centre of the village. There is a café and restaurant to the left and a covered market to the right. The Pl de l'Indépendance which follows is littered with more cafés, and beyond stands a late 17th-century fort with a fine gate and marble inscription. Opposite and of the same period, a colonnade shades a fine group of fountains. Behind it rise the satisfying proportions of a square minaret. The outbuildings of the mosque are more recent and house the tomb of Sidi Ali Lechbab, a mujhadeen or holy warrior during the corsair war.

The third fort used to be a prison but now contains workshops and boat-builders. The road continues to the harbour café, a friendly place in a dark clapboard hut overlooking coloured fishing boats, which bob gently in the shallow water.

Sidi Ali el Mekki Beach

From Ghar el Melh, a road carries on through 3 km of almost Caribbean scenery to a new concrete fishing harbour, which has a café and shelters some larger deep-sea fishing boats.

Shortly before the port, a bumpy track to the left leads a further 3 km to the beach of **Sidi Ali el Mekki**. On the shoreline, five palm trees have incongruously grown up in the middle of the beach, and, though dying, provide a langorous and whispering focus for one of the most beautiful beaches in Tunisia. Despite its proximity to both Tunis and Bizerte, this long stretch of white sand is served only by a number of straw huts for rent and summer cafés.

At sunset, the combination of viscous blue Mediterranean, and the orange glow of Cap Farina is outstandingly sensual, and it is an ideal time to visit the two marabouts on the headland. The **tomb** of Sidi Ali el Mekki hugs the mountain and looks at first more like a fortress than a place of burial. Strong exterior walls hide a warren of caves and passages hewn from the mountain wherein lies the marabout's grave. It is a popular place of pilgrimage and non-Muslims are discouraged from visiting the tomb itself, but the view from the terrace is well worth the short climb from the shore path.

Two kilometres further on, marking the end of the Cap Farina headland, is the white cupola of Sidi Haj Bareck, attended by a lone shepherd with his dogs and herds. Here you are welcome to visit the tomb, which is draped in a green shroud and full of devotional items—alarm clocks, plastic flowers, shell pictures and gaudy scarves.

The headland was known to the Romans as *Promontorium Pulchri*, the beautiful promontory. With Cap Bon, it comprises the two welcoming horns that flank the great crescent bay of Tunis, with Carthage at its heart. It also marked the southernmost limit to which Roman ships were permitted to sail, as agreed in treaties with Carthage from as early as 507 BC. This demarcation lasted until Scipio landed his troops here in 204 BC on his way to the decisive confrontation with Hannibal at Zama.

Raf Raf

On the other side of the headland lies Raf Raf beach and the nearby town of Raf Raf. Unless you want to climb over the back of Cap Farina you must retrace your steps beyond Ghar el Melh to the Raf Raf road. The town itself is of interest only as a staging post to the beach.

Raf Raf beach, signposted *Raf Raf Plage*, is a long white crescent, backed at one end by a village and at the other by dunes and pine woods. It faces the island of **Pilau**, a barren outcrop that looks like a listing rusty battleship. If anything, the situation is more dramatic than Sidi Ali el Mekki though seaweed and debris from summer weekends can be off-putting. There is one moderately priced hotel, the **Dahlia**, which stays open throughout the year, has an unlicensed fish restaurant and 10 rooms upstairs. In the summer a scattering of beach café-grills and the smarter Café Patisserie el Andalous open up for business. A walk to the top of Jebel Nadour gives splendid views south over the Gulf of Tunis and west to Bizerte. The lazy and mobile can drive up a reasonable road, unsignposted about 2 km out of town.

Raf Raf to Bizerte

This road keeps well inland, passing through the local administrative centre, **Ras Jebel**. There is a lively **market** here on Fridays in Place Hassen Belkhoja, and a basic hotel, the **Okba Ibn Nafi**, on the road of the same name.

Continuing west, the road bypasses **Cap Zebib**, a promontory scarred by quarrying which shelters a small fishing harbour, on its way to the hillside village of **Metline**. Once a pretty place, divided in two by a stream and surrounded by terraced gardens, like much of Tunisia it is now in the process of being rebuilt with breeze-blocks and concrete.

Following the Bizerte signs will take you below the village of **El Alia**. Its uninspiring, cubist exterior hides an undisturbed heart of narrow streets clinging to the side of Jebel Hakina and rare glimpses of unmodernized architecture. Originally a Roman site, El Alia was settled by Andalucian refugees in the 16th and 17th centuries. The whitewashed houses, picked out in aquamarine and blue, the vivid blue of interior courtyards and heavy doors patterned with nails retain a recognizable Moorish flavour. El Alia used to be famous as the centre of the teazle trade, items much demanded by Tunis hat-makers to comb out their red felt.

BIZERTE

Bizerte has a long town beach, a 17th-century walled medina overlooking a celebrated old corsair harbour, and a convenient French-built new town. It is not overwhelmed with tourists but has half a dozen fish restaurants and as many hotels, good transport facilities and quieter

Minaret of the Great Mosque, Bizerte

197

beaches to both east and west. It is the obvious base from which to explore the northern region, but the city itself has a slightly listless air, and business has never recovered from the departure of the French Navy, stationed at a base on the shore of Bizerte's lake. The streets are gently decaying and only come alive briefly for the evening passeo.

History

Bizerte sits astride a canal leading to the enormous natural harbour of Lake Bizerte. It is fated to be a port, and has attracted a full cast of invading armies. As a result, Bizerte's military history is depressingly active—a recurring cycle of destruction and restoration.

Hippo Diarrhytus

The Phoenicians were the first to build here and to dig a canal linking Lake Bizerte to the sea. Their settlement was destroyed by Agathocles in 310 BC when, to divert attention from the Carthaginian siege of his own beleaguered city of Syracuse, he landed in Africa. He established a Greek colony here named Hippo Diarrhytus and though it lasted only a few years, the name stuck.

The Romans followed in the footsteps of Agathocles, sacking the second Phoenician city in the same year that they destroyed Carthage, and settling the port with disbanded soldiers. This foundation lasted over 800 years, becoming one of the chief naval bases of the Byzantine fleet, and surviving until the Arab invaders learned how to build their own fleet in 698. The Byzantine garrison promptly sailed away, leaving the town to the tender mercies of the invaders.

Muslim Bizerte

Rebuilt in the 9th century by the Aghlabids, Bizerte was later favoured by the 13th-century Hafsid Caliph El Mustansir, who built a palace here and enclosed a vast hunting park to the south. During the 16th-century Hapsburg-Ottoman Mediterranean war, possession of Bizerte was a barometer of fortune. It was taken by the Spanish in 1510, Barbarossa managed to establish a garrison here by 1534, Charles V sacked it the next year and held the fort until El Eluj Ali, the Bey of Algiers, retook it in 1569. Next on the scene was Don Juan of Austria who, after the battle of Lepanto, held it for 12 months before it fell to the Turkish Bey of Tunis.

The shape of the old city today was established in these last few decades of the 16th century. It was improved upon by Youssef Dey, who ruled from 1610–37. He welcomed the last tide of Muslim refugees from Spain to Bizerte, built the present defences and fitted it up as a major corsair base. It survived various European assaults during the 17th and 18th centuries, before being devastated by government forces after a tax rebellion in 1864, and swept by a triple killer—famine, plague and cholera—in 1873.

A French Naval Base

When the French arrived in 1882, they carved out a new canal and built a naval base on the shores of Lake Bizerte, supported by docks and an arsenal at Menzel Bourguiba. In November 1942 Axis troops occupied Bizerte to forestall the advance of the Allies from Algeria. It became a major target for Allied bombing, and from April 1943 not a single merchant ship made it safely to the docks. Shattered, the city gave a very subdued welcome to the US forces when they took it on 7 May.

The Bizerte Crisis of 1961

After the war, Bizerte became a favourite port of call for Europeans, its streets lined with boutiques and bars where prostitutes and drugs were readily available. This happy state of late colonialism came to an abrupt end in the Bizerte crisis. Whilst French rule of Tunisia ended in 1956, the occupiers refused to give up their military bases and arsenals round Bizerte, although the town itself was under Tunisian authority. In May 1961, as part of the Algerian war, the French bombed the Tunisian border town of Sakiat Sidi Youssef. Tunisian fury was further aggravated by the extension of the Bizerte air base in July. Diplomatic protests and demonstrations further escalated feelings, and encouraged the new Tunisian National Guard to fire on a French helicopter.

Retaliation was savage. French troops stormed the National Guard barracks, mortared the medina and in one notorious incident shot a crowd of stone-throwing children. When they returned to their barracks 48 hours later, they left behind over 1300 Tunisian dead. Talks held the following year led to the French evacuation on 15 October 1963. Bizerte remains a garrison town, for the French bases were promptly occupied by Tunisian forces, and it is still the most important military base in the land.

GETTING AROUND

By Train

Bizerte train station is a conspicuously new building some 500 m west of the main bus station on Rue de Rinja, tel (02) 31070. There are four trains a day to Tunis, currently making the 1½-hour journey at 05.40, 08.10, 13.45 and 18.30.

By Bus

There are two bus stations in Bizerte, three minutes' walk apart. The main **Société National de Transport**, serving Tunis and destinations south, is on Quai Tarik Ibn Zaid, tel (02) 31132, whilst the **SRT** is on Rue d'Alger, tel (02) 31222.

There are over a dozen buses to Tunis, 11 to Ras Jebel, five to Mateur, three to Jendouba, three to El Kef and one to Ghar el Melh, and a direct evening coach to Sousse. Two buses a day leave the main station for Tabarka.

The most useful of the local yellow-striped buses are nos. 1 and 2 which ply the coastal corniche road, leaving from outside the Musée Océonographique. Every quarter of an hour the no. 9 leaves the main station for Menzel Abderrahman. Bus no. 6 for Bechateur and no. 16 for Ras Engelah leave hourly from Houmt Shorfa, a square on Blvd Hassan en Nouri.

By *Louage*/Taxi

All *louages* leave from the Rue d'Alger, beside the gardens. For *taxi bébé*, as local taxis are known, go to the pavement surrounding the Syndicat d'Initiative booth on Av President Habib Bourguiba.

By Car

There are plenty of hire offices in Bizerte, so you can shop around. At the moment Avis at 7 Rue d'Alger, tel (02) 33076, seems marginally the cheapest. Otherwise, try InterRent at 52 Av d'Algérie, tel (02) 39018; Hertz on Pl des Martyrs, tel (02) 33679; Europcar on Rue ibn Khaldoun, tel (02) 31537; and ABC on Av Habib Bourguiba, tel (02) 31220. Prices are all in the region of 20 dn a day with mileage of around 0.2 dn per km, or 300 dn for a week's unlimited mileage. Insurance and tax are extra.

By Bike
Ben Khalil's shop, tel (02) 31622, opposite the Agil garage on Av Habib Bourguiba, rents out bicycles for 3.5 dn a day, and motorbikes for 15 dn a day or 4 dn an hour.

TOURIST INFORMATION
The **Syndicat d'Initiative** booth on Av President Habib Bourguiba, tel (02) 32703, is well stocked with pamphlets and a slightly out-of-date town map.

The **Post Office** is on Av d'Algérie, opposite the Café Radar, and there is a **Tunis Air** office in an airplane-shaped building at 16 Av Habib Bourguiba, tel (02) 32201.

There are plenty of **banks** scattered about the new town and they take it in turn to open on Saturday morning. You will find the Banque Nationale de Tunisie on Rue du 1er Juin, and the Société Tunisienne de Banque behind the Artisanat, in front of the old port.

The Old Port

The heart of Bizerte and its chief visual attraction is the old harbour—a basin lined by the blue and white houses of the **medina** and the yellow stone walls of the **kasbah**. Minarets peer above the roofline to add their reflection to the still, dark water. The entrance to this old pirate haunt was guarded on both banks by artillery bastions which still stand.

For the last 150 years the harbour has been used only by fishermen whose gaily painted boats line the quay or stand dry on the dock for repair. The harbour is best seen in the evening when crowds mill around it and the setting sun catches the full luminosity of the scene. As the light fades, tables are moved out on to the quays from otherwise reclusive cafés. After the evening call to prayer, blue, red and white fishing boats nose their way through floating debris to the open sea, their lights flickering on the horizon like a mirror to the stars.

Place Lahedine Bouchoucha

The old harbour used to be one of two quick-flowing channels connecting the sea to Bizerte's inland lake. They made an island of the dilapidated block of houses that now surrounds the *Artisanat*, an island that was once the smartest quarter of the medina. It contained the customs offices, the richest Jewish merchants' houses and the residences of the European consuls. A French consul, residing here from 1686, spent most of his time negotiating ransoms for his countrymen with the Muslim corsairs.

The second canal was filled in and now forms the wide avenue of **Place Lahedine Bouchoucha**. It is the liveliest street in the area, and separates the warren of the medina from the regular grid plan of the French new town. The minaret of the **Mosque of Rbaa** rises above it, next to which is the entrance to the fish market. This is a place of enormous activity, resounding with the cries of the stallholders, skilled filleting operations and much sluicing of water.

The **medina** begins on the other side of Place Lahedine Bouchoucha where an elegant black and white arch frames the dry **fountain** of Youssef Dey. A marble plaque on this Jerayna spring, capped in 1642, invites those who pass to drink from the fountain, an agreeable standby until the drinker is able to taste the waters of Paradise.

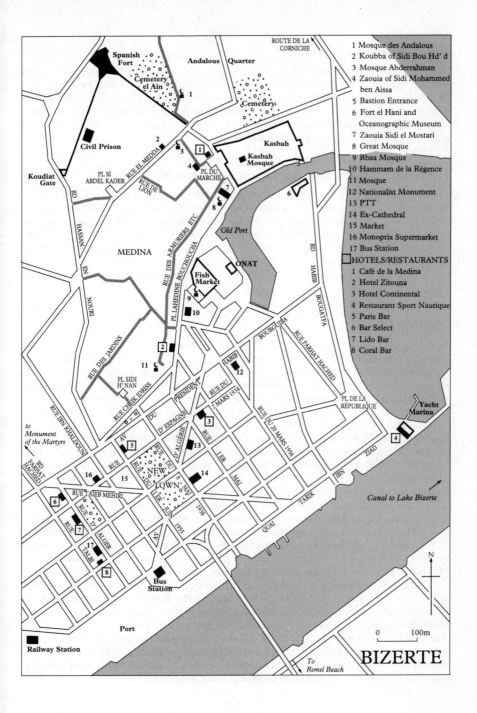

1 Mosque des Andalous
2 Koubba of Sidi Bou Hd'd
3 Mosque Abderrahman
4 Zaouia of Sidi Mohammed ben Aissa
5 Bastion Entrance
6 Fort el Hani and Oceanographic Museum
7 Zaouia Sidi el Mostari
8 Great Mosque
9 Rbaa Mosque
10 Hammam de la Régence
11 Mosque
12 Nationalist Monument
13 PTT
14 Ex-Cathedral
15 Market
16 Monoprix Supermarket
17 Bus Station

HOTELS/RESTAURANTS
1 Café de la Medina
2 Hotel Zitouna
3 Hotel Continental
4 Restaurant Sport Nautique
5 Paris Bar
6 Bar Select
7 Lido Bar
8 Coral Bar

BIZERTE

The Kasbah

The long wall of the kasbah stretches to the west of the old port. For a cannon's-eye view from the artillery terrace of the **north bastion**, walk along the wall to the studded door on the left. The quarter within can only be reached through an arch just below Pl du Marché, which leads straight to the attractive façade of the **Kasbah Mosque**. Alleys hung with buttress arches and painted with contrasting shades of blue wait to be explored. Glimpses of sparkling, deep blue interior courtyards beckon like underwater caverns.

Fort Sidi El Hani and the Oceanographic Museum

The opposite bank of the canal is protected by the fortress of **Sidi el Hani** and its mosque. It has recently been restored and a small **Museum of Oceanography** installed in the rooms. A 200-ml ticket allows you to inspect a dozen fish tanks, holding a shy crayfish, some mussels, flying fish, a sea turtle and purple-headed eels that swim sensuously in and out of broken amphorae necks. Other odds and ends include a mosaic of a sura from the Koran, whale bones, an exhibition of knots and some bottled zoological specimens that are too disturbing to examine closely. The upper gallery of the fort has been turned into a café where you can recover from the exhibits.

The Medina

This, the old city, suffered greatly from the Allied bombing in 1943, and many of the buildings are sadly modern. Until then, Bizerte was still a compact 17th-century town, guarded by four land gates that used to be locked at dusk. The medina held more than a dozen mosques and two dozen religious brotherhoods. The man who presided over the religious life of the city, the Mufti of Bizerte, made judgements that were of national consequence.

Best preserved is the area around the **Great Mosque**, beginning in Pl de la Medina. Sitting with your back to the kasbah, the alley in the right-hand corner of the square leads to the **Zaouia of Sidi Mohammed ben Aissa**. The entrance door is surrounded by painted tiles and the interior is currently being restored, but you are welcome to enter the small central courtyard filled by an orange tree and the scent of jasmine. The domed and painted plaster decoration of the sheik's tomb-room is on the right, his catafalque draped in green cloth. Coming out of the zaouia, **Hammam es Seghir** is on the left.

Pass through the animated din of the **Souk des Forgerons**, the blacksmiths' market, to approach the **Great Mosque**. Its well-proportioned minaret and Turkish-style hanging gallery are framed by street arches and form the single most satisfactory image in the medina. The mosque was built in 1652 by Mohammed Dey, the Agha of Bizerte, when the city was at the height of its corsair prosperity. Beside it is the high stone doorway of the **Zaouia of Sidi Mostari**, finished in 1672 and the oldest and most respected teaching college in Bizerte.

From the Great Mosque, a continuous and tortuous alley runs the length of the medina. It is known under different names, Rue des Menusiers, the Rue des Bouchers and Rue des Armuriers, all of which appear to have little effect on the woodworkers, tourist bazaar and secondhand machinery and clothes stalls that line its way. If you keep straight on, you meet Rue Cheik Idriss where the Bab Jedid, the New Gate, used to stand. Just beyond is the entrance to what used to be the enclosed cemetery and **Zaouia of Sidi H'nan**. It has been colonized by a **flea market**, where displays of old locks, legal textbooks, housecoats and battered copies of muscle and girlie magazines await inspection.

Another well-preserved piece of the 17th-century medina is to be found on **Rue de Lion**, beneath the Spanish fort.

The Andalous Quarter

Muslim refugees from Christian Andalucia arrived in waves from 15th–17th centuries, and contributed greatly to the strength and effectiveness of the corsair fleet. Not only did they burn with a desire for revenge, they also brought practical knowledge of the Christian coastline and trading routes. They tended not to be involved in the actual sailing, which was done by Christian renegades or Greek converts, but made up the boarding and raiding parties.

They were also a fractious and troublesome lot, and were encouraged to settle outside the city walls. Nothing much is left of their settlement, centred on the **Mosque of the Andalous**, immediately below the cemetery of El Ain. Twice a week however, the open space outside the kasbah walls becomes a lively **market**.

The Fort of Spain

The hilltop fortress which goes by this name was in fact built by the great Turkish commander of Algiers, El Eluj Ali, and was mistaken for Spanish by his compatriots when they routed Don Juan of Austria from it in 1574. The fort commands an excellent view over Bizerte and in summer theatrical performances are held in its courtyard. The rough ground enclosed by the city walls below used to be the cemetery of Sidi Bou Hdid, whose white koubba is on the Rue el Medda. A civil prison now occupies one corner of it.

The Monument of the Martyrs

The Bizerte crisis of July 1961 is commemorated by two monuments. There is a greyish-black mausoleum, flanked by fountains of dubious taste in a dusty square of the new town, incomparable with the extravagant **monument** on a hill to the south of the town. Follow the signs off Av Habib Bourguiba and up Blvd Farhat Hached. A towering concrete triumphal arch rises above the unmarked tombstones of 1000 martyred dead. On either side of a processional staircase is a vivid stone carving in best socialist-heroic style by Michael Simeonov. It depicts the French invasion in 1881, the massacre of July 1961 and the final French departure in 1963. The names of the dead are painted in gold on black stone pinned to the walls of a dry moat beneath the monument.

WHERE TO STAY

MODERATE

First choice is **Le Petit Mousse**, a small family hotel with a good restaurant that overlooks a bit of rocky beach about 6 km from the centre of town on the Rue de la Corniche, tel (02) 32185. Each room has its own sea-view balcony.

There are five other large hotels along the beach front, most of which are massive package establishments. Best are the **El Kebir** and its neighbour the **Residence Ain Meriem**, both set in fine gardens with a good stretch of beach. The Ain Meriem, tel (02) 37615, rents out family-sized apartments, for five or seven people, with a fridge and cooker.

On the other side of town, above Remel Plage, the **Auberge de Remel**, tel (02) 32574, has a restaurant, a busy bar and rents out spacious barrel-vaulted double rooms with cold showers.

CHEAP

Cheaper beach options are also to be had at Remel Plage. There is a **campsite** here, shaded by pine trees and just below the dunes, where you can also rent spartan cells.

The choice in town is between two basic hotels. The **Zitouna** is on the edge of the medina at 11 Pl Lahedine Bouchoucha, tel (02) 38760, and its rooms are arranged round a central courtyard. The best hammam in town, **Bain de la Régence**, is diagonally opposite. The **Continental** is in the new town at 29 Rue de 2 Mars 1934, tel (02) 31436. It is a darker but slightly upmarket alternative, and the price of a bed includes free use of the hot showers.

EATING OUT

The best restaurants are all on the seafront and serve largely European food, while those in town leave much to be desired. Snacking at cafés on Av Habib Bourguiba usually produces a better meal than a town restaurant. Do not miss the Patisserie Berhauma opposite Tunis Air, which serves thirst-quenching lemonade, freshly squeezed orange juice, coffee, cheese pies and cakes.

Smartest of all is **Restaurant Eden**, tel (02) 39023, on Rue de la Corniche, almost opposite the Corniche Hotel. The house speciality is *langouste* stuffed with seafood at 17.5 dn a kilo, but the grilled squid at 3.5 dn and sole in orange sauce are equally good.

Le Petit Mousse Hotel runs a fish grill and pizza oven in the garden during the summer months or you can eat at any time of the year in the popular upstairs dining-room. They serve six oysters for 3.8 dn, followed perhaps by a filling bowl of *spaghetti aux fruits de mer* for 3.8 dn. However full, you ought to try the house speciality, *Glace Nougat á l'Antillerie* at 1.8 dn.

Restaurant Le Sport Nautique overlooks the yacht harbour and fire boats moored in the ship canal, at the end of Quai Tarik ibn Ziad, tel (02) 32262. It is a good place to settle down for a boozey lunch, with *brik aux fruits de mer* for 1.8 dn and a cold bottle of Blanc de Blanc for 4.5 dn.

In the summer months there are three other fish restaurants at the far end of the Rue de la Corniche to try. The **Zairouna Restaurant** is housed in a 1950s-style igloo, tel (02) 32120. Perched above the sea is **La Belle Plage Restaurant**, and a bamboo shack serves barbecued fish on **Plage des Grottes** at the far end of the Corniche.

There are two popular pizza houses in town, **La Mammina** at 1 Rue d'Espagne and the older and better-established **La Mamma** at 27 Rue ibn Khaldoun. The **Restaurant du Bonheur** on Rue Taalbi is one of the few cheap licensed places in town and serves a menu of fish and Tunisian dishes for under 2 dn.

NIGHTLIFE

Bizerte is a great place for café life. There is a good collection along Av President Habib Bourguiba, one well sited in Pl de la Medina and in the cool of the evening tables are brought out beside the old harbour.

The bars in Bizerte's new town are almost invisible by day, but when fully open for evening business they are impossible to miss, alarmingly full and exclusively male. The **Café Bar Lido** on Rue d'Alger is the most civilized, its pavement tables filled with smartly dressed groups playing chess, backgammon and card games. The **Canal Bar**, on the corner by the SRT bus station is well placed for a quick beer or an *anise* sipped slowly between buses.

Nightclub/discos operate in all four of the big beachfront hotels, the **El Kebir** being the best. In July and August a **youth festival** takes place and Tunisian bands play in the Spanish fort, the old church and in a hall above the old port.

SPORTS

Riding on the beach is organized from a stall between the Nador and El Kebir hotels on Rue de la Corniche, starting at 8 dn an hour. You can also take a ride in a **pony trap** from here, out to the more remote coves at the far end of the Corniche. There are facilities in front of the Nador Hotel for **waterskiing, windsurfing** and **parascending.**

Around Bizerte

To the West: Cap Blanc and Ras Engelah

Cap Blanc and Ras Engelah, the two headlands west of Bizerte, compete for the title of the most northerly point on the African continent. They both make rewarding expeditions, though the chances of solitude increase as you progress further west.

Cap Blanc

At the end of Route de la Corniche, the beach slowly gives way to a shoreline of rocks punctured by sandy inlets, including **Plage des Grottes**, with a bamboo-shaded café-restaurant. Just beyond, two right turns lead to views of Cap Blanc, one leading under the base of Jebel Nadour, the other up a rocky track to the 261-m summit. The headland fully justifies its name—it is an improbable chubby, white extension, crowned by two hills that drop vertical cliffs into the sea.

Ras Engelah, Bechateur and Sidi Abd el Ouabed

To get to Ras Engelah beach, follow Av Farhat Hached out of town and climb up the hills to the west, taking the Bechateur road. A signposted tarmac road branches off and winds down through a cleft in the limestone hills, past a marabout's shrine and down to the sea. At the shore the track to the left leads to the headland and a charming black and white Moorish lighthouse. The track to the right bumps over pastureland behind the long sandy beach.

If you stay on the road you reach **Bechateur**, a village clustered around the shrine of Sidi Daoudi, built from the easy quarry left behind by previous inhabitants. The whole hilltop is studded with unexcavated Roman ruins, the ground broken by numerous water cisterns.

The road carries on beyond the village to the sea. At the fork take a right to Sidi Abd el Ouabed. It is a small sandy cove beneath a fortress-like lookout post, reached only down a 20-m sand slide. On the cliff of a neighbouring cove there are the faint ruins of a village.

To the South: Jebel Ichkeul National Park and the Lakes

The shores of Lake Bizerte are sorely disappointing. The west bank is largely military and the south industrial, with Menzel Bourguiba's belching iron mill. However, Lake Ichkeul beyond has been turned into a national park and is well worth a visit.

Lake Bizerte

The village of Tinja, 10 km from Bizerte along the western shore, straddles the **Oued Tinja** which connects Lake Ichkeul to Lake Bizerte. The river is strewn with nets for trapping migrating eel and mullet, but is also controlled by a complex dam system vital to the survival of the Jebel Ichkeul National Park. Dams on the rivers feeding the lake increasingly threaten this important winter bird sanctuary, by drawing off more and more water for irrigation and raising the salt level in the lake. About 15,000 aquatic birds, mostly from Eastern Europe, currently depend on Lake Ichkeul for the winter (see also p. 79).

The Jebel Ichkeul National Park
Five kilometres from Tinja on the P11 to Mateur, a right turn leads to **Jebel Ichkeul National Park**. In the marshland to the right, water buffalo graze amongst the disparate herds. The first pair of *Bubalus Bubalis* was given to Hussein Bey by the King of Sicily in 1729 and sent out to Jebel Ichkeul, then a Beylical hunting park. Their breeding was encouraged in the 1830s by Ahmed Bey who used them to haul his artillery carriages, and they have always provided 'sport' for visiting dignitaries who shoot them up the backside to preserve the head as a trophy. The herd was nearly wiped out by trigger-happy members of the American Army in 1943, and by 1963 there were only three surviving females. They were served by an Italian bull, and this herd is their descendants.

Turning right beneath a quarry into the park, the gravel road runs along the foot of the mountain through hamlets of stone huts thatched with marshland reed. Only 120 families are licensed to remain with their domestic herds in the park, and there are plans to stop quarrying the sacred mountain altogether. Hawks coast over limestone outcrops and marshland, and the mountain is the home of porcupine, wild boar and clouds of butterflies.

The road continues through a forlorn group of vaulted whitewashed buildings, a hammam marking the 40°C thermal springs of **Sidi ben Abbes**, which were used even before the Phoenicians arrived. It then climbs a wooded spur to reach the **Eco Museum**, a stone hall with exhibits covering every aspect of the park. Outside there is an excellent view over the shimmering extent of the lake. Skeins of pink flamingos and hawks can be spotted throughout the year, but for the enormous range of wildfowl from Eastern Europe, you should come at dawn or dusk between November and February.

To the East: Remel Plage and Menzel Abderrahman

Remel Plage
A high drawbridge crosses the ship canal east of Bizerte, and a left turn to **Remel Plage** is signposted after a kilometre or so. This beach is wilder than that along the corniche, fringed with sand dunes and shipwrecks, and bordered by a pine forest.

Menzel Abderrahman
For a picnic in unspoilt countryside, take an immediate right turn over the bridge for **Menzel Abderrahman**, founded in the 9th century by the Aghlabid Sultans. The route passes through rolling countryside, wooded by mature olive groves and well-tended smallholdings. The lake shore is dotted with small fishing jetties and fish traps.

From Bizerte to Tabarka

Between Bizerte and Tabarka lies a poor area of mountains, mines and villages, and a series of reclusive beaches. Most travellers cross the region in a few hours' bus ride, and any time spent here passes in a time-warp. Unchanged farming methods, with teams of ploughing oxen and thatched haystacks, appeal back to a 19th-century romanticsm, and forward to today's concern for sufficiency and the environment.

History

The northern hill tribes who inhabit this area have long been renowned for their poverty and aggression. The soil is unrewarding, and few governments have been able or interested enough to impose their rule. The two chief market towns, Mateur and Béja, were known as the Gates of Barbary, the frontiers of central government beyond which stretched the government of the tribes.

The whole area is often referred to as Khroumirie, but three distinct tribal leagues inhabited the area: from east to west, the Moghod, the Nefza and the Khroumir. The tribes were divided into *khams*, or fifths, which were themselves composed of divisions. These divisions governed a couple of hamlets and centred on a *djemma*, where a council of about 40 men gathered to make communal decisions. They were led by an elected *amihn*.

In times of common danger these small republics elected a leader, an *amihn el ulemma*. In 1855, the Nefza were threatened by the army of Ahmed Bey, and the tribe united and massacred the 300 soldiers whom they trapped in a mountain pass. As recently as 1881, the French used the lawlessness of the Khroumir as the excuse for their invasion of Tunisia. Though there was no nationwide resistance, the Khroumir united under the charismatic leadership of Sidi Abdullah ben Jenet, a marabout with a reputation for the miraculous cure of fevers, and vigorously opposed them.

The relative isolation of these Berber tribes has allowed a number of distinguishing features to remain. There is a high incidence of tattooing, on arms and calves in the case of men, and the forehead and chin in women. The Barbary horses are also smaller and leaner than their Arab counterparts, their compact frames reflecting their agility. Only their forefeet are shod, in completely circular shoes. In social terms, the fact that Berber women do not inherit property means that the birth of a daughter is a blessing, auguring only potential wealth from her bride price, rather than the dissolution of family land.

The Berbers also had a strong tradition of paying blood money for murder. The murderer had to pay between 600–800 piastres (when the poll tax was 17 piastres) to the offended tribal community. He was then driven out, his house destroyed and all his goods confiscated. Tribal law was satisified, but the honour of the family could only be assuaged in blood. Sometimes these feuds would leave families with no adult man alive, but the grieving widows married quickly to have their dead husbands avenged.

GETTING AROUND

There are two routes from Bizerte to Tabarka. By bus you travel south through Menzel Bourguiba and Mateur before picking up the P7 and heading west into the hills. If you have your own car the C51 is a slower, prettier route which joins the P7 at **Tamra**, two-thirds of the way to Tabarka.

The C51 to Tamra

Travelling along the western shore of Lake Bizerte towards Tinja, look out for the road to **Teskaia**, 12 km south of Bizerte, which climbs into calm country dotted with old colonial farmhouses and fine views over Lake Ichkeul. As the pasture wears thinner, crop land is replaced by slopes of heather and woodland, and poor, assertive highland girls try a form of hard sell on the roadside. Compact villages give way to small groups of houses, surrounded by pens and herds of sheep, goats and cattle.

Cap Serrat

Forty kilometres from Bizerte a right turn leads to the shore at **Cap Serrat**. The dirt road, through eucalyptus and a rolling scrubland of wild olives and juniper, gradually deteriorates into a sandy track, leaving you to walk the last few hundred metres to the shore. Here stretches a sandy bay with a lone fisherman's hut, and beyond, at the far end of the bay, cliffs capped by a lighthouse plunge dramatically into the sea.

The village of Cap Serrat lies behind the far end of the second beach. There is a school and a café-cum-store amongst the low group of white houses. A pothole of a road, just navigable at 15 kph, leaves the village after the school for the increasingly awkward 13-km drive to **Plage Sidi Mechrig** (see below).

The Route through Mateur to Tamra

Buses from Bizerte skirt between Lakes Bizerte and Ichkeul on the way to **Mateur**, a rural market town. Though badly damaged by fighting in 1943, Mateur maintains its historic trading position as one of the two 'Gates of Barbary'. Before the French Protectorate, merchants planning to trade in the hills would first lodge in a Mateur fondouk, while they negotiated a letter of safe conduct from one of the sheikhs of the religious brotherhoods.

Mateur is now locally famed for its **cheeses**, and for the **Friday market** out by the railway track on the road to Béja. The bus station is at the eastern foot of the town, below the curious steeple of a defunct colonial church and an extensive Muslim cemetery. Walk up through the sleepy shaded café square to Av Mohammed Ali and its central market. Beyond is the old **mosque**, its stumpy minaret rising opposite the painted doors of two surviving **zaouia**. The green door is that of the Aissaouia brotherhood, which now echoes to the chants of an infants' koranic school.

Beyond Mateur, the P7 climbs into the bleaker terrain of the Moghod massif, pocked with zinc and lead mines. Sixteen kilometres into the hills, a plinth commemorates the fighting which took place from November 1942 to April 1943 to secure Bald and Green Hills. Now tranquil-looking places, on 29 November 1942 these two hills flanking the road hid German troops who decimated the first company of Argyll and Sutherland Highlanders to venture towards them. Fighting continued throughout the long muddy winter.

Sejnane, a small village beside a worked-out mine, is famed for its 'Sejnane Ware', often crude, maroon and black glazed maternity figures, which were part of a local tradition of modelled pottery. They were 'discovered' in a nearby hamlet in the 1970s and from this prototype a new range was created by the potters of Tunis and Nabeul. Eleven kilometres west of Sejnane, the P7 and C51 converge at Tamra.

Plage Sidi Mechrig

A right turn in Tamra puts you on the 17-km road to **Plage Sidi Mechrig**, the first 7 km of which is tarmac. In clearings amongst the mature stands of pine, eucalyptus and cork grow unexpected crops of cabbages and tobacco, protected from goats by brushwood fences. The village of Sidi Mechrig contains a shop but no hotel, despite persistent rumours. The beach is an unexceptional sandy crescent, often quite dirty, but perched above it on a rocky promontory are the striking ruins of a **Roman bathhouse**—no more than three intact arches but a perfect foil for the horizontal sea. Behind, partly excavated from the sand, is a mosaic bath surrounded by graves.

Cap Negro

Back on the P7, the turning for **Cap Negro** is again to the right, about 7 km west of Tamra. The 20-km track is a good three-quarters of an hour's drive, and forks five times. At the first four junctions turn right, but at the fifth, before a tiled farmhouse, take the left up a steep hill. The ground worsens, but the *maquis* which clings to the thin topsoil is brimming with variety: dwarf oak, rosemary, oleanders, juniper and so-called strawberry trees. In the distance, plumes of smoke rise mysteriously from the forested hills signalling the hidden fires of itinerant charcoal burners. The last 5 km up and down to the sea is nothing less than hair-raising.

Cap Negro consists of four holiday houses, some fishing shacks and a National Guard post which occupies the ruins of a 16th-century French coral factory. The French were ejected in 1741 by Younes, the son of the reigning Bey, on a successful campaign that also won back Tabarka from the Italians. Apart from the allure of the clear turquoise water and a small sandy beach, the most remarkable feature of Cap Negro is its rock formation. From the top of the promontory lines of resistant strata are visible, heading out to sea like underwater battlements.

Nefza

Back on the P7, the road runs beneath a railway viaduct to the left of which is a series of well-preserved haouanets or grave-chambers. They were used by the Berbers from the 2nd century BC, and are only found in the north of the country, rarely more than a day's walk from the sea.

The town of Nefza has always been the local market centre, a friendly place that comes particularly alive with colourfully dressed and bejewelled hill women for the **Wednesday market**. Their bright red checks and tartan costumes are held together, without a stitch, by massive silver brooches and countless Hands of Fatimah. The Monoprix store can usually supply your hamper with both cheese and wine.

Plage Zouiraa

A few kilometres beyond Nefza, a tarmac road leads 13 km down through pine forest to a beach known as **Plage Zouiraa**. A magnificent long, wide sandy stretch, it is backed by high dunes and a café operates here in the summer.

On to Tabarka

At Ras Rajel, directly opposite the Agil petrol station, there is a **Commonwealth War Cemetery**. A large cross, adorned with a sword, provides the focus for 500 gravestones set in an immaculate walled garden. The elegant white slabs are carved with regimental crests and a few lines of endearment. Most of the dead are from the fighting in March 1943 and all were pitifully young.

After Ras Rajel there is a chance of a swim at **Bechouch Beach**. Look out for the track that creeps through a square bridge under the railway embankment, just before the bridge over the river. A left turn at a T-junction leads through a citrus plantation and on to the beach.

Tabarka

Tabarka is an elegant French creation, a version of their own Mediterranean coast in Africa. Tree-lined avenues separate white stucco houses with blue shutters and red-tiled roofs. Set against the rising backdrop of the wooded slopes of the Khroumir mountains, to the east a long sandy beach stretches beyond the horizon, and to the west there are intimate rocky coves. The town has a fishing port, half a dozen restaurants, a few hotels, an old fortress and an even older history.

For as long as guidebooks have been written, there have been dire warnings of an apocalyptic end to the peace and tranquillity of Tabarka. An airport, a 27-hole golf course, a yacht marina and a 5-star hotel are the newest threats. So far there is no sign of ruin, and Tabarka's history has shown it to be a place adept at absorbing foreigners.

History

Isolated on Tunisia's north coast, Tabarka's history has been dominated by her port since the Phoenicians first established a trading post here around 800 BC. In Roman times, its traditional exports of timber and minerals were augmented by Chemtou marble, wild beasts for the amphitheatre, minerals and corn.

Roman Thabraca's intrinsic importance developed in the 3rd century, when it became an early centre of Christianity. Even during a period of great persecution, in AD 255 we hear of Victorius, Bishop of Thabraca, presiding over a town of numerous chapels, churches and convents. The Christian era lasted until the 7th century, when the town was destroyed by Arab fleets. Well into the 11th century, El Bekri writes of ancient monuments of admirable construction, ruins of the churches which survived.

Offshore fishing by visiting boats from Pisa, Marseille and Catalonia, who dominated the area during medieval times, was disrupted by the renewal of Muslim sea power under the Barbary corsairs in the 15th century. Tabarka became the occasional haunt of Khar el Din, the legendary pirate known as Barbarossa. In one of the numerous petty engagements of the corsair war his deputy, Dragut, was captured by a Genoese galley. Dragut served as a galley slave for four years before Barbarossa could arrange a suitable ransom, negotiated through no less a figure than Emperor Charles V of Spain. In 1544, Dragut was freed and in exchange Barbarossa handed over the Isle of Tabarka to one of the chief banking families of Genoa, the Lomellini. It remained in their possession for 250 years. They and the French, who already held two nearby trading posts and coral factories at La Calle (El Kala in Algeria) and Cap Negro, were expelled in 1741 by an army led by Younes, the son of Bey Ali Pasha.

Tabarka was one of the first objectives of the French invasion from Algeria in 1881. They built the causeway connecting the island to the mainland, built a road over the Khroumirs, laid out the town and added a railway. Their investments did little to enliven the town, which subsided quickly into its current tranquil state. Indeed, so removed was Tabarka from the action, that Habib Bourguiba was sent into internal exile here, staying in Room 1, Hotel de France.

GETTING AROUND

By Air
The airport currently under construction is due for completion in 1992. Until then the closest airport is Tunis.

By Bus
The SNT bus station is one road uphill from Av Habib Bourguiba on Rue du Peuple, and runs eight buses a day for Tunis, half of them via Béja and half though Mateur, where you can change for Bizerte. They also run a daily service to Ain Draham and one direct to Bizerte.

The local bus station operates near the Corail Restaurant on Av Habib Bourguiba. They run a daily bus to El Kef, via Ain Draham and Jendouba, one to Jendouba and two to Ain Draham. There is also an early morning service to Bizerte.

By *Louage/*Taxi

All the town taxis and *louages* leave from near the main roundabout, dominated by the massive sculpture of Habib Bourguiba.

By Car

You can hire cars from the Esso garage at the entrance to the town. The costs are standard, at 20 dn a day, plus mileage, insurance and tax or 150 dn for three days' unlimited mileage.

TOURIST INFORMATION

Tabarka's main street, Av Habib Bourguiba, contains most of the **restaurants, coral shops,** the **PTT, Tourist Office** (only open in the summer) and **banks**. The parallel Rue du Marché, towards the sea, has the **food, fish and vegetable markets**. The **Friday souk** is held between the port and the old railway station.

The Isle of Tabarka

Tabarka's most spectacular monument is the **Genoese fort** which crowns the hill of what used to be the Isle of Tabarka. It was built by the Lomellini family in the 16th century and constantly updated to keep abreast of improvements in artillery. The interior of the castle is currently undergoing restoration, but views from the battlements, inside which stands a black and white lighthouse, are imperious; with the opalescent sea breaking on the rocks hundreds of metres below, the position feels impregnable. Whichever way you clamber up, you will find remains of buildings, both fortifications on the clifftops and houses on the gentler slopes.

The Museum

The town museum is housed in **La Basilique,** just up the hill from the Café Andalous (open 09.00–12.00, 14.30–17.30; adm). This basilica started life as a 3rd-century Roman water cistern and was only converted into a church by the missionary White Fathers in the 19th century. It now exhibits local crafts, contemporary pottery, saddlery, jewellery and musical instruments, though the heart of the collection is the Christian funerary **mosaics** from the 4th and 5th centuries, which were uncovered in the **Chapelle des Martyrs**. There is a lifesize photograph of the most celebrated Tabarka mosaic (held in the Bardo), which has proved valuable in fathoming early Christian architecture.

Roman Thabraca

Opposite the museum and over a wall is a small exposed area of excavation, the remains of the Roman main street and its row of shops. There is another patch of exposed excavation in the town square. Just below Borj el Jedid, the military post above Tabarca, stands **Borj**

211

Messaoud, another Roman cistern converted into a Tunisian artillery fortress in the 18th century. It has recently been made safe and is used for events in the summer festival.

Les Aiguilles

Following Av Habib Bourguiba to its conclusion leads to a natural rock formation known as **Les Aiguilles**, the Needles. These naturally sculpted pinnacles, which rise 20 m into the sky, form the natural destination of the evening passeo.

SPORTS AND EQUIPMENT

Tabarka is the best place in Tunisia to learn to **scuba dive**, having some excellent diving fields as well as an efficient and friendly school, the **Yachting Club of Tabarka**, just behind the harbour. The postal address is Porte de Pêche, BP 8110, Tabarka, tel (08) 44478. To join the club costs 12 dn, on top of which a course of dives will cost 120 dn. This will take a beginner down to depths of around 30 m. If you are already competent, bring your certificate along and, having joined the club, each dive will cost you 15 dn.

The club also rents out boats, both wooden and rubber for 150 dn a day. Snorkels can be rented or bought from the **Magasin Sinbad d'Equipment Marine**, a shop that faces the port and also sells cork floats, line and hooks.

FESTIVALS

Tabarka is well known in Tunisia for its **summer festival**, the so-called *Université de l'Été*. Hundreds of students come to pursue a life identical to any other holiday-maker, spiced with music, debates and comedy reviews in the evenings.

The **coral festival** in July is little more than a promotion for the town's coral shops. Coral fishing is now severely restricted. The depleted beds are under government protection, and over-collection means that specimens are now only found at potentially hazardous depths.

WHERE TO STAY

EXPENSIVE

The **Mimosa**, which commands wonderful views of the town and castle from its terraced garden, has a selection of cool and spacious rooms.

MODERATE

There are two equally good hotels in town, both overlooking the far end of Av Habib Bourguiba. The older **Hotel de France**, where Habib Bourguiba stayed during his exile in 1952, is slightly more expensive, but rooms come with their own bathrooms. The **Hotel Corail**, which has communal showers, is more likely to have rooms free.

CHEAP

For those who cannot afford either of these, try the simple **Mammia**, two roads uphill, or the **Hotel du Port** in front of the port.

EATING AND DRINKING

The liveliest café in town is the **Café Andalous**, next door to the Hotel de France, a tiled extravaganza full of antiques and card games. The bar of the Hotel de France is usually friendly for a drink, but can get very lively. To savour the rare event of men and women calmly drinking and talking together, go to the garden of the Mimosa Hotel, though be prepared for slow service.

The licensed **Restaurant des Agriculteurs**, tucked behind a corner café on Av Habib Bourguiba, serves delicious spicy seafood dishes for around 3.5 dn and a good *salade mechouia* for 2 dn. Another good cheap meal can be had opposite at the **Restaurant Corail**, though it does not have a licence. The food at the **Hotel de France** is less inspired, but in summer the chance of being served the 4-dn menu, washed down with wine, on tables in the wisteria-clad courtyard more than makes up for it.

For cheaper grill cafés, try the side streets above Av Habib Bourguiba, and particularly the **Restaurant El Hana**, where a meal of fish and vegetables comes to just 2.3 dn.

Around Tabarka

Below Melloul village, which is 7 km west of Tabarka and serves as the border post with Algeria, you can swim in Melloul Bay. A very eroded track leads down from the village café to the rocky beach used by half a dozen fishing boats.

The Galite Archipelago

The most adventurous expedition is out to Galite, a volcanic archipelago of half a dozen islands 50 km northeast of Tabarka. **La Galite**, the largest isle, is about 5 km long and 2 km wide, and is reported to have faint traces of Roman settlement and some enduring rock-cut Phoenician graves. The only way out there is to befriend a fisherman or hire a fishing boat, though you may be told that it is now an official nature reserve.

La Galite witnessed the final scene of the North African campaign. A small British naval force was sent to liberate this last piece of North African territory and came into the tiny harbour to be greeted by Monsieur le Maire. Complete with tricoleur sash, he was escorted by the village elders who all made moving speeches, so moving that one of the speechmakers was overcome by his rhetoric and fell into the harbour. The proceedings were interrupted while he was hauled ashore.

Those with a shark phobia may be discouraged by the 1200-kg great white shark that was caught off La Galite in December 1988.

Ain Draham

The approach to Ain Draham from Tabarka spirals dramatically up the valley of the Oued el Kebir. The driving is made even more exciting by local children playing 'chicken' with the cars, and going in for some aggressive roadside salesmanship with their pine nuts.

Ain Draham, which means the 'spring of money', sits in a col between two mountains. It is an ex-colonial hill resort, surrounded by pine and cork forests, and was used by the French to escape the summer heat of the plains. The reason for its continuing popularity hangs on practically every café wall. In Tunisia, framed reproductions of alpine scenery seem to have an almost mystical quality, as if depicting paradise on earth. Unless you have sweltered for half the year, however, the cool, scented winds of Ain Draham will probably have less of an appeal.

French settlement began with a fort established to keep an eye on the undisciplined Khroumir tribes. The surrounding slopes were soon dotted with dreary mock-alpine chalets, haunted by the ghosts of chaperoned daughters going on path-bound walks in the hope of a chance meeting with a suitable bachelor. Throughout the Algerian Resistance (1956–64), Ain Draham was a vast refugee camp; now it is like a suburb in a pine forest. The drive across the mountains from Tabarka to Djendouba should not be missed, however, and cool air and solitude are to be had at the isolated **Hotel les Chênes**, 8 km south of Ain Draham.

GETTING AROUND
All Ain Draham's public transport leaves from the T-junction in the centre of town. There are daily buses to El Kef and Jendouba, and three buses a day for Tabarka. *Louages* also leave frequently for Tabarka and Jendouba, but be prepared for some competitive seat-grabbing.

TOURIST INFORMATION
A walk up the main street towards the **Beauséjour Hotel** naturally leads past the half dozen cafés, sandwich stalls and souvenir shops that make up the centre of the town. The **PTT** is just beyond the Beauséjour and the STB **Bank** is opposite the mosque with the brick-faced minaret. In summer the **municipal pool** is open, two blocks below the youth hostel, a long yellow bungalow with a high-pitched roof, on the other side of town.

Walks
The two obvious introductions to the area are to walk up to the summits of the two mountains that flank Ain Draham. The eastern peak, **Jebel Bir** (1014 m), is approached from the track behind the brick-faced mosque though the way is circumscribed by barracks and military zones. The views north down the Oued el Kebir valley are immediately rewarding.

The western summit, **Jebel Fersig**, is approached on a tarmac road known as the **Col des Ruines**. It is a loop that swings off the Tabarka road about 500 m north of Ain Draham and twists through an attractive old cork wood, sprinkled with chalets, to a spring and overgrown viewing terrace. From here, on a broad gravel track, it takes half an hour to reach the top.

The season for boar hunting is from the end of September to February, so out of season there is no danger in exploring the mountain tracks that stretch east from Ain Draham. These could take you across to Béja, Nefza or down to Tabarka, but only appeal to hardened all-day walkers.

Boar Hunting
The Hotel Les Chênes offers a comprehensive service for those who wish to hunt boar, including running the hunters to and from the airport. They suggest a weekend trip, which includes two days of hunting, or a week's stay with five days in the forest. As prices continually change, you are advised to telephone the hotel on (08) 47211/315, or telex them on (08) 80025. It is wise to book several months in advance as schedules become very full. There are also a number of time-consuming formalities which have to be adhered to in order to license the hunter and his gun, and to arrange export licences for trophies.

WHERE TO STAY AND EAT
MODERATE
The **Hotel les Chênes** is the place to head for if you are looking for isolation and a certain decaying sporting lodge charm. Entirely alone, just beside the Jendouba road 8 km south of

Ain Draham, you can ask the local bus or *louage* to drop you off. Try to get rooms 31, 32 or 33, which have large balconies overlooking the surrounding forest. As there is no *à la carte* menu it is safe to go for full board—38 dn a double—otherwise a meal is 5 dn a throw. Licensed, with a pool and the inevitable stuffed boars, the hotel will often allow camping if you ask politely; tel (08) 47211/47315.

In Ain Draham there are two hotels. The **Hotel Beauséjour**, tel (08) 47005, is creeper-covered and old colonial in look. The patron's family has now expanded to fill all the bedrooms, so guests are lodged in the **Hotel Khroumir**, a wholly-owned subsidiary 20 m behind. The restaurant is still in the ground floor of the main block, the menu of the day costs 4.5 dn, and an excellent ice cream is served on the terrace.

Less preferable is the **Hotel Rihana**, a large modern affair with a bar and restaurant on the loop road at the edge of the town, tel (08) 47391.

Around Ain Draham

Hammam Bourguiba

The tarmac road to Hammam Bourguiba starts at the village of **Babouch**, 5 km north of Ain Draham. The woods around here were some of the wildest and least explored in the country when the French arrived in 1881. Within 20 years they had shot the last native lion and by 1932 the panther had also been hunted into extinction. It was a bad period for conservation elsewhere as well. The last crocodile in a Saharan oasis was killed in 1930, the last addax and the last oryx antelope shot soon after the turn of the century.

Babouch has a border post with Algeria, but the road to Hammam Bourguiba branches off and leads 10 km to the open valley of the Ouled Barbar tribe who have their weekly market on Thursdays. **Hammam Bourgiba** began when the President had a chalet built below this tribal hamlet, above an open-air thermal pool, but everything has now been absorbed into an hotel.

The hotel has an appalling atmosphere, a mixture of hospital and country club, and the hot spring has been obscured and channelled into a pseudo-medical cellar complete with showers, massage rooms and a mineral pool. A few vestiges of the old Roman baths are displayed by the hotel door. If this appeals, a double room costs 25 dn, use of the thermal bath 2.4 dn, and a massage 3 dn.

Beni M'Tir and Fernana

The turning to the **Beni M'Tir dam** is about 9 km south of Ain Draham, 1.5 km from the Hotel les Chênes. The route through cork and oak woods is splendid but the lake itself, being a hydro scheme, is not for swimming.

The village of **Fernana**, on the edge of the forest zone, has a curious history. The name means cork tree in Arabic, and a massive cork oak once stood here and acted as an oracle for the Khroumir tribes. Questions were addressed to the tree and from the responding rustle of the leaves, an answer was formed. Its last oracle was to approve of the border raid that resulted in the French invasion of 1881.

215

The Mejerda Valley, from Tunis to Mejez el Bab

The main road from Tunis to Mejez el Bab, the P5, runs considerably south of the **Oued Mejerda**. To follow the river itself, take the old minor road or the train, which follows this longer and slightly prettier route through **Tebourba**.

To Mejez el Bab via Tebourba

Leaving Tunis on the road to Mateur, the P7, the remains of the great **Roman aqueduct** which brought fresh water from the hills at Zaghouan to Carthage can be seen. **El Battan**, 'the dam', 34 km from Tunis, was named after the ruins of a Roman dam over the Mejerda. In the early 17th century, a new bridge/dam was built on the Roman foundations, with a series of mills. Overlooking the millpond, a Beylical palace, barracks and storehouses were also added, but are now in a state of total decay.

Tebourba

Tebourba, named after its Roman predecessor **Thuburbo Minus**, had its heyday at the height of Beylical rule, from the 16th to the 18th centuries, when as an administrative centre it commanded the roads to both Mateur and Mejez. It is now a quiet backwater and a centre of wine-making, not without some charm. The **market square** is lined with cafés, booths and the entrance to the covered market, its skyline disturbed by small minarets, which peek on to the square. The streets behind retain even more of their Beylical feel, enhanced by the soft patina of whitewash, tinged with blue. Find someone to show you the **Zaouia of Sidi ben Aissa**, an 18th-century religious college, where a koranic school works in conditions of unusual calm beneath the carved plaster dome.

Longstop Hill

From Tebourba, the C50 follows the railway line to Mejez el Bab. At the hamlet of **El Heri**, a small monument reads 'Longstop Hill. 23/24 Dec 1942 Coldstream Guards; 24 April 1943 Argylls, Surreys, Kents, Northern Irish Horse'—a cryptic memorial to some of the heaviest fighting in the Tunisian campaign. 'Longstop' was the English name for the rough wooded spur that runs along the north of the valley, and commanded the road east to Tunis. The Allies failed to capture it in December 1942, thus halting their advance on the capital for the winter. When they attacked again on a fine, still Good Friday morning in 1943, three brigades of crack Panzer Grenadiers were dug in, defending their position. The summit was stormed by the Argyll and Sutherland Highlanders, but out of an entire battalion they were reduced to 40 men. To capture the whole ridge, the fighting continued for four days.

The P5 to Mejez el Bab

Massicault Commonwealth War Cemetery

This melancholy memorial lies 30 km from Tunis, sloping uphill from the road to two pavilions which flank a 'Cross of Sacrifice', an old crusading symbol. There are 1578 men buried here beneath a perfect parade of white headstones, 130 of them never identified. A group of headstones near the entrance gives some idea why not: beneath it lie the remains of the crew of an anti-tank gun, whose five bodies were inextricably muddled in the carnage of their death. The burials date mostly from late April–May 1943, the final bloody push to Tunis when, during one engagement, 150 German paratroopers under the command of a sergeant repelled an attack with the loss of just three men, but destroyed nine tanks and 300 Royal Fusiliers.

Sidi Medien and the Goubellat Plain

Almost 20 km beyond the cemetery, a left turn to Sidi Medien takes a loop road through the fertile Goubellat plain to Mejez el Bab. Sidi Medien, a small farming hamlet, sits above the **Oued el Hamar**. On the far side of the river bed lie the extensive but undistinguished remains of Roman **Colonia Vallis**. The summit of the small hill is crowned by the remains of a temple and, beneath it in various stages of decay, lie baths, part of an aqueduct and some water cisterns.

Following the course of the river, the road swings round to the red-tiled roofline of Goubellat, once the centre of a large colonial settlement in one of the most fertile areas of Tunisia. The rightful owners are back in possession but they live amongst the shadows of colonial architecture. The spire of the Romanesque stone church is still as prominent as the new minaret. A right turn in town twists through low hills and descends to Mejez el Bab.

Mejez el Bab

Mejez el Bab is a dusty sprawling town of 12,000 inhabitants and a strategic bridging point over the Mejerda, which commands the last narrow gap in the hills before Tunis. Routes from Algeria and the west converge here, and in December 1942, the Axis Commander-in-Chief, Kesselring, sent a terse rebuke to General Nehring, quoting the wisdom of Hannibal: 'He who holds Membressa holds Carthage.' Nehring knew enough history to know that the ancient city of **Membressa** was the modern railhead of Mejez el Bab.

Very little remains of this Roman past, for that which had survived into the 20th century was destroyed in the fierce fighting and bombardments of the Second World War. The narrow congested bridge contains fragments of its old Roman counterpart, and the garden of the nearby government offices is littered with fragments—a broken pillar or two and a number of stone inscriptions.

GETTING AROUND

By Train

The train station is several kilometres from the centre of town, and you will need to find a taxi to take you there. There are seven trains a day to Tunis and Béja, six of which continue to Ghardimao and one to Algeria.

By Bus and *Louage*

Buses to Tunis, Béja, Jendouba and El Kef leave frequently from the large open bus station by the bridge. *Louages* to Béja and Tunis, and *taxis rurals* which will take you to the surrounding villages, also leave from the bus station.

WHERE TO STAY AND EAT

If you get stuck in Mejez el Bab, there is a cheap hotel, the **Membressa**, just across the bridge from the bus station. They serve good barbecued meat, fish and salad in the outdoor restaurant.

Around Mejez el Bab

Chaouach

For a good view of the Mejerda Valley and a slice of rural life, visit the hill village of Chaouach on the limestone escarpment northwest of Mejez. *Taxis rurals* ply the route regularly. If you are driving yourself, turn to the north by the Hotel Membressa. Just beyond the railway bridge, the road to the hills is signposted 'Toukabeur'.

At **Toukabeur** the main road bends around a series of barrel-vaulted stables and work-shops—old Roman cisterns put to good use. The older part of **Chaouach**, 3 km beyond, sprawls within walls that were once a Byzantine fort. The terrace by the mosque, right on a cliff edge, has the best view and benches made from Roman pillars, possibly from a temple on the same spot. Below march olive trees, camouflaging two ruined Roman arches, part of the ancient town of **Sua**.

Mejez el Bab Commonwealth War Cemetery

Three and a half kilometres southwest of Mejez, on the road to Testour, is the largest of Tunisia's eight Commonwealth war cemeteries. The shaded garden, lawn and flanking pavilions are in striking contrast to the dust and traffic of Mejez, and make a reflective place to hide from the afternoon heat. There are almost 3000 tombstones here and a memorial to the 2000 soldiers of the First and Eighth British Armies who were never recovered from the battlefields of North Africa.

The architect, Hubert Worthington, seems to have exceeded his brief in claiming that the reason for these deaths was 'to set free North Africa'. Seen from a Tunisian perspective, it was a civil war between their colonial overlords and other Christians, unfortunately waged on their soil and with some of their citizens. Many of the comments in the visitors' book marvel at the state of the garden. Since foreigners have long commented that the only true religion practised in England is gardening, it seems a fitting tribute to the British dead that they should be swathed in such a requiem of shade, colour and scent.

Though it is very peaceful now, spare a moment to ponder on this description of the devastation at Fort McGregor near Mejez el Bab: 'The little hill was a mass of twisted blasted corpses. Those that had fallen, both British and German, in the original attack had been pounded to bits by artillery and lay in untidy heaps in weapon pits, holes and out in the open. It was a sight that one hopes to forget but never can.' (A soldier from B Company)

The Road to Béja

Modern **Oued Zarga**, the blue river, is a savage and mournful village on the main road, moved here when the Sidi Salem Dam drowned the old village. This lay below the hill to the east, beside a signposted **British War Cemetery**. The cemetery, beside a half-drowned village in the shade of a half-demolished colonial church, has a haunted feel. There are 239 British and Indian soldiers buried here, looking over the flooded valley, with dead trees emerging above the water level. Here also the rebellion of September 1881 against the French invasion began, when 11 European railway workers were burned alive.

Continuing to Béja, the road passes close to the lake before climbing into undulating hills. To the north is the vivid silhouette of **Jebel Munchar**, 'the Saw'. Munchar's atmosphere is malignant. Memories linger from the defeat of the mercenaries in 238 BC. As recorded by

Polybius and repeated by Flaubert, the mercenary army were trapped by the Carthaginians in the defile of a mountain called 'the Saw'. In desperation they descended to cannibalism, and when their ten leaders came out to negotiate with Hamilcar he crucified them. The leaderless army were then slaughtered, but Hamilcar disdained to tire his troops and sent in his elephants to trample them to death.

Béja

Béja is not everyone's idea of a holiday town. It is a quietly prosperous agricultural centre of about 30,000 people, and has one bar, two cinemas and a reputation for work rather than leisure. At its heart however, Béja nurses an unchanged medina, a place of mosques and markets virtually untouched by tourists.

History

Béja is a natural marketplace on the border between the pastoral economy of the hills and the corn-growing plains, and has therefore been consistently fought over and despoiled.

An outpost of Carthage in the 6th century BC, it passed into the domain of the Numidian kings four centuries later. Even then it was the acknowledged centre of the corn market, a rich prize which attracted the attention of the expansive Romans. Early in the Jugurthine War it surrendered, but later rebelled and massacred the Roman soldiers garrisoned there. The officers of the garrison had their throats cut as they sat at a banqueting table, guests of the town's leading citizens. The leaderless soldiers were then attacked in the street, and stoned to death from the rooftops by women and children. Two days later the Romans took their revenge, and the 'large and wealthy town was completely destroyed' (Sallust).

Later sieges are less well documented. The town was sacked by the Vandals in 448, and fortified by the Byzantines in the 6th century when it was named after Justinian's wife, Theodora. It bounced back from a series of Arab sackings in the 9th–11th centuries, to be described by the Arab geographer El Idrissi in 1154 as 'a beautiful city, built in a plain with not a city so important or more rich in cereals in the whole of the Maghreb'. The role of market continued, and Béja became one of the two 'Gates of Barbary', mediating between the government in Tunis and the lawless Berber tribes of the northern highlands (see p. 207).

GETTING AROUND

By Train
The train station lies downhill from the Béja's central square. It is on the line which runs from Tunis to Algeria via Ghardimao, and there are seven trains a day to and from the capital. In the other direction, six trains continue to Ghardimao via Jendouba, and one carries on to Algeria.

By Bus
The bus station is below the railway line on the main Jendouba road. There are 18 buses a day to Tunis and eight to Jendouba, of which three continue to Ain Draham. There is one direct

bus for El Kef and one for Teboursouk, as well as four for Tabarka, four for Bizerte and two for Sousse.

By *Louage*/Taxi
The *louage* station is over the railway line from the bus station and turn right on to the road which runs beside the tracks. The most regular destination is Tunis, but some *louages* operate to Jendouba.

TOURIST INFORMATION
There are **banks** and a **PTT** on Béja's central crossroads by the church, but the town is not geared up for tourism. Try to cash cheques and make telephone calls somewhere else.

The Medina

Right in the centre of Béja stands the French colonial **church**, a strange hybrid with a minaret-like steeple, complete with stork's nest. The flower-covered koubba beside it is no thoughtful folly, but the **tomb of Sidi Abu Arbaa** which predates the whole ensemble.

The main thoroughfare of the medina, **Rue Kheireddine**, leads off to the right of the church, and is entirely bordered by shops. Morning and evening, the street is a sea of three colours: white—the haiks of the women and the walls; red—the old men's skull-caps; and blue—the painted woodwork and canopies. Steam from huge vats of soup wafts spices and shimmering confusion into the mêlée, and above the roofs, you catch glimpses of a stubby, whitewashed minaret here, the green-tiled dome of a holy tomb there.

Just as you enter Rue Kheireddine, you pass the **song-bird shop** on the right, stocked by boys who trap finches in the woods round the kasbah. The first major turning on the left leads to **Pl Abdel Kader**, a cobbled area shaded by trees, and thence to a larger auction square, lined with cafés.

Markets
Opposite is **Rue el Attarine**, the entrance to a parallel set of souks. Here you will find secondhand clothes, dry goods, spices and chickens, each giving a distinctive aroma to its quarter. Continuing parallel to Rue Kheireddine, another arch announces **Souk en Nehasach**, a narrow street lined with blanket merchants. Their goods are all supplied by local weavers, the work is of excellent quality and the prices are low. Beneath the blankets you find more intriguing old pieces—swatches of killim, saddle bags and highly original weaves; some of the best buys in Tunisia are to be had here. Leather and heavy-weave pack saddles for mules and donkeys are made in the neighbouring alleys.

Water gate and Koranic School
Souk en Nehasach leads back to Rue Kheireddine. Continuing up here, look out for a left turn to the **Bab el Ain**, or water gate. Out of an old stone wall pours a spring of cool, clear water, protected from harm by the marabout's tomb behind. To the right, on Pl Khemis Bedda, a crumbling green-tiled roof, like a crushed felt hat, crowns the **Zaouia of Abdel Kader**. Once the home of a religious brotherhood, it continues part of its old function as a koranic school for poor children. As well as being instructed about Islam, they are given basic

secular schooling, food and often clothes. The teachers are welcoming and happy to show you the interior courtyard, carved dome and tomb-room.

The Kasbah
The crowning kasbah is still occupied by soldiers and best appreciated from the town. For 1400 years this Byzantine fortress has been sacked and restored by succeeding waves of invaders, and old habits die hard.

The Colonial and Commonwealth War Cemeteries

The new town does not have much to offer, though the Colonial and Commonwealth war cemeteries have a certain charm. You will find them just beyond the *louage* station on the road beside the railway line. Where the **war cemetery** is an immaculate stretch of garden, the neighbouring colonial graves are a riot of decay, pecked over by the custodian's chickens, ducks, turkeys, goats and amicable sheep. From the number of Italian memorials, it seems that Sallust could have written two millennia later that Béja was 'the most frequented market in the whole kingdom; many Italians used to settle there for purposes of trade'.

WHERE TO STAY AND EAT
The **Hotel Phénix**, 37 Av de France, tel (08) 50188, is cheap and the best on offer. It occupies a first-floor corridor, has a dozen large bedrooms with old comfortable beds, a prolific, hot, communal shower and a barely functioning lavatory. The current price is 9 dn a double. If by some freak this is full, the **Hotel de France** is on Pl Chedly Rhaidem behind the Phénix.

The **Café el Hana** in the same square serves good strong coffee and *pain au chocolat* for breakfast.

Beneath the Hotel Phénix is the **Brasserie Phénix**, Béja's only licensed bar and restaurant (closed Fri). Until you have been here, you have not seen drunk male camaraderie at its height. Simple grilled meat or fish, salad and wine are yours for no more than 6 dn a head.

Opposite the Phénix, the **Restaurant La Belle Époque** is run by a large and genial patron. Ask him for the specials of the day, as he prides himself on introducing traditional Tunisian food to the few tourists that come his way.

Around Béja

There are three possible directions in which to head to escape the midday heat and lassitude of the town for a picnic, though they are pretty awkward without your own transport. Leaving town past the bus station, a left turn to Nefza leads over the **Khroumir hills**, along oleander-strewn riverbeds, to the north coast. The shores of **Sidi Salem lake** to the south are peaceful and deserted, but the fine Roman bridge that once stood here, the *Pont de Trajan*, has disappeared beneath the recently dammed water.

Belalis Major

Despite its name, this is only a minor Roman site. Most of it is at ground level or below, but it is a romantic and picturesque spot where you can picnic in the shade of fig trees, beside an ancient forum.

To get there, take the Mateur road and turn right up a farm track after the 8-km milestone. Five hundred metres up the track, towards a cypress hedge, you reach the custodian's house. Walk to a clump of four fig trees which identify the **House of the Priest**. The mosaics have been taken away for restoration, but Christian symbols and inscriptions remain on the paving in the courtyard.

On your way to the next clump of half a dozen fig trees beside the paved **forum**, you pass the **baths**, identifiable by a deep well and a **maze mosaic**, whose red and black labyrinth leads to a central panel where Theseus is slaying the Minotaur. The crudely carved stelae lying around, depicting men in togas carrying animals, commemorate the fulfilment of a vow to make a sacrifice to the wrathful Saturn, a god whose influence seems to have persisted here well into the Christian era. On the other side of the forum, a single white pillar stands in the ruins of a small **church**. Beneath another pillar is a small cruciform baptismal font.

Beside the cypress hedge on the far edge of the site are the confused traces of a larger church or **cathedral**. Two white pillars peek above the walls of the **fort** which surround it. These walls date from the Islamic period, and this may be one of the few pockets where Christianity survived in North Africa, until the Almohads and Bedouin Arabs exterminated the faith in the 12th century. Look out for a fine early carving of a raven and a griffin on a block of white marble.

Bou Salem

Bou Salem is another agricultural town, with a **market** on Thursdays. It is the creation of the French, but the site marks the marketplace of two neighbouring Bedouin tribes, the Ouled Chahia and the Ouled Bou Salem. Eleven kilometres north of Bou Salem, perched on limestone hills, is the village of **Balta**. Its minareted mosque presides over ruined Roman walls, rock-cut tombs and dolmens scattered amongst olive trees. The sites are nothing special, but these villages are a good excuse to get away from the main routes and do a bit of walking, for example, to the summit of **Jebel Bou Goultrane** (903 m), directly behind Balta.

Between Bou Salem and Jendouba, two considerable tributaries, the Oued Tessa and Oued Mellègue, join the Mejerda.

Jendouba

Twenty three kilometres from Bou Salem the young town of Jendouba, with its hotels and banks, is the obvious place from which to explore the nearby Roman sites of **Bulla Regia** and **Chemtou**. Its straight avenues have grown up beside the French-built railway station and a road bridge over the Mejerda. Jendouba has always been the site of a weekly market; it was previously known as Souk el Arba, the Wednesday souk.

As any of Jendouba's 15,000 residents will tell you, 'Jendouba's big problem is water'. For a town that sits on Tunisia's only full-time river, it is somewhat ironic, but the tap water is notoriously noxious. Consequently, the road from the clean spring at Bulla Regia, the old Roman town 8 km north, is full of mules pulling cartloads of jerry cans.

GETTING AROUND

By Train
The railway station is right at the centre of town, beside the Hotel Atlas, the PTT and the banks. Trains leave for Tunis five times a day and a similar number run to Ghardimao on the Algerian border, one of which continues to Algeria.

By Bus
Buses leave just north of the railway line on the road to Ain Draham, with regular departures for Tunis, Ghardimao, Ain Draham, Teboursouk, El Kef, and hourly buses to Bulla Regia.

By *Louage*/Taxi
Louages and taxis congregate on Pl 7 Novembre 1987, the roundabout at the western end of town. Here you will find *louages* to El Kef, Ain Draham, Ghardimao and Tunis, and can bargain the price of a round trip to Bulla Regia and Chemtou.

WHERE TO STAY
If Jendouba seems hot, quiet and tedious by day, it does come alive in the evening outside the cafés, in bars and at the shops.

MODERATE
Stay at the **Hotel Atlas**, on Rue du 1er Juin 1955. It is unexciting, but the rooms are clean and comfortable and there is a popular garden bar. A double costs 15 dn with basin and bidet, or a little more with a shower.

CHEAP
The other alternatives are cramped and airless, but the best is the **Saha en Noum** (which translates as 'sleep well') Pension on Blvd Khemais el Hajeri. A bed here is a mere 3 dn.

EATING OUT
The restaurant in the Hotel Atlas ranks as one of the worst in Tunisia, so it is certainly worth going out to eat. The **Restaurant Africa** on Rue Hedi Chaker is a perfect contrast, though be certain to point at what the locals are eating rather than being pushed into tourist food like steak and chips. It is licensed and busy, though there is a calmer backyard, shaded by a bamboo awning and decorated with murals.

Bulla Regia

The ruined Roman city of **Bulla Regia** lies at the foot of **Jebel Rabia** on the edge of the flat fertile valley of the Mejerda. The site is fed by a spring of cool, clear water which breaks from the foot of the mountain. People had been living here since at least the 4th century BC, but the luxurious villas for which it is celebrated date only from the 1st and 2nd centuries AD.

Where the inhabitants of modern Jendouba speak wistfully of the cool winds of Ain Draham, the aristocrats of Bulla Regia retired underground to while away the heat of a midsummer's day. Though the above-ground ruins are extensive, they are desolate, and it is their contrast with the cool, inviting chambers below that gives Bulla Regia its magic. Bulla Regia was well known for its opulent lifestyle. In 399, St Augustine complained of its easy welcome to strangers, and its louche reputation as a hang-out for actors and prostitutes.

There were darker, more possessive, passions at play as well. The first excavation in 1906 found an iron collar riveted round the neck of a female skeleton. The collar was inscribed: *Adultera meretrix: tene me quia fugavi a Bulla Regia*, Adulterous prostitute: hold me, because I ran away from Bulla Regia.

History

The 4th-century BC town of Bulla earned its qualifying 'Regia' (of the king) in the 2nd century BC, when it became the seat of the Numidian King Micipsa. As Carthaginian power waned, so his father Massinissa had absorbed this prosperous agricultural community into his kingdom. During the struggle to preserve the Numidian kingdom from the encroachments of Rome, Micipsa's heir Jugurtha was finally defeated 25 km from here.

The city passed effortlessly into the Roman orbit, but the Punic and Numidian culture of its citizens was only slowly eclipsed. During the Byzantine era (535–647), the site was still heavily inhabited, as the two basilicas and fort testify, but after the Arab invasion it appears to have been used principally as a burial ground.

GETTING THERE
The ruins are north of Jendouba, 6 km along the Ain Draham road and 2 km east. Taxi drivers from the town are happy to drop you and pick you up later at a prearranged time, and it should not cost more than 4 dn. Alternatively, take the hourly bus from the bus station.

The Museum

Tickets for the site and museum are sold at the museum, and both are open from 08.00 to sunset. In the heat of the day, the guardian will show you a tap from which cool fresh spring water gushes.

In the first room there is a mesmerizing black bas-relief carving of a Numidian cavalryman from the 1st century BC. These fierce warriors formed the backbone of Hannibal's army.

Carving of Numidian cavalryman, 2nd century BC

224

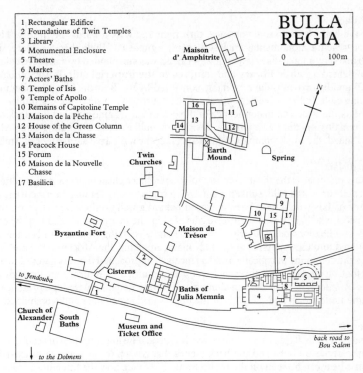

1 Rectangular Edifice
2 Foundations of Twin Temples
3 Library
4 Monumental Enclosure
5 Theatre
6 Market
7 Actors' Baths
8 Temple of Isis
9 Temple of Apollo
10 Remains of Capitoline Temple
11 Maison de la Pêche
12 House of the Green Column
13 Maison de la Chasse
14 Peacock House
15 Forum
16 Maison de la Nouvelle Chasse
17 Basilica

BULLA REGIA

0   100m

Maison d' Amphitrite

Twin Churches

Earth Mound

Spring

Byzantine Fort

Maison du Trésor

Cisterns

Baths of Julia Memnia

Church of Alexander   South Baths

Museum and Ticket Office

back road to Bou Salem

to Jendouba

to the Dolmens

At Zama, the only battle he ever lost, the Romans had managed to procure more of them than he had. The carving shows the horseman's long hair tied back in a fillet, and details of the bridle and stirrup-less saddle. From coins discovered on the site, portraits of the Numidian kings have been blown up to bring these somewhat distant characters, Massinissa, Jugurtha and Juba I to life on the walls.

The second room contains a 2nd-century tomb, a mosaic head of Medusa, and two 3rd-century female statues, a pair of grim matriarchs firmly clutching their tasselled purses of household keys.

The Site

Baths of Julia Memnia
Opposite the museum, the site entrance faces the monumental ruins of the **baths of Julia Memnia**, with **cisterns** stretching away to the west. Pass through the narrow passage straight ahead and you arrive on a major Roman **street**. To the right is the entrance to the baths, built at the end of the 3rd century AD and named after the Syrian wife of the Libyan Emperor Septimius Severus. The entrance hall and central *frigidarium*, with its flanking cold baths, are well preserved.

225

Royal Palace

Leaving the baths by the same entrance, turn right and walk towards the theatre. Halfway there, you reach a monumental enclosed space, signposted 'Bibliothèque'. Here, a large garden flanked by a moat-like trench of water tanks was surrounded by a massive colonnade which contained a **public library** and **temples to the imperial cult**. It was probably the original Numidian **royal palace**, suitably converted by the Romans into a loyalist middle-class dining club. In the far eastern corner of the courtyard is a surviving Corinthian capital which shows the scale and magnificence of the colonnade. A nine-pointed interlocking **star mosaic** remains on the pavement—a design not unlike those decorating later Moorish palaces. Indeed, the whole complex seems to presage the walled palace gardens of Andalucia.

Temple of Isis

Continuing on towards the theatre, an irregular open space clusters below it. It is dotted with temple enclosures, the odd sunken pool and terraced steps leading to sanctuaries. The **sanctuary of Isis** would have been enclosed behind a wall up the seven steps on the left. Here, novices who had proved themselves devoted to 'the many-named goddess' by offering sacrifices and libations daily, adoring her statue and abstaining from sex and certain foods, were initiated into the mysteries of the holy night. Apuleiùs, the African writer and initiate, describes the ceremony in typically mystical terms: 'I approached the very gates of death and set one foot on Proserpine's threshold, yet was permitted to return, rapt through all the elements. At midnight I saw the sun shining as if it were noon; I entered the presence of the gods of the underworld and the gods of the upperworld, stood near and worshipped them.'

Theatre

The **theatre** is Bulla Regia's most impressive building. The lower portion of seating survives, as does the orchestra bowl and the back niches that rise up to the stage. A much-restored mosaic of a bear can be seen on the orchestra floor. Notice how the three lower rows of the seats are wider and of lower pitch. They would have been separated from the rest of the audience by a low wall and were reserved for the small group of leading citizens.

The 60-m theatre was built during the reign of Marcus Aurelius (161–80 AD). Though there are plenty of available sloping hills on which it could have been terraced in the Greek style, here the monumental Roman technique of building on arched vaults is used. The theatre was decorated with statues of Ceres, a hybrid goddess part Greek Demeter and Kore, part Punic Tanit. She was at the centre of North African religious life, her cult day was a public holiday all over North Africa and lavish entertainments were performed in her honour. Just north of the theatre was a **bathhouse** reserved for actors, where their trefoil-shaped tub can still be seen.

Forum

Walking uphill, you pass an open-air **market** on the left, a small but elaborate courtyard, its entrance flanked by booths which would have served as shops stalls. You then enter a large, desolate rectangular plot that used to be the **forum**, the centre of the city's commercial, political, judicial and religious life. To the west are the remains of the **Capitoline temple**, where the central trinity of Jupiter, Juno and Minerva were worshipped. To the east lie knee-high traces of the **basilica** which served as the law courts. North is the **temple of Apollo**, and it was here that a magnificent collection of statues were found where they had fallen from their plinths. The statues remain together in the Bardo and make the most ravishing gallery in the museum.

The Villas

Walk north from the forum, past the ancient **spring** which is fenced off and enclosed in a modern pumping house. The villas are clustered together in the smart quarter of town. Eight have been excavated and there are at least a dozen more waiting to be uncovered. The major villas are labelled, and the guardian, who keeps the keys to their underground chambers, will probably show you them himself. If you want to have a good look at their confused topography, you can climb to the top of the earth mound made by the archaeologists and try to match our map with what you see.

THE HOUSE OF THE GREEN COLUMN

Here the central courtyard shows traces of an ornate water channel that gurgled around a central garden. As in Moorish gardens today, the Romans evidently loved the soothing trickle and sense of coolness that running water creates. In two rooms to the east of the house, sizeable fragments of painted wall plaster can be seen. Imagine the effect of a brand-new mosaic floor and bright coloured walls in this red, green, blue and yellow design. Then in the larger rooms and courtyards add statues, furniture and the smell of garden flowers.

LA MAISON DE LA PÊCHE

Dating from Hadrian's reign, this is the oldest of the surviving villas, and its underground architecture is in its infancy. There are a number of small rooms, and circulating air is insured by 18 air vents which pierce the walls. A small fountain pool was added to the courtyard at a later date, and faces a room with the remains of a **fishing mosaic**. Notice the ingenious use of interlocking terracotta tubes to create vaults and arches. Lighter and more flexible than stone, these could be shaped as the architect required and were easy to plaster over as their surface was textured to hold mortar. Beware the guardian telling you they were hot and cold water pipes.

LA MAISON D'AMPHITRITE

The House of Amphitrite lies on its own, further up the Roman road. Down in this small underground villa, built during the reign of Antoninus Pius (138–61 AD), lie the most startling mosaics in Bulla Regia. The central room, a domed and vaulted dining-room, contains a large mosaic of **Venus**. Her pink flesh seems almost alive as she is supported above the waves by two eager sea creatures, one of whose head-claws she is affectionately tweaking. Over her head, cupids are holding a wreath, and her supporters, riding dolphins, carry her prized possessions, a mirror and a jewel box. The entrance hall floor is dominated by a striking mosaic portrait of the goddess, set into a deep black background. The niche in front of it cries out for a marble statue. On either side of the dining-room two smaller rooms contain humble geometric designs and traces of painted wall plaster.

LA MAISON DE LA NOUVELLE CHASSE

Returning to the main block of villas, you will recognize this one by the **hunting mosaic** which adorns the ground floor. The outlines of half a dozen graves have disturbed the entirety of the picture, but there is almost more than enough left: plenty of blood, a lion hunt, a lion and panther fighting, two servants carrying a dead python, plus more gore. The border is a more accomplished, dark-green composition. Hunting horns and floral bracts enclose brilliant medallions of boars' heads, hounds, rabbits and deer.

LA MAISON DE LA CHASSE
Immediately to the south is the Maison de la Chasse, the House of the Hunt. The hunting mosaic has long since gone, but the house has the most sophisticated set of underground rooms. Twenty-two steps lead down to a central courtyard enclosed by superbly bow-shaped columns. The capitals are Corinthian, but have been carved with virile African lotus leaves instead of the traditional acanthus. The hexagonal gaps constructed in the stonework above relieve the columns of carrying unnecessary extra weight. The dining-room contains the customary inverted T-shape mosaic, with profuse floral decoration. Unusually, this room has been placed at an angle to the courtyard, to give each guest an interesting perspective at dinner. A well, sunk through the floor, allowed for constant wetting to bring the mosaics alive. Handsome red columns mark out the upper courtyard.

THE HOUSES OF THE PEACOCK AND THE TREASURE
There are two other excavated houses with underground rooms nearby. The House of the Peacock, *La Maison du Paon*, has been relieved of its peacock mosaic, and the Treasure House, *La Maison du Trésor*, is further south. A stash of coins was found in the underground rooms, where, unusually, the dining-room has been placed in the open courtyard. Its formal vine-leaf mosaic was once, no doubt, reflected by a ceiling of vines shading the midday sun.

Christian Basilicas
Two Christian churches, built during the Byzantine period (534–647 AD), lie on the western edge of the villa quarter. At the western end of the larger of the two adjacent basilicas, a marble **baptismal font** in the shape of a cross lies beneath two pillars. Fonts played an important role in the early church, as their prominent physical position bears out. New converts first attended church as listeners and were taught their catechism, but only entered the church fully having received communion after baptism. The process took anything from two to five years. Priests of the time are reported to have become increasingly worried by the sprees of debauchery to which catechists succumbed just before baptism. For, once baptized, it was thought that you could only be forgiven your sins once. At the eastern end of the basilica rises the dais which would have held the altar.

In the smaller chapel to the north, look out for the **mosaic** between two standing columns. It features a chalice flanked by two peacocks, symbols of incorruptible flesh and eternity. If you wet the mosaic you will see fragments of glass, added to the blues and greens to give a translucent glow.

The Byzantine Fort and Rectangular Building
Walking back towards the road, you can take in the **Byzantine fort** on your way. It is an unusually small square building and rather well jointed compared to the normal hurried fortresses the Byzantines threw up. Fitted with electricity, it is now used by the visiting French and Tunisian archaeological teams.

Passing in front of the rows of cisterns, you will come to a curious rectangular building, its walls decorated with a delicate lozenge pattern, and the interior supported by rows of square columns. Its date, somewhere between the 1st century BC and 1st century AD rules it out as a church, and no one has come up with a satisfactory suggestion.

South Baths, Church of Alexander and Dolmens
South of the road, the ruins of the **south baths** are heaped beside a visible lone pillar. The pillar belongs to a small square building next door, known as the **church of Alexander**. It began life as a kiosk for the distribution or sale of corn and oil, perhaps Bulla Regia's civic dole

office. Under the Byzantines it was converted into a chapel, but was destroyed by fire during the Arab conquest.

The oldest traces of Bulla Regia lie beyond, on the limestone outcrop south of the field ahead. A large number of **dolmens**, tombs or urn shelters formed from unshaped slabs of stone poised on some smaller blocks, litter the hillside. Unless you are an expert, however, you will probably only recognize them by the white numbers painted beside them by archaeologists.

Chemtou

The scattered remains of the Roman city of **Chemtou** lie beside the Mejerda River. A few farmers' huts nestle amongst the largely unexcavated ruins, from which rise the monumental shells of the city's baths, bridge and basilica. Though impressive, the real distinction of Chemtou lies in the twin-peaked outcrop of stone that overlooks the site. It is crowned by a sanctuary and bitten into by ancient quarries, for this ridge was the sole source of a prized veined marble, known as *antico giallo*. A precious commodity, it was a monopoly of the emperors, who bestowed Chemtou marble columns on their favourite palaces and most favoured cities.

History

Chemtou marble was being cut by the Numidians in the second century BC, though the first shipment to Rome was not until 78 BC. This quickly created a demand which called for a more commercial method of exploitation, and the quarries were placed under imperial management, with a procurator and a workforce of slaves. The ruins of the theatre, amphitheatre and baths are not signs of the most civilized labour camp of all times. They belonged to the city of Chemtou and the slaves were housed in separate barracks out of sight and sound on the other side of the hill.

After his victory at Actium in 27 BC, Augustus began disbanding his enormous army and securing the existing imperial frontiers. He settled Chemtou with ex-soldiers, but the visible ruins are a couple of centuries later, from the great period of building in the 2nd and 3rd centuries AD. During the late Empire, Chemtou had its own bishop, but the spread of Christianity made no difference to conditions amongst the slave workforce. The quarry was reopened in the 19th century after centuries of disuse, but since 1970 the only digging has been archaeological.

GETTING THERE
Chemtou lies 16 km off the main Jendouba to Tabarka road, opposite the turning to Bulla Regia. The road continues, after Chemtou, as a gravel track for the 14 km to the Roman ruins of Thuburnica, where it sweeps round to Ghardimao. Either hire a taxi from Jendouba or try going the back route. Take a *louage* to the village of **Oued Melliz** on the Ghardimao road and walk 3 km towards the clearly visible incised hills to the north.

The Site

Approaching Chemtou from the Bulla Regia road, you pass an impressive length of aqueduct which delivered water 30 km from the heart of the Mejerda mountains. In times of drought, it was stored in a massive cistern, still hidden in the hills and known locally as Medinet el Ard.

Baths and Theatre

The unmistakable mass of the **baths** lies next, in monumental disrepair. To the southwest is the gaunt structure of the **theatre**, rising like a modernist honeycomb with stairways and vaults beckoning down to the lower levels. As at Bulla Regia, it uses no natural hills and follows the Roman method of creating a free-standing theatrical bowl.

Nympheum and Forum

Halfway up the neighbouring hill stands a lonely apse, the **nympheum** where the aqueduct once disgorged its water in a temple grotto dedicated to the genie of the spring. Lower on the hill is another much larger apse, that of the **basilica** which dwarfs the paved area of the **forum** beside it. It served as the city's law court before it was transformed in the 6th century into a church. The centre of the forum has been excavated by a joint German and Tunisian team to reveal a pair of royal tombs from the Numidian period. The lower courses of the dry-stone **tower** they have revealed are interesting as rare survivors from this period, but more so as an indication of the brutality of the original Roman conquest. Power was asserted in the most graphic form, by levelling the tombs of the old dynasty to provide the foundation for a new town centre. Every morning throngs of an urban multitude walked over the graves of princes.

Roman Bridge

Down in the deeply incised river bed are the piers of a **bridge** built during the reign of the Emperor Trajan. Originally the piers would have been reflected in a tranquil pool, for this stretch of river also doubled as a millpond. The remains of a millrace can be seen downstream, a large block of stone incised from top to bottom with three channels.

Walking further around you reach a colonial courtyard which is now an **archaeological depot**, its yard filled with fragments of statues, mosaics and inscriptions from the site. It is not open, but there are plans to turn it into a museum. For the moment, all you can get are tantalizing glimpses through the front gate.

Marble Quarries

Moving up towards the gaping holes in the hillside, you pass a small French chapel that adds a touch of 19th-century ruin to the buried Roman city. In the three main **quarry bowls** there are signs of half-finished work—a column from the Roman period half carved out, and numbered blocks from more recent French operations. By their clean slicing the French have exposed the random array of colour and pattern that made Chemtou marble so celebrated, fields of honey-orange strata crossed with thin veins of the darkest wine.

Hilltop Sanctuary

Climb carefully above the cliff-edged bites of the works to reach the summit. Here lie the confusing remains of a hilltop sanctuary, an ancient open-air **altar** to Baal which was first dressed in stone during the reign of the Numidian King Micipsa. Enclosed and turned into a temple dedicated to Saturn by the Romans, it was transformed into a church by the Byzantines in the 6th century, then despoiled, and finally excavated and half-restored by a German archaeological team. The outer walls of the Roman temple of Saturn were decorated with large Hellenistic medallions which were pushed down the hill, possibly by monks, but are now safe in the archaeological compound.

From the sanctuary you have a good view east over the Mejerda valley and some of the lesser remains. Just to the south you can pick out an unexcavated **amphitheatre**, a cross-vaulted building now in use as a farm stable, and numerous **cisterns**. To the north is the regular grid of the **mining camp**, both a prison for the slave labour force and a skilled workshop for carving and polishing marble. It was a completely self-contained community: excavations have revealed lodgings, temples, baths and worn work benches. Just beside it are traces of a 6th-century Byzantine church.

Ghardimao

West of Jendouba the road and railway line follow the Mejerda river upstream towards the Algerian border and the town of Ghardimao, 34 km away. This small market centre is the most important **border crossing** between Tunisia and Algeria, and the Trans-Maghreb Express train rolls through every afternoon.

In the 19th century it used to be a centre for **tobacco farming**. At that time Tunisian cigars were considered almost the equal of Cuban and its cigarettes were established alongside the admired blends of Turkey and Egypt. Surprisingly, tobacco had a long fight to enter the Muslim world. Right into this century the Senussi of Libya maintained the death penalty for anyone even smelling of cigarettes.

Today, if the town can ever be considered to bustle, it does so with the queues, taxis and paperwork of a border crossing. Apart from involving yourself in this, there are two reasons to come to Ghardimao: to look at the ruins of **Thuburnica**, 11 km to the north or to walk in the wooded **Feija hills** to the northeast.

GETTING AROUND: STAYING A NIGHT
The Trans-Maghreb Express currently stops at Ghardimao at about 16.00, though this may change when the planned route to Casablanca comes into operation. Until then it leaves Ghardimao for Souk Ahras 70 km west, on the way to Constantine and Algiers.

Buses and *louages* leave about 200 m from the railway station. There are frequent *louages*, mostly to Jendouba and at least one direct bus to Tunis. Opposite the station is the cheap **Hotel Tuburnic**, a two-storey building with 26 bedrooms, a bar and restaurant which is an adequate base for exploring the area. A double room costs 10 dn.

Around Ghardimao

Thuburnica

To find these Roman ruins, 11 km from Ghardimao, leave the town on the Algeria road. After a short while, a right turn to the north takes you over the Mejerda River. The tarmac gives way to a gravel road which crosses two more bridges, before arriving at a Roman one. Alternatively, carry on on the farm track from Chemtou.

The ruins of Thuburnica, a town founded by the Roman general Marius and settled by Campanian veterans after his victory over King Jugurtha in the 1st century BC, are on the wooded hillside above. The modern hamlet of **Henchir Sidi Ali Belgacem**, clustered round the holy man's tomb, lies beside the road ahead.

The **Roman bridge** is in astonishing condition. It is 10 m high and not a stone is out of place in its arch. The joints are much finer than present-day Tunisian workmanship and look as good as new.

A drive through the olives leads up to a **colonial mansion** occasionally used by visiting archaeologists. Its driveway houses a collection of Punic and Roman **stelae** and the custodian may show you around the empty house. Punic stelae have been set above the fireplace in the drawing-room, and into the terrace outside. Through a vista of twisted olive trunks rear monuments of brilliant orange stone, and a sense of discovery makes up for the simplicity of the remains.

Here rises a **mausoleum**, there a **triumphal arch** with empty niches and a crudely carved keystone which balances on age alone. There is a squat rectangular building with double apses, perhaps a stumpy legal **basilica**, and two **temples**. From inscriptions found in situ, one has been identified as a temple to Juno, Concord and the presiding spirit of the town. The other is dedicated to the Four Seasons, Mercury Sobrius and the Pantheus Augustus or imperial cult. There are also numerous remains of houses and the ubiquitous water cisterns. On the hill above the ruins, farm buildings mask the ruins of an old **Byzantine fort**.

The Feija Hills

There is spectacular walking to be had in these hills, but you must get clearance from the police and customs as the track there skirts the Algerian border for most of the way. Take the Algeria road, and after 4 km turn north up a gravel road which climbs for 12 km to the forestry station (Maison Forestière) of Feija. There you should ask for the path up **Kef Nechka**, a rocky outcrop half an hour's walk to the south. Steps have been cut into its side, and from the top you get a magnificent view down over the flat lands of the Mejerda. An hour's walk beyond the Forestry Station, the Ain Soltane youth hostel will put you up in the summer.

Part VII
THE TELL

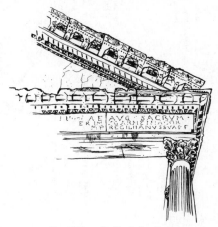

Detail from the Capitol at Dougga

The Tell is an amorphous highland region, enlivened by monumental evidence of its past. The high open plains rise gradually to the Algerian border, and are studded with ruined ancient cities. Magnificent temples, solitary mausoleums and triumphal arches vie for attention with the remains of opulent public baths, latrines, forts and churches, boasting lip-shaped baptism pools paved in mosaic.

This Roman prosperity was based on wheat. The northern Tell has always received enough rain to grow it, while the southern half of the region is too dry and supports only rough grazing. Conflict between the way of life in these two climatic belts, between the settled farmers and the nomadic herdsmen, has largely defined the region's history. The late Roman Empire was the high noon of the farming culture, when sophisticated farming methods and a steady export market supported hundreds of towns across the region. The desert frontier was patrolled to keep the wild tribes at bay, and to control the passage of nomad herds over farming land.

By the 12th century, the towns of the Tell lay empty. Nomads in their woven tents grazed their herds nearby and moved on, leaving the monuments untouched since they had no use for building stone. No merchandise could be safely transported across the area except on pack animals rented from, and with the protection of, one of the tribes, and the nomad cavalry made and broke the authority of Sultans. By the mid-19th century the great tribes of the Tell, the Drid, Frechich, Majeur and Zlass numbered 200,000, a quarter of the national population.

It was not until after the French invasion in 1881 that the region returned to sedentary farming, and colonial farmsteads and railway stations still abound. French scholars also excavated and restored many of the Tell's monuments, encouraged by a colonial administration that thought itself the true heir of Rome. Since independence, the development of

233

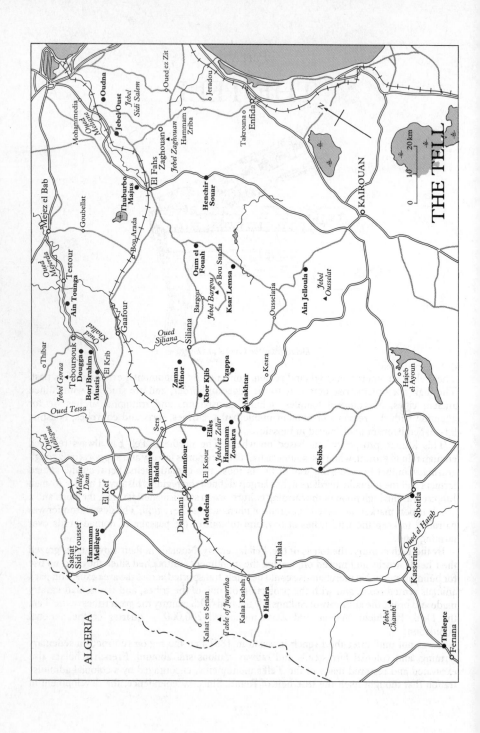

THE TELL

both farming and archaeology in the region has continued, and wheat is still the bedrock of the north's comparative prosperity.

The ruined Roman cities of Sbeitla and Dougga are the twin stars, their magnificent temples familiar from posters, brochures and postcards. There is such an embarrassment of riches at these two alone, that the evocative ruins of Haidra, Makhtar and Medeina remain almost completely unvisited. In addition there are a further two dozen monuments, from megalithic tombs to Byzantine forts, where you can feel like an explorer.

The Tell's mountains are predominantly gentle, but around Jebel Zaghouan, Jebel Bargou, Jebel Chambi and at the Table of Jugurtha, true natural drama unfolds. At El Kef, an ancient citadel, ruins combine with good walking country, hotels and food, to make the most attractive base for a longer stay. For those in the Tell over the summer, there is a festival of Andalucian music in the 17th-century town of Testour in late June, and classical plays are staged in the Roman theatre at Dougga in August.

Tunis to El Fahs

The Bled El Fahs is a rich agricultural region south of the plain of Tunis, on the edge of the Tell. At its centre is **El Fahs**, the chief market town and transport centre of the region. The attractions lie outside it, at the old urban centres of Roman **Thuburbo Majus** and the 17th-century, hill-top town of **Zaghouan**, which has the area's only hotel.

On the way, you might have time to see the lesser-known sites along the road from Tunis to El Fahs. These include the crumbling ruins of a 19th-century palace at **Mohammedia**, the **Roman aqueduct** over the Oued Meliane, the remains of the Roman town of **Oudna** and the ancient and modern thermal baths at **Jebel Oust**.

Mohammedia

From central Tunis, it is 16 km on the P3 to Mohammedia, the first excuse to stop. Three great blocks of gaunt mud-coloured ruins, the shell of a 19th-century Beylical palace, dominate the skyline of the town. Any decoration has long since rotted away and the inhabitable parts are divided amongst squatters. Only the roadside palace mosque survives, in use and good repair, but it is not open to non-Muslims.

Mohammedia is used to rotting palaces, for this is at least the second. The first, which crowned the hill beyond the town quarry, was built by Mohammed Bey but was deserted after three years, in 1759, before it had even been finished. The same saga of conspicuous consumption was repeated by Ahmed Bey, who spent five years building the immense pile in the middle of town in time for his death in 1847. It was an old tradition of the Beys that the house they died in could not be lived in by a successor, so it too was abandoned.

To the right of the road as you climb through Mohammedia, is a covered channel, part of the Zaghouan to Carthage **aqueduct**. This reveals itself with growing majesty as you descend into the valley of the Oued Meliane. The aqueduct is a testament to the magnificence of the Roman Empire's public works. Much cited by historians and praised by urban planners, it is also a monument to the expense spared by pipeline technology.

Elegant and romantic in ruin, the aqueduct was state-of-the-art engineering at the time of its construction in the 2nd century AD. Fresh water at Zaghouan gushed from springs at 289 m and flowed along a gentle gradient all the way to the cisterns at Carthage. As the crow flies it is 56 km, but the aqueduct, necessarily following the contours, flows 132 km. Selecting a quicker and cheaper route used to be a favourite game for surveyors, but Emperor Hadrian, who ordered its construction, was just the man to defy cost accountants. It has required constant upkeep, but a catalogue of patchwork brick, pise and concrete has added to its aura of antiquity. It was still running 500 years after its inauguration though it never completely recovered from damage during the Arab siege of Byzantine Carthage in 698. The Fatimids in the 10th century and the Hafsids in the 13th restored certain lengths, as did the Beys, adding new sources and diversions.

Oudna

For a pleasant half-hour stroll over the deserted Roman ruins of Oudna, bear left off the main road and follow the diminishing arches of the aqueduct. Having passed Oudna station, take a left turn at the Y-junction and after a dry river bed turn right, up a farm track, towards a white-towered farmhouse on the hill. This is perched in the centre of the ruins.

The scrubby hill behind the farmhouse has a reliable spring whose water was delivered by an aqueduct to a succession of vast cisterns that cluster around to form a castle of water reservoirs. Above the farm are the remains of the **aqueduct**; below it are the enormous ruins of the city's great **baths**. A monolithic jumble above ground, the **cellars** and underground **cisterns** are still largely intact though you will have to scramble under precarious blocks and banks of earth with a torch to explore them fully.

Oudna was the creation of Emperor Augustus, who settled discharged soldiers from the Third Legion here, giving each 200 *iugera* of land, a measurement based on what a *iugum*, a yoke of oxen, could plough in a day. The soldiers proved bad farmers, however, and within a generation most of the lots were bought up to create large and efficient estates.

Oudna was only a day's ride from Carthage and seems to have been consistently prosperous. The low ruins of a couple of large private houses are found round towards the lower knoll. Eleven of these villas have so far been excavated, revealing over 60 **mosaics**, a full range of changing styles from the 1st–4th centuries AD. The grandest house, that of the Laberii, had over 40 rooms and the splendid mosaic from its hall is now prominently displayed in the Bardo Museum in Tunis: it is an Arcadian view of the delights of rural life with scenes of ploughing, shepherding, hunting and trapping made during the reign of the philosopher Emperor, Marcus Aurelius. There are plenty of geometrical mosaics in situ, but all the pictorial ones have been removed.

Crowning the crest of the knoll are the ruins of the **amphitheatre**, a great ruined bowl with a frozen cascade of massive stone blocks. Below, beside the farm track, are the skeletal ruins of a **Roman bridge**, the haunt of a pair of breeding small owls.

Jebel Oust

The left turn to Zaghouan off the main P3 road also passes the ruins of a **Roman hammam**, and its modern equivalent, a health spa. Both feed off the 58°C water that bubbles, steaming, from a spring on the flank of Jebel Oust.

Romans seeking good health would spend a night at Jebel Oust in *incubatio*, a vital part of their cure, which accounts for the more than 220 rooms in the complex. Arriving at the mountain, they would follow the long cleansing ritual of a Roman bath, and drink the cooled waters before visiting the shrine erected above the source of the hot spring. There they would pray and present offerings to Aesculapius, the god of healing, and Hygeia, the goddess of health. Cleansed physically and spiritually, they would spend the night in a nearby cell, hoping in the morning for a strong recollection of their dreams, the usual method by which the gods communicated with mankind. These might be specific, instructions to avoid certain types of food and behaviour, but like today, more often than not they required professional interpretation. A number of dream text books have survived, showing ancient dreamers to be sexually more frank and less obsessed by royal families than we are today.

Visiting the site now, the most conspicuous remains are the two **central pools** which were once enclosed by colonnades. Both the small round and the much larger rectangular bath are caked in an almost nightmarish layer of calciferous deposit like the inside of some ever-boiling kettle.

The other feature of the baths not to be missed are the **mosaics** and **marble floors**. Heading towards the road from the round pool, you come across a room with a startling *opus sectile* floor, a kaleidoscope of white, red, yellow, green and grey marble surrounding an eight-pointed star. Beyond are two adjacent rooms with a simple mosaic design executed in marble and terracotta that remains bright and equal to the best of modern Tunisian carpets. Two rooms away lies the **Room of the Four Seasons**, containing the only surviving figurative mosaic. Winter announces herself with an olive branch from the December harvest; autumn with a pruning hook and bunch of grapes harvested in September; summer keeps cool with a fan and a peacock feather; spring delicately holds a seedling. Throughout the maze of rooms are marble steps and traces of marble veneer that once covered the walls. They created a sumptuous, clean and cool interior in sharp contrast to the dense steam, mineral vapours and sweating humanity of the baths.

Walking uphill, you come across interior walls haphazardly dividing large mosaic-paved courtyards, and olive presses occupying baths and cisterns, evidence of later habitation. In a clearing above stands the site of the old **sanctuary of Aesculapius and Hygeia**, capping a deep red gash whence the hot spring flowed. A baptismal font was inserted into the heart of the temple when the sanctuary was Christianized in the 6th century. Walking towards the modern hotel, you pass over faint traces of a triple-apsed **Byzantine church**.

Zaghouan

Jebel Zaghouan's massive bulk dominates this red-roofed town, which sits on an escarpment beneath red cliffs and forested slopes. The mountain hides the ruins of a **Roman water temple**, while the town boasts a handful of religious buildings. At its heart is the clean white minaret of the **Mosque of Sidi Ali Azouz** and the green-tiled dome of the **zaouia** beyond. Above the road, overlooking well-watered gardens, are a dirty yellow church tower and an extravagantly decorated, modern Islamic neighbour.

Zaghouan is an intimate hill-town, with cobbled streets and small enclosed squares which smack of the European Mediterranean. As far back as Roman times the town was an Italian enclave, populated by the people of Chiusi who fled from the civil war and settled here in 82 BC. It was revived by an influx of Andalucian settlers in the 17th century, who established a successful if unglamorous national reputation for producing ordinary unglazed dishes. The town has not got much bigger and, with a population of under 9000, still feels more like a village.

GETTING AROUND

Enfida and El Fahs have better transport connections than Zaghouan and also have train stations, so it is often easier to catch a *louage* to one or other and continue your journey from there. Local buses are frequent but also a bit erratic. There should be two a day for the 1¼-hour journey to Tunis, three for the 2¼-hour journey to Kairouan and two each to Enfida, El Fahs, Sousse and Nabeul.

The Town

Walking up from the main road, the square in front of the old church and Post Office has a view north over gardens and out to Jebel Oust. A few springs, embellished with Andalucian tiles, are scattered throughout the town and along narrow Rue Sidi Ali Azouz which runs the length of the escarpment. From here, steep paved alleys run down in both directions to the lower town. At the far end of the road, the **zaouia** makes a good target for a walk or a sketch, its exterior walls and dome linked with an old outer gate. If you can find someone to show you inside, there is a traditional carved plaster ceiling, and walls lined with glazed tiles.

Just above the Enfida ringroad stands a **triumphal arch** in good condition. It is at the social hub of the town, its neighbouring stairway connecting popular cafés to the bus stop.

The Water Temple or Nympheum

A signposted road leads uphill from the town to this open-air Roman sanctuary. Though the nympheum is a remarkable survivor, the nymph who guarded the spring has long since left. Modern pumps extract the water from ever deeper levels; the courtyard is covered in concrete; the temple is smeared with graffiti and smells of urine. There is, however, a pleasant vine-shaded café by the site for replenishing strength.

The nympheum was built in the 2nd century AD by Emperor Hadrian at the same time that the aqueduct to Carthage was being laid out. The outer semi-circular wall is well preserved but a number of more or less well-meaning additions confuse its original design. It was built to honour the nymph, the guardian of the spring, and to ensure a continual supply of her clear water for Carthage. The central cella, the small temple still visible at the back, rose above the spring and was adorned with veneers of coloured marble. The courtyard was paved and partly enclosed by a colonnade, bits of which survive. This had a vaulted roof and mosaic floor. The 12 surviving niches on the outer wall held statues of sister nymphs.

The spring which bubbled noisily in the central cella, echoing round the courtyard, was carried by an underground drain into the double kidney-shaped pool below. Its steps and shape ensured a swirl of water, a dramatic water garden with a practical purpose. It doubled as a settling pool before the water was tapped off to run down the sealed aqueduct to Carthage. The entrance to this underground world is just to the right of the pool, and the sloping tunnel of the aqueduct is safe but constricting.

Hadrian was famous for his travels and his Greek learning, and possibly modelled Zaghouan on the much older temples of Pisidian Antioch and Xanthos. The measurements at Zaghouan reveal a love of classical order: the width of the colonnade is a quarter that of the courtyard, the temple door exactly twice as high as the depth of the shrine. It is Rome at its best, not innovative except for bringing the art of Greek Asia to the mountains of North Africa. A study has concluded that the masons were all locals, since they used the Carthaginian ell (51.4 cm) as the basic measurement, rather than Roman lengths. The stone is cut from local quarries, an aged grey in comparison to the magnificent heights of living rock that rear above.

WHERE TO STAY AND EAT

MODERATE

About halfway between the town and the nympheum is the **Hotel les Nymphes**, a reclusive place brushed by pine-scented breezes in the hot summer months. The central green-tiled building holds a bar, sitting-room and restaurant. The rooms, a series of four-bed apartments, are 50 m below, set in a small garden with good views. Telephone in advance, on (02) 75094, as it has been known to close unexpectedly, and the only nearby possibilities are the **Zaghouan youth hostel** or the pseudo-medical atmosphere of **Hotel Thermes** at the Jebel Oust spa.

Walks around Zaghouan

The limestone hills around Zaghouan make one of the best places for walking in Tunisia. The summits and higher slopes provide striking views over the Gulf of Tunis, or east over the Gulf of Hammamet. The lower hills also have their own gentler charm, a confusion of scents from the mixed woodlands of Aleppo pine, kermes oak, wild olive, fig, broom and the low shrubs of the *maquis* like rosemary, cistus and heather. They provide cover for over a dozen species of breeding birds, best seen at dusk, though birds of prey remain strikingly visible spiralling up on currents of mountain air. Easily identifiable are ravens, buzzards, white Egyptian vultures, kestrels, cliff-nesting peregrines, kites and booted eagles as well as rarer raptors like lanner, Bonelli's and short-toed eagles, together with the odd golden eagle and griffon vulture passing through.

Jebel Zaghouan

Jebel Zaghouan is the central and the largest mountain in the area with a summit of 1295 m and a mass of outriding ridges to be explored. The easiest approach to the summit is along the 3-km dirt road to **Sidi Bou Gabrine** from the nympheum. It doglegs back to the aerial post, and passes below the central peak as it doubles back.

Zriba

To the southeast, 5 km from Zaghouan on the road to Enfida, is a turning marked **Hammam Zriba**. Walk up through the first settlement to reach **hot mineral baths**, good for the skin, which block the entrance to a gorge. The baths are popular, housed in a pretty building with three green domes to the fore and a mass of white roof behind. Men enter on the left, women on the right. The approach road is clustered with apartments, cafés and *casse-croûte* stalls. The gorge beyond is where Flaubert walked to get the right feeling for his description of the massacre of the mercenaries in *Salammbo*.

If feeling more adventurous, skirt the messy banks of the fluorine mine, and follow the track for **Haute Zriba**, a Berber mountain village nestling between limestone outcrops. It is a more reclusive version of Takrouna and Jeradou, which are further to the east but over-visited (see pp. 132–3).

Oued ez Zit

Northeast of Zaghouan are two hills divided by a col from which two streams, the Oued el Hamma to the north, and the Oued ez Zit to the south, flow. The western mountain is **Jebel Sidi Salem** whose summit is 506 m high and to the east is the slightly higher **Jebel ez Zit** at 751 m.

The village of Oued Zit, literally the 'river of olive oil', is 16 km from Zaghouan. Walking up the river bed you pass a colonial villa, built like a koubba. Now occupied by a farmer, the neighbouring building is the terrace of a Roman temple whose fluted pillars are slowly being excavated. A stairway leads below the sanctuary to a subterranean vaulted cistern divided in two. Intact and empty, its darkness is pierced by skylights. The head of the col is a 7-km walk, passing two esteemed, mineral-rich springs. At the pass you can branch west, passing the extensive white **zaouia of Sidi Salem** on your way to conquer the low wooded peak.

Jebel Ressas

The 795-m peak of **Jebel Ressas** is another 18 km towards Tunis. The tranquillity and soul of the mountain have been destroyed by the two mines that eat into its lower slopes, now and then rocked by blasting and smothered in great clouds of dust. La Laverie, as the mines are known, are ugly, but have produced lead since Carthaginian times. You might conceivably be tempted by Tunisia's only **gliding club** here. For details phone (01) 906712/255762.

Thuburbo Majus

This elegant Roman city is signposted 3 km before El Fahs off the Tunis road, and is open from dawn to sunset. The road sweeps past a triumphal arch before reaching the entrance where, apart from the ticket office, you will find a welcome and refreshing hand-pump in the middle of the car park. There are a number of coin salesmen who will pursue you for some time with tales of woe, but who may be useful for pointing out the major buildings.

History

Thuburbo, a distinctly un-Roman name, was given to this site by the Berber population who first settled it. It was spared complete destruction after supporting Carthage in her defeat in 146 BC, and was first officially colonized by the Romans in 27 BC, when a group of veterans was settled here. It was not until the 2nd century AD however that Thuburbo Majus began to equip itself with the prerequisites of a proud Roman city—a forum, capitol, baths and other temples. Many of the most important buildings were restored and added to in the 4th century, and from this time temples began to be transformed into Christian churches.

With the Vandal invasion in 407, the town's decline began, though the ruins continued to be used by local farmers and shepherds for pressing oil and sheltering flocks. During the First World War German POWs helped in the excavations.

The Site

Capitol and Forum

Walk straight to the four beckoning columns of the **Capitoline temple** and you arrive in a massive open space, the old **forum**. Built at the heart of the city between AD 161–92, a forest of green marble pillars once surrounded the paved forum on three sides, but only a few remain. The fourth side was occupied, then as now, by the contrasting pale stairway of the Capitoline temple, built in AD 168 and one of the most impressive left in Africa. Originally, there were six of these massive fluted columns, 9 m high, each crowned by a Corinthian acanthus-leaf capital. Behind them, now disappeared, the solid rectangular sanctuary

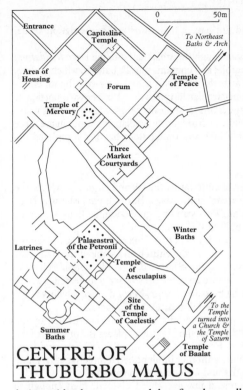

Entrance
Capitoline Temple
To Northeast Baths & Arch
Area of Housing
Temple of Peace
Forum
Temple of Mercury
Three Market Courtyards
Winter Baths
Latrines
Palaestra of the Petronii
Temple of Aesculapius
Site of the Temple of Caelestis
To the Temple turned into a Church & the Temple of Saturn
Summer Baths
Temple of Baalat

CENTRE OF THUBURBO MAJUS

contained a 7-m statue of the god Jupiter, the head and foot of which were recovered and are now in the Bardo Museum in Tunis. The Capitoline temples were symbols of the Empire, occupied by the three principal deities of the state. Jupiter was the supreme god, protector of city and state, and guardian of public morality. Other members of this trinity were Juno, his wife and protectress of the Roman people, and Minerva, the protectress of commerce and industry. From on top of the temple, look down into what were once the **treasure chambers**. The olive press is a much later addition.

Temple of Peace

Surrounding the forum are a number of other temples. Looking from the capitol, the low courtyard on the left is the **Temple of Peace**. It is ironic to find a small relief carving of Pegasus, the winged horse, here, for he was the mascot of the Third Augustan Legion who guarded the Saharan frontier.

This temple is typically African in design, with a large courtyard dwarfing the small sanctuary chamber or cella which juts out from the back wall. It is a style which reflected the importance of ritual and priesthood in African worship.

Temple of Mercury and Market

Opposite, to the right looking from the capitol, is the **temple of Mercury**, easily identified by its coronet of marble pillars which form a rare circular peristyle in the temple courtyard. The corners of the outer walls are formed by semi-circular niches, and the inner sanctum beyond has all but disappeared.

Mercury, god of merchants, looked down on the town's **market area**. Built in the late 2nd and early 3rd centuries, it consists of three courtyards: one plain, one including the two standing lotus-leaf capitals on pillars, and the other surrounded by shops on three sides.

Summer Baths

An impressive line of grey marble columns and monumental walls to the southwest of the market mark the remains of the **summer baths**. The colonnade surrounded the **palaestra of the Petronii**, named after a wealthy family who donated this exercise yard to the city in AD 225. Before going to the baths, men would run, wrestle and box in the courtyard. There is an entrance, flanked by two columns, into a small **temple of Aesculapius**, the god of healing. An inscription found here prescribed ritual purity to its suppliants. For three days before entering the sanctum barefoot, they should not have a haircut or bathe, indulge in sexual intercourse, nor eat pork and beans.

Entering the baths from the *palaestra*, pass through the small hall into the large *frigidarium* or cold room, on the left. It was lined with marble, and contains mosaic baths in which bathers would plunge. The *tepidarium*, where warm baths were taken, is recognized by its eight-pointed star mosaic. The neighbouring semi-circular latrine with its impressive portico of columns originally had no entrance from the baths. Sitting over a trench of flowing water against the back wall, you relieved yourself while peering through pillars to statues in the three niches on the wall. Scented sponges for ablutions and under-floor heating completed the picture of companionable splendour.

Temples of Caelestis, Baalat and Saturn

Southeast of the baths lie a confusing series of courtyards, the second largest of which, the **temple of Caelestis** is now a minefield of treacherous holes. Beyond, enclosed in a large courtyard sanctum, is the **temple of Baalat**. Two standing grey columns flank nine pale stone steps which led to the inner temple, built in the 2nd century AD.

Uphill from here, taking a small road that turns into a path, lie the remains of an old temple and courtyard, later turned into a church. The nave of the church and some of the slate-grey pillars that divided it in three can still be seen in the courtyard. The old temple cella was transformed into a baptistery, and the other end into an apsed presbytery, with benches where the priests would have sat during services. The massive masonry beyond the presbytery to the right is all that remains of the original three-arched entrance to the sanctum.

The highest point of Thuburbo Majus, just outside the town gates, is crowned by the yellow stone blocks of a **temple of Saturn**, 'the God, the Holy, who places the braziers of the heavens in the firmament, the Prince of Days'. From here views stretch to El Fahs and Jebel Zaghouan beyond. Looking towards the capitol is another unidentified temple sanctuary and, beyond that, the ruins of the **northeast baths** and a ruinous town gateway.

Walking towards El Fahs, you come across a massive apsed **cistern**, high enough to provide a sufficient head of water to power fountains and the baths. Above it, is the doughnut mound of the old **amphitheatre**, its stonework buried. The statue bases, plinths and inscribed stones seen here were brought from the forum when the amphitheatre was turned into a fortress in the 6th century.

Heading back to the forum, but leaving the temple of Baalat well to your left, you come upon the magnificent entrance portico of the **winter baths**, four of the pink columns still standing. Twisting past an olive oil basin, you arrive at the heart of the baths, a huge rectangular *frigidarium* with its plunge pool and light-grey columns. The trench of the latrine is straight ahead, and the hot rooms are off to the right. Passing through into a later addition, there is a sumptuous dressing room, the *apodyterium*, with three marble columns made of Chemtou marble, pitted with crystal holes and veined with seams of blood-red.

Returning to the carpark from the forum, the ruins to your left were once houses, some of which predate the Roman settlement. Head for the group of grey columns which surrounded a courtyard, and are themselves surrounded by a mosaic cloister.

El Fahs and Around

El Fahs is a market town, with a Saturday souk. The **Lanterne Restaurant**, right off the road from Tunis in the town centre, is decorated in Swiss alpine style and serves excellent soups and stews.

242

Heading south or west from here, there are no hotels anywhere but more than a dozen small sites to reward the intrepid. These are described in four routes from El Fahs: to **Kairouan**, to **Ousselatia**, to **Makhtar** and to **El Krib**.

GETTING AROUND

By Train
Three trains a day run through El Fahs on their way between Tunis and Kalaa Kasbah.

By *Louage*
The only *louages* you can be sure of finding in El Fahs ply the routes to Tunis and Zaghouan.

By Bus
There are seven buses to Tunis a day and nine to Zaghouan. From Zaghouan a couple of buses a day wind down to the coast, stopping at Enfida and Hammamet on the way to Nabeul. Buses leave daily for Kairouan at 08.30 and 15.00. Seven departures pass through Siliana on the way to Makhtar. There are also two buses a day to El Krib, leaving at 08.00 and 15.00.

El Fahs to Kairouan

The P3 road climbs from the plain of Fahs and twists through limestone uplands before opening out onto the steppe, at first dotted with olive groves. As you approach the walled city of Kairouan it becomes appreciably flatter and bleaker.

The only place worth stopping is **Henchir Souar** to have a look at some rare if smudged examples of Neolithic cave art. The first is on the sheltered face of a rock 25 m above the road, below a quarry and surrounded by goats and piles of old machinery, almost directly opposite the milestone marking 65 km to Kairouan, 25 km to El Fahs. Three ochre designs can be made out, an animal, a stylized man and a linear hand. The second example is a little further along the road, painted on the orange stone of an open cave in a cleft of rounded rocks just above a hamlet. A stream runs below the rocks which have a striking natural sanctity, though the paintings, a line of red fingers and a fox-like animal, are less impressive.

El Fahs to Ousselatia

The point of this 80-km journey, apart from striking landscape, is the astonishingly well-preserved Byzantine fortress of **Ksar Lemsa**. It is awkward if you are dependent on public transport, for there is no regular bus service from El Fahs and not enough traffic on any of the roads to make hitching an easy option.

Leaving El Fahs on the signposted road for Siliana, the P4 climbs quickly into the pine-wooded hills of the Tell. After 16 km, turn left at the roadside village of **Sidi Aoudiat**, and climb steeply to **Oum el Fouah**, a hamlet of barrel-vaulted huts housing a few dozen families of shepherds, above the ruins of ancient **Seressi**. Two 3rd-century AD **triumphal arches** made from local pale stone frame the scant ruins, which cluster round a mountain stream, in summer its bed a sharp line of oleander blossom. The track through the ruins passes below the remains of a **temple** and above traces of a **Byzantine fort** and the last flicker of a **theatre**. The water source at least remains consistent, and a modern well has been sunk at the head of the stream where women draw water that once supplied a city.

Ksar Lemsa

The **fortress of Ksar Lemsa** sits at the foot of an escarpment of bleak limestone, the long face of Jebel Serj. Its four corner towers stand as the Byzantine military engineers built them in the 6th century, enclosing a courtyard entered through a northern gate. Three of the walls are high, and have had their battlements restored, but the eastern curtain wall has been completely destroyed. A black line on the inside of the courtyard wall marks the level of debris removed in a 1968 excavation to reveal details of the Byzantine interior. These waist-high walls give an oddly domestic feel, almost of a hamlet sheltering behind cliffs rather than an army barracks. The water collection system is peculiar: a drain running along the northern wall flows down into a large shallow tank outside what would have been the eastern wall. It is an almost frivolous piece of engineering that seems out of place in this military building.

Ksar Lemsa was built to guard the city of **Limisa**, traces of which survive in the custodian's garden, a small open-air museum of carving, and in the remains of a theatre, just beside the garden wall. The most interesting piece has been propped up beside the path to the ksar—a gravestone which was in later ages reused as an oil mill, as the grooves on the reverse side show.

Ousselatia and Aggar

Continuing down the Malouf valley there is a T-junction 23 km later, with Kairouan to the east, and **Ousselatia** 12 km to the west. Ousselatia's broad avenue and the silhouette of the colonial church testify to its origins. The French founded the town in 1927 and established the olive and almond groves that now proliferate.

Before the protectorate, the valley was the grazing ground of one of the most powerful tribes of the Bedouin Arabs, the Zlass, divided into two clans, the Ouled Shabib and the Ouled Hilal. In the valley, a sedentary population coexisted with the Zlass and, in return for protection from other tribes, guarded the Zlass grain stocks when they moved to other grazing grounds. This string of tight villages can still be seen clinging to the spring line at the foot of the **Jebel Serj** escarpment, their ancient olive groves spilling a little out into the plain. The most southerly, Sidi Amara, was known in the Roman period as **Aggar**, and is sited below a natural pass through the wall of Jebel Serj, the gorge of **Foum el Afrit**.

Following the road west from Ousselatia for 9 km you are warned of the approach of Aggar by **Ksar Krima**, a two-storey mausoleum that looks north up the valley. The indistinct ruined mound of Aggar is chiefly memorable for the great number of altar-shaped *stelae* that rise from the ground at odd angles like a set for a Gothic horror. A trial trench has been dug below the ruins of a Byzantine fort in an attempt to find the forum, exposing stone as fresh as if it had been carved yesterday. There are only two other recognizable features, a jumble of collapsing benches from the theatre, half-consumed in a hedge of prickly pear, and the **martyrs' cemetery**. A few of the dead from the armed struggle for independence in 1954 are buried where they fell, now shaded by cypress and enclosed in a whitewashed wall. The chief delight is in Foum el Afrit where a rickety colonial bridge fords the **Oued Jilf** beside the six spans of a majestic, but long-broken Roman bridge.

This rocky road continues to Siliana (see below). The road to Kairouan from Ousselatia climbs out of the Malouf valley on to the pine-wooded highlands of Jebel Bou Dabbous and Jebel Ousselatia. This pass is perennially fought over, and most recently commemorated by a menhir to three distinct periods of fighting in the Second World War. The village of **Ain Jelloula** sits at the foot of the mountains on the edge of the steppe land, and the nearby dry banks of the **Oued Hamra** are lined with a mixture of Roman and 18th-century ruins. Ain Jelloula was a victim of the long succession war of 1729–40 that divided the country between the Hussainiya and the Bashias. The Zlass were Bashia, the city of Kairouan was the centre of the Bashias, and poor Ain Jelloula was caught in between.

El Fahs to Makhtar

It is 100 km from El Fahs to Makhtar on the P4. An early bus can get you to Makhtar with time to have lunch, see the ruins and move on to the greater comfort offered by El Kef or Kairouan. Along the P4 there are three possible side trips, off to the Berber mountain village of **Ain Bou Saadia,** to the 3rd-century BC **battlefield of Zama** or to the isolated hamlet of El Ksour studded with ruins from Roman **Uzappa.**

Ain Bou Saadia
A left turn at Bargou, 46 km from El Fahs, puts you on the 30-km road to Ain Bou Saadia. Driving up the steep, sheltered valley cut into Jebel Bargou, you feel that you have entered a lost Berber kingdom. The inhabitants depend on the small leafy gardens mingled with olive groves in the valley floor, and their flocks of sheep and goats which graze the severe hills. Until the arrival of electricity in the last few years, they lived in concentric stone villages which still cling to the slopes and make obvious objectives for walks.

Ain Bou Saadia holds a special place in the consciousness of Tunisians, as the site of some of the fiercest fighting during the struggle for independence in 1954. A graveyard in the pine forest, signalled by red and white kerbstones just before you enter the village, commemorates the dead. At the bottom of the village is a forlorn **mini-spa** built in the 1950s around a once opulent spring, now usually dry and echoing to the sound of a petrol-pump. The tarmac road peters out beyond the village, turning into a bumpy but passable track that continues through the forest wilderness 18 km to Sidi Said, back on the road towards El Fahs.

Siliana
From Bargou it is 19 km to Siliana, the administrative centre of the region, which sits bang in the centre of the Siliana valley. Before the 20th century, it was a weekly camping ground where the Thursday market, the Souk el Khemis, was held. Even today the marketplace, surrounded by cafés, restaurants, bus and taxi stations, remains the hub of the community. Across the main street the square in front of the PTT building has been turned into a shady garden ornamented by a martial Roman torso, columns and the odd carved gravestone.

Zama Minor
Just off the Siliana–Makhtar road there is a turning marked Zama, which leads 9 km to a hillside hamlet, famous as the site of the battle where Scipio defeated Hannibal, at the end of the Second Punic War.

The ruins of Roman **Zama Minor** are not impressive. The modern farming hamlet nestles among a few broken columns, carved stones, a still-working underground Roman well and three vast cisterns whose floor is wide enough to be ploughed by tractors and sewn with wheat. The villagers are happy to see visitors, who will be offered handkerchiefs pregnant with old coins, the first stage in a long bargaining process.

It is not these that draw a visit so much as the chance to speculate on one of the most decisive battles of the world. Polybius remarks that here 'the Carthaginians were fighting for their very survival and the possession of Africa, the Romans for the Empire and sovereignty of the world.' Before the battle of Zama the Romans, restricted to an uneasy suzerainty over an assortment of allies in southern Italy, had an essentially defensive foreign policy. After Zama their ambition knew no limits. In little more than 50 years they had totally destroyed two of the greatest cities of the ancient world, Carthage and Corinth.

It is also a contentious battle: theories abound over the actual site, the routes of the two armies, their camps and where the melodramatic meeting between Scipio and Hannibal on the eve of the battle took place. This much is known: by the summer of 202 BC a Roman army under Scipio had marched up the Mejerda valley turning south at the Oued Tessa to enter the Siliana plain. Hannibal moved inland from the coast, attempting to intercept Scipio before he could be reinforced by Massinissa, Rome's Numidian ally, who was bringing a great force of native cavalry. By the time he made camp here at Zama, Hannibal realized that he had failed. It was a decisive blow, for in all his previous campaigns the Numidian cavalry had been under his command. Realizing his great disadvantage, he offered to meet Scipio.

Out from the ranks rode the two commanders, escorted by a dozen horsemen who stopped to allow the generals to meet alone. An attempt to patch up a truce failed and they rode back to make their dispositions for the battle. Hannibal, realizing his weakness in cavalry, gave orders that his own force should pretend to flee in order to draw Massinissa and his cavalry away from the battle. This done, he sent forward his squadron of 80 elephants in an attempt to shatter the Roman formations. But Scipio had drawn up his forces in echelon and the unwieldy beasts passed harmlessly through the prearranged gaps. Hannibal had divided his infantry into three divisions. Keeping his experienced veterans from Italy in reserve, he threw his first division of 12,000 mercenaries against the Roman legions, followed later by his regiments of Carthaginians. Their defeat was of no concern. They were mere cannon-fodder to tire the Romans and blunt their weapons. His shattered forces attempted to withdraw, but Hannibal ordered his veterans to present their lances and not to allow them to retreat. Faced with certain death from their own army, they were forced back against the Romans. The field grew slippery with blood, the legions weary of the slaughter. Only then did Hannibal command his veterans, fresh and untired from the day, into the assault. The fighting was bitter but the Roman front held, and before Hannibal could get in a decisive blow Massinissa and his cavalry returned to the battle. He fell on the unprotected Carthaginian rear and the Numidian cavalry began a slaughter that left 20,000 corpses. His army annihilated, Hannibal managed to escape to safety behind the walls of Sousse.

Uzappa

Twenty-five kilometres beyond Siliana is a left turn marked **Essafina**. This leads 10 km through limestone uplands, punctured by caves and dry valleys, to a remote hamlet that faces the alluring slopes of **Jebel Ballouta**, haunt of wild boar and megalithic tombs. Scattered amongst the few houses are the vestiges of ancient **Uzappa**. Foremost amongst these is a magnificent **arch** of golden stone, the monumental entrance to a **temple** dedicated to Liber Pater, one of the cult names for Bacchus. Its well-preserved façade has flanking engaged columns, topped by Corinthian capitals which include eagles and leering human faces in their design. Overlooking a tributary stream are the remains of a **triumphal arch**, and by the school is an unidentified **colonnade**. On the rugged hill above the village are traces of a **fort**, and on a neighbouring crag, deeply incised into the rock, is a worn **relief carving of Bellona**, the Roman goddess of war and pagan patroness of soldiers. Tarmac only reached here in 1989, and electricity was promised in 1990, so visitors are rare enough to be treated to the full force of Tunisian hospitality. If you want a natural adventure, try camping beneath apple trees by the river or walking in the hills.

Off the P4, Ksar Mdouja is 3 km after the Essafina turning. It is an ancient **mausoleum** whose lower chamber is still covered by its original vaulted roof. Beyond, a small ruined **fort** guards a spring, which still flows almost imperceptibly into a series of Roman troughs, 6 m long and worn by 2000 years of use. The road twists up to meet the El Kef–Kairouan road. Turn left for Makhtar, 6 km south.

El Fahs to El Krib

This 83-km route is strewn with the ruins of a chain of Roman towns, mostly unexcavated mounds of little interest, which coincide with the red-tiled roofs of French colonial towns, stations and farmhouses. Seventy years of the protectorate transformed the region from lightly worked, communally held tribal land into a few efficiently run private estates.

Leaving El Fahs on the Siliana road, take a right turn marked **Bou Arada** and **Gaafour**. Bou Arada has a few Roman bits tastefully displayed at its central crossroad. A 100-m walk down the Mejez road brings you to a **zodiac mausoleum**, enclosed in a garden strewn with finely carved tombstones and entered through the remains of a 2nd-century AD triumphal arch. The mausoleum has an altar-shaped roof and a frieze of boats and ox skulls; below are carved the signs of the zodiac, all save two. About 3 km further north there is a 10-km farm track to the right to the village of **Ftiss**—ancient Avitta Bibba, complete with ruined temples, arches, mausoleum and the inevitable cisterns.

Gaafour, 30 km from Bou Arada, is the biggest town of the region and a weathered colonial creation. The French built the town beside the **koubba** of Sidi Bou Argoub, itself on faint traces of ancient Thimisua, which overlooks the banks of the Oued Siliana. From Gaafour it is 21 km to El Krib and **Mustis**.

The Road to El Kef

Testour

The old town of Testour, 22 km from Mejez el Bab, is the most undisturbed of the Andalucian settlements in Tunisia. Its skyline is pierced by minarets, and the wooden balconies of its main street match the blue of the evening sky. It was built in the 17th century by refugees from Philip III's expulsion of all Moorish citizens from Spain in 1609. They were not welcomed in the Sahel, and settled in pockets around and in Tunis, in this case on the ruined site of Roman Tichilla, given to them by the Bey. By the end of the 17th century, Testour was a production centre for ceramic stewpots, vases, pans and rounded Andalucian tiles, which are still produced on a small scale. Money also came from silk spinning, fed by the local mulberry groves.

Although not many tourists visit Testour, the people are wary of those that do, and the welcome, apart from childen asking for pens, is muted. The mosques and shrines are usually closed, as is the town's one hotel, so unless you are lucky enough to be 'adopted', Testour is inevitably seen in passing. If you come on a Friday you will coincide with the **market** when crowds also build up to attend the week's sermon at the noon prayers. Otherwise, aim for the week-long **festival of traditional Andalusian music**, called malouf, which is staged at the end of June. Tickets, precise dates and news of any other events can be extracted from the cultural centre, housed down a side street, and also exhibiting a few dusty musical instruments.

Arriving from the east, the town is heralded by an extensive cemetery, scattered on the hill to the south. A large component of the Andalucian refugees were Sephardic Jews, expelled with the Muslims from Spain. They have their own graveyard, but the once thriving Testour community has now dispersed. Rabbi Es Saad Fradj Chaoua, a distinguished scholar born in the Mellah, the ghetto of Fez in Morocco, wandered around the scattered communities of Israel but died at Testour. The celebration of his death is an excuse for the old Jewish families of Testour to return for a holiday. The cemetery gate also serves as a *louage* and bus stop, and beside it a road sweeps into the heart of the old quarter, to an orange-tree square in front of the old mosque. Here you can sip tea beneath the shade of trees at the tables of the **Café el Borri**, or in the jasmine-scented courtyard of the **Café Andalous**.

The minaret of the **Great Mosque** dominates the town. It was built within ten years of the refugees' arrival, and would originally have been more severe. The multi-coloured octagonal summit is a recent addition, very exuberant and Tunisian with its hour clock and seals of Solomon. The other **minarets** of Testour are also typical examples of Mudejar, the late Muslim architecture of Spain: a strong, square brick tower, pierced by ascending double windows to light an inner staircase and surmounted by a simple round lantern, topped by a cone.

The true glory of the mosque, usually hidden from tourists, is the courtyard, known as the *sahn*, enclosed by a simple colonnade with Corinthian capitals, some of the columns recycled from local Roman ruins. Jasmine falls from the tiled roof and in one corner stands a sundial raised on a platform beside a sugar-loaf column. Another side courtyard was added to allow women separate access to the prayer hall.

From the two cafés, the central avenue runs parallel to the Mejerda River which can occasionally be seen down one of the side streets, lined by low houses that fall down to the river bank. Most are still whitewashed and tiled in Spanish terracotta, picked out with blue woodwork, and create a striking picture of old Spain. Of the other visible minarets, only one is in regular use—the attractive brick building known as the **Mosque of Sidi Abdul Latif**. Beyond this, a street on the left, Rue du 26 Fevrier 1953, leads past the **Mosque of Sidi Nasser el Garouachi** to his 18th-century **zaouia**, an attractive rambling progression of whitewashed walls surrounding a green-tiled, hatlike koubba. If the zaouia is closed, you can get a good view from the main road. The street gate, flanked by benches, opens into an enclosed courtyard and a tree-filled quadrangle lined with pilgrims' lodgings. From there you enter the domed koubba itself, decorated with carved plasterwork.

Jebel Skhira

The lush gardens that surround Testour are watered by the slow-moving Mejerda River and the industry of the Andalucians. Furthermore, Tunisia's most recent and ambitious hydro scheme, the **Sidi Salem Dam**, a few kilometres northwest of Testour, has stopped flooding, irrigated an extra 50,000 hectares and provides a little electricity on the side. The unnatural grandeur of the concrete dam is hidden behind a striking outcrop of land, the **Jebel Skhira** escarpment. Its cliffs change colour with the hour of the day and form the lodestone of the region.

Just out of Testour towards Mejez there is a temporary-looking bridge that spans the Mejerda. The road that crosses soon becomes a farm track, passing through alternating

248

groves of olive, citrus and pomegranate, with beds of corn and vegetables grown in their shade. The track then skirts across rough land towards the sculpted massif of Jebel Skhira, now dotted with the small garden plots of a village, where once there was an ascetic university. Its rough caves and natural arches sheltered pious Muslims, escaping from the world to seek God on the slopes of the holy mountain. Turn left at the village crossroads to visit the dam itself.

EATING OUT
Apart from the cafés in the old town, there is the **Hotel Zeidoun** at the El Kef end of new Testour. The rooms are, in theory, being redecorated but the bar and restaurant are still open. Telephone (08) 68033 to check the situation.

Ain Tounga

It is an easy mistake to think that once you have seen one ruined Roman town you have seen them all. It is even easier on your way to the glories of Dougga to whisk past **Ain Tounga** whose dominant feature—a Byzantine fort—can be seen from a passing window. However, the site rewards a half-hour of your time. It is 8 km from Testour, overlooked by a great Byzantine keep beyond which, on the slopes of **Jebel Laouej**, are the thinly scattered ruins of **Thignica**. The city reached its heyday at the end of the 3rd century, a time of discord for much of the Roman Empire but continued prosperity for the two provinces that comprised Tunisia.

Thignica was at the centre of a region heavily dominated by the personal estates of the emperors. Known as *saltus*, these were enormous land holdings, substantially increased when Nero executed the six largest landowners in Africa to obtain their estates. They were run by procurators and a staff of slaves, who let the land to middlemen, *conductores*, who in turn sublet to freeborn tenants, *coloni*, who were the nucleus of the system. In exchange for the land, the *coloni* made over a third of their harvest and a couple of days' labour a year to the *conductores*. The *coloni* were encouraged by the emperors to bring more land under cultivation. If they planted olives on marginal land known as *subseciva*, literally 'oddments', they were rewarded with a 10-year tax holiday and all rights over this land other than its sale. An inscription survives of a complaint against the local procurator who used soldiers to extract increased shares of the harvest. The emperor's reply, inscribed on an altar, orders the procurator to conform to the traditional shares.

Ain Tounga is also important for our knowledge of the cult of Saturn. There are 118 known sites of **Saturn worship** in Tunisia, of which only 10 have been excavated. One of these, at Ain Tounga, unearthed 538 *stelae*, over a fifth of the total for the whole of Africa. In almost biblical phraseology worshippers inscribe the details of their sacrifice 'life for life, breath for breath, blood for blood', addressing Saturn as 'Holy, the God, the prince of days, who places the braziers of the heavens in the firmament'. Priests of Saturn were veiled and wore no shoes, or iron, and their tunics were stitchless. Their hair was tied by a headband, their tunic by a knotted sash, all covered by a fringed cloak from which hung a crescent pendant.

The Site
The 6th-century **Byzantine fortress** is one of the best preserved in Tunisia, vying with Haidra and Ksar Lemsa. It has never been excavated, which leaves the true height of its walls, its five towers and two gates still hidden by piles of stone and debris. Inside, amongst the usual

spoilia of inscriptions and lintels used by the Byzantines, an entire Roman arch has been looted to make an internal entrance for the tall southwest tower. An inscription in Latin, contemporary with this, is a reminder of the polyglot world of the Byzantine Empire where Greek, Syriac and Latin all held sway as literary languages.

Some 2nd-century Roman baths lie about 200 m west of the citadel. The central hall, the *frigidarium*, is flanked by two symmetrical chambers, each once supported by six massive pillars, creating an overawing sense of civic grandeur.

Directly above the citadel spans a **triumphal arch**, and beyond it is an excavated portion of the city. A well-paved street climbs uphill, passing to the right a house with an intact cellar, and to the left a house with a large courtyard which has been tentatively identified as a *schola*, halfway between a club and a municipal institution. Above are the ruins of a **temple**, its enormous columns lying half unearthed and fragmented at the foot of the sacred terrace.

Further round the hill is the distinctive semi-circular wall of a **theatre**. Its two side entrance tunnels are easily identified, but there are peculiarities in its structure which suggest a later attempt at fortification.

It is well worth climbing the half-wooded slope of Jebel Laouej, whose summit is strewn with fragments of an **old sanctuary**. The view down the Mejerda valley is exalting. Further along the crest of the ridge a recent excavation has disinterred the platform and apse of another **temple**, once enclosed on its hilltop by a sumptuous colonnade.

Teboursouk

Teboursouk, a township of 8000 inhabitants, has spilled out of its Byzantine fortress which for centuries provided protection to traders and travellers. In the 18th century, 2500 people lived securely here, trading in wheat bought from local tribes like the Ouled Abu Salem and the Jundubah. Stretches of the wall remain, and within are substantial parts of the medieval street pattern, known locally as the *Cité Ksar*. The Thursday souk is still held below the walls and a few soup kitchens sell *chorba* and sheeps' heads to the hungry. The new town spreads rapidly in all directions from the old heart and beside the road is a bank, new political party headquarters, the covered market and a few cafés. Before the Byzantine fortress was built here in the 6th century, the Roman city of **Thubursicum Bure** spread over the hillside slopes.

GETTING AROUND
There are six buses a day to Tunis, just under 2½ hours away; and six to El Kef, a ride of 2 hours plus. There are also daily buses north to Béja and south to Siliana.

There are sometimes *louages* and *taxis rurals* in Teboursouk's market square, but there are no regular taxis here. If you want to visit Dougga, you will have to be prepared to walk 6 km to the ruins.

WHERE TO STAY
MODERATE
Below the town, just off the main road is the **Hotel Thugga**, the only efficient hotel between Tunis and El Kef, and the natural base for exploring Dougga and the many minor sites in the surrounding hills. The hotel is modern, and is enlivened by a collection of antique carvings. For added character ask for one of the smaller, barrel-vaulted rooms in the second courtyard. To reserve a room call (08) 65800/65713.

EATING OUT

Avoid the lunchtime crowds of tour groups at the hotel. The 5-dn *menu du jour* is often the same for both lunch and dinner, and though never inspiring is perfectly adequate once a day when washed down with the local wine from Thibar, just over the hill to the north. After dinner at the bar, look out for Teboursouk's answer to Dylan Thomas, an incomprehensible but poetic farmer.

If it is not Friday you can eat and drink at the restaurant bar hidden below the carpark at Dougga. They serve good fresh brochettes, fish and salad on a terrace with peaceful pastoral views. The other alternative is the cheap snack cafés by the road in Teboursouk.

Dougga

Dougga is reason enough to visit Tunisia. It is one of the most striking and evocative ruined cities in the Mediterranean world, and occupies a natural limestone bowl. The higher slopes are studded with the ruins of temples, and the massive columns of the temple of Saturn advertise its glories for miles around.

For the casual visitor, there is no need for guides or maps, as the main buildings are all triumphantly conspicuous. The enthusiast will have a whole day of exhausting unravelling ahead, but even a minimal hour-long tour should include the **theatre**, the **capitol**, the **baths of Licinius**, the loo in the **Cyclops' baths**, the **Trifolium brothel**, **Arteban's mausoleum**, the **temple of Juno Caelestis** and the **temple of Saturn**. Pick these out on the map and any information under the headings below, as the itinerary outlined here demands at least a couple of hours.

History

Judged by architecture and elegance alone, Dougga appears to have been a great city. Yet even at the height of the Empire its population was never more than 5000, smaller than present-day Teboursouk. It was not an important market or agricultural centre, nor did it play a military or administrative role as it only came under full Roman law in the late 3rd century AD. But though there were plenty of richer and larger cities, Dougga had a social, cultural and religious pre-eminence, fuelled by a long history which the others could not hope to touch. It contains more temples than any other city in North Africa, and in its heyday must have seen an almost continuous succession of processions, dinners, public performances and masques in honour of the gods. Its baths were numerous and vast, its brothels elegant, its temple precincts busy with supplicants, like a mixture between Bath, New Orleans and Lourdes.

Dougga is one of the oldest towns of the Tunisian interior. It started as a walled citadel, the capital of a Numidian principality which survived both the Carthaginian and Roman conquest intact. The Carthaginians only started to conquer the fertile zones of inland Tunisia from the middle of the 5th century BC. It was an uneven business, and though frontier posts were established as far west as Tebessa in Algeria, most of the Tell remained in Numidian hands, tied to Carthage by dynastic alliance. As early as the 4th century BC, according to the historian Diodorus, Dougga had a certain grandeur. Gradually the influence of Carthage came to dominate in matters of religion and language, but the princely mausoleum that survives from the 2nd century BC shows the sophistication and continued independence of the native principality. The seizure of Dougga by the Numidian King Massinissa in 155 BC saved it from

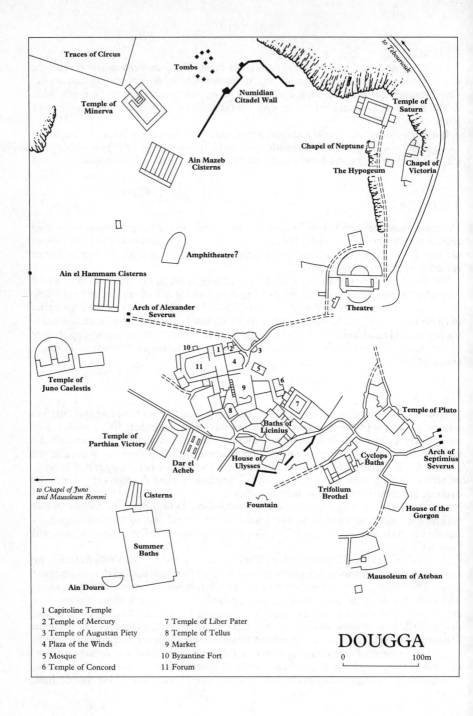

Traces of Circus

Tombs

Numidian
Citadel Wall

Temple of
Minerva

Ain Mazeb
Cisterns

Temple of
Saturn

Chapel of Neptune

The Hypogeum

Chapel of
Victoria

to Teboursouk

Amphitheatre?

Ain el Hammam Cisterns

Arch of Alexander
Severus

Theatre

Temple of
Juno Caelestis

10   1 2

11   4   3

5

9   6

8   7

Temple of Pluto

Temple of
Parthian Victory

Dar el
Acheb

Baths of
Licinius

House of
Ulysses

Cyclops
Baths

Arch of
Septimius
Severus

to Chapel of Juno
and Mausoleum Remmi

Cisterns

Trifolium
Brothel

House of the
Gorgon

Fountain

Summer
Baths

Mausoleum of Ateban

Ain Doura

1 Capitoline Temple
2 Temple of Mercury
3 Temple of Augustan Piety
4 Plaza of the Winds
5 Mosque
6 Temple of Concord

7 Temple of Liber Pater
8 Temple of Tellus
9 Market
10 Byzantine Fort
11 Forum

DOUGGA

0   100m

destruction by his allies, the Romans. Following the defeat of Carthage nine years later, a flood of Punic refugees settled the city, which remained just outside Rome's boundaries.

Its key role on the border was recognized by the Roman general Marius, the conqueror of Numidia, who secured the quiescence of Dougga by planting two new military colonies at Thibar and Uchi Majus nearby. The official absorption of Numidia into the Empire, a generation later in 46 BC, was therefore a painless affair. Dougga, or Thugga as it became known, was partially settled by Roman colonists but inscriptions record early intermarriages with the indigenous population. The town kept its own laws, magistrates and traditions and the great period of building, paid for by local aristocrats in the 2nd century, testifies to its esteem.

But Dougga kept faith in the old gods for too long to be either wise or fashionable. It was still building new temples in the late 3rd century AD and became an increasingly isolated pagan outpost in a Christian landscape. There is only one clear trace of Christianity in the city, a small 5th-century mortuary chapel.

The Byzantine conquest of Tunisia in the 6th century finished Dougga. Under the Christian missionary zeal of the Emperor Justinian the remaining temples, oracles and philosophical schools all over the Mediterranean were closed. Dougga's temples were pillaged for stone to make a rude fortress over the forum. The town degenerated into just another farming village, existing in the lee of a castle. Certain buildings were still occupied in 1954, when the inhabitants were rehoused in 'Nouvelle Dougga' to make way for the archaeologists.

The Site

Four kilometres along the road from Teboursouk, a left turn to Dougga passes below the columns of the temple of Saturn to arrive at a partly shaded carpark, complete with soft-drink salesmen and potential guides. Tickets can be bought from the wandering ticket seller, dawn to dusk.

The Theatre

Rising immediately above you is the most complete Roman theatre in Tunisia, used every summer by a touring company from the Comédie Française. It was built in the Greek style, carved into the natural gradient of the hill. The *cavea* of stone seats held 3500, small by 2nd-century standards when the theatre of Pompey in Rome held 27,000. Today, the largest theatre in the world, the Colon in Buenos Aires, holds only 5000. The wide seats at the bottom of the *cavea* were reserved for the chairs of dignitaries who arrived just before the start of the play. Below is a small orchestra pit used by the choirs. The actual stage, known as the *proscaenium*, extends beyond the *pulpitum* wall, customarily decorated with alternating rectangular and semi-circular niches, statues and fountains. The Corinthian columns of the backdrop or *scenae* stand now in a picturesque attitude of ruin. The central gate, the royal, was reserved for principal actors, one side gate used by those acting the parts of people from the town, the other by those acting strangers.

The Roman theatre season began with the festival of Cybele, the mother goddess, on 4 April and ended with the people's games in September. There was a popular and flexible programme in Latin—debates, lectures, farce, pantomime, circus and comedy. The tragedies were Greek and the repertoire had been established in the 1st century BC. Masks hinting at the characters' fate were worn, coloured brown for men and white for women. Dress was also dictated: a white robe signified an old man, yellow a courtesan, purple for the rich, red for the poor, multicoloured for uncertain youth and a short tunic for a slave. To counterbalance the continued use of Greek, a language unknown to the mass of the audience, the producers created the germs of a new art form, bringing choirs on to the stage, adding fantastic scenery and props, clipping the dialogue and fostering soloists. These stars dominated the stage, with singing that alternated between the pathetic and the passionate and acting that bordered on mime touched by the exhilaration of ballet.

The Plaza of Winds, the Temple of Mercury and the Market
Joining the paved road ahead, look out on your left for the temple of Augustan Piety, dedicated to the Roman virtue of 'pietas', a superstitious respect for the gods. It was a simple apse flanked by a pair of Corinthian pillars built in the reign of the Emperor Hadrian over an old shopping booth. This whole city centre, the plaza, temple and market, was all built in the second century by the Pacuvius family.

Step down to enter the Plaza of the Winds, a public space with an elegant circle carved into the paving recording the names of the 12 winds. To the right, up four steps is a ruined shrine of Mercury, the god of commerce. A portico at the head of the stairs enclosed the temple precinct and three distinct chapels. This may prove the African origin of the cult of the 'Thrice great Hermes', a monotheistic mystery religion, which in the 3rd century almost overshadowed Christianity. The small domed mosque to the east of the plaza is built over an old temple to Fortune.

South of the Plaza of Winds, suitably overlooked by the temple of Mercury, is the *marcellum*, or marketplace. It is now a bleak open space littered with boulders, but would have been separated from the plaza by a portico and lined by a colonnade of expensive boutiques surrounding a fountain. In the southern face of the market you can trace the outline of an apse, dedicated to Mercury—an elegant reflection of the larger temple.

The Capitol
The star attraction of Dougga is the Capitoline temple. It is not size, age or originality of architecture that makes it such an exciting building, but the surving elegance of its carved Corinthian portico, baked gold by the African sun, cut by dark shadows and set against an aching blue sky. The inscription on the architrave is to the ruling trinity, Jupiter Optimus Maximus, Royal Juno and August Minerva, who also ruled from the Capitoline hill in Rome. It was a late addition to Dougga, which already honoured all three gods in older and larger sanctuaries, and was built in the reign of Marcus Aurelius. The worn carving on the pediment is not Jupiter raping Ganymede but the apotheosis of Antoninus Pius, the previous emperor, being taken up by an eagle to join the immortals. Inside the *cella*, which would have been used for dinners held by the college of priests, are three niches for the statues of the gods. Lying in dust on the floor is a massive marble head of Jupiter, blinded by Christian monks and neglected by the 20th century. The high raised podium of the temple concealed three crypts where wills and sacred objects were safely stored.

We owe the preservation of the capitol to the fact that it was included in the later Byzantine fortress. The remains of this fortification still cut across the forum, obscuring the ante-capitol, a clear space the same size as the temple complete with an altar, placed at the other end of this public square. It was used for official sacrifices, declarations and oaths.

The Forum
The forum is an open space, enclosed by the walls of the later Byzantine fort, at the foot of the old Numidian citadel. The fort was built hurriedly in AD 540 with stone from the surrounding

temples and public buildings, but was not a military post, rather a shelter for the population of the town during raids. All you can recognize of the Roman public square is the base of the Corinthian colonnade, but standing here at the end of the 3rd century, the skyline would have been broken by the roofs of temples to Saturn, Jupiter, deified Massinissa and Tiberius, by two triumphal archs, the law courts, a town hall and a number of colossal imperial statues, not to mention the capitol.

The Temples of Tellus and Parthian Victory and the Dar el Acheb

There are three lesser edifices in the confused area of ruin in the sloping ground below the market. In the southern face of the market a staircase leads down to the temple of Tellus, a ruined courtyard facing a row of three chapels, built in the late 3rd century. The large central one contains three niches for statues of Tellus Mater herself, Telluno her male counterpart and Ceres. Tellus Mater watched over the fruitfulness of the soil and the germinating seed. Brides sacrificed to her before entering their husbands' house and she shared in the rites before the harvest. Echoes of her worship are still found in Tunisia, where corn dollies are woven from the last of the harvest and ploughed into the first furrow of the following crop.

From this temple head down across a villa to the Dar el Acheb, recognizable by a Corinthian column to the left of the doorway. It is an extensive rectangular courtyard with central bins and flanking porticoes built during the reign of Marcus Aurelius. Its function is not known, but it is possibly a combined workshop and marketplace run by a guild, complete with a sanctuary to its patron.

Turn left out of the Dar el Acheb and face a 30-m long undeciphered semi-circular monument, possibly an ornate fountain in honour of an imperial family. Immediately behind are the ruins of a temple erected by the Emperor Caracalla to victory over the Parthians. The road beside it carries the remains of another forgotten monument, a massive Corinthian pilaster colonnade.

The Temple of Liber Pater

Returning to the Plaza of Winds, take a left and wind past the mosque. On your left two Corinthian pillars flank a flight of seven steps up into the small temple of Concord, its inner courtyard leading to an apsed shrine. Concord was a sort of official patroness of Roman Tunisia. Augustus refounded Carthage in her name, *Colonia Concordio Julia Carthago*, a symbol to heal the hatred still simmering after the destruction of the city and the civil war.

Next door is a much larger temple complex known as Liber Pater. It has an enclosed colonnaded courtyard and five distinct shrines to the northwest, but an almost domestic atmosphere, for it was the house of the Gabini before they converted it into a sanctuary in Hadrian's reign. The larger apsed shrine is believed to have held the cult statue of Liber Pater, the 'Free Father', an Italian deity who later became confused with Bacchus/Dionysus, though his rites had a stronger archaic concern with the powers of regeneration. His feast day, *Liberalia* on 17 March, was the day when adolescents first donned their adult male clothing, the *toga virilis*. According to inscriptions discovered, Frugifer, an African version of Pluto and a patron of Dougga, and his brother Neptune were honoured in other shrines here. Immediately below the sanctuary is a small temple theatre, an intimate space where religious rites and mimes were performed.

Baths of Licinius

Opposite this temple is the small lobby of the 3rd-century baths of Licinius, whence two flights of stairs lead down into a colonnaded, open-air courtyard, decorated by a statue. This was the principal entrance hall, a social gathering spot before passing into the square vestibule, which opens directly on to the central nave of the baths, the *frigidarium*. The vestibule also has a service tunnel entrance and was the start of a long chain of hot rooms, now largely featureless apart from traces of the hypocaust system for heating the walls and floor. Bathers passed through the *sudatoria* (sweat rooms) before progressing into a small and then the recognizable large *calidaria* (hot rooms) which had small steam baths set in the outer wall. They would then have moved into the wedge-shaped *tepidarium* and back into the elegant rectangular space of the *frigidarium* lined by cold pools and sitting areas. At the other end of the *frigidarium* an intact arched colonnade leads into another vestibule with its own symmetrical set of hot rooms, another service tunnel and on the left the elegant 16-pillared *palaestra* or gymnasium. The baths were not all a cult of the body, and the public also thronged here to see their friends, and visit the associated libraries and shops. The symmetry of the baths was aesthetic rather than practical, and different opening hours rather than walls kept the sexes apart here.

Leaving the baths by the service tunnels you come out into a street which passes through a residential quarter whose villas once boasted a glittering collection of mosaics. Over 10 separate pieces are now lodged in the Bardo, though there are still some admirable geometric designs and lesser portraits worth a quick inspection. The richest collection was found in the villa almost directly opposite the bath exit, known as the House of Ulysses after a mosaic much reproduced by the Tunisian Tourist Board.

Trifolium Brothel
Walking below the baths, cut down opposite the Liber Pater theatre to the *Maison du Trifolium*, a purpose-built brothel from the 3rd century AD. Its entrance used to be advertised by a herm, a stone column decorated with an erect penis, but this has been removed to leave two simple columns flanking a hall, whence a staircase leads down into a sunken courtyard of baked stone and dead weeds. Around the courtyard are numerous small booths for the prostitutes, empty but still conjuring up a langorous orientalist dream world. In a corner of the garden is a vaulted chamber, a clover-leaf dining room, which gives the house its name, and has its own back passage to the kitchen. Now empty, it would once have been thick with the mingled perfume of wine and scent, sprinkled with couches judiciously angled to frame a temporary stage.

Cyclops' Bath
Next door is the Cyclops' bath, a small ruinous neighbourhood bathhouse which was directly connected to the Trifolium. Its chief attraction is a *forica* or public latrine, immediately to the left of the main entrance. Admittance cost one *as*, a trifling fee for the use of this horseshoe bench with a dozen neat key-hole slits cut into the stone in companionable proximity. A sewer ran below, a trench of fresh water trickled by your feet for ablutions and the gay sound of a fountain splashed away in the corner. Though there are no traces now, there would have been metal brackets between the holes both as a support and a demarcation, and the wall above would have held niches with statues of heroes and deities like Fortune, the goddess of health and happiness. The *forica* was a mixture of delicacy and coarseness that has no modern analogy: a place where people met, conversed and exchanged invitations to dinner without embarrassment. The baths themselves, squeezed into an odd plot of land, have none of the usual symmetry, but you can recognize the *frigidarium* with its rectangular pool. Beside it is an *exedra*, a dressing-room, whose floor was covered by a mosaic of three, sweaty, muscle-bound cyclopes hammering away in Vulcan's forge (now in Room XII of the Bardo).

The Temple of Pluto and Arch of Septimius Severus

Coming out of the baths turn right and head down a paved street. The ruined sanctuary of Pluto, one of the patrons of Dougga, is to the left just before the broken arch.

The arch of the Emperor Septimius Severus was built in AD 205. It was the most impressive of the town gates, decorated with Corinthian pilasters, and threw a 15-m arch above the main road that leads up from the Carthage to Tebessa highway. On the left is the broken inscription, its carving of palm bark a suitable reminder of the Emperor from Libyan Sabratha.

House of the Gorgon

Walking back from the arch, take the road downhill to the pyramid-capped mausoleum, popping into the House of the Gorgon on the way. It is a spacious villa with a network of cool capacious cellars under the living rooms. Look out for the swastika mosaic in the principal room with its damaged central medallion. This showed Perseus with the Gorgon's head until it was mutilated by Christians, fortunately a minority in Dougga but well established in this house if the number of their oil lamps found in the cellar is anything to go by.

Mausoleum of Ateban

This Libyo-Punic tomb is one of the most important monuments in Tunisia. It is the only survivor from the Punic era, a precious relic whose fusion of Libyan, Egyptian, Greek and Persian styles forms the basis for all reconstructions of Carthaginian architecture.

It was built for Prince Ateban, son of Iepmatath, son of Palu during the reign of King Massinissa, somewhere around the year 200 BC. The most immediately apparent influence is Egyptian: discard the three stages of vertical wall and you find that the summit and three flights of steps fit together to form a perfect pyramid. The middle storey is clearly Greek with its fluted Ionic pilasters supporting a simplified entablature. The carved rams' horn capitals on the corners of the lower and upper storey and the window-like haouanets appear to have been drawn from native traditions. From Persia came symbolic animal carvings: the surviving carvings of four-horse chariots represent the journey of the soul through the heavens. The four sirens that once perched on the angles of the pyramid patrolled the four quarters of the sky, and a lion on the apex symbolized the final purity of the sun.

There is also a strong English involvement with this building, a mixture of vandalism and scholarship. Thomas Read, the consul in Tunis, demolished it in 1842 in order to extract a bilingual inscription, in Punic and Libyo-Phoenician. This allowed Libyan to be deciphered for the first time in the British Museum. Fortunately the French archaeologist Poinssot, using a sketch made in 1765 by James Bruce, was able to rebuild it in 1910.

Walk to the Temple of Juno Caelestis

Potter back uphill and take the farm track down to the left, passing below a plain apse with three niches, a fountain-cum-nympheum that disgorged water stored in Ain el Hammam cisterns. The track then passes through the scattered ruins of the public **summer baths**, built at the end of the second century. Only the eastern quarter has been excavated, revealing large pedestals and capitals that give some indication of the grandeur and expansive scale. These were at least four times the size of the baths of Licinius, and with the forum provided the main axis of public life in Dougga.

Just beyond on your left, partly hidden behind a wall of prickly pears is **Ain Doura spring**, surrounded by animal dung and the cracked pillars of a colonnaded apse. Refreshed by this ancient source, walk uphill through twisted olives. The ruins of the **chapel of Juno** are hidden behind a prickly pear hedge set in a little olive grove of their own. It is a domed four-apsed oratory where a statue of the goddess presided over the city of the dead. Call the sovereign lady under any of her contemporary titles, Mary or Fatimah, and this oratory would continue to have its trickle of suppliant widows in any Mediterranean graveyard. On the hill above can be seen the remains of a mausoleum, built to house the urns of the Remmi, who with the Magnia were the chief families of the town. Stumbling up the farm track, past the tombstones of lesser citizens, like a weary supplicant you approach the temple sanctuary of Juno of the Heavens.

Temple of Juno Caelestis

Enclosed by a bowl of hills and surrounded by olives, the ruined temple of the queen of the gods offers an architectural microcosm of its surroundings. A colonnaded semi-circular courtyard half encloses a high sanctuary which is completely encircled by free-standing columns. A portico of 14 Corinthian columns would have looked out over the agricultural plain. It is the most harmonious and studiedly elegant temple in Dougga, a piece of pure Hellenism in Africa. The temple was built on virgin land in the early 3rd century AD when the Severan dynasty, an imperial family of Punic origin, showed favour to any city who honoured their patron goddess. To make the point even more clearly the names of other towns and provinces who supported the cult of Juno Caelestis were inscribed on the entablature of the outer colonnade and their symbols included in carvings on the portico.

Walk to the Temple of Saturn

Above the temple of Juno is an **arch** raised to a Severan Emperor, Alexander Severus, in gratitude for giving Dougga the privileges of a *municipium*. It is a slight, almost perfunctory affair, as befits what was little more than a cemetery gate. Just above is the **Ain el Hammam** cistern, whose five long reservoirs were fed by an aqueduct from el Hammam spring, 12 km west of the city. In a corner of the cisterns a marabout is buried, marked by a whitewashed stone. Tradition has it that the villagers took to living underground amongst the hidden world of cisterns, drains and canals to escape the Hilalian invasion in the 11th century.

Uphill the depression on the right has been somewhat enthusiastically identified as an **amphitheatre**. Above are seven vaulted reservoirs were known as **Ain Mazeb** after a reliable local spring, itself a hidden asset of the Numidian citadel who venerated its guardian nymph. The corner of the reservoir almost touches the **temple of Minerva** set within an enormous and barely recognizable courtyard. Only three pillars of the colonnade still stand, beside the temple podium, sole traces of the 2nd-century enlargement of this ancient hilltop shrine. To the northwest of the temple was the site of the circus, a race track marked out by low dry-stone walls. The spectators sat al fresco on the bare surrounding rocks. To the north by the cliff face is a cluster of dolmens, simple arrangements of large stone slabs that covered funerary urns. These tombs have been dated from between the 3rd and 1st century BC, so they were still used well after Arteban's mausoleum had been built. To the east, complete with traces of two towers, a 130-m stretch of the wall of the Numidian citadel survives. Follow the traces of this above the cliff face to bring you to the temple of Saturn.

The Temple of Saturn

The view through the four columns of the temple of Saturn is a classic Tell vista over grain fields to the forested heights on the other side of the valley. It is the oldest view in Dougga, since a cave found here, dedicated to the worship of Baal, predates the Numidian citadel. The present temple, built by the Emperor Septimius Severus in AD 195, dressed the original sanctuary in a classical façade but respected the original plan. The standing columns held a false portico behind which stretched a high-walled colonnaded courtyard entered through a small door. At the back of this courtyard are the ruins of three sanctuaries, the central one dedicated to Saturn. Just in front of it are a pair of crudely carved footprints, which once held *vestigia*, a pair of finely carved footprints of the god, probably in metal, a symbol with multiple references. For the simple and superstitious they were thought to be the actual marks left by Saturn whilst visiting the temple, to others an indication to approach the shrine in bare feet and humility, to others a warning that though the gods are invisible, they are everywhere. The holy of holies, a series of connected grottoes now exposed in the centre of the courtyard, was originally entered by a stairway to the left. Numerous stelae and urns filled with burnt sacrifices were found here.

The Hypogeum and Chapel of Victoria

Beside the temple of Saturn is another of the town's cemeteries and a scattering of broken urns, stelae and sarcophagi. A small apse, set almost into the hill and approached by three steps was a wayside chapel of Neptune, the god to approach for those fearful of earthquakes. Below that is an *hypogeum*, a crypt whose cellar is still chock full of stone sarcophagi and one or two niches for urns. A brief excavation has revealed a mixture of Christian and pagan symbols—signs of tolerance or double insurance? Further down the hill lie the remains of the **Chapel of Victoria**, a combined chapel and crypt. It is the only positively Christian building in Dougga, a clumsy irregular structure that may have grown up around a martyr's grave. Flanking steps lead to the altar with corresponding stairs down into a small crypt. It was built in the early 5th century with stones robbed from the theatre and the temple of Saturn, when Dougga as one would wish to imagine it had already decayed.

Out from Teboursouk

The Road to Béja and Bou Salem

From Teboursouk the road for **Bou Salem** climbs over **Jebel Goraa**, recognizable by its radio mast and cliffy summit. Just before the top, 10 kms out of Teboursouk, a blue and white factory on the right is the bottling plant for **Ain Melliti**, a mineral water drunk the length and breadth of Tunisia. A pipe runs down from an enclosed spring on the right of the road, and fragments of the 2nd-century Roman town **Numluli** rise to the northeast.

Thibar

Continuing over Jebel Goraa, the village of Thibar lies 2 km down the Béja turning. It centres on the farm and agricultural college of the White Fathers, an order founded in the 1870s by Cardinal Lavigerie to work in Africa and spread the Christian message by example rather than conversion. Thibar, known as the Domaine de Saint Joseph, originally started as an orphanage, funded by the farm, college and vineyard, but the last White Father left Thibar, and Tunisia, in January 1976. Their large, quasi-fortified farmyard is a riot of animals, and the

Domaine is still one of the most important producers of Tunisian wine. Here they produce *Thibar, Clos de Thibar, Chateau Khanguet* and *Thibarine*, a digestif made to a secret monkish recipe.

Follow the green sign to the **British War Cemetery**, another strange quiet 'corner of some foreign field that is for ever England', next to the Catholic cemetery and seminary garden. The restaurant opposite the Domaine bottling factory will make you a spicy *casse-croûte*.

Djebba

Opposite the turning to Thibar, a road winds right up under Jebel Goraa to Djebba. The Romans, who knew it as Thiggiba Bure, mined here for galena, which contained a small proportion of silver, and calamine which they used to make brass. The works were only finally closed 50 years ago.

In the cliffs above are caves, one of which is known as the **Cave of the Seven Sleepers**. It is named after the seven brothers who hid from the persecution of Emperor Decius in a cave where they miraculously fell asleep for 200 years, waking only when Christianity had become the official religion. The story is corroborated by a verse of the Koran, and throughout the Muslim world there are dozens of rival locations.

Looking into the fields around, it is possible to guess the chief ingredient of Thibarine liqueur, with gnarled fig trees splayed across most of the small walled fields, and new groves still being planted.

Suttu/Henchir Chett and Uchi Maius

The south face of Jebel Goraa is also puckered by caves and cliffs turned orange with age. Beneath the mountain is an inhabited Roman villa, known as **Henchir Chett**, sole remnant of the town of **Suttu**, and a few kilometres beyond are the remains of another Roman settlement, that of **Uchi Maius**.

Heading out towards Dougga, take the road that branches off to the right, signposted to Souk el Jemma. Take a right turn 11 km later and then after 1 km fork right and follow a track up to Henchir Chett, a fortress-like house below the mountain. It is a working farmhouse, surrounded by dung heaps and orchards, but by hanging around and smiling a lot you may be invited to have a look inside. The paved courtyard contains fragments of columns, a beautiful Corinthian capital and a number of Roman tombstones used to support a series of later arches. The central tower-like chamber is now a cowshed, but this quiet outpost of antiquity shows how little the essential conditions of a share-cropping tenant farmer have changed in 16 centuries.

Returning to the Souk el Jemma road, after some 4 km look out on the right for a hill littered with dressed stones. This was **Uchi Maius**, a town settled by the veterans of Marius' 2nd-century BC campaign against Jugurtha. The site has never been excavated and is just an olive grove, littered with fragments of pottery and carved stone, where pillars lie propped against trees and the atmosphere is disturbed only by herds of cows and tortoises. It is a perfect **picnic spot**, a place where every ruin or mound is a potential temple or a palace of the imagination. Only one half of a **triumphal arch** is immediately recognizable, though above it is a series of immense **cisterns**. On the summit of the hill rests a neglected **mosque**, its prayer hall supported by Roman columns. Within the graveyard wall nestles a **temple sanctuary**, and the crest of the hill is marked by the traces of a defensive wall.

On to El Kef

Along the El Kef road is the modern roadside village of **Nouvelle Dougga**, to which the original inhabitants of Dougga were moved to make way for the archaeologists. Half a kilometre past Nouvelle Dougga, a hedge of cypress opens up and a farm track leads to **Borj Brahim**, a square Byzantine fort in good condition. It is partly occupied by a farm, but you are welcome to inspect the interior and climb the stone stairs that lead to the summit of the northeast tower. From here you look down inside the walls to a 19th-century colonnade, built to house a detachment of cavalry to guard this post on the Tunis to El Kef road. The Byzantines used a Roman inscription from Emperor Septimius Severus in the wall, and Lt Bentley from the British First Army added his name and unit to the stone when Borj Brahim was on the front line in December 1942. The ploughed fields towards Dougga are only a few feet thick, the fertile earth resting on the roof of a vast series of cisterns.

Mustis

The ruins of Mustis are 19 km from Teboursouk by the modern town of El Krib, where a Tuesday market animates this otherwise self-sufficient farming community.

Mustis was a much younger city than Dougga, founded by the Roman general Marius at the end of the 2nd century BC but was much larger and busier. It sat right on the crossroads of Roman Africa's two great highways, the routes from Carthage to Timgad and from Annaba to Sousse.

Coming from Teboursouk a **triumphal arch** to the left of the road signals the ruins, which are a little further on the right, dominated by a 6th-century AD Byzantine fortress on the hill. The first building you see from the entrance is the **temple of Ceres**, the great mother goddess whose festival was one of the chief events of the African year. Its original form has been disturbed by the Byzantines who also made this block of the city into a fort. The only entrance is now from behind on to its pillared courtyard. Two half-statues crown the temple above some carved sphinx figures. Beyond is the **temple of Apollo**, the god of reason, music and learning.

Beside the temple of Ceres through a triple arch runs a paved street, climbing up to the fortress but passing the **temple of Pluto** on the way. The street is lined with shops, the stone portals marked with the grooves by which the storekeepers secured their goods with heavy shutters and bars. In front of the austere temple of Pluto, god of the dead, but probably honoured here more as lord of mineral wealth and the patron of miners and quarrymen, sit two pieces of an olive oil press. On top of the first is a grooved slab where a millstone would have turned to crush the olives into a pulp, which would then have been shovelled out along the channel. The second part of the process, represented by the pear-shaped stone upright against the wall, entailed packing the olive pulp into sacks, placing them on top of one another and squeezing them under a heavy vice, the oil trickling out into the circular drain and out along the neck.

To the west of the temple there is the complete floor plan of a grooved **olive mill**, including the stone vat in which the oil would have been left to settle. Just to the south of this lies a **villa**, built around a columned courtyard with a surviving staircase climbing to a second storey. North of the oil press is a **Byzantine church**, contemporary with the fort. Its plan is typical: a nave divided into three aisles leads to a semi-circular apse beside which is a round marble font. On the left as you enter the church, steps lead down into the cool underground chambers of an earlier **villa**.

Entering the **Byzantine fortress**, you are plunged back into the 6th century, into the world of Belisarius, his eunuch deputy Solomon and their master Emperor Justinian. The outer walls, the interior barracks and cisterns seem only recently deserted, and reveal the energy and determination of the Byzantine Empire. The monuments of the old Roman city must have been almost levelled to provide the stone to build the enormous thick walls of the fortress. It is ironic that the Byzantines, who saw themselves as the heirs of the old Roman Empire, should have defeated the Vandals in order to perform such state-wide vandalism themselves. An inner wall in the far left-hand corner of the fortress is a monstrous jackdaw's nest of carved and inscribed stones.

The most exquisite things are to be found in the second cistern. Beyond a geometric **mosaic** found in the church, complete with peacocks and a chalice, stand fragments of **half pillars**, one deeply carved with vines and another flowing with a serpentine pattern inspired by ears of wheat. They would have made a fitting tribute to Ceres in her temple. Looking from the battlements, the lintels of unexcavated houses extend to the north and west, and the foundations of another **triumphal arch** mark the western limits of the town.

Borj Messaoudi

Eight kilometres from El Krib, on the edge of the village of Borj Messaoudi, is the **koubba of Sidi Moussa**, where an old Aleppo pine has grown to shade the whitewashed walls. The recent dead are buried around the koubba amongst the barely perceptible contours of the Roman city of **Thacia**, and newly married couples visit the shrine to circle the tomb, light a candle and pray, placing the fertility of the new union under the protection of the saint.

Hammam Baida

Directly opposite the shrine is the road to Souk el Jemma. For six days a week it is hardly a hamlet, but every Friday it becomes a **market** town of tents, complete with stable yards for donkeys and Peugeot trucks. Sitting above the fertile agricultural plain through which the Oued Tessa flows, Souk el Jemma has its own curious water supply. An outcrop of limestone rises beside the road and hides within its contours a cave filled with hot sulphurous water, the natural **Hammam Biada**, popular with local farmers and known to the Romans as **Aptucca**. There is no charge to use this gift of God; just grab the blue nylon rope and drift into a darkened cleft of hot water and acrid fumes. A separate channel fuels the ladies' hammam, a more organized and reclusive affair, consisting of stone chambers, ditches, doors and marginally cooler water.

Back on the main road to El Kef, after it crosses the Oued Tessa it begins a gradual climb up the **Khanguet el Kedim col**, a twisty passage flanked by **Jebel Berkane** to the north and Jebel Kebbouch to the south. In summer, scent from pines mixes with the colour of the oleanders on the river bed, beckoning travellers to delay, though a hundred years ago spurs would have been applied to hurry through this notorious haunt of bandits. About 5 km before the Kairouan crossroads, keep an eye open for a bridge, just a few metres from the ruins of its Roman predecessor. Once at the crossroads, known locally as **Borj el Aifa**, you are on the high plateau of El Kef, 17 km east.

El Kef

El Kef is the capital of the Tell. The medina clings to a hillside, capped by the high walls of a **kasbah**, and looks out across fertile plains and mountains. At sunset the mountains, stretching west into the distance, are silhouetted against a fiery sky and evoke a sense of the vast continent beyond.

As well as the kasbah, there is a good local museum and amongst the scattering of ruins you can find the most complete and mysterious Roman building in the country and the best preserved Byzantine church. There are a number of idiosyncratic hotels and restaurants in the town, which, untouched by tours, has kept an atmosphere of open friendliness. It has good transport connections and makes the ideal base from which to explore the monuments in the Tell or to take less demanding walks in the surrounding countryside.

History

Fifty-thousand-year-old tools have been found in the caves and woodland surrounding El Kef, and once here it is easy to understand what attracted these early settlements. Situated at the end of a limestone escarpment with commanding views of the plains below, the land is riddled with caves and dotted with perennial springs.

Although El Kef was a Carthaginian fortress in 450 BC, it first enters history books after the First Punic War (264–241 BC). The Carthaginians had been defeated by the Romans and forced to pay huge indemnities. As a result, their mercenary army went unpaid, and was exiled to El Kef. Within a year it rebelled, and the ensuing Mercenary War was a truceless conflict of legendary brutality.

In his account of the war, Polybius also mentions El Kef's fame as a place of temple prostitution. Strong religious leanings and a military connection have stayed with the city to this day. The Roman colony established by the Emperor Augustus at the time of Christ was known as Sicca Veneria, a name derived from Venus, the goddess of love, in devotion to whom priestesses were trained in her subtle arts. When Christianity came to Africa, El Kef became a stronghold for the new faith, and its bishop is mentioned as early as AD 256.

The kasbah fortress was built in the early 6th century when the Byzantine Empire was imposing its control. It fell to the Arab invasion in the 7th century but remained the strongpoint of the region, embroiled in a continuous succession of border and dynastic wars. One of the most dramatic of these came in 1705 when an Algerian army invaded, captured the ruling Bey in battle just outside El Kef and advanced to lay siege to Tunis. Resistance was led by Hussein ibn Ali Turki, the son of an El Kef garrison officer, whose tomb can be seen here in the medina. Hussein organized the defence of Tunis and mobilized the tribes, sending the invaders back to Algeria three months later. His 30-year reign has a curious symmetry, ending with a battle fought just outside El Kef against an Algerian army.

Border fighting flickered on, and by 1860 the population numbered a mere 3000. As the only urban centre in the west, however, El Kef still had an extensive religious and intellectual influence. The nine *zaouia* in the medina were linked to well over 60 lodges that operated amongst the nomad tribes.

In 1881 a French force stepped neatly and quietly into the shoes of the Turkish garrison, followed in good time by mining engineers and estate managers in the town. At the end of 1942 El Kef served as headquarters for de Gaulle's Free French. Here they waited until Christmas Eve when the assassination of Darlan, the Vichy commander of North Africa, marked an Allied purge which gave them control of the colonial administration.

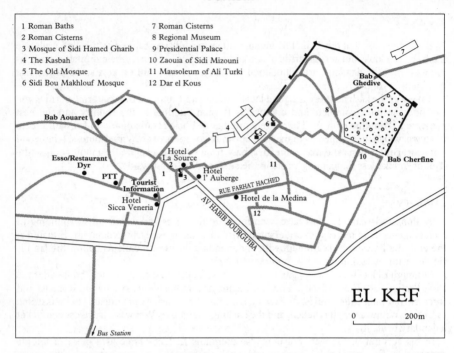

1 Roman Baths
2 Roman Cisterns
3 Mosque of Sidi Hamed Gharib
4 The Kasbah
5 The Old Mosque
6 Sidi Bou Makhlouf Mosque

7 Roman Cisterns
8 Regional Museum
9 Presidential Palace
10 Zaouia of Sidi Mizouni
11 Mausoleum of Ali Turki
12 Dar el Kous

EL KEF

0   200m

The French–Algerian war was in full flow when Tunisia was given independence in 1956. El Kef's kasbah was perfectly sited for observing a number of Algerian resistance encampments in the area. The French garrison therefore failed to depart and only did so after local tribesmen picketed the heights of Jebel Dyr and sniped away at them continuously.

GETTING AROUND

By Bus
El Kef's bus station is downhill from the body of the town, below the **Sicca Veneria Hotel** and on down a wide street, tucked in below the signposted **Monoprix**. From here there are hourly buses to Tunis from 05.00, stopping at Teboursouk and Mejez el Bab on the way. Buses north to Jendouba currently leave hourly between 06.00 and 10.00 and then at 14.00 and 16.00. Buses to Kairouan, stopping at Makhtar, leave twice a day and there are three a day for Kasserine, connecting to Sbeitla and Gafsa. Buses for Sakiat Sidi Youssef on the Algerian border currently leave at 06.00, 10.00 and 14.00.

By *Louage*
You can pick up *louages* for all destinations at the bus station.

By Car
Hertz have opened a car hire office in El Kef, opposite the main entrance to the Sicca Veneria Hotel on Rue Salah Ayeche, tel (08) 22059. Prices are higher than elsewhere, with a week's unlimited mileage in a Fiat Uno costing 320 dn, or 23 dn a day plus 230 ml per kilometre. Both these prices are before insurance and 17% tax.

TOURIST INFORMATION
The Association for the Protection of the Medina (A.S.M.) acts as an informal **tourist office** and café on Rue Hedi Chaker. It is covered with old prints and photographs, and cabinets of musty books. They will advise you how to find the sights of El Kef, and how to get into anything that is proving difficult.

The only **bank** which seems to change money is the STB, on Rue Salah Ayeche opposite the Sicca Veneria. To get to the **Post Office** carry on walking a few hundred metres from the centre of town.

The spring
At the heart of El Kef is the spring that has supplied the various cities with water for the last couple of millennia. Now known as **Ain el Kef**, it is also referred to as Ras el Ain, the head of the waters. Modern pumping has reduced the once profuse flow, but there is usually a trickle to be heard in its paved and shaded courtyard. Beside the spring is a locked niche, containing a small altar to Lalla Ma, the Lady of the Waters. The survival of this spirit, the last remaining allusion to the Punic goddess Ashtarte, shows the vital role of water and its equitable distribution in an arid country. In summer the courtyard becomes an open-air café in the evenings. The town park and municipal swimming pool below mark the old course of the stream.

Roman Baths and Byzantine Church
Beyond the **mosque of Sidi Hamed Gharib**, beside the spring, lie some exposed ruins from **Sicca Veneria**. An impressive hexagonal chamber, enclosed by double arches marks a Roman bath complex. A fountain filled the central hexagonal pool, which lapped water into the surrounding paddling pools, each with its own drain. This was reflected by an apse at the other end of the hall, where a fountain played. Reminiscent of a *nympheum*, the corridor behind it leads into a dark tunnel to the cisterns.

Beside this exuberant display of water power, the Byzantines built a small **church**. The eastern altar apse can just be made out, nestling against one of the outer walls of the hexagon. Archaeologists are undecided whether the hexagon was then used for baptism. Patches of **mosaic paving** survive and a number of engraved Christian gravestones litter the floor of the nave.

Across the road are the **cisterns**, the keys for which are kept by the guardian who will doubtless find you. You descend into a vast, partly excavated cavern supported by 54 columns.

The Kasbahs
Looming above the town and proudly flying the red crescent and star of Tunisia, are the two kasbahs, enclosed in one outer wall. The lower courses of the smaller of the two forts are recognizably Byzantine, its walls made from the despoiled Roman town below. In 1740, Ali Bey began the construction of the larger and higher kasbah beside it. A force of archaeologists and skilled craftsmen have recently taken over, and though work is very much in progress, you can still enter by the gate above **Bou Makhlouf square**.

As you walk into the kasbah, a row of cannons on your right face cisterns on the left. Ahead is the gate of the old kasbah, constructed largely from Roman *spoilia*. Its walls enclose a small courtyard and give fine views over the town below. Immediately beneath the walls to the south are the old cavalry stables.

Coming out of the old kasbah, ask to see the old **Turkish prison** on your left. Two large chambers held prisoners of either sex waiting to be judged. The commonest form of punishment was the *bastinado*, beating the soles of the feet, and was supposedly carried out in the smaller chamber. A small passage leads to five solitary confinement cells.

The old Turkish drawbridge into the new kasbah is being restored, and will lead through an elaborate S-bend into the main courtyard. The ramparts are also being restored, a library and museum built and the existing open-air theatre improved. Further schemes involve the restoration of the highest Ramadan tower, where a cannon will sound the end of the daily fast, and the building of a cinema, restaurant, café and hotel. If all this is not an elaborate pipe dream, it should be well worth the price of a bed.

The Old Mosque
Beside where the stairs from the kasbah meet Bou Makhlouf square stands an austere stone building. The removal of its minaret and the display of Roman and Punic statuary in its gardens add to the confusion surrounding its history.

Although it is certainly one of Tunisia's oldest places of Muslim worship, in use since the 8th century, it was built about 400 years earlier, but no one knows what for. Within lie two principal spaces, a magnificent open courtyard with a shaded colonnade, whence a gate leads into an extraordinary barrel-vaulted room in the shape of a cross. The apse contains three niches, and niches with troughs line the transept on both sides. In each corner hides a small dark room. The plain, beautifully dressed stone, the generous proportions and the aura of mystery and darkness suggest at least some public function. Archaeologists have thankfully given up, leaving room for the imagination. Here in ancient Sicca Veneria it is tempting to suggest some form of early Christian temple prostitution, but more prosaic minds moot a marketplace or the centre for the distribution of the city's dole.

The Mosque of Sidi Bou Makhlouf
Above the clean stonework of the Old Mosque, worn stairs approach the **Mosque of Sidi Bou Makhlouf**. Flanked by whitewashed courtyards and green doors, and crowned by an octagonal minaret and a pair of sculpted domes, the mosque is the archetypal image of Muslim El Kef. The interior is an elaborate honeycomb of sculpted plaster in the Moorish taste.

Sidi Bou Makhlouf Mosque, El Kef

266

Sidi Bou Makhlouf began life as the zaouia of the Aissaouia brotherhood, one of the more notorious of the 16th-century Sufi fraternities. The founder is buried in Morocco, but his mystical practices were taught here by his disciples. After prolonged dancing, the spirit is open to God and the body insensible to pain. In past years adepts would demonstrate this by self-mutilation and even by eating poisonous plants and animals. The brotherhood was closed down, however, in the reforming days after independence and the building is now a normal mosque.

During Ramadan, it is the centre of events, and there is a religious **festival of Sidi Bou Makhlouf** in July. All around the mosque are courtyards which used to house pilgrims to the zaouia. Many are being restored, and one behind the building is developing into a craftsmens' fondouk, where already there are stone carvers and makers of traditional musical instruments.

The Mausoleum of Ali Turki and the Jewish Quarter
Steps lead steeply downhill from Bou Makhlouf Square, directly below a corner shop, the Epicerie Bou Makhlouf. The cobbles divide to encircle the **mausoleum of Ali Turki**, father of Hussein ibn Ali Turki, founder of the Husseinite dynasty. The state of disrepair seems unbelievable for such an important figure, but then which of us knows where George I's father lies? You can peer through windows or the key-hole, across the overgrown courtyard and into the rubbish-filled tomb room.

Continuing downhill on the right-hand flight of stairs, you dive into what used to be the old Jewish quarter, passing the highly dilapidated **synagogue** on your left. There is a faint echo of its past in the continuation of traditionally Jewish crafts. Tailors and jewellers line the wide, lower stretches of Rue Bahiri Babouch leading to Av Habib Bourguiba.

Dar el Kous/church of St Peter
To find the restored ruins of this 4th-century church, walk along Av Habib Bourguiba and turn left just before the Patisserie du Nord. You enter through metal gates 30 m up the street on the right.

After you have passed through a small courtyard, the church begins with a vaulted narthex, in which non-communicants would worship. Three doors lead into the body of the church, which was divided by rows of pillars into three aisles. The **presbytery apse** at the far end of the nave is the best preserved in Tunisia. The raised seats around the wall were used by priests during the service, and above their heads you see the restored half-dome, an elaborate scallop design bearing a cross on the keystone. These seats were divided by columns, echoing the two flanking columns still in place.

The Zaouia of Sidi Mizouni
On the eastern edge of the old town, just below the President's palace, rises the elegant Andalucian minaret of the **Zaouia of Sidi Mizouni**. This branch of the learned Qadriya brotherhood was founded in 1834, and still boasts an impressive religious library and a koranic school for children. There is a good view from its neighbouring garden, an oasis of shade, colour and scent.

The Regional Museum of Popular Art and Traditions
Walk up past the President's palace to reach the town museum on a roundabout within the old walls (open Tues–Sat, 09.15–15.30, Sun 09.00–14.30; adm.). It is devoted to the rural life of the Bedouin and the hill farmers.

The building which houses the museum is sometimes still called the Zaouia of Ahmed ben Ali bou Hadjer, who came from Oran in Algeria and founded a zaouia of the Er Rahmania Brotherhood here in 1784. Otherwise it is named after one of his descendants, a leading nationalist, Ali ben Issa, who was buried in one of the rooms in 1956.

Passing through an open courtyard, straight ahead is the tomb room, filled with displays of wedding dresses, cosmetics and jewellery. Even today, most Tunisian women make their own shampoo and many of their own cosmetics, particularly kohl and henna, and you will recognize many of the ingredients in local souks.

The other door from the courtyard leads to the main exhibition of the rural Bedouin and Berber way of life. In the centre of the room, a large tent takes pride of place, filled with carpets, chests, implements and a coffee pot boiling over an orange bulb. The collection of domestic pottery demonstrates one of the great problems faced by Tunisian archaeologists, for the modelled pottery of the countryside has not changed appreciably since the Neolithic revolution 4000 years ago, and is therefore difficult to date.

The display of weaving shows killim carpets, strips of tenting, cushions, saddles, bags and sacks. The tribal looms had to be highly portable and are no more than 60 cm wide. Any genuine rural killim or tent is made of many strips, laboriously sewn together.

Vital to a shepherd's life are his whistles and pipes. The music echoes across the hills to locate and lead the herd, and also provides a sense of companionship in an otherwise lonely occupation.

Cooking centres on the grindstone and couscous pot, and the essentials of earthenware pottery. The olive barely features in the lives of these inland farmers, for this was the land of rancid butter, not oil.

Another courtyard, planted with basil and mint, leads into an exhibition of the horseman, a tradition which goes back to the stirrup-less Numidian cavalry and the Arab conquest. You can see intricate embroidered saddlery, the influence of Moorish Spain in the development of a high Western saddle, and learn just how to wear your Arab scarf.

Large Roman Cisterns and Colonial Cemetery

Opposite the museum and across the roundabout, a passage leads to the city's old mountain gate, known as **Bab Ghedive**. Ghedive was the town's governor, who in 1881 opened the gate to the advancing French, thus surrendering the hub of Tunisia's western defences without a shot being fired.

The gate retains some of its medieval essence, since you pass from the packed medina within its walls straight out into an empty wilderness of stone, a quarry where you half expect to find a colony of diseased lepers. Ahead of you lies a series of eleven vast cisterns, still intact, with their own stone staircase. Take a torch if you want to get beyond the initial public lavatory and explore where the first French garrison played billiards and exercised in a makeshift gymnasium.

Beyond, on the right of the road, is the old colonial cemetery, a twisted hectare of neglect. Many of the tombs have been broken into, and most of the bodies returned to Europe. The excavated walls of the **church** below it are not French but Roman.

WHERE TO STAY

MODERATE

If you think it is better to be in the eyesore than looking at it, the functional rooms in the **Hotel Sicca Veneria** may have their advantages. However, its best feature, the restaurant, can be sampled while staying elsewhere. Each room has a bathroom and guaranteed hot water, and you can choose between a quiet room with a balcony, or a view of the kasbah and the bustle of downtown El Kef without.

CHEAP

El Kef is renowned for having the most sumptuous and affordable bedroom in Tunisia, in the **Hotel de la Source**, above the central mosque. It is a T-shaped family room with four beds. To shoulder height the walls are covered in old geometric tiles and above, the vaulted ceiling is covered with decorative plasterwork. It is only marginally more expensive than the other rooms in the hotel and is well worth it.

The **Hotel de la Medina**, at 18 Rue Farhat Hached, tel (08) 20214, is spotless, almost clinical and the maid even whips away your dirty clothes when you are not looking. Less attractive than both is the **Hotel Auberge**, just off the beginning of Av Habib Bourguiba, tel (08) 20036, which has the dubious attraction of a bar on the first floor.

EATING OUT

The downstairs restaurant at the **Sicca Veneria** serves inventive Tunisian food, instead of the bland mélange in most hotels of its kind. Try *knef*, braised tender lamb in a delicate rosemary-infused broth, served with rice and vegetables or *kamounia*, a meat stew flavoured with cumin, both 3.5 dn. The **Esso Restaurant** or **Restaurant Dyr**, depending on which entrance you use, is above the garage, tel 08 20785. Here a large plate of *salade niçoise* costs 1.6 dn and a succulent, tender *brochette* with spiced rice and vegetables 3.6 dn. It also has a licence and a rowdy bar.

The unlicensed **Café Restaurant El Andalous** is the best of the cheaper places, and all its main dishes cost 1 dn. Try *shakshuka*, chickpeas, tomatoes, onions and peppers stewed toegether, or *koucha*, lamb with potatoes in a spicy sauce. The two other licensed restaurants are the **Restaurant Venus** on Rue Farhat Hached and as a last resort the restaurant of the **Hotel Auberge**.

For coffee and croissants in the morning, the **Café Ben Chaabane**, in the terrace of shops on Av Habib Bourguiba. The **Patisserie du Nord** opposite make delicious almond cakes. In the evening settle down with a hookah at the **Café de la Source**.

Around El Kef

Sidi Mansour

Walk out beyond the Roman cisterns by the radio mast at the top of town (see above), and take a steep left at the beginning of the old Italian graveyard. A tarmac road climbs to the crest of a small hill and winds down for 1 km or so to the **Mosque of Sidi Mansour**, the courtyard of which is smoothly paved with Roman stones. Beside the mosque, strange caves, part quarry, part natural, line the upper cliffs of a deeply eroded river bed. A track runs 3 km directly up the rising escarpment beyond, passing springs and herds on the way, to an absorbing view towards Barrage Mellègue.

Barrage Mellègue

The monumental dam is a 10-km walk and there is a hotel, the **Hotel Restaurant du Lac**, tel 08 46103, beneath it. A bed costs 7 dn half board, and fish is good at 2 dn, washed down with beer or wine in the shady garden, as long as you do not mind being just downstream from several million tons of water. There are regular buses and *louages* back to El Kef from the main square at Barrage Mellègue.

Hammam Mellègue
Here is a chance to bathe in a communal marble tub used by the Romans and fed by natural hot mineral water. Take the road out to Sakiat Sidi Youssef, and turn right to Hammam Mellègue. The last 4 bumpy kilometres wind down a steep escarpment, whose slopes are scarred with the glitter of green and red minerals, into the Mellègue valley. All this prepares you for the slightly salty water which bubbles out beside the cold green river at 50°C.

What it does not prepare you for are the four original **Roman baths**, one of which is still in use. Three of the baths are open to the elements, surrounded by walls and arches. The fourth is hidden in the stone bathhouse, a cavernous place lit by natural skylights and entered through lofty wooden doors, and has turned the colour of rust with use. If you are a mixed-sex party, arrive at midday, so that the women can bathe before the approximate 14.00 change-over time. Nearby cisterns suggest that the Roman complex would have had the usual cold pools as well as hot.

Sakiat Sidi Youssef
It is 42 km from El Kef to the high, windswept border town of Sakiat Sidi Youssef. Though Sakiat occupies the site of the Numidian fortress of Naraggara, the only reason to come here is to ponder on a rather more recent event. On 8 February 1958, at a point in the Algerian War when the French troops on the ground were feeling let down by the government in Paris, an unauthorized bombing raid was made on an FLN camp, based in Tunisia at Sakiat. The raid was not only on the wrong side of the border, but in the process tens of Tunisian civilians were killed. This incident, and the public outcry which followed, brought to a head the military crisis within the French Army in Algeria, and forced the French to recall de Gaulle to the presidency in order to diffuse the possibility of a separatist coup in Algiers. The bloody episode of the bombing is commemorated by a long swathe of steps leading up a hillside on the edge of town to a slender white arch encased in brick and decorated by a sombre plaque bearing the names of those who died.

From El Kef to Kairouan

Makhtar is halfway between El Kef and Kairouan, and makes an enticing day trip from either. Morning buses stop here at around 08.00, leaving plenty of time to see the ruins and have lunch before catching the afternoon bus on. If you want to witness a Makhtar sunset or visit some of the minor sites like Elles, Zannfour, Kbor Klib, Kesra, Uzappa and Hammam Zouakra, you could stay a night or two at Makhtar's hotel. It offers comfortable beds, wine and grilled food, but the plumbing is only suitable for hardened travellers with no bowel problems.

From El Kef take the P12 route to Kairouan. Le Sers, 33 km on, is an agricultural centre on the banks of the Oued Tessa. Quite distinct and further south is the small hamlet of **Vieux Sers**, sitting on a crossroad which leads off to the megalithic tombs of Elles and Roman ruins at Zannfour.

Zannfour

Little more than 2 km down the Vieux Sers-Elles road, turn right towards a mosque and continue along the plain to a small river canyon. Zannfour is the name of the scattered hamlet, built from pale local stone on the opposite bank of the river. On the same spot stood the Roman city of **Assuras**, now little more than a large barley field, riddled with stones. Above, like surrealist sculptures in the American prairies, rise two **arches** wrapped in scaffolding and a **temple**. Further inspection reveals a **mausoleum**, now half buried by the height of the ploughed land around it, knee-high traces of two **Byzantine forts** and a great crescent of **theatre** seats. Another **arch**, only half-surviving, is over the brow of the hill. The temple is worth sketching, two faces of its once monstrous cella are still decorated with a fine frieze of ox skulls laced with garlands. Roman Assuras was established by Augustus who settled disbanded soldiers here, a policy that diminished his vast armies, defended frontiers and secured the subjection of the provinces.

Elles

Locally pronounced 'Les', this village is 9 km from Vieux Sers, and is esteemed for its fruit and olive trees. It sits above a spring which irrigates the orchards and is the centre of constant ferrying as jerry cans are filled and strapped on to donkeys. Elles was a prosperous town in the Roman period and a few scattered pediments and pillars can be seen in the dust or reused in farmhouse walls.

Above the village rises a crescent of hills covered in **megalithic tombs**. There are dozens of these massive structures, mostly compact groups of tombs formed by six or eight chambers. It appears that they were built in the 2nd and 3rd centuries BC when a number of highland Numidian principalities existed in various states of alliance with Carthage. The tombs may have been built for the noble clans that dominated these petty tribal states, which were strong in cavalry and rich from the corn trade.

The most famous group is to the left behind a hedge as you walk up the village. It was covered by a rising terrace of massive steps, making it look like a truncated, perhaps even a complete, pyramid. This is not unlike the only surviving Libyo-Phoenician architecture from the 2nd century BC, the elegant mausoleums at Dougga and Makhtar, which consist of monolithic tomb chambers crowned by pyramids. The other celebrated group is above the village on the right of the valley, looking like a small Stonehenge.

Kbor Klib

Back on the El Kef–Kairouan road, 4 km after Vieux Sers, the Siliana turning leads 10 km to two ancient buildings. Just over the brow of the hill is a two-storey Roman mausoleum known as **Ksar Toual Zouamel**, but before that the hilltop is dominated by a great rectangular mass of solid stone, 15 m by 40 m, pierced by two blind alleys and fronted by a smaller square detached plinth. It is known as **Kbor Klib**, but no one knows for certain who built it, or why. The odds-on favourite is Julius Caesar, who could not publicly celebrate his victory over fellow Romans in the civil war, but could and did mark his defeat of their foreign ally, King Juba II of Numidia. The plinth probably supported a massive trophy made of captured weapons, and the blind alleys were spanned by arches to create a single terrace on which sat three distinct temples. All we know for certain is that there was a frieze composed of massive medallions, alternating between a shield bearing a profile of the goddess Diana, and suits of Macedonian armour.

Makhtar

Makhtar rivals El Kef as a place to witness spectacular sunsets. The hills stand out as darkening silhouettes against the western glow of the dying sun, which fills the clear evening sky with a fusion of fire and ripened corn.

It is the ruins of **Mactaris**, however, that draw a steady flow of visitors. The ancient and modern towns are separated by a Roman arch that marks the spring and old native village of Bab el Ain. The new town is a dull grid of low houses, founded in 1887, which is entertaining only for as long as it takes to shop for a picnic in the central market. The streets are either whipped by strong cold winter winds or embalmed in the baking dry heat of the summer. For compensation there is an aura of mystery. The Carthaginians established a tophet, a place for the fire sacrifice of their children, by the Bab el Ain gate and the town's water has a mild hallucinogenic quality the first time you drink it.

GETTING AROUND

Buses from El Kef and Kairouan arrive and depart somewhere between 07.00 and 08.00 in the morning and again shortly after 14.00. On an alternative axis there is a service between Kasserine and El Fahs that passes through Makhtar. This timetable is even more flexible, so ask locally for details. The bus stop is just opposite the licensed Hotel Mactaris.

History

In 1964 the tophet was found by archaeologists, confirming that Makhtar had been a centre of Carthaginian influence, possibly the capital of the inland province of Pagus Thuscae which contained 50 towns. Dates are uncertain for the Carthaginian conquest of inland Tunisia, which started in earnest in 480 BC, but was a patchy and uneven process.

After the battle of Zama in 202 BC, when Hannibal was defeated by Scipio, the balance of power shifted dramatically, and Massinissa, a loyal ally of Rome, rose to become King of all Numidia. In 155 BC he annexed Makhtar, thus saving it from destruction in the last Punic War, and his successors welcomed Carthaginian refugees fleeing from the Roman conquest. No archaeological evidence has been found pre-dating the 2nd century BC, and it is possible that it was these refugees who established the tophet, which the Romans had elsewhere suppressed.

Makhtar remained outside the Roman Empire until 44 BC, and the dismantling of the city walls in AD 30 hints that the process of absorption into the Empire was not entirely peaceful. Well into the 2nd century AD, Punic was still used here rather than Latin for official inscriptions. But the prosperity of the late 2nd century, when the baths, arches and a new forum were built, transformed Makhtar into a recognizably Roman town. A symbol of this era is the story of the 'Mactar Reaper', a local boy who made good through hard work, recorded in verse on a stone that is now lodged in the Louvre.

In the 5th century Makhtar briefly served as the capital of a native principality before the Byzantines restored the frontier. The town was then but a shadow of its pagan past, its baths converted into either forts or churches. Islamic coins and glazed oil lamps bear testament to continual occupation until the Hilalian Arabs destroyed the city in the 11th century.

The Museum

Opposite the Bab el Ain arch, the museum is open every day from 09.00–12.00, 14.00–18.00 (17.30 in winter); adm. It serves as the entrance to the site, but if it is closed, walk round to a gap in the hedge to the left. The surrounding shady garden bristles like a packed cemetery with carved stone. The museum contains three dark and dusty rooms, showing exhibits from the Libyo-Punic, Roman and Christian eras.

On the gravestones in the first room are carved birds, leaves and Punic symbols. The crescent moon is associated with Tanit, the great Carthaginian goddess; the pine cone with Baal, who in his first manifestation as a rain god of the Lebanese mountains was linked with their cedar forests. The pomegranate and the scythe are attributes of Baal Hammon. In parts of Tunisia a farmer will still crush a pomegranate in his hands as he turns the first sod with the plough. The peacock is an ancient symbol of the goddess of love and of incorruptible flesh. The bug-eyed depiction of humans, their clothes in stiff folds, is characteristic of 1st-century AD North African carving and continues well into the 2nd century. As the Roman influence became stronger, so the freshness and naive mystery of the carving disappears and is replaced by more sophisticated, but comparatively soulless figures.

Passing to the second room beneath a Roman lintel, dedicated by the Juventutes club to the Emperor Domitian, you find a rare example of Latin carved in its written, cursive form. There is also an entertaining collection of 2nd- and 3rd-century **Roman heads**: of the Emperor Septimius Severus as the god Serapis; of Aesculapius, the god of healing, as himself; of Saturn carved in the local bug-eyed style; and a young women with her veil slipped back to reveal a well-dressed head of hair.

The third room contains cabinets of familiar terracotta **oil lamps**, **coins** and some Christian grave **mosaics**. Here you can also pick out the change and continuity of symbols: birds flit in and out of every culture, but the wine cup of Bacchus reappears as the Christian chalice. On coins, the sunburst that surrounds the bust of the divine pagan emperors is retained in the official Christian period before it is transformed into the Byzantine halo. Horses appear on Muslim glass weights just as they do on the earliest Carthaginian coinage; oil lamp design remains constant, though the addition of a green glaze creates an instantly recognizable Islamic look.

The Site

Forum and Triumphal Arch
Climb up through the pillared nave of a 6th-century Christian **church** behind the museum, to the relatively modest **amphitheatre** which lies to the left. Up the hill is the 'new' **forum**, built at the same time as the great **triumphal arch**, during the reign of the Emperor Trajan, as you can just make out from an inscription on its farther face. In the far corner of the forum from the arch, marked by four fluted columns, is the **marketplace**, with an intact dedication to Mercury, the presiding god of commerce, communication and crooks.

Temple of Hathor Miskar
From here, a short walk across stony ground leads to excavations that have revealed a **Punic temple** to Hathor Miskar and a palatial villa, known as the **House of Venus**. At the first area of digging look for dark orange boulders, which lie in what would have been the temple courtyard. The head-height area of mortared building stone marks the temple **sanctuary**, its south-facing apse just discernible.

Though visually scant, this dig revealed the longest Punic text in North Africa, an inscription recording the restoration of the temple in the 2nd century AD which shows the town still governed by Carthaginian law and magistrates. Beyond, covering a much greater area is the House of Venus. Its courtyard surrounds the remains of a central **fountain pool**,

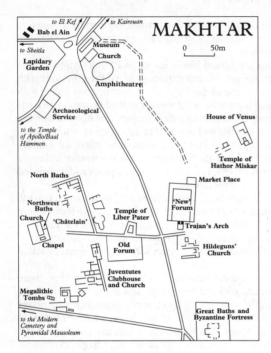

MAKHTAR

0   50m

to El Kef
Bab el Ain

to Kairouan

to Sbeitla
Museum
Church
Lapidary
Garden

Amphitheatre

Archaeological
Service

House of Venus

*to the Temple
of Apollo/Baal
Hammon*

Temple of
Hathor Miskar

North Baths

Market Place

Northwest
Baths
Church   'Châtelain'
Temple of
Liber Pater
'New'
Forum

Chapel
Old
Forum
Trajan's Arch

Juventutes
Clubhouse
and Church
Hildeguns'
Church

Megalithic
Tombs

*to the Modern
Cemetery and
Pyramidal Mausoleum*
Great Baths and
Byzantine Fortress

though only a few posts carved with lozenges now stand. The mosaics found here, of birds and of Venus, are on display in the museum.

Hildeguns' Church

Returning to the Trajanic arch, the confusing pile of stonework around it is the remains of a Byzantine fort. Beside the arch, to the left, are the hip-high walls of a basin, once fed by a fountain. Twenty metres beyond the arch on the left are truncated pillars that divided the nave of **Hildeguns' church**, named after a man of Vandal descent buried beneath a mosaic tombstone by the entrance. The church shows signs of a series of reorganizations which has left the **baptistery** behind the apse. This is typical of the early church where adult baptism, the ritual that marked full membership of a Christian community, was accorded an importance equal in its solemnity to the initiation procedure of contemporary mystery cults. The mosaic baptismal font was sunk into the ground, and above it was a stone canopy held up by four columns. Its apse is decorated with a mosaic scallop shell, a motif suitably borrowed from Venus' miraculous birth from the waves.

The Great Baths

Makhtar's great 2nd-century baths rise monumentally beyond, though the visible exterior dates from the 6th century, when the Byzantines converted them into a fortress. The entrance leads into a paved square courtyard, the exercising hall or *palaestra*, which was surrounded by columns capped by the richly carved entablature that now lies on the floor. Five square pillars crowned by engaged Corinthian capitals, still divide the *palaestra* from an apsed *exedra*, where friends could sit, talk or idly follow the path of the black and white maze on the floor. From the *exedra* you enter the central hall of the baths, an immense *frigidarium* where even today the walls soar 18 m into the air. Its roof would once have been vaulted. The central well dates from the Byzantine fortress.

The floor is paved with a blue and green wave mosaic, which when wet would have undulated in contrast to its fiery red and orange borders. Traces of the marble which lined the walls can be seen jutting out from the floor. The long cold pool, partially hidden by three open arches to the east, completes a picture of overblown magnificence. Other parts of the bath are in worse repair, but you can make out several of the smaller hot rooms to the west and the south. Looking at the area behind the *exedra* you can see that the mosaic design continues under walls, for what was once a vast public space has been crudely partitioned to create smaller rooms.

274

The Old Forum

Returning to the Trajanic arch, follow the paved Roman road left to the **old forum**, its steeper gradient scored to prevent slipping. Overlooking the forum, on the right as you enter, is the **temple of Liber Pater**, a manifestation of Bacchus popular in North Africa, where one lonely column makes do for a whole portico. Though the current structure was restored by the guild of fullers in AD 180, it is an ancient place of worship, and beneath it two staircases lead down to a vaulted crypt, itself built above a natural cave which it protects with its weight-distributing structure. Who knows what bibulous rituals were enacted in this dark hidden grotto in the name of the god of wine?

The road continues along the length of the forum to a T-junction, above which stand the knee-high ruins of a triple-apsed building, known as **'Chatelain'** after a French archaeologist. There are a number of buildings like this in Tunisia but no one has worked out what they were for. The basins of varying size which lie scattered in the courtyard have inspired some guesses: a centre for the distribution of dole in corn and oil, a launderette or a fishmonger.

Northwest Baths

The wide spanning arch which rises from the earth beyond marks an unexcavated section of the northwest baths. Steps lead down into a paved exercise hall, the *palaestra*, and the three arches, now blocked up, would have led directly into the *frigidarium*. There a Christian **church** was inserted and you can still see the nave and apse of this late arrival. The numerous posts, crowned by curious cubes, would have held a balustrade making a straight and narrow path along the nave to the altar. Walking out through the door of the church there is a small square **chapel**, complete with altar, which almost certainly housed the precious relics of a holy man, the koubba of a Christian marabout.

The Juventutes Clubhouse

Returning to the T-junction in the old forum, continue straight on down to a shaded forest of pillars which marks out some pretty grey ruins. This too has two distinct periods of occupancy: first, as the clubhouse of the Juventutes, and secondly as a **church**. The Juventutes was an institution under the protection of the god of war, found throughout the Empire, a sort of special constabulary and boys' athletic association combined. If it sounds a bit fascist that is no great surprise, for the Roman Empire was the ultimate fascist state. It was run for the benefit of a small aristocracy, who sustained the illusion of 'national unity' with a constant diet of scapegoats, public works, circuses and athleticsm, backed up by skilful propaganda and a ruthless military machine.

The clubhouse is very agreeable. Entering from the road you pass through a small hall into an open-air courtyard, its colonnade still in excellent shape. In the church period a wall was built at the far end to curtain off a small chapel, complete with altar and pillars. Off the courtyard were various rooms, including a communal latrine of which one key-hole seat remains.

The main rectangular room of the club is beyond, and was converted into a nave, furnished with pillars and embellished with an apse. This is banked up with seating for the priests who officiated at the central altar, made from a 3rd-century tomb.

The Cemetery

The surrounding ruins are confusing. To the north was a Christian graveyard, to the south a quadruple-apsed room, looking like a four-leaf clover and surrounded by niches and troughs—another unknown 'Chatelain'-type building. To the southeast, a few gravestones propped up against a wall signal a **cemetery** which has been in continual use from the 3rd century BC to the 20th. If you can take the smell, examine the **megalithic tomb** beyond. Its six porches lead into four monolithic burial chambers, now sprinkled with snail shells and the odd turd. Excavators found 44 bodies in one chamber, the result not of a mass burial, but of its use as a bin by grave robbers. The modern graveyard is in a walled compound beyond the hedgerow above which peeks the pyramidal roof of a well-preserved two-storey **mausoleum**, its upper chamber open to the sun, the ground floor decorated with carved pilasters.

The Temple of Apollo

Outside the site itself there are a number of other odd things to look at. Almost opposite the museum, hidden by modern houses, is the **mausoleum of the Julii**, usually a bit rubbish-strewn, showing a scene of ox sacrifice on its lintel.

Taking the road that leads up from the museum towards the other mausoleum, you pass two bungalows belonging to the archaeological service, signalled by a Roman brothel sign, a *stele* bearing a large erect penis. The inaccessible gardens behind contain a much more impressive selection of stones than the half-hearted lapidary garden below the road.

Carrying on up the road, and taking a dirt track ahead through houses, you arrive at traces of a large **temple to Apollo** where the road bends round to the left. An expansive paved courtyard, a couple of pillars and some dressed stones from the sanctuary indicate the basic plan. It follows the African tradition of a succession of courtyards, rather than classically focusing on the sanctuary building itself. This was the site of a **Punic temple to Baal Hammon**, the supreme male deity to whom the Carthaginians sacrificed their children. Beside it is a small **colonial graveyard** beneath the arches of a **Roman aqueduct** where some Italians and French have chosen to be buried under recycled classical plinths.

WHERE TO STAY

In the evening, the **Hotel Mactaris** serves a meal of grilled steaks, chicken, chips and salad either in the bar or in the upstairs hall. A comfy bed but desperate plumbing are yours for 4 dn.

Around Makhtar

Makhtar stands at the centre of some of the most handsome country of Tunisia, rolling hills divided by watercourses and valleys that create intimate vistas within a largely bleak and overawing high plateau. In a 20-km radius from Makhtar there are half a dozen reclusive sites, none of them easily accessible by public transport or likely to be other than of minority interest. Zannfour, Elles and Kbor Klib are described from the road to El Kef, Kesra on the road to Kairouan, and Uzappa on the road from El Fahs.

Hammam Zouakra

Despite its name Hammam Zouakra has no baths, but you can see traces of the **Roman town** where Makhtar's aqueduct began, and over 30 **megalithic tombs** lying on the far bank of the Oued el Hammam.

Take the Sbeitla road and 6 km later a right turn to Souk el Jemma, 'Friday market'. Turn left before you reach the barracks, and continue down a dirt track for 8 km to Hammam Zouakra. Amongst ancient olives stands a lonely **triumphal arch**. Excavations down to the foundations of the arch have exposed a massive fluted column of Chemtou marble that hints at the magnificence of a buried temple. The only other distinct monument is a ruined **mausoleum**, perched above a tributary stream, displaying in its interior hall the niches in which funerary urns would have been placed.

The older burial places are on the other side of the river, beyond traces of a Roman bridge. At first they look like strata of resistant rock emerging from the river bank, but are massive slabs of stone, carefully fitted and jointed to create **cave-like tombs**. The work is remarkably fine, the joints kissing perfectly after thousands of years without mortar or bolts. The tombs follow a consistent design. Roof boulders, as much as 2 m by 3 m, are supported by the slabs of the side walls, an occasional rough pillar and by a pair of menhirs at the front, which leave an overhanging lintel that forms a 'chapel' porch. The entrance was sealed by a face of stone, the joints often carefully hidden, though these are now mostly broken or have been removed by later users. The back wall is often the hillside itself. The tombs are rarely single, but in groups of four, six and eight, with a common front.

All this you can see for yourself: all theories are merely enlightened speculation. You would have to have some good reason for burying with such effort. The chapel porches suggest some commemorative ritual, perhaps a feast for relatives with a libation poured to the spirit of the ancestor. The grouping of the tombs suggests an extended family, perhaps clans of Numidian nobles. Their strength suggests the dead may have been buried with something worth guarding but no urns or bones have yet been found. All the tombs have been pillaged and reused in later centuries as stores, graves, houses and lately as rubbish tips, making any evidence found questionable. Currently the construction date is put at the 3rd century BC, a late testament to the megalithic, 'big stone', civilization. Even on the outer fringes of civilization like Britain, stone circles were built around the 12th century BC.

One treat remains. Above the tombs and to the left is one of the most individual **village stores** in Tunisia.

To Kairouan

The obvious place to break this 104-km journey is at the Berber village of **Kesra**, 84 km from Makhtar. It is an ancient site, known to the Romans as Chusira, and one of the few places in this part of the Tell with a continuous history of settlement. The village, perched safely on the edge of a mountain, is surrounded by fruit trees and contains a number of springs, a mosque and two cafés. Dotted around the edge of the settlement are several koubbas commemorating a galaxy of local holy men—Sidi Ameur, Sidi el Hajml, Sidi Bou Guendou, and, to the south of the village, Sidi Ahmed ben Abdallah. Two flights of stone steps climb up from the centre to a natural terrace with fine views. Above, some inhabited farm buildings occupy the fragmentary remains of an old **Byzantine fort**. If you want the excuse for a longer walk, ask to be shown the path north from the terrace which leads 3 km to **Henchir Jemal**, where there are a number of megalithic tombs.

Back on the main road, 9 km from Kesra, is a short tunnel and a celebrated rock formation, the needles of **Dechrat el Gharia**. Dropping down through the last belt of wooded hills, the arches of **Cherichira aqueduct** appear on the left. This is a 10th-century Arab construction which brought fresh water from mountain springs 40 km across the plain to the Aghlabid basins at Kairouan.

From El Kef to Sbeitla

Between El Kef and Sbeitla are two sites of interest, the Roman ruins of Althiburos at Medeina and the sparse remains of Sufes at Sbiba. Take the road for Dahmani, visible as you descend from El Kef, snaking its way into the distance across the plain. Dahmani centres on the Pl de l'Indépendance, surrounded by shops and restaurants, where *louages* congregate. On one side of the square is an anonymous hotel, a colonial building with blue shutters and balconies above a ground-floor café. It charges 2.5 dn a night, and provides cold showers and a mucky hole as a loo. Three trains a day leave for Kalaa Kasbah in the west, and all destinations to Tunis to the east, from the station by the main through road.

Althiburos

To get to this Roman site, at the present-day village of **Medeina**, take the road west to **Djerissa** for 6.4 km, and in sight of a small hamlet, beneath a conical hill to the left, a stop sign indicates the appropriate left turn. Crossing a river bed and bearing right 2 km later, the road leads to Medeina school, and a late 3rd-century **triumphal arch** beyond it marks the beginning of **Althiburos**.

There has been continuous settlement at Medeina, due to the springs which feed the area. Situated in a natural amphitheatre, the site is surrounded by villages and the noises of everyday life—shepherds, cocks, washing and donkeys—bring the ancient city to life.

It was founded in the 2nd century BC as a Punic outpost in tribal Berber lands. Sited on the military road between Carthage and Tebessa, Althiburos blossomed as a Roman city during the reign of Hadrian (AD 117–38). The impressive civic centre with its **theatre** and **capitol**, date from the apex of the Empire at the end of the 2nd century. Large houses were still being built here into the 4th century, and both Catholic and Donatist Christians worshipped in the city. Fortified after the Byzantine invasion, Althiburos crumbled to become the sleepy village of Medeina after the Arab invasion.

Cross the river bed, and stick to the track until you approach the prominent remains of the **capitol**, where a Roman street leads between the bases of an **arch** dedicated to Hadrian by the grateful citizenry. To the left, two staircases lead into the completely paved **forum**; it is littered with massive Corinthian capitals, richly carved from golden stone and it takes little imagination to recreate this impressive public square. It would also have been adorned with civic statues, and the base of one, complete with inscription and foot-holes on top for the sculpture, still stands in the centre. It once held a dignitary called Marsyas, whose fame lives on at the beginning of the fourth line of the inscription.

Walking across the forum, in the direction of the marabout on the hill, steps lead up into a **temple**, once completely enclosed by the outer wall. The small courtyard in front contains a pool for washing. Beside the temple to the right is a large **house**, notable for, and named after, the 16 column bases found in its spacious central courtyard. As everywhere, the columns have disappeared, but nine of the bases are here with bas-relief carving on their sides. The designs mix Berber symbols such as lozenges, pomegranates and pine cone, with Latin orna-mentation. The bases once supported a stone wall around the courtyard.

Back across the forum, the steps which would have led up into the now precarious ruins of the **Capitoline temple** no longer exist. The street in front is lined with its deeply carved entablature, and there is Corinthian relief carving on the standing inner sanctum wall.

Continuing towards the visible arches of the **theatre**, down the Roman street between the bases of another arch, you come to a monumental fountain on the street corner to the right. Its four niches once held statues, and water played into the stone pool, draining downhill into a lower, cruder trough for animals.

Turning left at this crossroads, you come to a curious building whose walls are lined with niches. If you mentally destroy the central wall which was added later, you are left with a square room, its centre taken up with a large stone water tub, its walls incised and a round vaulted annexe leading off. The prosaic suggest that it had some industrial use, but perhaps it was a fish restaurant, where clients caught their own meal from the pond, or a jeweller's shop with display niches.

The **theatre** is now showing its age, and if you are superstitious you may not want to chance walking beneath its precarious arches. Beyond, you can make out the crumbling remnants of a couple of **mausoleums** in the old burial quarter of the city.

Returning to the forum, scramble down to the obvious remains of two excavated buildings on the other side of the river, passing a terraced house which is on the point of tumbling into the river bed itself. The lower of these two buildings is a palatial **house**, built around a courtyard and known after its **mosaic of the Muses**, now in oblivion, that is, the Bardo cellars. Stairs at one end of the courtyard lead down to cool summer living quarters, where niches in the upper stones acted as ventilation shafts.

The building above, once a private house, was transformed into a **public bath** complex during the 4th century. Even today it is a beautiful ruin. The entrance staircases show signs of balustrades, and it was from the large entrance hall, flanked by mosaic bath tubs, that the magnificent boat mosaic in the Bardo was extracted. This vast work shows 25 different types of sea-going vessel, including naval, military, commercial and fishing boats and, though rather out of place in this landlocked town, is thought to have been commissioned by a grain merchant. He recognized the fine dividing line between the legitimate users of the sea and pirates by including some of corsair vessels in his floor.

The building's central courtyard is a riot of symmetrical fountains and pools, and the many rooms which surround it contain still more basins and baths for ablutions. The complex is known as the **building of Aesculapius**, after a vanished mosaic celebrating games held in honour of the healing god. All the rites associated with Aesculapius involved copious bathing, and some of the unidentified rooms may have been bedrooms where the ill would hope to receive messages from the god in their dreams.

Sbiba

Continuing south on the Sbeitla road from Dahmani, the agricultural town of **El Ksour**, with its octagonal minaret, is the home of Safia water, Tunisia's 'Evian'. The road ploughs on through fertile agricultural ground, through the village of **Rohia**, where a pretty sculpted dome of a marabout lies in gardens to the east.

A signposted left turn in Sbiba takes you into the town centre, the **Pl du Souk**, an appropriate hub for a town which seems to live and breathe trading. Come here on a Thursday or Friday morning and you could be in the Tunisia of a hundred years ago. Though there are some Roman remains, the town's most memorable sight is the old stone **fondouk**, still buzzing on market days, where passing merchants would have stowed their goods and stabled their horses on long journeys. Nowadays, donkeys wait patiently in the shade of its walls for their masters to return from marketing, and tea is brewed for those about to journey home. Beyond the fondouk, the most impressive remnant of Roman **Sufes** is a semi-circular **nympheum**, from which the water of the local spring once gushed. In the fertile gardens below lie the orange stone remains of Sufes **baths**, rising above orchards which stretch into the distance. Visible from the nympheum through a screen of eucalyptus trees looking north, are the distinguishing pillars of a Christian basilica which was transformed in the 7th century into a **mosque**. The mosque took the name of the Arab conqueror of Tunisia and founder of Kairouan Sidi Oqba, who local tradition insists camped here.

Sbeitla

The modern town of Sbeitla would pass unnoticed by tourists if it were not for the ruins of Roman **Sufetula**. Above the town, between the road to Kasserine and the Oued Sbeitla, a towering yellow stone **triumphal arch** announces a glittering site, including three ghostly orange **temples** which make up the capitol. If you see nothing else Roman in Tunisia, they are well worth aiming for.

Modern Sbeitla's 5000 inhabitants constitute approximately half the population of the Roman settlement, and their town boasts a fraction of its civic delights. All you are likely to be interested in is the bus station and two hotels.

History
Despite the splendour of Sbeitla's ruins, little is known of their history. The earliest inscription dates from the reign of Vespasian (AD 69–79), suggesting that the Romans built the town from scratch beside the spring. It grew more important after Sousse and El Jem rebelled and were punished in the 3rd century, but only in the 7th century did it achieve any real fame.

In 646, the Patriarch Gregory rejected the authority of his Byzantine emperor in Constantinople, and proclaimed himself Emperor. At the same time he moved his seat of power from Carthage to Sbeitla. The following year the first of the Arab armies, 20,000 men led by Abdallah ibn Saad, sacked the town, killed the self-styled Emperor and looted his considerable riches. Sbeitla was the last of the victories in this wave of conquest, but 20 years later the Arabs were to have a more lasting success.

GETTING AROUND

By Bus
The bus station at the end of the road from Kairouan. Six buses a day leave for Tunis, travelling via Makhtar. There are five daily departures for Kairouan, connecting with regular departures for Sousse and Monastir. For neighbouring Kasserine, there are 11 buses a day, two of which continue to Gafsa. Five buses also currently depart for El Kef, three stopping at Sbiba en route. To visit nearby Sidi Bou Zid for the weekend market, there are three buses a day.

By *Louage*
Louages also leave from the bus station, and most ply the route to Kasserine. On market days, you may find *louages* to other destinations. Markets take place on Thursday at Kasserine, Thursday and Friday at Sbiba, Saturday and Sunday at Sidi Bou Zid, Monday at Makhtar, Tuesday at Hajeb el Ayoun (halfway to Kairouan) and Wednesday in Sbeitla itself.

The Museum

In Sufetula museum (open dawn to sunset; adm) opposite the site entrance there is the customary collection of 2nd-century red **pottery and oil lamps,** mostly from the necropolis which lies buried on this side of the road. Also *in memoriam* are the collection of **headstones,** known as *stelae,* which feature crudely carved men and women, whose wide eyes date them to the 1st centuries BC and AD (see Makhtar museum for further information).

More interesting is the **mosaic** of the Triumph of Venus, set against a green sea, and three fragments of **statues.** The headless Diana is dedicated to Faustina, the wife of Emperor Antoninus Pius, and the bust of Creperia Innula comes from Haidra. The statue of Bacchus, reclining on a panther, was discovered in the nearby theatre.

The Site

Byzantine Forts

The entrance booth on the site is built in the lee of a square 6th-century **Byzantine fort.** A second fort to the left has a rough stairway, added later when the fort was used as a house, which gives access to the walls. The neat Byzantine plan inside is rather muddled. Sixteen rooms line the exterior wall, only one opening on to the central courtyard, whose 12 piers would have supported a second storey. Water was provided by an underground cistern, sited below the only round pier.

Walk to the Great Baths

The **church of Saints Gervais, Protais and Tryphon** is just 10 m further, but only its restored gateway remains. Examination of the stones revealed that it was built from pillaged classical blocks in the last few turbulent decades of Christian Tunisia. Two rows of double columns once divided the nave in three, and a dressed boulder bears the footings for an altar. Nearby, a lone post crowned by a dice device is all that remains of the balustrade which surrounded the altar. The small area of white mosaic behind the altar marks the priest's inner sanctum, the presbytery.

Beside the church, slap in the middle of the Roman road, rise the menhir-like columns of a **Byzantine oil press.** On the round millstone, raised in the centre, the olives were first crushed. A mule, slave or donkey plodded slowly round, dragging a heavy millstone which pulverized the flesh and stones. This mixture was then transferred to *scourtins,* the bags still used in modern oil mills. These were packed on top of one another in the centre of the slab of stone marked out with a circular runnel. Levers, steadied by the massive upright stones, compressed the *scourtins.* Three or four ratchets, each exerting different degrees of pressure, are still visible in the inner groove. The oil dribbled into the circular channel and down into the central basin. Oil presses are usually found in pairs, so that the procedure of packing the *scourtins* could be done whilst the other press was oozing away.

Off to the left are some over-restored **private baths,** with a good example of 6th-century **mosaic** work in one pool. This crude, late style used large stones and single colours on a white background with refreshing naivety, giving the yellow, black and red fish a cartoon quality. The central black one was a swordfish, but has recently lost its sword.

Turning right after the oil press, follow a long Roman street to the shoulder-high ruins of a **fountain,** built in the 4th century AD. In its heyday, the surrounding groove in the pavement would have housed the sides of a stone basin. The water was shaded by a canopy, supported

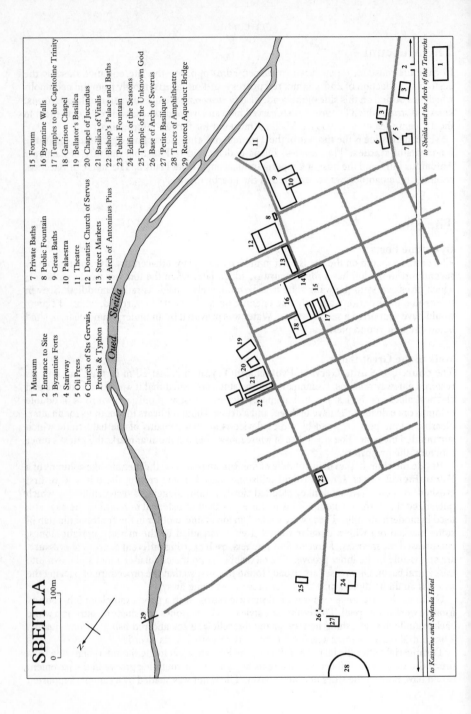

SBEITLA

0   100m

1 Museum
2 Entrance to Site
3 Byzantine Forts
4 Stairway
5 Oil Press
6 Church of Sts Gervais,
   Protais & Typhon

7 Private Baths
8 Public Fountain
9 Great Baths
10 Palaestra
11 Theatre
12 Donatist Church of Servus
13 Street Markets
14 Arch of Antoninus Pius

15 Forum
16 Byzantine Walls
17 Temples to the Capitoline Trinity
18 Garrison Chapel
19 Bellator's Basilica
20 Chapel of Jucundus
21 Basilica of Vitalis
22 Bishop's Palace and Baths
23 Public Fountain
24 Edifice of the Seasons
25 Temple of the Unknown God
26 Base of Arch of Severus
27 'Petite Basilique'
28 Traces of Amphitheatre
29 Restored Aqueduct Bridge

Oued   Sbeitla

to Sbeitla and the Arch of the Tetrarchs

to Kasserine and Sufetula Hotel

by columns which divided and emphasized a backdrop of six niches. Resist the attractions of the **forum** for the moment, and turn right.

The Great Baths

The entrance to these baths was once flanked by two columns leading to a small hall which, then as now, was dominated by an inscription to one Carpentius, doubtless the munificent benefactor who built the baths for the city. Passing through two larger halls, you reach the central *palaestra*. Here athletes exercised, boxers and wrestlers demonstrated and friends sparred in the fierce sunlight. Truncated double columns mark its colonnade.

To the left of this is the paved floor of the *frigidarium*, the cold room, a splendid 45-m long rectangle flanked by two square pools in good condition. In the pool which still sports three columns, look out for the niche to the right whence a fountain played into the pool. On the other side of the *palaestra*, the plan of the baths is repeated, though the exigencies of the site did not allow for the usual strict symmetry. You can make out the rectangular *frigidarium*, still paved and containing a square pool. Beyond stretch rambling and ruinous hot rooms, always the first to decay because of the raised floors, which made way for underfloor heating.

The Theatre

Carry on downhill to the theatre, which is in a state of romantic ruin perched above the dry river bed. It was built in the Greek style, using the lie of the land for the tiered seating, at the end of the 3rd century AD. Little more survives than the prestigious front two rows of seats, reserved for leading citizens. The orchestra pit, where choruses sang, is intact and above a restored line of niches marks the front of the stage, or *proscaenium*, though it should be about twice its current height. It was here that the statue of Bacchus now in the museum was found. All the great plays were first staged in honour of the god of wine, dance and merriment. At the back of the stage rises the picturesque ruin of the columned backdrop. The central entrance, known as the principal or royal, was reserved for the leading actor.

The Church of Servus

Returning towards the forum, just beyond the fountain is a curious building known as the **church of Servus**. Its four unstable corners hang in the air above a field of broken columns; a few columns have been re-erected to suggest its colonnade. Originally a temple to some unknown god, the building was converted into a church, and the pool you find within was once the baptistery. To the right a raised floor with slots for a balustrade marks out a small chapel, used for consecrating sacred oil used in baptism. This must have been a church of the Donatists, an early but intense schism based in Algeria and parts of western Tunisia. Its followers believed that the sacraments were only as holy as the priest who consecrated them, a not unreasonable view, but one which alienated North African converts from the pomp and hierarchy of the established Church. Donatist churches are distinguished by the added emphasis given to areas used for complicated baptismal rituals, by which they set great store. The apsed **presbytery** of the church, filled with four sarcophagi, is one of its few identifiable landmarks.

The Forum

Walking up to the arched gateway which gives on to the forum and Capitoline temples, you pass the ruins of four small **markets** on the right. The three-bayed **arch** is a classic piece of architecture from the golden era of the 2nd-century Antonine dynasty. It was dedicated to the Emperor Antoninus Pius and his two adopted sons in AD 139. The two flanking niches would have held statues, as would the summit.

During the Roman period, this arch was not hemmed in by the massive walls you see today. These were part of a Byzantine fortress which served as the local army headquarters. It was constructed around the forum in AD 550 by Belisarius to protect the fledgeling Byzantine hegemony from persistent attacks by local Berber kings.

The 2nd-century **forum** within retains much of its dignity. Broken columns face the three massive temples ahead, and part of the huge entablature they supported can be seen on the right. To the left are numerous bases and inscribed plinths which once held a gallery of past emperors, a dignified civic Madame Tussaud's. The small apsed building to the left of the temples is thought to have been the municipal council chamber.

The three triumphant **temples** ahead of you form one of the most memorable views in Tunisia. Ideally, you should linger in Sbeitla overnight, to watch their shifting colours at dusk and when first lit up by rosy-fingered dawn. It is unusual to find separate temples to the Capitoline trinity, Jupiter, Juno and Minerva, for elsewhere they were worshipped in one temple, and it is not known why the relatively impoverished town of Sufetula should have been thus blessed.

The larger central temple was dedicated to Jupiter, king of the gods. Set back slightly, it never had a stairway, being linked to its flanking sister temples by two arched walkways. In front of the temple, at the tribune, all the most solemn oaths and civic proclamations were declaimed, and important sacrifices made. The capitals on the temple to Jupiter are more elaborate than the classically Corinthian ones on either side.

All the temples still contain niches on the back wall from which statues of the gods would have presided over sacred feasts, ritually prepared by their colleges of priests and priestesses. The three rectangular niches on the side walls were filled by lesser personifications. Juno, for example, had a galaxy of different titles by which she could be appealed to at different stages of childbirth. The crypts below were filled with the holy of holies, temple treasures donated by worshippers and ancient cult objects. Deep in olive country, the temple to Minerva, creator of the olive, might have contained a black Madonna, the chance growth of an olive tree in the form of a female figurine, revered as a cult statue. The portal of the Jupiter temple preserves its lintel and open hemisphere. When the doors were closed, the only light that entered came through here, reflected off the carved ceiling of the massive porch.

Bellator's Basilica

Leaving the forum via the dark tunnel that cuts majestically between the temples, the ruins just outside the corner of the Byzantine fortress wall are of a **Byzantine church**, possibly the garrison's chapel. Continuing right towards the single palm tree, the solid rectangular shape to the left is known as the **basilica of Bellator**.

This is the most ancient site in Sufetula, though the present ruins are those of a 3rd-century cathedral. Beneath it lie traces of a temple courtyard, which some believe to be the old temple of Baal Hammon, the head of the Phoenician pantheon. Two lines of paving within the solid walls mark the line of the columns which divided the nave into three. The altar has had several positions in the cathedral, reflecting shifts in the doctrine and practice of the church in Africa, and leaving two apses. The one by the street is full of sarcophagi, and was possibly an early martyr's chapel. The other, above the altar, served as a presbytery. As a result of these altar movements, a square fragment of the original **mosaic** can still be seen, a crude eclectic design which mirrors the motifs used in Berber carpets and killims to this day.

The Chapel of Jucundus and Vitalis' Basilica

Next door, encased in some outer ruins, is a courtyard known as the **chapel of Jucundus**. Originally, this was the baptistery of the cathedral, and it contains a lip-shaped basin, once covered by a stone canopy, supported by the surviving corner pillars. When a new cathedral was built next door in the 6th century, the baptistery was converted into a saint's shrine and the relics of Jucundus were placed in the hollow column that still sits in the centre of the font.

Cross the street beside the chapel, to enter that 6th-century cathedral, the **basilica of Vitalis**. Its pillars have vanished and indeed the central basin, decorated with a fish **mosaic**, belongs to a house that was knocked down to build the cathedral. Throughout, fragments of domestic mosaic exist under the layer laid down in the 6th century by the church, and show how decorative techniques deteriorated between the 3rd and 6th centuries.

At either end of the nave are two raised apsides. The altar stood in the nave near the presbytery apse, the one with wide steps. The other, distinguished by smaller circular steps was a martyr's chapel, and once held a single massive sarcophagus.

The most striking element of this cathedral, however, is the **baptistry**, housed directly behind the presbytery but approached through a chain of small halls, which formed part of the processional ritual which developed around baptism in North Africa. The baptismal basin was covered by a canopy held up by four columns. In excellent condition, and covered in mosaic, the **font** itself is composed of a delightful series of contoured bays and steps. The symbolism of a second birth was played out in this vulva-shaped bath. Converts emerged from the waters of the mother church into a new life within the Christian community.

Beside the cathedral are the ruins of the **bishop's palace** and the ruins of a small bath complex, believed to be part of this episcopal quarter. The road beyond leads past some ruins of lesser interest. To the left lies another 3rd-century **fountain** partly obscured by the wall of a later house.

Walk to the Amphitheatre

Further on the right are the perilous ruins of a **temple** to an unknown god. In front are the remains of the **shrine of a marabout**, attracted later to this holy place.

Directly opposite is the **Edifice of the Seasons**, neither a house nor a temple. The visible columns decorate a large apsed chamber that opened off the dining-room. The lintels, carved with vines, are handsome, as are the proportions of the outer courtyard. Ringed with booths, the ensemble is mooted to have been the property of a guild of craftsmen, with workshops, a communal dining-room and the council chamber of the masters. The two corridors beside the dining-room, plastered for holding water, might have combined air conditioning with a shrine to the water nymphs.

Continuing on the road towards the Sufetula Hotel, you pass through the base of the **arch of Severus**, most of whose component stones lie scattered in a greater arc to the left. Beyond, the building misnamed *Petite Basilique* is in fact a courtyard house. Scant traces of the **amphitheatre** beyond are misleadingly labelled the *Arc de Sèvres*.

Below the hill to the right is a heavily restored Roman **bridge/aqueduct**, which brought water straight from the spring to the city. A modern pumping station to the right provides an audible continuum.

The Triumphal Arch

At the far end of the site, next to the modern town, is a magnificent arch. Bas-relief Corinthian columns reflect the free-standing columns on the face of the arch. It was built during the reign of Diocletian, at the end of the 3rd century, and dedicated to the Tetrarchs, an ill-conceived institution which divided the Empire and resulted in prolonged civil war and the eventual triumph of Constantine in 309. The arch defined the official limits of the city, which was never walled.

WHERE TO STAY

EXPENSIVE
While there is a swimming pool at the Bakini, it is nothing compared to that of the **Sufetula Hotel**, which looks back towards the town over the ruins. Rooms are built round an interior courtyard, or in blocks in the well-tended garden. It is only slightly more expensive than the Bakini.

MODERATE
The **Hotel Bakini**, on the edge of town by the turning to Kairouan, is a distinctly kitsch place, with a plague of weeping pierrots in the dining-room.

CHEAP
For a cheap bed, the **Hotel Bar Ezzohour**, opposite the bus station, may suffice, though it is more of a bar than a hotel.

EATING OUT
The food in both these hotels is designed for lunchtime coach groups and is correspondingly bland. They both tend to be packed out in the middle of the day, so escape to the **Restaurant Erriadh**, just up from the Ezzohour. A good spicy lunch here costs around 1.5 dn.

Around Sbeitla

The Road to Kairouan

This dull road crosses the southern steppe, which is flat and arid without the fascination of real desert. It is the domain of nomadic herders who are still the most efficient users of this land. The only conceivable stop is at **Hajeb el Ayoun**, a village 3 km down a turning by an Agil garage. The village holds a Tuesday market, though you can sniff out a good spicy lunch for 1 dn any day of the week. Its busiest time of the year is July, when the great flocks of the steppe are shorn and the wool sold to merchants. A few gardens, strung along the **Oued el Hateb** watercourse below the village, nestle beside unearthed remnants of a Roman past.

The Road to Sfax

This is a numbingly flat journey of 163 km, mostly across arid grazing, the last third through a rigid geometry of olive trees. Ruin enthusiasts may want to visit **Ksar el Baroud**, 8 km before Jelma to the left at the first major crossroads. Just beside the road is a chunky mass of Roman **bathhouse** masonry and a recently excavated **church**, complete with mosaics, a lip-shaped baptistery and intact sarcophagi.

At the next major junction, you could take the turning to **Sidi Bou Zid**, once the unofficial capital of the nomad tribes, where they met under the protection of the saint's tomb to arrange war, peace and marriage. It is worth a look on Saturday or Sunday morning, market days, and there are relics from Roman Gamouda, two capitals and a headless emperor, exhibited on the central roundabout. The unlicensed **Hotel Restaurant Chems** offers double rooms at 9 dn, tel (06) 30515.

The Table of Jugurtha and Haidra

South of El Kef, the P17 runs parallel to the Algerian frontier at a distance of some 16 km. It is wild and mountainous countryside, but there are two uplifting forays to be made—one up the extraordinary mountain known as the **Table of Jugurtha**, the other to the undisturbed ruins of **Haidra**.

Table of Jugurtha
The Table of Jugurtha is a massive slab of stone, rising like brown cliffs of Dover above the surrounding sea of heathland. There are *louages* from El Kef direct to the village of **Kalaat es Senan** at the foot of the mountain. On the way, Tajerouine boasts a hotel for the needy, and is 28 km from Kalaat es Senan. To get to the mountain, take the 4-km track from Kalaat es Senan. A Jacob's ladder, cut into the living rock, climbs to the flat summit. The plateau, with views in all directions, is as close as you will come to the heavens, an ideal site for the marabout of Sidi Abd el Jouad.

Halfway up, the stairway ducks under a surprising Byzantine gateway. Jugurtha, the Numidian king, is reputed to have garrisoned this natural fortress from 112–105 BC. Its other name, the **fortress of Senan**, is more recent. From the mountain, Senan, a local bandit leader, managed to check the advance of Beylical tax-collecting troops. He added to the mountain's natural fortifications and built massive cisterns on top to supply his troops with water over long periods of siege.

Haidra
Kalaa Kasbah is a dusty phosphate mining town, little more than an industrial railway shunting yard, though there are three daily trains to and from Tunis. Buses and *louages* on the El Kef to Kasserine route also run through the town.

The isolated ruins of Haidra lie 18 km west of Kalaa Kasbah. With spectacular Roman **mausoleums** and a haunting **Byzantine fortress**, they are well worth the hitch, and the road has its fair share of lorries heading for the Algerian border not far beyond. On the way along the valley, notice the prominent **koubba** and modern **cemetery** on the left, which sit on an ancient place of worship, once a temple to Baal and later to Saturn.

History
Thanks to an abundant spring in the Oued Haidra, this unprepossessing scrubland has supported several generations of towns since the 1st century BC. On a national frontier to this day, Haidra's principal role has been as a military centre. The **fort** you see today is 6th-century Byzantine, and the northern end was refortified in the 1840s by Bey Ahmed I. It sits opposite a French frontier fort built in 1886, and somewhere nearby lie the buried remains of a 1st-century BC Roman fortified garrison, Ammaedara.

This territory was briefly controlled by Carthage and then the Numidian Berbers before being garrisoned in 30 BC by the Third Augustan Legion, who patrolled the frontiers of the Roman empire. By establishing fixed frontiers and farmland, the legion deprived the nomads of their traditional transhumant existence, moving flocks between summer and winter pastures. This, more than anything else, provoked indigenous resistance, and it was from

Ammaedara that the Romans led part of their campaign against the revolt of the local rebel, Tacfarinas. He was finally killed in Algeria in AD 24, and by AD 75 the area around Ammaedara was subdued and the legion's headquarters had moved west, to Timgad in Algeria.

Ammaedara, sited on a crossroads leading to Carthage, Tebessa, El Kef, Gafsa and Sousse, flourished as a civilian town, peopled by veterans of the legion. The archaeological evidence of five churches attests to a vibrant Christian community, beset by the schisms and liturgical arguments which raged in the early church. A period of Vandal occupation (439–533) was superseded by the Byzantine invasion, when the whole area was heavily fortified by Solomon, Belisarius' formidable eunuch general. The town appears to have survived until the 9th century, and was reused to defend Tunisia against the French in Algeria in the early 19th century. By the late 1880s, the French had their own border post here, though the village beyond remained little more than a few huts until 1939.

Haidra has never been subject to systematiç archaeological exploration, though the Italian doctor in Kalaa Kasbah, Dr Dolcemascolo, did his best between 1925–40. Most of the prominent visible structures date from the Byzantine period, while the glories of the Roman town are tantalizingly hinted at by a series of half-buried buildings.

The Site
The dangerously eroded single pillar that stands at the top of a stairway was at the heart of the old Roman town. This, because of its immense size, is thought to be the **Capitoline temple**, where Jupiter, Juno and Minerva were worshipped. The ground around is littered with its fallen columns and massive Corinthian capitals. In front, the old **forum** is now dissected by the modern road, but broken pillar bases trace the line of its former sweeping colonnade.

Below the forum, the yellow limestone building attached to the top of the fortress is known as the **'building with five windows'**. Archaeologists have long puzzled over its use, and believe it was the **Roman law court**. Traces have been found of a square room divided by two rows of pillars and a second transversal room, similar to the plan of other contemporary courts.

The square courtyard to the right of the Capitoline temple is the semi-excavated Roman **marketplace**. Bases of pillars trace a colonnade, and remnants of stalls can be deciphered beneath the soil round the edges.

Climb up behind the temple to reach the confusing ruins of the **baths**, most of which are way below ground. The eastern section of the baths, above ground, is thought to be the cold rooms. To the west, copious cellars indicate room for heating services but are now used as public toilets. They would have subsisted beneath the hot rooms, the haunt of furnaces, complex terracotta pipe systems and wood-hauling slaves.

Returning to the forum, walk past the French fort and straight on to the twin spanning arches of a ruin known as the **'building of the troughs'**. It belongs to a group of North African buildings that have long puzzled archaeologists. Here you will find an apse, a nave, in this case divided in three, but also a number of stone troughs, each with a hole near the top lip. The most likely explanation is that they were distribution points for some form of dole payments, or an office for the collection of taxes in kind.

On one side of the building is a courtyard, with remnants of its fluted and spiralled colonnade lying abject on the ground, and traces of a pool at its centre. Walk through the more recent building on the other side to the **Vandal chapel**. Enter the building, with its solid southern wall, through the only unblocked original door. It has been dated to the Vandal occupation by tombs found in the floor, to the right of the column which stands in the nave. Other Christian tombstones found here attest to the continued existence of a pagan imperial cult known as the Eternal Flame. The pillar by the door is an old pagan funerary stone, its inscription excised.

Little survives of the Roman **theatre**, a mound of earth 150 m east of the chapel. An internal corridor running round the back of the bowl of seats, the first rows of seats and the orchestra pit remain. Beyond the theatre to the northeast stands a modest **square mausoleum**, three steps leading up to the lower storey, which is decorated with engaged Corinthian pillars on the corners.

Due south the **arch of Septimius Severus** beckons. Built over the road from Carthage, parts of which are still paved, the arch has survived astonishingly well, thanks to the rough stone fort built around it by the Byzantines. The delicate porticoes thrown out on each corner of the arch are typical of its early 3rd-century date. The Corinthian columns are surmounted by a pleasing, simple entablature. Originally, there would have been a further band of stone

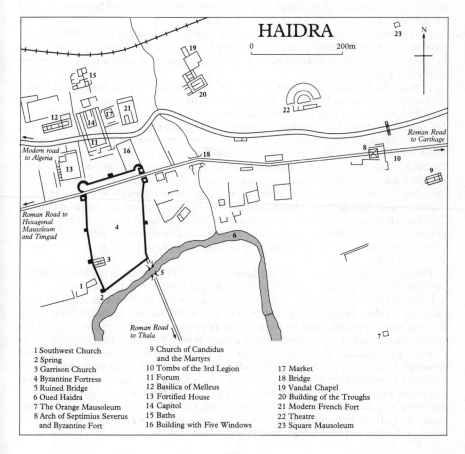

HAIDRA

0   200m   N

Roman Road to Carthage

Modern road to Algeria

Roman Road to Hexagonal Mausoleum and Timgad

Roman Road to Thala

1 Southwest Church
2 Spring
3 Garrison Church
4 Byzantine Fortress
5 Ruined Bridge
6 Oued Haidra
7 The Orange Mausoleum
8 Arch of Septimius Severus
  and Byzantine Fort

9 Church of Candidus
  and the Martyrs
10 Tombs of the 3rd Legion
11 Forum
12 Basilica of Melleus
13 Fortified House
14 Capitol
15 Baths
16 Building with Five Windows

17 Market
18 Bridge
19 Vandal Chapel
20 Building of the Troughs
21 Modern French Fort
22 Theatre
23 Square Mausoleum

above the inscription. To the left of the arch, inside the town limits, you will find a cistern, built by the Byzantines, to water the soldiers defending the fort.

The road to Carthage was once lined with imposing white mausoleums, memorials to soldiers of the Third Legion. The bright white foundations have been unearthed, and scattered between are split-column tombstones, commemorating Italian, Gallic and African soldiers.

Below the cemetery is the 4th-century **church of Candidus and the Martyrs**. The nave is littered with columns, bases and capitals. The chapel had two distinct phases. At first it had an apse in the west, but this was later transformed into a martyrs' chapel, and a new apse added to the eastern end of the nave. In this eastern apse, entered up four steps, traces of the *synthronos*, or bench where the priests sat, remains hugging the wall. The whole nave was divide by two rows of columns into three separate vaulted aisles. In the later Byzantine phase, the floor was covered in mosaics, paid for by Candidus and Adeodata, whose generosity was commemorated in the floor itself. In the martyrs' chapel in the western end of the nave a low stone wall, decorated with carved lozenges, enclosed a mosaic, dedicated to the local martyrs of Emperor Diocletian's persecution of the Christians in AD 305. Since no bodies were found buried here, this constituted a memorial rather than a cult site.

The **Orange Mausoleum** which stands on the edge of the Oued Haidra is visible for miles around. The base is partly destroyed by grave robbers, but the front still bears a faint inscription. The top floor takes the form of a miniature temple, its portico supported by four Corinthian pillars.

To reach the **Byzantine fortress**, cross a narrow gorge on a **Roman bridge** which once supported the main road from Carthage. Although this massive fort has never been fully excavated, its dignified walls still manage to convey something of the monumental severity of a 6th-century military outpost, an isolated imperial bastion in a hostile tribal sea. The southern wall of the fort drops almost straight into the river, its western corner covering the vital spring, which supplied massive cisterns within. The road from Gafsa crossed a bridge straight into the citadel through the fortified southeastern gate. You can see traces of the **bridge** in the river bed, and of the old road on the far bank passing through a ruined arch. Stairways led up on to the battlements, whose wide catwalk was supported by arches along the inside wall.

Built against the walls in the southwest corner is the apse of the fortress' **garrison church**. Two green marble columns held the key arch at the front of the apse, a presbytery in which the priests sat during the services. From the nave, divided in three by rows of pillars, the soldiers would have witnessed the mysteries of their religion, little different from the orthodox services of today.

The semi-circular bastions on the northern part of the fort were rebuilt in 1840, replacing a set of two fortified gates, through which the road from Carthage to Tebessa passed.

Just outside the fort, in the southwestern corner, lies another small **church**. Little is known about the building, because being so close to the spring and the river bed nobody was buried here for fear of pollution, and so there are no dated gravestones. It appears to have been rebuilt and fortified by the Byzantines, who closed up all three eastern doors in the process.

Walk up the length of the citadel's western wall, passing through the remains of a **fortified house** and over the modern road to the columns of the **basilica of Melleus**, the Catholic cathedral. It was the largest church in Haidra, begun in the late 4th century, but it underwent significant changes over the following centuries. By the 6th century, the church's pre-eminence was assured with the burial here of both the Vandal Bishop Victorinus and the Byzantine Catholic Bishop Melleus. Beneath one of the two altars a reliquary was also found which, according to a 6th-century inscription, contained the remains of St Cyprian.

In 1969, the church was restored, its walls partly rebuilt, Corinthian columns re-erected and the arches in the courtyard rebuilt. To the west of the church is a courtyard, once porticoed and later used as a cemetery. The long nave of the church, divided in three but with prominence given to the larger centre aisle, bears traces of two altars.

Along the old Roman road to Timgad in Algeria is a **hexagonal mausoleum**, perched right above the river bed, which marks the town's western cemetery.

Kasserine

If Kasserine exists at all in the popular consciousness it is remembered, erroneously, as a battle in the Second World War. Two American tank brigades were destroyed by Rommel near Sidi Bou Zid, whereupon the American army retreated north up the Kasserine pass where they were reinforced by French and British units. Despite low cloud cover which prevented a massacre by Axis fighter planes, the Americans lost 6500 men, 183 tanks and 700 trucks, compared with a handful of German casualties. Patton, their new commander, summed up: 'The boys' morale was so low it could have passed under a snake.'

Kasserine is a gritty unattractive town, a ribbon development that stretches 5 km along the main road, punctuated by a train station, a cellulose factory, two dry river beds and a military barracks. The modern town is entirely French, but it is an old site. The name Kasserine derives from 'the two ksour', an Arab reference to two surviving **Roman mausoleums**, and on the hill south of the town are scant remains of Roman **Cillium**. Now it is the market and government centre of the southern steppe, one of the poorest and most neglected regions of the country, with a strong political nerve of its own. In April 1906, three Christian monks were killed here in an outburst of fanaticism that threatened to spread throughout the country, and the 1984 bread riots that swept the country started here.

But Kasserine does have its uses. It has characterful hotels in every price range, and much better transport facilities than Sbeitla, which makes it a good base for visiting Haidra. It is the unofficial rendezvous for trans-Saharan groups and appeals to hill walkers and boar hunters, as **Jebel Chambi**, the highest mountain in Tunisia, rises immediately to the west of the town.

The Roman Mausoleums
The mausoleums of Kasserine are much cited in travelogues but their present sunken, belittered and befumed roadside condition has reduced their charm. The first, with only two standing walls, is just past the first dry river bed. The second, the **mausoleum of Flavius Secundus and Petrouan**, just after the larger bed of the Oued ed Darb, is much more impressive. It is a three-storey memorial with engaged Corinthian columns, whose summit was originally crowned with a cock. On the roadside ground wall you can read 110 lines of verbose verse praising the mausoleum and its rich owner, one Flavius Secundus: 'Marvel at this building and be staggered at the wealth which has caused this monument to rise to the heavens.' His remains were joined by the urns of other members of his family, including Petrouan, who added the inscription on the first storey.

Cillium

Leaving Kasserine on the Gafsa road keep an eye out for the circular Hotel Cillium on the left. Above its terraced garden lie the ruins of Cillium. It is a site with more atmosphere than architecture, but there is a **triumphal arch**, some rock-cut **tombs** and a compact theatre overlooking the Oued ed Darb valley. The theatre, which uses the natural slope of the land in the Greek fashion, was built in the 1st century to hold an audience of 2500. It is associated with the Roman writer, Pliny the Elder, who was procurator of Africa during the reign of Vespasian when Cillium became a *municipa*. The triumphal arch may well have commemorated its further advance in status to a *colonia* in the 3rd century. In winter, the siting of the town is explained by springs gushing out of the hill, now tapped to supply the modern town below. On the summit are traces of three rectangular enclosures, almost certainly **Byzantine forts**, and patches of mosaic which archaeologists have variously identified as baths, villas and a church.

Like Kasserine in the 20th century, Cillium in the 6th century found itself in the hub of war. A Byzantine army conquered Tunisia from the Vandals in a quick campaign, only to face the harder task of subduing the Algerian and Tunisian hinterland. Solomon, the eunuch Byzantine commander, set out to restore imperial authority in 539, with a five-year plan for the fortification of Tunisia. Four years later this was put to the test by Antalas, King of the Aures, who had united the tribes as far away as Libya for a joint assault. Solomon won the first battle at Tebessa in Algeria, but for the second time in his career his troops mutinied in the hour of victory. Deserted by his army, Solomon stood his ground, dying in the defence of Cillium. Antalas went on to destroy the mutineer army at El Kef but the tribes, flushed by success, then fell to fighting amongst themsleves.

Jebel Chambi

There is obvious appeal in climbing the 1544-m peak of the highest mountain of Tunisia, though it is a mere foothill of the Monts de Tebessa, just over the border in Algeria. The easiest approach is to be driven out on the Thala road and 11 km later take a left turn, passing through the hamlet of **Borj Chambi**. A track 3 km later on the left climbs round the back of the mountain, passing below the wooded summit, and rejoins the main road to Gafsa.

SHOPPING FOR ESPARTO

Aside from fleeces, the southern steppe produces a second cash crop, painstakingly gathered from over 1.5 million arid acres by the women of the plains. They harvest the tufty clumps of esparto grass which are bundled into bales and sold to the depot in Kasserine. From there the annual crop of 70,000 tons is exported to Europe to make fine paper or processed at the Kasserine works into cellulose.

The left-over esparto grass is woven into **mats** and shopping **baskets**. Look out for them in the centre of town, at the Tuesday **souk**, the Cillium Hotel or in Gafsa.

WHERE TO STAY AND EAT

MODERATE

The **Cillium**, Route de Feriana, tel (07) 70682, is a circular 1950s hotel with a bar, restaurant and pool, on the edge of ancient Cillium and looking out on Jebel Chambi.

On the Sbeitla edge of town is the cheaper **Hotel Pinus** with a bar and a cool, dark restaurant covered in murals.

CHEAPER

In the centre of town by the bus station, the **Hotel de la Paix**, tel (07) 71465, costs 9 dn and has its own à la carte restaurant. Two doors down is the **Bar en Nouar**.

Around Kasserine

North to Haidra

The journey north to Haidra takes you through the infamous Kasserine pass, a narrow valley cut by the **Oued el Hattab** through two mountains. Beyond the pass you enter a high plateau fringed by wooded hills. Thinly populated now, a succession of half-buried villas and the more visible menhirs of oil presses testify to the vanished olive groves and prosperity of the Roman period.

Twenty-four kilometres south of Thala is the site of an heroic British defeat that deserves to be remembered with that of the Light Brigade. As Rommel's Tenth Panzer Division chased the retreating Americans up the pass, it destroyed two British tank regiments, the Lothians and Lancers. The Allied line then consisted of a few pieces of US artillery which had been ordered to withdraw. At dawn on 22 February 1943, the colonel of the Lothians led a suicidal attack with his last 10 tanks. They managed to persuade Rommel that Allied reinforcements were arriving in great numbers and that afternoon he ordered a general withdrawal.

Thala

Thala is made up of stone-walled, red-tiled houses that cascade down two hills overlooking the plain to the north. It has a bank, several cafés and the **Hotel Bouthelja**, a cheap modern hotel with a restaurant. The *louage* station is immediately below the stone minaret on the main road.

Right in the centre of the town is an excavated square of **Roman ruins**, thought to be a town mentioned by Sallust in *The Jugurthine Wars*. The ground plan of a **church** can be recognized, surrounded by a sanctuary wall left over from the **temple** that used to occupy the area. The Christians had even less respect for the pagan dead, and dug up their carved gravestones to use as a bannister. Just north of Thala, marring its image as a mountain idyll, are **quarries** mining local white stone, and 12 km further is Kalaa Kasbah and the turning to Haidra (see p. 287).

South to Gafsa: Thelepte and Feriana

From Kasserine the P17 sweeps south across 106 km of the southern steppe to reach Gafsa. Only Byzantine enthusiasts will want to stop for the ruins of **Thelepte**, known locally as *Medinet el Kedima*, the old town. The road and the railway plough though the heart of what was once the military headquarters of the province of Byzacena, now a massive acreage of ankle-high pottery, marble and stone. It covers 5 km between the railway station of Thelepte and the modern town of **Feriana**. Watch out for one or two deep wells as you walk round the crumbled perimeter of an enormous rectangular **Byzantine citadel**. Tucked away by the river bank is the remains of a **theatre** and, overlooked by Roman quarries again in use, are the great mortared walls and apses of a set of **baths**. For all the silence of its stone, 6th-century Thelepte survives through the autobiography of one of its citizens, St Fulgentius (467–532). If you plan to read this amongst the ruins, there is a basic roadside hotel and restaurant, the **Mabrouk**, in Feriana.

Part VIII

THE CHOTT EL JERID

Harvesting Dates

The Chott el Jerid marks the beginning of true desert culture. It is the largest in a series of reddish, barren salt flats, called 'chotts', that stretch from the Mediterranean deep into Algeria. Nothing can survive on this sterile mud, but on its periphery gush springs which give birth to celebrated date palm oases, such as Tozeur and Nefta, giving the Chott the name 'Jerid', meaning palm. Beyond these islands of fertility rise barren sun-baked hills, cut through by canyons, like those at Midès and Seldja, which expose their contorted sedimentary layers. The *hammada*, a pebble-strewn monotony that covers most of the region, provides grazing for drifting herds of camel and goat, accompanied by knots of brown nomad tents. Around Douz, to the south, lie areas of erg, of shifting windblown sand, piled up in towering golden crescents, which satisfy the most romantic desert imagination.

There are few man-made sites in the Chott: at Gafsa, a pair of monumental Roman pools fed by warm springs, and at Tozeur and Nefta, the distinctive architecture of their brick-built medinas, a decorated geometric pattern. Otherwise, the region offers the arid splendours of its scenery, and a chance to examine life in the desert: walking from the mountain oasis of Tamerza to the cliff-top eyrie of Midès; bathing in the open-air hot springs of Tozeur; and learning something of the Bedouin way of life as you trek across the sand desert from Douz on the back of a camel.

Desert Life and Nomads

For those who work in the oasis gardens, water, its ownership, division and use, are all-important. In the great oases the system of canalization is so complex that the French engineers who attempted to improve conditions quite failed to even unravel its mysteries.

294

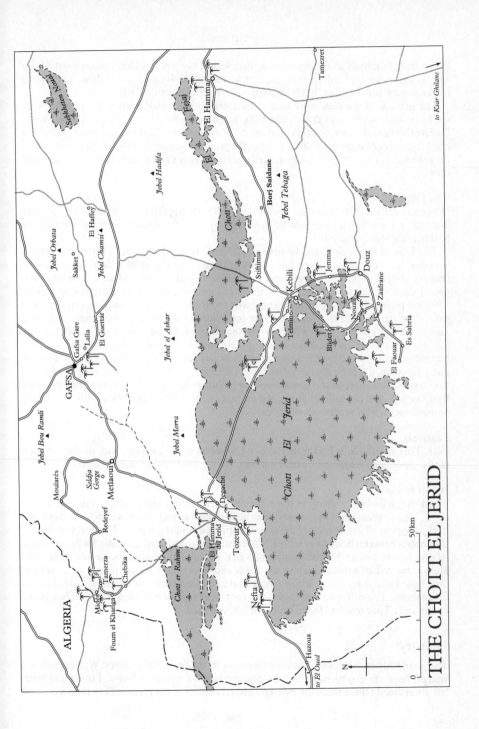

THE CHOTT EL JERID

Water from hundreds of springs must be distributed to every last plot; sewage must not be wasted; and water from salt springs must be channelled safely out of the gardens. The system requires constant attention, but is ultimately dependent on mutual trust.

The nomads of the area move south with their flocks in early March, to catch the brief spring pasture in the sand desert, and back to the oases for summer in the relative shade. During this time the men go off to tend any cornland sown by the tribe, and those left behind must find fodder for the animals. In autumn the group moves north, to scrub that has survived the summer on the north of the Chott, and in winter it is back at the oasis, harvesting dates and olives.

The Date Palm

'They feel delight in their mutual love, and ... this is clearly shown by the fact that they lean towards one another, and cannot be bent back by even the strongest winds.' (Ammianus Marcellinus, 4th century AD)

The king of the region, and its major cash crop, is the date palm. There are a myriad varieties, but they only produce full, sugary fruit, such as the 1000 tons of *deglat-en-nour* (fingers of light) produced a year here, in a narrow climatic band, and have therefore been prized since antiquity. The trees are majestic natural pillars and are either male or female. They are productive for up to 150 years, starting to fruit at 5–6 years old. Between April and June, they are 'mated': the pollen-bearing male flowers are cut from male trees and hung amongst clusters of unfertilized dates on the female trees. As these begin to ripen in autumn, the best varieties are enclosed in a sack to protect them from insects, sand and rain. The date harvest stretches from November through to February, depending on the type. As well as fruit and an income, the palm provides date honey, animal fodder in the stones, an aphrodisiac in the flowers, fibre for rope and shoes, wood for building and *laghami*, a potent palm wine made from the sap. And beneath the shade of their fronds, the palmery gardens are able to produce pomegranates, figs, vegetables and corn.

Festivals

Both Tozeur and Douz host festivals over Christmas and New Year, with displays of local crafts, games and traditions—camel fighting, racing, sand hockey and fantasias.

When to Go

Think carefully before going in the summer, when midday temperatures can rise to over 40°C. The heat makes those unused to it bad-tempered, and restricts activity to dawn and dusk, stopping all exploration of the more isolated parts of the region. The best time to visit the chott is between November and early May, when you will need a sweater for the evenings. Always ensure you have a good supply of water. In very hot weather you should drink eight pints a day. When driving, keep to the roads and tracks, as it is easy to lose your sense of direction. Four years ago a British family drove off for a picnic in the desert and their car broke down. The driver walked back down the track to get help but his family got hot, bored and thirsty. They too decided to walk, got lost and died.

History

The Jerid's historical identity has been forged by its rigid physical features. Water supply is a vital prerequisite to settlement, and the concentration of springs at Gafsa, Tozeur and Nefta has always made these three the rich agricultural centres of the region. They form a political community screened from the steppe by a chain of mountains to the north, and by the Chott to the south. The Jerid was never an important entrepôt for trans-Saharan trade, as the caravans had to avoid the Great Eastern Erg, the sand desert which stretches for some 400 miles to the south. However, it was well placed to catch the east–west traffic, principally used by pilgrims en route to Mecca, but which also linked it to the trading oases of Ghadames and Biskra.

At the first sight of weak central government, the Jerid has been quick to assert its independence. It is the archetypal rebel base, capable of supporting a dissident court, isolated enough to be safe and yet close enough to threaten the centres of power. Despite these advantages, and the general Muslim tendency to adopt new dynasties from the desert, the Jerid has failed in all its coups.

The Roman Frontier
The Jerid first appears in a characteristic role, as the southern base for Jugurtha's long guerrilla campaign against Rome. Having defeated him, the Romans established the Chott as their southern frontier. They created a line of posts to guard the open plain, which stretches west of the Jerid to the Aurès mountains, against the Lawata, a great nomad confederation. A precious insight into life at the time is given by the Albertini tablets, a set of household records from AD 496, which were found 65 km west of Gafsa. They could have been written now, with their concern over odd parcels of land, water rights, looms and dowries. The clothing and jewellery described are more Berber than Roman, but the striking difference from today lies in the tablets' description of great olive groves in what is now desert.

A Kharijite Oasis
After the Arab conquest in the 7th century the Jerid, in common with the other Saharan oases, was quick to embrace the Ibadite creed. It stressed a puritanical equality among the Muslim community of believers, and had a strong political attraction for the Berbers, who under its banner rebelled against their Arab overlords.

For centuries the Jerid seethed with this revolutionary creed, vacillating between the leadership of Kharijite Imams and the orthodox Aghlabid Emirs at Kairouan. In the mid-9th century, the region even boasted its own improved Kharijite variation, the Nafathiyya. It also produced the archetypal southern rebel, Abu Yazid, 'the man with the donkey', around whom layers of myth have been woven. In 943 he led a Kharijite rebellion from the Jerid, which within six months had overrun the entire country, save the capital. Legend recalls that whilst Abu Yazid besieged the walls of Mahdia, the Fatimid Sultan sat contentedly by the fountain in his palace garden, playing with an eel, for Yazid's arrival had been predicted 30 years before. The Sultan took his time, checking the exactness of the prophecy, and then sent out his soldiers to catch and skin alive the man who was endangering the dynasty. Abu Yazid's corpse was stuffed with straw and given as a toy to two caged monkeys.

Jerid Principalities
In the 11th century, the Beni Hilal and Sulaym Bedouin flattened cities, burned orchards and destroyed watercourses and cisterns, before establishing petty kingdoms amongst the remnants of agricultural life. The defeat of these Arabs in Algeria a century later allowed the Almohad dynasty from Morocco to extend their Empire over Tunisia. Their authority over the south was brief, for the Beni Ghaniya, a dynasty of governors from Majorca who were violently opposed to them, moved to the Jerid in 1184 and gathered the tribes in rebellion. By 1203 the Beni Ghaniya were in virtual control of Tunisia, and though defeated by the Almohads three years later, they survived as bandit princes for another half century. The

297

Hafsids, with the odd exception, exercised only distant suzerainty over the Jerid, leaving its cities to be ruled by local dynasties.

Turkish Reunification

In the 16th century, the Turks reincorporated the Jerid into Tunisia. Every November, the Bey du Camp left Tunis for the Jerid, arriving in time for the date harvest, and usually returned to the capital by March. He received tribute, mostly in dates and wool, which was collected by the various Sheikhs and Caids and presented to him in his camp. He also settled oustanding disputes and presented these local leaders with expensive garments from Tunis in return for their loyalty. For the rest of the year, they were left to govern themselves.

In the 19th century Nefta and Tozeur each had a population of 8000, the same size as Sousse, the fourth city of the nation. Until European imports flooded the market, the Jerid was famous for its weavers. Tozeur produced the best burnous, Nefta was a centre for pottery as well as turning out a fine line in a mixed wool and silk cloth for haiks, and Gafsa was known for its *farashiya*, long bright-coloured garments.

The French Colonial Regime and Phosphates

Before they brought doctors, electricity and radios to the Chott, the French brought phosphate mining. It was, and still is, easily the most important industry in Tunisia, though predictably the local workers were poorly paid and treated badly by the European foremen. All this yielded important political dividends, for the Muslim miners of Metlaoui were at the vanguard of both the labour movement and the independence struggle, and by 1956 the mountain region was on the brink of armed revolt.

The Jerid Today

Since the 1960s, soil conservation has increased the area of worked ground in the oases, and a profitable tourist industry has been created. As ever, it is water, or the lack of it, that sets the pace in the south. Too great an exploitation of artesian wells has lowered the water table, and the seven-fold population increase this century has only added pressure to the often conflicting requirements from the gardens, mines, hotels and houses.

Gafsa

Gafsa is the largest town in the region, spreading out from an ancient central medina. At the heart of the old quarter are a pair of Roman pools, still filled by bright aquamarine hot water. On the edge of the town is a working palmery, rarely visited by tourists, and not far away are more palmeries, hot springs and the Berber villages of Jebel Orbata to explore.

History

Gafsa's strategic position is immediately apparent from the barren hills that rise insistently above the town's roofscape. It guards a gap in the escarpment that elsewhere separates the world of the steppe from the Sahara. At this important juncture, the Capsian Stone Age culture, 10,000–6000 BC, developed, named after Capsa, the Roman name for Gafsa (see p. 35).

The antiquity of human settlement in this area is also mirrored by robust Phoenician myths about the town, which they believed was created by Melkarth, as a walled city of 100 gates known as Hecatompylos. During the Carthaginian era, the town was a Berber stronghold known as 'Kafaz', the walled. It fell to the Romans in 106 BC. Marius suprised the town with a forced march from El Kef, his troops making water containers from the skins of the cattle they ate. Although the town surrendered, 'it was set on fire, the adult men massacred, the remainder of the population sold into slavery and the booty divided among the soldiers.' (Sallust)

Roman Capsa was, by the reign of Trajan (98–117), a prosperous colonial possession. Fortified by the Byzantine eunuch general Solomon in 540, it was renamed Justiniana after the Emperor. Though the town was originally taken by the Muslims in 668, it is also reputed to be one of the sites of the last stand of Al Kahena, the Berber queen, in 703.

A kasbah was first built on the present site in 1434, by the Hafsids. Little more than 100 years later, in 1556, Dragut secured its allegiance for the Ottomans, and with some rebuilding it remained largely intact until, in 1943, during the Tunisian campaign in the Second World War, an Allied arsenal exploded, taking much of the building with it.

Gafsa last hit the headlines with a mysterious affair in January 1980. During the night of 27 January, the town was taken over by guerrillas. It took the Tunisian army several days to regain control, with the death of over 20 soldiers and 20 civilians. The group, who called themselves the Tunisian Armed Resistance and declared that they aimed to free Tunisia from the 'dictatorship' of the socialist Destour Party, have never been properly identified. Links with Libya were serious enough for diplomatic relations between the two countries to be suspended. Thirteen of the 60 people brought to trial were hanged on 17 April 1980, amidst much protest at home and abroad. Whatever the nature of this attempted coup, it is no surprise that it began in the south, the country's poorest region, where four years later bread riots, which spread throughout Tunisia, erupted.

GETTING AROUND

By Train

There is one train a day in both directions to and from Tunis, via Sfax, and another to Metlaoui. The railway station, tel (06) 20335, is a couple of kilometres out of town, in a suburb called Gafsa Gare. To get there, take a taxi from outside the Maamoun Hotel.

By Bus

Gafsa's bus station hides in a yard behind the Hotel Tunis, with a narrow entrance on Pl du 7 Novembre 1987 beside the Café Patisserie Elafrah. Seven buses a day head for Tunis, Kairouan and Kasserine, five for Gabès, four for Kebili, Tozeur, Nefta and Sfax and three for Redeyef. Local buses operate from Pl du 7 Novembre 1987 itself.

By *Louage*/Taxi

Local taxis wait outside the Maamoun Hotel. *Louages* operate to Tunis, Sfax, Gabès, Tozeur, Metlaoui and Kasserine, again from Pl du 7 Novembre 1987, on the side known as Rue du 13 Fevrier 1952.

TOURIST INFORMATION

Gafsa's **Tourist Office** is not always open but is to be found on the open space in front of the Roman pools, tel (06) 21664. The large **PTT** dominates the same end of Av Habib Bourguiba, a number of **banks** surround Pl du 7 Novembre 1987, and the **police station** is next to the Hotel Khalfallah.

WHAT TO SEE

Gafsa lends itself to a gentle stroll, taking in the kasbah, palmery, Great Mosque and Roman pools in one sweep. From Pl du 7 Novembre 1987, walk past the Mosque of Sidi Bou Yaccoub on Av Taïeb Méhiri, take a left on to Av Amor Ben Slimane and later onto tree-lined Rue Farhat Hached. This meets Av Habib Bourguiba at the corner of the **kasbah**, now partly housing the law courts, partly in decay, and closed to visitors. Its monolithic pale walls are sadly unimpressive, their restoration giving them the look of a two-dimensional film set.

Immediately behind the kasbah and neighbouring cinema rise the first of the oasis' **100,000 palms**. Gafsa is a little too far north for the best-quality eating dates, but compensates with famously good pistachios. The road at the edge of the palmery passes the **Great Mosque**, into whose vast courtyard, adorned with pillars from all ages, you will not be permitted. The best view of its octagonal minaret is from the Roman pools a little further on.

Turning left onto Rue Ali Belhaouane shortly after the mosque, there is a cluster of olive oil presses, busy after the harvest from November and February. A narrow dirt track to the left, almost opposite the Hotel Hedili, leads into the heart of Gafsa's residential quarter, past some sturdy examples of traditional oasis architecture—the house at no. 31, for example, with its massive wooden doors and palm trunk ceilings.

This track leads directly to the **Roman pools**, two deep stone enclaves, each with steps leading to pure green water which bubbles out at 31°C. Sipping a coffee from the nearby *Café des Piscines Romaines*, you can watch the fishes, and the sand bubbling up between weathered rocks where the springs rise. The wall of one pool still bears a faint Roman inscription, over the arch which once framed a spring. Water from the far end of the other pool drains into a hammam. To wash here, walk through the arcade of the Dar el Bey, supported by ancient capitals, and through the door on the left.

Returning to Rue Ali Belhouane, continue back to the town centre through the market area, at its busiest for the Wednesday souk. The local speciality is woven alfa mats and baskets.

WHERE TO STAY

EXPENSIVE

The **Hotel Maamoun**, on the Gabès road, tel (06) 22740/433, is much patronized by tour groups, small and large. It is also the most expensive in town. Avoid the Hotel Jugurtha in the neighbouring oasis of Sidi Ahmed bou Zarrouk. Once highly rated it now has the atmosphere of a tomb and sits in an increasingly suburban oasis.

The **Gafsa Hotel** with its entrance on Rue Ahmed Snoussi, tel (06) 22676/468, offers lashings of hot and cold water, air conditioning or heating.

CHEAP

A cheap bed can be found in one of the **Tunis Hotel**'s 18 rooms, on the southern face of Pl du 7 Novembre, tel (06) 21660. The **Hotel Khalfallah** on Av Taïeb Méhiri, tel (06) 21468, is much cleaner, and its downstairs bar and restaurant are amusingly busy.

EATING OUT

The licensed **Restaurant Semiramis**, part of the Gafsa Hotel with its own entrance on Rue Ahmed Snoussi, is the best in town, and serves excellent stuffed squid, steamed lamb and 'Doigts de Fatimah', a Tunisian spring roll. A slap-up dinner for two, with wine, costs around

15 dn. To eat and drink outside the hotels, try the **Restaurant de Carthage**, beside the Tunis Hotel.

The **Café des Palmiers**, beside the Gafsa Hotel in a large concrete hanger, is an archetypal boisterous North African drinking bar.

For breakfast, the **Café Patisserie Elafrah**, on Rue 13 Fevrier 1952, to the left of the bus station entrance, serves croissants, orange juice and coffee.

Around Gafsa

Gafsa Gare is a passenger station, a suburb, an oasis and a marshalling yard that sends crushed grey phosphate rock, extracted from the mountains behind Metlaoui, to Sfax. After the station, a signposted left turn to **Lalla** leads to an idyllic but unsophisticated palmery market garden. Follow the signs to **Restaurant Ain Sultan** to arrive at the heart of the oasis. The restaurant is really more of a bar, whose shaded terrace overlooks springs gushing hot mineral water. Further into the palmery gardens, there are natural warm pools in which to wash.

Jebel Orbata is an area of sparse highland olive groves, Berber hamlets and eroded kasbahs. Beyond the oasis of El Guettar, 18 km from Gafsa on the Gabès road, the left turn to Sakket and Sened runs beneath the escarpment and heads for a gap in the saw-edge ridge. The hillsides here are pitted with caves, so heavily eroded and with such a confusion of sedimentary layers that the rock appears to be dripping down the slopes.

The tarmac stops at the village of Oulad Bouttamrane, and the nearby hill is crowned by two marabouts' koubbas and a ruined ksar, with a fine view into the neighbouring valley.

Further along the Gabès road, a left turn to Ettalah, 46 km later in the roadside village of Belkhir, just after the mosque, leads to another picnic spot by an **old Turkish fort**, 5 km up the road. As a digestif, walk through the crack in the mountains behind to a reclusive palm garden.

Metlaoui and the Seldja Gorge

Before the end of the last century, Metlaoui was little more than a nomad encampment, occasionally swelled by caravans from Algeria which had taken a short cut down the course of the Oued Seldja. Today, it is a phosphate mining town of 27,000.

Phosphates were first found in the region by Philippe Thomas in 1885. He was a vet and an amateur fossil collector who made his discovery in the course of studying diseased goats in the Seldja gorge. Some 10 years later the efficacy of phosphate fertilizers was discovered, and the Compagnie des Phosphates de Gafsa (CPG) set up.

GETTING AROUND
By Train: There is a daily service between Metlaoui and Gafsa, the train continuing to Tunis via Sfax. In the other direction, three trains a day wind up the gorge to Redeyef, whence *louages* ply the road to Tamerza.
By Bus: At least seven buses leave Gafsa for Tozeur, stopping at the main square in Metlaoui. Buses also run from Metlaoui through Moularès to Redeyef *throughout* the day.
By Louage: You can also reach Tozeur by *louage* from the centre of the town.

301

WHAT TO SEE

Metlaoui's one mainstream tourist attraction is Le Lézard Rouge, the revamped 19th-century Beylical train that leaves from the train station for the dramatic run up the **Seldja gorge** just northwest of the town. This trip, through the deep, straight-sided orange gash in the hills, is run by Transtours whose office is beside the station. It starts at 10.30 and costs 8 dn.

If you would rather explore the canyon at your own pace, there is a local train to Redeyef at 15.05. For just over 1 dn you can hop off at the Seldja halt, miles from anywhere and surrounded by cliffs, spend two hours exploring in solitude, and catch the next down train which arrives back at Metlaoui at 19.10.

To drive to the entrance of the gorge, take the Tozeur road, and after the green and white school, take a right turn to Thiljas. Avoid the Shell oil rig, and wind up to the pumping station by the watercourse of the Oued Seldja. From here you can walk up the dry course into a narrow defile, the *coup de sabre*. This 'sabre cut' was made by the legendary El Mansour. Having eloped with the beautiful princess Leila, he needed a matrimonial bed, and with a single blow of his sword he created the river bed's defile. Above the dry waterfall are traces of Roman dams which used to supply now vanished gardens, and the canyon reveals itself with every step beyond.

WHERE TO STAY AND EAT

The **Hotel Ennacim** is at the Tozeur end of town and for a mediocre room it charges 13 dn a double. You can either eat there, in its busy restaurant-cum-watering hole, or try an excellent couscous at the **Restaurant al-Djazia** towards Gafsa.

Tamerza, Midès and Chebika

The mountains northwest of Metlaoui contain some of Tunisia's most alluring scenery, concentrated around a group of three oases near the Algerian border. Tamerza, Midès and Chebika all sit beside ancient rivers which have, over the millennia, worn contorted courses deep into the hills.

Until the 19th century, the villages were astride the main east–west caravan route. During the Roman Empire it was controlled by a line of posts and an 800-strong garrison in the fort of Aid Maiores, outside the Algerian oasis of Negrine. As well as having a strict defensive role, these posts also stopped the nomad herds from moving into the farmed steppe land until the harvest was over. A tablet of custom duties records the traffic at the imperial frontier: slaves, horses and mules imported at $1\frac{1}{2}$ denarii, raw hides at $\frac{1}{2}$ denarii a 1 cwt, with exports like an amphora of wine or *garum* charged 1 sesterce, half that for 10 lb of sponges.

Isolated from modern trade routes, the villages are now dependent on their palmery gardens. The people are poor, but are consoled by a communal lifestyle. Payment is still made in kind—dates in return for a sheep from a nearby bedouin flock—and favour repays favour. While the men rely on one another for distribution of water in the oasis gardens, women prepare the daily couscous cooperatively, lending to those who have none. As recently as the mid-1960s a villager at Chebika had this to say about money: 'We've seen that; yes, we have. But ... God doesn't intend it to stay at Chebika. It travels. They have money in other places.'

GETTING AROUND

A tarmac road loops north from Metlaoui, through these border villages, and continues as a track across Chott Rahim to Tozeur. There are buses and trains from Metlaoui to Redeyef, and *louages* from there to Tamerza. At Tamerza the source of public transport dries up, and you must hitch to reach Chebika and Tozeur or back track.

On the road from Metlaoui to Moularès and Redeyef, the downside of the phosphate industry becomes increasingly apparent. Layers of grey dust have settled everywhere and the hills are torn to pieces. After Redeyef, the scenery rapidly improves as the road crosses a vast plain, with a sharp escarpment on the left and a range of hills far off to the right.

Tamerza

The road winds enticingly down into the valley of Tamerza, past a brown koubba and the old village, which was finally deserted in 1969, after catastrophic flooding, and is now melting back into the earth. Built out of mud bricks, like the Byzantine bishopric and the Roman fort that occupied the site before, it would disappear without trace were it not for recent conservation work.

The modern village lines the road. The police station and the bank are at the centre of the settlement, and shortly afterwards a blue sign points left to the Hotel des Cascades, and the eponymous waterfall.

Walking up river from the hotel,you can explore the old village, which is decorated with patterned brick and contains a decaying koubba beneath a white dome on the corner of two streets. Opposite the village, across the river bed below, rise some of the springs that feed the river and a further area of palms. A couple of kilometres downstream from the hotel there is an even more dramatic waterfall (p. 304) and keen walkers can follow the river bed right down to Foum el Khanga.

Walk to Midès

Midès, right on the Algerian border, can be reached by a track off the Redeyef road, by donkey from the Hotel des Cascades, or on foot, the most dramatic approach. Leave Tamerza on the Tozeur road, where the tarmac crosses over the river bed turn right up into the Oued el Oudei gorge. The bed gradually narrows and twists to become a tight, constricting gorge of polished rock.

After about $2\frac{1}{2}$ hours walking you will see the old village of Midès towering above, like an impregnable castle in the sky. It once served as an outpost on the Roman frontier, well protected by gorges on three sides. The buildings are being saved from total ruin by the Tourist Board, though the villagers rejected a recent Belgian offer to turn it all into a hotel. Many of the one-room houses, each with courtyard, are furnished with built-in daises for sleeping and gypsum Ali Baba jars for keeping dates. The houses in the centre have become quiet souvenir shops, selling minerals, dates, oranges and petrified wood, and nearby the mosque and marabout of Sidi Bou Sia are kept in good repair. The palmery, divided into small parcels of land known as *hussah*, supports figs, pomegranates, chillis, beans and houmous, shaded by dates.

Foum el Khanga

Where the road to Tozeur fords the river, walk past a souvenir shack to another waterfall, which falls from an eroded lip of rock. Eight kilometres through this gorge of fragile, shattered rocks, is Foum el Khanga, on the Tozeur road.

Chebika

Chebika nestles on a sandy spur beneath a steep escarpment, 5 km beyond Foum el Khanga on the Tozeur road, its palmery almost hidden in the gorge below.

The site served as an 'ad speculum' on the Gabès to Tebessa road in the days of the Roman Empire. Observers would report the size and make-up of caravans on the route with a mirror (*speculum*), flashing the sunlight in a form of morse to the next post. Ironically, when the anthropologist Jean Duvignaud came to the village in 1960, none of the villagers had ever seen their own reflection, and the grocer's new mirror was causing a stir. In his book, *Change at Chebika*, he tells of the unchanged lifestyle he found in the village which was originally known as Ksar el Shams, the castle of the sun, and later as Chebika, the narrows. When Duvignaud arrived, an elderly Chebikan described the village as 'a pebble in the desert, an agglomeration of poor people and stones'. By the time his team of researchers had left the villagers had seen pictures of themselves in an international magazine, and were challenging the government to improve their lot.

From the cafés at the head of the new village, a path leads to the elegant cascade at the foot of the escarpment. Tepid spring water flows out, chuckling, into the palmery, the home of shoals of frogs. For dramatic views of the palmery and of the hidden valley beyond, climb up past the koubba of Sidi Sultan in the old village, and through a cleft in the hill above. Sidi Sultan, 'the holy man beloved of women', is a mysterious figure, a marabout who requested that when he died, he be strapped on to a camel, and that wherever the camel stopped he be buried.

The arid valley behind Chebika makes another good walk, and is a mine for fossils. Beds of rock entirely made of compressed seashells have fallen over the years from the high cliffs on both sides.

On to Tozeur

Passing a small palmery, guarded by a ruined ksar, the road heads out across the Chott er Rahim. The 42-km journey to El Hamma du Jerid is enlivened by occasional camel herds, mirages and some sandy patches requiring attentive driving. El Hamma and its palmery offers a local restaurant on the right and natural hot hammams in barrel-vaulted brick buildings further on the left. It is another 9 km to Tozeur from here.

WHERE TO STAY AND EAT

The only hotel in the area is the **Hotel des Cascades** at Tamerza, tel (06) 48520. Its setting, in the heart of the sandy palmery, is one of the best in Tunisia. Lofty palms rise over its large, clean swimming pool. The bamboo bedrooms are sandwiched together, and cost 16 dn a double, which includes powerful hot showers. When working at capacity (over 150 beds), the hotel loses much of its charm, however, so avoid Christmas and Easter. The evening meal is graceless and institutional, but unfortunately there is nowhere else to eat at night, unless you stock up for picnics beside the river by moonlight. By day do not miss lunch in the unlicensed **Restaurant Typische** on the road to the hotel. It serves cheap and excellent vegetable couscous.

In Midès, looking on to the old village, is the **Café Camping de l'Oasis**, offering shaded tent space and a water tap. The café sells Fanta, coffee and tea, and will occasionally prepare meals. If you intend to camp, however, you should bring all your food with you, as the village is not well stocked.

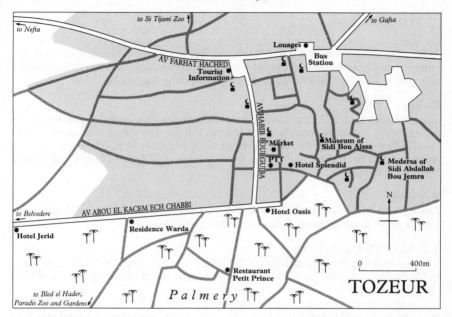

Tozeur

'At Tozer particularly ... there is a great Traffick carried on by the general Merchants, who travel once a Year into the Country of the Ethiopians, and bring with them from thence, a number of Blacks who they usually exchange for Dates at the rate of one Black for two or three Quintals.' (Thomas Shaw in the 18th century)

Tozeur is still the main market and administrative town of the Jerid, spread out on dead land above a large palmery which it shares with a number of neighbouring villages. Immediately south of the palmery lies the flat salt-sodden wasteland of the chott. Its principal attractions are simple: walks in the date palmery, where the water still flows according to a system of distribution created in the 13th century; bathing in natural hot water springs and ambling through the distinctive architecture of the old town, made from thin hand-made sand bricks. This style is borrowed from Mesopotamia, purportedly brought to the Jerid by an Abbasid army in the 8th century, and dresses the façades with mesmerizing geometry.

Water distribution in the oases, measured in parcels of time rather than by volume, is so important here that water minutes are actually sold at auction. Only about 15% of the land is worked by its owners. The rest of the oasis is tended by share-croppers, known as *khammes*, after the fifth (khamsa) of the harvest they traditionally receive from the absentee landlords, though because of the relatively high value of the date harvest this is more like an eighth. Despite an increased quantity of trees, and a better price, however, date farming is becoming less profitable, and more owners are finding themselves farming their own land. As a result, the community of *khammes* is diminishing, and more men from the Jerid are being forced into the nearby mines or to look for work abroad.

GETTING AROUND

By Air

Tozeur airport, off the road to Nefta, has regular flights to Tunis and Jerba, connecting with international flights to London. The only foreign destination served direct is Paris. For more information, visit the Tunis Air office on Av Habib Bourguiba, tel (06) 50038.

By Bus

The bus station is on Av Farhat Hached, towards Gafsa from the central T-junction and on the right. One bus a day journeys to the Algerian frontier, two a week continuing on to El Oued. There are five a day for Nefta, seven for Gafsa and three for Kebili. Local buses run hourly to Degache. Further afield, there are daily buses to El Kef and Gabès, and three to Tunis via Kairouan.

By *Louage*

Louages leave from a courtyard almost opposite the bus station on Av Farhat Hached. The most common destinations are Gafsa via Metlaoui, and Nefta.

TOURIST INFORMATION

The **Syndicat d'Initiative** is at the top of Av Habib Bourguiba. They arrange the usual tours, to Midès, Nefta, Kebili, Douz and the Lézard Rouge train at Metlaoui, for a fixed tariff pinned up in the office.

The main **tourist office** is on Av Abou el-Kacem Chabbi, tel (06) 50503. Nearby, between the Continental and Jerid Hotels, you can pick up a colourful **pony-trap** or **camel** to explore the outer reaches of the oasis, settling a price before embarking.

Mehari Voyages, at the Centre Commercial de Tozeur on Av Farhat Hached towards Nefta, tel (06) 50387, fax (01) 783060, is one of the most efficient package tour organizers, with a Paris office, tel 45747435, fax 45721696. Their tours start at 85 dn per person for three days' travelling and an eight-day tour for 228 dn per person.

The **Post Office (PTT)** is on the market square, left at the bottom of Av Habib Bourguiba, tel(06) 50000. **Banks** abound throughout the town, the **police station** is on Av Farhat Hached, towards Gafsa, and the **Monoprix** supermarket out on the Nefta road.

The Old Town

From the Hotel Splendid, a web of sandy alleys leads through Tozeur's old quarter, little changed since the 14th century when it was built by the Ouled el Hadef tribe. Here decorative building techniques are at their most exuberant, with towering façades patterned by bas-relief zigzags, lozenges and chevrons, brick platforms for lying around on and covered alleys shaded from the sun.

Walk down Rue des Jardins, and turn left at Rue de Kairouan. A little way down on the right is the entrance to the **Museum of Folklore and Popular Art** (open 09.00–12.00, 14.00–17.30, every day except Mon; adm), occupying the ancient koubba of Sidi Bou Aissa. The building itself lends the museum great charm, but the exhibits are largely a collection of colonial furniture masquerading as something older. Worthy of attention are the wooden doors in the courtyard, containing separate entrances for men, women and children, and the room containing the belongings of a bride-to-be. In the third room a book, assembled by a French civil servant, P. Penet, contains the secrets of Tozeur's water distribution. The system was originally conceived by the town's Imam, Ibn Chabbat, in the 13th century, and was

Geometric Brickwork in the Medina

handed down orally until this study was published in 1911–12. Even then, the French admitted defeat in actually administering the system.

Continue down Rue de Kairouan to noisy Av Ibn Chabbat. Turning right, and right again down Rue de Bizerte you re-enter the maze of brick, and can happily lose yourself for hours, stopping to sketch or read in a patch of quiet shade.

The Palmery

Tozeur's oasis is the largest and most important in the region, covering over 2500 acres, and slowly increasing, thanks to reclamation schemes on the edge of the chott. For a first foray into the palmery, walk to **Paradise**, an unlikely flower garden, at its best in early spring. The well-marked route which begins near the Hotel Residence Warda is negotiable by car, but it makes a shady and gentle 2.5-km stroll. On the way, you pass through the hamlet of **Bled el Hader**, site of the Roman Thusuros, a town on the ancient caravan route from Biskra to Gabès, which saw hides, slaves and animals passing to the coast, purple dye and imported clothing returning to the Berbers of Algeria. The mosque, itself built in the 11th century, is separated from an older ruined minaret by a paved courtyard, now the local football pitch. The massive stones on which the minaret is based are Roman. Ibn Chabbat, Imam and creator of Tozeur's watering system in the 13th century, is buried in a tomb beyond the minaret.

At the decaying **koubba of Sidi Ali Bou Lifa** beside a sacred jujube tree further on, a right turn leads to Paradise. The garden of oleander, bougainvillaea, hibiscus and roses, protected by the shade of fruit and palm trees, was created by local horticulturalist Amor Rahouma. The associated zoo is a useful place to visit to check up on local species of snakes, lizards, raptors and mammals. The manager specifically asked that any English people likely to become depressed by caged animals should stay away. There is a rainbow of homemade flower syrups for sale at the bar, made from violets, roses, bananas, pomegranates and pistachios; the effect is subtle and thirst-quenching, and may encourage you to buy a bottle.

307

Back at the jujube tree, another road leads on through the palms and back to the Restaurant Le Petit Prince. A small detour will take you out for a lunar walk on the surface of the chott. It is an alien, life-denying place, supporting only a species of monstrous asparagus. Miniature conical volcanoes occasionally appear, caused by deep pockets of subterranean gas and water forcing their way to the surface.

The Si Tijani Zoo
Tozeur's second zoo is found by walking down Av Farhat Hached towards Nefta, turning right at the Mobil petrol station and following the signs, tel (06) 50003. (Open 08.00–18.00, every day; adm).

The collection of animals, all of which, except the lion and baboon, come from Tunisia, was started by Si Tijani, local hero and jack-of-all-trades who died recently. He is most renowned for catching snakes and scorpions in the desert and for supplying laboratories across Europe with the animals or just their venom. He also acted as a mediator between the outside world and the people of the area. If there was a building project to be completed, Si Tijani found the labour force; if an academic was visiting, Si Tijani was his guide, effecting suitable introductions. Some of the esteem in which he was held is explained by his name, which links him to a prestigious dynasty of Sufi sheikhs. It is debatable whether a zoo in which camels drink Coke for the amusement of tourists is a fitting tribute, though his son who runs the place obviously enjoys it.

The Belvedere
At the end of Av Abou el-Kacem Chabbi, you will see the newly constructed **Cultural Centre**, a collection of folk exhibits and shops just up the hill. Continue straight on into the palmery until you arrive at a strange, weathered outcrop, Tozeur's equivalent of Hanging Rock. From the top of this belvedere, the view shows the vast extent of the palmery and the chott stretching south beyond the horizon.

Tozeur's campsite is at the foot of the rock, and back along the palmery track on the right is a refreshing natural swimming pool, in a dell surrounded by sand and shaded by palms. Behind the belvedere, very hot water leaks into two small basins, where your aching bones could be cured, if you can withstand the temperature (women in morning, men in afternoon).

FESTIVALS
Tozeur holds an oasis festival over Christmas, with exhibitions covering many aspects of palmery life, such as agriculture and weaving, and including camel racing and demonstrations of marriage ceremonies.

HAMMAMS
The town's hammam is beside the Hotel Essada, but even in the winter, the waters in the natural pool by the belvedere are warm enough for a wash.

SHOPPING
Av Habib Bourguiba is a riot of carpets, cascading over the shops' brick façades. One of the best shops, with a full selection of contemporary carpets and some of the more muted older designs is *Bella Italia* at the top of the street opposite the Syndicat d'Initiative. Take part in the age-old process, and buy some *deglat-en-nour*. Avoid the presentation boxes, which are often

old and full of maggots, and inspect the fruit before you buy. There are also hats and baskets woven from palm fronds, and the multicoloured essences made from flowers in the Paradise garden to be conjured with.

WHERE TO STAY

MODERATE
Tozeur's smarter hotels are filled by package tours. The **Hotel el Jerid**, Av Abou el-Kacem Chabbi, tel (06) 50488/50554, is the best of a bad bunch, its only excitement being a thermal swimming pool.

CHEAP
The **Residence Warda**, Av Abou el-Kacem Chabbi, tel (06) 50597, is new, spotless, air conditioned and good value. It is right on the edge of the palmery and family run. The **Hotel Splendid**, Rue de Kairouan, tel (06) 50053/50293, is slightly decrepit, with small bedrooms and a noisy bar. It has the advantage of a swimming pool (2 dn for non-residents) and a licensed restaurant.

The **Hotel Essada**, just of Av Habib Bourguiba, tel (06) 50097, is very basic and cheap. Tozeur's **campsite** at the belvedere is tiny and crowded, the only compensation being the nearby natural warm pool.

EATING OUT

Licensed Restaurants
Le Petit Prince is signposted off Av Abou el-Kacem Chabbi on the edge of palmery. The cooking is overrated, but the setting is good, and your meal can be eaten on a table looking on to the palmery. Dawdle here over *ojja merguez*, fish and a bottle of Gris de Tunisie; around 15 dn for two.

Unlicensed Restaurants
There is little to choose between the **Restaurant de la République**, under an arcade off Av Habib Bourguiba, and the nearby **Restaurant du Paradis**, next to the Essada Hotel. They are both cheap and serve up the standard fare.

In a class of its own, gastronomically speaking, but even cheaper, is the **Restaurant du Sud**, opposite the Agil petrol station on Av Farhat Hached. They serve exquisite couscous and stews in immaculate surroundings.

Nefta

Arriving in Nefta for the first time, it may seem a mean and desolate, one-road town, lined with sand-coloured houses. This main street obscures a warren of striking brick-built houses to the south and the town's main palmery. To the north is Nefta's most famous site, the Corbeille, where several thousand palm trees shimmer at the bottom of a massive natural sand-bowl.

Medieval Nefta was one of the three religious centres of Tunisia, and a skyline of domes crowns the Corbeille. While the Zitouna Mosque in Tunis and the Great Mosque of Kairouan preserved Orthodox Islam, Nefta harboured Tunisia's mystical tradition. The two poles of sanctity are the Koubba of Sidi Bou Ali, deep in the main palmery, and the Zaouia of the Qadriya. Sidi Bou Ali el-Nefti died here in 1213. Born in Morocco, he travelled to Nefta to lead the local Berbers out of their heretical ways, and allegedly planted the first date trees at Nefta. He is petitioned by the local community with the age-old grievances of oasis life, at his tomb deep in the main palmery.

The highest dome on the Corbeille belongs to the Zaouia of the Qadriya, the oldest and most widespread of the Sufi brotherhoods. It was founded in the early 12th century by Abd el-Qader el Jilani, whose tomb is still an object of pilgrimage in his hometown of Baghdad. Sufism is a branch of Islam which seeks direct experience of union with God, when the believer will become 'the hearing with which he seeth and the hand with which he fighteth and the foot with which he walketh'. Each follower chooses a master, or *sheikh*, who prescribes a regime of chanting, praying and dancing, designed to bring the follower to unity with God (see Islam, p. 56–60). Like Christian monasteries, the zaouia would also have housed visitors, taught children, looked after the poor and been a stable focus for the community when in conflict with central government.

GETTING AROUND

By Bus
There is a bus every day, currently leaving at 10.00, for the Algerian border. Three buses a day make the dash to Tozeur, where connections for other cities can be made. There is a 23.00 departure for Tunis from Nefta, which also picks up passengers at Tozeur.

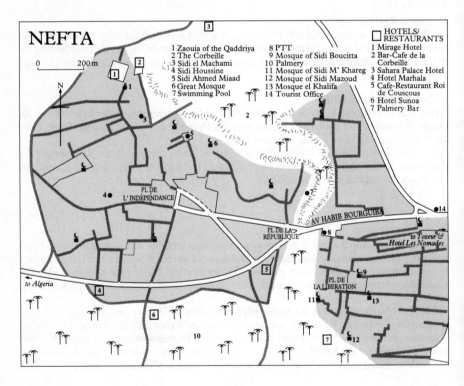

NEFTA

0   200m

N

1 Zaouia of the Qaddriya
2 The Corbeille
3 Sidi el Machami
4 Sidi Houssine
5 Sidi Ahmed Miaad
6 Great Mosque
7 Swimming Pool

8 PTT
9 Mosque of Sidi Boucitta
10 Palmery
11 Mosque of Sidi M' Khareg
12 Mosque of Sidi Mazoud
13 Mosque el Khalifa
14 Tourist Office

HOTELS/
RESTAURANTS
1 Mirage Hotel
2 Bar-Cafe de la Corbeille
3 Sahara Palace Hotel
4 Hotel Marhala
5 Cafe-Restaurant Roi de Couscous
6 Hotel Sunoa
7 Palmery Bar

PL DE L' INDÉPENDANCE

PL DE LA RÉPUBLIQUE

AV HABIB BOURGUIBA

to Tozeur & Hotel Les Nomades

to Algeria

PL DE LA LIBERATION

By *Louage*
Louages regularly leave for Hazoua on the Algerian border. Nefta's hotels always contain a number of people heading for El Oued and the Algerian Sahara as well, so you may get a lift that way.

TOURIST INFORMATION
Nefta's **Tourist Office** arranges a variety of excursions, at fixed tariffs displayed on the wall. It is on the north side of Av Habib Bourguiba, tel (06) 57236. A camel ride through the oasis makes a good initiation, before trying a more long-term aquaintance at Douz, and costs 5.5 dn an hour. The same by donkey costs 4.25 dn, and in a pony-trap 4.5 dn. They also run landrover excursions to Chebika and Midès, 25 dn, and over to Douz and Kebili, 25 dn.

The **PTT** is on the south side of Av Habib Bourguiba, next to the **police** and there are banks on both sides of the street, and a quaint, mobile **Banque de Sud** in a specially modified bus.

The Corbeille
Exploration of Nefta should start with coffee at the Café de la Corbeille, next to the Hotel Mirage, looking out over a sea of palm fronds. The Sahara Palace Hotel is better to look out of than on to, and it is difficult to imagine it being Brigitte Bardot's 'favourite hotel', though as a local girl (she came from an Italian family that had settled in Tunisia) she may have her reasons. Hidden beneath the palms below are a series of springs, some hot, some cold, and a bathing pool used by women in the morning, men in the afternoon. The non-volcanic hot springs around the Chott el Jerid are some of the most prolific in the world. The water rises from rocks deep below the surface, heated by faulting and intense folding; despite the salty chott it contains very few dissolved minerals and is therefore excellent for irrigation.

The Ridge of Domes
To get down to the Corbeille, take the sandy track on to the right-hand lip of the bowl. The first dome, immense and pregnant, marks the Zaouia of the Qadriya, also known as Sidi Brahim after the Qadriya sufi who is buried here. Its ancient whitewashed walls, irregular and bulging, conceal a tomb room, mosque, teaching and lodging facilities. Unfortunately, the guardian is unlikely to let non-Muslims enter.

Keeping to the path, pass the single dome of Sidi el Machami high above. Turn left and wander downhill past well-restored façades, concealing inner decay, to a sandy square dominated by the dome of Sidi Ahmed Miaâd.

After the square, turn left, left again and right, through a long covered arch, to reach the immaculately whitewashed Great Mosque, its main dome, which serves as minaret, decorated with koranic calligraphy, laid out in brick. Beyond, the cliffs over the Corbeille give an excellent view of the palms, shading boisterous figs.

Returning to the mosque, follow its walls round to the green door, and immerse yourself back into the town, diagonally opposite. Walk downhill to an open area, and turn right for Pl de l'Indépendance, the daily marketplace, with animated cafés, and at the end of the street the whitewashed bastion of the tomb of Sidi Houssine.

Returning through the market square, continue straight on to Pl de la République, the site of the Wednesday **souk** on the main road. The public **hammam** looks straight on to it, and 70 m behind the bathhouse, behind a whitewashed wall on the right, is a small public swimming pool.

The Palmery and Southern Medina

For a first trip into Nefta's main palmery, take the path beside the PTT which hugs the concealing plain walls of the southern medina. At the far end rises the Mosque of Sidi M'khareg, with its tapering whitewashed minaret. Architectural details are picked out in duck-egg green, matching the paintwork of the doors and windows.

While the tops of the nearby palm trees are still close, look out for incongruous pottery jars nestling amongst the fronds. They are collecting palm milk, the sap of the tree, usually to be fermented into *laghami*, palm wine. Cutting into the living heart of plant and milking it kills productivity, so only low-quality, male trees are tapped. Plunge down the second track into the trees and turn left for the famed marabout of Sidi Bou Ali, much visited by the local population and which is the focus of a *moussem*, or religious *fête*, on the third day after Aid el Kebir.

Returning to the edge of the houses, halfway between the mosques of Sidi M'khareg and Sidi Mazoud, a path leads down to Nefta's secretive drinking hole, the palmery bar. The walls of the Mosque of Sidi Mazoud encircle a koubba and shrine to the marabout as well. Grillwork windows give tantalizing glimpses of the shaded garden beside the saint's tomb.

Any of the paths into the southern medina lead between houses built without architects. The thin bricks are made from baked mud and sand, and the numerous cool, dark passages are the width that a palm beam can sustain. Many of the houses' blind façades are decorated by a relief pattern in brick, a tradition imported from Mesopotamia during the early Arab invasions. The patterns used are typically Berber, lozenges and chevrons, and match the decorations on local carpets and tattoos. At the centre of this warren of housing is a pretty, brick-faced square, Pl de la Libération, sandwiched between the minarets of the Mosque el Khalifa and the Mosque of Sidi Boucitta, and next to the vegetable market.

Le Marché des Roses du Sahara

Ten kilometres west of Nefta, coachloads of tourists are deposited on the chott at a place known as the Marché des Roses du Sahara, a mineral market. It is one of the many thousands of places from which you can view mirages, which are particularly strong at the end of the afternoon.

WHERE TO STAY

EXPENSIVE

The newest hotel in Nefta, **Hotel Sunoa**, is in the Zone Touristique, tel (06) 57449/57416/57355, behind the Marhala. It looks like a Scottish castle and contains a bar like a nightclub in Bahrain. It scores top marks for incongruity, has dull bedrooms but an interesting restaurant.

The **Sahara Palace Hotel** has partly ruined the Corbeille in pursuit of a unique view, but has little to justify its high prices (77 dn a double) apart from an alluring swimming pool. The small non-group dining-room serves bland international food at a price.

MODERATE

Le Marhala Touring Club Hotel, at the Algerian end of the main street, tel (06) 57127, is housed in an extraordinary barrel-vaulted barn. Hideous from the outside, it is delightful inside, with friendly staff and rooms round a covered courtyard, containing a small tiled swimming pool. Mediocre food is served rather early in the licensed restaurant. The hotel does get very booked up, so ring to reserve or get there early in the day.

Second choice is the **Hotel Les Nomades**, south of Av Habib Bourguiba as you enter the town from Tozeur, tel (06) 57052. The rooms are spacious and clean, furnished with raised beds and rush matting. It has a swimming pool, a bar and a restaurant.

EATING OUT

There are a number of good, cheap places to eat in Nefta, all of them cheap. The **Café de la Corbeille**, when the coachloads have left after sunset, becomes a lively grill restaurant. Sitting there with a drink as darkness falls, you may be offered *fool*, delicious hot beans flavoured with cumin.

Restaurant La Mamma, opposite the Mobil petrol station in centre of town, though not always open, serves delicious spicy stews, to be mopped up with bread. For couscous, go to **Restaurant le Roi de Couscous**, opposite Pl de la République.

The palmery bar, down a path between the two mosques on the edge of the southern medina, is worth stumbling around in the dark to find. Sitting beneath the palm trees, watching dark figures and Mobylettes converging from all over, you will be served barbecued meat, salad and chips with your wine or beer.

Tozeur to Kebili—the Road across the Chott

Degache

This road first passes through Degache, a small oasis community. The remains of the old town lie behind the ruined ksar on the main road, just opposite the *louage* stop and **PTT**. Its three minarets each illustrate a different Islamic tradition. The four-domed tower beside the koubba is of a type only seen in the northern Chott. The square brick tower is typical of the Maghreb, and the hexagonal shape, though decorated in a local style, was brought to Tunisia in the 16th century by the Ottoman Turks.

WHERE TO STAY

Degache's **Camping de l'Oasis** is the best campsite in Tunisia, with clean, hot and cold showers and loos. A bed in a bungalow or a night in one of their bedouin tents or your own tent costs 3 dn per person. It's situated in a fertile palmery garden, owned by the local Chief of Police, Badhi Tahar, and is run by his charming henchman, Alloui Bengassem, who also cooks excellent 3-dn meals. Twice a week the garden gets its allowance of water for the 244 date palms, and Alloui will happily give you an introductory course in palmery gardening. There is a useful **Taxi Brousse** kiosk at the entrance to the campsite, which arranges expeditions as well as simple journeys, and will also change money. The municipal **swimming pool** is conveniently just across the main road.

Zaouiet el Arab

The next village in this continuous oasis, separated from Degache only by a river bed, is Zaouiet el Arab. A track to the right after the Horchani Date Factory winds into the edge of the palmery to a **9th-century mosque**, recently restored to its original crisp clean lines. There is a fresh vigour in its plainness, which contrasts with the bold decoration of its four cupolas. The stone base of minaret is Roman. The mosque is surrounded by the melted mud ruins of the ancient ksar of Zaouiet el Arab. Continuing on the main road, the koubba of Sidi Mohammed Krisanni, whose role protecting an old spring has been usurped by pumping equipment, is cared for by an atmospheric resident madman.

313

The Koubba of Sidi Bou Hellal

Just as the road leaves the palmery for the open chott, there's a turning to the left, signposted to Deghoumes. After about 2 km take a track left towards the visible white koubba and *mosque* on the edge of the mountain ridge. Sidi Bou Hellal, buried in the high double-arcaded mausoleum crowned with a dome, is a venerated local saint, with a popular moussem. Even more intriguing are the remains of a deeply decayed town, with a number of rock-cut oil presses, on the spurs behind, divided by a series of gorges.

Crossing the Chott

A dead straight causeway road has been built across the Chott el Jerid, to ensure easy crossing at all times of the year. Local legend serves up a myriad tales of disaster on the thin salt crust which masks black mud, including the complete disappearance of a caravan of 1000 camels, but except in the rainy season it is negotiable on foot almost everywhere. Halfway across the blue salty surface, a series of souvenir shops and cafés signal **El Mensof**, an ancient resting spot where a spring fills crystal-clear, salt-encrusted dykes. The surface of the chott is totally barren and yet it is never quite still, the heat vibrating like a swarm of invisible insects and creating endless mirages.

In 1876, a certain Captain Roudaire put forward a plan to dig a canal from the Gulf of Gabès to the Chott el Jerid, inciting much absurd talk of 'Nefta—Port de Mer', the perfect colonial holiday spot. Inspired more by legend than by science, he wanted to flood the plain and recreate the legendary bay of Triton, birthplace of Poseidon, across which Jason and his Argonauts sailed. This may be a memory from the Saharan wet period when a river, known as the Western Nile, flowed from the Hoggar Mountains in Algeria to fill the chotts and flow out into the Gulf of Gabès. When de Lesseps, builder of the Suez Canal, surveyed the area a major problem was discovered—that all but the most far western chott were above sea level. A company was nevertheless formed to dig a 150-mile canal but only raised enough interest to excavate a moat beside the Oued Akarit estuary. In 1962, the Americans suggested that their Ploughshare Programme to investigate the 'peaceful use of nuclear weapons' might be used to blast a lake in the Chott, creating, according to their estimates, minimal, and certainly containable, radiation. That too was shelved, and today the surface is used for nothing more malignant than sailsurfing, which you can book from the Hotel el Jerid in Tozeur, tel (06) 50488/50554.

The southern 'shore' of the Chott is signalled by a scattering of oases with the odd, scenic koubba, perched on a sand dune, shaded by palm trees. Nothing remains of the Roman border settlements which once existed, except two very disappointing, now concrete, pools in the village of Mansoura to the left of the road.

South of the Chott

A third of Tunisia is desert, but only the southwestern corner is covered by sand. The two main oases south of the Chott, Douz and Kebili, are market towns for the scattered communities in the smaller neighbouring palmeries. They have also recently become tourist destinations, servicing the European desire to experience the majesty and desolation of the wind-sculpted sand desert.

Kebili

Kebili has always been the main administrative oasis in the area, and the centre of the Nefzaoua Berbers, descendants of the Nasamons who were pillaging Roman border settlements back in the 1st century BC. Converted to Islam in the 8th century, they like all the south became firm partisans of the Kharijite creed, providing troops whenever there was a chance of pillaging the fat lands to the north. The 11th-century invasion by the Beni Hilal nomads curtailed the range of the Nefzaoua, expelling them from the best desert pastures and increasingly confining them to the oases. By the 14th century they were predominantly date farmers, small-scale shepherds and suppliers of slaves to the coastal markets. They were a community always on the fringe of the nation who as late as the mid-19th century were still rebelling against Tunis at the cost of massive fines and temporary exile.

Sandwiched between hills, palmery and chott, Kebili is a narrow dusty town with little to interest the traveller. Bored soldiers from the surrounding barracks monopolize the café tables in the main Pl du 7 Novembre 1987, at the heart of the town. There is a **bank** here and a good local restaurant, **Restaurant El Bacha**, for lunch. Up until the 19th century, the town was a renowned trading place for slaves from the Sudan (a generic Arab term for all of the land south of the Sahara). The prominent negro features of some of the local population, which gathers for the Tuesday **market**, serve as a reminder.

Around 20 November, Kebili holds a festival of the date harvest. Any Tourist Office should be able to provide the exact date, which changes each year. The bus and *louage* station is on the right of the road out to Douz, and serves Tozeur, Douz and Gabès.

WHERE TO STAY

MODERATE

The town's one intriguing feature is its hotel, Borj des Autruches, tel (05) 90233, signposted from the centre but perched alone on the edge of the desert, with romantic, desolate views. It is named after a failed attempt to breed ostriches here at the turn of the century, both for their meat, feathers and eggs, and for their fat which is said to have strong therapeutic powers. The hotel has just been renovated, and all its facilities, including swimming pool, bar and restaurant, improved. Its distinguishing trait, however, is its hot water, which comes direct from a neighbouring mineral spring. Half-board is sensible since the hotel is some way from the town and the rooms, each with a shower, are immaculate.

Douz and Beyond

Along the road between Kebili and Douz the desert of the European imagination begins: random dunes crowned by clumps of palms, and doomed attempts to prevent drifting across roads with fences of tatty palm fronds. As the tarmac speeds on towards the Great Eastern Erg, a massive sea of sand, the oases become sparser, starting with bustling Douz and petering out beyond the almost treeless El Faouar.

These oases are the home of tribes who claim descent from the 11th-century invaders, the Beni Hilal. Different nomad tribes attached themselves to the various oases, traditionally serving as shepherds and protectors of the sedentary population. The M'Razig are to be found at Douz, the Ghrib at El Faouar, the Adhara at Zaafrane and the eponymous Sabria at Es Sabria. Altogether, there are an estimated 15,000 nomads, a number which the

315

government's sedentarization programme, creating oasis communities for each tribe with schools, medical clinics and housing, is continually reducing.

GETTING AROUND
Six minibuses a day run between Douz and Kebili, from the bus station near the Tourist Office in the centre of Douz. There are three buses on as far as Zaafrane, but after that no public transport. Two buses also leave Douz for Tunis, and two for Gabès, one of which originates at Zaafrane.

Douz

Douz is a surprising tourist centre, a camel-coloured town in a dusty oasis, focused on the market square to the left of the road from Kebili. It is the self-styled 'gateway to the Sahara', and makes an excellent base for a trip into the dunes, providing you come with no false illusions of covering unbroken ground. With time to spare, it is possible to escape for days into the desert with one of the experienced local guides, carrying nomad tents and your own food, moving by day from one water source to another.

A frenetic market takes place in Douz on Thursdays, but for the rest of the week the shops and cafés beneath the arcade do a gentle business, in leather goods and woollen blankets. In the corner is a shop offering a made-to-measure, overnight service in suede desert shoes.

The roundabout at the centre of town is the hub of the tourist trade. The road to the west runs past an enclosure which towards sun-down is suddenly animated with camels and calèches, waiting for the invasion of westerners wanting a perfect desert sunset. It turns into the palmery, passing all the major hotels and Douz's well-worn sand dune on its way to Zaafrane and beyond.

EXCURSIONS INTO THE DESERT
The best camel excursions from Douz are organized by Zaid Ali Zaid, who can either be contacted at the **Camping Nomade el Nouail** (see below) or in his office next to Douz' **hammam**, tel (05) 95584. Zaid organizes tours of up to 10 days, but for those who have never tried riding a camel, an experimental half-day trip is recommended first. As saddle sores threaten to weaken resolve, bear in mind the recent words of a M'Razig tribesman: 'the charm of the desert is destroyed by engines. The pace of a man and a camel walking is more suitable.'

If you want to explore the region by car, **Douz Tourist Office** and café, run by Mohammed Mansour, offers desert excursions by Landrover as well as on camels. From here, eight people can visit a site that really needs four-wheel drive, the sand-enveloped Roman fort at Ksar Ghilane, for 120 dn, or take a trip to the villages around Matmata. Camel rides, anything from a half-day to five days in the open desert, are also on offer. As a last resort try **Abdul Moula Voyages**, on the right as you approach the Tourist Office.

FESTIVALS
If you are in the area at the time, do not miss Douz' Saharan festival over Christmas and New Year. Over a week, in the purpose-built stadium by the Hotel Mehari, everything from camel fights and fantasias to marriage dances and weaving displays are put on.

WHERE TO STAY

EXPENSIVE
There are plans for at least three new hotels in Douz by 1992, all for the mini-safari market. At the moment, the **Hotel Mehari** is the most exciting, tel (05) 95145, and has a mineral pool and a good restaurant.

MODERATE
In the middle of the palmery lie a nest of hotels. Try the **Hotel Saharien**, tel (05) 95339/95337, which has a swimming pool and holds nightly folk dancing displays in the height of the season.

CHEAP
For the more independent-minded, choose from two cheap small hotels in town. The **Hotel 20 Mars** is clean, with 20 rooms around a small patio, above the café of the same name on the market square. The brand-new **Hotel Belhabib**, tel (05) 95309, outside the market square and downhill, has clean bedrooms but avoid its restaurant.

EATING OUT
There are a couple of restaurants in town worth eating at. The new **El Kods**, near the Tourist Office is clean and cheap, but go to the **Ali Baba**, at the Kebili end of town, for atmosphere.

Beyond Douz

El Nouail
About 5 km along the road, a right turn leads to **Camping Nomade el Nouail**, a combination of tents and bungalows set in deep sand, 12 dn per person for half-board. The restaurant is good, but at least twice a week the place is infested with Club Mediterranée holiday-makers, so before you arrive check at their office in Douz (see above).

From Nouail the road continues 35 km to Kebili through a string of palmeries, Klebia, Chokria and Blidette, which are completely unvisited by tourists.

Zaafrane, Sabria and El Faouar
Zaafrane is a sand-engulfed oasis settlement. Its low bank of dunes, looks out over an infinite desert. The **hotel** here is one of the smallest and most isolated in the region, and its staff are charming and helpful. Half-board costs 12 dn per person, lunch 2.5 dn, and the restaurant is licensed.

Twelve kilometres beyond Zaafrane the road splits. The left fork leads to Sabria, a government-aided area of sedentarization for the Sabria tribe. Beyond the village is a perfect white koubba surrounded by dunes and palms, but the village children are demanding.

The other fork continues to the **Hotel El Faouar**, (05) 95085. This is another, largely tented hotel, which has the advantage of a pool and facilities for free sandskiing. One of the 400-odd beds will cost 10 dn with dinner and breakfast. Camels rides from here are 5 dn an hour.

Watch out on the road that connects El Faouar and Kebili, as it passes close to the chott and can become boggy.

East from Kebili—to Gabès

This 122-km journey follows the southern shore of the narrow Chott el Fejaj, and runs parallel to the absorbing contours of Jebel Tebaga to the south. A left turn just 4 km out of Kebili leads to Stiftimia, a small palmery on the edge of the chott, famous for its excellent *ftimi* dates, second in quality to *deglat-en-nour*. Hot sulphurous springs rise in the dusty central square.

Only Borj Saidane, an inaccessible National Guard post, interrupts the deserted road. Built like a prototype toy fort by the French, it was once used as a hotel.

El Hamma

El Hamma, 86 km from Kebili, has been a market town since the 15th century, when it saw its share of the trans-Saharan trade. Today the daily market deals in tourist items rather than slaves, and a busy local souk takes place on Mondays. The town is also long-famed for its hot waters, and was known by the Romans as *Aquae Tacapitanae*. The hammam is currently being rebuilt, but contains a male and female side. Drinking is ill-advised, not least because, as Leo Africanus described, the water tastes 'like brimstone so that it will nothing at all quench a man's thirst'.

The Back Road to Matmata and Ksar Ghilane

For those who want to avoid Gabès and take an adventurous drive to Matmata, just beyond El Hamma a broad dirt road follows a half-buried oil pipeline south. After 40 km a left turn at the crossroads leads 20 km to the tarmac road at Tamezret near Matmata, with some rocky patches. The right turn opposite leads to a hamlet, often empty except for the owner of **Café Djelilli** and her children. She serves refreshing peanut tea in a desert front garden filled with chickens and rabbits.

Continuing straight on down the pipeline and navigable only by four-wheel drive, you eventually arrive at **Ksar Ghilane**, a ruined Roman border fort surrounded by mountains, sand and a tented hotel. For the middle of the desert it can be pretty noisy though the fort, natural bathing pool, night sky and scenery are well worth the journey.

Part IX

JEBEL DEMER AND THE ISLE OF JERBA

Ghorfas of Ksar Ouled Soltane

The arid coastal plain of the south, its sandy shore broken by oases, is protected from the full effect of the Sahara by the Jebel Demer, a crescent of rugged mountains. On the slopes of these mountains perch an extraordinary series of honeycomb structures; dry-stone-walled fortresses, communal granaries and village citadels. Underground houses tucked into the high valleys complete an unworldly landscape. This settlement pattern is the product of a peculiar local history that saw the indigenous Berber tribes take refuge in the hills to escape from invading nomads. The Isle of Jerba functioned as another refuge, but otherwise it is the antithesis of the mountains. Its whitewashed buildings peer out of a green backdrop, for Jerba is flat, lightly wooded with olive trees and date palms and relatively well-watered.

When passing through Gabès treat yourself to a good meal and look in at the museum. If you want to look at the underground houses of the Matmata hills, ignore the main town and concentrate on Haddej and the Oued Barrak valley. From the hotels at Medenine and Tataouine you can explore a web of villages, with ksour and kalaa hidden away in isolated valleys, though if you attempt this in the summer months, the heat will put severe restrictions on any walking. All the ksour have their own character, but an ideal itinerary would include Ksar Toujane, Ksar el Hallouf, Douirat and Ksar Ouled Soltane. For a beach holiday head straight for Jerba, which it seems impossible to spoil, despite some effort.

History

Time and time again this area has been plunged into tribal conflict. Much of the strife has been a simple competition over grazing, though rivalry between Cain and Abel, the gardener and the shepherd, has also contributed to the bloodshed.

The five centuries of Roman rule were the heyday of the gardening culture. In 46 BC Julius Caesar took over the Emporia, a chain of sophisticated Carthaginian trading cities that had dominated the coast for the previous 500 years. Roman military security, colonization and dry farming techniques increased the area of cultivation on the coastal plain right to the military frontier, the Limes Tripolitanae, established along Jebel Demer. South of this frontier was the territory of unconquered nomads who controlled the Saharan trade routes.

In the 5th century the desert frontier, neglected by the Vandals, was broken open by the Lawata, a confederation of Berber desert tribes, who raided deep into central Tunisia. The camel, which had been successfully bred in North Africa since the 3rd century, gave these nomads new strength and mobility. The Lawata proved eager converts to Islam in the 7th century, and were recruited in large numbers into the Arab armies during the 50-year struggle to conquer northern Tunisia. Once the Arabs had established themselves as a privileged ruling class, the southern Berbers became disaffected, and within a few decades had become strong partisans of the puritan Kharijite creed.

The nemesis of the southern Berbers began in 1051. Two Arab tribes, the Beni Hilal and the Beni Sulaym, who between them perhaps numbered a quarter of a million, moved west from Egypt. They were prepared to exterminate rivals, ruin irrigation works and burn orchards in order to make pasture for their herds. The Beni Hilal crushed the army that guarded Gabès in 1052 but it was the Ouled Debbab, a faction of the Beni Sulaym, who eventually settled on the southern coastal plain. Two of the Berber tribes of the Sahara, the Touareg and Nefzaoua, survived, but other shattered Berber groups sought refuge in Jerba or in the hills of Jebel Demer. Some, with continual vigilance and strong citadels, kept their language and their independence. The majority gradually adopted Arab speech and entered into relationships with the tribes on the plains. At its best these were simple exchanges between shepherd and farming communities. However, the natural vulnerability of orchards and standing crops often encouraged a strong nomad tribe to impose a near-feudal protection racket, and some of the weaker Berber communities drifted into virtual serfdom.

By the 14th century the division between Berber and Arab had become confused, rather in the same way as that between Celts and Saxons in Britain. This was further altered in the 16th century by Si Moussa ben Abdallah, a noble missionary from the western Sahara who founded the Ouerghamma. This was a tribal confederation, revitalized by Islam but rooted in the Berber culture of the hills, composed of pure Berbers, Arabic-speaking Berbers and Arabs. The Ouerghamma eclipsed the old supremacy of the nomad tribes of the plains but concentrated their energy on dominating Jebel Demer.

Control of the area vacillated between the rulers of Tripoli and Tunis but in the late 17th century it was decisively integrated into the Tunisian state by the Muradite Beys. Ghadames, the key oasis on the trans-Saharan route, remained under the control of Tripoli, which jealously guarded its new monopoly. The region was effectively cut off from the caravan trade. The Ouerghamma, who could by then field an army of 5000 warriors, were exempted by the Beys from tax in exchange for policing the southern frontier.

Ancient tribal and village rivalries dominated southern politics even on great national questions. The French subdued the area in 1881–8, leading to an exodus of 30,000 tribesmen who preferred Libya. They gradually made their peace and returned, though there was a brief Turkish-backed flare-up during the First World War. During the spring of 1943, the Tunisian campaign produced a dazzling display of pyrotechnics on the coast, with the almost continuous running battles of Medenine, Mareth and Oued Akarit.

320

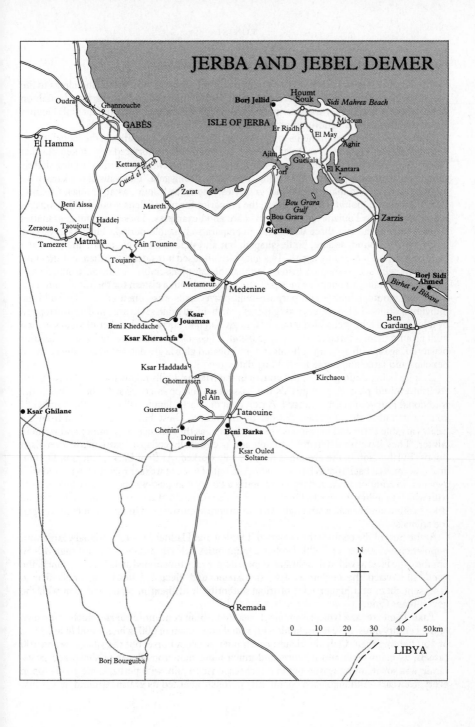

Berber Architecture, Culture and Cultivation

Spoken Berber is now known by a tiny minority of the people in the south, and clings to life only through place names. It was rare even in the 19th century, when linguists found it only on Jerba, where a few Berber manuscripts turned up, in the three citadels of Chenini, Douirat and Guermessa and a handful of other villages.

The most enduring monuments to the Berber culture are the buildings in the Jebel Demer. The old hillforts are known as 'kalaa'. They were built with unmortared dry-stone walls that follow contours rather than impose any rigid geometry. The favourite location is along slightly sloping escarpments, protected at the lower end by a strong gate. The walls of old kalaa have often been reused to make communal granaries, known as 'ksour', as at Joumaa, Chenini, Beni Barka and Douirat. In some cases, the granaries form a nucleus around which villages have grown; Ksar Toujane and Guermessa are good examples. These communal granaries evolved during the last three centuries, a comparatively stable period. They have varying ground plans: round, square, bottle-shaped, but always face into a courtyard and present a blank outer wall pierced by a gate. The gate often housed a resident guardian and itinerant craftsmen, who set up shop on Friday, Jamma, the day of assembly. A flat space outside was chosen as a msalla, an open-air mosque, and equipped with a cistern for the ritual ablutions. Later marabouts' koubbas and purpose-built prayer halls were often added. To build the individual vaults of a ksar, known as 'ghorfas', earth-filled grain sacks are piled up and topped by a loose hurdle of green olive branches, to give a good curve. A chamber of stones is then built around them, mortared with local gypsum. The sacks are then emptied and the interior plastered, again with gypsum. The more sophisticated ghorfa are decorated and stocked with benches and large amphorae for holding dates and oil.

Despite being underground, the houses in the Matmata hills follow the traditional North African ground plan. A gate guards the passage to the open courtyard around which the traditional four rooms are arranged. A rich man or a large family will extend the number of courtyards rather than increase the size of the rooms. These houses are created from the easily carvable earth and in response to the climate, as they are cool in summer and warm in winter. They have no defensive function and occasionally collapse, particularly after flash floods. Further south, the ground is not so easily worked. At Beni Barka, Chenini, Douirat and Guermessa, back rooms have been hacked out of lines of weaker rock and plastered with gypsum. In addition to an underground house a family may possess one or more brown tents with which to follow the herds. On the Jefara plain you might also see a few conical huts made from bamboo and brush, a strikingly African structure mostly used in the summer or as a pen for animals.

At the turn of the century the villages of Douirat and Haddej were exceptionally large with populations in excess of 2000. Berber communities seldom numbered more than 40–50 families, the level at which their brand of local democracy functioned at its best. A council, the *miad*, supervised the customary law, the *kanun*, and elected a headman, or sheikh, to represent them at a higher level of tribal authority, lead them in battle and deal with the government Caid.

Take Tamezret as a typical example. It is a stone-built concentric village which at the turn of the century housed 50 households with a total population of 500, which could field a force of 100 fighting men. Only the richest seven men owned a horse, but the village owned 100 camels, as many cows and donkeys and much more numerous flocks of sheep and goats. Grain was sown not by season but in direct response to rain, with perhaps one good crop in every five years. Although each community jealously guarded its grazing ground, it was first come first served when it came to cultivating the plain. At the first hint of rain the village would empty, leaving it guarded by old men. Not until late summer when the crops were harvested and the flocks fattened would the village reassemble, the season for trading, marriage and raiding.

In the Sahara, rainfall is infrequent but invariably violent, its destructive power aggravated by massive runoff from the barren mountain slopes. As a result the higher valleys have long been terraced with dry-stone walls known as *jeser* or *katra*. They are primarily designed to hold back the soil, but also facilitate irrigation. The walls are higher than soil level which allows any alluvium brought down to settle and holds back a good pool of water which sinks in. The side walls nearest the hillside are ramped and strengthened, dissipating the destructive force of a torrent into a wide, even and shallow cascade down on to the next level. Frequent channels tap natural runoff into underground cisterns, both at the valley level and on the mountain slopes. These gardens also face the danger of too strong a sun, but a carefully graded hierarchy provides protection, an ancient oasis technique described by Pliny: 'in the midst of the sand the soil is well cultivated and fruitful ... beneath the high palms are olives and under that a fig tree. Under the fig tree grows a pomegranate and beneath that again a vine. Moreover beneath these are sown corn, then vegetables or grass.'

Another resource of the industrious Berbers is temporary emigration. Young men would seek work in coastal towns, living with great frugality in order to earn enough money to marry, and to buy a horse or an orchard on their return. French officers penetrating the remotest communities in the 19th century were continually surprised by villagers who knew the language and streets of Marseille. This tradition grows ever stronger, and many of the small-town grocers in Tunisia are from Jerba, the railway and market porters from Douirat, the peanut vendors from Tataouine; Tunis' newspaper sellers come from Chenini and Ghomrassen men are famed for their doughnuts throughout the country.

Gabès

Forget the tourist brochure nonsense about Gabès being the only Maghreb oasis on the sea. It is the largest town in the south with a military base and a future firmly fixed on the nearby power and chemical industries at Ghannouche. It is a focal point of travel with good bus connections, a train station and plenty of car hire offices. Gabès has hotels and restaurants for an enjoyable night's stop-over, which is enough time to check out the Jara market, the museum and perhaps take a walk in the palmery gardens.

History

Gabès has a long history but few monuments. The advantage of its fertility has been offset by its strategic position, in a 30-km gap between the sea and salt marshes, directly in the path of any invader. There is no trace of the Carthaginian trading Emporia and the Roman town of Tacape. The city's golden period was from the 9th to the 11th centuries when it held a Great Mosque, a lighthouse and the celebrated palace of El Aroussien, all protected by a wall, a moat and a garrison in the kasbah. As well as being a centre for silk-weaving and leather work, it also served as an entrepôt for both trans-Saharan and Meccan caravan routes. This important role fed its historical pretensions, and Islamic Gabès claims to have been founded in the 7th century by Sidi Boulbaba, a companion of the Prophet.

The city was destroyed by the Hilalian Arabs in 1052. For the next 400 years, the oasis supported a series of petty dynasties before slipping into complete decline by the time the Turks and Spaniards fought over the ruins in the 16th century. By the 19th century the oasis had a head count of 4500 and a tree count of 200,000 date palms. It was divided by fierce rivalry between the villages of Menzel, Jara and Chenini, whose intrigues extended in a web of alliances with the tribes of the region. For instance, the Naffat nomads who grazed the land between Sfax and Gabès owned 3000 palms in Chenini and 63 in Menzel but would not touch anything from Jara. Conversely, the nearby Hazem tribe owned trees in Jara and Chenini but nothing in Menzel. The future shape of the town was decided when Jara allied itself to the rising power of France. Menzel and Chenini joined the tribal army of Ali ben Khalifa, which attempted to defend the oasis against the French occupation in 1881. They failed, and the new town grew on the road between the French barracks and Jara, which was also rewarded with the closure of the markets at Menzel and Chenini. Since then Gabès has been damaged twice, during the fighting in 1943 and then by a flood in 1962.

GETTING AROUND

By Train
The train station, on Rue Mongi Slim, is the end of the line. There are two daily trains to Sfax, and on Saturday and Sunday a direct train to Gafsa leaves at 17.00.

By Bus
The western end of Av Farhat Hached is the bus station, both sides of the road cluttered with cafés, stalls and the offices of the three bus companies. There are frequent buses for Sfax, of

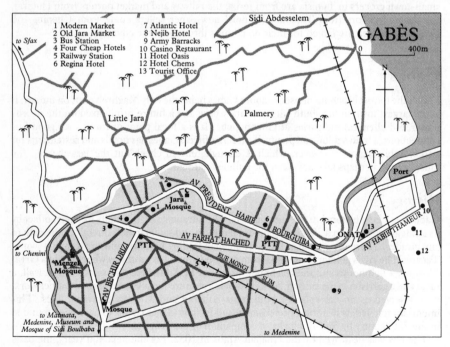

1 Modern Market
2 Old Jara Market
3 Bus Station
4 Four Cheap Hotels
5 Railway Station
6 Regina Hotel
7 Atlantic Hotel
8 Nejib Hotel
9 Army Barracks
10 Casino Restaurant
11 Hotel Oasis
12 Hotel Chems
13 Tourist Office

GABÈS

which a couple go on to Sousse, and eight direct departures for Tunis, the last three of which go overnight leaving from 22.30. There are also five buses a day for Kebili, and four morning buses for Gafsa where you can pick up connections to Tozeur.

Local buses leave for neighbouring Chenini in the oasis every hour. There are six a day for Matmata (bear in mind that the last bus back from Matmata leaves at 17.00). A daily bus for Toujane, via Mareth, currently leaves at 15.00. There are seven buses a day for Houmt Souk in Jerba, one of which goes via Zarzis, and six daytime departures for Medenine and Tataouine.

By *Louage*
The *louage* station, opposite the ONAT on Av Farhat Hached, is busiest in the early morning with regular runs to Sousse, Sfax, Tunis and Medenine.

Car Hire
The offices of Hertz, tel (05) 70925, Avis, tel (05) 70210, and Europcar, tel (05) 72829, are all on Av Farhat Hached and local firms like Najar Chaabane, tel (05) 70216, and Touregs, tel (05) 70093, are on Av Mongi Slim. Najar Chaabane specializes in landrovers.

TOURIST INFORMATION AND TOURS
The **Tourist Information Office** is in a booth in the middle of Av Habib Thameur, the beach road. All useful shops, offices, cafés, hotels and restaurants are likely to be on the two long avenues that cut across the town, Av Habib Bourguiba and Av Farhat Hached. There are four **banks** at the eastern end of Av Habib Bourguiba, and the main **Post Office (PTT)** is on the western end of Av Farhat Hached, opposite the ONAT, a state-run showroom for crafts and other artisan goods. There is also a Catholic chapel at 25 Rue d'Algérie, tel (05) 20026.

The two main **tour companies** in Gabès are Sahara Tours at 57 Av Farhat Hached, tel (05) 70930 and Najar Chaabane, tel (05) 70212, whose offices are at the garage nearest the railway station on Av Farhat Hached. They run the usual week-long package tours of the Tunisian south for about 260 dn per person.

Jara Market
The old self-contained village of Jara was at the western end of Av Habib Bourguiba, though now, apart from the old market, it is indistinguishable from Gabès town. The old marketplace which sprawls down to the river bank is still a satisfyingly archaic place with its rickety beams, cobbled blacksmiths' and jewellers' streets and dark courtyards broken by pools of strong light. Its pavements overflow with displays of basketwork, palm-frond hats and burgeoning alfa sacks of Gabès henna which manage to obscure the tackier souvenirs. The central Jara mosque, immediately opposite the market, was rebuilt in 1952, following war damage. Jara's oldest mosque, which was endowed with 737 palms, by far the largest grove in the oasis, is **Sidi Driss** just the other side of the river in Little Jara. It is seldom open, particularly to tourists, but is a restoration of an 11th-century mosque, destroyed in the 1962 floods, which had a galleried courtyard and a prayer hall with seven aisles divided by horseshoe arches, supported by Roman columns. Sidi Driss was built by the Beni Jami, a petty Arab dynasty of Hilalian origins.

Sidi Boulbaba and Gabès' Museum of Arts and Popular Traditions
The Mosque of Sidi Boulbaba and the museum are on the edge of Gabès, a short taxi ride or an unattractive 2.5-km walk from the bus station. Go down Av Bechir Dziri, which runs

beside the Artisanat and PTT, then turn right after the bridge over the Oued Gabès flood dyke, and uphill towards the minaret of the neighbourhood mosque which is opposite the museum and shrine.

Sidi Boulbaba, the barber of the Prophet Mohammed, is believed to have founded Gabès in the 7th century, establishing a ribat on the ruined Roman city of Tacape. The large graveyard that surrounds his own tomb, and the constant trickle of pilgrims bear testament to his local importance. The shrine and mosque are modern, the open courtyard aping the enclosed 17th-century building destroyed in the war.

Beside the shrine is an elegant pale stone building, once Sous Medersa, a residential college built around a central courtyard where students, the *tolba*, which literally translates as the reciters, could study the Koran and Islamic law for seven years. It was built in 1692 by Mohammed Bey, the Muradite prince who campaigned in the south. Since 1969 it has housed the **Museum of Arts and Popular Traditions**, which provides an excellent introduction to the lifestyle of the contemporary Jebel Demer communities (open 09.00–12.00, 14.00–17.00 every day, except Mon; adm). Its serene central courtyard, empty but for a sun clock to determine the hours of prayer, is bordered by a triple-arched colonnade.

The first six cabinets explain techniques for preparing and dyeing wool, for weaving cloth and killims, and North Africa's passion for embroidery. There are some fine samples of traditional blankets, killims and haiks, the natural dyes bleeding into the stripes and lozenges of the simple decorative patterns.

The medersa's old prayer hall, its mihrab arch partly obscured on the left, is now a hall of marriage, with displays of bridal costumes, jewellery and trousseaux. A second room off one of the two smaller courtyards displays agricultural tools and hand mills. The final display in the museum covers the diet of the south, based on a trinity of alfalfa sacks containing corn, large gypsum amphorae for dates and smaller ones for olive oil. In addition these communities relied on rancid butter, red peppers, dried fish, figs, honey and meat for feast days. A second small courtyard contains a collection of Roman ossuary boxes and loos.

Gabès Oasis

The oasis of Gabès, seldom less than a kilometre wide, stretches for 6 km along the Oued Gabès to the sea. It is quite pretty to walk in, though its attractions have been exaggerated. The 300,000 date palms that shade a neat patchwork of irrigated garden plots are grown primarily for wood and crop shelter. Gabès, with its sea breezes and muggy air, is not hot or dry enough to produce exportable dates and those which do grow are usually fed to animals or used as manure. The gardens, with their kaleidoscopic variety of crops, are fascinating, but the Oued Gabès and its subsidiary irrigation ditches have become open sewers.

Chenini

The western part of the oasis, upriver from the town's drains and the Sfax road, is the most attractive area criss-crossed by a grid of sandy paths. Be warned however that Chenini palmery, on the far western edge, is firmly established on the package-tour itinerary. A line of horse-drawn carriages stands ready for coach parties just beyond the bus station.

If you would also like to go there, catch a horse carriage for around 6dn, the hourly local bus or walk. Cross the Oued Gabès ditch and then follow the tarmac Chenini road marked by a modern minaret. Three kilometres later, having passed through the hamlets of Sidi Merouane, Chemassa and Oued el Haj, take a left turn at Al Aouadid, strolling down towards the river, past the Café des Cascades. Ahead lie souvenir stalls clustering around a concrete water tank built beside fragments of an old dam. Beside it is a Nile crocodile/American alligator **farm** which is gradually turning itself into a small zoo. From here by palmery path or road walk along to the Hotel Chela Club, at the foot of Chenini village. Continue up to the high-banked Oued Gabès, passing two more dams before reaching Ras el Oued, the hillock at the head of the valley, with its view back over the Chenini palmery.

The Port and the Beach
East of the town centre, past the well-guarded barracks compound, is a fishing harbour and strip of sandy beach. Two package hotels and the Casino café restaurant exist in the summer, the swimmers presumably indifferent to Oued Gabès' effluent and the Ghannouche generating and chemical works 6 km due north.

WHERE TO STAY

EXPENSIVE
If you want a prompt, hot bath use Gabès' business hotel **Hotel Nejib**, tel (05) 71286, an otherwise institutional affair on the eastern edge of Av Farhat Hached.

MODERATE
The **Atlantic**, on the eastern end of Av Habib Bourguiba, tel (05) 20034, is a large ex-colonial hotel with balconies that has been recently refurbished and now has its own café and restaurant. If you do not mind the company of groups, look at the **Chela Club** outside Chenini village, tel (05) 27442, which has 50 stone bungalows, a bar, Gabès' only swimming pool and a restaurant set in the middle of a palmery garden.

CHEAP
If you are stopping off between buses there are four cheap hotels by the bus station: the **Ben Nejima** at 66 Rue Ali Djemel, tel (05) 72095, the noisy **Medina** on Rue Djilani, tel (05) 74271, the **Mrabet** and the **Keilani**, tel (05) 72320. None of them is recommended for women alone.

EATING OUT

Most of the licensed restaurants are along Av Farhat Hached: the elaborate and expensive **El Mazar**, tel (05) 72065, **L'Oriental** at no. 11, tel (05) 70098, the overrated **de l'Oasis**, tel (05) 70098 and the **Le Pacha**, tel (05) 72418, the cheapest and quietest in town, where *ojja*, couscous and wine for two costs 13dn. Av Habib Bourguiba's restaurants are cheaper and mostly unlicensed, like the **Amori** and the **Bonne Bouffe**. The restaurant in the ground floor of the **Tacapes Hotel**, tel (05) 70700, is a popular local choice, with good food and wine for two at around 16 dn.

BARS

Gabès' bars are dominated by the garrison which makes them even busier and more macho than normal. Outside the restaurants, the most relaxing place for a drink is the bar at the Nejib Hotel. The last chance to build up a stock of wine for picnics in the south is from the secretive off-licence that operates on Av Habib Bourguiba, three doors from the Rue de Nifzaoua turning.

From Gabès to Matmata

The road to Matmata sweeps out of Gabès past another large military barracks, crossing a dry plain before reaching the modern settlement of Nouvelle Matmata on the crossroads between the oasis of El Hamma and the half-underground village of Beni Zelten, beneath a ruined ksar at the foot of the Matmata hills. The road then climbs up into rounded hills where the odd patches of orchard and terraced garden are tucked out of sight, to give the impression of a succession of bleak, barren, eroded bluffs. Hidden here are a number of reclusive underground houses.

Tijma and Haddej

The hamlet of Tijma is recognizable by the roadside Maison Fatma, a well-established second-generation underground souvenir shop, and the Restaurant Barette, a drop-off point for coach tours and camel rides. It also marks the turning for Haddej, which used to be the largest village. In 1890 it had 3000 inhabitants to Matmata's 500, and also served as the seat of the Khalifa of Matmata, a deputy of the Caid of Gabès. Haddej was devastated by the 1969 flood and though many of the houses are still lived in there are even more that are deserted and free to be explored in the company of persistent village guides. Ask to be shown the underground olive oil press and the marriage house, with its long-dining room and hidden upstairs chamber where the bride would wait for her husband.

Matmata

The underground houses of Matmata are one of the most famous and popular sites in Tunisia. They were first recorded in the 4th century BC when Herodotus lists the Berbers of the region as troglodytes. At the turn of the century they formed a nearly invisible village, the open courtyards of the 50 underground houses appearing like so many craters in a punctured moonscape. This prospect is now obscured by above-ground building, though many are still in use and three of the largest have been converted into hotels. The village children will be delighted to show you underground, at a price. Matmata's fame was boosted by *Star Wars* which opens with Luke Skywalker's sunken desert home, and used the Sidi Driss hotel for the alien jazz club sequence.

The Matmata hills are the home of one of the oldest identifiable Berber tribes in the south, the Hammama des Matmata. They were part of the Lawata confederacy that raided the southern borders of the Roman Empire. The Matmata occupied a weak defensive position, on the lowest and northernmost edge of Jebel Demer and so they were quick to assimilate with the dominant nomads of the plain and speak Arabic. The town is now a disappointing place, swamped with coaches, cameras, touts and camel treks, which are replaced at dusk by jeep convoys of adventure tourists. However, you can still see the less exploited face of the area by exploring the underground houses of Haddej and by walking and picnicking in the Oued Barrak valley.

GETTING AROUND
Sotrogames run the bus route to Gabès: six currently leave between 07.15 and 17.00. There are buses to Techine at 12.30 and 17.30, a direct bus to Tamezret at 13.30, and a morning and evening bus that pass through on their way to Taoujout.

Around Matmata

Oued Barrak Valley

Taking the road past the Hotel les Berbères, walk, drive or hitch east along the helter-skelter tarmac road. After 3 km it dips down to cross the Oued Barrak valley, which drains north towards the oasis of El Hamma and is lined by a number of small villages with underground houses, above which tower a succession of hilltop ksour. **Sidi Mettar**, which is just above the turning onto the Oued Barrak track, is a modest hamlet of underground houses, a mosque halfway up the hill and a ksar of caves and ruined dry-stone walls that stretches along the escarpment above. A well-maintained koubba rewards the climb. By following the mountain tracks from here, or walking down the valley track, you could continue on to **Ksar Sidi Ayed** with its gleaming white mosque and cluster of koubbas. Two kilometres beyond it stands a school house, the sole building above ground in the village of **Beni Aissa**.

Tamezret, Taoujout and Zeroua

In the 19th century these three villages beyond Oued Barrak were the only pure Berber speaking communities left in these hills. Their long tradition of independence was only broken after an early rebellion against the French. Tamezret, 10 km from Matmata, is a tightly packed stone village on a low hill within which is hidden the tomb of Sidi Haj Yusuf. The café at the summit has an excellent all-round view from its roof and a brew of delicious almond tea. From Tamezret a road twists 4 km north to Taoujout, a similar pretty stone village, that clings to several protruding hill spurs with a proliferation of koubbas and grocery shops. It is connected to Matmata by two buses a day, morning and evening, both of which wait at least half an hour in the village before going back. Two other tracks lead off from Tamezret. The track to the northwest winds 6 km to Zeroua, the least visited of the three stone villages. Due east it is a bumpy 20-km drive over rocks to the Ksar Ghilane/pipeline road.

East from Matmata

Leaving southeast from Matmata the road climbs up between hills that are part of a military base which was established in the 17th century by Mohammed Bey on his return from disciplining Ghomrassen. A 5-km walk along this track is rewarded by a magnificent view and the venerable atmosphere of the sanctuary of **Lalla Telkoussat** perched on an outcrop of rock. The track continues for another 18 km or so to the Ksar of Toujane (described from Mareth), with signposted turnings to some hill hamlets of lesser interest, Technine with a café and Zuerten which has a ruined ksar.

WHERE TO STAY

MODERATE

The **Matmata**, a new-above ground hotel, is a useful walking base, tel (05) 30066. It has 32 bedrooms with bathrooms, a pool and a restaurant.

CHEAP

Even if the bedrooms and restaurants of the three underground hotels are block booked by tour groups, noisy with evening entertainments, you are usually free to look around the courtyards and have a drink. The **Marhala Touring Club**, tel (05) 30015, is the smallest and by far the prettiest of the three, with its palm-wood gate, jasmine-scented courtyard and bar. The **Berbères**, tel (05) 30024, is larger and the **Sidi Driss** the dirtiest, but it is also the one with the greatest chance of a spare bed, tel (05) 30005.

Gabès to Medenine

The route from Gabès to Mareth cuts across a number of well-watered valleys. Teboulbou oasis is almost contiguous with Gabès but Kettana a little further on has a separate identity, lined with bamboo huts selling fruit, dates from the Jerid and the local crops of grapes and pomegranates. From the Oued Ferch river bed, by the Restaurant Selmi in Kettana, you can walk up to the village of Sidi Salem or downstream to Zrigue by the coast.

Mareth and Ksar Toujane

Mareth, a dusty roadside town with a Monday market, was made famous by the line of defences which once extended from the coast to the Matmata hills here. This Mareth Line was built in 1938 by the French against Mussolini's Italian army stationed in Libya, but was used by Rommel's Afrika Korps against Montgomery's Eighth Army. The *Johannides*, an epic by the Byzantine poet Corippe, celebrates an earlier battle at Mareth, the victory of John Trogliata over the Lawata nomads in 546.

As you enter Mareth from Gabès, an 8-km road cuts along the edge of the palmery to the village of **Zarat**, whence a track leads down to the beach and a new fishing port. On the southern edge of the palmery, just before the turning to Jorf, a dirt road heads inland for the modern village of Ain Tounine at the foot of the hills. The road on up the hill to **Ksar Toujane** has thoughtfully been tarmacked. It is a stone-built village with working olive mills that perches on the edge of the hills overlooking the plain. The ruined kalaa that rises immediately above the village has exhilarating views from its small plateau of polished rock, bordered by perilous vertical walls. It is approached by a path that snakes up the valley on its other side, passing village cisterns and washing pools on the way up to a captured spring. Two hairpin, signposted roads lead from the village, either southeast 30 km to Ksar Metameur, or northwest 23 km to Matmata, passing turnings to the small hamlets of Zmerten and Technine.

On the southern edge of Mareth, 1 km before the Jorf turning you might catch a glimpse of a small pyramid, a monument to the Free French forces of General Leclerc who died at Mareth. Jorf, the ferry port to the island of Jerba is 47 km from Mareth.

Mareth to Medenine

A British monument to Field Marshal Montgomery was erected 3 km south of Mareth's tributary, the Oued Zigzaou, and in the process a prehistoric site was discovered, uncovering tools contemporary to those at Oued Akarit. The next oasis of Ain el Arram has turned up an even richer collection of flint tools, for the ground around the spring was used as a knapping ground for hundreds of thousands of years. The palmery also boasts over a dozen marabouts and the zaouia of Sidi Yahia, one of a large number of holy men who originated in the western Sahara.

Twenty kilometres south the road sweeps past the village and spring of Koutine, the fount of its own brand-name mineral water. Just 4 km outside Medenine, a left turn leads up to Metameur.

GETTING AROUND AND WHERE TO STAY
One bus a day to Toujane via Mareth currently leaves Gabès at 15.00. Mareth has a cheap hotel, the **Hotel du Golfe**, for the offbeat traveller set on visiting Zarat and Ksar Toujane.

Ksar Metameur
Walking up between the village bakery and school, the crest of the village is occupied by a long ghorfa courtyard, Ksar Metameur, which is partly and discreetly occupied by the most attractive hotel in the region. The **Hotel el Ghorfa**, tel (05) 40294, is run by Drifi Hachem who also organizes trips to the more reclusive ksour of Jebel Dahar, many totally untouched by tourists, and perching precipitously in a dramatic landscape. You camp by night in the ksour, travelling by camel, donkey or bicycle in the hands of a delightfully opinionated and informed guide. He will need two to three weeks to organize a tour for a minimum of 10. There are all sorts of variations, and a three-day trip costs about 60 dn.

Medenine

Medenine is a dusty crossroads and market town studded with modern administrative buildings. There is little to indicate its age, for the old town was summarily bulldozed in the modernization of the 1960s. Until then Medenine, apart from an arcaded market square, was composed of a dazzling collection of 35 interlocked ksour up to six storeys high, the ultimate expression of the region's distinctive architecture. For four centuries it served as the capital of the Ouerghamma confederacy, after they abandoned their citadel at Ghomrassen in the 17th century. By building at Medenine in the centre of the Jefara plain, they gave a dramatic demonstration of their new power.

The remains of three ksour have survived, with such an anarchy of levels, vaults, doorways and stairways that they still startle the sturdiest surrealist. The first ksar has become a tourist shopping yard, and the other two are used as a vegetable markets. To find them take the Jorf road and 150 m later turn left, opposite a line of old wells.

GETTING AROUND

By Bus
The bus station is in the centre of town, on Rue 18 Janvier by the Jorf turning. A dozen buses leave for Gabès between 06.00 and 21.15, six for Houmt Souk via Jorf, four via Zarzis. Between three and five buses serve Tataouine during the day and three go to Tunis, currently at 08.00, 11.30 and 21.15. There is one bus a day to Ghomrassen/Ksar Haddada, currently at 14.00, and four small buses to Beni Kheddache at 08.00, 10.00, 12.00 and 16.00.

By *Louage*
Opposite the bus station, *louages* collect for Tataouine, Jerba, Tunis, Sfax, Gabès and Zarzis.

WHERE TO STAY AND EAT
There are three hotels in Medenine, none of which is used to tourists. Truckers use the **Motel Agip**, by the petrol station at the Gabès end of town, which also has a very busy restaurant. A double room costs 20 dn, and dinner for two with wine 14 dn. Passing Libyans tend to use the unnamed new hotel, above a café at the Tataouine end of town, which charges

6 dn a bed. Visiting technicians and bureaucrats put up at the **Hotel Sahara** at Rue du 2 Mai, off Pl des Martyrs, beside the PTT, which has a restaurant and double rooms at 12 dn.

To the Isle of Jerba

There is nothing to be gained by going to Jerba on the El Kantara causeway, via Zarzis. Islands should be approached by boat, and Zarzis just is not worth the detour. Jorf is the **ferry point** to Jerba and has a café where you can wait for the ferry to do its 15-minute crossing. Ferries run half-hourly from 05.00–20.00 and hourly between 20.00–24.00 and 02.00–04.00; they cost nothing for passengers and 600 ml for a car. The road from Medenine to Jorf crosses 50 km of the flat, almost featureless Jefara plain, and passes close to the Roman ruins of Gigthis.

Gigthis

Break the journey at Gigthis for a walk by the sea, amongst jumbled Roman ruins. Gigthis' charm lies in the colour of its carved stone, which is lost in the midday light but comes alive in the subtler light of the evening and morning. There is a tattered signpost for the turning to the ruins just before the roadside village of Bou Grara. Open from dawn until sunset, with tickets from the guardian's hut.

History
Gigthis was a minor member of the Emporia, the chain of Carthaginian trading towns along the Gulf of Syrtes that benefited from the trans-Saharan trade. It now looks an odd site for a port, but its sheltered position on the shore of a virtually inland sea was an advantage in the days when shallow-draughted galleys preferred to row within sight of the shore.

The Emporia was peacefully absorbed into Massinissa's expanding Numidian kingdom in 202 BC and later passed into the Roman Empire after Julius Caesar's victory over Juba I at Thapsus in 46 BC. Most of the ruins date from civic improvements in the 2nd and 3rd centuries AD, and the city died suddenly in the middle of 5th century, sacked by the Lawata Berbers. A fort built by the Byzantines on the cliff in the 6th century was reoccupied in the 10th century. Later ages left only a few rude huts on the site of the old forum.

The Ruins
Go directly to the forum beneath the upright green fluted columns. This, the central public square, was paved in gold, pink and red stone now partly strewn with sand and scattered with fragments of its colourful portico of red limestone columns, pink marble bases and Corinthian capitals. A double flight of stairs climbs up on to the prominent temple podium, badly restored with one of its columns erected upside down, which was once presumed to be the capitol. However, a sundial found by the steps and a statue of Serapis/Helios suggest a temple to the sun god, whose worship developed into the cult of the unconquered sun. This rivalled Christianity in the late 3rd century and gave us Sunday as our holy day.

The north face of the forum had a busy skyline. There was a temple to Melkarth, the Punic Hercules, a temple to Concord whose sanctuaries were often used as town halls, and a sanctuary to Apollo beyond the small arch. On the south face, only a temple to the imperial cult of the *genius* of Augustus has been identified. The seaward edge was occupied by a market and a basilica for the law courts. Behind these the large yellow paved courtyard marks a temple to Liber Pater, the god of wine and renewal, whose sanctuary must have been the most impressive in town with a portico supported by 28 enormous Ionic columns of golden stone. Going further towards the sea there is another large, but unidentified, temple courtyard, opposite a small shrine to Aesculapius, the god of healing, before you reach the ruined sea gate. Fragments of the harbour wall can be seen protruding out into the silted shore, north of which is stretches its modern equivalent. On the cliffs above the palm trees are traces of the 60-m square Byzantine fort, and a mosque and koubba beyond.

About 150 m south of the forum, the other side of the dry river bed, are the confused remains of houses, a public bath, a square market, a crescent of shops and some surrounding inns. Continuing uphill through figs, vines and young olives for about 400 m you should stumble on the enclosure of Mercury, near an L-shaped bungalow. The *cella* with its flight of rock-cut steps, flanked by chapels to Minerva and Fortune, can be identified but it is the golden-coloured ruins, delicately carved Ionic capitals and entablature that beckon.

Beni Kheddache and Ksar Jouamaa

On the hilltops around Beni Kheddache sit a handful of crumbling ksour, destinations for exploratory walks. For drivers, a track leads on across the plain to Ksar Haddada, a mere 24 km from Foum Tataouine.

To the west of Medenine the C113 road crosses sandy scrubland before approaching the sculpted mountain plateau of Jebel Dahar. The foot of the escarpment is dotted with orchards of olive and figs, and white houses whose roofs are laden with storage pots and sacks. The village of **Ksar Jedid**, off to the right was built at the turn of the century and is worth a visit on Friday, market day.

As the road climbs up into the mountains, the blank walls of **Ksar Jouamaa** appear in the distance like a castle with round crenellations. A signposted track leads directly up to the ksar. A mosque and koubba stand outside an arch, which leads into the courtyard of ghorfas built on a projecting spit of high land.

Jouamaa's history is preserved in tribal genealogies. El Khzouri, one of the seven sons of Si Moussa, the saintly 16th-century founder of the Ouerghamma confederacy, presided over the entire region. His three eldest sons took the rich grazing grounds of the plains and left the youngest, Ahmed, with nothing but a *haouia*, a worn camel saddle, as his inheritance. However, the saddle is an ancient symbol of tribal chieftainship and through courage and determination Ahmed managed to establish a tribe, which he named the Haouia. They farmed and grazed in the valleys of the Oued Demer, and above it he built Ksar Jouma to store their goods. Only the booths on either side of the gate were inhabited, by a resident guardian and itinerant blacksmiths and carpenters. The date on the arch, 1178/1764, records the date of some restoration work.

The village of **Beni Kheddache**, perched at the foot of a mountain 8 km further into the hills, was the headquarters of the government-appointed Khalifa of the Haouia tribe. It holds a market on Mondays and Thursdays in the French-built arcade and has a school and a post office. Above the market are the remains of the old four street ksar, where a handsome sandy-coloured minaret rises above the remaining rows of delapidated ghorfas.

Ksar Zemmour and Ksar El Hallouf

Ksar Zemmour and Ksar el Hallouf are two of the more spectacular and approachable of the many ksour in the immediate area. Follow the tarmac road that leaves from the top of the village beyond the marketplace, over the hill until you reach a triangular marker, by a green and white mosque. Take a right turn down over the dry river bed and another right 100 m later for the rough track that snakes uphill to the rambling ruins of **Ksar Zemmour**.

Ksar El Hallouf is 4 km up the dirt track to the left of the triangular marker, perched on the summit of a hill which has a commanding view over the small groves and underground houses of its valley. It is a fine example of the transition between a kalaa and a ksar, its natural defences strengthened by an impressive gatehouse and a still-venerated koubba.

Ksar Kherachfa, Ksar Ouled Mahdi and Ksar Haddada

In a landrover or cautiously driven car it is possible to take the back track to Ghomrassen, via Ksar Haddada. This passes by turnings for the even rougher tracks to Kherachfa and Ouled Mahdi, two distinctive and well-preserved circular ksour. Ksar Kherachfa was built by Ali el Kerchoufi who, in the legends of his descendants, first arrived from Tripolitania as a tenant, but then drove his master out of these hills, forcing him to take refuge in Metameur. Later he welcomed a party of Mahadha tribesmen to his new lands. At first they used Kherachfa for the safe storage of their grain, but in time they built the neighbouring Ksar Ouled Mahdi.

Leaving Beni Kheddache for Medenine, take the first signposted track to the right, then a left at the Y-junction to cross the plateau of small sand dunes and alfa grass before climbing up to the hamlet of Ksar Jeraa. A rough track to the left before Jeraa leads 8 km to Kerachfa and a track to the left just after Jeraa leads 3 km to Ouled Mahdi.

At Ksar Jeraa, take the right turn below the ruined circular ksar and then the centre track of three which eventually slips down into a widening valley dotted with underground houses. The conspicuous silver dome of the mosque at Ksar Haddada makes a useful landmark. The actual ksar is in good condition as it is has been converted into a hotel. It is usually block-booked by tour groups, but you are welcome to use the bar and usually left free to clamber around the bedrooms; 7 dn per person if there is a bunk spare. For neighbouring Ghomrassen see p. 338.

Foum Tataouine

The area around Tataouine is one of the most exciting places to explore in Tunisia. Tataouine is a Berber word meaning the springs, and until the French built a military post here in 1892 it was nothing but a gorge, or *foum*, cut through the northern edge of Jebel Abiod by Oued Tataouine. The colonial headquarters was originally at Douirat, but Tataouine soon proved a more convenient centre, its primacy locally confirmed when it attracted the Ouderna tribe's camel market. On the twin pillars of commerce and the military it has since grown into a town of 30,000, and its streets and marketplaces fill on Mondays and Thursdays with merchants from all over the south.

Travel books in the colonial era had a recurring theme, that France was following in the footsteps of the Roman Empire. The French headquarters were decorated with a pair of Roman statues that had been found in the wall of a tomb 3 km away (the fossilized wood and neo-Punic inscriptions never got any attention). They are still there, but since independence the building has been occupied by the Tunisian army.

GETTING AROUND

By Bus

The bus station is on Rue 1 Juin 1955, just above the main road. Four buses a day make the hour's journey north to Medenine, and there is a direct bus to Gabès, currently at 05.30. A direct bus for Tunis, a 10-hour journey, leaves Hotel La Gazelle at 20.00. There are two buses a day for Houmt Souk on Jerba, one via Zarzis, the other via Jorf. In addition, there is one bus for Remada and four buses to Ghomrassen. Irregular services also run to Maztouria.

By Taxi

Taxis make up for the lack of bus services and can be hired with a little bargaining for the day. Large blue and yellow striped *louages* make regular runs to Medenine and Gabès, while red top taxis serve local destinations. Peugeot half-trucks, *taxis rurals*, ply the off-piste tracks to mountain villages. All leave from a square on Rue Farhat Hached.

WHAT TO SEE

Everything in town happens along two parallel streets, Av Habib Bourguiba and Rue Farhat Hached, which are above the main Medenine to Remada road. At the beginning of Av Habib Bourguiba, no. 39, is Megbli Mokhtar, tel (06) 60040, one of the best places in Tunisia to buy killims and old pottery. The banks, shops and twice weekly market are on Pl Ali Belhouane, halfway along Av Farhat Hached. The Tourist Board organizes a fairly bogus festival of the ksour, held every year around Easter.

WHERE TO STAY AND EAT

MODERATE

Hotel La Gazelle, at the southern end of Av Habib Bourguiba, tel (06) 60009, is an expansive, slightly decaying ex-colonial hotel with vaulted bedrooms, working showers, a bar and a restaurant.

CHEAP

Choose between **Hotel de la Paix** which has 14 rooms and a small sun terrace and the down-market **Hotel Ennour** on Av Habib Bourguiba. A bed in a room above its lively café restaurant costs a mere 3 dn per person.

Ksar Megelba and Ksar Degrah

A 500-m stroll south from Hotel La Gazelle brings you to two ksour on the edge of Tataouine. To the west of the road, the village and ksar of Megelba climbs the hill; to the east, just above the signposted turning to Beni Barka, is Ksar Degrah. Its entrance arch leads into a long courtyard of sturdy two- storey ghorfas, a downhill extension of the smaller, older ksar, where traces of flights of stairs can be made out on the walls.

Around Tataouine

On the edge of the mountain plateau to the west of Tataouine are the three celebrated Berber citadel villages of Chenini, Douirat and Guermessa. They all deserve to be seen at dawn or dusk, particularly Chenini which is the most beautiful and the most visited of the three. To the east, in the valleys cut into Jebel Abiod, there are dozens of ksour, all quite empty of tourists.

You can continue with your own explorations, after a look up the Oued Zondag valley at Beni Barka, Maztouria and Ksar Ouled Soltane.

Chenini

Two kilometres south of Tataouine is the turning for the 18-km drive to Chenini, approached across a palm-scattered plain. The flat agglomeration of square white houses making up the new village sits beneath the escarpment of the old town, at this distance only detectable by its hilltop white mosque. Around the shoulder of the hill, you catch the first full view of Chenini, draped in a horseshoe col where every sound is echoed and shared by the community. Terraces of half-cave houses stretch along like an emormous amphitheatre on three levels. The sky is patrolled by hawks and pigeons, gliding on the winds produced at the saddle of the mountain.

The kalaa, built according to one inscription in 1193, sits above the white mosque at the summit of the escarpment. Its decayed walls are filled with individual ghorfa, some of which are still used for storage but most are in decay. Scramble up along clifftop paths to peer into empty but still complete chambers fitted with lockable wooden doors, ornamented with great gypsum jars for storing dates, sacks for corn and Jerban amphorae for olive oil. The vaults are decorated with relief patterns, individual combinations from the traditional Berber repertoire of lozenges, stripes, hands, script and arabesques. From the knife-edge summit there is a spectacular view, down across the dry mountainous plain or further into the mountains.

At the bottom of the village there are a couple of grocery shops and the *Relais Chenini* which serves a three-course meal for 3 dn and rents out space in the dining-rooms at night for 2 dn a person. The other choice of accommodation is the **Seven Sleepers Campsite**, below the road between the old and new village. This is named after a cave beside an old underground mosque, the Jamma Qedima, about 1 km down the road, which like many sites in North Africa is associated with the myth of the seven sleepers. They were seven men who hid in a cave during the 3rd-century persecution of Christians by the Emperor Decius, and only awoke during the reign of the Emperor Heraclius to become early converts to Islam.

The Back Road from Chenini to Douirat

Follow the dirt road below Chenini for the back track to Douirat, a delightful 15-km drive up a palm-shaded valley, past underground houses and terraced gardens up into the bleaker landscape of the plateau. Keep an eye out for the signposted left turn (the right turn is for those who want to get lost in the desert, somewhere in the direction of Ksar Ghilane), and motor 8 km on to Douirat.

Douirat

To get to Douirat from Tataouine, drive south on the Remada road for 9 km to Ksar Ouled Debbab, built by the dominant nomadic tribe of the southern Jefara plain as a store house equidistant from their principal clients. Once a hotel, wreckage and roadside litter now dominate.

The road opposite the ksar leads to Douirat. The village lies level with the surrounding table-top hills, eroded stacks and volcanic silhouettes on the skyline. It was founded by Ghazi ben Douaieb, a merchant and holy man from the Saharan oasis city of Tafilalet in Morocco. He came to the local Beni Mazigh tribe 500 years ago and was offered as much land as could be covered by a camel's skin, and like Dido before him he cut it up into the thinnest thread and encircled the whole valley of Douirat. The outwitted Beni Mazigh quit the region, and their ksar is still visible in ruin on the hills opposite Douirat. Ghazi cemented good relations with Chenini by marrying a daughter of the town and established the first trading links with the oasis of Ghadames, in Libya. At its height Douirat had the largest market in the south, a population of 2000 and another 2000 inhabitants settled in 20 hamlets scattered around. Only those out of sight of the village, up the gorge or along the track to Chenini, are still inhabited, but old patches of Douirat land, water holes and gardens, now in Algeria and Libya, attest to the mercantile energy of the descendants of Ghazi.

The village is capped by a fortress, a kalaa, that once boasted a 30-ft-high wall. It was later converted into a communal granary and used as a marketplace. The interior gradually filled, like an enormous wasps' nest, with a warren of ghorfas. It is now a decaying, potentially dangerous mass of cascading stone, out of which appear tumbling arches, walls and hidden chambers. The village extends in a double crescent below, its two layers of terraced houses half-built into seams of softer rock. A mass of stone-walled forecourts, gates and outhouses, sheltering underground rooms plastered with decorated gypsum, wait to be explored. Three buildings are kept in good repair: the white minareted mosque below the ksar, an underground camel-driven oil press to the right of the ksar and to the left a msalla, an open-air mosque with an underground ablution chamber. Below Douirat stretches a cemetery, the head and foot stones melting into the barren expanse, like mole hills around half a dozen dirt-white koubbas.

Guermessa

Travel 2 km south of Tataouine, turn right, ignoring the Chenini turning to the left. Drive on through **Ras el Ain**, the head of the spring, a scattering of well-heads and barrel-vaulted houses set in a terraced valley of date palm and olives. The high ground to the north is known as **Jebel Tlalett**, a name strongly reminiscent of the Roman frontier fort of Tabalatti, which was listed in the early 3rd-century *Itinerary of Antonin*, an extensive A–Z of the Roman Empire. Imagine the archaeologists' excitement when they found this fort which they could accurately date from coins discovered in the foundations. It was built in 263 and restored in 355.

At the summit of the valley, just beside the road, rise the immaculate rounded exterior walls of **Ksar Ferch**, next to a white koubba and barrel-vaulted mosque. Its austere and regular courtyard, lined by large double ghorfas, was built in 1911 and seems more Mexican than North African. Look out for the intact traditional olive oil press. Shortly after Ksar Ferch is a left turn (signposted in Arabic to Guermessa and Chenini 23 km) which leads 5 km to the modern village of Guermessa, nestling at the foot of the old.

Ksar Guermessa
Though architecturally the least impressive of the three citadels, Guermessa more than compensates for this by its natural grandeur and lack of tourists. Migration into the new village, with its electricity and water, is not yet complete, and the long terraces of old Guermessa, perched on either side of the central mosque and below the double summit, are still inhabited. As evening descends, a procession of water-laden mules makes its noisy ascent up the paved mountain path. The villagers still work on small terraced plots in the region or tend communal herds, though for three generations the big money has come from men working as porters in the markets and railway station in Tunis.

The larger pinnacle of the twin summit is the old kalaa, a natural citadel whose rock walls are virtually unadorned. The people of Guermessa call themselves the sons of Hamza. Eight hundred years ago they left their native land around Kairouan to follow Sidi Hamza ben Brahim ed Dahmani. This holy man came from Seguiat el Hamra, the red river in the western Sahara, and led them to their old village, a kalaa whose vestiges can be found 10 km northwest, on the slopes of Jebel Qedim. The tribe fell under the overlordship of the Arab Zorgane, and during a time of comparative stability built the present chaotic jumble of ghorfas but the kalaa is now all but completely decayed.

Ghomrassen and Ksar Haddada

Ghomrassen, a town of 10,000, is strung along the bottom of a deep, narrow valley, reached by turning left off the Medenine road, some 5 km out of Tataouine. In the evening the central market is a bustle of women shopping in magenta haiks and more static groups of men haggling, or lounging by taxi ranks and on café terraces. It survives on the energy and loyalty of its emigrant citizens who are famed throughout Tunisia for their doughnuts. The cliff-like walls of the valley are pitted with caves, ksour and koubbas, mostly now overlooked by modern concrete and used as goat pens.

Ghomrassen has always been important in the region, a centre of the Hamdoun Berbers well before the Hilalian invasion in the 11th century. Here they retained a great hatred for the Arabs of the plain, and Tijani, writing in the 15th century, recalls that the valleys twin kalaa, of Nifik and Hamdoun, were the best fortified in the south. In the 16th century, Si Moussa established his zaouia here and won the first adherents for his new Ouerghamma confederation from the Hamdoun. The valley traditionally received its name from Si Moussa, whose first action had been to plunge his head in the river, 'nghom rasi', in ritual ablution before prayers. Ghomrassen remained the centre of the Ouerghamma for a hundred years before a Libyan marabout led the tribe down from the hills and founded Medenine.

Climbing uphill out of the town (first left for Guermessa and Ksar Ferch), take a right turn 4 km later for Ksar Haddada. This small village, complete with oil press and a showy mosque, squats below a four-square ksar, now used as a hotel. Its ghorfa bedrooms are usually block-booked by passing tour groups but by day it is empty, the well-preserved gateway and impressive interior open for inspection. The ksar was used for storage by four tribes: the Haddada and their 'cousins' the Hamdoun from Ghomrassen, and two other tribes claiming exotic origins in Morocco and Libya. (See p. 334 for the route from Beni Kheddache.)

East of Tataouine: the Ksour of Jebel Abiod

Jebel Abiod, the white mountain, has a tangled geography. It is an area where the plain and the mountains mingle, territory shared between the farmer and the herder. As a result it has witnessed petty tribal squabbles and periods of almost genocidal warfare, remembered in a body of often conflicting legends and genealogy. By the 16th century the traditional division between Arab nomad and Berber farmer had become blurred as the area was wholly Arab-speaking with a checkered pattern of land holding.

Beni Barka
A left turn on the southern edge of Tataouine, marked Beni Barka and Maztouria, leads up the Oued Zondag valley into the heart of Jebel Abiod. After 0.5 km, take a right turn up a 3 km

track to the village of Beni Barka. It stretches like a white necklace below a ruined ksar, whose crumbling jagged walls appear to be teased up from the rock. The village adheres to old traditions, and even the row of modern houses sits on a seam of softer rock into which the back rooms are hacked.

From the summit of the ksar there is an extensive view over Tataouine and the mountains. Looking south you can just make out the ruins of Kalaa Blidet el Meguedmine which nestles around a volcanic plug. This was the fortress of a Berber tribe who claimed to have been overlords of Chenini until they were defeated by one Mansour, a name they ever after avoided giving to their sons.

The Maztouria Ksour

Further up the road, stretching on both sides of the Oued Zondag, is the sinuous palmery of Maztouria. The village is overlooked from the west by a row of three rectangular ksour, whose strength and regularity has given them the separate classification of *kherba* from the local word for ruin. The first *kherba* has an elegant gatehouse, with an intact beamed and stone-paved passage, flanked by rows of stone seats. The second *kherba*, which dates from the 11th century, is known variously as Kedim or Zenata. It is the presumed model for the half-dozen similar ksour in the area, and though the most ruinous, it has the thickest walls and most elegant masonry. Fortunately its vaulted gateway is now being restored. The ghorfas in the courtyard have some of the best decorated and inscribed vaults in the south, containing not only traditional Berber, but also Jewish and Kharijite influences. The third *kherba* is an oddity. It has a beamed gatehouse with an upper chamber, and a modern keep in the centre of its three-storey ghorfa courtyard, reached by a delightful network of irregular rustic stairways, and a floor of polished bedrock.

Tamelest

Five kilometres upriver is the small village of Tamelest, the hill above crowned by the scant ruins of Ksar Ouled Chehida. Initially, this served as the fortifed village of the Berber Gelawi tribe, whose old underground houses can still be seen on the slopes below the ksar. It then passed into the hands of the Arab Ouled Chehida, who grazed the plains immediately south of Jebel Abiod but required a ksar to store the tribute they received from the Berber Gelawi and Atemma tribes.

Sedra or Bou Ziri Ksar, on the other side of the valley, presents a more spectacular ruin. Drive 2 km beyond Tamelest and take the right turn which sweeps up close to the ksar. Sedra served for 600 years as the citadel of the Atemma before the tribe became clients of the Arab Ouled Chehida and Ouled Debbab tribes. The line of underground houses below the ksar are now deserted. The road continues, only to peter out after 7 km in a dusty, windswept village.

Ksar Ouled Soltane

Back on the main valley road, Ksar Ouled Soltane, around which a village has crystallized, is just 5 km from Tamelest, up a left turn at the Y-junction beyond the village. The ksar is one of the best preserved and most delightful in the region. Its two compact courtyards of four-storey ghorfas, eccentric staircases and wooden perches, are still partly in use. Be here around the midday Friday prayers to see the place at its liveliest. The first courtyard is more than 400 years old, and the second was built around 1850. It is named after a faction of the Arab Ouled Chehida tribe. On the horizon to the northeast of Ouled Soltane are three rocky promonotories once capped by fortified villages, from left to right: Tazeghanet, Techtout and Beni

Oussine. They predate the 11th-century Hilalian invasion but apart from a few underground houses are in total ruin. In 1911 they were heavily bombarded, for they sheltered the core of a revolt against the French which was backed by arms smuggled in from Turkish Libya.

Gettofa and Khrachoua

You may need a guide to find Gettofa, 8 km east of Tataouine, just off the track that passes through the hamlet of Beni Yekrzer and ends at Ksar Khrachoua. Gettofa has three parts. Ksar Kedim is an ancient fortified hilltop village belonging to the Berber Atteba tribe, with the 900-year-old mosque of El Azemma, and the three-storey Kasbah Arusa which is haunted by a couple who were poisoned here on their wedding night. Just to the west of the empty village are two other ksour, the 400-year-old Ksar Ajerda and Ksar Jelata, dated by an inscription to 1726.

Ksar Khrachoua was the home of Zaterna Berbers until the 16th century, when it was occupied by the Khrachoua who built the present four-storey ghorfas. The Khrachoua were allies of the powerful nomad tribes of the plain but not pure Arabs. At least half the tribe were by origin Berber nomads from the Libyan desert. This ksar is sometimes known as Kerbet el Khrachwa to distinguish it from another ksar of the tribe, known as Retbat el Khrachwa which was built in the Jefara plain, 40 km due south of Smar.

South of Tataouine

Borj el Khadra, the southernmost point of Tunisia, is 365 km from Tataouine, about the same distance that separates Tunis from Gabès. This considerable expanse is controlled by army garrisons at all the airstrips and principal waterholes in the desert. The only part of this region open to civilians is the road south from Tataouine through Remada to Dehibat, the recently opened border post with Libya. It is a long and unstimulating drive controlled by army checkpoints, and is of little interest unless you are aiming for Libya, or wish to see more of the hostile desert terrain without other tourists spoiling the view.

Three tribes of nomadic Arabs, the Dehibat, Traifia and Makhalba, have for centuries grazed the sparse plains of southernmost Tunisia and used its few waterholes. They had no kinship with the powerful Ouled Debbab to the north, and claimed to have been descended from the original 7th-century Arab invasion. They coexisted with the Berbers in the mountains and oases. The farmers gave their flocks into the care of the nomads who received a simple payment of corn and oil in return for the shepherding. This stable pattern was broken by the Ouderna, one of the seven sub-tribes of the Ouerghamma confederation. They wrested control of the hills from the Arabs and imposed such a brutal overlordship that the ksour were deserted.

Remada

The road south of Tataouine is dominated by the high plateau of the Jebel Demer to the west. The only break in the monotonous 90-km journey to Remada comes at Bir Thalatine, a village with mosque and café. Remada is a large village ringed by small patches of palmery garden, watered principally by artesian wells on the edge of the Oued Dhib river bed. The main street leads to a martyrs' monument and military barracks, its walls built on the ruins of a Roman fort from the Limes Tripolitanae. Remada's most distinctive sight, on the road out to the south, is a curious tamarisk-shaded group of 15 mudbrick koubbas, the old slaughter houses. Civilian life, such as it is, is focused on shady Pl de l'Indépendance, where you can buy shoes, shepherds' crooks and drink coffee with curious off-duty soldiers in the café. Dehibat, with its ruined ksar, on the Libyan border is a further 47 km.

The Brega Legend

The road to Borj Bourguiba, southwest of Remada, is military territory. The arid French military post was renamed after its most famous prisoner, who was held here in internal exile for a year. The legend of the Brega tribe, who dominated the surrounding land from Brega Ksar between the 11th and the 17th centuries, tells the tale of their exodus from the area in 1672. It also tells of a fragile and violent existence, torn between powerful local tribes and the wrath of central government.

Each year, Aissa ben Trif, the chief of the Traifa nomads, overlords of the Brega, demanded an increasingly onerous tribute. In 1672 he demanded that his great tent be filled with the soft white woollen blankets for which the Brega women were famous. Each family wove a blanket, but on the appointed day there was still room for one more blanket in the cavernous tent. To fill it, Ben Trif's slaves tore the haik off the daughter of the Sheikh of Brega, and that night the Sheikh fled this humiliation, leaving only a wooden bowl behind in his empty house. Next morning, the villagers peered under the bowl and found two pigeons, one of which was plucked. In its claw was a scrap of paper, declaring that 'those who leave will find a land of freedom, those who remain here in the shadow of the Traifa will find themselves without clothes or feathers.' That night the villagers burned the village and left. When the Traifa arrived next morning they found only the wooden bowl. They lifted it and one pigeon flew off in freedom, but the other was left cowering in the shadows. Aissa ben Traifa sent his fastest messenger to speak to the Sheikh, who stopped only long enough to curse that '...your men be killed in battle, ... your women be possessed by slaves and your flocks turned into burnt meat.' Before the year 1672 was out, the Brega were safely installed on the slopes of Jebel Bargou in the Tell, and the Traifa faced vengeance at the hands of Murad III. The Bey's army left nothing behind but dead men and burnt flesh, and took the women as prostitutes to the army barracks.

As to the truth, the Traifa were in fact decimated by government troops from Tripoli, not Tunis, and the Brega fled for the north, but only because the Traifa could no longer protect them from the Ouderna.

The Jefara Plain

There are two roads, from Medenine and Tataouine, that sweep across the high plateau of Jefara to Ben Guerdane. The Jefara is a land of herds and tents, though two years out of five there might be enough rain to plant wheat in the more sheltered depressions. It is traditionally the territory of the Ouled Debbah, an Arab tribe descended from the Beni Selim who held sway here from the 13th century. On the Tataouine road, the C111, there are ruined mud-brick ksour at Gheriani and Ksar Bhir, and better preserved ghorfas in the villages of Kirchaoua and Smar. Smar contains the only café on the 75-km journey, looking out over a central garden square.

These few settlements offer little evidence of the power and wealth of the Ouled Debbah as you cross the desolate plain. Many of the inhabitants, even now, live in round tents beside breeze-block houses, and the entire landscape has an air of transience. The Ouled Debbah, rather than build ghorfas on the plain, stored their corn underground. Wheat was packed in *rwani*, alfa sacks, and hidden in silos known as a *retba*, watched over by a shepherd given the role of guardian, the *rettab*.

Ben Guerdane

Ben Guerdane was founded by the Touzaine nomads, a branch of the Ouerghamma confederation, who built a ksar here to guard the produce of their client cultivators. The French expanded the area of olive cultivation, added some dreary colonial villas, but created a pleasant centre with a market square, overshadowed by the beautiful minaret and concertina dome of the old mosque.

The town now faces a second transformation. Since the reopening of the Libyan border, it has been transformed from a dead-end farming town into one of the liveliest markets in Tunisia. On Sundays, it is Tripoli at Ben Guerdane as Libyans and migrant workers stream across the border to shop. The market overflows on to the road which is lined with a staggering profusion of tacky carpets, plastic flowers, toys and pottery as well as grocery stalls, grill cafés and money-changers fanning great wads of notes. Hotels and restaurants in the centre proliferate, where once the Hotel Pavilion Vert and the Cafe el Oums had a monopoly.

Birhet el Bibane

North of Ben Guerdane the olive groves give way to a flat marshy flood plain that stretches east. To the east is the Birhet el Bibane, a shallow blue plain of seawater filled with oysters, flamingoes, wintering heron, egrets, spoonbills and smaller waders. The Birhet is almost sealed from the sea by two long spits. Where these threaten to meet, an island holds the shimmering white fort of Sidi Ahmed Chaouch.

Zarzis

Zarzis is a colonial creation, a motley collection of bungalows and a large, occupied barracks. It is not a great place for an independent beach holiday, though travel agents, who stress the sponge fishermen, the encirling olive groves, white sand and isolation have no problem filling up five large, package hotels. These are set in gardens well to the north of the town, attracting clusters of car hire firms, tour agents, restaurants and souvenir stalls. Central Zarzis is worth a visit on Friday, market day, and to see the signpost for Cairo, '2591 km' away. The old Turkish fort was demolished in 1978 to make way for a new mosque, and the archaeological museum in a disused church has been closed for years. Mouansa, a village just inland, is dominated by the twin trades of olive oil and weaving wool, has a good local market on Wednesday and no day-glo tourists.

If you do decide to stop over, use either the cheap **Hotel l'Olivier** in town, tel (05) 80637 or the beach-front **Amira Hotel**, below Hotel Zita, which has a dozen large bedrooms, a bar and a restaurant.

From Zarzis, it is a simple 20-km trip through olive groves to El Kantara (Continent), where the 7-km causeway to Jerba begins.

THE ISLE OF JERBA

Jerba, with its intensively cultivated farms, sprinkled with palm, fig and olive trees, seems luxuriant compared to the mainland. The traditional architecture of the island offers a low,

A Jerban Mosque

whitewashed silhouette of sunken weavers' workshops, four-square farmyards with blind outer walls, known as *houch* and a large number of small mosques. These are shorn of decoration, the angles and edges aged into gentle curves by layer upon layer of whitewash. At night the stumpy minarets and buttressed prayer halls are illuminated by strings of white bulbs.

The island's fertility, despite an outward appearance of ease, is only maintained by continuous labour. There is on average only 8 in of rain a year, and every available surface has been put to use as an *impluvium*, catching and channelling rain into underground cisterns. From the ubiquitous well-heads comes water that is mostly too salty for anything but the hardiest of crops. The majority of Jerba's water comes by pipeline from the mainland, across the El Kantara causeway. The dates grown here are of inferior quality, suitable only for animal consumption, and the yield from the often ancient olive trees is low. The sandy earth is not fertile enough to provide food for the island's 75,000 inhabitants, let alone for the tourists who fill the 40-odd hotels which line the beach at Sidi Maharès. Though tourism has created around 6000 new jobs, half the male population of Jerba continue the tradition of emigration, many following in the islanders' time-honoured occupation as grocers. One saving grace is the abundance of fish and squid in the waters around Jerba, where the shallowness of the sea discourages big commercial operators.

For the visitor, however, Jerba is still the land of the Lotus Eaters. The entire island is fringed with sandy beaches, and 'when you get there, there is, thank God, nothing on earth to do.' As well as the tourist development at Sidi Maharès, Houmt Souk, the island's only real town, has a clutch of good hotels and restaurants, and makes an excellent base from which to escape to deserted beaches during the day. The handful of island sights are easily explored by bike or moped for the island is only 29 km by 27 km, the roads are quiet and only one set of hills exceeds 50 m. The history of Jerba's much depleted Jewish population is kept alive at the 20th-century synagogue of La Griba, the Jerban tradition of pottery continues at Guellala and a number of corsair forts punctuate the extremities of the island.

343

History

The Lotus Eaters, a Literary Distraction

Jerba is one of the many islands that claims to be the land of the Lotus Eaters, briefly but tantalizingly described in Homer's *Odyssey*. Ulysses and his crew were distracted from their voyage after tasting the divine nectarous fruit of the Lotus, which caused 'insatiate riots in the sweet repasts, nor home nor other cares intrude'. It is a pretty enough description of narcotic bliss, which many authors insist refers to *laghami*. This is a crude alcoholic drink made from fermented palm sap which for a confirmed wine drinker like Ulysses would have had few attractions. Lotus fruit is also unlikely to refer to marijuana which was commonly consumed as a tea by boat crews to lull away the tedium of a sea voyage. Herodotus is sometimes used to back up Jerba's claims. In his description of the Berber tribes there is this passage: 'Within their territory a headland runs out into the sea, and it is here that the Lotus Eaters dwell, a tribe which lives exclusively on the fruit of the lotus. It is about the size of a mastic berry, and as sweet as a date. The Lotus Eaters also make wine from it.'

Phoenician Gifts

The Phoenicians in the 6th century BC brought enduring gifts to Jerba—the skills of metalwork, weaving, dyeing and pottery that still stand the island in good stead. In the Carthaginian and Roman period the island supported four independent towns: Tipasa, Haribus, Girba and Meninx. Meninx was the principal town as well as a general name for the island. It means the land of receding waters. The island's 2-m tide is nothing to those used to the Atlantic but is the largest in the Mediterranean. The island was connected to the mainland by a causeway and enjoyed brief celebrity as the birthplace of Gallus and his son Volusianus, a short-lived dynasty of Roman Emperors who reigned from 251–60. Scant ruins, beside the El Kantara causeway, revealed a large church with a cruciform marble baptistery, a lone but magnificent testimony to Jerba's Byzantine period, now on prominent display at the Bardo.

The Island of Ibadites

Jerba was the first part of Tunisia to accept Islam, conquered by Oqba ibn Nafi on his way north to found Kairouan. Following the short-lived overthrow of orthodox Arab rule by the Berber Kharijite revolt in 740, the extremist Ibadite creed remained in control of the desert fringe until hunted down by Fatimid armies in the 10th century. The survivors fled to Jerba, which became a sanctuary (a separate group survived at Mzab, an oasis of the Algerian Sahara), and save for two small Jewish villages was to remain exclusively Ibadite until the 17th century. They were known mockingly as the Khames, the fifths, for there are only four recognized orthodox creeds. The Jerbans have all the puritan attributes: industrious, self-reliant, mean and clannish, with a strong sense of communal solidarity, qualities compounded by continual threats of invasion.

The first and most terrible of these was that of the Hilalian Arabs in the 11th century. In the 12th century it came under Roger II, the Arabic-speaking Norman king of Sicily and in 1284 Roger de Lauria, the Aragonese viceroy of Sicily, built a fort on the island. Not until 1338 did the vigorous Hafsid ruler, Abu Bakr, expel the Spanish.

A Corsair Base

Jerba was used by pirates from the 14th century but gained added notoriety from 1500 when it became the base of El Aruj and his younger brother Barbarossa (see p. 46). In 1510 the Spanish struck back, but were repulsed by the islanders led by their sheikh. Reinforcements were summoned from Sicily and 1500 men landed later that year, on 30 August, but they were trapped by a salty well and massacred. Eight years later Christian raiders seized a galley off Jerba and presented Pope Leo X with Al Hassan ibn Mohammed, better known as Leo Africanus the author of *A History and Description of Africa*.

Dragut's Kingdom

In 1541–2 Barbarossa surrendered Tabarka to free his lieutenant Dragut who had served four years on the rowing bench of a Genoese galley. In return Dragut suppressed a revolt of Jerban sheikhs in 1550 and the following year whisked his fleet out of a Genoese trap by having the galleys dragged over the Jerban causeway.

In the next seven years Dragut carved out a new province for the Ottoman Empire, stretching inland to Gafsa and Kairouan and up the coast to Sfax. To disarm this growing threat Philip II of Spain ordered the invasion of Jerba, but the invasion fleet took two years to organize and four months to sail from Sicily to Jerba. Dragut, reinforced with an Ottoman fleet which had just completed a record crossing, from Istanbul to Jerba in 20 days, returned from a raiding trip and caught the Spanish completely unprepared, loading up with Jerban olive oil. He destroyed over half the ships and beseiged the stranded Spanish garrison for two months, rewarding their brave fight by using their skulls for a commemorative pyramid.

Tunisian Jerba

Jerba was only reconquered by the Tunisians in 1604. Jerbans began to work and travel on the mainland, though even now they seldom marry outsiders. The island had a measure of self-government from Tunis under dynasties of local Caids, but the Beys kept local politicians on their toes. In 1738, for instance, Caid Said Jallud was executed, his extensive family ruined and authority given to their rivals, the Banu Ayyad.

Jerba's tradition of independence was mirrored by the career of its most famous son, Salah ben Youssef. His radical pan-Arabism and opposition to Habib Bourguiba led the islanders to boycott the first elections in 1956.

GETTING AROUND

By Air

Jerba-Mellita airport is 8 km west of Houmt Souk, tel (05) 50233, and runs scheduled flights to Tunis, Tozeur and Monastir on Tunis Air. The Tunis Air office is on Av Habib Bourguiba, tel (05) 50159. The Syndicat d'Initiative on Pl des Martyrs offers a 'Tunis Shopping' tour on Thursdays for 75 dn, and two days and a night in Tozeur and Nefta, on Mondays and Tuesdays for the same price.

By Bus

The bus station in Houmt Souk is behind the Tunis Air office, on Rue Mosabh Jarbou, tel (05) 50233/50076.

The most useful local buses include: the no. 10, for Midoun and a trip round the island, the no. 11, which runs hourly along the coast as far as Cap Taguermès, the no. 12 which makes the journey to Ajim and the boat for the mainland four times a day, the no. 14, seven a day, which travels to Er Riadh and Guellala, and the no. 15 to the airport.

Services for the rest of the country are currently as follows: two buses a day for Gabès and Sfax, and one for Sousse, all in the morning. The two early evening departures for Tunis can be full, so book as far as possible in advance. There are also three buses a day for Medenine and two for Tataouine.

By Taxi

The blue island taxis are thin on the ground, but the best place to try to find one is on Av Habib Bourguiba. *Louages* also congregate here, near the Tunis Air office, mostly making journeys to Gabès and Medenine, but sometimes to Sfax and Tunis.

Car Hire

There is a plethora of car hire firms on Jerba. Topcar seems to have one of the best deals, at 265 dn a week, unlimited mileage plus tax and insurance. They have agencies in the large hotels and a head office in Houmt Souk, on Rue du 20 Mars, tel (05) 50536. Hertz's office is on Av Abdelhamid el Kadhi, but charges start at 336 dn a week for unlimited mileage, or 24 dn a day plus mileage. The speed limit on the island is 70 kph.

Bicycle and Motorbike Hire

Both of these are excellent ways of getting around Jerba. Even the most rusty cyclist will be able to manage the island's few inclines. Intercar at 173 Av Abdelhamid el Kadhi, tel (05) 51155, rent bicycles at 1 dn an hour, 6 dn a day and Mobylettes at 4 dn an hour, 15 dn a day. Most of the hotels also rent out bicycles; try the Sindbad in Houmt Souk, and out on Sidi Maharès beach, opposite the Hotel Strand, is a 'Location de Moto' shop where you can hire trail bikes, at a price.

TOURIST INFORMATION AND EXCURSIONS

Jerba's main **Tourist Office** is near the Old Fort on the road out of Houmt Souk towards Sidi Maharès beach, tel (05) 50016/ 50544. They are closed on Friday and Saturday afternoons, and all day on Sundays. The **Syndicat d'Initiative**, also a tourist office, is on Pl des Martyrs, off Av Habib Bourguiba, tel (05) 50157, and is also closed on Sundays.

The **PTT** is next to the Syndicat d'Initiative on Pl des Martyrs and there are **banks** the length and breadth of Av Habib Bourguiba. Stalls on this main road also sell foreign language newspapers during the season.

Before considering a **tour** of southern Tunisia, see if you are able to do it independently of an organized trip with its fixed routine of meal times, photo opportunities and staged events thinly disguised as an adventure. If you are unable to travel any other way, go to the Syndicat d'Initiative, which books a variety of itineraries through **Transtours**. These range from overnight landrover excursions to Kebili and Douz for 60 dn, an overnight trip to Ksar Ghilane for 60 dn and a three day tour of the Chott el Jerid for 85 dn.

For longer trips, try **AfricaTours**, on Av Abdelhamid el Kadhi, tel (05) 50291. They run an eight-day tour of the entire south for 250 dn, three-day trips for 100 dn, plus a variety of shorter excursions.

Houmt Souk

Houmt Souk literally means 'the marketplace' and is the only town of any size on the island. At its heart are a series of white, arcaded squares, bristling with café tables and shaded by rambling clusters of magenta bougainvillaea. Hidden away beside the squares is the maze of the souk, some stalls, traditionally selling the most valuable goods, in covered alleyways known as *qaysarriya*, others in open squares or along open streets. This marketplace has been taken over by the tourist trade, though at one time the only foreigners it would see were merchants, staying in one of the fondouks nearby, bargaining wholesale for goods that made the island famous: blankets, coral, cloisonné and sponges.

Religious Buildings

The three major religious buildings in Houmt Souk were all built for orthodox Muslims who did not share the puritan creed of the islanders. They are worth taking a quick look at, though the interior prayer halls are closed to non-Muslims. The Hanefite Mosque of the Turks is not far from the Hotel Sable d'Or. The minaret is a sympathetic combination of traditional architecture with a touch of decoration, a band of koranic inscription picked out in black and topped by a precarious lantern. Travellers to southern Tunisia in the 19th century were obssessed by apparent connotations of phallic worship enshrined in these lanterns. Looking at them, it is obvious that the obssession said more about the European observers than it ever did about the southern Tunisians.

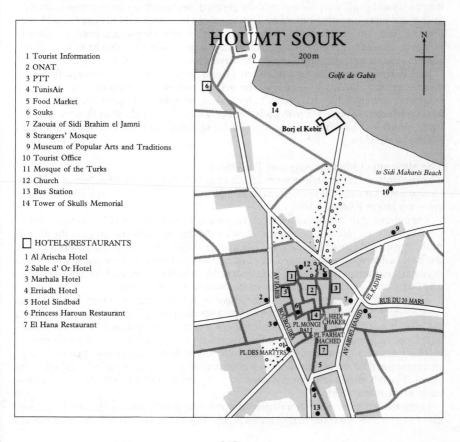

HOUMT SOUK

1 Tourist Information
2 ONAT
3 PTT
4 TunisAir
5 Food Market
6 Souks
7 Zaouia of Sidi Brahim el Jamni
8 Strangers' Mosque
9 Museum of Popular Arts and Traditions
10 Tourist Office
11 Mosque of the Turks
12 Church
13 Bus Station
14 Tower of Skulls Memorial

☐ HOTELS/RESTAURANTS
1 Al Arischa Hotel
2 Sable d' Or Hotel
3 Marhala Hotel
4 Erriadh Hotel
5 Hotel Sindbad
6 Princess Haroun Restaurant
7 El Hana Restaurant

Golfe de Gabès

Borj el Kebir

to Sidi Maharès Beach

347

The other two buildings, the Zaouia of Sidi Brahim el Jamni and the Stranger's Mosque flank Av Abdelhamid el Kadhi by Rue de Bizerte. The zaouia was founded in 1674, but was not completed until the early years of the next century, by Bey Murad ben Ali. Its walls are so solid they give the impression of a military garrison rather than the tomb of a holy man. By contrast, the Stranger's Mosque is a riot of cupolas and carving.

Borj el Kebir
(Open 08.00–12.00, 14.00–17.00, every day except Sun; adm)
The history of this fortress, also known as Borj Ghazi Mustapha, celebrates Jerba's maritime importance through the centuries. Originally built in the mid-15th century by Abu Fares el Hafsi, it was reinforced by the Spanish in 1560, and again under Dragut, by one Ghazi Mustapha, after he had expelled them. Beneath it, and now visible thanks to an archaeological dig in the central courtyard, is a 13th-century fortress built by the Sicilian admiral Roger de Lauria, who in turn built on Roman foundations. The bloodiest episode in the history of the fort was Dragut's two-month seige in 1560. When the corsair finally stormed Borj el Kebir, he massacred the Spaniards and piled their skulls up about 500 m away towards the port. The long bones and pelvis were used to hold the pyramid together; it was strengthened with dabs of clay and given a yearly whitewash. This gruesome memorial, said to have been 11 m in diameter, was only dismantled in 1848, when Jerba's Maltese population made a successful plea to be allowed to bury the bones. The pyramid is now commemorated by an insignificant concrete monument, standing alone on the waste ground between fort and port.

Borj el Kebir marks the eastern end of Houmt Souk's port, and is entered through a massive gateway, flanked by cannons. The dog-leg hall, or *sqifa*, gives on to a rectangular courtyard, surrounded by massive walls and a series of round and square towers. Passing a motley collection of pottery, a path leads through cool passages and out on to the walls of the castle, which look on to the sea over the remains of a moat. In the northern wall lies Ghazi Mustapha's koubba.

The Museum of Popular Arts and Traditions
Clearly displayed in the 18th-century zaouia of Sidi Zitouni, on Av Abdelhamid el Kadhi, Houmt Souk's museum is open from 09.00–12.00, 14.00–17.30 (15.00–18.30 in summer), every day except Fridays; adm.

The entrance hall, a high vaulted room, contains clothing from across the island, including some valuable old pieces of Jerban silk, showing the different sartorial habits of the island's Arab, Berber and Jewish populations. The picture of circumcision, normally performed by the local barber when a boy is aged six or more, shows a second child breaking a pot full of sweets at the moment of incision. This is designed to draw the attention of the jinn, evil spirits, who love blood, so that they do not enter the body of the young boy.

The second room displays a treasure trove of Jerban jewellery, made by the Jewish community and mirrored by an intricately carved wooden ceiling. The floor too, covered with old tiles, is worth a look. A staircase leads down to a reconstruction of a Jerban potter's workshop, half-underground to keep the clay moist. The two following courtyards and the room off them contain a display of Jerban pottery. The most characteristic type is the huge amphorae, used for storing anything from grain to clothing because of the lack of wood on the island. Though made within the last hundred years, these jars are exactly the same as those made in the Roman period.

In the vaulted tomb room, is a display of woodwork, from saints' catafalques to looking-glasses and chests. The saint in the koubba is famed for curing the mentally ill, and is reputed to be able to compel a dead woman to haunt her husband, should the husband make such a request.

Not far from the museum, continuing in the direction of the beach of Sidi Maharès, is one of the many weaving huts or *hanouts* in the island. Its triangular end-walls are connected by an undulating, corrugated roof and buttressed walls, like a chunky Toblerone. The men working inside are happy to have visitors, continuing to talk over the muted clack of wood on wood. The building is buried half-underground to keep it cool in summer and warm in winter.

The Port
In the morning and evening Houmt Souk's small port buzzes with the engines of returning and departing fishermen. In the winter squid season, you will notice thousands of plain pottery jars lined up on the quays. Squid like rocks to hide in, and in this sandy water they will get into anything you put down. In the morning, the fishermen simply pull the pots up with sleeping octopus inside. Occasionally you will still see sponges being brought from boats, black and slimy, until the algae have dried and been removed. Many of the fishermen are happy to take day excursions, at a price which should be fixed before you leave. Ask about excursions to Flamingo Island, tel (05) 50488, though these are normally booked in large groups.

Borj Jellid
The road to the airport leaves Houmt Souk from a turning near the PTT, and continues to the northwestern point of the island, about 12 km from the centre of town. Here, looking out over productive fishing waters and a small harbour, stands Borj Jellid, a ramshackle fort originally built in 1745 by Ali Pasha and transformed into a lighthouse in 1970. Out to sea, the tops of palm fronds appear above the waterline, describing large arrow shapes. These are fish-traps, which encourage the fish to swim up towards the tip of the arrow, where a net lies waiting to be checked daily by the fishermen. Taking the track along the edge of the beach back to town, there are miles of untouched sea-front to enjoy.

The Island

Four other roads fan out from Houmt Souk across the island. Two head roughly southeast, covering the beaches, hotels and the villages of Midoun and Aghir. The other two link Jerba to the mainland, via the causeway at El Kantara and the ferry at Ajim. Off the El Kantara road, the Jewish synagogue at La Griba and the potting village, Guellala, are both worth a visit. All the sites of the island can be visited in one day, if you rent a car, but it is more fun taking your time, by bus or by bike.

Midoun, Aghir and the Tourist Beaches
About 7.5 km from Houmt Souk on the road signposted to Plage Sidi Maharès, the best beach on the island begins, and is unspoiled and peaceful for a couple of kilometres before the beach hotels. Because of the shallowness of the water, it is impossible to swim on the south and east of the island, and this is therefore one of the best spots for sunbathers in search of silence. With the Ulysse Palace Hotel, the build-up begins, and continues for 17 km to the village of Aghir, itself little more than its Youth Hostel. The quietest area in the stretch is Cap

Taguermês, between the Sidi Yati and Tanit hotels, down a turning 19 km from town. Three kilometres beyond Aghir on the road to El Kantara, a track leads off to the left, to Borj Kastil, the remains of a fort built on the promontory in 1285 by Roger de Lauria, during the 50-year Sicilian occupation of the island.

A road from Houmt Souk and a number from the beaches lead inland to Midoun, a small town entirely overrun by package tourism. Every afternoon at 15.30 there is a Jerban wedding procession, and at the modern *café touristique* a camel walks pointless, picturesque circles around the well, lifting its salty contents. Try to time a fleeting visit to coincide with the market, on Friday morning, and there is a *maasera*, an underground olive mill north of the town. It is off the road to Tourguenès, 100 m from the hospital and behind the well on the left. The millstones are 300 years old, though the building has been frequently retouched.

La Griba Synagogue, Guellala and El Kantara

It is 25 kilometres from Houmt Souk to El Kantara and its causeway to the mainland, passing the characteristic, fortified Mosque Umm et Turkia at El May on the way. Six kilometres from the capital, a right turn leads to Er Riadh, which at the turn of the century still housed a Jewish community and was known as Hara es Seghira, the Little Ghetto, a sister to the larger Hara Kbira, near Houmt Souk.

Jerba's Jewish community has dwindled to around 1000, emigration to Israel and Jerba's limited opportunities being the major reasons. It claims to be one of the earliest in the world, founded after the exile from Jerusalem in the 6th century BC, and replenished by Jews fleeing the holy city after it was taken by Titus in AD71.

Those that remain, largely old men and women, perhaps do so because of the **El Griba (Marvellous) Synagogue**. Just outside Er Riadh, it is one of the most holy Jewish buildings in North Africa, the site of a pilgrimage on 22 and 23 May which fills its neighbouring pilgrims' hotel. The present synagogue was built in the 1920s, but the site was supposedly chosen in 600 BC, when a holy stone fell from heaven, and a mysterious stranger, a girl, appeared to direct the building. To round off the myth, the last Jew on Jerba is charged with locking the synagogue and throwing the key back up to heaven. Except during Sabbath services on Saturday mornings, the synagogue welcomes visitors, making sure that their heads are covered, and tries to fleece them at every turn. The building is not beautiful, weighed down by dark wood panelling, tiles and stained glass, but it has a memorable atmosphere created by the elderly Jews who sit inside all day. A guide might give you a brief glimpse of El Griba's pride, a *Torah* with extravagant claims to antiquity.

The road through Er Riadh continues a further 11 km to the pottery centre of the island, **Guellala**, a group of houses and smoking kilns. Clay continues to be extracted from the hills above the town, which are pock-marked with staircases leading deep underground. Daily charabancs of tourists have adversely affected quality, but the showman and enthusiast Ben Mahmoud Ramdan is worth a visit. His emporium is hidden behind a large pair of blue Andalucian studded doors, and you can watch him at the wheel, take a look at the underground oil mill and press (*maassera*) and buy one of the irresistibly kitsch magic camels.

A road from Guellala continues back to the main road at the village of Sedouikech. Just north of El Kantara, by the turning to the eastern beaches, stony ground marks the ruins of Meninx, a town established by the Carthaginians as a centre for the production of purple dye from murex shellfish. The town continued this trade during the Roman era, supplying imperial purple for the courts at Rome, and became an important centre of Christianity. The plain marble cruciform baptistery in the Bardo, the model for George Sebastian's bath-tub in Hammamet, was found here.

The Carthaginians also built a causeway to the mainland from El Kantara, which lasted until Dragut, in 1551, breached it in order to escape from the Genoese. After independence, the route was restored and a vital but unsightly water pipeline added.

Ajim

The 21-km journey from Houmt Souk to the ferry at Ajim crosses Jerba at its flattest and least interesting. Ferries cross every half-hour 05.30–20.30, hourly 20.30–23.30 and at 01.00, 03.00 and 04.30. If you have to wait, you can eat under a raffia umbrella at the Restaurant Complex de l'Oasis. Once famed for its sponge fishing, Ajim is now just an all-purpose fishing port and transport centre.

FESTIVALS

In August, a *festival d'Ulysses* takes place in Houmt Souk, concentrating on the songs, dances and traditions of the island.

HAMMAMS

At the port end of Av Habib Bourguiba, next to the Tunisian craft shop, the ONAT, Hammam Ziadi is well used to foreigners. For 2 dn you not only get clean, you get scraped and pummelled by the masseur; men in the mornings, women in the afternoons.

There is also a hammam 30 m from the Zaouia of Sidi Brahim el Jamni, on Rue de Bizerte.

SHOPPING

Houmt Souk means marketplace, and the centre of the town is a maze of shops, complemented by pavement salesmen. Jerba was once famed for coral and rich cloisonné jewellery, made by the Jewish community in a Byzantine style. Today's offerings are less opulent, but some of the filigree silver work is still good value. The workshop and shop called Main de Fatimah, just off Pl Hedi Chaker, is a good place to acquaint yourself with the local style, before plunging into the souk. Another local speciality to consider is blankets, which are of superb quality. On Av Abdelhamid el Kadhi, there is a family-run antique and carpet business called Hadji, opposite the offices of InterRent. Here you can find fine painted furniture, old killims, puppets and silk.

The market for buying picnics, on the corner of Av Habib Bourguiba and Av Abdelhamid el Kahdi, is partly open every day, but market days, when it is brimming with goods and people, are Monday and Thursday mornings.

WHERE TO STAY

In Houmt Souk

MODERATE

The **Hotel Sables d'Or**, at 30 Rue Mohammed Ferjani, tel (05) 50423, is one of Tunisia's best hotels. Most of its 12 well-decorated rooms open on to the first-floor balcony of a central courtyard. The rooms all have showers and basins, though the loos are communal, and are kept spotless by the brothers who run the place.

Several of Houmt Souk's other hotels occupy converted fondouks, where foreign merchants would have lived, their goods stored and pack animals securely stabled round a guarded courtyard, while trading on the island. The recently renovated **Hotel Erriadh**, just off Pl Hedi Chaker, tel (05) 50756, is the most expensive. It has elaborately tiled walls, 28 immaculate bedrooms with bathrooms, air conditioning and heating.

CHEAP
The basic **Hotel Marhala**, on Rue Moncef Bey, tel (05) 50146, surrounds a pretty old courtyard and once served as a fondouk as well. The prettiest, with a well in the centre of the courtyard, is the **Hotel El Aricha**, behind the Catholic church on Pl de l'Eglise, tel (05) 50384. Because of its bar it is a bit more noisy, but prices are similar to the Marhala. A fourth fondouk hotel, the **Sindbad**, is on Pl Mongi Bali opposite the PTT. It is rather darker than the others, but can be resorted to if the others are full.

On the Beach
Most of beach hotels are crowded together on Plage Sidi Maharès, with little to chose between them.

EXPENSIVE
At the top end of the market try the **Hotel el Menzel**, on Plage de la Séguia, tel (05) 57070, one of the smartest on the island, with 85 dn rooms arranged in a series of houses, designed with an eye to the local architecture on a promontory leading to the sea. Each has its own private balcony, bathroom and sitting-room, and the hotel provides watersports of all kinds.

MODERATE
Cheaper but still very civilized, and a fair distance from any others at the end of Sidi Maharès beach on Cap Taguermês, is **Hotel Sidi Yati**, tel (05) 57016. The 44 clean, bright and simple bedrooms are ranged round a series of blue and white courtyards. The restaurant is good, and the manager sells the hotel on its peacefulness. As a result there are no watersports facilities, but there is a swimming pool. Walking further down the beach, you will find waterskiing and windsurfing catered for at the **Hotel Tanit**, where they are happy to rent the facilities to outsiders.

CHEAP
If you want to camp by the beach, the best **campsite** is next to the **Club Sidi Ali Hotel** beyond Cap Taguermês. The hotel also has bedrooms in stone huts on the beach which it rents out and a restaurant, open in the evenings only.

EATING OUT
Out on the beachfront there is little to choose from, though the restaurant at the **Hotel Sidi Yati** stands out and the Hotel Strand should be avoided. There are a host of different restaurants to sample in Houmt Souk, from cheap cafés on Av Habib Bourguiba to sophisticated fish restaurants.

Houmt Souk's licensed restaurants are relatively expensive and most of them are clustered around Pl Hedi Chaker. Of these, **Restaurant du Sud**, tel (05) 50479, just off the square is the best, though it can get a bit noisy as the staff seem to relish large parties. **Restaurant Méditerranée**, tel (05) 50702, on the corner of Rue de Bizerte and Moncef Bey, on the other hand, is small, tranquil and has excellent service. Both cost about 15 dn for two without wine,

20 dn with. The other place in town you should try is **Restaurant el Hana**, on Pl 7 Novembre 1987, tel (05) 50568. It is slightly cheaper, and serves a delicious *soupe de poisson*, and good fresh fish for up to 5 dn a dish. The restaurant's popularity is compensated for by a rash of tables outside. The smartest restaurant on the island is the **Princesse de Haroun**, on Houmt Souk's port. You should book a table in advance on (05) 50488, and save your pennies for lobster, exceptional squid and a good selection of wine.

Of the cheaper crowd, the **Restaurant du Sportif**, Av Habib Bourguiba, serves a good three-course meal for under 4 dn. Other restaurants nearby are equally good value, as is the busy place opposite Hotel Sables d'Or, on Rue Mohammed Ferjani.

GLOSSARY OF HISTORICAL, ARCHITECTURAL AND ARABIC TERMS

Abassids: the 2nd dynasty of Caliphs who ruled the Muslim world from Baghdad from 750–1258.

Abd (pl. **Abid**): a slave or servant, and by inference a negro. It is widely used to create names in conjunction with one of the 99 names of God, as in Abdal-Aziz, servant of the Mighty.

Aesculapius: Roman equivalent of the Greek god of healing, Asclepius, also equated with the Carthaginian vegetation and corn god, variously known as Eshmoun or Adonis (a corruption of the semitic for 'my Lord, my Master'), whose cult celebrated the mysteries of death and rebirth. The Carthaginian deity was of extraordinary beauty, born of a Cedar tree, into which his mother Tanit had transformed herself. He is often depicted holding a spear on the watch for the wild boar that is fated to kill him each spring.

Aghlabids: rulers of Tunisia from 750–910.

Aid: a feast, as in Aid es Seghir, the small feast, at the end of Ramadan and Aid el Kebir, the large feast, that commemorates the sacrifice of Abraham.

Ain (pl. **Aioun**): a spring or waterhole.

Aissa: the Arabic name for Jesus.

Aissaouia: a Sufi religious brotherhood, founded in Morocco in the 17th century.

Ali: the cousin and son-in-law of Mohammed by his marriage to Fatimah, and the founder of Sufism. He became the 4th Caliph but his reign was responsible for the split between the Sunni, Shiite and Ibadite sects.

Almohad: the unitarians. An Islamic reform movement which developed into a North African Empire and ruled Tunisia between 1159–1230.

Andalucia: the Muslim area of southern Spain, from 714–1493. Recurring disputes with the Christian kings of Spain saw a continuous flow of refugees from these cultured states to Tunisia, until the last migration in 1610.

Arabesque: loose description of Islamic decoration.

Baal Hammon: Lord Hammon, the two horned god of the sky and fertility was the principal male god of the Carthaginians, whom the Romans equated with Saturn and the ancient North African god Ammon. He is depicted as a dignified and bearded old man seated on a high-backed throne. Pine cones and pomegranates were sacred to him, and he was worshipped with gifts of bread and wine served on a gold table, sacrifices of male animals and in times of danger by a *moloch*, a fire sacrifice of boys.

Bab: a gate.

Bachiya: one of the two opposing sides into which the towns and tribes divided during the 18th-century succession war. Their adversaries were **Hassinya**.

Baraka: a blessing or holy luck. A gift passed down through saintly dynasties, and obtained by pilgrims at the shrines of saints.

Basilica: a large apsed building built by the Romans as law courts and used as a model for the first churches.

Bes: known by the Greeks as Ptah Pataikos, the Phoenician dwarf, and frequently used as a ship's figurehead. This Carthaginian god was depicted as a dwarf with bow legs, prominent belly and protruding tongue. He often wears a leopard skin loincloth, an ostrich feather headdress and a skull necklace. He was a buffoon, fond of dancing and fighting but also presided over childbirth, women's toilet and could chase away evil spirits, bad dreams, snakes and poisonous insects.

Bey: originally an Ottoman military title. In Tunisia from 1591–1637 it designated the military official in charge of imposing law and raising taxes from the interior. From 1637–1881 it was the title used by the reigning member of the Muradite and Husseinite dynasty, whose heir was often designated the Bey du Camp and fulfilled its earlier functions. From 1881–1956 the Beys were mere window dressing for the French colonial regime.

Beni: the sons of, often used in the description of a tribe. The Berber equivalent is **Ait**.

Bir: a well.

Borj: a fort.

Burnous: a man's heavy, woollen, hooded cloak.

Cadi: a judge of Muslim law (sharia).

Caid: the chief magistrate of a town, province or tribe.

Caliph/Khalifa: the successor to the Prophet's leadership of the Muslim community. The Almohad and Hafsid dynasties were the only Tunisian ones to use the title, which implies a claim to the sole leadership of the entire Muslim world.

Capitol: the main temple complex in a Roman town, named after the temples to Jupiter, Juno and Minerva on the Capitoline Hill at Rome.

Cella: the inner sanctuary of a Roman temple.

Chechia: a hat traditionally made by Andalucians in Tunisia from knitted white wool, that is washed, beaten and reduced to its proper size by repeated dyeing and drying. Normally red, they are then scraped, pressed and brushed with a teazle.

Cursive: the most common style of flowing rounded Arabic script.

Damascene: a decorative inlay, usually of silver or copper on iron or brass.

Dar: a house, building or palace. City quarters are often named after the most distinctive house of the quarter.

Dey: an uncle, a Turkish officer in command of 100 men and the title of rulers of Tunisia between 1591–1705 after which it referred to the officer in charge of Tunis

Donatism: a 3rd-century Christian schism, created by a bishop of Carthage, which insisted that the sacrament was only as good as the person who administered it.

Dragut: celebrated corsair captain, 1485–1565. Originally called Torghoud, he was born the son of a Turkish peasant, trained as a Mameluke in Cairo and then captained a corsair boat operating off Alexandria before joining Barbarossa in North Africa.

Erg: dunes or region of dunes in a desert.

El: the remote head of the Carthaginian pantheon, the father of years, who existed before the world and dwelt by the far western shore.

Eshmoun: see Aesculapius.

Fantasia: a display of horsemanship featuring small charges, dramatic halts and the firing of muskets.

Fatimah: the only surviving daughter of Mohammed. The central female cult figure of Islam who absorbed many earlier beliefs, like the Hand of Fatimah, an ancient good luck symbol. The Fatimid dynasty claimed descent from her.

Fiqh: the Islamic legal code. There are four traditional codes acknowledged by the orthodox Muslim: Malekite, Hanefite, Chafiite and Hanbalite.

Fondouk: a courtyard in which merchants would stay, living in rooms on the first floor, above their stabled animals and goods. Also an artisan and trading centre.

Forum: the central square in a Roman town, the focal point of the town's commerce, law, politics and religion.

Gandoura: a simple cotton tunic worn by men.

Garum: a fish paste, made of salt and rancid, mashed tuna intestines, beloved by the ancient Romans.

Ghorfa: a barrel-vaulted chamber for storing agricultural produce in a ksar.

Habous: money endowed for the upkeep of religious buildings and associated charity, confiscated in Tunisia in the first years of independence to be administered by the state.

Hadith: the collected sayings and actions of the Prophet as remembered by his companions.

Hafsid: Tunisia's ruling dynasty from 1230–1574.

Haik: a large cloth used by women to cover themselves in the street, a predominately urban habit. They are white in the north, black in the south.

Haj: the title earned by those who make the pilgrimage to Mecca

Hammam: public baths.

Hanefite: one of the four schools of Sunni law and the one followed by most Ottoman Turks. Hanefite mosques are distinguished by octagonal minarets.

Hara: the old Jewish quarters of Tunis and Jerba.

Hegira: the Islamic era, which began with the flight of Mohammed from Mecca to Medina in July 622. The Muslim calendar is based on a lunar rather than a solar year and is therefore 11 days shorter than each Gregorian year.

Henna: a red dye is made from the powdered leaves of the henna tree for hair and creating intricate patterns on hands and feet.

Hilali: a nomadic Bedouin tribe which, with the **Sulaym**, left the Arabian peninsula in the 11th century and destroyed the achievements of centuries of civilization in North Africa in one destructive sweep.

Husseinites: the dynasty who ruled Tunisia from 1705–1957, the last 76 years as puppets of the French.

Ibadites: a Kharijite sub sect who took refuge in Jerba.

Ibn Khaldoun: Tunisian historian and sociologist, 1332–1406, and the country's greatest literary figure—see under Literature.

Ifriqiyya: the name given by the Arabs to Tunisia, plus useful bits of Algeria and Libya on either side.

Imam: the leader of communal prayers, used by Shiites to describe the political leader.

Jebel/Djebel: a mountain. A Jebella is also a city dweller's label of contempt for countrymen.

Jedid: new, often applied to gates.

Jellaba: a large cotton or wool coat with sleeves and a hood, worn by men.

Jihad: the struggle and by extension, holy war, against the enemies of Islam.

Jinn: invisible spirits, referred to in the Koran, that can be malicious or helpful.

Kaaba: a square sanctuary in Mecca, supposedly situated on the spot were Abraham erected his altar. Inside, amongst other things, is a black stone meteorite, venerated from antiquity. Muslims pray towards the Kaaba and circle it seven times before kissing it as the culmination of the pilgrimage.

Kalaa: drystone walled hillfort.

Kasbah: the citadel of a town or a rural fortress. The meaning of the word has been extended to describe any defensive building.

Kharijite: an early puritanical faction of Islam that believes that the community of Islam is restricted to the active body of worshippers and governed by an elective leadership. This creed was especially attractive in 739 when the Berbers wished to retain Islam but overthrow their harsh Arab rulers.

Khatib: a preacher who delivers the **khutba**, the sermon after noon prayers on Friday.

Killim: a woven rug, known when embroidered as a **mergoum**.

Kohl: powder ground from sulphur of antimony. Applied to the eyes, it stimulates a watery sheen that protects against soot and sand.

Koran: the word of God dictated in Arabic to Mohammed by the Archangel Gabriel and later compiled into the Muslim holy book.

Koubba: a dome, and, by extension, a saint's tomb.

Kurughlis: the children born to a native mother and a Turkish soldier

Ksar (pl. **Ksour**): a fortified village. The Arabic noun is derived from the Latin 'Caesar'.

Kufic: the angular hieratic style of Arabic script used mostly in stone carving and named after Kufa in Iraq.

Lalla: lady, a title of respect used for a female saint or woman of dignity.

Leo Africanus: 16th-century author of *A History and Description of Africa*—see under Literature.

Maghreb: literally, 'setting': the region that comprises Tunisia, Algeria and Morocco.

Mahalla: an armed tax-collecting expedition.

Malekite: the school of law widely followed in North Africa, formulated by the 8th-century Malik ibn Anas.

Mameluke: officials, acquired as child slaves from the Christian provinces of the Ottoman Empire and trained to fill high government positions.

Maqsara: a wooden screen in a mosque that protect rulers from assassination.

Marabout (pl. **murabitun**): a holy man and hence the shrine that covers his tomb.

Mauretania: the kingdom of Mauretania was divided by the Romans into two provinces, Mauretania Cesariensis and Mauretania Tingitana. Present day Mauritania is a country below Morocco.

Mecca: the sacred Muslim town in Saudi Arabia.

Medersa: a residential school for the study of the Koran and religious law, which proliferated from the 13th century.

Medina: a walled city or old quarter. Named after the city where Mohammed fled to avoid persecution in Mecca.

Merlons: decorative battlements.

Mihrab: a niche in a place of prayer which indicates the direction of Mecca.

Minbar: a pulpit-like staircase in mosques used for the noontide Friday sermon.

Mohammed: founder of Islam, who is believed to be the greatest and last in the succession of prophets, including Abraham, Noah, Moses and Jesus, who called man to the one God.

Mouloud: the feast celebrating Mohammed's birthday on the 12th day of the Muslim month of Rabi at-Tani.
Moussem: an annual popular pilgrimage to the tomb of a saint and by extension any festival or outdoor entertainment.
Muezzin: the call to prayer, and also the caller.
Mufti: Islamic lawyer who issues judgements known as *fatwa*.
Muradite: ruling dynasty of Beys from 1637–1702.

Nador: a watchtower.
Nasrani: a Christian.

Omayyads: the first dynasty of Caliphs who ruled the Islamic world from Syria between 660–750.
Oued: a river.
Ouerghamma: a tribal confederation that dominated southeast Tunisia from the 16th century. The **Ouderna** were their most militant and aggressive faction.

Palaestrum: exercise yard/gymnasium.
Pasha: Ottoman governor of Tunisia from 1574–1590, after which it became a purely honorific title.
Phoenicians: merchants from half a dozen cities on the coast of Lebanon who settled the Tunisian coast from 1000 BC and introduced the higher civilization of the Near East. From their chief city at Carthage they dominated the western Mediterranean from 6th–2nd centuries BC.
Pise: packed earth used to make walls and roads.
Ptah Patèque/Pataikos: see **Bes**.
Punic: the adjective used to describe all things emanating from Phoenician Carthage—see Phoenicians.

Ramadan: Muslim month of fasting, the ninth lunar month of the year. No food, drink or sex is allowed during daylight hours. Travellers, the sick, the old, the pregnant and children are exempt.
Ribat: a fortified monastery, usually built from 7th–10th centuries to protect the coast from Vikings and Christians and as bases for raiding Sicily and Italy.

Sanhaja: one of three tribal groupings of Berbers, occupying the Saharan fringe.
Sebkha (pl. Sebkhet): inland lake, lagoon or seasonal salt-marsh.
Shahada: the profession of faith: *La illaha ill'Allah, Mohammed rasul Allah*—there is no God but God and Mohammed is his Prophet.
Sharia: the Islamic code of law, as revealed in the Koran and Hadith.
Sheikh: the leader of a religious brotherhood, tribe or village.
Sherif/Sharif (pl. Shorfa): a descendant of Mohammed.
Shia/Shiite: the major heretical sect in Islam, whose believers, Shiites, consider that the Caliphate should have been inherited by the children of Ali and Fatimah.
Sidi/Si: a male honorific title, often used to denote a saint.
Souk: a market.
Stele (pl. stelae): tombstone.
Sufi: the group of related mystical brotherhoods, who cultivate techniques of chanting and dancing to attain an ecstatic union with God.
Sultan: ruler, a word of Turkish origin.

358

Sunna: orthodox Islamic dogma followed by Sunnis.
Sura: a verse of the Koran.

Tanit: the principal goddess of the Carthaginian religion, often worshipped in conjunction with Baal Hammon and addressed as the consort or face of Baal. She had numerous lesser attributes, which allowed the Romans to equate her with Juno, Venus and Minerva. The symbol of Tanit is a triangle with outstretched, supplicating arms and a vestigial head. She is also represented by a crescent moon or with her head surmounted by a disk between two horns.
Tolba: students, and by implication koranic reciters.

Ulema: a council of professors of Islamic law, who are consulted to approve of new laws.
Umma: the Muslim community of believers.

Vizier/wazir: a minister, as in *wazir al akbar*, prime minister.

Wadi: a dry river bed or watercourse.
Wali: a friend, as in wali Allah, a friend of God, hence a saint.

Zaouia/Zawiya: a complex attached to the tomb of a saint, where mystical studies, charity and prayer take place.
Zirids: the Berber dynasty which ruled Tunisia from 973–1060.

CHRONOLOGY

Keydates

814 BC	Foundation of Phoenician Carthage
202	Romans win Second Punic War against Carthaginians at Battle of Zama
146	Romans destroy Carthage and set up province of Africa Proconsularis
46	Caesar defeats Pompey in Civil War at the Battle of Thapsus
AD 238	El Jem and Sousse rebel and are sacked by Romans
312	Emperor Constantine converts to Christianity
439	Vandals capture Carthage
533	Belisarius conquers Vandals
670	First Arab invasion and foundation of Kairouan by Oqba ibn Nafi
698	Hassan ibn Numan completes Arab conquest
739	Kharijite revolt of Berbers against ruling Arabs
800–909	Golden Century of the Aghlabids
915	Fatimids triumph and found Mahdia
1051	Invasion of Hilalian Arabs
1520–80	Hapsburg-Ottoman War leaves Tunisia in Ottoman hands
1705	Hussein ibn Ali Turki establishes the Husseinite dynasty (1705–1881)
1881	French occupy Tunisia
1934	Foundation of Neo-Destour party at Ksar Hellal
1956	Tunisia gains independence from France
1957	Foundation of the Republic by Habib Bourguiba
1987	7 November 'Doctor's Coup'—Ben Ali becomes President

List of Rulers

Carthaginian Empire, 6th century BC to 146 BC

Numidian Kings, 202 BC to 46 BC

202–148	Massinissa
148–118	Micipsa
118–105	Jugurtha
108–81	Hiarbas
108–61	Hiempsal II
60–46	Juba I

Africa Proconsularis, a province of the Roman Empire, was ruled by governors at Carthage from **146 BC– AD 429.** A separate southern province, Byzacena, was created in AD 309.

146–27	Senate and People of Rome
27 BC–AD 14	Augustus
14–37	Tiberius
37–41	Gaius Caligula

41–54	Claudius
54–68	Nero
68–69	Galba, Otho and Vitellius
69–79	Vespasian
78–81	Titus
81–96	Domitian
96–98	Nerva
97–117	Trajan
117–138	Hadrian
138–161	Antoninus Pius
161–180	Marcus Aurelius (161–9 with Lucius Verus)
178–193	Commodus
193–211	Septimius Severus
211–217	Caracalla (211–12 with Geta)
217–218	Macrinus
218–222	Heliogabulus
222–235	Alexander Severus
235–238	Maximinus
238–284	20 short-lived Emperors
284–305	Diocletian (and Tetrarchy)
306–337	Constantine (sole ruler from 311)
337–361	Constantine II (with Constans until 350)
361–363	Julian the Apostate
364–378	Valens
375–383	Gratianus
375–392	Valentinian II
379–395	Theodosius I
395–423	Honorius
425–455	Valentinian III

Vandal Kings, ruled from Carthage, 429–533

429–477	Genseric
477–484	Huneric
496–523	Thrasamund

Byzantine Emperors appointed Exarchs of Carthage, 533–698

527–565	Justinian
565–578	Justin II
578–582	Tiberius II Constantine
582–602	Maurice
602–610	Phocas
610–641	Heraclius
641–668	Constans II
668–685	Constantine IV
685–695	Justinian II
695–698	Leontius

643–705	Arab conquest
705–800	Wilaya of Ifriqiya ruled by Emirs of the Ommayad and Abbasid Caliphate

Aghlabid Emirs, 800–910

800–812	Ibrahim ibn al Aghlab
812–817	Ibrahim II
817–837	Ziyadat Allah I
841–856	Mohammed I
856–863	Abu Ibrahim Ahmed
863–864	Ziyadat Allah II
864–875	Mohammed II
875–902	Ibrahim II
902–903	Abdullah II
903–909	Ziyadat Allah III

Fatimid Caliphs, 910–969

(902–910	Abu Abdullah)
910–934	Ubayd Allah
934–946	Al Qaim
946–953	Ismail al Mansur
953–975	Al Muizz

Zirid Emirs, 973–1148

973–984	Yusuf Buluggin ibn Ziri
984–996	Al Mansur
996–1016	Badis
1016–1051	Al Muizz

Almohad Caliphs, 1159–1230

1159–1162	Abdel Moumen
1163–1184	Abu Yacoub Youssef
1184–1199	Yacoub el Mansour
1199–1213	Mohammed en Nair
1213–1223	Youssef el Mustansir
1223–1229	Al Ma'mun

Hafsid Caliphs, 1230–1574

1228–1249	Abu Zakariyya
1249–1277	Al Mustansir
1277–1279	Abu Yahya al Wathiq
1279–1283	Abu Ishaq
1284–1295	Abu Hafs
1295–1309	Abu Asida
1309–1311	Abu Bagu
1311–1318	Ibn al Lihyani
1318–1347	Abu Bakr
1347–1369	Abu Ishaq ibn Bakr
1370–1394	Abu Abbas
1394–1434	Abu Faris
1435–1488	Abu Amr Othman
1490–1494	Abu Yahya

1494–1526	Mohammed al Hassan
1526–1542	Al Hasan
1542–1573	Ahmed
1574	Mohammed (taken to Istanbul)

Deys and Muradite Beys, 1574–1705

1574–1590	Ottoman Pashas
1594–1610	Dey Othman
1610–1637	Youssef Dey
1631–1666	Hammouda Pasha I
1666–1675	Murad Bey II
1675–1684	Bey Mohammed el Hafsi
1684–1702	Muradite princes
1702–1705	Dey Ibrahim al Sharif

Husseinite Beys, 1705–1881

1705–1740	Hussein ibn Ali Turki
1734–1756	Ali Pasha I
1756–1758	Mohammed ar-Rachid
1758–1781	Ali Pasha II
1781–1813	Hammouda Pasha II
1813–1814	Othman ibn Ali
1814–1823	Mahmoud
1823–1835	Hussein II
1835–1837	Mostafa
1837–1854	Ahmed I
1854–1859	M'hammed
1859–1882	Mohammed es Sadok

French Protectorate, 1881–1956, ruled by French resident general with puppet Beys

1882–1902	Ali III
1902–1906	Mohammed al Hadi
1906–1922	Mohammed an Naasir
1922–1929	Mohammed al Habib
1929–1942	Ahmed II
1942–1948	Mohammed al Moncef
1948–1957	Mohammed al Amin

Independence 1956

Tunisia declared a republic 25 July, 1957.

Presidents:

| 1957–1987 | Habib Bourguiba |
| 1987– | Ben Ali |

LANGUAGE

The official language of Tunisia is Arabic, and a very small percentage of the population in the south also still speak an indigenous Berber language. Most of the people you are likely to meet will also speak fluent French, a hangover from colonial times, but one which is now causing problems. Whole magazine issues and countless newspaper articles address the problem of how to curb office 'Frarabic', a language spoken by officials and on the telephone which jumps, word by word, between Arabic and French, and is not only difficult for the uninitiated to understand, but is rotting both languages from the inside.

With two languages already under their belts, many Tunisians also speak a third, either English or German. They will be surprised enough if an English speaker addresses them in French, but speaking even a few words of Arabic causes merriment and instant friendship, and could make a difference to your stay. By showing interest and learning a little, you will not only be unusual but it will also help to chip away at some of the prejudices and barriers that separate our cultures.

Below you will find a useful core of Arabic words and phrases also translated into French, followed by more complicated phrases in French only and a section to help you in restaurants, translated into both languages.

Arabic

Written Arabic is the same from Iraq to Morocco, and throughout the Arab world newspapers and television presenters speak a universal modern language, similar to that spoken in Cairo. However, spoken Tunisian Arabic, a form of Maghrebi Arabic, is unique, as are the hybrids spoken in neighbouring Libya and Algeria, and there are no phrase books for it. If you know Arabic of any kind, it will of course be useful, but don't expect conversation to be easy.

Pronunciation
Arabic is a universally guttural language, but this does not mean that it should be hard sounding. As a general rule, hard consonants should be pronounced as far back in the throat as possible, thereby softening them slightly. In particular:

'gh'   should sound like a purring 'gr', from the back of the throat, a hardened French 'r'

'kh'   like a Gaelic 'ch', is pronounced again at the back of the throat, as in the Scottish 'loch'

'j'   again a softer sound, like the French pronunciation of the letter in 'Frère Jacques'

'ai'   should sound like the letter 'i' as you would pronounce it when reciting the alphabet

'h'   there is a strong 'h' in Arabic which is very difficult for English speakers. It's breathy but hard, and comes from somewhere at the back of the throat that you were hitherto unaware of. The only answer is to find someone to coach you.

The accents used in the following list of Arabic words and phrases show which syllable should be stressed.

ENGLISH	FRENCH	ARABIC
Useful Words and Phrases		
Yes	Oui	Naam/Ih
No	Non	La
Please	S'il vous plaît	Birábee
Thank you	Merci	Barakaláufik/Shókran
Not at all	De rien	Afón
(Very) good	(Très) bon	Béhi (yéssir)
Bad	Mauvais	Mish béhi
That's life	C'est la vie	Máalesh
Okay	Okay	Béhi
I don't understand	Je ne comprends pas	Ma fahímtsh
Slowly, please	Lentement, s'il vous plaît	Shwai shwai
What?	Quoi?	Shoo?
Come in	Entrez	Tfáddal
I/you	Je/vous	Ana/ínta
And	Et	Wa
Watch out!	Attention!	Rud Bálek!
Go away!	Allez-vous en!	Imshee/bárra!
Meetings and greetings		
Sir	Monsieur	Si/Sídi
Madam	Madame	Lálla
Hello	Bonjour	Asláama/Saláam Aláykum
How are you?	Comment allez-vous?	Kifelháal?/Labáis?
Fine	Très bien	Elhúmdulila/Labais
Not well	Pas très bien	Mish béhi
Good morning	Bonjour	Sbah el khir
Good night	Bonne nuit	T'sbah la khir
Sleep well	Dormez bien	Léela saiéeda
Goodbye	Au revoir	Bslémah
Until we meet again	A la prochaine	Il'allickáh
Shopping		
Money	Argent	Floos
How much?	Combien?	Kadésh?
Too much	C'est trop	Yéssir
I would like	Je voudrais	N'hebb
This is no good	Ce n'est pas bon	Mish béhi
Numbers		
1	un	wáhad
2	deux	tnéen
3	trois	tléta
4	quatre	árba

365

ENGLISH	FRENCH	ARABIC
5	cinq	khámsa
6	six	sítta
7	sept	séba
8	huit	thmánia
9	neuf	tíssa
10	dix	áshera
11	onze	ahdásh
12	douze	itnásh
13	treize	thletásh
14	quatorze	arbatásh
15	quinze	khamstásh
16	seize	sittásh
17	dix-sept	sebatásh
18	dix-huit	thmantásh
19	dix-neuf	tissatásh
20	vingt	ashréen
21	vingt et un	wáhad wa ashréen
22	vingt-deux	tnéen wa ashréen
30	trente	thletéen
40	quarante	arbaéen
50	cinquante	khamséen
60	soixante	sittéen
70	soixante-dix	sebaéen
80	quatre-vingts	thmanéen
90	quatre-vingts-dix	tissaéen
100	cent	mía
200	deux cents	miatéen
300	trois cents	thléta mía
400	quatre cents	árba mía
1000	mille	elf
2000	deux milles	elféin
3000	trois milles	thlétat aláaf

French

There are three accents in French used to modify vowel sounds, and a fourth which makes no difference to the pronunciation:

‘´’ makes 'e' a short vowel, and should be pronounced 'ai'.

‘`’ lengthens an 'e' and has no discernable effect when found over an 'a'.

‘ ¸’ is sometimes found below a 'c' and softens it to an 's'.

‘^’ above a vowel has no effect on pronunciation.

One other major rule of pronunciation: remember never to pronounce the last consonant in any word, unless it is followed by an 'e'. In addition, bear in mind that any vowel followed by an 'n' takes on a nasal twang, as if they were followed by a hint of a 'g' ('Hong Kong').

366

ENGLISH	FRENCH
Directions and Travel	
Do you speak English?	Parlez-vous anglais?
I am lost	Je suis perdu
...hungry	J'ai faim
...thirsty	...soif
...tired	Je suis fatigué
...sorry	Je m'excuse
...ill	Je suis malade
Where is (are)...?	Ou se trouve(nt)...?
...the loos (male/female)	...les toilettes (hommes/femmes)
...the telephone	...le téléphone
...a restaurant	...un restaurant
...a hotel	...un hôtel
...a garage	...un garage
...a doctor	...un docteur
...a chemist	...une pharmacie
...the hospital	...l'hôpital
...the police station	...le commissariat de police
...a bank	...une banque
...the post office	...la poste
...the airport	...l'aéroport
...the bus station	...la gare d'autobus
...the railway station	...la gare
...the beach	...la plage
Turn left/right	Tournez à gauche/à droite
Straight on	Tout droit
North	Nord
South	Sud
East	Est
West	Ouest
Crossroads	Un carrefour
Street/road	La rue/la route
Square	La place
How many kilometres to...?	C'est combien de kilometres à...?
It is near/far	C'est proche/loin
Bus	Le bus
Train	Le train
Plane	L'avion
Ship	Le bateau
When is the next ... for ...?	A quelle heure part le prochain ... pour ...?
Where does it leave from?	D'ou est-ce qu'il part?
Platform/track	Quai
How long does it take?	Combien de temps faut-il?
How much is the fare?	C'est combien le voyage?
A ticket for ..., please.	Un billet pour ..., s'il vous plaît
One-way	Aller simple
Return	Aller-retour

Time

What time is it?	Quelle heure est-il?
... o'clock	... heure
What day is it?	Quel jour est-il?
Monday	Lundi
Tuesday	Mardi
Wednesday	Mercredi
Thursday	Jeudi
Friday	Vendredi
Saturday	Samedi
Sunday	Dimanche
It is too early/late	C'est trop tôt/tard
Now/later	Maintenant/plus tard
Yesterday/today/tomorrow	Hier/aujourd'hui/demain
What time does ... open/close?	A quelle heure ouvre/ferme ...?
... the museum	Le musée
... the site	Le site

In Restaurants

The most common Tunisian dishes are described in the Eating Out section in the first chapter of this book (pp. 28–30). The vast majority of menus will also be in French. In the less touristy places, where the menu tends to be verbal, the best thing to do is to go into the kitchen and take a look at what's on offer.

ENGLISH	FRENCH	ARABIC
Give me	Donnez moi	Attíni
That's enough	Ça suffit	Izzi
Big/small	Grand/petit	Kebír/seghír
Hot/cold	Chaud/froid	Haar/báared
Bread	Pain	Khobs
Olives	Olives	Zitoun
Oil	Huile	Zit
Salt	Sel	Mílah
Pepper	Poivre	Lébzar
Sugar	Sucre	Súkar
Cheers	Santé	B'sméllah
The bill, please	L'addition, s'il vous plaît	Khseb, birábee

To Drink

Water	L'eau	Meh
Coffee	Café	Káhwa
Tea	Thé	Tei
Milk	Lait	Haléeb
Orange Juice	Jus d'orange	Jus d'orange
Beer	Bière	Bíira

ENGLISH	FRENCH	ARABIC
Wine	Vin	Sharáb/hamra
red	rouge	ákhmar
white	blanc	áb'yith
rosé	rosé	bordoukháli

To Eat		
Meat	**Viande**	**Lahm**
chicken	poulet	
lamb	agneau	
mutton	mouton	
beef	boeuf	

Fish	**Poisson**	**Huud**
anchovy	anchois	
brill	barbue	
barracuda	brochet	
bream (gold)	daurade	
bream (bronze)	pageot	
perch	loup de mer	
whiting	merlan	
grouper	merou	
mullet	mulet	
red mullet	rouget	
tuna fish	thon	

Fruit	**Fruit**	**Ghaláa**
Vegetables	Légumes	Khódra

FURTHER READING

General

Knapp, W. *A Survey of North West Africa*. Wilfrid Knapp wrote the 3rd Edition in 1977, (earlier editions by Neville Barbour) to provide the best introduction to North Africa.

Knapp, W. *Tunisia*, (Thames and Hudson 1970).

Mansfield, P. *The Arabs*, (Penguin 1985). An up-to-date and approachable survey of the Arab world, followed by national case histories.

Perkins, W. *Tunisia, Crossroads of Islamic and European Worlds*, (Croom Helm).

Ancient History

Brown, P. *Religion and society in the age of St Augustine*, (Faber 1971).

Harden, D. *The Phoenicians*, (Thames and Hudson 1962).

Lane Fox, R. *Pagans and Christians*, (Penguin 1986). A fascinating picture of the Mediterranean spiritual world of 2nd to 4th century AD.

Livy, *The War with Hannibal*, (Penguin).

MacKendrick, P. *The North African Stones Speak*, (Croom Helm 1980). A quirky, archaeologist's-eye view of the Roman period, with four chapters on Tunisia.

Picard and Picard *The Life and Death of Carthage*, (Sidgwick and Jackson 1968). An authoritative review by the French archaeologists who excavated Carthage and Makhtar.

Polybius, *The Rise of the Roman Empire*, (Penguin 1979).

Procopius, *The Vandalic War*, (Penguin).

Raven, S. *Rome in Africa*, (Longman 1984). A good introduction to Roman North Africa.

Sallust, *The Jugurthine War*, (Penguin 1982).

Warrington, B.H. *Carthage*, (Pelican 1964). An accomplished history, satisfyingly well written for the general reader and innovative enough for the specalist.

Islamic and Modern History

Abun Nasr, *A History of the Maghreb in the Islamic Period*, (CUP 1987). Constantly updated and refined, this is the primary source for Tunisia's Islamic history. It's initially a confusing read, however, and demands some familiarity with the region.

Anderson, L. *The State and Social Transformation in Tunisia and Libya, 1830–1980*, (Princeton).

Bovill, E.V. *The Golden Trade of the Moors*, (OUP). This traces the influence of trans-Saharan trade. Written by an amateur rather than a scholar, it has a fresh enthusiasm and has inspired many.

Brown, L.C. *The Tunisia of Ahmed Bey 1837–1855*, (Princeton 1974). The first half of this book provides an excellent picture of the pre-protectorate society.

Ibn Khaldoun *The Muqaddimah: An Introduction to History*, (RKP 1987). (See page 72).

Messenger, C. *The Tunisian Campaign*, (Ian Allen 1982). Packed with photographs and maps, but perilously close to an official history.

Morsy, M. *North Africa*, (Longman). An approachable and short regional history, the obvious start before tackling Abun Nasr.

Salem, N. *Habib Bourguiba, Islam and the creation of Modern Tunisia*,(Croom Helm 1985).

Zartman, W. ed. *Man, State and Society in the Contemporary Maghreb*, (Pall Mall, 1973). A collection of speeches, essays and commentaries which is worth dipping into.

Travel

Little has changed since the end of the 19th century when Rankin angrily complained, 'I assure you I have read about a dozen extremely bad books about Tunisia'. He disparagingly records the essential baggage of the travel writer, 'in one pocket a French guide book and in the other a copy of his immediate predecessor's work'. He then went straight on to add his own bad book to the pile. Celebrated writers such as André Gide, Aldous Huxley, Norman Douglas and Alexandre Dumas have all written about Tunisia, but have left nothing to enthusiastically recommend. This, therefore, is half a reading list and half a black-list.

Africanus, Leo *Description of Africa*, late 15th century, (Hakluyt Society, 1896).

Al Idrisi, Mohammed *The Book of Roger* or *A Description of Africa and Spain*, (Leyden 1866). A geographical account written for Roger II of Sicily in the mid-12th century.

Bruce, J. *Travels to Discover the Source of the Nile*, (1790). This famed early traveller passed through Tunisia on his way south and east.

Barth, Dr. H. *Travels in North and Central Africa (1845–1855)*. The unsung scholar-hero of Saharan exploration was among the first to map out the ruins of the Tunisian interior on his way south.

Brunn, D. *Cave Dwellers of Southern Tunisia*, (1898; Darf reprint). An informed account by a Danish anthropologist of the life of the Berber tribes in the Matmata hills.

Dumas, A. *Tangier to Tunis*, (Peter Owen 1959). An account of an officially sponsored PR tour through North Africa in 1846, though Dumas overdoes things by commandeering a French warship as his cruise ship.

Graham, A. and Ashbee, H.S. *Travels in Tunisia*, (1887).

Hess Wartegg, Chevalier de *Tunis: The Land and the People*, (Chatto and Windus 1899). An intriguing and largely unprejudiced account of the last years of Beylical rule.

Ibn Battuta *Travels in Asia and Africa, 1324–1354*, (RKP 1983). The Muslim Marco Polo gives Tunisia a passing glance in his description of the pilgrimage route to Mecca from Morocco.

Johnston, Sir H. *A Journey through the Tunisian Sahara*, (Geographical Journal Vol XI, June 1898 pp 581—608). An entertaining glimpse of 19th century enthusiasms, with spurious speculation on phallic worship and the origin of the races.

Shaw, Dr. T. *Travels and Observations in Barbary*, (1757).

Temple, Sir Greville *Excursions in the Mediterranean*, (1835).

Playfair, R.L. *Handbook for Travellers in Algeria and Tunis* (Murray 1891). One of the first guidebooks, by the same British consul who compiled an exhaustive North African bibliography.

20th-Century Travellers

Two books that stand out for their knowledge and affection for the country were both written by Americans and are well worth tracing:

Anthony, J. *About Tunisia*, (Geoffrey Bles 1961). This gives a refreshingly candid account of a lesser diplomat's life in the country just before Independence.

Martin, D. *Among the Faithful*, (Michael Joseph 1937). An account of the author's two years in Kairouan in the '30s. Remarkable in that she allows her description of Tunisian family life to stand untainted by Western moralising.

Broughton Brodrick, A. *Parts of Barbary*, (Hutchinson 1943). Dated but still entertaining.

Carrington, R. *East from Tunis*, (Chatto and Windus 1957). A chatty, informed chronicle of a trip from Tunis to Cairo in 1955.

Douglas, N. *Fountains in the Sand*, (OUP 1986). A short visit to southern Tunisia in 1912 described with the author's familiar ability, intolerance, racism and self-importance.

Dunbar, I. *The Edge of the Desert*, (Phillip Allan 1923), with illustrations by the author.

Furlonge, G. *The Lands of Barbary*, (John Murray 1966).

Gide, André *Amyntas*, (Ecco Press 1988). A series of sensual vignettes from extensive travels through Algeria and Tunisia at the turn of the century by a future Nobel Prize Winner.

Hammerton, T. *Tunisia Unveiled*, (Robert Hale 1959). A competent but uninspiring account of the main tourist sites.

Huxley, A. *In a Tunisia Oasis*, in a collection of stories called *The Olive Tree* (Chatto and Windus 1939).

MacCallum, A. *Barbary. The Romance of the Nearest East*, (Thornton Butterworth 1921). Random speculations by an M.P. on literature and the future of French colonialism in North Africa.

Mariner, J. *The Shores of the Black Ships*, (William Kimber 1971). A drab diary of day trips from a yachting holiday masquerading as a study of the Phoenicians.

Petrie, G. *Tunis, Kairouan and Carthage*, (Heinemann 1908/Darf 1985), with 48 charming illustrations.

Rankin, Lt. Col. Sir Reginald, *Tunisia*, (Bodley Head 1901). A gun-room monologue—the colonel's thoughts and experiences on his sporting tour.

Sitwell, S. *Mauretania*, (1939). Some thoughts on the benefits of colonial rule whilst motoring through North Africa.

Anthropology

Berque, J. *Arab Rebirth: Pain and Ecstasy*, (Al Saqi 1983). A stimulating essay by a leading French scholar on the new Arab culture emerging after colonialism.

Duvignaud, J. *Change at Shebika*, (Penguin 1978). A fascinating survey of the changes in a small oasis community in the 1960s, written for the layman.

Gallagher, *Medicine and Power in Tunisia, 1780–1900*, (CUP 1974). This discouraging title hides a fluent social history of 19th-century plagues.

Gellner, E. *Muslim Society*, (CUP 1985). A disparate collection of essays and reviews by a respected North African anthropologist.

Mernissi, F. *Beyond the Veil: the Sexual Ideology of Islam* (Al Saqi 1985). Based on Moroccan research, this is an entertaining and provoking study and relevant to Tunisia. Including the Prophet's sex life, letters to an 'agony aunt' and much more...

Minority Rights Group *Arab Women*. The MRG reports are usually concise, sober and hard hitting. This is one of their woolliest.

Tillion, G. *The Republic of Cousins: Women's Oppression in Mediterranean Society*, (Al Saqi 1983). A celebrated analysis of the root causes of oppression.

Valenski, L. and Udovitch, A. *The Last Arab Jews*, (Harwood Academic Publishers 1985). A study of the Jewish community on the Island of Jerba.

(Auto-biography

Bradford, E. *The Sultan's Admiral—Life of Barbarossa*.

Brown, P. *Augustine of Hippo*, (Faber 1967). Supersedes Rebecca West's 1933 biography.

Lewis, N. *Jackdaw Cake*, (Hamish Hamilton 1985). Celebrated travel writer's autobiography, of which the last third is set during the North African campaign.

Nicholson, N. *Alex: The Life of Field Marshal Earl Alexander of Tunis*, (Weidenfeld and Nicholson 1973). The Tunisian campaign is covered in pp 171–192.

Saint Augustine, *Confessions*, (Penguin 1961).

Art

Dunbabin, R. *The Mosaics of Roman North Africa*, (OUP 1978).

Hill, D. and Golvin, L. *Islamic Architecture of North Africa*, (Faber and Faber).

Hubert, C. *Islamic Ornamental Design*, (Faber and Faber 1980).

Hutt, A. *North Africa—Islamic Architecture*, (Scorpion 1977).

Khatabi, A. and Sigilmassa, M. *The Splendours of Islamic Calligraphy*, (Thames and Hudson 1976).

Mitchell, D. *Islamic Achitecture*, (Thames and Hudson).

Royal Academy *The Orientalists*, (Royal Academy Catalogue). The inspiration of the Arab world on Delacroix, Vernet, Ingres, Formentin.

Said, E. *Orientalism*, (Penguin 1978). A counterblast to the Western image of Arab culture engendered by the paintings of the Orientalist school.

Talbot Rice, D. *Islamic Art*, (Thames and Hudson 1986).

Ward Perkins, J.B. *Roman Imperial Architecture*, (Pelican 1981).

Islam

The Koran, (Penguin 1974/OUP).

Lings, M. *What is Sufism?* (Mandala 1981).

Guillaume, A. *Islam*, (Penguin 1954).

Mortimer, E. *Faith and Power*, (Faber and Faber). A study of the role of Islam in the political life of six countries.

Nigosian, S. *Islam—The Way of Submission*, (Crucible 1987). An excellent, clear survey for newcomers to the subject.

Shah, I. *The Way of the Sufi*, (Penguin 1986).

Literary History

Haywood, J. *Modern Arabic Literature 1800–1900*.

Kritzeck, J. ed. *Anthology of Islamic Literature*, (Penguin).

Nicholson, R. *Literary History of the Arabs*.

Fiction

Apuleius, *The Golden Ass*, (Penguin 1950). (See page 71).

Flaubert, G. *Salammbo*, (Penguin 1987). Archetypal orientalist fantasy: a tale of cruelty, treachery, luxury and unchecked sexuality, based on the revolt of the Carthaginian Mercenaries.

Mellah, F. *Elissa*, (Quartet 1990). A ponderous reconstruction of Dido's voyage from Tyre to found Carthage.

Virgil *The Aeneid* (Penguin 1974). Books I and IV cover the founding of Carthage and Dido's tragic love for Aeneas.

Memmi, A. *The Pillar of Salt*. The most famous Tunisian writer is discounted by Arabist purists as he writes in French, is Jewish and lives mostly in Paris.

There are two Tunisian publishing houses, Editions Sindbad and Editions Salammbo, that

373

print French translations of Arabic fiction, and fiction originally written in French. If you want to stay with English there are a number of Egyptian and Moroccan writers whose work addresses many themes common to all North Africans.

Bowles, P. trans. *Five Eyes*, (Black Sparrow Press). A collection of short stories by five contemporary Maghrebi writers.

El Saadawi, N. *Woman at Point Zero* (Zed 1982). A controversial Egyptian feminist, whose understanding of the predicament of Muslim women is both tragic and hopeful.

Mahfouz, N. *The Beginning and the End* and *Midaq Alley* or indeed anything by Mahfouz (Doubleday). The Egyptian Nobel Prizwinner for Literature is 'kaleidoscopic, Dickensian, brilliant'.

Serhane, A. *Messaouda*, (Carcanet 1986). A raw semi-autobiographical account of the brutalisation of a growing boy in a poor Moroccan village.

Flowers and Birds

Etchecopar, R.D. and Hue, F. *The Birds of North Africa* (Oliver and Boyd 1967), trans. by P. Hollom.

Henzel, Fitter and Parslow, *The Birds of Britain and Europe with North Africa and the Middle East*, (Collins).

Polunin, O. and Huxley, A. *The Flowers of the Mediterranean*, (Hogarth Press).

Cooking

Boxer, A. *Mediterranean Cookbook*, (Penguin 1981).

Edwards, J. trans. *The Roman Cookery of Apicius*, (Rider).

Haroutunian, A. der *North African Cookery*, (Century).

Roden, C. *A New Book of Middle Eastern Food*, (Penguin).

INDEX

Note: Page references in *italics* indicate illustrations; references in **bold** indicate maps.

Abu Yazid 43, 102, 164, 189, 297
accommodation, *see* camping; hotels
Acholla 64, 108, 167
adventure tours 3, 346
Agathocles, Greek military leader 37, 124, 142,
  193, 198
Aggar, Roman remains 244
Aghlabid rule 42–3, 150, 177, 183, 187–8, 198
agriculture 55, 74–7, 130–1, 195, 206, 231, 233–5,
  320
Ain Bou Saadia, Berber village 245
Ain Draham 21, 213–15
Ain el Arram, prehistoric site 330
Ain Jelloula village 245
Ain Tebournok, Roman remains 130
Ain Tounga (Thignica),
  Byzantine fort 62, 249–50
  Roman remains 250
air travel,
  domestic 10, 85, 152, 160, 169, 210, 345
  international 1–2, 84
Algeria, border 6, 55, 231, 232
Almohad rule 44–5, 66, 72, 83
alms 15, 58
Althiburos, Roman remains 278–9
Aousja village 195
Apuleius 71, 226
Arab Conquest 42, 65, 82, 116–17, 124, 160, 193
Arabic 65–6, 71–3
architecture,
  Berber xi, 322–3
  Byzantine 61–2, 185
  courtyard plan 63, 142
  Islamic ix, xi, 62–3, 97, 153–4, 184–5
  Mudejar 147, 248
  oasis 300, 306, 312
  Phoenician 61
  Roman 61, 179
  Romanesque 90, 217
art, modern 25, 68–9, 156
Augustine of Hippo, St 41, 70–1, 116, 121, 223

Babouch village 215
Balta village, Roman remains 222
banks 13, 88, 127, 153, 160, 170, 184, 200, 214,
  220, 265, 299, 306, 311, 315, 325, 335, 346
Barbarossa 46, 83, 198, 210, 344–5

bargaining 22–3, 90, 188
Barrage Mellègue 269–70
Bay of Tunis 81–123, **82**
beaches xi
  Bay of Tunis 123
  Cap Bon peninsula 126, 129, 133, 136, 137, 145,
    147
  Jebel Demer and Isle of Jerba 342, 343, 349–50
  north coast 190, 192, 196, 206, 208–10
  Sahel 148, 150, 163, 167, 173, 176
Béja 219–21
  accommodation and restaurants 221
  colonial and Commonwealth war cemeteries 221
  history 219
  kasbah 221
  Medina 220
  souks 220
  transport 219–20
  Zaouia of Abdel Kader 220–1
Bechateur, Roman ruins 205
Bechouch Beach 209
beggars 15
Belalis Major, Roman site 221–2
Belisarius, Byzantine general 41, 116, 167, 262,
  284, 288
Belkhir, Turkish fort 301
Ben Ali, Zine el Abidine 54, 55, 148, 152
Ben Guerdane, market 342
Beni Aissa, underground houses 329
Beni Barka, ruined ksar 338–9
Beni Khaled market 130
Beni Kheddache village 333
Beni M'Tir dam 215
Berbers 190, 315
  history 36, 41–4, 70, 83, 207, 209, 320, 328–9
  villages 132, 133, 239, 245, 322–3, 335–6, 340
bicycles 12, 127, 134, 176, 200, 346
Bir Thalatine village 340
birds 78, 79, 113, 124, 138, *143*, 143, 205–6, 239,
  342
Birhet el Bibane, plain 342
BIZERTE xi, 190, 197–205, **201**
  accommodation and restaurants 203–4
  Andalous Quarter 203
  Fort of Spain 203
  fortress Sidi el Hani, Museum of Oceanography
    62, 202

375

Great Mosque *197*, 202
  history 198–9
  kasbah 202
  medina 200–3
  Monument of the Martyrs 203
  Mosque of Rbaa 200
  nightlife 204
  old port 200
  sports 205
  tourist information 200
  transport 199–200
  Zaouia of Sidi H'nan 202
  Zaouia of Sidi Mohammed ben Aissa 202
  Zaouia of Sidi Mostari 202
Bled el Hader (Thusuros), mosque 307
boar hunting 21, 214
Borj Brahim, Byzantine fort 62, 261
Borj el Aifa 262
Borj el Khadra 340
Borj Messaoudi, koubba of Sidi Moussa 262
Bou Arada, zodiac mausoleum 247
Bou Salem, market 222
Bourguiba, Habib ibn Ali 19, 51, 52, 53–4, 55–6,
  58, 96, 148, 160, 162, 175, 189, 210
Brega tribe, legend 341
Bulla Regia,
  basilicas 228
  Baths of Juli Memnia 225
  dolmens 229
  forum 226
  history 224
  Museum 224–5
  Roman remains 35, 223–9, *224*, **225**
  Royal Palace 226
  Temple of Isis 226
  theatre 61, 226
  transport 224
  underground villas xi, 227–8
bus travel 11
Byzantine rule 19, 41, 60, 65
  in Bay of Tunis 116
  in Cap Bon peninsula 124
  north coast and Mejerda valley 198, 224, 228
  in Sahel 142, 160
  in the Tell 243, 250, 253, 261–2, 288, 292

calligraphy 61, 62, 65–7, 69, 106, 153, 161, 172
camel rides 7, 21, 129, 136, 176, 311, 316, 317
camping 27–8, 129, 147, 204, 215, 304, 308, 309,
  313, 317, 336, 352
cannabis 16
Cap Blanc 205
Cap Bon peninsula ix, 124–47, **125**
  accommodation and restaurants 129, 131, 136–7,
  138, 140, 144, 146, 147

Cap Farina 192, 196
Cap Negro 209
Cap Serrat xii, 208
Cap Zebib 197
Capsian culture 36, 173, 298
carpets, buying 15, 24–5, 188, 308
cars,
  hire 11–12, 88, 127, 134, 152–3, 160, 170,
  199–200, 211, 264, 325, 346
  travel 84–5
CARTHAGE ix, 37–9, 61, 64, 113, 114–21, *116*
  accommodation and restaurants 121
  American Military Cemetery 121
  amphitheatre 121
  Antonine Baths 118–19
  Basilica of St Cyprian 121
  Byrsa Hill 119–20
  history 31, 37–42, 70, 114–17, 124
  Mago Quarter Architectural Park 118
  Museum of Oceanography 117
  National Musem of Carthage 120
  Park of Roman Villas 119
  Punic Harbours 117–18
  Roman and Palaeo–Christian Museum 118
  Roman theatre 119
  Salammbo Tophet 105, 114, 117
  transport 117
Carthaginians 105, 140–2, 263, 350–1, *see also*
  Phoenicians
catacombs 157, 167
cave paintings 36, 243
Cedria Plage 112
ceramics 25, 67–8, 105, 136, 208
Chaoach village 218
Chebba, beaches 167
Chebika village 304
Chemtou 229–31
  hilltop sanctuary 230–1
  marble quarries xi, 229, 230
  Nympheum and Forum 230
  Roman bridge 61, 230
  Roman theatre 61, 230
Chenini,
  hill citadel xi, xii, 335–6
  palmery 326–7
Cherichira aqueduct 277
Chott el Jerid 294–318, **295**
  accommodation and restaurants 300–1, 302, 304,
  309, 312–13, 315, 317, 318
  crossing 314
  desert tours xi, 316
  history 296–8
  salt-flats xii, 314
Christianity 40–1, 43, 59, 65, 70, 105, 116, 253,
  288

Cillium,
  accommodation and restaurants 292
  Byzantine forts 292
  Roman theatre 291–2
cinema 21
climate 7, 9, 73–4, 124, 233, 296, 323
clothes,
  buying 25
  suitable 9, 18
coffee 32
coins,
  Islamic 68, 189, 273
  Roman 25, 245
Commonwealth War Cemeteries 132, 209, 216–17,
    218, 221
consulates 4, 14–15
corsairs 47, 59, 83, 195, 198, 203, 210, 344–5
crafts 23, *see also* metalworking; woodworking
credit cards 13
crime 85
cuisine 28–30
currency 13
Customs 6–7, 15, 232
Cyprian, St 41, 70, 116, 290

Dahmani 278
Dar ben Abdallah, architecture 62
date palm 75, 76–7, *294*, 296, 305, 315, 318, 343
Dechrat el Gharia, rock 'needles' 277
Degache 28, 313
Dehibat, ruined ksar 341
desert tours xi, 7, 21, 316
Destour Party 51–2, 162, 299
diving 22, 133, 157, 211
Djebba (Thiggiba Bure), Cave of the Seven
    Sleepers 260
Donatism 40–1, 278, 283
DOUGGA 251–9, **252**
  Capitoline temple *233*, 254
  history 251–3
  Phoenician remains 61, 257
  Roman remains xi, 61, 235, 253–9
  Roman theatre 20, 253–4
Douirat village 322, 336–7
Douiret, hill citadel xi, xii
Douz,
  accommodation 317
  desert tours xi, 7, 316
  festival 20, 316
Dragut, corsair 46, 169, 175, 210, 299, 345, 348,
    351
drink 30–2

Ech Chaffar, beach 177
El Alia village 197
El Battan 216
El Fahs 235, 242–3
El Faouar, oasis 317

El Hamma, market 318
El Haouaria,
  Falconry Festival 20, 143
  Roman quarries ix, 118, 142–3
El Heri, Longstop Hill memorial 216
El Jem,
  accommodation and restaurants 181
  Archaeological Museum 180
  history 40, 42, 64, 178–9
  Roman amphitheatre xi, 26, 60, 61, 178, 179–80
  second amphitheatre 181
  transport 179
EL KEF xi, 263–9, **264**
  accommodation and restaurants 268–9
  Ain El Kef spring 265
  Bab Ghedive 268
  Byzantine churches 62, 265, 267
  history 35, 37, 263–4
  kasbahs 263, 265–6
  Mausoleum of Ali Turki 267
  Old Mosque 266
  Regional Museum of Popular Art and Tradition
      67, 267–8
  Roman baths 265
  Sidi Bou Makhlouf Mosque *266*, 266–7
  tourist information 265
  transport 264
  Zaouia of Sidi Mizouni 267
El Ksour 279
El Mensof 314
El Nouail, camping 317
electricity 16
Elles, megalithic tombs 61, 271
embassies 14–15, 89
embroidery 93
Enfida,
  museum 65, 132
  war cemeteries 132–3
Eurocheques 13
European influence 49–52, 68–9, *see also* France;
    Spain

Fatimid rule 43–4, 62, 71, 163, 164, 165, 183
fauna 78–80, 215
Feija hills 231, 232
Feriana, Byzantine citadel 293
Fernana village 215
ferries 2–3, 84, 113, 169, 332, 351
festivals 20, 247–8, 296, 308, 312, 315, 316, 351
fish, as goodluck symbol ix, 26, 180
fishing xii, 22, 157, 176
flora 77–8
food 26, 28–30, 190, 221, 269
football 21, 136
fossils 26, 304
Foum el Afrit gorge, Roman bridge 244

Foum el Khanga 303
Foum Tataouine 334–5
France, influence 49–53, 56, 72–3, 130, 148, 169, 209–10, 214, 233, 298
Ftiss (Avitta Bibba), Roman remains 247

Gaafour, koubba of Sidi Bou Argoub 247
Gabès 323–7, **324**
  accommodation and restaurants 327
  Chenini palmery 326–7
  history 320, 323–4
  Jara market 325
  Mosque of Sidi Boulbaba 325–6
  Museum of Arts and Popular Traditions 67, 325–6
  nightlife 327
  oasis 326
  port and beach 327
  tourist information 325
  transport 324–5
Gafsa 298–301
  accommodation and restaurants 300–1
  Great Mosque 300
  history 35, 36, 173, 298–9
  kasbah 299, 300
  Roman pools 300
  tourist information 299
  transport 299
Gafsa incident 53, 55, 299
Galite Archipelago 213
Gammarth 123
gas 16
geography 73–4
Gettofa, ksar 340
Ghadames, history 45, 320
Ghar el Melh, forts 192, 195–6
Ghardimao 231
Gheriani, ruined ksar 341
Ghomrassen 338
Gigthis, Roman remains 332–3
gladiators 179–80
golf 21, 109, 128, 136, 157
Gordian, governor of Carthage 40, 178
Goubellat 217
Grombalia, wine festival 130
guides 15–16, 143, 184

Hached, Farhat, trade union leader 52, 96, 169, 175, 176
Haddej village, underground houses 328
  history 322
Hafsid rule 45–6, 72, 83, 104, 183
Haidra 287–91, **289**
  basilica of Melleus 290–1
  Byzantine remains 62, 290–1
  fort 62, 290

history 287–8
  Orange Mausoleum 290
  Roman remains 288–90
Hajeb el Ayoun village, market 286
Hamilcar Barca, Carthaginian military leader 38, 219
Hammam Biada (Aptucca) 262
Hammam Bourguiba 215
Hammam Lif 111, 112
Hammam Mellègue, Roman baths 270
Hammam Zouakra,
  megalithic tombs 61, 277
  Roman remains 276–7
Hammamet ix, 126–9
  accommodation and restaurants 129
  festival 20, 128
  Kasbah 127
  Medina *124*, 127
  Roman Pupput 128
  sports 21, 128–9
  tourist information 7, 127
  transport 126–7
hammams xii, 9, 108, 157, 184, 236–7, 239, 262, 270, 308, 311, 318, 351
Hammouda Pasha I 48, 90, 95, 101, 187
Hammouda Pasha II 48–9, 91, 172, 180
hang gliding 22
Hannibal 38, 124, 175, 224–5, 245–6
haouanets (grave chambers) 61, 140, 209
Hassan ibn Numan 42, 82, 91, 113, 116, 123, 181
Haute Zriba 239
health matters 17
Henchir Chett, Roman villa 260
Henchir Jemal 277
Henchir Souar, cave paintings 243
Hergla 133
hitchhiking 12, 243
holidays,
  religious 19, 59
  secular 18
horseriding 21, 109, 129, 130, 136, 157, 176, 205
hotels xi, 27
Houmt Souk, *see* Isle of Jerba
Hussein ibn Ali Turki 48, 84, 97, 98, 183, 186, 267
Husseinite rule 48–9, 84, 98, 183, 263
hydrofoils 3, 138

Ibadites 160, 297, 344
Ibero–Maurẹtanian culture 35–6, 173
Ibn Khaldoun 71, 72, 89, 99
independence 52–3, 96, 148, 245
insurance, travel 17
Islam 19, 49, 56–61, 65–6, 154
  religious life 58
  see also Ramadan; Shiism; Sufism
Isle of Chikli 113

Isle of Jerba xi, 332, 342–53, *343*
  accommodation and restaurants 351–3
  Aghir village 349
  Ajim 351
  beaches 343, 349–50
  El Kantara 350–1
  Guellala, pottery 343, 350
  hammams 351
  history 344–5
  Houmt Souk xi, 346–9, *347*
    Borj el Kebir 62, 348
    Borj Jellid 349
    Museum of Popular Arts and Traditions 67,
      348–9
    port 349
    religious buildings 347–8
  Jewish population 101, 343, 348, 350
  La Griba synagogue 343, 350
  Midoun 350
  shopping 351
  tourist information 346
  transport 345–6
Italy, influence 50
itineraries 33–4, 319

Jara, mosques 325
Jebel Abiod, ksour 335, 338–9, 338–40
Jebel Ballouta 246
Jebel Bir 214
Jebel Bou Goultrane 222
Jebel Bou Korbous 146
Jebel Bou Kornine 111–12
Jebel Chambi 292
Jebel Demer and Isle of Jerba xi, 319–53, **321**
  accommodation and restaurants 327, 329–30,
    331–2, 334, 335, 342, 351–3
  history 319–20
Jebel ez Zit 239
Jebel Fersig 214
Jebel Goraa 259–60
Jebel Ichkeul National Park and Museum 205–6
Jebel Laouej, sanctuary 250
Jebel Munchar 218–19
Jebel Nadour 195, 197, 205
Jebel Orbata 301
Jebel Oust, thermal baths 235, 236–7
Jebel Rabia 223
Jebel Ressas 22, 240
Jebel Serj 244
Jebel Sidi Abiod 144
Jebel Sidi Salem 239
Jebel Skhira 248–9
Jebel Tlalett 337
Jebel Zaghouan 100, 122, 123, 237, 239
Jefara plain 322, 341–2
Jendouba 222–3

Jeradou 132
jewellery 26, 93, 351
Jews 49, 83, 101, 112, 123, 248, 339, 343, 348, 350
Jorf 332
Juba I of Numidia *38*, 39, 163, 225, 332
Jugurtha 38, 39, 224–5, 231, 287, 297
Junci, Roman site 177

KAIROUAN ix, 181–9, **182**
  accommodation and restaurants 188–9
  Aghlabid basins 187–8
  Bir Barouta 186
  carpets 15, 24, 188
  festivals 188
  Great Mosque 14, 43, 62, *184*, 184–5
  history 42–4, 181–3
  Medina 185–8
  Mosque of the Three Gates 186
  shopping 188
  souk 186
  tourist information 7, 16, 184
  transport 183
  Zaouia of Sidi Abidel Ghariani 186
  Zaouia of Sidi Amor Abbada 187
  Zaouia of Sidi Sahab 187
Kalaat el Andalous 192
Kalaat es Senan 287
Kasserine,
  battle 291
  Roman Mausoleums 291
Kbor Klib 271
Kebili oasis 35, 315
Kechafa Echaabma, beaches 167
Kef Nechka 232
Kelibia 3, 138–40
  castle ix, 139
  Punic tombs 139–40
  Roman remains 139
  transport 138–9
Kerkennah Isles 150, 174–6
  accommodation and restaurants 176
  activities 22, 176
  Chergui 175–6
  Gharbi 175
  history 175
Kerkouane, Phoenician ruins ix, 61, 140–2
Kesra village, Byzantine fort 277
Khanguet el Kedim col 262
Kharijites 42, 102, 297, 315, 320, 339, 344
Khroumir hills 221
Khroumirie Tribes 206–9
kif 16
killims 24–5, 94, 188, 220, 335
Kirchaoua, ghorfa 341

Koran 56, 57, 58, 65–7, 189
Korba, souk 137
Korbous,
    Ain el Atrous 145
    Ain Oktor 146
    Kalaa Sghira 145
    spa 146
Ksar Bhir, ruined ksar 341
Ksar Degrah 335
Ksar el Baroud 286
Ksar el Hallouf 333–4
Ksar Ferch 337
Ksar Ghilane, Roman fort xii, 316, 318
Ksar Guermessa 337–8
Ksar Haddada 334, 338
Ksar Hellal 51, 162
Ksar Jedid, market 333
Ksar Jeraa 334
Ksar Jouamaa 333
Ksar Kherachfa 334
Ksar Krachoua 340
Ksar Krima 244
Ksar Lemsa, Byzantine fort 62, 243–4
Ksar Mdouja, mausoleum and fort 247
Ksar Megelba 335
Ksar Menara, Roman mausoleum 131
Ksar Metameur 331
Ksar Ouled Mahdi 334
Ksar Ouled Soltane, ghorfas 319, 339–40
Ksar Sidi Ayed, mosque 329
Ksar Toual Zouamel 271
Ksar Toujane 330
Ksar Zemmour 333–4
kufic script 65–6, 67, 68, 171, 186, 187, 189

La Goulette ix, 2, 82, 113
    kasbah 62, 113–14
    restaurants and accommodation 114
La Marsa, villas and palaces 123
La Skhira 178
Lake Bizerte 205–6
Lake Ichkeul 205–6
Lake of Tunis 113
Lalla, oasis garden 301
Lalla Telkoussat sanctuary 329
Lamta (Leptis Minor) 163
land holding 74–5
    cultivation 75–7
Latin 41, 70–1, 116, 273
lavatories 16
leather goods 26, 93–4, 186, 220
Lebna 138
Leo Africanus 72, 318, 345
Leptis Minor, see Lamta (Leptis Minor)
Liber Pater cult 255, 275, 333

Libya, border 4–6, 55, 177, 342
Limisa, remains 244
literature 69–73
louages 11
Louis, St 45, 120, 122

Maamoura, beach 137
Macomades Minores, Byzantine site 177
Mahdia ix, 163–6
    accommodation and restaurants 166
    Borj el Kebir fortress 62, 165–6
    Great Mosque 14, 62, 165
    history 46, 164
    Medina 164–5
    Skifa el Kahla 164
    transport 164
Mahrès 177
Makhtar 270, 272–6, 274
    Cemetery 275–6
    Great Baths 274
    Hildeguns' church 274
    history 272
    Juventutes Clubhouse 275
    megalithic tombs 61, 276
    Museum 272–3
    Old Forum 275
    Phoenician remains 273–4, 276
    Temple of Apollo 276
    tophet 272, 276
maps 12–13
Mareth village 330
Marsa ben Ramdan beach 145
Massicault Commonwealth War Cemetery 216–17
Massinissa 38, 38–9, 224–5, 246, 251–3, 272, 332
Mateur, market 208
Matmata, underground houses xi, 328
Maztouria, ksour 339
Medeina village, Roman Althiburos 278–9
Medenine,
    ksour 331–2
    Roman theatre 61
Mejerda Estuary 192–7
Mejez el Bab 217
    Commonwealth War Cemetery 218
Menzel Abderrahman 206
Menzel Bou Zelfa, orange festival 130
Menzel Temime 137, 138
mergoums 24, 188
metalwork 26–7, 90
Metlaoui 35, 301–2
Metline vilage 197
Midès village xii, 303, 304
minerals 26
Mohammed, prophet 56, 57
Mohammed es Sadok 50
Mohammedia,

Beylical palace 49, 235
  Roman acqueduct 235–6
Moknine, Museum of Local Art and Folklore 67,
  162–3
Monastir 159–62
  accommodation and restaurants 162
  Bourguiba Family Mausoleum 161–2
  Great Mosque 161
  history 159–60
  Medina 162
  Mosque of Sidi Ali el Mezzeri 161
  Museum of Islamic Art 161
  Ribat of Harthema 62, 159, 160–1
  transport 160
  Zaouia of Sidi Douib 161
mopeds 12, 127, 134, 200
mosaics 63–5
  in Cap Bon peninsula 128
  in Carthage 118
  in North Coast 193–4, 211, 227
  in Sahel 154–6, 166, 173, 180
  the Tell 236, 237, 262, 279, 284–5
  in Tunis 104, 106–8
mosques 14, 63
Mouansa, market 342
museums xi, 14
music 73, 99, 122, 247–8
Mustis,
  Byzantine fort 62, 262
  Roman remains 261–2

Nabeul ix, 126, 133–7
  accommodation and restaurants 136–7
  Museum 135
  Neapolis 135–6
  shopping 25, 136
  sports 21, 136
  transport 134
National Tourist Board 7, 27
Nefta 309–11, 310
  accommodation and restaurants 312–13
  the Corbeille 311
  Koubba of Sidi Bou Ali 309–10
  Marché des Roses du Sahara 312
  palmery and southern medina 312
  Sufi centre 59, 310
  tourist information 7, 311
  transport 310–11
  Zaouia of the Qadriya 310, 311
Nefza, market 209
Neo-Destour Party 51–4, 148, 162
newspapers 20
nightlife 32–3, 111, 129, 159, 174, 204, 327
nomads 78, 178, 233, 244, 286, 294–6, 315–16,
  320, 340
Normans 44, 344

North Coast and Mejerda Valley xi, 190–232, 191
  accommodation and restaurants 196–7, 203–4,
    212–13, 214–15, 217, 221, 223, 231
Numidians 36, 38–9, 177, 219, 224, 224–5, 229,
    246, 251–3, 271, 272, 332
Numluli, Roman remains 259

olives 74, 76, 133, 148, 281
opening hours 13–14
Oqba ibn Nafi, Arab leader 42, 181, 184, 344
Ottomans and Hapsburgs 46–7, 59, 62, 83, 160,
    198
Oudna, Roman remains 64, 235, 236
Oued Akarit 35, 173, 178
Oued el Hamar, Roman remains 217
Oued el Hattab, Roman remains 293
Oued el Khatef, hanaounets of Harouri 140
Oued ez Zit 239–40
Oued Fouara 130
Oued Hamra, Roman ruins 245
Oued Meliane, Roman acqueduct 235
Oued Melliz 229
Oued Zarga village, war cemetery 218
Oued Zigzaou, prehistoric site 330
Ouerghamma tribal confederation 320, 331, 333,
    338, 340, 342
Ousselatia 244
overland travel 2

package tours 4
para-gliding 21, 129, 157, 205
parks and gardens 77
passports 4, 5, 9, 12
Pheradi Maius, Roman remains 131
Phoenicians ix, 36–7, 60, 63–4, 69–70
  in Bay of Tunis 111, 114–15
  in Cap Bon peninsula 140–2
  in Chott el Jerid 298–9
  in Jerba 344
  in north coast 192–4, 198, 210
  in Sahel 148, 150, 159, 165
  see also Carthaginians
photography 16–17
Pilau island 196
Plage Ejjenine 147
Plage Sidi Mechrig, Roman bathhouse 208
Plage Zouiraa 209
Police 15, 127, 134, 153, 184, 232, 299, 306, 311
Port el Kantaoui 21, 133
Post Offices 13–14, 88, 127, 134, 153, 170, 184,
    200, 265, 299, 306, 311, 325, 346
prehistory 35–6, 243, 263, 271, 277, 298, 330

radio 20
Raf Raf, beach 192, 196–7
Ramadan 19, 58, 59, 186

Raouad 113, 123
Ras el Ain 337
Ras Engelah, beach 205
Ras Jebel, market 192, 197
Rass ed Dreck, beach 144
Regulus, Roman military leader 37–8, 124, 140
Rekkada, museum 189
religious services 108–9, 157, 170
Remada, koubbas 340–1
Remel Plage 206
restaurants xi, 28–30
Rohia village 279
Roman remains xi, 5, 60
  in Bay of Tunis 105
  in Cap Bon peninsula 135
  in Chott el Jerid 300, 318
  in Jeber Demer 332–3
  in north coast 193, 211–12, 217, 221–2, 223–32
  in Sahel 163, 177, 179–80
  in the Tell 235–6, 238, 240, 240–2, 243–4,
    245–7, 249–50, 251–9,   260, 261–2, 265,
    271, 272–6, 278–9, 293
Romans, history 38–41
  in Bay of Tunis 115, 116
  in Cap Bon peninsula 124
  in Chott el Jerid 297, 299
  in Jebel Demer 320
  in north coast 198, 210, 219
  in Sahel 163, 178
  in the Tell 233, 246, 287–8
Rtiba beach 145

Sabria, oasis 317
Sahel, the ix, 148–89, **149**
  accommodation and restaurants 148, 158–9, 162,
    166, 173–4, 176, 181, 188–9
sailsurfing 22, 129, 314
Sakiat Sidi Youssef 270
Salakta,
  catacombs 167
  museum 166
sand yachting 22, 314
Saturn worship 67, 242, 249, 258–9
SBEITLA 280–6, **282**
  accommodation and restaurants 286
  basilica of Ballator 284
  basilica of Vitalis 285
  Byzantine remains 62, 65, 281, 284
  Capitoline temples 67, 284
  Great Baths 283
  history 281
  museum 281
  Roman remains xi, 235, 280, 281–6
  transport 280
  triumphal arch 285–6

Sbiba,
  basilica-mosque 280
  fondouk 279
  Roman remains 279–80
Scipio, Roman general 38, 39, 163, 245–6
Second World War 52, 128, 139, 153, 169, 178,
    198, 208, 213, 216, 217, 261, 291, 293, 299,
    320
  cemeteries and memorials 112, 121, 122, 132–3,
    209, 216–17, 218, 221, 260, 330
Sedra, ruined ksar 339
Sejnane, ceramics 208
Seressi, Roman remains 243
sex 17–18
SFAX ix, 167–74, **168**
  accommodation and restaurants 173–4
  Archaeological Museum 172–3
  Bab Jebilli 171
  coast 173
  Dar Jallouli Museum 171–2
  Great Mosque 62, 67, 170–1
  history 167–9
  Kasbah 171
  Medina 170–2
  New Town 169, 172–3
  nightlife 174
  shopping 27, 171
  tourist information 170
  transport 169–70
Shiism 43, 44, 164, 165, 183
shopping 22–7, 156, 171, 292
Siagu, Roman remains 130
Sidi Abd el Ouabed 205
Sidi Ahmed (Borj Younga), ribat 177
Sidi Ahmed Chaouch, fort 342
Sidi Ali el Mekki, beach 192, 196
Sidi ben Abbes, thermal springs 206
Sidi Bou Hellal koubba 314
Sidi Bou Said ix, 113, 121–3
  metalwork 27, 122
  restaurants and accommodation 122–3
Sidi Bou Zid, market 286–7
Sidi Daoud 144–5
Sidi Mansour Mosque 269
Sidi Mechrig, Roman baths *190*
Sidi Mettar, underground houses 329
Sidi Rais 146
Sidi Salem lake 221
Siliana 245
Skanès, beach 159
Smar, ghorfa 341
Soliman 146–7
Souk el Jemma 262
souks 22–3, 90, 156, 163, 171, 220
SOUSSE ix, 150–9, **151**
  accommodation and restaurants 158–9
  Catacombs of the Good Shepherd 155, 157

festivals 157
Great Mosque 14, 43, 62, 67, 153–4
hammams 157
history 40, 64, 150–2
Kalaout el Koubba 62, 156
Kasbah Museum of Antiquities 154–6
Medina 153–7
Mosque of Bou Ftata 156
nightlife 159
religious services 157
ribat 62, 150, 154
Sofra Cistern 156
sports 157
tourist information 7, 153
transport 152–3
Spain, influence 46–7, 83, 113, 164, 195, 248
spas 112, 146, 245
sports xi, 21–2, 157
Stiftimia palmery 318
Sua, Roman remains 218
Sufism 53, 58–9, 72, 96, 104, 183, 267, 310
Suttu, Roman villa 260
swimming pools 103, 109, 122, 147, 174, 176, 304,
        309, 311, 312–13
Syndicats d'Initiative 7

Tabarka xi, 190, 209–13
accommodation and restaurants 212–13
festival 73, 212
fortress 62, 211–12
Genoese fort 211
La Basilique museum 211
Les Aiguilles 212
Roman remains 211–12
sports 21, 22, 212
tourist information 211
transport 210–11
Table of Jugurtha mountain xii, 287
Takrouna village 133
Tamelest, ksar 339
Tamerza village 303, 304
Tamezret village 329
organisation 322–3
Taoujout village 329
Tataouine (Foum Tataouine) 334–5
tax, 'tourist' 6
taxis 11, 217, 218
Tazerka, beach 137
tea 32
Tebessa, history 37
Tebourba (Thuburbo Minus), Zaouia of Sidi ben
        Aissa 216
Teboursouk 250–1
Technine village 329
telephone 14, 127, 153, 184
television 20–1

Tell, the xi, 233–93, **234**
accommodation and restaurants 150–1, 239, 242,
        249, 268–70, 276, 278, 286–7, 291, 292,
        293
temperatures 9, 296
tennis 21, 109, 129, 136, 157, 176
Terence 41, 70
Tertullian 70, 116
Teskaia 207
Testour 247–9
accommodation and restaurants 249
Great Mosque 248
music festival 73, 235, 247–8
Thaenae (Thyna, Thina), ruins 167, 177
Thala, Roman ruins 293
Thapsus, battle 39, 163
Thelepte, Byzantine ruins 293
Thibar, British War Cemetery 260
Thibar village 259–60
Thuburbo Majus 240–2, **241**
amphitheatre 242
Capitol and Forum 240–1
history 240
mosaics 64
Roman baths 241–2
Roman bridge 61
temples 241, 242
Thuburnica,
Roman bridge 61, 231
Roman remains 231–2
Tijma hamlet 328
time 18
tipping 15
tophets 105, 115, 117, 150, 155, 272, 276
Touaregs 70, 320
Toukabeur, Roman remains 218
Tourbet el Bey, architecture 62
Tourist Offices 7, 12, 88, 134, 160
Tozeur **305**, 305–9
accommodation and restaurants 309
belvedère 308
desert tours xi, 7, 306
medina *307*
Museum of Folklore and Popular Art 306
Old Town 306–7
palmery 307–8
shopping 308–9
Si Tijani Zoo 308
tourist information 306
transport 306
train travel 10, 302
travel agents 3–4
travel, transport 1–2, **8**, 10–12, 84–8
traveller's cheques 13
Tuis, Zitouna Mosque 43

TUNIS 86–7
accommodation 109
Al Jellaz cemetery 103, 104
Anglican Church of St George 101
Bab el Bahr 89
Bab el Bouhour 92
Bab el Djemilla 88
Bab el Souika Quarter 88, 101–2
Bachiya Medersa 62, *92*, 92, 103
Bardo Museum ix, 62, 63, 67, 104–8
Belvedere Park 103–4
cafés 91, 95, 96, 103, 104, 110–11
Dar el Bey 95
Dar Hussein palace 83, 99
Dar Lasram 102
Dey Othman Palace 97–8
El H'Laq Mosque 100
Es Slimaniya Medersa 93
festivals 108
Great Mosque 62
Hammam des Teinturiers 97
Hammam Kachachine 93
hammams 108
Hammouda Pasha Mosque and Mausoleum 94–5
Harmal Mosque 97
history 45, 47, 49, 50, 82–4
Kasbah Mosque 62, 96
Kouba of the Khorassan 83
Medersa el Acharia 102
Medersa en Nakhla 92
medina ix
Mosque des Teinturiers 62, 97
Mosque of the Ksar 83, 99–100
Mosque of Sidi Mahrez 102
Mosque of Youssef Sahib et Tabba 101
Msid el Koubba 98
Musée du Sidi Bou Khrissan 96–7
Museum of Arts and Traditions (Dar ben Abdallah) 88, 98
Museum of Modern Art 68, 103
'New Town' 50, 51, 84, 88, 89–90
northern medina 100–3
religious services 101, 108–9
restaurants 100, 104, 110
Sadiki College 50, 51, 96, 160
Sahib et Tabaa Mosque 62
St Croix church 90
shopping 25, 108
Sidi el Beshir Mosque 97
Sidi Youssef Mosque *81*, 95
slave market 93–4
souks 91–4, 95, 100, 102, 103, 108
southern medina 97–100
sports 109
tomb of Princess Aziza 94
Tourbet el Bey 84, 98–9
Tourbet Laz 96

tourist information 88
transport 84–8
Zaouia of Sidi Behassen ech-Chadli 104
Zaouia Sidi Brahim 102
Zaouia of Sidi Kassem el Zellij 96
Zaouia of Sidi Mahrez 83, 102
Zitouna Mosque 14, 82, 88, 90, 91
Zitouna University 45, 49, 83, 91, 95

Uchi Majus, Roman remains 260
Utica,
history 39, 64, 193
Museum 193–4
site xi, 192, 194–5
Utique, market 192
Uzappa, Roman remains 246–7

Vandals 41, 71, 116, 132, 167, 219, 240, 288–9
Vieuz Sers, hamlet 270
visas 4, 5, 6

walking xii, 22, 214, 222, 231, 232, 235, 239–40, 303, 304
water 31, 272, 294–6, 298, 305, 306, 343
water-skiing 21, 129, 136, 157, 205
watersports 21, 136, 157
windsurfing 21, 136, 157, 176, 205
wines ix, 30–1, 130, 140, 146, 260
women,
attitudes to 17–18
travelling alone 27, 171, 188
woodworking 27, 91, 108

Youssef Dey 47–8, 83, 93, 95, 198, 200
youth hostels 232, 349

Zaafrane, oasis 317
Zaghouan 237–9
accommodation and restaurants 239
mosque and zaouia of Sidi Ali Azouz 237, 238
Nympheum 238
Zama, battle 38, 225, 245–6, 272
Zama Minor, Roman remains 245–6
Zannfour (Assuras), Roman remains 271
Zaouiet el Arab village, mosque 313
Zarat village 330
Zarzis, beach 332, 342
Zembra, island 143
Zembretta, island 143
Zeroua village 329
Zirid rule 44, 161, 164, 183
zoos 103, 307, 308
Zriba, thermal baths 239
Zuerten village, ksar 329

Other Cadogan Guides available from your local bookshop or from UK or USA direct:

From the UK: Cadogan Books, Mercury House, 195 Knightsbridge, London SW7 1RE.
From the US: The Globe Pequot Press, 138 West Main Street, Chester, Connecticut 06412.

Title

Australia .... ☐
Bali .... ☐
Berlin .... ☐
The Caribbean.. ☐
Ecuador, The Galápagos & Colombia .... ☐
Greek Islands .... ☐
India .... ☐
Ireland .... ☐
Italian Islands .... ☐
Italy .... ☐
Mexico .... ☐
Morocco .... ☐
New York .... ☐
Northeast Italy .... ☐
Northwest Italy .... ☐
Portugal .... ☐
Prague .... ☐
Rome .... ☐
Scotland .... ☐
South of France: Provence, Côte d'Azur, Languedoc-Roussillon .... ☐
South Italy .... ☐
Southern Spain: Andalucia & Gibraltar .... ☐
Spain .... ☐
Thailand .... ☐
Turkey .... ☐
Tuscany, Umbria & The Marches .... ☐
Venice ....

Name ....

Address ....

.... Post Code ....

Date .... Order Number ....

Special Instructions ....

....

Please use these forms to tell us about the hotels or restaurants you consider to be special and worthy of inclusion in our next edition, as well as to give any general comments on existing entries. Please include your name and address on the order form on the reverse of this page.

Hotels

Name ....

Address ....

Tel.. Price of double room ....

Description/Comments ....

....

....

Name ....

Address ....

Tel.. Price of double room ....

Description/Comments ....

....

....

Name ....

Address ....

Tel.. Price of double room ....

Description/Comments ....

....

....

Name ....

Address ....

Tel.. Price of double room ....

Description/Comments ....

....

....

Restaurants

Name ....

Address ....

Tel... Price per person ....

Description/Comments ....

....

....

Name ....

Address ....

Tel... Price per person ....

Description/Comments ....

....

....

Name ....

Address ....

Tel... Price per person ....

Description/Comments ....

....

....

Name ....

Address ....

Tel... Price per person ....

Description/Comments ....

....

....

General Comments